EXPLORING SOCIO-CULTURAL THEMES IN EDUCATION

READINGS IN SOCIAL FOUNDATIONS

SECOND EDITION

JOAN H. STROUSE
Portland State University

Merrill
Prentice Hall

Upper Saddle River, New Jersey
Columbus, Ohio

Library of Congress Cataloging-in-Publication Data

Strouse, Joan.

   Exploring socio-cultural themes in education : readings in social foundations / Joan H. Strouse.—2nd ed.

     p. cm.

   Rev. ed. of: Exploring themes of social justice in education. c1997.

   Includes bibliographical references and index.

   ISBN 0-13-016454-2

   1. Educational sociology. 2. Educational anthropology. 3. Social justice—Study and teaching. I. Strouse, Joan. Exploring themes of social justice in education. II. Title.

LC191 .S754 2001

306.43—dc21

                                              00-028363

Vice President and Publisher: Jeffery W. Johnston
Editor: Debra A. Stollenwerk
Editorial Assistant: Penny S. Burleson
Production Editor: Mary Harlan
Design Coordinator: Diane C. Lorenzo
Cover Design: Jason Moore
Cover Photo: Super Stock
Text Design: Clarinda Publication Services
Production Coordination: Cliff Kallemeyn, Clarinda Publication Services
Production Manager: Pamela D. Bennett
Director of Marketing: Kevin Flanagan
Marketing Manager: Amy June
Marketing Services Manager: Krista Groshong

This book was set in Garamond by The Clarinda Company.

The cover was printed by Phoenix Color Corp.

10 9 8 7 6 5 4

ISBN: 0-13-016454-2

With Love For
_____

My Life Partner,

Bill Greenfield

My Parents,

Bette Wolf Strouse

1922-1989

Lawrence Klein Strouse

1918-1991

My Niece and Nephew,

Jessica Strouse

David Strouse

You have taught me so much

PREFACE

The aim of this book is to help teachers become critically informed about the process of teaching and schooling in the United States. This book is designed to actively engage students in the process of developing a personal perspective for themselves on the function of schooling in our society and on the special responsibilities teachers have to consider the broader implications of the enterprise of formal education as it occurs in this country. Whether they are prospective teachers or more experienced educators, readers will find much here to challenge their assumptions about schools and teaching. And, it is hoped, in coming to personal terms with the perspectives offered here, both groups will approach their responsibilities with a new sensitivity to the social justice challenges and complexities of teaching.

THE RATIONALE FOR THIS BOOK

Teaching is very demanding work, work that is not well understood or appreciated by the public at large. Public education, as the social bedrock supporting virtually all other occupations and institutional structures in our society, depends increasingly on teachers' willingness to commit themselves to serving the public good, believing that they *can* make an important difference in the lives of children, particularly the growing numbers of children representative of those in U.S. society who have been marginalized by virtue of their social class, gender, and/or linguistic, racial, or cultural heritage. If teachers are to be *good* teachers, they need to understand the roots of our system of public schooling, the assumptions upon which it rests, and the degree to which it is intended to serve all children equitably and effectively. This book's purpose is to help teachers develop a personally meaningful understanding of the foundations of U.S. education and implications for their effectiveness as professional educators.

WHAT'S "SUBJECT MATTER" GOT TO DO WITH TEACHING?

If all teachers had to do was teach subject-matter content, their work would be challenging, of course, but nevertheless relatively simple compared to what they actually find themselves doing. The prevailing approach to both preservice and inservice teacher education is usually grounded in such an assumption, requiring that teachers "complete" certain subject-matter courses and college majors. They learn how to design lesson plans, manage classrooms, and use specific teaching techniques, and are generally required to demonstrate a minimum level of proficiency at these tasks under the guidance of a supervising teacher in their local public school system. Indeed, in many states teachers are even now required to demonstrate subject-matter proficiency on national tests, and there is a strong movement afoot to increase emphasis in subject-matter expertise and content learned as standards of proficiency for teachers and for students in schools. There is no doubt that both can be important. However, what too often gets ignored by teacher-educators (as well as by pundits telling educators how to improve our country's public school system) is that children and the communities in which they live are tremendously diverse and becoming increasingly so.

Exploring Socio-Cultural Themes in Education: Readings in Social Foundations doesn't deny the need for teachers to be grounded in the subject matter of their teaching specialty, classroom management techniques, and good pedagogical practices. There is no question that these are important to good teaching. However, what is often missing in the education of teachers in general, and in the perspectives teachers bring to their daily work, is a personalized understanding of the broader function of school in society, the principles upon which it was founded, the rhetoric on which it is sustained, and the unintended but nevertheless negative consequences of our system of schooling for those it exists to serve and who are most in need of what formal education can make possible in our society.

The readings in this book encourage beginning and experienced teachers alike to examine the present system and its effects on children and the broader social structure and to challenge themselves to develop their capacity to make a real difference in the lives of children. Schools offer the possibility of social justice—and teachers themselves are the critical link in that equation. What are the issues of social justice that confront teachers daily in their classrooms? What are teachers' commitments to teaching in ways that respond to the life experiences of the children in their classrooms?

PERSPECTIVES ON SCHOOLING IN AMERICA

This book offers prospective as well as experienced teachers a unique opportunity to read many original source materials written by authors representing divergent points of view and a broad historical spectrum in the field of education. It introduces students to this broader view of education,

enabling them to understand the roots of many of the challenges confronting contemporary educators and providing them with the basis for developing a personal philosophical perspective on the work of teaching, the function of schools in our society, and the relationships between education, productivity, community, and the changing social, cultural, linguistic, and ethnic landscape of our society and its impact on schools, children, and teaching. While a number of the articles selected for inclusion might seem "old" to many readers, their message is of enduring importance to understanding the challenges faced by contemporary educators.

KEY THEMES

Several key themes integrate the readings. These are reflected in questions such as:

- What are the relationships between culture, society, and education?
- What are the dynamics of daily life in schools as institutions in particular organizational and community contexts?
- In what ways are gender, language, culture, race, social class, and the relationship between school and work important to our education?
- What orientations and strategies can teachers adopt that will enable them to become more transformative educators?

STRUCTURE OF THE TEXT

The book is divided into seven parts: "Education as Cultural Transmission," "Social Structure and Education," "Socialization and Progress," "Legitimation and Reproduction," "School Life," "Education and Societal Inequality," and "Transformational Educators." Each part contains two or three contributions by distinguished and well-recognized educators of historical or contemporary significance. An introduction to each part highlights the key ideas and issues reflected in the readings. At the end of the readings are questions intended to guide the reader in examining the critical issues and to stimulate discussion of the ideas and their implications for contemporary teaching and schooling. The seven parts are briefly reviewed below.

EDUCATION AS CULTURAL TRANSMISSION

What are the values embedded in school curricula, the roles of teachers and students, social relations within the school, and the way the classroom and the school are organized and governed? Practices usually thought of as "normal," because they are so much a part of our experience and accepted ways of doing things, often are not examined or questioned. Yet it is these very practices which are, in subtle and informal ways, the primary means by which schools transmit and embed culture in our society. Given deliberate consideration, what values can teachers point to that are transmitted by the curriculum and other aspects of the ways in which we conduct schooling in our society? While many would have us believe that schools and teaching are "value free," they simply are not. What values should (and should not) be promulgated by our public schools? What are teachers' rationales for their perspectives regarding this crucial function of schooling?

SOCIAL STRUCTURE AND EDUCATION

Most Americans believe that the success of one's effort in formal education is based on achieved rather than ascribed attributes like race, class, native language, or gender. It is assumed by the public at large, including most legislators as well as most public educators, that the availability of a free public education gives everyone an equal chance to advance and to become a satisfied and productive citizen reaping all of the social and economic benefits of being *fully American*. Is this truth or fiction? The readings in this section engage students in an examination of how societal, school, and teacher expectations often undermine the rhetoric that sustains our belief in schools as the great "leveler" in our society. What are the *functionalist principles* upon which public schools in the United States are grounded, and do these serve all citizens well? Often left out of

the picture are the devastating effects of intergenerational poverty, poor health, institutionalized racism, a climate of violence, social neglect, and family and community turmoil. Do schools serve mainly to perpetuate the existing class structures and divisions in our society? *Conflict theorists* argue that public schools serve to maintain the privileges and power of the elites in society. If race, class, and gender *do* make a critical difference, what about teachers' expectations of children? What are teachers' perspectives on children of color, English-language learners, or poor children? What difference do their expectations of children make in U.S. schools?

SOCIALIZATION AND PROGRESS

What is the role of school in society? Is it the purpose of our nation's public schools to train the next work force generation, to shape the moral development of children, to teach the academic skills needed to pursue higher education, or to be agents of social change, as has been tried in the desegregation of schools and the teaching of safer sexual practices? While it is clear that schools are major influences on the moral and technical socialization of children, and teachers are critical socializing agents, to what ends should the efforts of schools be directed? The readings in this part reveal the *hidden curriculum* of schools and encourage teachers to reflect on their beliefs about what children should learn in school and who should be making that decision.

LEGITIMATION AND REPRODUCTION

The readings in this part lead teachers to examine the role of schools in maintaining and legitimizing the existing social structure in the United States. The readings offer both theoretical and concrete examples of how schools function as instruments of class domination. By encouraging a critical examination of whose interests are being served by schools, who gets ahead and why, the readings challenge educators to consider how they will either reinforce or work to change the status quo. Teachers are invited to explore radically different ways of thinking about schools and education, and about the functions of school in society, and to entertain the potential of significantly different models of schooling and their implications for curriculum, the roles of teachers and students, and the interplay of school and community.

SCHOOL LIFE

Excerpts from two ethnographies of schooling and a discussion of education in a multicultural society comprise the readings in this part. They illustrate how influential the teacher is and how often teachers and students are on different wavelengths in terms of their understandings of rules, roles, and expectations; in other words, how different the cultures are that are shaping children and the cultures of schooling in the United States. What is life in schools like from the student's perspective? What dilemmas must teachers face as they struggle to balance their efforts to meet the needs of both low- and high-achieving students: Should the teacher give a lot to a few or a little to many? What kind of knowledge counts most for teachers—and why is this form of knowing so alien to so many students? What teachers do to enable themselves to keep abreast of the continuously changing reality of school life can make a tremendous difference for them as they search for the best way to be fair and effective as teachers. These readings examine the assumptions and stereotypes teachers have of children, particularly children of color and children of the poor, and help us understand how influential teachers can be in helping (or hindering) student learning and development.

EDUCATION AND SOCIETAL INEQUALITY: RACE, GENDER, CLASS, AND ETHNICITY

Despite the tremendous strides that have been made during this century, much work remains to make schools truly equitable places where all children can learn. U.S. demographics are changing rapidly, and teachers find themselves facing ever-increasing diversity in their classrooms—a diversity taking many forms, including ability,

race, social class, language, and culture. Schools have always had difficulty succeeding with all students, particularly those who differ from the traditionally predominantly white, middle-class student body. While the vast majority of teachers in public schools reflect this historically dominant profile, the student profile is changing rapidly. Whether it be a learning disabled or physically or emotionally challenged student, a refugee whose native language is not English, or a student of color, the mix of students in contemporary classrooms presents teachers with a tremendous set of new challenges. The readings in this part will help new as well as experienced educators anticipate the changing classroom reality they face as contemporary teachers.

The increasingly culturally diverse communities that our public schools serve require that teachers be able to see beyond the latest teaching fad, the current curriculum or pedagogical controversy, or the school governance crisis of the moment. Teachers who do in fact see the bigger picture, who have a personally meaningful understanding of how teaching and schooling *can* make a difference in the lives of all children, *are* the teachers who will be most successful in serving our nation's students, particularly the ones from the historically marginalized groups least likely to benefit from traditional schooling. Teachers who have a historically rooted sense of their special role as a public educator will be the teachers most likely to succeed with children despite the odds against these students.

It is teachers such as these that this book seeks to inspire and encourage. Our profession needs to foster the development of a new kind of educator—one prepared to be thoughtful and reflective and able to remind themselves and others of the historical and social significance of their work as public school teachers in a democratic society. The issues and dilemmas addressed in this book reflect the enduring challenges facing educators. Public school teachers who come to an early understanding of these broader issues will be better able than their contemporaries to teach and succeed in the emerging school milieu.

TRANSFORMATIONAL EDUCATORS

While the challenges are indeed great, there are teachers who actively are engaged in teaching aimed at *transforming* the lives of students. These teachers are truly passionate about their work and adopt an activist orientation toward their teaching. Unwilling to stop at merely teaching "subject matter", these teachers are responsive to their students—to their cultural and social class backgrounds, to their life experiences and the limitations of their life circumstances. Evident in the efforts of such teachers is their desire to empower students, to engage students in a reflective and critical dialogue that goes beyond the classroom to a consideration of the broader conditions within our society—conditions the students themselves experience on a daily basis but perhaps have never really examined nor understood. The readings in this part reflect actual teaching practices and circumstances in a variety of public schools and community contexts. They are offered here as examples, not of the one best way to teach, but as illustrations of the many different ways in which teachers strive to achieve their individual visions of good teaching.

Reading and thinking about the implications of the ideas in this book will help teachers become more reflective about their practice—to think through the broader implications of the curriculum, the social relations that are fostered in schools, and the images of self, other, and society that are embedded and reinforced in traditional schooling practices. As a result of grappling at a personal level with the very real dilemmas inherent in our current system of public education, teachers will face the necessity to choose, for themselves, how they will practice their craft. Will they sustain the present system, or practice in ways that will enable schools to serve all students more equitably and effectively?

The purpose of this book is to heighten teachers' awareness of the bigger issues at stake and to stimulate them to reflect on their duty as professional educators to "educate" their students—that is, to prepare them to teach in a way that enables their students to benefit fully from their public schooling experience.

STUDY QUESTIONS

At the end of each part are a series of questions. These are not the sort of questions that have definitive answers. Rather, their purpose is twofold: to provide the reader with a preview of some of the major ideas to be explored in the readings, and to stimulate students to explore the implications of the readings as they discuss their thoughts and feelings with their classmates and with the instructor. Given the concerns their reflections on these questions yield, how might they orient themselves in the classroom, as a teacher? Would they have schools or the roles of teachers and students change in some respect? How, and why? Given what they have read, what are some alternative or competing perspectives? Questions in this section include both matters of primary concern to prospective or inexperienced teachers as well as issues typically found to be of more interest to the experienced professional.

FIELD AND PRACTICUM EXPERIENCES

The book concludes by offering suggestions for field and practicum experiences. These obviously can be adapted to the particulars of any given instructional setting. These experiential, school- and community-based components of learning can become a powerful supplement to the readings and class discussions in providing concrete examples of the ideas explored in this book.

The intention in having students participate in several different field experiences is to give them the opportunity to find out firsthand about life in schools beyond the pedagogical dimensions of classroom teaching. Whether a beginner or experienced in the classroom, spending some time talking deliberately with a teacher-colleague or principal about what it is like to be in that role can help provide a personal perspective on what it means, in a phenomenological sense, to be a teacher. The insights occasioned by a field experience will enable students to see the broader picture of teaching and schooling and the complex interplay between the community, school, and classroom that bears upon teaching and learning.

Similarly, a more extended experience, such as a practicum for the prospective teacher that involves the student in a concrete and recurring interaction with one or more children in a school or classroom setting, can be an especially enlightening learning experience. The primary purpose of the practicum is to enable prospective teachers to develop their awareness of the many factors influencing their work, to reflect on the effects of these influences on what occurs in a classroom, and perhaps to speculate about what courses of action a teacher might take to build on the positive influences and ameliorate those with negative effects. The equivalent for a more experienced teacher might be to arrange to "trade" teaching assignments with a colleague at another grade level or in a school that is culturally, racially, or socioeconomically different from one's usual or previous experience as a teacher.

SUGGESTED READINGS

At the end of the book is a bibliography of related readings that faculty and students may want to consider as they probe deeper into the ideas, theories, and concepts presented within this book.

CHANGES IN THE SECOND EDITION

The biggest change in this new edition is the addition of Part 7, "Transformational Educators," which offers examples of the ways in which teachers themselves come to grips in positive and transformative ways with the social and cultural realities of teaching. While it is relatively easy to find flaws within the current educational system, there are too few examples of how beginning and experienced educators can, in fact, respond to these conditions in a positive and effective way. Part 7 provides examples of how teachers can help *all* children learn without lowering standards, without

blaming the kids, their families, or the communities in which they live, without watering down the curriculum, and without leaving some children out of the teaching-learning "loop," or by simply "keeping things quiet" until the bell rings and the children leave. Given the magnitude of the challenges described in Parts 1–6, it is important to offer new teachers as well as seasoned but perhaps discouraged veterans hope that something positive can in fact be done to help kids do well in public educational settings. Part 7 includes examples of what it is possible for a teacher to accomplish (in a transformative sense) in a variety of settings reflecting different school and community contexts and different age groups of children. One of the points to be made with the inclusion of these portraits is that the effects of such efforts not only have payoffs for children but have a transformational impact on teachers as well. Readings in Part 7 draw on contributions by William Bigelow, Gloria Ladson-Billings, and Mike Rose.

Other changes in the second edition, based on feedback from students and instructors, include: the replacement of material by Feinberg and Soltis with discussions of functionalism and conflict theory by Hurn and empirical examples of those concepts in a study by Anyon; a comprehensive discussion of multicultural education by James Banks; a reordering of the chapters in Part 3, "Socialization and Progress," wherein Dewey's general observations on the effects of schooling are followed by Dreeben's explanation of particular norms learned in school, and concluding with Grant and Zeichner's discussion of the importance of teachers being reflective in their practice; and inclusion of additional suggestions for student activities and field work. I am especially indebted to my students for many of these improvements, and anticipate that readers will find these changes satisfying.

SUGGESTIONS FOR INSTRUCTORS AND STUDENTS ABOUT USING THIS BOOK

The text is designed for a "Socratic" approach to teaching whereby the students assume a major responsibility for their learning, for engaging and exploring the ideas presented. The instructor's role is that of guide, facilitator, critical questioner, or devil's advocate. That is, the instructor supports students in helping them clarify their ideas, get beyond their taken-for-granted assumptions, and explore new terrain. This is a text that calls for active engagement by the students *and* the instructor in the material being explored. Because the issues explored by the readings are highly value-laden, and because there are no easy answers in any objective sense, the readings invite alternative and competing perspectives and interpretations.

This invitation to inquire into and consider such value-laden questions will be exciting to students, in the sense that it will get their "juices" flowing. It will also be scary and, for most, a first-time experience with authentic thinking and feeling in the context of their experience of formal schooling. Their past experience will most likely have been that of passive vessel rather than active thinker. Thus it is important that the instructor encourage students to take personal risks in stating their feelings and expressing their thoughts about some very complex and important issues. Toward this end, it is important that the instructor be supportive and reinforcing as students seek to understand their thoughts and feelings and to give voice to them in a public arena such as a classroom. Students within a class will not all be of a similar mind in considering these questions, and instructors can anticipate that discussion of these questions will bring out strongly held and very divergent viewpoints among students. Instructors and students alike will be challenged regarding their tolerance for ambiguity and their ability to be respectful of the viewpoints of others.

There is no special "magic" to the order in which the selections proceed. However, my 15 years' experience in teaching a course that uses these materials satisfies me that the current order "works" very well. Nevertheless, it may not work for every instructor, and I encourage you to rearrange the various parts into a sequence that fits with your logic of inquiry into these matters.

Also, some selections are longer than others and it may be necessary for instructors to "jigsaw" some of the readings — that is, rather than require that every student read all of the material in its entirety, that reading responsibilities be divided among members of the class, with students assigned to read and report key concepts for different selections.

ACKNOWLEDGMENTS

My teaching career spans several decades. During this period I have "field tested" (with past and present students) several iterations of the text you now hold in your hands. This second edition was changed and revised significantly based on student feedback and comments; I am grateful for your assistance. I hope my former students are continuing to educate children and create democratic classrooms in the spirit of these readings.

I want to thank my editor, Debbie Stollenwerk, who brought humor and reasonable deadlines to this work. Penny Burleson, editorial assistant, has been a constant source of support and information gathering. I would also like to acknowledge the reviewers of this book: Tom Callister, Whitman College; Malcolm B. Campbell, Bowling Green State University; Deane Curtin, Gustavus Adolphus College; Jeanne Ellsworth, Plattsburg State University of New York; Stephanie Evans, California State University, Los Angeles; and Jim Kauffman, University of South Carolina, Aiken.

I am fortunate to have friends, mentors, and colleagues who have supported me and my career over the years. Thank you all so much. Special recognition and deep gratitude are given to those who have helped and encouraged me as I wrote this: Richard Ruiz, Amy Driscoll, Seema Kapani, Manya Shapiro, Karen Brooks, Leslie Rennie-Hill, Teri Venker, Doug Sherman, Ray DeMarco, and Sabaii Dee. Bill Greenfield, husband extraordinaire, deserves his own formal acknowledgment, for without him this couldn't have been done!

Manzanita, Oregon

COMPANION WEBSITE

DISCOVER THE COMPANION WEBSITE ACCOMPANYING THIS BOOK

THE PRENTICE HALL COMPANION WEBSITE: A VIRTUAL LEARNING ENVIRONMENT

Technology is a constantly growing and changing aspect of our field that is creating a need for content and resources. To address this emerging need, Prentice Hall has developed an online learning environment for students and professors alike—Companion Websites—to support our textbooks.

In creating a Companion Website, our goal is to build on and enhance what the textbook already offers. For this reason, the content for each user-friendly website is organized by topic and provides the professor and student with a variety of meaningful resources. Common features of a Companion Website include:

FOR THE PROFESSOR

Every Companion Website integrates **Syllabus Manager**™, an online syllabus creation and management utility.

- **Syllabus Manager**™ provides you, the instructor, with an easy, step-by-step process to create and revise syllabi, with direct links into Companion Websites and other online content without having to learn HTML.
- Students may logon to your syllabus during any study session. All they need to know is the web address for the Companion Website and the password you've assigned to your syllabus.
- After you have created a syllabus using **Syllabus Manager**™, students may enter the syllabus for their course section from any point in the companion website.
- Class dates are highlighted in white and assignment due dates appear in blue. Clicking on a date, the student is shown the list of activities for the assignment. The activities for each assignment are linked directly to actual content, saving time for students.
- Adding assignments consists of clicking on the desired due date, then filling in the details of the assignment—name of the assignment, instructions, and whether or not it is a one-time or repeating assignment.
- In addition, links to other activities can be created easily. If the activity is online, a URL can be entered in the space provided, and it will be linked automatically in the final syllabus.
- Your completed syllabus is hosted on our servers, allowing convenient updates from any computer on the Internet. Changes you make to your syllabus are immediately available to your students at their next logon.

FOR THE STUDENT

- **Topic Overviews**—outline key concepts in topic areas
- **Electronic Bluebook**—send homework or essays directly to your instructor's email with this paperless form
- **Message Board**—serves as a virtual bulletin board to post—or respond to—questions or comments to/from a national audience
- **Chat**—real-time chat with anyone who is using the text anywhere in the country—ideal for discussion and study groups, class projects, etc.
- **Web Destinations**—links to www sites that relate to each topic area
- **Professional Organizations**—links to organizations that relate to topic areas
- **Additional Resources**—access to topic-specific content that enhances material found in the text

To take advantage of these and other resources, please visit the *Exploring Socio-Cultural Themes in Education* Companion Website at

www.prenhall.com/strouse

CONTENTS

PART
1

EDUCATION AS CULTURAL TRANSMISSION

The selections in Part 1 raise three basic questions for the reader:

- What are the key values reflected in U.S. culture?
- How is contemporary U.S. culture transmitted and maintained?
- What are the roles of schools and teachers in promulgating these values, attitudes, and beliefs, or in fostering changes in them in anticipation of our society's future needs?

The discussion by George Spindler provides a good introduction to the concept of culture and its transmission. It is especially useful because in his descriptions of the cultural practices and transmission processes of societies and groups unfamiliar to us, Spindler provides the reader with a perspective that is helpful in illuminating processes for cultural transmission and maintenance. What is especially difficult to understand about one's own culture is that the values, attitudes, and beliefs that constitute the culture are so familiar to us that they are hard to discern; they are "common sense" and so taken for granted as to remain hidden from us most of the time. Spindler's rich descriptions of cultural beliefs and practices not our own help one ask: How does U.S. society differ from those he describes? What similarities do they share? What are the ways educators shape the values, beliefs, and attitudes of children in the United States?

Similarly, the discussion by Conrad Arensberg and Arthur Niehoff is helpful to us in describing some of the more dominant U.S. cultural values. Although these authors have written the piece to help readers understand how their values might differ from those of another culture, its importance to us is in focusing our attention on the key values associated with being American and being successful in our society today. While many other forces are shaping our values, beliefs, and attitudes, historically we have relied to a great extent upon our public schools as primary vehicles for transmitting and maintaining our culture. Schools socialize young children and adolescents to adopt orientations and dispositions that will enable them to contribute to maintaining and improving this society.

As a prospective teacher, you need to understand our core cultural values and how they are transmitted through public schooling. It also is important that you understand the special character of U.S. society and the challenges and opportunities that its increasingly heterogeneous population brings to the schoolhouse door. We are a society of multiple subcultural groups, and each group carries with it a natural desire to maintain its special heritage and identity, as reflected in different languages, races, religions, and cultural traditions. We are increasingly a multicultural society, and often the values and beliefs of divergent groups bubble up in the form of school curricula designed to celebrate and honor these differences, rather than seeking to homogenize them. What are our core cultural values? Are new cultural values emerging as these diverse cultural groups interact and influence one another? Are some traditional values becoming less central as society changes and evolves? What effects are mass communication and other highly advanced forms of technology having on our values, beliefs, and attitudes? What is the role of public education in transmitting and maintaining our society's core cultural values? Do public school teachers have a responsibility to help prepare young children and adolescents for a technologically sophisticated but largely unforeseeable future? What role does mass public education have in transmitting or changing our culture?

As you read and think about these issues, you should keep several key concepts in mind: culture; the management of cultural discontinuity and compression; cultural recruitment and maintenance; and cultural change. The idea of culture is easy enough to grasp: Many describe it as "the ideas, values, beliefs, and assumptions of a particular group or society." The culture of a particular group, especially one's own, is more difficult to understand because it is embedded in everything we do, in our notions of common sense, in what we take for granted as the way things are. The next two readings are designed to illustrate the meaning of culture, offer a framework for understanding U.S. cultural values, and focus attention on the historical role public schools have played as a primary source of cultural transmission and maintenance in our society.

The reading by Spindler offers examples of the ways culture is transmitted in different social groups. He examines the educational functions of initiation rites in small, homogeneous societies and shows how techniques like cultural discontinuity and compression come into play in transmitting and maintaining culture. He further illustrates the purpose of education in modern cultures for bringing about cultural change, showing us both how schools serve a recruitment function to maintain aspects of the culture and how they also serve as agents of cultural discontinuity aimed at fostering cultural change and development.

Discontinuity in cultural transmission refers to the abrupt and often dramatic changes in roles that children and adolescents experience at certain stages in their journey to adulthood. Such transition points are of relatively brief duration in societies such as those described by Spindler. The discontinuity in cultural transmission of the sort Spindler describes has the effect of maintaining and validating the culture, thus resulting in cultural continuity. Spindler goes on to explain that the equivalent in developed Western society has a different effect. That is, a kind of cultural discontinuity occurs wherein traditional values and norms are not reinforced: Schools in part strive to recruit students to a cultural system that does not yet exist, or is emerging (Spindler, 1973, p. 304). To further paraphrase and extend Spindler's ideas to our contemporary situation in the United States, public schools function to recruit people both into the current system and to specific roles. They also strive to maintain the cultural system; to keep the system and roles working (Spindler, 1973, p. 303).

In a society like ours, what is the purpose of education? Can public schools effectively serve the purpose of maintaining our culture while introducing values and beliefs that challenge the accepted traditions in the effort to prepare us for the future? An example of such an effort is the 1954 Kansas Supreme Court *Brown v. Board of Education of Topeka* decision aimed at providing access to equal educational opportunities for African Americans through school desegregation. Another example is the passage by Congress in 1972 of Title IX of the Education Amendments to the Civil Rights Act, which is intended to guard against discrimination on the basis of sex from participating in or benefiting from any education program or activity receiving federal assistance. These and other federal laws illustrate legislation that has had a profound impact on the nature of schooling in the United States and, ultimately, can be expected to have a sustaining influence on who our public schools serve and upon the cultural values and beliefs that are promulgated as a result. In a marked departure from the past, more children today attend integrated schools, girls now are more likely than ever to play on a varsity sports team, and children with disabilities and limited English proficiency are more likely than in the past to be served in public schools. Because these changes challenge the cultural status quo, some communities have not accepted them easily. In this sense, as Spindler suggests, schools function as ". . . intentional agents of cultural discontinuity, a kind of discontinuity that does not reinforce the traditional values or recruit youngsters into the existing system" (1973, p. 303).

A critical aspect of cultural transmission and maintenance, however, is that, as Spindler says, "People must believe in their system" (1973, p. 303). The public school system is organized to foster recruitment into the existing cultural system. To ensure maintenance of the cultural system, the schools are organized to socialize students to the values, beliefs, and attitudes critical in maintaining the cultural system. Teachers, as crucial socialization agents, and as members of the profession our society has charged with responsibility for public schooling, have a moral duty to be deliberate in deciding what values, beliefs, and attitudes to cultivate through their teaching. It is entirely possible that a public school teacher may be asked to teach secular values or organizational attitudes (HIV education, life skills, being a good "team player," being punctual and following rules, etc.) that are at odds with his or her personal beliefs (children should be encouraged to be spontaneous and creative; sex education is a parental responsibility).

What are U.S. cultural values, and what values, beliefs, and attitudes should public schools be teaching? Many argue that schools should not teach values. Often, what such advocates really mean is that schools should not be teaching values with which they disagree. This is a tough issue. Just what values should schools be teaching, and who gets to decide? Is it possible for a teacher to be neutral? Should a teacher even strive to be neutral?

Some cultural values are taught as an explicit goal of the school and are such that few would disagree with them (work hard, be honest, respect people and property), but many cultural values are hidden within the curriculum, latent but nevertheless potent in their influence on young children and adolescents. Examples of these include habits of work, such as punctuality and persistence; habits of thought, such as don't be critical or questioning of authority; the idea that winning is what counts; the idea that only certain kinds of knowledge are important; the idea that some things are "for girls" and others are "for boys"; a hierarchical model of work; and so forth.

The second reading in this section, by Arensberg and Niehoff, offers a road map to our cultural values. Although the language used in their article is now dated, these are values that most mainstream Americans, from any part of the country, still subscribe to in their day-to-day lives and in their general cultural orientation. Among these are: the importance of material well-being; a propensity to classify acts as good or bad; the inclination to clearly differentiate work from play; the notion that time is money and that time is scarce and worth saving; the belief that problems can be identified and overcome; the attitude that with enough effort, individuals can experience success; valuing of the pragmatic over the mystical; the idea that nature can be "harnessed"; and the belief that all people should have equal opportunities to achieve. These by no means reflect all the values that might be attributed to U.S. culture, nor are they necessarily the most central. As Arensberg and Niehoff propose, however, our history as a people has significantly influenced our character as a society and has left a distinctive cultural imprint.

The worldview one brings to teaching is a product of one's education, experience, and personal background. As a teacher, you will approach that responsibility with a particular orientation, one reflecting your personal integration of the values you hold sacred, the secular values to which you subscribe as a member of the larger society, and the values you have been socialized to as a professional educator. What you teach, how you teach, and your view of and response to students will depend on this constellation of values. Your responsibility is to be aware of your values and of how they intrude into your work.

Students, too, will come to the classroom with their own special set of values: orientations that reflect their family upbringing, ethnic background, religious beliefs, social class, and childhood experiences. Sometimes the orientations of the children in your classroom will be compatible with your own attitudes, values, and beliefs; often they will differ. What is your duty as a teacher—to require the child to adapt or to respond to the child as presented? Will the child suffer because he or she behaves in a culturally different (and by your standards, inappropriate) manner? Whose cultural values shall prevail?

As you read the next two selections, think of the purpose of public schooling in our society. Is it designed to maintain the cultural system as it presently exists or to change certain aspects? Who decides what values count? As a teacher working with children and adolescents from diverse backgrounds, what is your responsibility relative to the transmission and maintenance of the cultural values required to sustain U.S. society? What cultural values will you strive to teach the children in your charge? Why?

THE TRANSMISSION OF CULTURE

GEORGE D. SPINDLER

This chapter is about how neonates become talking, thinking, feeling, moral, believing, valuing human beings—members of groups, participants in cultural systems. It is not, as a chapter on child psychology might be, about the growth and development of individuals, but on how young humans come to want to act as they must act if the cultural system is to be maintained. A wide variety of cultures are examined to illustrate both the diversity and unity of ways in which children are educated. The educational functions that are carried out by initiation rites in many cultures are emphasized, and the concepts of cultural compression, continuity, and discontinuity are stressed in this context. Various other techniques of education are demonstrated with selected cases, including reward, modeling and imitation, play, dramatization, verbal admonition, reinforcement, and storytelling. Recruitment and cultural maintenance are analyzed as basic educative functions. The chapter is not about the whole process of education, but about certain parts of that process seen in a number of different situations.

WHAT ARE SOME OF THE WAYS THAT CULTURE IS TRANSMITTED?

Psychologists and pediatricians do not agree upon the proper and most effective ways to raise children. Neither do the Dusun of Borneo, the Tewa or Hopi of the Southwest, the Japanese, the Ulithians or the Palauans of Micronesia, the Turkish villagers, the Tiwi of North Australia, the people of Gopalpur, or those of Guadalcanal. Each way of life is distinctive in its outlook, content, the kind of adult personalities favored, and the way children are raised. There are also many respects in which human communities are similar that override cultural differences. All major human cultural systems include magic, religion, moral values, recreation, regulation of mating, education, and so forth. But the *content* of these different categories, and the ways the content and the categories are put together, differ enormously. These differences are reflected in the ways people raise their children. If the object of cultural transmission is to teach young people how to think, act, and feel appropriately this must be the case. To understand this process we must get a sense of this variety.

THIS IS HOW IT IS IN PALAU

Five-year-old Azu trails after his mother as he walks along the village path, whimpering and tugging at her skirt. He wants to be carried, and he tells her so, loudly and demandingly. "Stop! Stop! Hold me!" His mother shows no sign of attention.

Source: *"The Transmission of Culture" from* Education and Cultural Process: Towards an Anthropology of Education, *copyright 1973 by George D. Spindler. Reprinted by permission of author.*

She continues her steady barefooted stride, her arms swinging freely at her sides, her heavy hips rolling to smooth the jog of her walk and steady the basket of wet clothes she carries on her head. She has been to the washing pool and her burden keeps her neck stiff, but this is not why she looks impassively ahead and pretends not to notice her son. Often before she has carried him on her back and an even heavier load on her head. But today she has resolved not to submit to his plea, for it is time for him to begin to grow up.

Azu is not aware that the decision has been made. Understandably, he supposes that his mother is just cross, as she often has been in the past, and that his cries will soon take effect. He persists in his demand, but falls behind as his mother firmly marches on. He runs to catch up and angrily yanks at her hand. She shakes him off without speaking to him or looking at him. Enraged, he drops solidly on the ground and begins to scream. He gives a startled look when this produces no response, then rolls over on his stomach and begins to writhe, sob, and yell. He beats the earth with his fists and kicks it with his toes. This hurts and makes him furious, the more so since it has not caused his mother to notice him. He scrambles to his feet and scampers after her, his nose running, tears coursing through the dirt on his cheeks. When almost on her heel he yells and, getting no response, drops to the ground.

By this time his frustration is complete. In a rage he grovels in the red dirt, digging his toes into it, throwing it around him and on himself. He smears it on his face, grinding it in with his clenched fists. He squirms on his side, his feet turning his body through an arc on the pivot of one shoulder.

A man and his wife are approaching, the husband in the lead, he with a short-handled adz resting on his left shoulder, she with a basket of husked coconuts on her head. As they come abreast of Azu's mother the man greets her with "You have been to the washing pool?" It is the Palauan equivalent of the American "How are you?"—a question that is not an inquiry but a token of recognition. The two women scarcely glance up as they pass. They have recognized each other from a distance and it is not necessary to repeat the greeting. Even less notice is called for as the couple pass Azu sprawled on the path a few yards behind his mother. They have to step around his frenzied body, but no other recognition is taken of him, no word is spoken to him or to each other. There is no need to comment. His tantrum is not an unusual sight, especially among boys of his age or a little older. There is nothing to say to him or about him.

In the yard of a house just off the path, two girls, a little older than Azu, stop their play to investigate. Cautiously and silently they venture in Azu's direction. His mother is still in sight, but she disappears suddenly as she turns off the path into her yard without looking back. The girls stand some distance away, observing Azu's gyrations with solemn eyes. Then they turn and go back to their doorway, where they stand, still watching him but saying nothing. Azu is left alone, but it takes several minutes for him to realize that this is the way it is to be. Gradually his fit subsides and he lies sprawled and whimpering on the path.

Finally, he pushes himself to his feet and starts home, still sobbing and wiping his eyes with his fists. As he trudges into the yard he can hear his mother shouting at his sister, telling her not to step over the baby. Another sister is sweeping the earth beneath the floor of the house with a coconut-leaf broom. Glancing up, she calls shrilly to Azu, asking him where he has been. He does not reply, but climbs the two steps to the threshold of the doorway and makes his way to a mat in the corner of the house. There he lies quietly until he falls asleep.

This has been Azu's first painful lesson in growing up. There will be many more unless he soon understands and accepts the Palauan attitude that emotional attachments are cruel and treacherous entanglements, and that it is better not to cultivate them in the first place than to have them disrupted and disclaimed. Usually the lesson has to be repeated in many connections before its general truth sinks in. There will be refusals of pleas to be held, to be carried, to be fed, to be cuddled, and to be amused; and for a time at least there will follow the same violent struggle to maintain control that failed to help Azu. For whatever the means, and regardless of the lapses from the stern code, children must grow away from their parents, not cleave to them. Sooner or later the child must learn not to expect the solicitude, the warm attachment of earlier years, and must accept the fact that he is to live in an emotional vacuum, trading friendship for concrete rewards, neither accepting nor giving lasting affection (Barnett 1960:4–6).

Is culture being transmitted here? Azu is learning that people are not to be trusted, that any emotional commitment is shaky business. He is acquiring an emotional attitude. From Professor Barnett's further description of life in Palau (Barnett 1960) we know that this emotional attitude underlies economic, social, political, even religious behavior among adult Palauans. If this happened only to Azu we would probably regard it as a traumatic event. He might then grow up to be a singularly distrustful adult in a trusting world. He would be a deviant. But virtually all Palauan boys experience this sudden rejection (it happens more gradually for girls)—not always in just this particular way—but in somewhat the same way and at about the same time. This is a culturally patterned way of getting a lesson across to the child. This culturally patterned way of treating the child has a more or less consistent result—an emotional attitude—and this emotional attitude is in turn patterned, and fits into various parts of the Palauan cultural system. What is learned by Azu and transmitted by his mother is at once a pattern of child training (the mother had it and applied it), a dimension of Palauan *world view* (Palauans see the world as a place where people do not become emotionally involved with each other), a modal personality trait (most normal adult Palauans distrust others), and a pattern for behavior in the context of the many subsystems (economic, political, religious, and so forth) governing adult life.

Azu's mother did not simply tell him to stop depending upon her and to refrain from lasting emotional involvements with others. She demonstrated to him in a very dramatic way that this is the way it is in this life (in Palau at least). She probably didn't even completely rationalize what she did. She did not say to herself, "Now it is time for Azu to acquire the characteristic Palauan attitude that emotional attachments are not lasting and the best way to teach him this is for me to refuse to carry him." Barnett says that she "resolved not to submit to his plea." We cannot be sure that she even did this, for not even Homer Barnett, as well as he knows the Palauans, can get into Azu's mother's head. We know that she did not, in fact, submit to his plea. She may well have thought that it was about time for Azu to grow up. Growing up in Palau means in part to stop depending on people, even your very own loving mother. But maybe she was just plain tired, feeling a little extra crabby, so she acted in a characteristically Palauan way *without thinking about it* toward her five-year-old. People can transmit culture without knowing they do so. Probably more culture is transmitted this way than with conscious intent.

Discontinuity between early and later childhood is apparent in the Palauan case. Most cultures are patterned in such a way as to provide discontinuities of experience, but the points of time in the life cycle where these occur, and their intensity, differ widely. Azu experienced few restraints before this time. He did pretty much as he pleased, and lolled about on the laps of parents, kin, and friends. He was seldom if ever punished. There was always someone around to serve as protector, provider, and companion, and someone to carry him, usually mother, wherever he might go. Much of this changed for him after this day at the age of five. To be sure, he is not abandoned, and he is still shielded, guided, and provided for in every physical sense, but he finds himself being told more often than asked what he wants, and his confidence in himself and in his parents has been shaken. He no longer knows how to get what he wants. The discontinuity, the break with the ways things were in his fifth year of life, is in itself a technique of cultural transmission. We will observe discontinuities in the treatment of children and their effects in other cultures.

HOW IS IT DONE IN ULITHI?

The Ulithians, like the Palauans, are Micronesians, but inhabit a much smaller island, in fact a tiny atoll in the vast Pacific, quite out of the way and fairly unchanged when first studied by William Lessa in the late forties (Lessa 1966). The Ulithians educate their children in many of the same ways the Palauans do, but differently enough to merit some special attention.

Like the Palauans, the Ulithians are solicitous and supportive of infants and young children.

The infant is given the breast whenever he cries to be fed or whenever it is considered time to feed him, but sometimes only as a pacifier. He suckles often, especially during the first three to six months of his life, when he may average around eighteen times during the day and night. The great stress placed by Ulithians on food is once more given eloquent expression in nursing practices. Thus, if both the mother and child should happen to be asleep at any time and it seems to someone who is awake that the baby should be fed, both are aroused in order to nurse the baby. . . .

The care of the baby is marked by much solicitude on the part of everyone. One of the ways in which this is manifested is through great attention to cleanliness. The infant is bathed three times a day, and after each bath the baby is rubbed all over with coconut oil and powdered with turmeric. Ordinarily, bathing is done by the mother, who, as she holds the child, rocks him from side to side in the water and sings:

Float on the water
In my arms, my arms
On the little sea,
The big sea,
The rough sea,
The calm sea,
On this sea.
[three sentences omitted]

An infant is never left alone. He seems constantly in someone's arms, being passed from person to person in order to allow everyone a chance to fondle him. There is not much danger that if neglected for a moment he will harm himself (Lessa 1966: 94–96).

Unlike the Palauans, the Ulithians do not create any special discontinuities for the young child. Even weaning is handled with as little disturbance as possible.

Weaning begins at varying ages. It is never attempted before the child is a year old, and usually he is much older than that. Some children are suckled until they are five, or even as much as seven or eight. Weaning takes about four days, one technique being to put the juice of hot pepper around the mother's nipples. Physical punishment is never employed, though scolding may be deemed necessary. Ridicule, a common recourse in training Ulithian children, is also resorted to. The child's reaction to being deprived of the breast often manifests itself in temper tantrums. The mother tries to mollify the child in a comforting embrace and tries to console him by playing with him and offering him such distractions as a tiny coconut or a flower (Lessa 1966:95).

Apparently this technique, and the emotional atmosphere that surrounds it, is not threatening to Ulithian children. We see nothing of the feelings of deprivation and rejection suffered by Azu.

The reactions to weaning are not extreme; children weather the crisis well. In fact, a playful element may be observed. A child may quickly push his face into his mother's breast and then run away to play. When the mother's attention is elsewhere, the child may make a sudden impish lunge at the breast and try to suckle from it. After the mother has scolded the weaning, he may coyly take the breast and fondle it, toy with the nipple, and rub the breast over his face. A man told me that when he was being weaned at the age of about seven, he would alternate sleeping with his father and mother, who occupied separate beds. On those occasions when he would sleep with his father, the latter would tell him to say goodnight to his mother. The boy would go over to where she was lying and playfully run his nose over her breasts. She would take this gesture good-naturedly and encourage him by telling him he was virtuous, strong, and like other boys. Then he would go back to his father, satisfied with his goodness (Lessa 1966:95).

We also see in the above account of Ulithian behavior that transmission of sexual attitudes and the permissiveness concerning eroticization are markedly different than in our own society. This difference, of course, is not confined to relations between young boys and their mothers, but extends through all heterosexual relationships, and throughout the patterning of adult life.

Given the relaxed and supportive character of child rearing in Ulithi, it is small wonder that children behave in a relaxed, playful manner, and apparently grow into adults that value relaxation. This is in sharp contrast with the Palauans, whom Barnett describes as characterized by a residue of latent hostility in social situations, and as subject to chronic anxiety (Barnett 1960:11-15).

> Indeed, play is so haphazard and relaxed that it quickly melts from one thing to another, and from one place to another, with little inhibition. There is much laughter and chatter, and often some vigorous singing. One gains the impression that relaxation, for which the natives have a word they use almost constantly, is one of the major values of Ulithian culture (Lessa 1966:101).

Particularly striking in the transmission of Ulithian culture is the disapproval of unusually independent behavior.

> The attitude of society towards unwarranted independence is generally one of disapproval. Normal independence is admired because it leads to later self-reliance in the growing individual, dependence being scorned if it is so strong that it will unfit him for future responsibilities. Ulithians talk a lot about homesickness and do not view this as improper, unless the longing is really for a spouse or sweetheart, the suspicion here being that it is really sexual outlet that a person wants. Longing of this sort is said to make a person inefficient and perhaps even ill. Homesickness is expected of all children and not deprecated. I was greatly touched once when I asked a friend to tell me what a man was muttering about during a visit to my house. He said he felt sad that I was away from my home and friends and wondered how I could endure it. Ulithians do not like people to feel lonely; sociability is a great virtue for them (Lessa 1966:101).

The degree and kinds of dependence and independence that are inculcated in children are significant variables in any transcultural comparison of cultural transmission. Palauan children are taught not to trust others and grow to adulthood in a society where social relationships tend to be exploitative and, behind a facade of pleasantness, hostile. Palauans are not, however, independent, and tend to be quite dependent for direction upon external authority (Barnett 1960:13, 15-16). The picture is confused in Palau by the greater degree of acculturation (than at Ulithi) and the threatening situations that the Palauans have experienced under first German, then Japanese, and now American domination. In American society, middle-class culture calls for independence, particularly in males, and independence training is stressed from virtually the beginning of childhood. But adolescent and adult Americans are among the most sociable, "joiningest" people in the world. Ulithian children are not taught to be independent, and the individual who is too independent is the object of criticism. Palauan children are taught a kind of independence—to be independent of dependency upon other people's affection—by a sudden withdrawal of support at about five years of age. But which is really the more "independent" adult? Palauans are independent of each other in the sense that they can be cruel and callous to each other and exploitative in social relationships, but they are fearful of independent action and responsibility, are never originators or innovators, and are dependent upon authority for direction. Ulithians are dependent upon each other for social and emotional support, but do not exhibit the fearful dependency upon authority that Palauans do.

This does not mean that there is no predictable relationship between the training of children in dependency or independence and the consequences in adulthood. It does mean that the relationship is not simple and must be culturally contextualized if it is to make sense.

Every society creates some discontinuities in the experience of the individual as he or she grows up. It seems impossible to move from the roles appropriate to childhood to the roles appropriate for adulthood without some discontinuity. Societies differ greatly in the timing of discontinuity, and its abruptness. The first major break for Azu, the Palauan boy, was at five years of age. In Ulithi the major break occurs at the beginning of young adulthood.

> The mild concerns of ordinary life begin to catch up with the individual in the early years of adulthood and he can never again revert to the joyful indifference of his childhood.
>
> Attaining adulthood is marked by a ritual for boys and another for girls, neither of which is featured by genital operations. The same term, *kufar*, is used for each of the initiations. . . .
>
> The boy's *kufar* is much less elaborate and important. It comes about when he begins to show secondary sex characteristics and is marked by three elements: a change to adult clothing, the performance of magic, and the giving of a feast. All this occurs on the same day. . . .
>
> The outstanding consequence of the boy's ritual is that he must now sleep in the men's house and scrupulously avoid his postpubertal sisters. Not only must he not sleep in the same house with them, but he and they may not walk together, share the same food, touch one another's personal baskets, wear one another's leis or other ornaments, make or listen to ribald jokes in one another's presence, watch one another doing a solo dance, or listen to one another sing a love song (Lessa 1966:101–102).

Brother-sister avoidances of this kind are very common in human societies. There is a whole body of literature about them and their implications and consequences. The most important thing for us to note is that this is one of the most obvious ways in which restrictions appropriate to the young adult role in Ulithian society are placed on the individual immediately after the kufar. Transitional rites, or "rites of passage," as they are frequently termed, usually involve new restrictions of this sort. So, for that matter, do the events marking important transitions occurring at other times in the life experience. Azu lost the privilege of being carried and treated like an infant, and immediately became subject to being told what to do more often than demanding and getting what

he wanted. One way of looking at Azu's experience and the Ulithian kufar is to regard them as periods of sharp discontinuity in the management of cultural transmission. Expressed most simply—what cultural transmitters do to and for an individual after the event is quite different in some ways from what they did before. Another way of looking at these events is to regard them as the beginning periods of cultural compression. Expressed most simply—cultural compression occurs when the individual's behavior is restricted by the application of new cultural norms. After the kufar, the Ulithian boy and girl cannot interact with their mature opposite-sex siblings except under very special rules. Azu cannot demand to be carried and is told to do many other things he did not have to do before.

In Ulithi the girl's kufar is much more elaborate. When she notices the first flow of blood she knows she must go immediately to the women's house. As she goes, and upon her arrival, there is a great hullabaloo in the village, with the women shouting again and again, "The menstruating one, Ho-o-o!" After her arrival she takes a bath, changes her skirt, has magic spells recited over her to help her find a mate and enjoy a happy married life, and is instructed about the many *etap* (taboos) she must observe—some for days, others for weeks, and yet others for years. Soon she goes to live in a private hut of her own, built near her parent's house, but she still must go to the menstrual house whenever her discharge begins (Lessa 1966: 102–104).

The discontinuity and compression that Ulithian young people experience after the kufar are not limited to a few taboos. Adolescence and adulthood obviously come rushing together at young Ulithians, and the attitude of the community toward them undergoes a rapid change. The boy and the girl are admitted to a higher status, to be sure, and they are given certain rights and listened to with more respect when they speak. But a good deal is expected of them in return. Young men bear the brunt of the heaviest tasks assigned by the men's council. For their own parents they must help build and repair houses, carry burdens, climb trees for coconuts, fish, make rope, and perform all the other tasks commonly expected of an able-bodied man. Young women are similarly called upon to do much of the harder work of the village and the household. Older people tend to treat these very young adults with a sudden sternness and formality lacking when they were in their childhood. The missteps of young people are carefully watched and readily criticized, so that new adults are constantly aware of the critical gaze of their elders. They may not voice strong objections or opinions, and have no political rights whatsoever, accepting the decisions of the men's and women's councils without murmur. Altogether, they are suddenly cut off from childhood and must undergo a severe transition in their comportment towards others about them. Only in the amatory sphere can they find release from the petty tyranny of their elders (Lessa 1966:104).

WHAT IS IT LIKE TO BE INITIATED IN HANO?

Like the Hopi, with whom they are very close neighbors on the same mesa in Arizona, the Hano Tewa hold an initiation ceremony into the Kachina[1] cult at about nine years of age. In fact, the Tewa and Hopi share the same ceremony. Further examination of this occasion will be instructive. Up until that time Tewa children are treated about the way the Hopi children are. They are kept on a cradleboard at first, weaned late, by middle-class American standards, and on the whole treated very permissively and supportively by mothers, mother's sisters, grandparents, fathers, older siblings, and other people in and about the extended family household, admonished and corrected by the mother's brother, and half scared to death from time to time when they are bad by the Kachinas, or the threat of Kachinas. Of course nowadays the continuity of this early period is somewhat upset because children

must start in the government day school at Polacca when they are about seven, and the teachers' ideas of proper behavior are frequently at variance with those maintained by Tewa parents. Excepting for school, though, Tewa children can be said to experience a consistent, continuous educational environment through the early years.

Things change when the initiation takes place at about age nine. A ceremonial father is selected for the boy, and a ceremonial mother for the girl. These ceremonial parents, as well as the real parents and for that matter everyone in the pueblo, build up the coming event for the child so that he or she is in a tremendous state of excitement. Then the day comes. Edward Dozier reports the initiation experience of one of his informants.

> We were told that the Kachina were beings from another world. There were some boys who said that they were not, but we could never be sure, and most of us believed what we were told. Our own parents and elders tried to make us believe that the Kachina were powerful beings, some good and some bad, and that they knew our innermost thoughts and actions. If they did not know about us through their own great power, then probably our own relatives told the Kachina about us. At any rate every time they visited us they seemed to know what we had thought and how we had acted.
>
> As the time for our initiation came closer we became more and more frightened. The ogre Kachina, the Soyoku, came every year and threatened to carry us away; now we were told that we were going to face these awful creatures and many others. Though we were told not to be afraid, we could not help ourselves. If the Kachina are really supernaturals and powerful beings, we might have offended them by some thought or act and they might punish us. They might even take us with them as the Soyoku threatened to do every year.
>
> Four days before Powamu our ceremonial fathers and our ceremonial mothers took us to Court Kiva. The girls were accompanied by their ceremonial mothers, and we boys by our ceremonial fathers. We stood outside the kiva, and then two whipper Kachina, looking very mean, came out of the kiva. Only a blanket covered the nakedness of the boys; as the Kachina drew near our ceremonial

[1] This word is sometimes spelled Katcina, sometimes Kachina. Voth, used as the source for the description of the Hopi ceremony, spells it Katcina. Dozier, used as the source for the Hano Tewa, spells it Kachina. Either is correct.

fathers removed the blankets. The girls were permitted to keep on their dresses, however. Our ceremonial parents urged us to offer sacred corn meal to the Kachina; as soon as we did they whipped us with their yucca whips. I was hit so hard that I defecated and urinated and I could feel the welts forming on my back and I knew that I was bleeding too. He whipped me four times, but the last time he hit me on the leg instead, and as the whipper started to strike again, my ceremonial father pulled me back and he took the blow himself. "This is a good boy, my old man," he said to the Kachina. "You have hit him enough."

For many days my back hurt and I had to sleep on my side until the wounds healed.

After the whipping a small sacred feather was tied to our hair and we were told not to eat meat or salt. Four days later we went to see the Powamu ceremony in the kiva. As babies, our mothers had taken us to see this event; but as soon as we began to talk, they stopped taking us. I could not remember what had happened on Powamu night and I was afraid that another frightening ordeal awaited us. Those of us who were whipped went with our ceremonial parents. In this dance we saw that the Kachina were really our own fathers, uncles, and brothers. This made me feel strange. I felt somehow that all my relatives were responsible for the whipping we had received. My ceremonial father was kind and gentle during this time and I felt very warm toward him, but I also wondered if he was to blame for our treatment. I felt deceived and ill-treated (Dozier 1967:59–60).

The Hano Tewa children are shocked, angry, chagrined when they find that the supernatural Kachinas they have been scared and disciplined by all their lives up until then, and who during the initiation have whipped them hard, are really men they have known very well in their own community, their clans, their families. To be treated supportively and permissively all of one's life, and then to be whipped publicly (or see others get whipped), would seem quite upsetting by itself. To find out that the awesome Kachinas are men impersonating gods would seem almost too much. But somehow the experience seems to help make good adult Hano Tewa out of little ones.

If the initiate does not accept the spiritual reality of the Kachina, and will not accept his relatives' "cruel" behavior as necessary and good for him (or her), he can stop being a Tewa. But is this a real choice? Not for anyone who is human enough to need friends and family who speak the same language, both literally and figuratively, and whose identity as a Tewa Indian stretches back through all of time. Having then (usually without debate) made the choice of being a Tewa, one is a *good* Tewa. No doubts can be allowed.

There is another factor operating as well. Children who pass through the initiation are no longer outside looking in, they are inside looking out. They are not grown up, and neither they nor anyone else think they are, but they are a lot more grown up than they were before the initiation. Girls take on a more active part in household duties and boys acquire more responsibilities in farming and ranching activities. And it will not be long before the males can take on the role of impersonating the Kachinas and initiating children as they were initiated. The ceremonial whipping, in the context of all the dramatic ceremonies, dancing, and general community uproar, is the symbol of a dramatic shift in status-role. The shift starts with just being "in the know" about what really goes on in the kiva and who the Kachinas are, and continues toward more and more full participation in the secular and sacred life of the community.

Dorothy Eggan sums it up well for the Hopi when she writes:

> Another reorganizing factor . . . was feeling "big." They had shared pain with adults, had learned secrets which forever separated them from the world of children, and now they were included in situations from which they had previously been excluded, as their elders continued to teach intensely what they believed intensely; that for them there was only one alternative—Hopi as against Kahopi.
>
> Consistent repetition is a powerful conditioning agent and, as the youngsters watched each initiation, they relived their own, and by again sharing the experience gradually worked out much of the bitter residue from their own memories of it, while also rationalizing and weaving group emo-

tions ever stronger into their own emotional core—"It takes a while to see how wise the old people really are." An initiated boy, in participating in the kachina dances, learned to identify again with the kachinas whom he now impersonated. To put on a mask is to "become a kachina" and cooperate actively in bringing about the major goals of Hopi life. And a girl came to know more fully the importance of her clan in its supportive role. These experiences were even more sharply conditioned and directed toward adult life in the adult initiation ceremonies, of which we have as yet only fragmentary knowledge. Of this one man said to me: "I will not discuss this thing with you only to say that no one can forget it. It is the most wonderful thing any man can have to remember. You know then that you are Hopi. It is the one thing Whites cannot have, cannot take away from us. It is our way of life given to us when the world began" (Eggan 1956:364—65).

In many ways the preadolescent and adolescent period that we have been discussing, using the Ulithian kufar and the Hano Tewa initiation ceremonies as representative cases, is the most important of all in cultural transmission. There is a considerable literature on this period, including most notably the classic treatment given by Van Gennep (1960, first published in 1909) and the recent studies by Frank Young (1965), Yehudi Cohen (1964), Gary Schwartz and Don Merten (1968), and Whiting, Kluckhohn, and Albert (1958). Judith Brown provides a cross-cultural study of initiation rights for females (Brown 1963). But these studies do not emphasize the educational aspects of the initiation rites or rites of passage that they analyze.

One of the few studies that does is the remarkable essay by C. W. M. Hart . . . based upon a single case, the Tiwi of North Australia, but with implications for many other cases. Hart contrasts the attitude of cultural transmitters toward young children among the Tiwi to the rigorous demands of the initiation period.

> The arrival of the strangers to drag the yelling boy out of his mother's arms is just the spectacular beginning of a long period during which the separation of the boy from everything that has gone be-

fore is emphasized in every possible way at every minute of the day and night. So far his life has been easy; now it is hard. Up to now he has never necessarily experienced any great pain, but in the initiation period in many tribes pain, sometimes horrible, intense pain, is an obligatory feature. The boy of twelve or thirteen, used to noisy, boisterous, irresponsible play, is expected and required to sit still for hours and days at a time saying nothing whatever but concentrating upon and endeavoring to understand long intricate instructions and "lectures" given him by his hostile and forbidding preceptors. [sentence omitted] Life has suddenly become real and earnest and the initiate is required literally to "put away the things of a child" even the demeanor. The number of tabus and unnatural behaviors enjoined upon the initiate is endless. He mustn't speak unless he is spoken to; he must eat only certain foods, and often only in certain ways, at fixed times, and in certain fixed positions. All contact with females, even speech with them is rigidly forbidden, and this includes mother and sisters (1963:415).

Hart goes on to state that the novices are taught origin myths, the meaning of the sacred ceremonials, in short, theology, ". . . which in primitive society is inextricably mixed up with astronomy, geology, geography, biology (the mysteries of birth and death), philosophy, art, and music—in short the whole cultural heritage of the tribe"; and that the purpose of this teaching is not to make better economic men of the novices, but rather ". . . better citizens, better carriers of the culture through the generations . . ." (Hart 1963:415). In this view Hart agrees (as he points out himself) with George Pettit, who did a thorough study of educational practices among North American Indians, and who writes that the initiation proceedings were ". . . a constant challenge to the elders to review, analyze, dramatize, and defend their cultural heritage" (Pettit 1946:182).

Pettit's words also bring into focus another feature of the initiation rituals implicit in the description of these events for the Ulithians, Hano Tewa, and the Tiwi, which seems very significant. In all these cases dramatization is used as an educational technique. In fact a ceremony of any kind is a dramatization, sometimes indirect and metaphoric, sometimes very direct, of the interplay of crucial forces and events in the life of the community. In the initiation ceremonies dramatization forces the seriousness of growing up into the youngster's mind and mobilizes his emotions around the lessons to be learned and the change in identity to be secured. The role of dramatization in cultural transmission may be difficult for American readers to appreciate, because the pragmatization of American schools and American life in general has gone so far.

These points emphasize the view of initiation proceedings taken in this chapter—that they are dramatic signals for new beginnings and, at various times before and throughout adolescence in many societies, the intensification of discontinuity and compression in cultural transmission. Discontinuity in the management of the youngsters' learning—from supportive and easy to rigorous and harsh; compression in the closing in of culturally patterned demand and restriction as the new status-roles attained by successfully passing through the initiation period are activated. Of course this compression of cultural demand around the individual also opens new channels of development and experience to him. As humans mature they give up the freedom of childhood for the rewards to be gained by observing the rules of the cultural game. The initiation ceremonies are dramatic signals to everyone that the game has begun in earnest.

WHAT HAPPENS IN GOPALPUR?

In the village of Gopalpur, in South India, described by Alan Beals, social, not physical, mastery is stressed.

> Long before it has begun to walk, the child in Gopalpur has begun to develop a concern about relationships with others. The period of infantile dependency is extended. The child is not encouraged to develop muscular skills, but is carried from place to place on the hip of mother or sister. The child is rarely alone. It is constantly exposed to other people, and learning to talk, to communicate with others, is given priority over anything else that might be learned. When the child does learn to walk, adults begin to treat it differently. Shooed out of the house, its training is largely taken over by the play group. In the streets there are few toys, few things to be manipulated. The play of the child must be social play and the manipulation of others must be accomplished through language and through such nonphysical techniques as crying and withdrawal. In the play group, the child creates a family and the family engages in the production of imaginary food or in the exchange of real food carried in shirt pockets (1962:19).

Children in Gopalpur imitate adults, both in the activities of play and in the attempts to control each other.

> Sidda, four years old, is playing in the front of his house with his cousin, Bugga, aged five. Sidda is sitting on the ground holding a stone and pounding. Bugga is piling the sand up like rice for the pounding. Bugga says, "Sidda, give me the stone, I want to pound." Sidda puts the stone on the ground, "Come and get it." Bugga says, "Don't come with me, I am going to the godhouse to play." Sidda offers, "I will give you the stone." He gives the stone to Bugga, who orders him, "Go into the house and bring some water." Sidda goes and brings water in a brass bowl. Bugga takes it and pours it on the heap of sand. He mixes the water with the sand, using both hands. Then, "Sidda, take the bowl inside." Sidda takes the bowl and returns with his mouth full of peanuts. He puts his hand into his shirt pocket, finds more peanuts and puts them in his mouth. Bugga sees the peanuts and asks, "Where did you get those?" "I got them inside the house." "Where are they?" "In the winnowing basket." Bugga gets up and goes inside the house returning with a bulging shirt pocket. Both sit down near the pile of sand. Bugga says to Sidda "Don't tell mother." "No, I won't." Sidda eats all of his peanuts and moves toward Bugga holding his hands out. Bugga wants to know, "Did you finish yours?" "I just brought a little, you brought a lot." Bugga refuses to give up any peanuts and Sidda begins to cry. Bugga pats him on the back saying, "I will give you peanuts later on." They get up and go into the house. Because they are considered to be brothers, Sidda and Bugga do not fight. When he is wronged, the older Bugga threatens to desert

Sidda. When the situation is reversed, the younger Sidda breaks into tears (Beals 1962:16).

In their play, Bugga and Sidda are faithful to the patterns of adult control over children, as they have both observed them and experienced them. Beals describes children going to their houses when their shirt pockets are empty of the "currency of interaction" (grain, bits of bread, peanuts).

This is the moment of entrapment, the only time during the day when the mother is able to exercise control over her child. This is the time for bargaining, for threatening. The mother scowls at her child, "You must have worked hard to be so hungry." The mother serves food and says, "Eat this. After you have eaten it, you must sit here and rock your little sister." The child eats and says, "I am going outside to play. I will not rock my sister." The child finishes its food and runs out of the house. Later, the child's aunt sees it and asks it to run to the store and buy some cooking oil. When it returns, the aunt says, "If you continue to obey me like this, I will give you something good to eat." When the mother catches the child again, she asks, "Where have you been?" Learning what occurred, she says, "If you bought cooking oil, that is fine; now come play with your sister." The child says, "First give me something to eat, and I will play with my sister." The mother scolds, "You will die of eating, sometimes you are willing to work, sometimes you are not willing to work; may you eat dirt." She gives it food and the child plays with its sister (1962:19).

This is the way the child in Gopalpur learns to control the unreliable world of other people. Children soon learn that they are dependent upon others for the major securities and satisfactions of life. The one with a large number of friends and supporters is secure, and they can be won and controlled, the individual comes to feel, through the use of food, but also by crying, begging, and working.

AND AMONG THE ESKIMO?

Eskimo children are treated supportively and permissively. When a baby cries it is picked up,

played with, or nursed. There are a variety of baby tenders about, and after the first two or three months of life older siblings and the mother's unmarried sisters and cousins take a hand in caring for it. There is no set sleeping or eating schedule and weaning is a gradual process that may not be completed until the third or fourth year.

How is it then that, as white visitors to Eskimo villages often remark, the Eskimo have managed to raise their children so well? Observers speak warmly of their good humor, liveliness, resourcefulness, and well-behaved manner. They appear to exemplify qualities that Western parents would like to see in their own children (Chance 1966:22). American folk belief would lead one to surmise that children who are treated so permissively would be "spoiled." Norman Chance describes the situation for the Alaskan Eskimo.

Certainly, the warmth and affection given infants by parents, siblings, and other relatives provide them with a deep feeling of well-being and security. Young children also feel important because they learn early that they are expected to be useful, working members of the family. This attitude is not instilled by imposing tedious chores, but rather by including children in the round of daily activities, which enhances the feeling of family participation and cohesion. To put it another way, parents rarely deny children their company or exclude them from the adult world.

This pattern reflects the parents' views of child rearing. Adults feel that they have more experience in living and it is their responsibility to share this experience with the children, "to tell them how to live." Children have to be told repeatedly because they tend to forget. Misbehavior is due to a child's forgetfulness, or to improper teaching in the first place. There is rarely any thought that the child is basically nasty, willful, or sinful. Where Anglo-Americans applaud a child for his good behavior, the Eskimo praise him for remembering. . . .

Regardless of the degree of Westernization, more emphasis is placed on equality than on superordination-subordination in parent-child relations. A five-year-old obeys, not because he fears punishment or loss of love, but because he identifies with his parents and respects their judgment. Thus he finds little to resist or rebel against in his dealing with adults. We will find rebellion more common in adolescents, but it is not necessarily a revolt against parental control.

By the time a child reaches the age of four or five, his parents' initial demonstrativeness has become tempered with an increased interest in his activities and accomplishments. They watch his play with obvious pleasure, and respond warmly to his conversation, make jokes with him and discipline him.

Though a child is given considerable autonomy and his whims and wishes treated with respect, he is nonetheless taught to obey all adults. To an outsider unfamiliar with parent-child relations, the tone of the Eskimo commands and admonitions sometimes sounds harsh and angry, yet in few instances does a child respond as if he had been addressed hostilely. . . .

After the age of five a child is less restricted in his activities in and around the village, although theoretically he is not allowed on the beach or ice without an adult. During the dark winter season, he remains indoors or stays close to the house to prevent him from getting lost and to protect him from polar bears which might come into the village. In summer, though, children play at all hours of the day or "night" or as long as their parents are up. . . .

Although not burdened with responsibility, both boys and girls are expected to take an active role in family chores. In the early years responsibilities are shared, depending on who is available. Regardless of sex, it is important for a child to know how to perform a wide variety of tasks and give help when needed. Both sexes collect and chop wood, get water, help carry meat and other supplies, oversee younger siblings, run errands for adults, feed the dogs, and burn trash.

As a child becomes older, more specific responsibilities are allocated to him, according to his sex. Boys as young as seven may be given an opportunity to shoot a .22 rifle, and at least a few boys in every village have killed their first caribou by the time they are ten. A youngster learns techniques of butchering while on hunting trips with older siblings and adults, although he is seldom proficient until he is in his mid-teens. In the past girls learned butchering at an early age, since this knowledge was essential to attracting a good husband. Today, with the availability of large quantities of Western

foods, this skill may not be acquired until a girl is married, and not always then.

Although there is a recognized division of labor by sex, it is far from rigid at any age level. Boys, and even men, occasionally sweep the house and cook. Girls and their mothers go on fishing or bird-hunting trips. Members of each sex can usually assume the responsibilities of the other when the need arises, albeit in an auxiliary capacity (1966:22–26).

Apparently the combination that works so well with Eskimo children is support—participation—admonition—support. These children learn to see adults as rewarding and nonthreatening. Children are also not excluded, as they so often are in America, from the affairs of adult life. They do not understand everything they see, but virtually nothing is hidden from them. They are encouraged to assume responsibility appropriate to their age quite early in life. Children are participants in the flow of life. They learn by observing and doing. But Eskimo adults do not leave desired learning up to chance. They admonish, direct, remonstrate, but without hostility.

The Eskimo live with a desperately intemperate climate in what many white men have described as the part of the world that is the most inimical to human life. Perhaps Eskimo children are raised the way they are because a secure, good-humored, resourceful person is the only kind that can survive for long in this environment.

IN SENSURON?

The people of Sensuron live in a very different physical and cultural environment than do the Eskimo. The atmosphere of this Dusun village in Borneo (not the Malaysian state of Sabah) is communicated in these passages from Thomas Williams' case study.

Sensuron is astir an hour before the dawn of most mornings. It is usually too damp and cold to sleep. Fires are built up and the morning meal cooked while members of the household cluster about the house firepit seeking warmth. After eating, containers and utensils are rinsed off with water to "keep the worms off" and replaced in racks on the side of the house porch. Older children are sent to the river to carry water home in bamboo containers, while their mother spends her time gathering together equipment for the day's work, including some cold rice wrapped in leaves for a midday snack. The men and adolescent males go into the yard to sit in the first warmth of the sun and talk with male neighbors. The early morning exchange of plans, news, and recounting of the events of yesterday is considered a "proper way" to begin the day. While the men cluster in the yard center, with old shirts or cloths draped about bare shoulders to ward off the chill, women gather in front of one house or another, also trading news, gossip, and work plans. Many women comb each other's hair, after carefully picking out the lice. It is not unusual to see four or more women sitting in a row down the steps of a house ladder talking, while combing and delousing hair. Babies are nursed while mothers talk and small children run about the clusters of adults, generally being ignored until screams of pain or anger cause a sharp retort of *kAdA!* (do not!) from a parent. Women drape spare skirts about their bare shoulders to ward off the morning chill. About two hours after dawn these groups break up as the members go off to the work of the day. The work tasks of each day are those to be done under the annual cycle of subsistence labor. . . .

Vocal music is a common feature of village life; mothers and grandmothers sing a great variety of lullabies and "growth songs" to babies, children sing a wide range of traditional and nonsense songs, while adults sing at work in the fields and gardens during leisure and social occasions and at times of ritual. Drinking songs and wedding songs take elaborate forms, often in the nature of song "debates" with sides chosen and a winner declared by a host or guest of honor on the basis of "beauty" of tone, humor, and general "one-upmanship" in invention of new verse forms. Most group singing is done in harmony. Adolescents, especially girls, spend much of their solitary leisure time singing traditional songs of love and loneliness. Traditional verse forms in ritual, and extensive everyday use of riddles, folktales, and proverbs comprise a substantial body of oral literature. Many persons know much ritual verse, and most can recite dozens of stylized folktales, riddles, and proverbs.

Village headmen, certain older males, and ritual specialists of both sexes are practiced speechmakers. A skill of "speaking beautifully" is much admired and imitated. The style used involves narration, with exhortation, and is emphasized through voice tone and many hand and body gestures and postures. Political debates, court hearings, and personal arguments often become episodes of dramatic representation for onlookers, with a speaker's phrase listened to for its emotional expressive content and undertones of ridicule, tragedy, comedy, and farce at the expense of others involved. The verse forms of major rituals take on dimensions of drama as the specialist delivers the lines with skillful impersonations of voices and mannerisms of disease givers, souls of the dead, and creator beings.

By late afternoon of a leisure day people in the houses begin to drift to the yards, where they again sit and talk. Fires are built to ward off the chill of winds rising off the mountains, and men and women circle the blaze, throwing bits of wood and bamboo into the fire as they talk. This time is termed *mEg-Amut,* after the designation for exchange of small talk between household members. As many as 20 fires can be seen burning in yards through Sensuron at evening on most leisure days and on many evenings after work periods. Men sit and talk until after dark, when they go into houses to take their evening meal. Women leave about an hour before dark to prepare the meal. Smaller children usually eat before the adults. After the evening meal, for an hour or more, the family clusters about the house firepit, talking, with adults often engaged in small tasks of tool repair or manufacture. By 8 or 9 P.M. most families are asleep; the time of retiring is earlier when the work days are longer, later on rest days (1965:78–79).

Children in Sensuron are, like Eskimo children, always present, always observers. How different this way of life is from that experienced by American children! Gossip, speech-making, folktale telling, grooming, working, and playing are all there, all a part of the stream of life flowing around one and with which each member of the community moves. Under these circumstances much of the culture is transmitted by a kind of osmosis. It would be difficult for a child *not* to learn his culture.

The children of Sensuron do not necessarily grow up into good-humored, secure, trusting, "happy" adults. There are several factors that apparently interact in their growing up to make this unlikely. In the most simple sense, these children do not grow up to be like Eskimo adults because their parents (and other cultural transmitters) are not Eskimo; Dusun cultural transmitters (anybody in the community that the child hears and sees) act like Dusun. But cultural transmitters display certain attitudes and do certain things to children as well as provide them with models. In Sensuron, children are judged to be nonpersons. They are not even provided with personal names until their fifth year. They are also considered to be ". . . naturally noisy, inclined to illness, capable of theft, incurable wanderers, violent, quarrelsome, temperamental, destructive of property, wasteful, easily offended, quick to forget" (Williams 1965:87). They are threatened by parents with being eaten alive, carried off, damaged by disease-givers. Here are two lullabies sung to babies in Sensuron (and heard constantly by older children):

> Sleep, Sleep, baby,
> There comes the rAgEn (soul of the dead)
> He carries a big stick,
> He carried a big knife,
> Sleep, Sleep, baby,
> He comes to beat you!
> or, as in this verse,
> Bounce, Bounce, baby
> There is a hawk,
> Flying, looking for prey!
> There is the hawk, looking for his prey!
> He searches for something to snatch up in his
>   claws,
> Come here, hawk, and snatch up this baby!
> (Williams 1965:88).

None of the things that the adults of Sensuron do to, with, or around their children is to be judged "bad." Their culture is different from Eskimo culture, and a different kind of individual functions effectively in it. We may for some reason need to make value judgments about a culture, the character of the people who live by it, or the way they raise children—but not for the purpose of understanding it better. It is particularly hard to refrain from making value judgments when the behavior in question occurs in an area of life in our own culture about which there are contradictory rules and considerable anxiety. Take, for instance, the transmission of sexual behavior in the village of Sensuron.

In Sensuron people usually deal with their sex drives through ideally denying their existence, while often behaving in ways designed to sidestep social and cultural barriers to personal satisfaction. At the ideal level of belief the view is expressed that "men are not like dogs, chasing any bitch in heat," or "sex relations are unclean." Some of the sexuality of Dusun life has been noted earlier. There is a high content of lewd and bawdy behavior in the play of children and adolescents, and in the behavior of adults. For example, the eight-year-old girl in the house across from ours was angrily ordered by her mother to come into the house to help in rice husking. The girl turned to her mother and gave her a slow, undulating thrust of her hips in a sexual sign. More than 12 salacious gestures are known and used regularly by children and adults of both sexes, and there are some 20 equivalents of "four-letter" English terms specifically denoting the sexual anatomy and its possible uses. Late one afternoon 4 girls between 8 and 15 years, and 2 young boys of 4 and 5 years were chasing about our house steps for a half hour, grabbing at each other's genitals, and screaming, *uarE tAle!* which roughly translated means, "there is your mother's vulva!" Adult onlookers were greatly amused at the group and became convulsed with laughter when the four-year-old boy improvised the answer, "my mother has no vulva!" Thus, sexual behavior is supposed to be unclean and disgusting, while in reality it is a source of amusement and constant attention . . . .

Children learn details of sexual behavior early, and sex play is a part of the behavior of four-to-six-year olds, usually in houses or rice stores while parents are away at work. Older children engage in sexual activities in groups and pairs, often at a location outside the village, often in an abandoned field storehouse, or in a temporary shelter in a remote garden (Williams 1965:82–83).

We can, however, make the tentative generalization that in cultures where there is a marked discrepancy between ideal and real, between the "theory" of culture and actual behavior, this conflict will be transmitted and that conflicts of this kind are probably not conducive to trust, confidence in self and in others, or even something we might call "happiness." We are like the people of Sensuron, though probably the conflicts between real and ideal run much deeper and are more damaging in our culture. In any event, the transmission of culture is complicated by discrepancies and conflicts, for both the pattern of idealizations and the patterns of actual behavior must be transmitted, as well as the ways for rationalizing the discrepancy between them.

How Goes It in Guadalcanal?

Many of the comments that have been made about child rearing and the transmission of culture in other communities can be applied to the situation in Guadalcanal, one of the Solomon Islands near New Guinea. Babies are held, fondled, fed, never isolated, and generally given very supportive treatment. Weaning and toilet training both take place without much fuss, and fairly late by American standards. Walking is regarded as a natural accomplishment that will be mastered in time, swimming seems to come as easily. Education is also different in some ways in Guadalcanal. There is no sharp discontinuity at the beginning of middle childhood as in Palau, nor is there any sharp break at puberty as in Ulithi, or at prepuberty as among the Hano Tewa or Hopi. The special character of cultural transmission in Guadalcanal is given by Ian Hogbin:

> Two virtues, generosity and respect for property, are inculcated from the eighteenth month onward—that is to say, from the age when the child can walk about and eat bananas and other things regarded as delicacies. At this stage no explanations are given, and the parents merely insist that food must be shared with any playmate who happens to be present and that goods belonging to

other villagers must be left undisturbed. A toddler presented with a piece of fruit is told to give half to "So-and-so," and should the order be resisted, the adult ignores all protests and breaks a piece off to hand to the child's companion. Similarly, although sometimes callers are cautioned to put their baskets on a shelf out of reach, any meddling brings forth the rebuke, "That belongs to your uncle. Put it down." Disobedience is followed by snatching away the item in question from the child and returning it to the owner.

> In time, when the child has passed into its fourth or fifth year, it is acknowledged to have at last attained the understanding to be able to take in what the adults say. Therefore, adults now accompany demands with reasoned instruction. One day when I was paying a call on a neighbor, Mwane-Anuta, I heard him warn his second son Mbule, who probably had not reached the age of five, to stop being so greedy. "I saw your mother give you those nuts," Mwane-Anuta reiterated. "Don't pretend she didn't. Running behind the house so the Penggoa wouldn't know! That is bad, very bad. Now then, show me, how many? Five left. Very well, offer three to Penggoa immediately." He then went on to tell me how important it was for children to learn to think of others so that in later life they would win the respect of their fellows.

> On another occasion during a meal I found Mwane-Anuta and his wife teaching their three sons how to eat properly. "Now Mbule," said his mother, "you face the rest of us so that we can all see you aren't taking too much. And you, Konana, run outside and ask Misika from next door to join you. His mother's not home yet, and I expect he's hungry. Your belly's not the only one, my boy." "Yes," Mwane-Anuta added. "Give a thought to those you run about with, and they'll give a thought to you." At this point the mother called over the eldest lad, Kure, and placed the basket of yams for me in his hands. "There, you carry that over to our guest and say that it is good to have him with us this evening," she whispered to him. The gesture was characteristic. I noted that always when meals were served to visitors the children acted as waiters. Why was this, I wanted to know. "Teaching, teaching," Mwane-Anuta replied. "This is how we train our young to behave" (1964:33).

It appears that in Guadalcanal direct verbal instruction is stressed as a technique of cultural transmission. Hogbin goes on to describe the constant stream of verbal admonition that is directed at the child by responsible adults in almost every situation. And again and again the prime values, generosity and respect for property, are reinforced by these admonitions.

The amount of direct verbal reinforcement of basic values, and even the amount of direct verbal instruction in less crucial matters, varies greatly from culture to culture. The people of Guadalcanal, like the Hopi, keep telling their children and young people how to behave and when they are behaving badly. In American middle-class culture there is also great emphasis on telling children what they should do, explaining how to do it, and the reasons for doing it, though we are probably less consistent in what we tell them than are the parents of Guadalcanal. Perhaps also in our culture we tend to substitute words for experience more than do the people of Guadalcanal, for the total range of experience relevant to growing up appropriately is more directly observable and available to their children than it is to ours.

Girls go to the gardens regularly with their mother from about the age of eight. They cannot yet wield the heavy digging stick or bush knife, but they assist in collecting the rubbish before planting begins, in piling up the earth, and weeding. Boys start accompanying their father some two or three years later, when they help with the clearing, fetch lianas to tie up the saplings that form the fence, and cut up the seed yams. The men may also allocate plots to their sons and speak of the growing yams as their own harvest. The services of a youngster are of economic value from the time that he is pubescent, but he is not expected to take gardening really seriously until after he returns from the plantation and is thinking of marriage. By then he is conscious of his rights and privileges as a member of his clan and knows where the clan blocks of land are located. As a rule, he can also explain a little about the varieties of yams and taro and the types of soil best suited to earth.

At about eight a boy begins to go along with his father or uncles when the men set out in the evening with their lines to catch fish from the shore or on the reef. They make a small rod for him, show him how to bait his hook, and tell him about the different species of fish—where they are to be found, which are good to eat, which are poisonous. At the age of ten the boy makes an occasional fishing excursion in a canoe. To start with, he sits in the center of the canoe and watches, perhaps baiting the hooks and removing the catch; but soon he takes part with the rest. In less than a year he is a useful crew member and expert in steering and generally handling the craft. At the same time, I have never seen youths under the age of sixteen out at sea by themselves. Often they are eager to go before this, but the elders are unwilling to give permission lest they endanger themselves or the canoe (Hogbin 1964:39).

The children of Guadalcanal learn by doing as well as learn by hearing. They also learn by imitating adult models, as children do in every human group around the world.

Children also play at housekeeping. Sometimes they take along their juniors, who, however, do not remain interested for long. They put up a framework of saplings and tie on coconut-leaf mats, which they plait themselves in a rough-and-ready sort of way. Occasionally, they beg some raw food and prepare it; or they catch birds, bats, and rats with bows and arrows. Many times, too, I have seen them hold weddings, including all the formality of the handing-over of bride price. Various items serve instead of the valuables that the grownups use—tiny pebbles instead of dog's and porpoise teeth, the long flowers of a nut tree for strings of shell discs, and rats or lizards for pigs. When first the youngsters pretend to keep house they make no sexual distinction in the allocation of the tasks. Boys and girls together erect the shelters, plait the mats, cook the food, and fetch the water. But within a year or so, although they continue to play in company, the members of each group restrict themselves to the work appropriate to their sex. The boys leave the cooking and water carrying to the girls, who, in turn, refuse to help with the building (Hogbin 1964:37–38).

Children seem to acquire the culture of their community best when there is consistent reinforcement of the same norms of action and thinking through many different channels of activity and interaction. If a child is told, sees demonstrated, casually observes, imitates, experiments and is corrected, acts appropriately and is rewarded, corrected, and (as in the Tewa-Hopi initiation) is given an extra boost in learning by dramatized announcements of status-role change, all within a consistent framework of belief and value, he or she cannot help but learn, and learn what adult cultural transmitters want him or her to learn.

HOW DO THEY LISTEN IN DEMIRCILER?

In Demirciler, an Anatolian village in the arid central plateau of Turkey, a young boy, Mahmud, learns by being allowed in the room when the adult men meet at the Muhtar's (the village headman) home evenings to discuss current affairs.

Each day, after having finished the evening meal, the old Muhtar's wife would put some small earthenware dishes or copper trays filled with nuts or chick-peas about the room, sometimes on small stands or sometimes on the floor, and the old man would build a warm fire in the fireplace. Soon after dark the men would begin to arrive by ones or twos and take their accustomed places in the men's room. This was the largest single room in the village and doubled as a guest house for visitors who came at nightfall and needed some place to sleep before going on their way the next day. It had been a long time since the room had been used for this purpose, however, because the nearby growing city had hotels, and most of the modern travelers stayed there. However, the room still served as a clearing house for all village business, as well as a place for the men to pass the cold winter evenings in warm comfort.

The room was perhaps 30 by 15 feet in size, and along one side a shelf nearly 15 inches above the floor extended about 2 feet from the wall and covered the full 30 feet of the room's length. The old Muhtar sat near the center of the shelf, waiting for his guests to arrive. As the men came in, the oldest in the village would seat themselves in order of age on this raised projection, while the younger ones would sit cross-legged on the floor. No women were ever allowed to come into this room when the men were there. The Muhtar's wife had prepared everything ahead of time, and when additional things were occasionally needed during the evening, one of the boys would be sent out to fetch it. Opposite the long bench was a fireplace, slightly larger than those in the kitchen of the other village homes, in which a fire burned brightly spreading heat throughout the room. The single electric bulb lighted the space dimly and so the shadows caused by the firelight were not prevented from dancing about the walls.

Mahmud would have been happier if the electric bulb had not been there at all, the way it used to be when he had been a very small boy. Electricity had been introduced to the village only a year ago, and he remembered the days when only the glow of the fire lighted these meetings.

As the gatherings grew in size, Mahmud heard many small groups of men talking idly about all sorts of personal problems, but when nearly all of the villagers had arrived, they began to quiet down.

The Hoca posed the first question, "Muhtar Bey, when will next year's money for the mosque be taken up?"

"Hocam, the amount has not been set yet," was the Muhtar's reply.

"All right, let's do it now," the Hoca persisted.

"Let's do it now," the Muhtar agreed.

And Mahmud listened as the Hoca told about the things the mosque would need during the coming year. Then several of the older men told how they had given so much the year before that it had been hard on their families, and finally, the Muhtar talked interminably about the duty of each Moslem to support the Faith and ended by asking the head of each family for just a little more than he knew they could pay.

Following this request there were a series of discussions between the Muhtar and each family head, haggling over what the members of his family could afford to give. Finally, however, agreement was reached with each man, and the Hoca knew how much he could count on for the coming year. The Muhtar would see that the money was collected and turned over to the Hoca.

The business of the evening being out of the way, Mahmud became more interested, as he knew that what he liked most was to come now. He had learned that he was too young to speak at the meetings, because he had been taken out several times the year before by one of the older boys and told that he could not stay with the men unless he could be quiet, so he waited in silence for what would happen next. After a slight pause one of the braver of the teen-aged boys called to an old man.

"*Dedem,* tell us some stories about the olden times."

"Shall I tell about the wars?" the old man nearest the Muhtar asked.

"Yes, about the great war with the Russians," the youth answered.

"Well, I was but a boy then, but my father went with the army of the Sultan that summer, and he told me this story" (Pierce 1964:20–21).

Is there any situation in the culture of the United States where a similar situation exists? When America was more rural than it is now, and commercial entertainments were not readily available for most people, young people learned about adult roles and problems, learned to think like adults and anticipated their own adulthood in somewhat the same way the Mahmud did. Now it is an open question whether young people would want to listen to their elders even if there was nothing else to do. Possibly this is partly because much of what one's elders "know" in our society is not true. The verities change with each generation.

At the end of the "business" session at the Muhtar's home an old man tells a story. The story is offered as entertainment, even though it has been heard countless times before. Young listeners learn from stories as well as from the deliberations of the older men as they decide what to do about somebody's adolescent son who is eyeing the girls too much, or what to do about building a new road. Storytelling has been and still is a way of transmitting information to young people in many cultures without their knowing they are being taught. Any story has either a metaphoric application to real life, provides models for behavior, or has both features. The metaphor or the model may or may not be translated into a moral. The elders in Demirciler do not, it appears, make the moral of the story explicit. In contrast, the Menomini Indians of Wisconsin always required a youngster to extract the moral in a story for himself. "You should never ask for anything to happen unless you mean it." "He who brags bites his own tail." A grandparent would tell the same story every night until the children could state the moral to the elder's satisfaction (Spindler 1971). People in different cultures vary greatly in how much they make of the moral, but stories and mythtellings are used in virtually all cultures to transmit information, values, and attitudes.

WHAT DOES CULTURAL TRANSMISSION DO FOR THE SYSTEM?

So far we have considered cultural transmission in cases where no major interventions from the outside have occurred, or, if they have occurred, we have chosen to ignore them for purposes of description and analysis. There are, however, virtually no cultural systems left in the world that have not experienced massive input from the outside, particularly from the West. This is the age of transformation. Nearly all tribal societies and peasant villages are being affected profoundly by modernization. One of the most important aspects of modernization is the development of schools that will, hopefully, prepare young people to take their places in a very different kind of world than the one their parents grew up in. This implies a kind of discontinuity that is of a different order than the kind we have been discussing.

Discontinuity in cultural transmission among the Dusun, Hopi, Tewa, and Tiwi is a process that produces cultural continuity in the system as a whole. The abrupt and dramatized changes in roles during adolescence, the sudden compression of cultural requirements, and all the techniques used by preceptors, who are nearly always adults from within the cultural system, educate an individual to be committed to the system. The initiation itself encapsulates and dramatizes symbols and meanings that are at the core of the cultural system so that the important things the initiate has learned up to that point, by observation, participation, or instruction, are reinforced. The discontinuity is in the way the initiate is treated during the initiation and the different behaviors expected of him (or her) afterward. The culture is maintained, its credibility validated. As the Hopi man said to Dorothy Eggan, "I will not discuss this thing with you only to say that no one can forget it. It is the most wonderful thing any man can have to remember. You know then that you are Hopi [after the initiation]. It is the one thing Whites cannot have, cannot take from us. It is our way of life given to us when the world began. . . ." This Hopi individual has been *recruited* as a Hopi.

In all established cultural systems where radical interventions from outside have not occurred, the major functions of education are *recruitment* and *maintenance*. The educational processes we have described for all of the cultures in this chapter have functioned in this manner. Recruitment occurs in two senses: recruitment to membership in the cultural system in general, so that one becomes a Hopi or a Tiwi; and recruitment to specific roles and statuses, to specific castes, or to certain classes. We may even, by stretching the point a little, say that young humans are recruited to be male or female, on the terms with which a given society defines being male or female. This becomes clear in cultures such as our own, where sex roles are becoming blurred so much that many young people grow up without a clear orientation toward either role. The educational system, whether we are talking about societies where there are no schools in the formal sense but where a great deal of education takes place, or about societies where there are many specialized formal schools, is organized to effect recruitment. The educational system is also organized so that the structure of the cultural system will be maintained. This is done by inculcating the specific values, attitudes, and beliefs that make this structure credible and the skills and competencies that make it work. People must believe in their system. If there is a caste or class structure they must believe that such a structure is good, or if not good, at least inevitable. They must also have the skills—vocational and social—that make it possible for goods and services to be exchanged that are necessary for community life to go on. Recruitment and maintenance intergrade, as you can see from the above discussion. The former refers to the process of getting people into the system and into specific roles; the latter refers to the process of keeping the system and role functioning.

MODERNIZING CULTURES: WHAT IS THE PURPOSE OF EDUCATION?

In this transforming world, however, educational systems are often charged with responsibility for bringing about change in the culture. They become, or are intended to become, agents of modernization. They become intentional agents of cultural discontinuity, a kind of discontinuity that does not reinforce the traditional values or recruit youngsters into the existing system. The new schools, with their curricula and the concepts behind them, are future oriented. They recruit students into a system that does not yet exist, or is just emerging. They inevitably create conflicts between generations.

Among the Sisala of Northern Ghana, a modernizing African society, for example, there have been profound changes in the principles underlying the father-son relationship. As one man put it:

> This strict obedience, this is mostly on the part of illiterates. With educated people, if you tell your son something, he will have to speak his mind. If you find that the boy is right, you change your mind. With an illiterate, he just tells his son to do something. . . . In the old days, civilization was not so much. We obeyed our fathers whether right or wrong. If you didn't, they would beat you. We respected our fathers with fear. Now we have to talk with our sons when they challenge us (Grindal 1972:80).

Not all of the Sisala have as tolerant and favorable a view of the changes wrought by education, however:

> When my children were young, I used to tell them stories about my village and about our family traditions. But in Tumu there are not so many people from my village and my children never went to visit the family. Now my children are educated and they have no time to sit with the family. A Sisala father usually farms with his son. But with educated people, they don't farm. They run around town with other boys: Soon we will forget our history. The educated man has a different character from his father. So fathers die and never tell their sons about the important traditions. My children don't sit and listen to me anymore. They don't want to know the real things my father told me. They have gone to school, and they are now book men. Boys who are educated run around with other boys rather than sitting and listening to their fathers (Grindal:83).

That these conflicts should flare up into open expressions of hostility toward education, schools, and teachers is not surprising. A headmaster of a primary school among the Sisala related to Bruce Grindal what happened when a man made a trip to a village outside Tumu.

> He parked his car on the road and was away for some time. When he returned, he saw that somebody had defaced his car, beaten it with sticks or something. Now I knew that my school children knew something about this. So I gathered them together and told them that if they were good citizens, they should report to me who did it and God would reward them. So I found out that this was done by some people in the village. When the village people found out their children told me such things, they were very angry. They said that the teachers were teaching their children to disrespect their elders. It is because of things like that that the fathers are taking their children out of school (Grindal:97–98).

The above implies that the new schools, created for the purposes of aiding and abetting modernization, are quite effective. Without question they do create conflicts between generations and

disrupt the transmission of the traditional culture. These effects in themselves are a prelude to change, perhaps a necessary condition. They are not, however, the result of the effectiveness of the schools as educational institutions. Because the curricular content is alien to the existing culture there is little or no reinforcement in the home and family, or in the community as a whole, for what happens in the school. The school is isolated from the cultural system it is intended to serve. As F. Landa Jocano relates concerning the primary school in Malitbog, a barrio in Panay, in the middle Philippines:

> . . . most of what children learn in school is purely verbal imitation and academic memorization, which do not relate with the activities of the children at home. By the time a child reaches the fourth grade he is expected to be competent in reading, writing, arithmetic, and language study. Except for gardening, no other vocational training is taught. The plants that are required to be cultivated, however, are cabbages, lettuce, okra, and other vegetables which are not normally grown and eaten in the barrio. [sentence omitted]
>
> Sanitation is taught in the school, but insofar as my observation went, this is not carried beyond the child's wearing clean clothes. Children may be required to buy toothbrushes, combs, handkerchiefs, and other personal items, and bring these to school for inspection. Because only a few can afford to buy these items, only a few come to school with them. Often these school requirements are the source of troubles at home, a night's crying among the children. . . . [sentence omitted] In the final analysis, such regular school injunctions as "brush your teeth every morning" or "drink milk and eat leafy vegetables" mean nothing to the children. First, none of the families brush their teeth. The toothbrushes the children bring to school are for inspection only. Their parents cannot afford to buy milk. They do not like goats' milk because it is *malangsa* (foul smelling) (Jocano 1969:53).

Nor is it solely a matter of the nonrelatedness of what is taught in the school to what is learned in the home and community. Because the curricular content is alien to the culture as a whole, what is taught tends to become formalized and unrealistic and is taught in a rigid, ritualistic manner. Again, among the Sisala of Northern Ghana, Bruce Grindal describes the classroom environment.

> The classroom environment into which the Sisala child enters is characterized by a mood of rigidity and an almost total absence of spontaneity. A typical school day begins with a fifteen-minute period during which the students talk and play, often running and screaming, while the teacher, who is usually outside talking with his fellow teachers, pays no attention. At 8:30 one of the students rings a bell, and the children immediately take their seats and remove from their desks the materials needed for the first lesson. When the teacher enters the room, everyone falls silent. If the first lesson is English, the teacher begins by reading a passage in the students' readers. He then asks the students to read the section aloud, and if a child makes a mistake, he is told to sit down, after being corrected. Variations of the English lesson consist of having the students write down dictated sentences or spell selected words from a passage on the blackboard. Each lesson lasts exactly forty minutes, at the end of which a bell rings and the students immediately prepare for the next lesson.
>
> Little emphasis is placed upon the content of what is taught; rather, the book is strictly adhered to, and the students are drilled by being asked the questions which appear at the end of each assignment. The absence of discussion is due partially to the poor training of the teacher, yet even in the middle schools where the educational standards for teachers are better, an unwillingness exists to discuss or explain the content of the lessons. All subjects except mathematics are lessons in literacy which teach the student to spell, read, and write.
>
> Interaction between the teacher and his students is characterized by an authoritarian rigidity. When the teacher enters the classroom, the students are expected to rise as a sign of respect. If the teacher needs anything done in the classroom, one of the students performs the task. During lessons the student is not expected to ask questions, but instead is supposed to give the "correct" answers to questions posed to him by the teacher. The students are less intent upon what the teacher is saying than they are upon the reading materials before them. When the teacher asks a question, most of the students hurriedly examine their books to find the correct answer and then raise their hands. The teacher calls on one of them, who rises, responds (with his eyes lowered), and then sits down. If the answer is wrong or does not make sense, the teacher corrects him and occasionally derides him for his stupidity. In the latter case the child remains standing with his eyes lowered until the teacher finishes and then sits down without making a response (Grindal 1972:85).

The nonrelatedness of the school to the community in both the content being transmitted and the methods used to transmit it is logically carried into the aspirations of students concerning their own futures. These aspirations are often quite unrealistic. As one of the Sisala school boys said:

> I have in mind this day being a professor so that I will be able to help my country. . . . As a professor I will visit so many countries such as America, Britain, and Holland. In fact, it will be interesting for me and my wife. . . . When I return, my father will be proud seeing his child like this. Just imagine me having a wife and children in my car moving down the street of my village. And when the people are in need of anything, I will help them (Grindal: 89).

Or as another reported in an essay:

> By the time I have attained my graduation certificate from the university, the government will be so happy that they may like to make me president of my beloved country. When I receive my salary, I will divide the money and give part to my father and my wife and children. . . . People say the U.S.A. is a beautiful country. But when they see my village, they will say it is more beautiful. Through my hard studies, my name will rise forever for people to remember (Grindal: 89).

As we have said, the new schools, like the traditional tribal methods of education and schools everywhere, recruit new members of the community into a cultural system and into specific roles and statuses. And they attempt to maintain this system by transmitting the necessary competencies to individuals who are recruited into it via these roles and statuses. The problem with the new schools is that the cultural system they are recruiting for does not exist in its full form. The education the school boys and girls receive is regarded by many as more or less useless, though most people, like the Sisala, agree that at least literacy is necessary if one is to get along in the modern world. However, the experience of the school child goes far beyond training for literacy. The child is removed from the everyday routine of community life and from observation of the work rules of adults. He or she is placed in an artificial, isolated, unrealistic, ritualized environment. Unrealistic aspirations and self-images develop. Harsh reality intrudes abruptly upon graduation. The schoolboy discovers that, except for teaching in the primary schools, few opportunities are open to him. There are some clerical positions in government offices, but they are few. Many graduates migrate in search of jobs concomitant with their expectations, but they usually find that living conditions are more severe than those in the tribal area and end up accepting an occupation and life style similar to that of the illiterate tribesmen who have also migrated to the city. Those who become village teachers are not much better off. One Sisala teacher in his mid-twenties said:

> I am just a small man. I teach and I have a small farm. . . . Maybe someday if I am fortunate, I will buy a tractor and farm for money because there is no future in teaching. When I went to school, I was told that if I got good marks and studied hard, I would be somebody, somebody important. I even thought I would go to America or England. I would still like to go, but I don't think of these things very often because it hurts too much. You see me here drinking and perhaps you think I don't have any sense. I don't know. I don't know why I drink. But I know in two days' time, I must go back and teach school. In X (his home village where he teaches) I am alone; I am nobody (Grindal:93).

The pessimist will conclude that the new schools, as agents of modernization, are a rank failure. This would be a false conclusion. They are neither failures nor successes. The new schools, like all institutions transforming cultural systems, are not articulated with the other parts of the changing system. The future is not known or knowable.

Much of the content taught in the school, as well as the very concept of the school as a place with four walls within which teacher and students are confined for a number of hours each day and regulated by a rigid schedule of "learning" activities, is Western. In many ways the new schools among the Sisala, in Malitbog, and in many other changing cultures are inadequate copies of schools in Europe and in the United States. There is no doubt, however, that formal schooling in all of the developing nations of the world, as disarticulated with the existing cultural context as it is, nevertheless is helping to bring into being a new population of literates, whose aspirations and world view are very different than that of their parents. And of course a whole class of educated elites has been created by colleges and universities in many of the countries. It seems inevitable that eventually the developing cultures will build their own models for schools and education. These new models will not be caricatures of Western schools, although in places, as in the case of the Sisala or the Kanuri of Nigeria described by Alan Peshkin (Peshkin 1972), where the Western influence has been strong for a long time, surely those models will show this influence.

Perhaps one significant part of the problem and the general shape of the solution is implied in the following exchange between two new young teachers in charge of a village school among the Ngoni of Malawi and a senior chief:

> The teachers bent one knee as they gave him the customary greeting, waiting in silence until he spoke.
> "How is your school?"
> "The classes are full and the children are learning well, Inkosi."
> "How do they behave?"
> "Like Ngoni children, Inkosi."
> "What do they learn?"
> "They learn reading, writing, arithmetic, scripture, geography and drill, Inkosi."
> "Is that education?"
> "It is education, Inkosi."
> "No! No! No! Education is *very* broad, *very* deep. It is not only in books, it is learning how to live. I am an old man now. When I was a boy I went

with the Ngoni army against the Bemba. Then the mission came and I went to school. I became a teacher. Then I was chief. Then the government came. I have seen our country change, and now there are many schools and many young men go away to work to find money. I tell you that Ngoni children must learn how to live and how to build up our land, not only to work and earn money. Do you hear?"

"Yebo, Inkosi" (Yes, O Chief) (Read 1968:2–3).

The model of education that will eventually emerge in the modernizing nations will be one that puts the school, in its usual formal sense, in perspective, and emphasizes education in its broadest sense, as a part of life and of the dynamic changing community. It must emerge if these cultures are to avoid the tragic errors of miseducation, as the Western nations have experienced them, particularly in the relationships between the schools and minority groups.

CONCLUSION

In this chapter we started with the question, What are some of the ways culture is transmitted? We answered this question by examining cultural systems where a wide variety of teaching and learning techniques are utilized. One of the most important processes, we found, was the management of discontinuity. Discontinuity occurs at any point in the life cycle when there is an abrupt transition from one mode of being and behaving to another, as for example at weaning and at adolescence. Many cultural systems manage the latter period of discontinuity with dramatic staging and initiation ceremonies, some of which are painful or emotionally disturbing to the initiates. They are public announcements of changes in status. They are also periods of intense cultural compression during which teaching and learning are accelerated. This managed cultural compression and discontinuity functions to enlist new members in the community and maintains the cultural system. Education, whether characterized by sharp discontinuities and culturally compressive periods, or by a relatively smooth progression of accumulating ex-

perience and status change, functions in established cultural systems to recruit new members and maintain the existing system. We then turned to a discussion of situations where alien or future-oriented cultural systems are introduced through formal schooling. Schools among the Sisala of Ghana, a modernizing African nation, and a Philippine barrio were used as examples of this relationship and its consequences. The disarticulation of school and community was emphasized. The point was made that children in these situations are intentionally recruited to a cultural system other than the one they originated from, and that the school does not maintain the existing social order, but, in effect, destroys it. This is a kind of discontinuity very different than the one we discussed previously, and produces severe dislocations in life patterns and interpersonal relations as well as potentially positive change.

REFERENCES AND FURTHER READING

Barnett, Homer G., 1960, *Being a Palauan*. CSCA. New York: Holt, Rinehart and Winston, Inc.

Beals, Alan R., 1962, *Gopalpur: A South Indian Village*. CSCA. New York: Holt, Rinehart and Winston, Inc.

Brown, Judith K., 1963, "A Cross-cultural Study of Female Initiation Rites," *American Anthropologist* 65:837–853.

Chance, Norman A., 1966, *The Eskimo of North Alaska*. CSCA. New York: Holt, Rinehart and Winston, Inc.

Cohen, Yehudi, 1964, *The Transition from Childhood to Adolescence*. Chicago: Aldine Publishing Company.

Deng, Francis Mading, 1972, *The Dinka of the Sudan*. CSCA. New York: Holt, Rinehart and Winston, Inc.

Dozier, Edward P., 1967, *Hano: A Tewa Indian Community in Arizona*. CSCA. New York: Holt, Rinehart and Winston, Inc.

Eggan, Dorothy, 1956, "Instruction and Affect in Hopi Cultural Continuity," *Southwestern Journal of Anthropology* 12:347–370.

Grindal, Bruce T., 1972, *Growing Up in Two Worlds: Education and Transition among the Sisala of Northern Ghana*. CSCA. New York: Holt, Rinehart and Winston, Inc.

Hart, C.W.M., 1963, "Contrasts Between Prepubertal and Postpubertal Education." In G. Spindler, ed., *Education and Culture.* Holt, Rinehart and Winston, Inc.

Henry, Jules, 1960. "A Cross-cultural Outline of Education," *Current Anthropology* 1, 267–305.

———, 1963, *Culture Against Man.* New York: Random House.

Hogbin, Ian, 1964, *A Guadalcanal Society: The Kaoka Speakers.* CSCA. New York: Holt, Rinehart and Winston, Inc.

Jocano, F. Landa, 1969. *Growing Up in a Philippine Barrio.* CSEC. New York: Holt, Rinehart and Winston, Inc.

Lessa, William A., 1966. *Ulithi: A Micronesian Design for Living.* CSCA. New York: Holt, Rinehart and Winston, Inc.

Mead, Margaret, 1949, *Coming of Age in Samoa.* New York: Mentor Books (first published in 1928).

———, 1953, *Growing Up in New Guinea.* New York: Mentor Books (first published in 1930).

———, 1964, *Continuities in Cultural Evolution.* New Haven: Yale University Press.

Peshkin, Alan, 1972, *Kanuri Schoolchildren: Education and Social Mobilization in Nigeria.* CSEC. New York: Holt, Rinehart and Winston, Inc.

Pettit, George A., 1946, *Primitive Education in North America.* Publications in American Archeology and Ethnology, vol. 43.

Pierce, Joe E., 1964, *Life in a Turkish Village.* CSCA. New York: Holt, Rinehart and Winston, Inc.

Read, Margaret, 1968, *Children of Their Fathers: Growing Up Among the Ngoni of Malawi.* CSEC. New York: Holt, Rinehart and Winston, Inc.

Schwartz, Gary, and Don Merten, 1968, "Social Identity and Expressive Symbols: The Meaning of an Initiation Ritual," *American Anthropologist* 70:1117–1131.

Spindler, George D., and Louise S. Spindler, 1971, *Dreamers without Power: The Menomini Indians of Wisconsin.* CSCA. New York: Holt, Rinehart and Winston, Inc.

Spiro, Melford, 1958, *Children of the Kibbutz.* Cambridge, Mass.: Harvard University Press.

Van Gennep, Arnold, 1960, *The Rites of Passage.* Chicago: University of Chicago Press.

Whiting, Beatrice B., ed., 1963, *Child Rearing in Six Cultures.* New York: John Wiley & Sons, Inc.

Whiting, John F., R. Kluckhohn, and A. Albert, 1958, "The Function of Male Initiation Ceremonies at Puberty." In E. Maccoby, T. Newcomb, and E. Hartley, eds., *Readings in Social Psychology.* New York: Holt, Rinehart and Winston, Inc.

Williams, Thomas R., 1965, *The Dusun: A North Borneo Society.* CSCA. New York: Holt, Rinehart and Winston, Inc.

Young, Frank, 1965, *Initiation Ceremonies.* Indianapolis: The Bobbs-Merrill Company.

AMERICAN CULTURAL VALUES

CONRAD ARENSBERG AND ARTHUR NIEHOFF

There are few truly isolated peoples in the world. Everywhere people with particular cultures and societies are in contact with people who are different from them. If they learn each other's languages and understand each other's customs, they are on the road to useful communication. However, when those in one culture believe that by introducing change they will help those in another to improve their lifestyle, they face another difficulty. People do not want the same things; they do not go about getting what they do want in the same ways. In this article, Conrad Arensberg and Arthur Niehoff show how American values have often frustrated those who would help change "underdeveloped" countries.

MISINTERPRETATION

In order to understand how ideas are transferred from one culture to another it is very important to know the role and characteristics of the change agents involved. Several of the cases in this manual indicate that a failure was due to the change agent's misinterpretation of the motives and needs of the hoped-for borrowers of the innovations. Such misinterpretations may result from the change agent's failure to learn enough about the receiving culture; but they may also rest on false suppositions, derived from assuming that conditions taken for granted in the home culture also exist in the other culture.

All men, in agrarian or industrial societies, have much in common in the solution of their problems. A peasant farmer in India and a commercial farmer in Texas are both pragmatic and must be shown that an improvement is genuine before they will adopt it, and a Lao farmer tries to get help from the supernatural in producing rain just as the American turns to prayer when a close family member is seriously ill. Nevertheless, it still does not follow that all the basic assumptions of people with different cultures are the same. Despite similarities, the unlikenesses are significant enough to block communication and thus impede change. If the change agent expects the people of the recipient culture to have precisely the same motivations or behaviors as are common in his culture, he is seriously risking failure of understanding.

The worst part of most such misapprehension of cultural realities is that it is unintentional. The individual does what is "natural" or what makes "common sense." He may not realize that his "natural" tendencies to action are inevitably limited by his own cultural experience, including his unconscious assumptions. To examine the cultural as well as individual premises of one's own actions is a difficult process. If one always stayed with people of the same background, this examination would never be necessary and most people would

Source: "American Cultural Values" from Introducing Social Change, copyright 1971 by Conrad Arensberg and Arthur Niehoff, eds. Reprinted by permission of authors.

probably be better off without doing it. However, if one is to deal with people of another culture, or simply to understand them at a distance, knowing one's own cultural assumptions is of the first importance. Thus, hybrid corn grown by Spanish-American farmers in Arizona was superior in terms of the Anglo-American economy and the change agent assumed the value of corn was the same. However, these Spanish-Americans valued it primarily for its taste and texture as a human food rather than as feed for animals. The United States administrators of Palau assumed that if individuals participated in an American system of electing public officials, democracy would be absorbed into the culture. However, the islanders interpreted leadership and social control differently, and manipulated their way around the "democratic" idea. In both cases the problems arose principally because of the cultural misperception of the planners who were putting mistaken reliance on "natural" and "common sense" assumptions which were relevant to the American scene but inadequate in contacts with people of another culture.

Culture creates unconscious blinders for all mankind. Other people do not act "naturally," that is, in accordance with a universal value system. Thus the American or other change agent must be given some opportunity of knowing himself as a product of American and Western culture. This means principally that he look analytically at his own assumptions and values. He should have some idea what influences his decisions and actions in introducing new ideas and what his reactions will be to difficulties among the people with whom he will be working. In short, he needs to know how being an American and a Westerner may help or hinder him in his mission.

In the age of cultural pluralism, what is meant by "American culture"? Is not the United States several streams of culture flowing side by side? There is probably more acceptance of this idea today than at any time since the founding of the country. And yet, there is still a national core, usually characterized as that of the middle class, having its origins in Western European culture. The language is English, the legal system derives from English common law, the political system of democratic elections comes from France and England, the technology is solidly from Europe, and even more subtle social values, such as egalitarianism (though modified), seem to be European derived. Thus, it seems justifiable to characterize the middle class value system of the United States, as derived originally from Europe but modified to suit local conditions, as the core of American culture.

All people born and raised in this country will have been conditioned by this national culture, although obviously the middle class will be most strongly marked. And though it is not implied here that there are no differences in other subcultural streams, it does mean that irrespective of region, national origin, race, class, and sex, there are points of likeness that will occur more frequently than among groups of people in other countries.

Where does this American character come from? As mentioned above, it seems to come from a European base that has been subsequently modified to meet local conditions. The values derived from life on the frontier, the great open spaces, the virgin wealth, and the once seemingly limitless resources of a "new world" appear to have affected ideas of freedom. Individualism seems to have been fostered by a commitment to "progress" which in turn was derived from expansion over three hundred years. Much of the religious and ethical tradition is believed to have come from Calvinist (Puritan) doctrine, particularly an emphasis on individual responsibility and the positive work ethic. Anglo-Saxon civil rights, the rule of law, and representative institutions were inherited from the English background; ideas of egalitarian democracy and a secular spirit spring from the French and American Revolutions. The period of slavery and its aftermath, and the European immigration of three centuries, have affected the American character strongly.

AMERICAN CULTURE

Is it possible to provide a thumbnail sketch of the most obvious characteristics of this system?

Most social scientists would probably agree to the following:

The number of people in America is considerable, compared to other countries, and they are located primarily in the cities and towns of a large area of diverse natural environments, still with considerable mineral and soil wealth and still not intensively exploited. There is an exceedingly elaborate technology and a wealth of manufactured goods that is now the greatest in the world.

Although the country has a strong agrarian tradition in which farming is still regarded as a family occupation, and although farming produces an extraordinary yield of foodstuffs and fibers, the nation has become urbanized and dominated by the cities. The farming population consists of less than 10 percent of the total, and agriculture has become so mechanized it can now be considered as merely another form of industry. Daily living is characteristically urban, regulated by the clock and calendar rather than by the seasons or degree of daylight. The great majority of individuals are employees, living on salaries paid by large, complex, impersonal institutions. Money is the denominator of exchange, even property having a value only in terms of its monetary worth. The necessities of life are purchased rather than produced for subsistence.

Because of the high standard of living and high level of technology, people have long lives. The birth rate is low but the death rate is among the lowest in the world. Thus, although there is a continuing expansion of population, it is much less rapid than in most of the agrarian nations.

Americans exhibit a wide range of wealth, property, education, manners, and tastes. However, despite diversities of origin, tradition, and economic level, there is a surprising conformity in language, diet, hygiene, dress, basic skills, land use, community settlement, recreation, and other activities. The people share a rather small range of moral, political, economic, and social attitudes, being divided in opinion chiefly by their denominational and occupational interests. Within the past decade there seems also to have been a separation of opinion based on age. There are some regional variations but these are far less than the tribal or ethnic pluralisms found in the new nations of South Asia and Africa. The narrow opinion range throughout the country seems to be primarily a product of the relatively efficient mass education system which blankets the country and the wide spread of mass communication, from which all people get the same message.

There are status differences, based mainly on occupation, education, and financial worth. Achievement is valued more than inheritance in determining an individual's position. Although in theory all persons have equal opportunities, certain limitations exist, particularly those based on ethnic background and sex. A Negro may be appointed as a member of the Cabinet, but it is improbable and he would not be elected as President at the present time. There are now Negro mayors, but there are still no Negro governors. Women also are prevented from serving in certain positions or occupations. Despite these limitations, most people move about freely; they change jobs and move up and down in status with considerable frequency.

The basic American kinship unit, though evidently weakening, is still the nuclear family of husband, wife, and children. Newly married couples set up their own small households and move several times in a lifespan. The family rarely has continuing geographical roots. Most couples have few children. Marital relationships are fluid and not particularly stable, with divorce quite common. Old people and unmarried adults usually live apart from their kin. Instead of strong kinship ties, people tend to rely on an enormous number of voluntary associations of common interest—parent-teachers' associations, women's clubs, social fraternities, church clubs, recreational teams, political clubs, and many others.

The general level of education is high, with literacy normal but not universal. From the age of five to eighteen the child usually is in an academic institution, learning the culturally approved goals of good health, character, and citizenship. Also, he learns basic and standard skills rather than any hereditary specialization—reading, writing, arithmetic, typing, liberal arts, driving cars, basic mechanics, housekeeping. Specialization comes later in the professional training that ordinarily takes place in college. More and more young people are extending their education through four years in college, although this is not yet legally required.

The moral tone of the country is heavily Calvinist Protestant but there are many other sects of Christianity, besides other religions and cults. Religious beliefs and practices are concerned almost as much with general morality as with man's search for the afterlife or his worship of deities. Family relations, sexual customs, man's relationship to other men, and civic responsibility are all concerns of religion. A puritanic morality has become generalized and secularized, part of the total culture rather than that of any single religious sect. Formal religion is compartmentalized, as are many other aspects of American life. A high percentage of the Protestants who form the bulk of the population attend church infrequently, and religious ideas are seldom consciously mixed with secular ones. The church serves a strong social function, being the center of many clubs and groups. Religion can hardly be considered a particularly unifying institution of American life. The spirit of the country is secular and rationalistic. Most people are not antireligious but merely indifferent.

MATERIAL WELL-BEING

The rich resources of America, along with the extraordinary growth of its industrial economy, have brought a widespread wealth of material goods such as the world has not seen before. There has been a wholesale development and diffusion of the marvels of modern comfort—swift and pleasant transportation, central heating, air conditioning, instant hot and cold water, electricity, and laborsaving devices of endless variety. The high value placed on such comforts has caused industries to be geared to produce ever greater quantities and improved versions. Americans seem to feel that they have a "right" to such amenities.

Associated with this attitude toward comfort (which has itself resulted in elaborate waste disposal facilities), and an advanced state of medical

knowledge, Americans have come to regard cleanliness as an absolute virtue. A most familiar slogan is, "Cleanliness is next to godliness," and although this is not heard as often as it once was, the word "dirty" is still one of the chief epithets in the language, as in "dirty old man," "dirty hippie," "dirty business," "dirty deal," etc.

Achievement and success are measured primarily by the quantity of material goods one possesses, both because these are abundant and because they indicate how much money an individual earns. This material evidence of personal worth is modified by the credit system; but still, credit purchases will carry an individual only so far, after which credit agencies will refuse to advance more without evidence of fundamental wealth.

Since there is little display value in the size of one's paycheck or bank account, the average individual buys prestige articles that others can see: expensive clothing or furniture, a fine car, a swimming pool, an expensive home, or one of the endless variety of devices that may have other functions but can also readily be seen by visitors—power mowers, barbecue paraphernalia, television, and stereophonic systems. A person's status is affected to a secondary degree by his level of education, type of occupation, and social behavior; but even these qualities seem to be significant only in terms of how much income they help him to obtain. Thus, a college professor who has earned his Ph.D. will have less status in the general community than a business executive or film actor who has no college education but commands a much larger salary.

People other than middle class Americans also value comfort and the saving of human labor, and one of the motivations to change everywhere is to perform traditional tasks more easily. However, many people of the world have found themselves unable to acquire so many laborsaving devices and have thus concentrated on the satisfaction of other needs; and it should be recognized that many of the spiritual or esthetic goals they pursue will outlast most of the machine-made devices treasured in America. But, their choices have been limited by their comparative poverty. Comfort in such circumstances has not been so highly valued; and in fact, Americans have been accused by this token of being excessively materialistic.

TWOFOLD JUDGMENTS

A special characteristic of Western thinking, fully reflected in American ways, is that of making two-fold judgments based on principle. The structure of the Indo-European languages seems to foster this kind of thinking and the action that follows. A situation or action is assigned to a category held high, thus providing a justification for positive effort, or to one held low, with justification for rejection, avoidance, or other negative action. Twofold judgments seem to be the rule in Western and American life: moral-immoral, legal-illegal, right-wrong, sin-virtue, success-failure, clean-dirty, civilized-primitive, practical-impractical, introvert-extrovert, secular-religious, Christian-pagan. This kind of polarized thinking tends to put the world of values into absolutes, and its arbitrary nature is indicated by the fact that modern science no longer uses opposite categories, in almost all instances preferring to use the concept of a range with degrees of difference separating the poles.

Judgment in terms of principle is very old and pervasive as a means of organizing thought in Western and American life. It may derive from Judeo-Christian ideas. In any event, it is deeply rooted in the religions that have come from this base as well as in the philosophy of the West. Its special quality should be recognized. More is involved than merely thinking in opposites. Other peoples have invented dual ways of thinking: the Chinese Yin-and-Yang, the Zoroastrian dual (though equal) forces of good and evil, male and female principles, and the Hindu concept of the forces of destruction and regeneration as different aspects of the same power. However, other peoples do not usually rank one as superior and thus to be embraced on principle as a guide to conduct.

This kind of thinking seems to force Americans into positions of exclusiveness. If one posi-

tion is accepted, the other must be rejected. There is little possibility of keeping opposite or even parallel ideas in one's thinking pattern. This is not the case in other cultures. In Buddhism and Hinduism disparate local beliefs exist alongside beliefs that are derived from the main theology. No one questions the fact that in Japan people may worship in a Buddhist temple as well as in a Shinto shrine; or that in the southern form of Buddhism, in Laos and Thailand, people propitiate the local spirits ("phi") as well as observe the ritual forms of Buddhism. This is quite different from the Christian attitude in which all that is believed to be supernatural but is not Christian is classified as superstition or paganism.

The average Westerner, and especially the American, bases his personal life and community affairs on principles of right and wrong rather than on sanctions of shame, dishonor, ridicule, or horror of impropriety. The whole legal system is established on the assumption that rational people can decide if things have been "wrong." The American is forced by his culture to categorize his conduct in universal, impersonal terms. "The law is the law" and "right is right," regardless of other considerations.

MORALIZING

One of the most basic of the twofold decisions Americans make is to classify actions as good or bad. Whether in the conduct of foreign affairs or bringing up children or dealing in the marketplace, Americans tend to moralize. Judging people and actions as absolutely right or wrong may have been a source of considerable strength in American history but it has also created pitfalls, particularly in the way it has influenced Americans in their relationship with other peoples. The attitude has frequently led Americans to indignation and even to warfare about the behavior of other peoples, Vietnam providing the most obvious recent example.

Every people has its own code of proper conduct. This is such an important part of any culture that some effort to understand it must be made. But this aspect of a cultural system is probably the most difficult to learn. And the greatest difficulties will occur if the outsider assumes that other people's basis of judgment is the same as his, or even that proper conduct will be based on moral rather than other kinds of principles.

In many other cultures, rank or esteem, the dignity of a person, the honor of an individual, compassion for an unfortunate, or loyalty to a kinsman or co-religionist may be the basis for judgment as to proper conduct. Most forms of sexual behavior may not be considered subject to moral considerations. The American, as an heir to the Western tradition, is familiar and comfortable with a code of conduct derived from absolute principles (mostly religious) and supported by a code of law enforced by central authorities. This entire code is supposed to be impersonal, and to a considerable extent it is. The morality tale of the honest, law-abiding policeman or judge who punishes his own law-breaking son probably does occur more frequently in America than in societies where kinship considerations are given more weight.

One other feature of this kind of thinking that can lead to considerable personal and public problems is that the American tends to overreact to the discovery that the ideal behavior he was taught to expect from parent, public servants, spouses, and other adults is not always present in real life. Some individuals react by becoming "tough" and "cynical" and "wise" to the corruption of the world. Others, particularly exemplified by the youth of the past decade, organize to eliminate by whatever means are available the "failures" of the older generation. This kind of thinking encourages the individual to believe that, whatever differs from the ideal version of high moral excellence is of the utmost depravity. It tends to direct the individual to see corruption and evil everywhere. And while such moralistic indignation may serve the culture well in some instances (as in the fight against pollution), it can also have negative consequences, particularly when the moralizer is trying to work with people of another culture.

WORK AND PLAY

Another kind of twofold judgment that Americans tend to maintain is based on a qualitative distinction between work and play. To most persons brought up in the present-day American environment of farming, business, or industry, work is what they do regularly, purposefully, and even grimly, whether they enjoy it or not. It is a necessity, and for the middle aged, a duty. A man is judged by his work. When strangers meet and attempt to establish cordial relationships, one of the first topics of discussion is the kind of work each does. It is a primary role classifier. Work is a serious, adult business, and a man is supposed to "get ahead" or "make a contribution" to community or mankind through his work.

Play is different. It is fun, an outlet from work, without serious purpose except possibly to make subsequent work more efficient. It is a lesser category, a later topic of conversation after one's occupation is identified. And although some persons may "enjoy their work," this is a matter of luck and by no means something that everyone can count on since all jobs contain some "dirty work," tedium, and tasks that one completes just by pushing on. Work and play are considered to be different worlds; there is a time and place for each, but when it is time for work, then lighter pursuits should be put aside. There is a newer emphasis in contemporary America on pleasure-seeking as a primary goal of life, but so far this seems to be an attitude espoused by a minority only, the young who have rejected the former goals of society and the retired old who have already completed their years of work.

The American habit of associating work with high or necessary purpose and grim effort and play with frivolity or pleasure seems to have a positive function in the American cultural context, but it may be quite out of place in another culture. For many peoples the times of most important work may also be times of festivity or ceremony. Work and play may be interwoven. A threshing floor may be a dancing arena, and building a new house or netting a school of fish may provide the occasion for a whole community to sing and joke together. Preparing the proper songs or dishes will be as "practical" an activity as cutting thatch or caring for nets.

The combination of work and play is not completely foreign to Americans, although urban industrial society does not seem favorable for it. The American frontier, and even Midwest farming communities until thirty or forty years ago, combined the two in their husking bees, houseraising and threshing parties. In the early decades of this century, before wheat combines and farms of large acreage dominated agriculture in the Midwest, farmers made the social and work rounds for several weeks in midsummer. Not only did they work together, but they also feasted, socialized, and even managed a considerable amount of courting. It was a point of pride for each farmer's wife to have the largest quantities of elaborate food available for the men when they came in from the fields. The unmarried girls made a particular effort to be there to search out the bachelors. It was a gay time as well as a time of hard work. It should also be pointed out that song and work has been well represented in the American past in the vast repertory of work songs that were once sung by occupational groups.

Basically, the nonindustrial societies have patterns of work and play that are closer to those known to preindustrial Americans; work and play are intermixed rather than distinct forms of activity.

TIME IS MONEY

Closely related to the American distinction between work and play is a special attitude toward time. Whenever Americans interact with people in nonindustrial countries, both quickly become aware that their outlook in regard to time is different. In many such countries the local people actually make a distinction in the spoken language, referring to *hora Americana* versus *hora Mexicana* or *mong Amelikan* versus *mong Lao*. When referring to the American version, they mean that it is exact, that people are punctual, activities are scheduled, time is apportioned for sep-

arate activities, and the measure is the mechanical clock; their own time lacks this precision.

Probably misunderstandings with people of other cultures occur most frequently in relation to work. For Americans, "time is money." Work is paid for in money and one should balance his work against time or through regular periods for a fixed salary. A person works for a stated number of dollars per hour and eight or ten hours per day for 40 or 48 hours a week. Work beyond the normal is "overtime." Play or leisure time is before or after work time. An employer literally buys the time of his workers along with their skills, and schedules and assigns work to be balanced against the gain he will obtain. In this way of thinking, time can be turned into money, both for the employer and employee, and work turned out faster than planned can release extra time for more work and more gain.

Equating work with time, using the least amount of time to produce the largest amount of work, expecting that time paid for will be marked by sustained effort, budgeting of man hours in relation to the cost of the end product—these are central features of the American industrial economy that have contributed a great deal to its productiveness. And although Americans may complain about the necessity of routine and the tyranny of the clock during working hours, they are thoroughly accustomed to such strictures. The activities of leisure—eating, sleeping, playing, courting—must take place during "time off." No wonder time to them is scarce and worth saving.

Such a precise concept of time is usually foreign to peoples of nonindustrial cultures. In most agrarian societies, especially in the villages, time is geared to seasonal requirements and the amount of daylight available. Many routines reflect, not hourly or daily repetitions based on wage labor, but the needs of individual and social life, the cycles of crops, fluctuations in daily temperature, and the round of ceremonial observances. The cities of these countries have all adopted the Western concept of time to some degree, although it is frequently noted that the rural pattern is still maintained in modified form in the urban context. Individuals simply do not keep hours or appointments precisely and are surprised when they learn that an American is irritated by a missed appointment.

EFFORT AND OPTIMISM

Americans are an active people. They believe that problems should be identified and effort should be expended to solve them. Effort is good in itself, and with proper effort one can be optimistic about success. The fact that some problems may be insoluble is very difficult for an American to accept. The high value connected with effort often causes Americans to cite the principle that "It is better to do something than to just stand around." This thinking is based on the concept that the universe is mechanistic (it can be understood in terms of causes and effects), man is his own master, and he is perfectible almost without limit (DuBois, 1955: 1233–1234). Thus, with enough effort, man can improve himself and manipulate the part of the universe that is around him.

This national confidence in effort and activity, with an optimism that trying to do something about a problem will almost invariably bring success in solving it, seems to be specifically American. Such an attitude is probably a product of the continual expansion of American culture during the past three hundred years, first along America's frontiers and later in its industrial growth. Obstacles existed only to be overcome, and bad conditions needed only be recognized to be rectified.

Effort and optimism permeate the life of the individual because of his cultural upbringing. Coming from an "open class system," where status is usually achieved rather than inherited, both privilege and authority should be deserved and won.

Effort, achievement, and success are woven through the fabric of American life and culture. Activist, pragmatic values rather than contemplative or mystical ones are the basis of the American character. Serious effort to achieve success is both a personal goal and an ethical imperative. The worthwhile man is the one who "gets results" and "gets ahead." A failure "gets nowhere" or "gets no results," for success is measured by results

(although there is a little "credit for trying"). The successful man "tackles a problem," "does something about it," and "succeeds" in the process. A failure is unsuccessful through his own fault. Even if he had "bad breaks" he should have tried again. A failure in life "didn't have the guts" to "make a go of it" and "put himself ahead."

This is a very severe code. No one is certain how widespread it is among Americans but it is probably recognizable to most. It indicates a culture in which effort is rewarded, competition is enforced, and individual achievement is paramount. Unfortunately, the code raises serious problems. One of the most important is that it calls all those in high positions successes and all those in low ones "failures" even though everyone knows the majority must be in lower positions. A code of this sort by its very nature creates much frustration in all those who have not been able to achieve high positions.

This traditional optimism of the American personality has been tempered to a certain degree in recent years, though primarily in the kind of goals sought rather than whether they can be achieved. Concentration on pragmatic effort seems unchanged, and even those Americans who are most disillusioned with the current state of affairs seem convinced that enough effort will produce success—for their new goals, however, rather than the old ones.

But it has become clear to everyone that whatever effort is expended, some situations are beyond the American's ability to control. Problems once thought to be simple are now seen to have a complexity not previously recognized. A weaker enemy cannot simply be bombed into submission with more and more explosives. Industrial production cannot be guided by the profit motive alone if one wants to breathe clean air and to swim in clean water. The inner city of an industrial nation cannot survive if it is abandoned by the well-to-do who move to the suburbs. These are some of the problems that have arisen because of a simplistic view of manipulation of the environment, both human and natural. Some pundits now feel they are beyond human correction, but although the optimism of the average man has probably been tempered in recent decades, his method of overcoming these obstacles is unchanged—simply put in greater effort.

The American overseas is prone to evaluate people and situations according to this code. When he observes that those in authority have achieved their position by means other than their own effort, he may become bewildered, angered, or cynical. He may quickly make an activist judgment and try to remedy the situation, using his own code. Or he may shift (usually unconsciously) from the notion of work as task-oriented, which many peoples share in their own fashion, to an emphasis on busy work, on hurrying and pressuring, on encouraging activity for its own sake.

To peoples in other parts of the world, a history of failure in recent times has been as compelling as the technological and economic achievements of America. Their experiences may have taught them to value passivity, acceptance, and evasion rather than effort and optimism. This will not be because they have no interest in getting things done but because of their history of reversals. They lack the confidence of the American.

Before taking action, other peoples may therefore make many preparations which the American, so concerned with technical efficiency, will consider unnecessary. These may consist in extensive consultation with others to build up a consensus, giving favors to win personal loyalties, trying to adjust proposed plans to religious and other traditional beliefs, and considering all alternatives, including the real possibility of not risking action at all. American demands for bustle and effort, for getting down to business, may not only be interpreted as nagging, pushing, and ill-mannered, but sometimes as downright frightening, especially when a wrong judgment could lead to personal disaster. After an initial failure, the American determination to "try again" or "try harder the next time" may seem particularly foolhardy. Merely to intensify one's effort and to try again on a bigger scale when resources are limited may appear as the most reckless compounding of original folly.

And as is not unusual, other peoples frequently do judge American behavior correctly.

The American passion to exert greater effort in the face of continuing difficulties has not always produced the hoped-for success. In Vietnam, for example, although an admittedly much weaker enemy clearly and early indicated that they would fight differently than in previous wars, the military heads of the United States went ahead with conventional bombing and ground maneuvers for almost ten years without ever altering their procedures significantly except to intensify them. At the end of this decade, the enemy seemed hardly any weaker than at the beginning. And it must be admitted that such a procedure is only possible for America because it has unprecedented wealth and industrial production.

The effort to which Americans normally commit themselves is expected to be direct and efficient. Americans want to "get down to business" and confine themselves to the problem or proposal specified. Misunderstandings have consequently occurred because other peoples, particularly Latins, have tended to be less direct. They indulge more in theoretical speech during conferences and discussions, refusing to confine themselves rigidly to the agenda at hand. All this indicates more concern with social values than is usual in the American manner of conducting affairs. Perhaps the impersonal, technological approach leads to more production but the social verities have their place also, and they are still significant in many parts of the world.

American assumptions about effort and optimism include a faith in progress and a constant view toward the future. Practically all life is arranged to fulfill the needs of children and of the generations to follow. There is a pervasive accent on youthfulness; the values exemplified in commercial advertising and entertainment almost always emphasize the young, and the old are not commonly sought out for their experience. Adults attempt to hold back middle and old age. In general, elderly people are bypassed, either left in old folks' homes or in isolated retirement, in both cases removed from practical affairs. An ironic aspect of the situation in the 1960s was the rejection by a considerable part of American youth of this idealized "youth culture." "You can't trust anyone over thirty," they say.

An accent on youthfulness is particularly American, although it seems to be shared to a lesser degree by other achievement-oriented industrial societies. In the agrarian nations or wherever tradition is important, people tend to equate age with experience. The old are treated with deference and the oldest male is usually the chief decision-maker of the basic kin unit.

Other cultures have had their periods of success, but it appears rare for progress to be a central value throughout the entire existence of a culture. It is only since World War II that American faith in the future has been modified significantly, with the realization that there are many undesirable consequences if technological progress is allowed to take place with few controls. But despite recent reversals, the general American attitude is still that the future should contain bigger and better successes, if not on this planet, then on others. This attitude also implies that the new and modern are better than the old and traditional. Technological and economic life must progress. No one—not even the strongest dissidents of the left or the right—expects to keep America as it is today or to return it to what it was yesterday.

MAN AND NATURE

The greater effort that normally marks the American's response to obstacles may sometimes seem shallow, irreverent, or premature to people in other cultures. Some obstacles deserve respect and there are limitations to what man can do, even if he is the cleverest manipulator of the environment to have appeared so far. The new ecological approach is an indication that the American is becoming aware of some limitations on his capacities, but whether this will deflect his value system in a basic way remains to be seen. Up to now, American man has attempted to conquer nature. It has been something to overcome, to improve, to tear down and rebuild in a better way. He has tried to "break the soil," to "harness" the natural resources, to treat the natural environ-

ment like a domestic animal. He has divided the plants and animals into categories of useful and harmful. Harmful plants are weeds and harmful animals are "varmints"—the first to be uprooted or poisoned and the second to be trapped, shot, or poisoned. American farmers and ranchers have been notorious for killing predators. The only kind of hawks they knew until recently were "chicken hawks" which were shot any time they appeared and their carcasses hung in long festoons on wire fences. Coyotes and bobcats are still trapped and hunted without compunction by Westerners, who can get bounties of a few dollars for the feet and ears of one of these animals. And although on occasion hawks and coyotes may kill a few chickens or sheep, they primarily live on mice, rats, rabbits and other small animals whose populations must be kept in balance by such predators. Even a weed is merely a "plant growing out of place" from man's point of view.

It must be admitted that many of the achievements of Americans are due to this conquering attitude toward nature. The enormous agricultural productivity is one such achievement, although credit must also go to the fact that there were large expanses of very fertile land available. But it must also be admitted that the American has paid and is continuing to pay high prices for these agricultural successes. Natural resources, particularly forests, water, and the air, have been squandered and despoiled over large areas. Nature's balance has often been upset. Such "wonder" insecticides as DDT are now under strong attack by conservationists as destroying many "useful" insects and birds, as well as for their effect on human health.

This conquering attitude toward nature appears to rest on at least three assumptions; that the universe is mechanistic, that man is its master, and that man is qualitatively different from all other forms of life. Specifically, American and Western man credits himself with a special inner consciousness, a soul, for which he does not give other creatures credit. In most of the non-Western world man is merely considered as one form of life, different only in degree from the others. The Western biologist also shares this view, which is the primary reason that traditional Western culture came into conflict with biological views in the nineteenth and twentieth centuries. In the so-called animistic religions, all living creatures are believed to have something corresponding to a soul, with no sharp dividing line between man and the other animals. Spirits are even attributed to plants and inanimate objects, such as soil, rocks, mountains, and rivers. In the Hindu and Buddhist world the belief in a cycle of rebirths strongly affirms man's kinship to nonhuman forms. In the cycle of existences man can become an insect, a mammal, another type of man, or even a form of deity. The validity of such beliefs is far less important than the fact that man's attitude toward nature is influenced by them (and after all, there is no more empirical basis for Christian beliefs than for Buddhism or Hinduism). Basically, most people (except Westerners) consider man and nature as one, and they more often work with nature than simply attempting to conquer it.

During long periods of trial and error, peoples of all cultures have worked out adaptations to their natural environment. These adaptations may lack much by Western standards but they do enable the inhabitants to survive, sometimes in quite difficult circumstances. Such people through experience have evolved systems of conservation, methods of stretching and restoring their slim resources, and elaborate accommodations to climate, vegetation, and terrain. Some such adaptations now embedded in tradition and religion are the Middle Eastern desert-derived pattern of Islamic ritual hygiene, austerity, and almsgiving; preindustrial Japanese frugalities in house structure, farming, and woodworking; and Southeast Asian village economies in the measured use of rice, bamboo, and fish. These and similar adaptations to natural environments are high developments in the balanced utilization of limited resources.

When, with a facile confidence that nature can be tamed by ever costlier mechanical devices, Americans and other Westerners attempt to brush aside the experience of centuries, it is perhaps temporarily exciting to the local people. However, they are not apt to be reassured if they have information about the realities of the envi-

ronment that is ignored by the rushing, pushing, self-assured newcomers, particularly since the local solutions sometimes outlast the glamorous innovations of the specialists. For example, a well-drilling project in Laos was based on a system that had been worked out in Florida where the water table is high the year around. The specialist drilled wells in one large area of Laos during the rainy season and found water almost every time, at a relatively high level. However, all these wells went dry during the dry season, since in Southeast Asia the water level drops markedly during this period. Most Lao probably knew this and would have revealed it if asked.

In environments that seem adverse (such as the rainy tropics, the arctic, or the desert), experience has shown that Western man's goods and machines rot, rust, freeze, or grit up all too quickly, requiring huge and costly effort merely to keep them going. This is not surprising since this machinery was developed primarily for use in a temperate zone where precipitation is spread more or less evenly throughout the year.

A graphic example of the lack of adaptability of Western machines has been observed during the military struggles in Southeast Asia in recent years. Tanks and other mechanized equipment were developed with the solid land forms of America and Europe in mind. However, their use has been drastically curtailed in the rice paddies of Vietnam and Laos. The mobile foot soldier, unencumbered with heavy gear, can slip through the soggy fields and marshes in constant readiness to fight while the tank or halftrack is bogged down in mud. The insurgent forces in Laos and Vietnam have made their greatest drives just before the heavy rains set in, knowing that the mechanized forces with American equipment will be mostly immobilized until the land dries again.

EQUALITY OF MEN

The tendency to moralize has been operative in supporting another important trait of American culture, egalitarianism. Americans believe all people should have equal opportunities for achievement.

This is more of a moral imperative than an actual fact of American life and has always been so. From the earliest times there have been some groups of people who were treated as inferior, and great differences of wealth, education, influence, opportunity, and privilege exist in the United States. Nevertheless, the experiences that Americans underwent along the frontiers and through the process of immigration did represent a huge historical experiment in social leveling. The legal and institutional heritage prescribes equal rights, condemns special privileges, and demands fair representation for every citizen. The latest efforts to obtain equal treatment for minority groups have been spearheaded by legal resolutions (Supreme Court decisions) and other re-emphases of the egalitarian nature of the society. Inequality, unless a product of achievement or lack of it, is considered to be wrong, bad, or "unfair."

There are, of course, ethnic minorities which have not been assimilated into the major society and which are treated unequally. The main disadvantaged groups now are of African, Mexican, and Amerindian ancestry. Although it is currently fashionable to regard this difference of treatment as based on race, other explanations are just as plausible. None of these groups really constitute a race and people with basically very similar appearances and genetic background (such as those of Italian, Spanish, Chinese, or Japanese ancestry) face much less discrimination. But these latter groups have attempted to adopt the Euro-American cultural pattern while Mexican-American and Amerindians have tended to maintain certain distinctive cultural patterns. The case of the Afro-American is probably unique, in that these people constitute the only group whose ancestors were held in slavery by the majority.

It is probable that the American attitude toward equality of treatment really means "within the major value system"; that is, people are, or should be, treated equally if they accept the basic beliefs and behavior of the social majority. In this sense, the American idea is similar to that of the Muslims, who have always taught that all men are equal under Allah; discrimination by race or any other criterion has been rare so long as one was dealing with acceptors of the faith, and within the ranks of believers the only significant feelings of superiority have been based on supposed relationships with the Prophet. People on a direct line of descent from Mohammed are considered higher than those on a more remote line.

There has been one other form of unequal treatment in American society, that between males and females. Although female liberation movements are fashionable now, the fact is that the American female is already in a position of more nearly equal treatment than in most other nations, and certainly those outside the West. In practice, women are barred from the highest positions and are discriminated against in certain professions. But there are few educational limitations and they can enter freely into economic affairs. Even marriage is considered to be a kind of partnership, an unusual arrangement among the vast range of cultures of the world.

Despite the remaining evidences of unequal treatment toward the unassimilated ethnic minorities and women, the basic American value judgment of equality among men (and women) has not changed. Open patterns of subordination, deference, and acceptance of underprivilege call forth sympathies for the "underdog" and American activist values call for efforts to do something about such matters. This impulse tempts Americans overseas to interfere directly in the life ways of other peoples. The American does not have the patience to deal with persons whose authority seems neither justified nor deserved, or to wait for the ordinary man who will act only when he has received the go-ahead from the figures of prestige or respect in his culture.

Another consequence of American egalitarianism is a preference for simple manners and direct, informal treatment of other persons. This can work to the American's advantage if kept within limits; but where people differ in rank and prestige, offense can be given if all are treated in a breezy, "kidding," impersonal manner. It is much better to try to acquire some of the local usages of long titles, elaborate forms of address and language, and manners of courtesy and deference, than to try to accustom other peoples to American ways. American "kidding" and humor are very special products of an egalitarian culture and generally work best at home.

Since all Americans are supposed to be equal in rights, and since "success" is a primary goal that can only be measured by achievement, a high value must be assigned to individuality. This accent on individual worth seems to be largely a heritage of frontier days and later economic expansion when there were plenty of opportunities for the individual to achieve according to his abilities. However, with population expansion and the filling up of the country, individuality has had to be limited to some extent. It is now known that the ravages of the natural environment are largely due to unchecked drives by industrialists toward individual achievement.

Although individual equality has been stressed throughout American history, the goals and ways of achieving success have been limited. The successful man was one who was better than everyone else but in a way similar to theirs; one might have more and better things than another, but they should be the same kinds of things. And with the full development of urban, corporate life, this similarity of goals seems to have evolved into personal conformity. The organization man has superseded the rugged individualist. Thus, individual self-sufficiency has steadily decreased. One indication of this development is a growing demand for security. And since Americans have abandoned the kinship system for this purpose, they now try to protect themselves with impersonal group insurance which they hope will cover all contingencies. In their efforts to attract new employees, corporations now advertise insurance benefits as much as the challenge of the work and the salary, and these "fringe benefits" are just as often the main concern of prospective employees. Americans buy insurance for the smallest items in their lives, even insuring household appliances against breakdown. Government too becomes more and more a giant insurance corporation, to its direct employees and to the citizenry in general.

HUMANITARIANISM

The American trait of coming to the aid of unfortunates is widespread and well known. It expresses itself in impersonal generosity which is activated by calls for help when unpredicted events of unfortunate or disastrous effect occur. Earthquakes, floods, famines, and epidemics are only a few of the kinds of events that strike a responsive chord in American society. At the end of both world wars American generosity was primarily responsible for getting European nations back on their feet. Not only are they generous, but Americans also show a tremendous amount of efficiency at such times, often more than in "normal" times.

A dramatic illustration of this competence was witnessed in the aftermath of a battle in Vientiane, Laos, at which time the capital was badly damaged. American diplomatic and assistance efforts in the preceding years had not been particularly impressive. In fact, the battle occurred principally because American diplomatic and military bureaus had come to the point of backing two opposing ideological factions of Laotians, supplying both groups with weapons. U.S. assistance efforts had been bogged down by a lack of cultural understanding of the Lao and by administrative problems in the aid mission itself. But after the capital had been heavily damaged by shelling, the American International Cooperation Administration, as well as other American groups in the city, went into action in a manner that was truly impressive. Although many areas had been flattened and an unknown number of people killed, within two to three weeks the city was on its feet again. Besides providing needed goods, the American officials thought nothing of working day and night, and their organizational ability was much more clearly demonstrated than in their inept efforts at military diplomacy which led to the battle. In three to four months, there was hardly a sign that the battle had taken place.

American humanitarianism is a characteristic that can hardly be criticized. It is of a special type, however, and contains one possible basis of misunderstanding in that it is usually highly organized and impersonal. For many other peoples humanitarianism is personal. They consequently do not share with everyone; they cannot. But through personal and kinship obligations, by religious almsgiving, and in other traditional ways, they give what they can. The American must not blind himself to the existence of these other patterns and also must perceive that other peoples are just not as rich as he is. The American tendency can hardly be praised if it is merely converted into a standard of negative judgment against other peoples' ways.

An American tends to condemn begging and the systems that support it, presumably because it involves personalized asking and giving. But it is worthwhile to look into the realities of such a system, as for instance that of *baksheesh,* the Middle Eastern begging tradition. The halt, lame, and blind line up with outstretched palm at the mosque or church door. The American is likely to condemn the cruelty of such a system, but in fact these people are being taken care of by their community according to traditional rules. Every member of the Islamic faithful is expected to give 10 percent of his income *(zaka)* in direct alms to the unfortunates who personally ask for it. This particular pattern of generosity is one that has been worked into the communal life of the society, in keeping with its meager resources. The difference between this system and the Community Chest is mainly one of organization and personalization.

STUDY QUESTIONS FOR PART 1

1. Spindler gives examples of cultural transmission from small, developing, homogeneous societies. Do such events of cultural transmission take place today within our contemporary American society? What are some examples of recruitment, discontinuity, and cultural compression in contemporary America?

2. Formal education is often encouraged in developing countries as a way to increase the standard of living and economic development in general. Does that work? What are your views of the pros, cons, and alternatives to such policies?

3. Arnesberg and Niehoff wrote about U. S. cultural values in the 1970s. In what ways are their assessments still accurate today? What would you add to their list? What would you delete?

4. How do you feel about those values? What values on the list are personally meaningful for you? Why? Are there values on the list that you personally find objectionable? Why?

5. In contemporary schools there tends to be little deliberate discussion of values embedded in the curriculum and in how the roles of teachers and students are defined. Why do you think this is so? What are the effects of this on teachers and students? What are some positive and negative consequences you would expect to be associated with a deliberate and on-going discussion of these values?

6. Should we have a national school curriculum? Why?

7. Do schools treat all students equitably? Explain what you mean by "equitable."

8. What might it mean to teach in a culturally responsive way? Should teachers teach all children in the same way, regardless of cultural diferences? Why?

9. Given the diversity of cultural groups and social classes in our society, what should be the major purpose of our public schools?

PART
2

SOCIAL STRUCTURE
AND EDUCATION

The previous readings offered a perspective on education as the transmission of culture and provided a framework for thinking about and understanding U.S. cultural values. The selections in Part 2 build on these themes and focus more directly on three broad, but related, questions:

- What is education?
- What societal needs does education serve?
- How are these needs met?

The first reading, authored by Durkheim, reflects what is called a *functionalist* perspective on education. This is the dominant set of assumptions underlying public schooling in our society. The next selection, by Hurn, discusses some of the limitations of the functionalist perspective and examines the *conflict* paradigm as an alternative view of the relationship between school and society.

Functionalism is a school of thought that seeks to explain social phenomena in terms of how the survival needs of society are served; in other words, how they help society adjust and adapt to changing social conditions. In the first selection, Durkheim (translated from French over 100 years ago—hence some of the awkward dated usage of language) argues that the basic function of education is to ensure that children grow up to become citizens and workers who function in ways that allow the continued survival of a particular society.

Two key ideas are associated with this theory: role differentiation and social solidarity. According to *role differentiation,* in modern societies there are many different roles that have to be filled. They are not all equally attractive or valued, nor do they all require similar knowledge, skills, or attitudes. Thus, one of the functions of the educational system is to be sure that people are able and trained to fill these different roles. *Social solidarity* ensures that there is a reasonable level of social stability among all the different people filling those different roles. The challenge here is that some roles have high prestige, status, and rewards, while others are relatively low in prestige, status, and rewards.

Functionalists believe that for society to survive, it requires both a sufficient degree of role differentiation to provide workers for all of the things that need to be done in a modern industrial society, and a sufficient level of social solidarity among those individuals for them to get along well enough to want to remain a member of the system. The way modern societies such as ours respond to this challenge is to have a system of universal, compulsory public education. Public education is assumed to provide a trained, ready, work force.

As discussed by Hurn, in the second selection, conflict theorists offer an alternative view. Marxist-oriented conflict theorists take functionalism to task, criticizing functionalism because " . . . it takes the interests and perspectives of the dominant social groups in society and elevates them to the status of universal norms. Having done this, it then uses these norms to measure the contributions of members of all other groups. In this way the interests of a particular social class are misrepresented as belonging to the society as a whole, and this misrepresentation then serves to maintain the privileged position of the members of that class" (Feinberg and Soltis, 1985, p. 46).

For conflict theorists, social class is the critical determinant of social power relations. The Marxian perspective is rooted in the idea that " . . . whenever people are related in different ways to the means of production we have a class society, and each particular class is defined in terms of this relationship" (Feinberg and Soltis, 1985, p. 49). In a capitalist society such as ours, the owners of private businesses constitute one social class, and the people who work in those businesses constitute another class. While in this contemporary time of specialized education and credentials social class distinctions are more complex than they once were, the reality is that the United States is a class society, and there are great disparities among the wealth of people in different classes and their capacity to provide for themselves and their family members. Obviously, a family that is very wealthy has many more alternatives regarding its choices of schooling for its children than does a single parent living in poverty or, for that matter, the typical middle-income wage earner.

In addition to these economic differences associated with one's relation to the means of production (owner, worker, jobless), there are other important differences connected with social class. Individuals in different classes typically have different values, beliefs (although some also are shared), and different perspectives on life in general. Class consciousness is a Marxian idea that refers to the general set of such orientations held by members of a particular social class. Two related concepts are hegemony and false consciousness. Hegemony refers to the condition wherein one class has power over another. False consciousness refers to a condition wherein members of the subordinate class " . . . express the point of view and share the values of the dominant class. . . . True consciousness of your own class is impeded by your acceptance of the values of the dominant class" (Feinberg and Soltis, 1985, p. 50).

While functionalists argue that public schooling reflects societal needs and assures " . . . the production of cognitive skills, the sorting and selection of talents, [and] the creation of an informed citizenry . . ." (Hurn, 1993, p. 47), conflict theorists "assert that we live in a divided and conflict-ridden society where groups compete for the control of the educational system. . . . Groups who compete for control of schooling use the rhetoric of social needs to conceal that fact that it is *their* interests and *their* demands they are trying to advance" (Hurn, 1993, pp. 57–58).

The functional perspective views the public schools as a more or less rational system for preparing and channeling youth toward occupations and social arrangements necessary for our society's general stability and productivity. In contrast, the conflict perspective views public schooling as a system that perpetuates an existing and inherently unequal social class structure that favors elites and disempowers the masses.

What do we mean by education? The reading by Durkheim provides a thoughtful analysis of the complexities of this question and helps us understand the different ways in which this question has been answered over the centuries. As you will see from discussions in class, this is not a resolved issue. Indeed, many of the reforms witnessed in recent years can be interpreted as different perspectives on the meaning of education. You need to think about how you would answer this question, because the way you answer it will have a large influence on your approach to teaching.

Durkheim makes a number of very important observations about education. Among them are the ideas that education varies by social class and locality; given the adult role to be filled by a child, beyond a certain age education needs to be more differentiated; for education to occur, children and adults must interact, with the adults influencing the children; a major objective of all education is to ensure that all children gain a basic understanding of what we know about human nature.

For Durkheim, the focus and primary function of education is to prepare children for their roles as workers and members of the larger society. Durkheim makes an important distinction between what he refers to as the "individual being" and the "social being." In his view, the purpose of education is to shape the social being: "a system of ideas, sentiments and practices which express in us, not our personality, but the group or different groups of which we are a part; these are the religious beliefs, moral beliefs and practices, national or professional traditions, collective opinions of every kind. Their totality forms the social being" (p. 72). Although Durkheim believes the development of the individual being is important, it is the socialization of children to membership in the larger group, outside the family, that is the critical function of education. What, then, is education? For Durkheim, "Education is, then, only the means by which society prepares within the children, the essential conditions of its very existence" (p. 71). Notice the functionalist point of view reflected in this observation.

What societal needs does education serve? The selection authored by Durkheim tells us that education serves two basic needs of society: (1) to be sure that children are prepared in adequate numbers to fill a wide variety of social roles needed for a complex modern society such as ours and to adapt and survive as the world's and our society's conditions change; and (2) to be sure that children acquire the attitudes, skills, and values needed to ensure that society can both achieve and maintain enough social solidarity to survive, and that workers and citizens believe in the system and want to remain a part of it. Conversely, adopting a conflict theorist perspective, does our system of public schooling really encourage the development of youth to its fullest capacity? Whose needs are being met by a public schooling system that perpetuates existing inequalities?

How are these needs achieved? For functionalists like Durkheim, there are two major ideas. One is that the major quality of the teacher is his/her moral authority. This, in combination with the teacher's belief in the importance of education and the relatively passive and vulnerable state of the child, gives the teacher an extraordinary amount of power to influence the child. The second critical way society's needs are achieved is through the role the State plays in education. Durkheim points out that the State has a vested interest in education and that it must intrude on a regular basis to remind the teacher of the values, attitudes, and sentiments the child is to be taught, in the interests of the State. "The role of the State is to outline these essential principles, to have them taught in its schools, to see to it that nowhere are children left ignorant of them, that everywhere they should be spoken of with the respect that is due them" (p. 81).

Alternatively, conflict theorists help us understand that "more of the same" is unlikely to advance our society toward a more meritocratic model, toward a more just and democratic way of life. Conflict theorists are less clear regarding *society's* needs, emphasizing the power differences and conflicting interests among different groups within our society and the inherent inequities perpetuated by the current system of education.

As you read the next two selections, give special thought to what education is, the connections between education and society, and the ways in which education meets society's needs. Also remember that these are competing views of education. Think about why you agree or disagree with the functionalist and the conflict perspectives. Can both these perspectives be true? What might be an alternative perspective? Finally, why is it so important for a teacher to have a good understanding of education and its purposes?

EDUCATION: ITS NATURE AND ITS ROLE

1. DEFINITIONS OF EDUCATION. CRITICAL EXAMINATION

The word "education" has sometimes been used in a very broad sense to designate the totality of influences that nature or other men are able to exercise either on our intelligence or on our will. It includes, says John Stuart Mill, "all that we ourselves do and all that others do for us to the end of bringing us closer to the perfection of our nature. In its most widely accepted sense, it includes even indirect effects on the character and faculties of men produced by things having quite a different objective: by laws, by forms of government, the industrial arts, and even by physical phenomena, independent of human will, such as climate, soil, and locality." But this definition includes elements that are quite disparate, and that one cannot combine under a single heading without confusion. The influence of things on men is very different, in their processes and effects, from that which comes from men themselves; and the influence of peers on peers differs from that which adults exercise on youth. It is only the latter that concerns us here, and, therefore, it is this meaning that it is convenient to reserve for the word "education."

But what is the specific nature of this influence? Various answers have been given to this question; they can be divided into two main types.

Following Kant, "the end of education is to develop, in each individual, all the perfection of which he is capable." But what is meant by perfection? It is, as has often been said, the harmo-

nious development of all the human faculties. To carry to the highest point that can be reached all the capacities that are in us, to realize them as completely as possible, without their interfering with one another, is not this an ideal beyond which there can be no other?

But if, to a degree, this harmonious development is indeed necessary and desirable, it is not wholly attainable; for it is in contradiction to another rule of human behavior which is no less cogent; that which has us concentrate on a specific, limited task. We cannot and we must not all be devoted to the same kind of life; we have, according to our aptitudes, different functions to fulfill, and we must adapt ourselves to what we must do. We are not all made for reflection; there is need for men of feeling and of action. Conversely, there is need of those whose job is thinking. Now, thought can develop only in detachment from action, only by turning in upon itself, only by turning its object entirely away from overt action. From this comes a first differentiation which is accompanied by a break of equilibrium. And behavior, in turn, as thought, can take a variety of different and specialized forms. Doubtless this specialization does not exclude a certain common base and, consequently, a certain balance of functions, organic and psychic alike, without which the health of the individual would be

---

Source: *Reprinted with the permission of The Free Press, a Division of Simon and Schuster, Inc. from* Education and Sociology *by Emile Durkheim, translated with an introduction by Sherwood D. Fox. Copyright 1956 by The Free Press.*

49

endangered, as well as social cohesion. We see, thus, that perfect harmony cannot be presented as the final end of conduct and of education.

Still less satisfactory is the utilitarian definition, according to which the objective of education would be to "make the individual an instrument of happiness for himself and for his fellows" (James Mill); for happiness is an essentially subjective thing that each person appreciates in his own way. Such a formula, then, leaves the end of education undetermined and, therefore, education itself, since it is left to individual fancy. Spencer, to be sure, tried to define happiness objectively. For him, the conditions of happiness are those of life. Complete happiness is the complete life. But what is meant by life? If it is a matter of physical existence alone, one may well say: that without which it would be impossible; it implies, in effect, a certain equilibrium between the organism and its environment, and, since the two terms in relation are definable data, it must be the same with their relation. But one can express, in this way, only the most immediate vital necessities. Now, for man, and above all for the man of today, such a life is not life. We ask more of life than normal enough functioning of our organs. A cultivated mind prefers not to live rather than give up the joys of the intellect. Even from the material point of view alone, everything over and above what is strictly necessary cannot be exactly determined. The "standard of life," as the English say, the minimum below which it does not seem to us that we can consent to descend, varies infinitely according to conditions, milieux, and the times. What we found sufficient yesterday, today seems to us to be beneath the dignity of man, as we define it now, and everything leads us to believe that our needs in this connection grow increasingly.

We come here to the general criticism that all these definitions face. They assume that there is an ideal, perfect education, which applies to all men indiscriminately; and it is this education, universal and unique, that the theorist tries to define. But first, if history is taken into consideration, one finds in it nothing to confirm such an hypothesis. Education has varied infinitely in time and place. In the cities of Greece and Rome, education trained the individual to subordinate himself blindly to the collectivity, to become the creature of society. Today, it tries to make of the individual an autonomous personality. In Athens, they sought to form cultivated souls, informed, subtle, full of measure and harmony, capable of enjoying beauty and the joys of pure speculation; in Rome, they wanted above all for children to become men of action, devoted to military glory, indifferent to letters and the arts. In the Middle Ages, education was above all Christian; in the Renaissance, it assumes a more lay and literary character; today science tends to assume the place in education formerly occupied by the arts. Can it be said, then, that the fact is not the ideal; that if education has varied, it is because men have mistaken what it should be? But if Roman education had been infused with an individualism comparable to ours, the Roman city would not have been able to maintain itself; Latin civilization would not have developed, nor, furthermore, our modern civilization, which is in part descended from it. The Christian societies of the Middle Ages would not have been able to survive if they had given to free inquiry the place that we give it today. There are, then, ineluctable necessities which it is impossible to disregard. Of what use is it to imagine a kind of education that would be fatal for the society that put it into practice?

This assumption, so doubtful, in itself rests on a more general mistake. If one begins by asking, thus, what an ideal education must be, abstracted from conditions of time and place, it is to admit implicitly that a system of education has no reality in itself. One does not see in education a collection of practices and institutions that have been organized slowly in the course of time, which are comparable with all the other social institutions and which express them, and which, therefore, can no more be changed at will than the structure of the society itself. But it seems that this would be a pure system of *a priori* concepts; under this heading it appears to be a logical construct. One imagines that men of each age organize it voluntarily to realize a determined end; that, if this organization is not everywhere the same, it is because mistakes have been made concerning either the end that it is to pursue or the means of attaining it. From this point of view, educational systems of the past appear as so many errors, total or partial. No attention need be paid to them, therefore; we do not have to associate ourselves with the faulty observation or logic of our predecessors; but we can and must pose the question without concerning ourselves with solutions that have been given, that is to say, leaving aside everything that has been, we have only to ask ourselves what should be. The lessons of history can, moreover, serve to prevent us from repeating the errors that have been committed.

In fact, however, each society, considered at a given stage of development, has a system of education which exercises an irresistible influence on individuals. It is idle to think that we can rear our children as we wish. There are customs to which we are bound to conform; if we flout them too severely, they take their vengeance on our children. The children, when they are adults, are unable to live with their peers, with whom they are not in accord. Whether they had been raised in accordance with ideas that were either obsolete or premature does not matter; in the one case as in the other, they are not of their time and, therefore, they are outside the conditions of normal life. There is, then, in each period, a prevailing type of education from which we cannot deviate without encountering that lively resistance which restrains the fancies of dissent.

Now, it is not we as individuals who have created the customs and ideas that determine this type. They are the product of a common life, and they express its needs. They are, moreover, in large part the work of preceding generations. The entire human past has contributed to the formation of this totality of maxims that guide education today; our entire history has left its traces in it, and even the history of the peoples who have come before. It is thus that the higher organisms carry in themselves the reflection of the whole biological evolution of which they are the end product. Historical investigation of the formation and development of systems of education reveals that they depend upon religion, political organi-

zation, the degree of development of science, the state of industry, etc. If they are considered apart from all these historic causes, they become incomprehensible. Thus, how can the individual pretend to reconstruct, through his own private reflection, what is not a work of individual thought? He is not confronted with a *tabula rasa* on which he can write what he wants, but with existing realities which he cannot create, or destroy, or transform, at will. He can act on them only to the extent that he has learned to understand them, to know their nature and the conditions on which they depend; and he can understand them only if he studies them, only if he starts by observing them, as the physicist observes inanimate matter and the biologist, living bodies.

Besides, how else to proceed? When one wants to determine by dialectics alone what education should be, it is necessary to begin by asking what objectives it must have. But what is it that allows us to say that education has certain ends rather than others? We do not know *a priori* what is the function of respiration or of circulation in a living being. By what right would we be more well informed concerning the educational function? It will be said in reply that from all the evidence, its object is the training of children. But this is posing the problem in slightly different terms; it does not resolve it. It would be necessary to say of what this training consists, what its direction is, what human needs it satisfies. Now, one can answer these questions only by beginning with observation of what it has consisted of, what needs it has satisfied in the past. Thus, it appears that to establish the preliminary notion of education, to determine what is so called, historical observation is indispensable.

2. DEFINITION OF EDUCATION

To define education we must, then, consider educational systems, present and past, put them together, and abstract the characteristics which are common to them. These characteristics will constitute the definition that we seek.

We have already determined, along the way, two elements. In order that there be education, there must be a generation of adults and one of youth, in interaction, and an influence exercised by the first on the second. It remains for us to define the nature of this influence.

There is, so to speak, no society in which the system of education does not present a twofold aspect; it is at the same time one and manifold.

It is manifold. Indeed, in one sense, it can be said that there are as many different kinds of education as there are different milieux in a given society. Is such a society formed of castes? Education varies from one caste to another; that of the patricians was not that of the plebeians; that of the Brahman was not that of the Sudra. Similarly, in the Middle Ages, what a difference between the culture that the young page received, instructed in all the arts of chivalry, and that of the villein, who learned in his parish school a smattering of arithmetic, song and grammar! Even today, do we not see education vary with social class, or even with locality? That of the city is not that of the country, that of the middle class is not that of the worker. Would one say that this organization is not morally justifiable, that one can see in it only a survival destined to disappear? This proposition is easy to defend. It is evident that the education of our children should not depend upon the chance of their having been born here or there, of some parents rather than others. But even though the moral conscience of our time would have received, on this point, the satisfaction that it expects, education would not, for all that, become more uniform. Even though the career of each child would, in large part, no longer be predetermined by a blind heredity, occupational specialization would not fail to result in a great pedagogical diversity. Each occupation, indeed, constitutes a milieu *sui generis* which requires particular aptitudes and specialized knowledge, in which certain ideas, certain practices, certain modes of viewing things, prevail; and as the child must be prepared for the function that he will be called upon to fulfill, education, beyond a certain age, can no longer remain the same for all those to whom it applies. That is why

we see it, in all civilized countries, tending more and more to become diversified and specialized; and the specialization becomes more advanced daily. The heterogeneity which is thus created does not rest, as does that which we were just discussing, on unjust inequalities; but it is not less. To find an absolutely homogeneous and egalitarian education, it would be necessary to go back to prehistoric societies, in the structure of which there is no differentiation; and yet these kinds of societies represent hardly more than one logical stage in the history of humanity.

But, whatever may be the importance of these special educations, they are not all of education. It may even be said that they are not sufficient unto themselves; everywhere that one observes them, they vary from one another only beyond a certain point, up to which they are not differentiated. They all rest upon a common base. There is no people among whom there is not a certain number of ideas, sentiments and practices which education must inculcate in all children indiscriminately, to whatever social category they belong. Even in a society which is divided into closed castes, there is always a religion common to all, and, consequently, the principles of the religious culture, which is, then, fundamental, are the same throughout the population. If each caste, each family, has its special gods, there are general divinities that are recognized by everyone and which all children learn to worship. And as these divinities symbolize and personify certain sentiments, certain ways of conceiving the world and life, one cannot be initiated into their cult without acquiring, at the same time, all sorts of thought patterns which go beyond the sphere of the purely religious life. Similarly, in the Middle Ages, serfs, villeins, burgers and nobles received, equally, a common Christian education. If it is thus in societies where intellectual and moral diversity reach this degree of contrast, with how much more reason is it so among more advanced peoples where classes, while remaining distinct, are, however, separated by a less profound cleavage! Where these common elements of all education are not expressed in the form of religious symbols, they do not, however, cease to exist. In the course of our history, there has been established a whole set of ideas on human nature, on the respective importance of our different faculties, on right and duty, on society, on the individual, on progress, on science, on art, etc., which are the very basis of our national spirit; all education, that of the rich as well as that of the poor, that which leads to professional careers as well as that which prepares for industrial functions, has as its object to fix them in our minds.

From these facts it follows that each society sets up a certain ideal of man, of what he should be, as much from the intellectual point of view as the physical and moral; that this ideal is, to a degree, the same for all the citizens; that beyond a certain point it becomes differentiated according to the particular milieux that every society contains in its structure. It is this ideal, at the same time one and various, that is the focus of education. Its function, then, is to arouse in the child: (1) a certain number of physical and mental states that the society to which he belongs considers should not be lacking in any of its members; (2) certain physical and mental states that the particular social group (caste, class, family, profession) considers, equally, ought to be found among all those who make it up. Thus, it is society as a whole and each particular social milieu that determine the ideal that education realizes. Society can survive only if there exists among its members a sufficient degree of homogeneity; education perpetuates and reinforces this homogeneity by fixing in the child, from the beginning, the essential similarities that collective life demands. But on the other hand, without a certain diversity all co-operation would be impossible; education assures the persistence of this necessary diversity by being itself diversified and specialized. If the society has reached a degree of development such that the old divisions into castes and classes can no longer be maintained, it will prescribe an education more uniform at its base. If at the same time there is more division of labor, it will arouse among children, on the underlying basic set of common ideas and sentiments, a richer diversity of occupational aptitudes. If it lives in a state of war with the surrounding soci-

eties, it tries to shape people according to a strongly nationalistic model; if international competition takes a more peaceful form, the type that it tries to realize is more general and more humanistic. Education is, then, only the means by which society prepares, within the children, the essential conditions of its very existence. We shall see later how the individual himself has an interest in submitting to these requirements.

We come, then, to the following formula: *Education is the influence exercised by adult generations on those that are not yet ready for social life. Its object is to arouse and to develop in the child a certain number of physical, intellectual and moral states which are demanded of him by both the political society as a whole and the special milieu for which he is specifically destined.*

3. CONSEQUENCES OF THE PRECEDING DEFINITION: THE SOCIAL CHARACTER OF EDUCATION

It follows from the definition that precedes, that education consists of a methodical socialization of the young generation. In each of us, it may be said, there exist two beings which, while inseparable except by abstraction, remain distinct. One is made up of all the mental states that apply only to ourselves and to the events of our personal lives: this is what might be called the individual being. The other is a system of ideas, sentiments and practices which express in us, not our personality, but the group or different groups of which we are part; these are religious beliefs, moral beliefs and practices, national or professional traditions, collective opinions of every kind. Their totality forms the social being. To constitute this being in each of us is the end of education.

It is here, moreover, that are best shown the importance of its role and the fruitfulness of its influence. Indeed, not only is this social being not given, fully formed, in the primitive constitution of man; but it has not resulted from it through a spontaneous development. Spontaneously, man was not inclined to submit to a political authority, to respect a moral discipline, to dedicate himself, to be self-sacrificing. There was nothing in our congenital nature that predisposed us necessarily to become servants of divinities, symbolic emblems of society, to render them worship, to deprive ourselves in order to do them honor. It is society itself which, to the degree that it is firmly established, has drawn from within itself those great moral forces in the face of which man has felt his inferiority. Now, if one leaves aside the vague and indefinite tendencies which can be attributed to heredity, the child, on entering life, brings to it only his nature as an individual. Society finds itself, with each new generation, faced with a *tabula rasa*, very nearly, on which it must build anew. To the egoistic and asocial being that has just been born it must, as rapidly as possible, add another, capable of leading a moral and social life. Such is the work of education, and you can readily see its great importance. It is not limited to developing the individual organism in the direction indicated by its nature, to elicit the hidden potentialities that need only be manifested. It creates in man a new being.

This creative quality is, moreover, a special prerogative of human education. Anything else is what animals receive, if one can apply this name to the progressive training to which they are subjected by their parents. It can, indeed, foster the development of certain instincts that lie dormant in the animal, but such training does not initiate it into a new life. It facilitates the play of natural functions, but it creates nothing. Taught by its mother, the young animal learns more quickly how to fly or build its nest; but it learns almost nothing that it could not have been able to discover through its own individual experience. This is because animals either do not live under social conditions or form rather simple societies, which function through instinctive mechanisms that each individual carries within himself, fully formed, from birth. Education, then, can add nothing essential to nature, since the latter is adequate for everything, for the life of the group as well as that of the individual. By contrast, among men the aptitudes of every kind that social life presupposes are much too complex to be able to be contained, somehow, in our tissues, and to take the form of organic predispositions. It follows that they cannot be transmitted from one generation to another by way of heredity. It is through education that the transmission is effected.

However, it will be said, if one can indeed conceive that the distinctively moral qualities, because they impose privations on the individual, because they inhibit his natural impulses, can be developed in us only under an outside influence, are there not others which every man wishes to acquire and seeks spontaneously? Such are the diverse qualities of the intelligence which allow him better to adapt his behavior to the nature of things. Such, too, are the physical qualities, and everything that contributes to the vigor and health of the organism. For the former, at least, it seems that education, in developing them, may only assist the development of nature itself, may only lead the individual to a state of relative perfection toward which he tends by himself, although he may be able to achieve it more rapidly thanks to the co-operation of society.

But what demonstrates, despite appearances, that here as elsewhere education answers social necessities above all, is that there are societies in which these qualities have not been cultivated at all, and that in every case they have been understood very differently in different societies. The advantages of a solid intellectual culture have been far from recognized by all peoples. Science and the critical mind, that we rank so high today, were for a long time held in suspicion. Do we not know a great doctrine that proclaims happy the poor in spirit? We must guard against believing that this indifference to knowledge had been artificially imposed on men in violation of their nature. They do not have, by themselves, the instinctive appetite for science that has often and arbitrarily been attributed to them. They desire science only to the extent that experience has taught them that they cannot do without it. Now, in connection with the ordering of their individual lives they had no use for it. As Rousseau has already said, to satisfy the vital necessities, sensation, experience and instinct would suffice as they suffice for the animal. If man had not known other needs than these, very simple ones, which have their roots in his individual constitution, he would not have undertaken the pursuit of science, all the more because it has not been acquired without laborious and painful efforts. He has known the thirst for knowledge only when society has awakened it in him, and society has done this only when it has felt the need of it. This moment came when social life, in all its forms, had become too complex to be able to function otherwise than through the co-operation of reflective thought, that is to say, thought enlightened by science. Then scientific culture became indispensable, and that is why society requires it of its members and imposes it upon them as a duty. But in the beginning, as long as social organization is very simple and undifferentiated, always self-sufficient, blind tradition suffices, as does instinct in the animal. Therefore thought and free inquiry are useless and even dangerous, since they can only threaten tradition. That is why they are proscribed.

It is not otherwise with physical qualities. Where the state of the social milieu inclines public sentiment toward asceticism, physical education will be relegated to a secondary place. Something of this sort took place in the schools of the Middle Ages; and this asceticism was necessary, for the only manner of adapting to the harshness of those difficult times was to like it. Similarly, following the current of opinion, this same education will be understood very differently. In Sparta its object above all was to harden the limbs to fatigue; in Athens, it was a means of making bodies beautiful to the sight; in the time of chivalry it was required to form agile and supple warriors; today it no longer has any but a hygienic end, and is concerned, above all, with limiting the dangerous effects of a too intense intellectual culture. Thus, even the qualities which appear at first glance so spontaneously desirable, the individual seeks only when society invites him to, and he seeks them in the fashion that it prescribes for him.

We are not in a position to answer a question raised by all that precedes. Whereas we showed society fashioning individuals according to its needs, it could seem, from this fact, that the individuals were submitting to an insupportable tyranny. But in reality they are themselves interested in this submission; for the new being that collective influence, through education, thus builds up in each of us, represents what is best in us. Man is man, in fact, only because he lives in society. It is difficult, in the course of an article, to demonstrate rigorously a proposition so general and so important, and one which sums up the works of contemporary sociology. But first, one can say that it is less and less disputed. And more, it is not impossible to call to mind, summarily, the most essential facts that justify it.

First, if there is today an historically established fact, it is that morality stands in close relationship to the nature of societies, since, as we have shown along the way, it changes when societies change. This is because it results from life in common. It is society, indeed, that draws us out of ourselves, that obliges us to reckon with other interests than our own, it is society that has taught us to control our passions, our instincts, to prescribe law for them, to restrain ourselves, to deprive ourselves, to sacrifice ourselves, to subordinate our personal ends to higher ends. As for the whole system of representation which maintains in us the idea and the sentiment of rule, of discipline, internal as well as external—it is society that has established it in our consciences. It is thus that we have acquired this power to control ourselves, this control over our inclinations which is one of the distinctive traits of the human being and which is the more developed to the extent that we are more fully human.

We do not owe society less from the intellectual point of view. It is science that elaborates the cardinal notions that govern our thought: notions of cause, of laws, of space, of number, notions of bodies, of life, of conscience, of society, and so on. All these fundamental ideas are perpetually evolving, because they are the recapitulation, the resultant of all scientific work, far from being its point of departure as Pestalozzi believed. We do not conceive of man, nature, cause, even space, as they were conceived in the Middle Ages; this is because our knowledge and our scientific methods are no longer the same. Now, science is a collective work, since it presupposes a vast cooperation of all scientists, not only of the same time, but of all the successive epochs of history. Before the sciences were established, religion filled the same office; for every mythology consists of a conception, already well elaborated, of man and of the universe. Science, moreover, was the heir of religion. Now, a religion is a social institution.

In learning a language, we learn a whole system of ideas, distinguished and classified, and we inherit from all the work from which have come these classifications that sum up centuries of experiences. There is more: without language, we would not have, so to speak, general ideas; for it is the word which, in fixing them, gives to concepts a consistency sufficient for them to be able to be handled conveniently by the mind. It is language, then, that has allowed us to raise ourselves above pure sensation; and it is not necessary to demonstrate that language is, in the first degree, a social thing.

One sees, through these few examples, to what man would be reduced if there were withdrawn from him all that he has derived from society: he would fall to the level of an animal. If he has been able to surpass the stage at which animals have stopped, it is primarily because he is not reduced to the fruit only of his personal efforts, but cooperates regularly with his fellow-creatures; and this makes the activity of each more productive. It is chiefly as a result of this that the products of the work of one generation are not lost for that which follows. Of what an animal has been able to learn in the course of his individual existence, almost nothing can survive him. By contrast, the results of human experience are preserved almost entirely and in detail, thanks to books, sculptures, tools, instruments of every kind that are transmitted from generation to generation, oral tradition, etc. The soil of nature is thus covered with a rich deposit that continues to grow constantly. Instead of dissipat-

ing each time that a generation dies out and is replaced by another, human wisdom accumulates without limit, and it is this unlimited accumulation that raises man above the beast and above himself. But, just as in the case of the cooperation which was discussed first, this accumulation is possible only in and through society. For in order that the legacy of each generation may be able to be preserved and added to others, it is necessary that there be a moral personality which lasts beyond the generations that pass, which binds them to one another: it is society. Thus the antagonism that has too often been admitted between society and individual corresponds to nothing in the facts. Indeed, far from these two terms being in opposition and being able to develop only each at the expense of the other, they imply each other. The individual, in willing society, wills himself. The influence that it exerts on him, notable through education, does not at all have as its object and its effect to repress him, to diminish him, to denature him, but, on the contrary, to make him grow and to make of him a truly human being. No doubt, he can grow thus only by making an effort. But this is precisely because this power to put forth voluntary effort is one of the most essential characteristics of man.

4. THE ROLE OF THE STATE IN EDUCATION

This definition of education provides for a ready solution of the controversial question of the duties and the rights of the State with respect to education.

The rights of the family are opposed to them. The child, it is said, belongs first to his parents; it is, then, their responsibility to direct, as they understand it, his intellectual and moral development. Education is then conceived as an essentially private and domestic affair. When one takes this point of view, one tends naturally to reduce to a minimum the intervention of the State in the matter. The State should, it is said, be limited to serving as an auxiliary to, and as a substitute for, families. When they are unable to discharge their duties, it is natural that the State should take charge. It is natural, too, that it make their task as easy as possible, by placing at their disposal schools to which they can, if they wish, send their children. But it must be kept strictly within these limits, and forbidden any positive action designed to impress a given orientation on the mind of the youth.

But its role need hardly remain so negative. If, as we have tried to establish, education has a collective function above all, if its object is to adapt the child to the social milieu in which he is destined to live, it is impossible that society should be uninterested in such a procedure. How could society not have a part in it, since it is the reference point by which education must direct its action? It is, then, up to the State to remind the teacher constantly of the ideas, the sentiments that must be impressed upon the child to adjust him to the milieu in which he must live. If it were not always there to guarantee that pedagogical influence be exercised in a social way, the latter would necessarily be put to the service of private beliefs, and the whole nation would be divided and would break down into an incoherent multitude of little fragments in conflict with one another. One could not contradict more completely the fundamental end of all education. Choice is necessary: if one attaches some value to the existence of society—and we have just seen what it means to us—education must assure, among the citizens, a sufficient community of ideas and of sentiments, without which any society is impossible; and in order that it may be able to produce this result, it is also necessary that education not be completely abandoned to the arbitrariness of private individuals.

Since education is an essentially social function, the State cannot be indifferent to it. On the contrary, everything that pertains to education must in some degree be submitted to its influence. This is not to say, therefore, that it must necessarily monopolize instruction. The question is too complex to be able to be treated thus in passing; we shall discuss it later. One can believe that scholastic progress is easier and quicker where a certain margin is left for individual initiative; for the individual makes innovations more readily than the State. But from the fact that the State, in the public interest, must allow other schools to be opened than those for which it has a more direct responsibility, it does not follow that it must remain aloof from what is going on in them. On the contrary, the education given in them must remain under its control. It is not even admissible that the function of the educator can be fulfilled by anyone who does not offer special guarantees of which the State alone can be the judge. No doubt, the limits within which its intervention should be kept may be rather difficult to determine once and for all, but the principle of intervention could not be disputed. There is no school which can claim the right to give, with full freedom, an antisocial education.

It is nevertheless necessary to recognize that the state of division in which we now find ourselves, in our country, makes this duty of the State particularly delicate and at the same time more important. It is not, indeed, up to the State to create this community of ideas and sentiments without which there is no society; it must be established by itself, and the State can only consecrate it, maintain it, make individuals more aware of it. Now, it is unfortunately indisputable that among us, this moral unity is not at all points what it should be. We are divided by divergent and even sometimes contradictory conceptions. There is in these divergences a fact which it is impossible to deny, and which must be reckoned with. It is not a question of recognizing the right of the majority to impose its ideas on the children of the minority. The school should not be the thing of one party, and the teacher is remiss in his duties when he uses the authority at his disposal to influence his pupils in accordance with his own preconceived opinions, however justified they may appear to him. But in spite of all the differences of opinion, there are at present, at the basis of our civilization, a certain number of principles which, implicitly or explicitly, are common to all, that few indeed, in any case, dare to deny overtly and openly: respect for reason, for science, for ideas and sentiments which are at the base of democratic morality. The role of the State is to outline these essential principles, to have them taught in its schools, to see to it that nowhere are children left ignorant of them, that everywhere they should be spoken of with the respect which is due them. There is in this connection an influence to exert which will perhaps be all the more efficacious when it will be less aggressive and less violent, and will know better how to be contained within wise limits.

5. THE POWER OF EDUCATION. THE MEANS OF INFLUENCE

After having determined the end of education, we must seek to determine how and to what extent it is possible to attain this end, that is to say, how and to what extent education can be efficacious.

This question has always been very controversial. For Fontenelle, "neither does good education make good character, nor does bad education destroy it." By contrast, for Locke, for Helvetius, education is all-powerful. According to the latter, "all men are born equal and with equal aptitudes; education alone makes for differences." The theory of Jacotot resembles the preceding.

The solution that one gives to the problem depends on the idea that one has of the importance and of the nature of the innate predispositions, on the one hand, and, on the other, of the means of influence at the disposal of the educator.

Education does not make a man out of nothing, as Locke and Helvetius believed; it is applied to predispositions that it finds already made. From another point of view, one can concede, in a general way, that these congenital tendencies are very strong, very difficult to destroy or to transform radically; for they depend upon organic conditions on which the educator has little influence. Consequently, to the degree that they have a definite object, that they incline the mind and the character toward narrowly determined ways of acting and thinking, the whole future of the individual finds itself fixed in advance, and there does not remain much for education to do.

But fortunately one of the characteristics of man is that the innate predispositions in him are very general and very vague. Indeed, the type of predisposition that is fixed, rigid, invariable, which hardly leaves room for the influence of external causes, is instinct. Now, one can ask if there is a single instinct, properly speaking, in man. One speaks, sometimes, of the instinct of preservation; but the word is inappropriate. For an instinct is a system of given actions, always the same, which, once they are set in motion by sensation, are automatically linked up with one another until they reach their natural limit, without reflection having to intervene anywhere; now, the movements that we make when our life is in danger do not all have any such fixity or automatic invariability. They change with the situation; we adapt them to circumstances: this is because they do not operate without a certain conscious choice, however rapid. What is called the instinct of preservation is, after all, only a general impulse to flee death, without the means by which we seek to avoid it being predetermined once and for all. One can say as much concerning what is sometimes called, not less inexactly, the maternal instinct, the paternal instinct, and even the sexual instinct. These are drives in a given direction; but the means by which these drives are expressed vary from one individual to another, from one occasion to another. A large area remains reserved, then, for trial and error, for personal accommodations, and, consequently, for the effect of causes which can make their influence felt only after birth. Now, education is one of these causes.

It has been claimed, to be sure, that the child sometimes inherits a very strong tendency toward a given act, such as suicide, theft, murder, fraud, etc. But these assertions are not at all in accord with the facts. Whatever may have been said about it, one is not born criminal; still less is one destined from birth for this or that type of crime; the paradox of the Italian criminologists no longer counts many defenders today. What is inherited is a certain lack of mental equilibrium, which makes the individual refractory to coherent and disciplined behavior. But such a temperament does not predestine a man to be a criminal any more than to be an explorer seeking adventure, a prophet, a political innovator, an inventor, etc. As much can be said of any occupational aptitudes. As Bain remarked, "the son of a great philologist does not inherit a single word; the son of a great traveler can, at school, be surpassed in geography by the son of a miner." What the child receives from his parents are very general faculties; some force of attention, a certain amount of perseverance, a sound judgment, imagination, etc. But each of these faculties can serve all sorts of different ends. A child endowed with a rather lively imagination will be able, depending on circumstances, on the influences that will be brought to bear upon him, to become a painter or a poet, or an engineer with an inventive mind, or a daring financier. There is, then, a considerable difference between natural qualities and the special forms that they must take to be utilized in life. This means that the future is not strictly predetermined by our congenital constitution. The reason for this is easy to understand. The only forms of activity that can be transmitted by heredity are those which are always repeated in a sufficiently identical manner to be able to be fixed, in a rigid form, in the tissues of the organism. Now, human life depends on conditions that are manifold, complex, and, consequently, changing; it must itself, then, change and be modified continuously. Thus it is impossible for it to become crystallized in a definite and positive form. But only very general, very vague dispositions, expressing the characteristics common to all individual experiences, can survive and pass from one generation to another.

To say that innate characteristics are for the most part very general, is to say that they are very malleable, very flexible, since they can assume very different forms. Between the vague potentialities which constitute man at the moment of birth and the well-defined character that he must become in order to play a useful role in society, the distance is, then, considerable. It is this distance that education has to make the child travel. One sees that a vast field is open to its influence.

But, to exert this influence, does it have adequate means?

In order to give an idea of what constitutes the educational influence, and to show its power, a contemporary psychologist, Guyau, has compared it to hypnotic suggestion; and the comparison is not without foundation.

Hypnotic suggestion presupposes, indeed, the following two conditions: (1) The state in which the hypnotized subject is found is characterized by its exceptional passivity. The mind is almost reduced to the state of a *tabula rasa*; a sort of void has been achieved in his consciousness; the will is as though paralyzed. Thus, the idea suggested, meeting no contrary idea at all, can be established with a minimum of resistance; (2) however, as the void is never complete, it is necessary, further, that the idea take from the suggestion itself some power of specific action. For that, it is necessary that the hypnotizer speak in a commanding tone, with authority. He must say: *I wish;* he must indicate that refusal to obey is not even conceivable, that the act must be accomplished, that the thing must be seen as he shows it, that it cannot be otherwise. If he weakens, one sees the subject hesitate, resist, sometimes even refuse to obey. If he so much as enters into discussion, that is the end of his power. The more suggestion goes against the natural temperament of the subject, the more will the imperative tone be indispensable.

Now, these two conditions are present in the relationship that the educator has with the child subjected to his influence: (1) The child is naturally in a state of passivity quite comparable to that in which the hypnotic subject is found artificially placed. His mind yet contains only a small number of conceptions able to fight against those which are suggested to him; his will is still rudimentary. Therefore he is very suggestible. For the same reason he is very susceptible to the force of example, very much inclined to imitation. (2) The ascendancy that the teacher naturally has over his pupil, because of the superiority of his experience and of his culture, will naturally give to his influence the efficacious force that he needs.

This comparison shows how far from helpless the educator is; for the great power of hypnotic suggestion is known. If, then, educational influence has, even in a lesser degree, an analogous efficacy, much may be expected of it, provided that one knows how to use it. Far from being discouraged by our impotence, we might well, rather, be frightened by the scope of our power. If teacher and parents were more consistently aware that nothing can happen in the child's presence which does not leave some trace in him, that the form of his mind and of his character depends on these thousands of little unconscious influences that take place at every moment and to which we pay no attention because of their apparent insignificance, how much more would they watch their language and their behavior! Surely, education cannot be very effective when it functions inconsistently. As Herbart says, it is not by reprimanding the child violently from time to time that one can influence him very much. But when education is patient and continuous, when it does not look for immediate and obvious successes, but proceeds slowly in a well-defined direction, without letting itself be diverted by external incidents and adventitious circumstances, it has at its disposal all the means necessary to affect minds profoundly.

At the same time, one sees what is the essential means of educational influence. What makes for the influence of the hypnotist is the authority which he holds under the circumstances. By analogy, then, one can say that education must be essentially a matter of authority. This important proposition can, moreover, be established directly. Indeed, we have seen that the object of education is to superimpose, on the individual and asocial being that we are at birth, an entirely new being. It must bring us to overcome our initial nature; it is on this condition that the child will become a man. Now, we can raise ourselves above ourselves only by a more or less difficult effort. Nothing is so false and deceptive as the Epicurean conception of education, the conception of a Montaigne, for example, according to which man can be formed while enjoying himself and without any other spur than the attraction of pleasure. If there is nothing somber in life and if it is criminal artificially to make it so in the eyes of the

child, it is, however, serious and important; and education, which prepares for life, should share this seriousness. To learn to contain his natural egoism, to subordinate himself to higher ends, to submit his desires to the control of his will, to confine them within proper limits, the child must exercise strong self-control. Now, we restrain ourselves, we limit ourselves, only for one or the other of the following two reasons: because it is necessary through some physical necessity, or because we must do it on moral grounds. But the child cannot feel the necessity that imposes these efforts on us physically, for he is not faced directly with the hard realities of life which make this attitude indispensable. He is not yet engaged in the struggle; whatever Spencer may have said about it, we cannot leave him exposed to these too harsh realities. It is necessary, then, that he be already formed, in large part, when he really encounters them. One cannot, then, depend on their influence to make him bow his will and acquire the necessary mastery over himself.

Duty remains. The sense of duty is, indeed, for the child and even for the adult, the stimulus *par excellence* of effort. Self-respect itself presupposes it. For, to be properly affected by reward and punishment, one must already have a sense of his dignity and, consequently, of his duty. But the child can know his duty only through his teachers or his parents; he can know what it is only through the manner in which they reveal it to him through their language and through their conduct. They must be, then, for him, duty incarnate and personified. Thus moral authority is the dominant quality of the educator. For it is through the authority that is in him that duty is duty. What is his own special quality is the imperative tone with which he addresses consciences, the respect that he inspires in wills and which makes them yield to his judgment. Thus it is indispensable that such an impression emanate from the person of the teacher.

It is not necessary to show that authority, thus understood, is neither violent nor repressive; it consists entirely of a certain moral ascendancy. It presupposes the presence in the teacher of two principal conditions. First, he must have will. For authority implies confidence, and the child cannot have confidence in anyone whom he sees hesitating, shifting, going back on his decision. But this first condition is not the most essential. What is important above all is that the teacher really feels in himself the authority, the feeling for which he is to transmit. It constitutes a force which he can manifest only if he possesses it effectively. Now, where does he get it from? Would it be from the power which he does have, from his right to reward and punish? But fear of chastisement is quite different from respect for authority. It has moral value only if chastisement is recognized as just even by him who suffers it, which implies that the authority which punishes is already recognized as legitimate. And this is the question. It is not from the outside that the teacher can hold his authority, it is from himself; it can come to him only from an inner faith. He must believe, not in himself, no doubt, not in the superior qualities of his intelligence or of his soul, but in his task and in the importance of his task. What makes for the authority which is so readily attached to the word of the priest, is the high idea that he has of his calling; for he speaks in the name of a god in whom he believes, to whom he feels himself closer than the crowd of the uninitiated. The lay teacher can and should have something of this feeling. He too is the agent of a great moral person who surpasses him: it is society. Just as the priest is the interpreter of his god, the teacher is the interpreter of the great moral ideas of his time and of his country. Let him be attached to these ideas, let him feel all their grandeur, and the authority which is in them, and of which he is aware, cannot fail to be communicated to his person and to everything that emanates from him. Into an authority which flows from such an impersonal source there could enter no pride, no vanity, no pedantry. It is made up entirely of the respect which he has for his functions and, if one may say so, for his office. It is this respect which, through word and gesture, passes from him to the child.

Liberty and authority have sometimes been opposed, as if these two factors of education contradicted and limited each other. But this opposition is factitious. In reality these two terms imply, rather than exclude, each other. Liberty is the daughter of authority properly understood. For to be free is not to do what one pleases; it is to be master of oneself, it is to know how to act with reason and to do one's duty. Now, it is precisely to endow the child with this self-mastery that the authority of the teacher should be employed. The authority of the teacher is only one aspect of the authority of duty and of reason. The child should, then, be trained to recognize it in the speech of the educator and to submit to its ascendancy; it is on this condition that he will know later how to find it again in his own conscience and to defer to it.

THEORIES OF SCHOOLING AND SOCIETY: THE FUNCTIONAL AND CONFLICT PARADIGMS

CHRISTOPHER J. HURN

THE FUNCTIONAL PARADIGM OF SCHOOLING

The functional paradigm of schooling is not the work of any one individual theorist, nor does it consist exclusively of the ideas of sociologists. In its most general form the functional paradigm has long been part of the conventional wisdom of liberal intellectuals in Western society and, to a large extent, part of the working assumptions of the great majority of all who have thought and written about schooling in Western societies until quite recently. Many of its assumptions are found in commencement addresses and political speeches on the benefits of education, as well as in textbooks on the sociology of education.[1]

MODERN SOCIETY—THE FUNCTIONAL VIEW

At the heart of the functional paradigm is an analysis of what adherents to the model see as the unique character of the modern Western world and the crucial functions that schooling plays in that world. The paradigm sees modern Western societies differing from most previous societies in at least three crucial respects.

THE MERITOCRATIC SOCIETY   In modern societies occupational roles are (and should be) achieved rather than ascribed. Contemporary intellectuals have long regarded the inheritance of occupational roles, and more broadly the inheritance of social status, as anathema. People believe high-status positions should be achieved on the basis of merit rather than passed on from parent to child. The children of the poor should have equal opportunity to achieve high status with more privileged children. And in all Western societies, particularly since World War II, governments have responded to this belief by trying to increase equality of opportunity: by expanding higher education, introducing universalistic rules for employment intended to discourage nepotism, and legislating elimination of discrimination on the basis of religion, race, and sex. The functional paradigm, therefore, sees modern society as *meritocratic:* a society where ability and effort count for more than privilege and inherited status. Although there is disagreement about just how far along this road to a perfectly meritocratic social order we have traveled, there is agreement that modern society is at least more meritocratic than most societies of the past.[2]

In part, this contention is a moral argument. It is simply wrong, we believe, that doctors or members of elite groups should enjoy overwhelming advantages in passing on inherited status to their children. Besides the moral argument, however, underlying the meritocratic thesis is a

---

Source: *"Theories of Schooling and Society: The Functional and Conflict Paradigms" from* The Limits and Possibilities of Schooling: An Introduction to the Sociology of Education *(3rd Ed.), by Christopher J. Hurn, copyright 1993. Reprinted with the permission of Allyn and Bacon, Inc.*

conviction that achievement is a far more rational way of allocating status than ascription. The theory maintains that modern society demands and requires far larger percentages of highly skilled people than ever before. The percentage of professionals in the United States labor force, for example, has multiplied about ten times since 1900. It is essential, therefore, that the most talented individuals be recruited for these demanding occupations. The health and the economic well-being of a society depend on the degree to which it can find and place its most talented individuals in the most demanding occupations. An increasingly meritocratic society is not only morally justified, but it is also a more rational and efficient society.

THE EXPERT SOCIETY   A second distinctive feature of the contemporary social order is closely related to these ideas about talent, efficiency, and rationality. The functional paradigm sees modern society as an expert society:[3] one that depends preeminently on rational knowledge for economic growth, requiring more and more highly trained individuals to fill the majority of occupational positions. Schools perform two crucial functions in this view. First, the research activities of universities and colleges produce the new knowledge that underpins economic growth and social progress. Second, extensive schooling both equips individuals with specialized skills and provides a general foundation of cognitive knowledge and intellectual sophistication to permit the acquisition of more specialized knowledge. Extensive education, therefore, becomes an increasingly necessary feature of any modern society. Skills that were primarily acquired on the job must now be acquired in specialized educational institutions. If schools cannot always teach the highly specific knowledge and skills required by an increasing number of jobs, they do provide a foundation of general cognitive skills that alone permits effective learning of more specialized knowledge. Since occupational skills change or rapidly become obsolete in contemporary society, individuals need an extensive general education as a foundation to learn new skills. They may also require later retooling educational programs

long after adolescence. Some progressive accounts of this argument, indeed, see schooling as lifelong learning and the whole society as a learning society. The crucial function of schools is not so much to teach specific useful vocational skills, but to teach people how to learn.

THE DEMOCRATIC SOCIETY   The functional paradigm portrays contemporary society as a democratic society moving gradually toward the achievement of humane goals: toward social justice, a more fulfilling life for all citizens, and the acceptance of diversity. Implicit in the functional paradigm, therefore, is a particular kind of political liberalism—a view that does not deny the evils and inequities of the present society, but does believe that progress has been made and will continue to be made. Increasing levels of education are at the core of this conception of progress. An educated citizenry is an informed citizenry, less likely to be manipulated by demagogues, and more likely to make responsible and informed political decisions and be actively involved in the political process. Education reduces intolerance and prejudice, and increases support for civil liberties; it is, in other words, an essential bulwark of a democratic society dedicated to freedom and justice. Finally, a more educated society will be a better society in another sense: a society dedicated not only to economic growth and material wealth, but also to the pursuit of social justice. The educated society is concerned with the quality of life and the conditions that make individual fulfillment possible.

SCHOOLING AND SOCIETY

The heart of the functional paradigm, therefore, can be seen as an explanation of why schooling is of such crucial importance in modern society. This explanation stresses the multiple functions that schools perform in modern society—the production of cognitive skills, the sorting and selection of talents, the creation of an informed citizenry—and it maintains that these functions could not be adequately performed without extensive and elaborate formal schooling. Thus the functional paradigm views the close relationship between schooling and future status in contemporary society as an essentially rational process of adaptation: a process where the needs of the increasingly complex society for talented and expert personnel are met by outputs from the educational system in the form of cognitive skills and the selection of talented individuals. And if only the most uncritical supporters of the paradigm would assert that such a process of social selection in schools is *perfectly* meritocratic or that disadvantaged groups have *identical* opportunities to those afforded to more privileged students, there is some general confidence that the direction of educational change has been in a meritocratic direction. From this perspective, the net effect of the expansion of schooling has been to increase the percentage of poor but talented students who reach high-status positions, with the assumption that further expansion of schooling will move us closer toward a society of equal opportunity. What schools teach is also, although imperfectly, a functional adaptation to the needs of the social order. As the nature of the modern economy increasingly demands (even in middle- or lower-status occupations) more sophisticated cognitive skills and flexibility and adaptability in the work force, so pedagogical techniques and curricula shift away from rote memorization and moral indoctrination to concern with cognitive development and intellectual flexibility. In this respect, the functional paradigm is by no means necessarily conservative in its implications for school practice, as its critics sometimes allege. Indeed, the argument that the new complex skills needed by modern society in turn require the transformation of traditional pedagogy and the traditional curriculum were virtually an article of faith among many functional theorists during the 1960s and 1970s.[4]

If the functional paradigm is not necessarily politically conservative, it certainly does portray the major features of contemporary society in fundamentally benign terms. Inequality, for example, is often seen as a necessary device for motivating talented individuals to achieve high-status positions. Although it is recognized by most observers that the correlation between ability and high status is far from perfect, they see the problem of inequality in contemporary society as one of erasing barriers to the mobility of talent rather than as a problem of redistributing wealth from high-status positions to low-status positions. That talent in turn tends to be conceived as one dimensional, underlying both success in school and success in life. And while liberals within this tradition argue there are vast reserves of untapped talent among disadvantaged groups, others more pessimistically conclude that such talent is inherently scarce. . . .

DIFFICULTIES IN THE FUNCTIONAL PARADIGM

The set of assumptions I have described is still influential among social scientists, policy makers, and educators, but it has lost some of the taken-for-granted character of a decade or more ago. The rate of educational expansion has declined; past projections of the need for college graduates have been confounded by a surplus of unemployed or underemployed degree holders. In the face of these developments it becomes more difficult to argue that industrial societies require ever-increasing percentages of highly educated individuals. But the difficulties of the functional paradigm are more fundamental than those posed by the current (and possibly temporary) imbalance between educational outputs and the supply of high-status jobs. In the past two decades a substantial body of research has developed that poses a challenge to almost all the main assertions of the paradigm—to the link between schooling and jobs, the assumption of an increasingly meritocratic society, and arguments about increasing opportunities for the mobility of talented, but underprivileged youth.

SCHOOLING, SKILLS, AND JOBS

In the functional paradigm, cognitive skills provide the crucial link between education and jobs. This is not to say that the major function of schools is to teach vocational skills that are directly relevant to job performance. The functional paradigm does assert, however, that the general cognitive skills and intellectual sophistication that schools develop have positive functions for the performance of adult occupations, and that, indeed, they are indispensable for the performance of growing numbers of middle- and high-status occupations.

To the extent that we can test such very general ideas, some evidence from United States research does not support them. Consider first the relationship between college grades and occupational status and future earnings. College grades are a rough and ready measure of the success with which an individual has learned the things that colleges attempt to teach. What should happen, therefore, according to the functional paradigm, is that college grades should predict occupational status and relative earnings. Those who do well in college should, other things being equal, obtain better jobs and make more money than those who did less well. Research on the relationship between college grades and occupational status and future earnings, however, has not been able to demonstrate such a relationship. In comparing bachelors degree recipients, grade point average in college does not predict either occupational status or future earnings with any degree of consistency.[5]

Direct measures of cognitive skills provide a second test of the hypothesis. Individuals whose test scores in school indicate high cognitive skills do indeed obtain better jobs and make more money in later life than individuals with lower cognitive skills. However, this relationship largely disappears when researchers control for educational attainment and family background. Christopher Jencks summarizes: "If we compare two men whose test scores differed by 15 points, their occupational status would typically differ by about 12.5 points. If they have the same amount of education and the same family background, their status will differ by only about 2.5 points."[6]

If the effect of cognitive skills on occupational status is problematic, studies of performance on the job provide little support for the functional paradigm. Even among teachers, the

correlation between grades in college and observer ratings of job performance average only between 0.2 and 0.3.[7] Among physicians, grades in medical school predict ratings of job performance only weakly in the early years of medical practice and not at all in later years.[8] How well people do in a particular job, as Ivar Berg has shown, can rarely be predicted by measures of how well they have learned what they were taught in school.[9]

These findings post a challenge to the functional paradigm. If increasing levels of education are somehow necessary for the performance of increasingly complex jobs, then there should be a relationship between cognitive skills (which schools presumably teach) and occupational status, earnings, and job performance. A large part of the explanation for the well-known correlation between educational attainment and occupational status should be that such educational qualifications reflect the possession of cognitive skills necessary or useful for effective role performance. But the evidence we have suggests that it is educational *credentials* as well as cognitive skills that predict future status and earnings. We know that employers prefer to employ college graduates, but there is no solid evidence that they make great efforts to hire people with the highest levels of cognitive skills. Nor is there evidence that once on the job those who have the highest skills perform better than those with lower skills.

These findings, therefore, suggest a different picture of the relationship between schooling and jobs than that provided by the functional paradigm. Instead of saying that educational institutions teach the skills that are necessary for the performance of complex occupations, it can be argued that educational credentials are used to ration access to high-status occupations. Employers who are faced with many potential applicants for a few jobs can use educational credentials as a convenient screening device that appears to be quite impersonal and fair. They can say that only college graduates or only holders of the M.A. degree are qualified to do the job. And, of course, as the percentage of the population with high levels of education credentials rises, so the standards for admission to a particular occupation rise also, not in response to any increasing complexity of the job itself, but as a reflection of the rise in average education levels in the population and the shifting supply and demand for particular jobs.

There is other evidence that supports this interpretation. There are, for example, great differences in the amount of education credentials required for entry into professional occupations in different Western societies. In Great Britain, for example, physicians qualify with three years less formal education than their U.S. counterparts. In much of Europe, only very recently have engineers and lawyers had to obtain college degrees before practicing their professions. In the United States, furthermore, entry requirements for many occupations—pharmacy, police work, physical therapy—have increased dramatically over the last twenty years. There are perhaps some grounds for asserting that new recruits to these jobs must know more than in the past, but it is also plausible that any occupation has much prestige to gain by attempting to raise its admission requirements. Police departments around the country may argue that the complex nature of modern police work demands at least two years of college as a preparation. Such arguments, however, seem self-serving. Raised standards increase the status of people already in the job and are crucial for claiming the high status of the occupation within the community at large. It is entirely understandable that police, pharmacists, physical therapists, and social workers (to name but a few occupations where educational requirements for admission have escalated in recent years) should argue that these occupations now require far more credentials than they did in the past. However, it is dangerous to confuse what may be self-serving justifications for new admission standards with an objective necessity for new recruits to have much higher levels of cognitive skills.

The link between schooling and jobs, therefore, is a good deal more problematic than the simple model implied by the functional paradigm. We cannot see rapidly escalating educational requirements as an obvious reflection of the increasing complexity of contemporary occu-

pations. Do people need a college degree to be efficient secretaries or to sell insurance? The need to ask the question suggests that the functional paradigm does not provide a satisfactory account. Those who have high levels of education do, of course, generally obtain higher-status jobs than those who have less education. But this does not seem to be because of the cognitive skills educated people learned in school. It is the possession of educational credentials, rather than the acquisition of the cognitive skills that those credentials denote, that seems to predict future status. The relationship between education and occupational status, then, is a good deal more complex and perhaps less rational than suggested by the functional paradigm.

SCHOOLING AND EQUALITY OF OPPORTUNITY

A second argument of the functional paradigm is that educational institutions sort and select talented people in a way, however imperfect, that is greatly superior to selection on the basis of such ascribed characteristics as parental social status, religion, or race. To tie occupational status closely to educational attainment, the paradigm suggests, will maximize society's chances of discovering its most talented individuals and placing them in the most important occupations. Implicit in this paradigm, therefore, is the idea that the expansion of education—more and more access to higher education for lower-class and minority students—will have the effect of increasing the chances of those individuals to gain access to high-status occupations. Educational expansion is not only morally justified, it is also a rational policy because it increases the discovery of talented individuals.

Research has challenged these arguments, too. It is true that measures of IQ are quite good predictors of school achievement. It is also true that IQ scores and occupational status and income are positively correlated.[10] But what prevents such findings constituting valid evidence for the meritocratic thesis is the strong relationship between all these variables and socioeconomic status. Samuel Bowles and Herbert Gintis, for example, show that when socioeconomic status is controlled, IQ exerts an only slight effect on earnings.[11] Controlling for IQ, by contrast, still leaves very large associations between socioeconomic status of parents and the incomes of their children. Bowles and Gintis show that those with the lowest socioeconomic status scores, but average IQ scores, have a 6 percent chance of being in the top one-fifth of all wage earners. Those with the same IQ scores, but from the highest decile of socioeconomic background have a 41 percent chance of being in the top one-fifth of all wage earners.[12] Jencks reports evidence supporting this general interpretation. He shows that much of the relationship between IQ and occupational status and future earnings disappears when we control for school attainment and for socioeconomic background.

Our society, then, is far from a pure form of meritocracy where intelligence or talent largely determine success in school, and where employers in turn use schooling as a rational way of sorting out the most talented from the least talented individuals. Socioeconomic status of the parents is a better predictor of future economic success than measured IQ. In part, this is because socioeconomic status predicts school achievement even when IQ is controlled; it is also because socioeconomic status predicts future adult status even after we take schooling and IQ into account.[13]

The evidence also raises questions about the argument that educational expansion increases meritocratic selection. If the expansion of schooling in the last fifty years has increased the relative chances of underprivileged youth to gain access to high-status jobs, we would expect a gradual decline in the relationship between parent's status and that of their children. What should happen, the meritocratic argument implies, is that high-status parents should experience increasing difficulty in passing on their high status to their children, and that more and more low-status children of high intelligence should be able to take their rightful places in prestigious occupations that demand unusual talent. Unless in-

telligence is inherited to a very high degree, it would follow that increasing educational expansion will increase the mobility chances of the underprivileged. Detailed treatment of this complicated issue will be postponed until Chapter 4, but the evidence for the United States indicates that the relationship between parent and child status has not declined in the last four decades. Parent social status remains about as good a predictor of a child's future status today as it was in the 1920s, despite enormous educational expansion and great efforts to ensure fairness and universality in selection procedures.[14]

Again, we are confronted with empirical evidence that is difficult to reconcile with the functional paradigm. No one would say, of course, that our society is perfectly open to talent or that IQ alone is the main determinant of income and status. But what should happen, according to the functional paradigm, is that we should be able to observe some reduction in the ability of privileged parents to pass on their advantages to their children. The fact that we do not observe this suggests that contemporary U.S. society is not a great deal more meritocratic than several decades ago.

QUALITY OF SCHOOLING AND EQUALITY OF OPPORTUNITY

Implicit in virtually all thought about education in the early 1960s was the theory that the quality of schooling available to different students was crucial to their future chances of occupational mobility. Poor students were severely handicapped by inferior schools, black students by the fact that most of the schools they attended were, quite simply, bad schools. Black students attended, for the most part, segregated institutions. Poor white students went to schools that hardly compared in facilities and resources with the schools attended by more privileged students. Inferior schooling compounded the initial handicaps of these students and led directly to the perpetuation of poverty and inequality in the next generation. In such books as Patricia Sexton's *Education and Income*, a direct line was drawn between inferior schools, reduced opportunities to learn, low prospects for higher education, and the persistence of inequality.[15] This vicious circle could be broken only by equalizing school resources for all students.

A great deal of empirical research has challenged this argument. A series of large-scale studies of schooling and its effects shows that student test scores are only weakly associated with measures of school quality, but powerfully associated with measures of student characteristics: socioeconomic background and IQ. Measures of teacher experience, pupil/teacher ratios, and the amounts of money expended per pupil all constituted some indications of what people meant when they talked about school quality. Yet none of these variables has proven to be of much help in predicting how well students will perform on particular tests.[16]

In research on school effects in a number of different countries, indicators of school quality have shown only a very weak or insignificant relationship with student performance on tests designed to measure cognitive learning.[17] And while such research has important shortcomings, which I shall discuss in later chapters, it does show that we can in no sense solve the problem of the unequal school achievement of different groups of students by equalizing school resources. Every study indicates that students from low-status families do less well on tests of cognitive achievement than more well-to-do students, but no study demonstrates that the gap can be substantially closed by providing what amounts to middle-class schooling for lower-class students.[18] Indeed, the history of research on school effects in the last ten years is a history of failure to confirm the proposition that eliminating differences in school quality can significantly close the gap in school achievement between students from different social origins. Results of research on school integration have provided, at best, equivocal positive findings. Most early studies tended to show mildly positive effects on black student performance. Although more recent studies do not necessarily contradict this assertion, a number of them indicate some negative effects of integration on

black self-esteem, and even on white achievement in majority black schools.[19]

No study has demonstrated that integrated schools reduce most of the gap between black and white school achievement. Nor has research on the effects of compensatory preschool education demonstrated the kind of clear-cut and lasting effects on later school achievement that its proponents hoped for. Although evaluation of such programs is exceedingly difficult, the most judicious conclusion is that strong positive effects on later school performance have not yet been demonstrated.[20]

While I shall have a great deal more to say about this research later in this book, this initial examination of the findings of large-scale research on school effects indicates serious difficulties for the orthodox interpretation of school reform and its effects on inequality. One assertion of the functional paradigm is that the expansion of schooling in modern society brings about an increasingly meritocratic social order. A closely related assertion is that better or higher quality schooling will reduce the advantages of privileged parents in passing on their high status to the next generation and increase the chances of underprivileged children to close the gap between themselves and more privileged students. Much of what we have learned in the last twenty years casts doubt on both of these assertions.

THE CONFLICT PARADIGM

I have shown that the model of schooling and society that dominated much thought about education until quite recently is beset with serious difficulties. Schools do undoubtedly teach cognitive skills and increase the intellectual sophistication of their students, but it is not clear that it is these skills that explain the relationship between schooling, occupational status, and earnings. The available evidence does not suggest that U.S. society is substantially more meritocratic than in the past. Nor is there much evidence to indicate that increased resources devoted to schooling have resulted in more favorable opportunities for the talented children of disadvantaged parents to obtain high-status positions. Simply put, the expansion of schooling does not seem to have worked in the way the functional paradigm suggests it should work.

The conflict paradigm offers a very different interpretation of schooling in its relationship to society. Like the functional paradigm, the conflict paradigm sees schools and society as closely linked—and, I shall argue, too closely linked—but it stresses the links between schools and the demands of elites rather than the needs of the whole society. It also stresses the connection between schooling and the learning of docility and compliance rather than the acquisition of cognitive skills. If the functional paradigm sees schools as more or less efficient mechanisms for sorting and selecting talented people and for producing cognitive skills, the conflict paradigm sees schools as serving the interests of elites, as reinforcing existing inequalities, and as producing attitudes that foster acceptance of this status quo.

THE INTELLECTUAL BACKGROUND

The functional paradigm took shape at a time when the climate of intellectual opinion was predominantly optimistic about the main features of contemporary society and its likely future evolution. Modern society was viewed as increasingly rational and meritocratic, a society where prejudice, racism, intolerance, and the ignorance that fostered these evils would gradually disappear. Schools taught, sustained, and nurtured essentially modern cosmopolitan values and attitudes. Schools, at least the best schools, worked to emancipate children from parochialism, from an unreflecting respect for the traditions of the past, and from ignorance and prejudice. The new mathematics of the late 1960s, with its stress on understanding the principles of logic rather than the mere acquisition of immediately useful skills, and the new English curriculum, with its use of modern novels that invited frank discussion of contemporary moral issues, both symbolized a commitment to modern, liberal, and cosmopolitan ideals. The best schools taught rationality; they developed the ability to handle moral complexity and to tolerate ambiguity. If the prisons of ignorance, prejudice and unthinking respect for the past prevented many parents from entering this new world, schools were agencies of emancipation for the next generation. In the modern world, schools do not merely reproduce the values, attitudes, and skills of the past, they are active agents in creating a more liberal, a more rational, and a more humane society.[21]

The attack on these ideas in the later 1960s and 1970s reflected a broader critique of their view of society, a disenchantment with the liberal vision of the modern world, and a rejection of the optimism of that world view. The ten years from 1965 to 1975 were a time of increasing skepticism about the benefits of science and technology and an increasing cynicism about the good intentions and moral purposes of established authority. The liberal model of modern society—a world admittedly full of serious imperfection, but nevertheless moving in a fundamentally progressive direction—was replaced, for more and more intellectuals, by a model of society requiring urgent and wholesale surgery to avoid disaster. The new, more skeptical vision saw greedy business corporations intent on destroying the environment, cynical and corrupt politicians concerned with their own power and privilege, and entrenched racism and sexism in virtually every social institution. Instead of a model of society where authority was based on expertise and competence, this radical vision defined a society where powerful elites manipulate public opinion to preserve their own entrenched position. Such elites might make symbolic or token concessions to pressures for reform, but such evils as racism, poverty, and sexism could only be eliminated by changing the distribution of power in the society.

Such were the new skeptical ideas that began to gain ground on the older liberal orthodoxy at the end of the 1960s. Although it would be misleading to claim that ideas like these became more popular than the liberal and optimistic ideas that underly the functional paradigm, they were hardly confined to those who considered themselves educational or political radicals. By the mid to late seventies, disillusionment with the liberal interpretations of schooling became quite widespread among educators and intellectuals. Large numbers of people were aware, for example, that major differences in school achievement by race and by social class persisted even after educational reforms designed to eliminate them. There was also emerging awareness of the large number of highly educated young people who could not find jobs commensurate with their qualifications. In other words, the system did not seem to work in the way that liberal common sense (and the functional paradigm) said it should work. The climate of opinion was ready for an alternative interpretation.

The conflict paradigm, even less than the functional paradigm, is not a unitary set of unambiguous propositions about the relationship between school and society. Indeed, disputes within the conflict paradigm, between Marxists and non-Marxists, or even between rival Marxists, are often more heated than arguments between functionalists and conflict theorists.[22] But we can nevertheless distinguish a set of broad assumptions to which most conflict theorists would subscribe, whatever their other differences, and with which few functional theorists would agree.

First, conflict theorists assert that we live in a divided and conflict-ridden society where groups compete for the control of the educational system. To argue that schooling reflects societal needs, therefore (as functional theorists maintain), is to miss this essential fact. Groups who compete for control of schooling use the rhetoric of societal needs to conceal the fact that it is *their* interests and *their* demands they are trying to advance. These elites may succeed in manufacturing consensus about the purposes and organization of schooling, but beneath the apparent consensus, conflict theorists believe, is always a struggle for power and status: *whose* values and ideals will be taught to the young, and *whose* children will obtain the most desirable jobs. Second, conflict theorists see this struggle between groups as unequal. Existing elites, though they must make compromises and bargains with other groups, almost always have the upper hand because of their superior resources and their con-

trol over the means of communication. Because of this, equality of opportunity has not been and is unlikely to be a reality within the confines of the present social order. The *rhetoric* of equality of opportunity conceals the fact that schools are organized in such a way as to make it inevitable that children of privileged groups will have great advantages over children of disadvantaged groups.

Finally, conflict theorists are skeptical of the view that the schools are linked to jobs in modern society primarily through the cognitive skills they teach. Rejecting the view that most work in modern society is intellectually highly demanding, conflict theorists emphasize instead that employers are more concerned with the attitudes and values of their future employees, particularly their loyalty, compliance, and docility, rather than their cognitive sophistication. From this perspective, therefore, while the *manifest* concern of schools is primarily with the teaching of cognitive skills, their fundamental business is to shore up the present social order by teaching appropriate attitudes and values. Again, the rhetoric of the official orthodoxy conceals the real nature of the relationships between schools and society.

These, then, are the ideas with which most, if not all, conflict theorists would agree. To understand the conflict paradigm more fully, however, we need to consider in some detail more specific theories, one neo-Marxist and the other non-Marxist.

THE NEO-MARXIST THEORIES OF BOWLES AND GINTIS

Samuel Bowles and Herbert Gintis's 1977 book *Schooling in Capitalist America* is probably the best known and most coherently argued statement of a specifically Marxist interpretation of schooling in modern society.[23] Published at a time when disillusionment with the liberal interpretation of schooling was beginning to be widespread, its radical interpretation of schooling has had a great deal of impact and stimulated extensive debate. That thesis is supported, furthermore, by a good deal of empirical evidence and closely reasoned argument—qualities that have not always characterized radical critiques of the functional paradigm.

Bowles and Gintis's central thesis is that schools serve the interests of the capitalist order in modern society. Schools reproduce the values and personality characteristics necessary in a repressive capitalist society. Although all schools must repress and coerce students to secure a compliant and efficient adult labor force, different schools accomplish this function in different ways. The values and qualities required by an efficient manual worker on the production line are different from the values and qualities needed by an executive of a large corporation. While the manual worker must be taught punctuality, the ability to follow instructions, and some degree of respect for superiors, the executive needs some degree of flexibility, an ability to tolerate ambiguity, and favorable attitudes toward change and innovation.

Therefore, schools whose graduates enter predominantly low-status occupations stress rule following, provide minimal discretion in choice of tasks, and teach obedience to constituted authority. Schools and universities that prepare students for elite positions, by contrast, encourage students to develop some capacity for sustained independent work, to make intelligent choices among many alternatives, and to internalize norms rather than to follow external behavioral rules. If we compare junior colleges with elite universities, for example, or the college preparatory tracks of a suburban high school with the vocational curriculum, we will find not only differences in curriculum, but also differences in the social organization of instruction. In junior colleges and in the lower tracks of a high school, students will be given more frequent assignments, have less choice in how to carry out those assignments, and will be subject to more detailed supervision by the teaching staff. By contrast, the college preparatory tracks of many suburban high schools and elite universities have a great deal more open and flexible educational environment. Such dissimilarities mirror both different class values (the preference of working-class parents for

stricter educational methods and the preference of professional parents for schooling that encourages initiative and independence) and the different kinds of qualities of personality needed for good performance in high- and low-status occupations. The social organization of particular schools—the methods of instruction and evaluation, the amount of choice and discretion permitted the students—reflects the demands of the particular occupations that their graduates will eventually obtain.[24]

REINFORCING INEQUALITY   Bowles and Gintis's major argument is that the educational system reinforces class inequalities in contemporary society. Different social classes in the United States usually attend different neighborhood schools. Both the value preferences of parents and the different financial resources available to different communities mean that schools catering to working-class students will teach different values and different personal qualities than schools serving higher-status populations. These latter schools are not better or freer in any absolute sense, but high-status schools communicate to their students the distinctive values and attitudes required by high-status occupations in modern capitalist societies. The great majority of occupations in contemporary society, Bowles and Gintis believe, require a loyal and compliant work force to perform tasks with little responsibility and discretion. Most schools, therefore, teach their students to follow orders reliably, to take explicit directions, to be punctual, and to respect the authority of the teacher and the school. Such schools, which satisfy the preference of most parents for discipline and good manners in their children, channel students to manual and lower-level white-collar occupations. But schools serving more elite groups are only superficially less repressive. Such schools encourage students to work at their own pace without continuous supervision, to work for the sake of long-term future rewards, and to internalize rules of behavior rather than depend on specific and frequent instructions. These qualities are essential to effective performance in middle- or high-status positions in large organizations. However, work in such organizations permits only limited freedom and autonomy. Workers may question specific procedures, but not the purpose of the organization; employees may be flexible and innovative, but they must be loyal. The capitalist society requires that all schools teach the values of individual achievement, material consumption, and the inevitability of the present social order. Free schools are therefore impossible in a repressive society.[25]

Bowles and Gintis decisively reject the meritocratic hypothesis, with its assumption that schools are efficient ways of selecting talented people. Instead, schools work to *convince* people that selection is meritocratic. It is essential for the legitimacy of the capitalist order that the population be convinced that people in high-status positions do deserve these positions, that they are more talented and harder workers than others. Schools are an essential prop of this legitimacy. Selection for particular tracks within a school must *appear* to be made on the basis of ability and intelligence, and such purportedly objective criteria as IQ and grades serve this function. But these criteria mask the fact that success in schooling, and of course success in later life, is strongly related to social class and shows no indication of becoming less closely related over time. The correlation between college graduation and social class in the last twenty years, they report, has remained unchanged despite the rapid expansion of higher education. Schools remain institutions that reproduce and legitimate existing inequalities between social classes. This state of affairs will continue indefinitely in capitalist societies unless capitalism itself is abolished. Reforms in the educational system alone cannot reduce inequalities in the life chances of different social classes. The premise of liberal educational reform—that educational expansion and improved schooling can create equality of opportunity—is false. Schools that liberate, diminishing rather than reinforcing the handicaps of inequality, can only be achieved after a revolution in the distribution of power and the ownership of the means of production in contemporary capitalist society. . . .

CONCLUSION

. . . In the modern world, it is agreed by both paradigms, schooling plays a much more important role than in any previous societies; in social mobility, in preparation for work, and in moulding common values and attitudes. But how are we to interpret this transformation? For functional theorists, the key to the explanation of this heightened importance of formal schooling lies in the distinctive needs of modern society. They see the expansion of schooling as an essentially rational adaptation to these needs. Not everything that schools teach is indispensable or even useful, of course, nor are schools ideally efficient in teaching cognitive skills, but the expansion of schooling is nevertheless best viewed as a response to new needs for sophisticated cognitive skills and cultural consensus. The world in general and the world of work in particular are more complex than in the past. It is therefore rational for public opinion to recognize that investments in education will equip the young for effective performance in that world.

For the conflict paradigm, such an interpretation misconstrues the relationship between schools and society and the nature of what schools primarily teach. It is the demands of elites, and not the needs of a society as a whole, that propel changes in schooling, and it is these demands for compliance and control over the mass of the population that shape the character of schools. In the Marxist version of the conflict paradigm, the changing character of capitalism and the struggle between capitalist elites and masses explains both the expansion of schooling and (from this point of view) its repressive character. Certainly employees need some levels of cognitive skills, but they also need a labor force willing to submit to the discipline of the work place, or, in the case of high-status jobs, employees who are willing to make the goals of corporate capitalism their own. Thus the primary link between schools and work is in the compliant and conforming values and attitudes schools convey rather than in the cognitive skills they teach. The hierarchical organization of schools, with their restrictive controls over student behavior, correspond to and reproduce the hierarchical organization of work. And although non-Marxist conflict theorists are less explicit about the correspondence of the organization of schooling with the organization of work, they too share its emphasis on elite control over the content of schooling and the irrational character of the escalation of educational credentials in recent decades. . . .

ENDNOTES

1. The clearest statement remains in Clark, *Educating the Expert Society.* For an account of the theoretical foundations of these ideas, see Talcott Parsons, *Structure and Process in Modern Societies* (New York: Free Press, 1960).

2. Bell, *The Coming of Post-Industrial Society.*

3. Clark, *Educating the Expert Society.*

4. Talcott Parsons, "The School Class as a Social System," *Harvard Educational Review* 29 (1959): 297–318.

5. Christopher Jencks et al., *Inequality* (New York: Basic Books, 1972), p. 187.

6. Ibid., p. 186.

7. Ibid., p. 187.

8. Ivar Berg, *Education and Jobs: The Great Training Robbery* (New York: Praeger, 1970), pp. 85–104.

9. Ibid.

10. See Otis Dudley Duncan, David Featherstone, and Beverly Duncan, *Socioeconomic Background and Achievement* (New York: Academic Press, 1972).

11. Bowles and Gintis, *Schooling in Capitalist America,* pp. 111–113.

12. Ibid. See also Christopher Jencks, *Who Gets Ahead?* (New York: Basic Books, 1979), pp. 115–121.

13. Jencks, *Who Gets Ahead?,* Chapter 3.

14. Peter Blau and Otis Dudley Duncan, *The American Occupational Structure* (New York: Wiley, 1967), pp. 81–113.

15. Patricia Sexton, *Education and Income* (New York: Viking, 1961).

16. The literature on this subject is vast. Perhaps the original Coleman Report itself, *Equality of Educational Opportunity,* and the reanalysis of the data in Jencks are the best sources. For a different interpretation of the evidence, see James Guthrie, et al., *Schools and Inequality* (Cambridge: M.I.T. Press, 1971).

17. Alan Purves, *Literature Education in Ten Countries* (New York: Wiley, 1973); Robert L. Thorndike, *Reading Comprehension in Fifteen Countries* (New York: Wiley, 1973); and L. C. Comber and John P. Keeves, *Science Education in Nineteen Countries* (New York: Wiley, 1973).

18. None of these data implies that if poor students attended schools that spent, for example, four times as much money as present-day schools, they would not do better. In this sense the research is dealing with questions of practical policy as much as with theory. See Philip Green, "Race and I.Q.: Fallacy of Heritability," *Dissent* (Spring 1976): 181–196.

19. Nancy St. John, *School Desegregation* (New York: Wiley, 1975).

20. Milbrey W. McLaughlin, *Evaluation and Reform: The Elementary and Secondary Education Act of 1965* (Cambridge: Ballinger, 1975).

21. The phrase *active agent* comes from Clark, *Educating the Expert Society.*

22. As the Marxist paradigm has lost popularity in recent years these disputes have assumed an increasingly doctrinal character.

23. Bowles and Gintis, *Schooling in Capitalist America.*

24. Ibid., Chapter 5.

25. Unless that is, the new revolutionary consciousness produced by free schools transforms the society. See their ambivalent comments on free schools, ibid., pp. 254–255.

STUDY QUESTIONS FOR PART 2

1. Durkheim, a Frenchman, wrote over a century ago about the need for education to create homogeneity among students and prescribed methodical socialization as the duty of educators. Is this perspective valid today? Why? Why not?

2. What is the role of the state and nation in education? As we move toward a more global society and an electronically shrinking world, is it important that the United States develop a *national* curriculum for our schools? What would you see as the advantages and disadvantages of such a system? Who would benefit; why?

3. Functionalists believe that formal education has the ability to equalize and level out other life conditions (poverty, ethnicity, gender, social class, etc.) and that by educating all citizens and giving everyone an equal opportunity to go to school, everyone will get a fair chance to achieve that of which they are capable. Do you believe that this is a reasonable premise and that it is working for the majority of children? Why?

4. What is the difference between achieved and ascribed status? Give three examples. What counts in schools? Why do you feel this way? What is the evidence to which you can point to support your view?

5. Should education be the act of giving out information and facts or should it try to influence what and how students think and believe? Many argue for clear content/subject standards. Do you agree with this stance? What is the reasoning behind your view?

6. Although children often are eager for more information, knowledge, and ideas, teachers often don't encourage this sort of inquisitiveness among poor children. Do you agree with this? Why?

7. What are the greatest areas of weakness (strength) of the functionalist perspective? Explain your thinking about this.

8. Is a high school degree today worth what it was 25 years ago? What contributes to the value of education in our society?

9. Does public schooling actually reinforce social inequality in our country? Explain the reasoning behind your answer to this question.

10. What would a functionalist or a conflict theorist have to say about the charter school movement? Do you agree with their assessment? Why?

PART
3

SOCIALIZATION AND PROGRESS

The following selections address several basic questions of the role of school in society and the connections between schooling and social progress:

- Should schools strive to change society or should they mirror society?
- What connections should there be between what is learned in school and the knowledge, skills, values, and attitudes needed to enable the U.S. work force to remain competitive in a global marketplace?
- Given our postindustrial era and the emergence of global and instantaneous electronic communication, what adaptations do you foresee for the work of teachers and the role of educators in our society?

The first selection, by John Dewey, offers a functionalist's view of the connections between school and society, emphasizing the role school plays in helping children make the transition from family to work and life in the broader community. He notes the importance of the school's role in developing within children the attitudes and values required for success as workers and adults. In the next selection, Robert Dreeben discusses in more concrete terms how these attitudes and values are shaped by the children's exposure to four critical norms during their school experience. The third selection, by Carl Grant and Ken Zeichner, argues that teachers have a special responsibility, indeed a duty, to be *reflective* as they fulfil their teaching responsibilities. That is, to be thoughtful and deliberate in their teaching, cognizant of their powerful influence as a teacher and the socialization effects of the experience of schooling on children, and aware of the attitudes and values they are reinforcing (or not) among the children in their charge.

Writing in 1899, John Dewey reflected on the connections between the changes he observed in the methods and curricula of schooling and broader changes in the larger society. His basic strategy was to see if he could find examples of changes in the school that mirrored changes in society. The Industrial Revolution had been under way for some time at this point, and many changes were to be observed in society: the shift from an agrarian, rural life to industrial, urban living; and an orientation to mass production, rapid global communication, and world markets in contrast to the former family-based model with service to the immediate community being the norm. Dewey concluded that these, and a multitude of lifestyle changes, had a major impact on the nature of school curricula and methods. The example he chose for illustrative purposes was the emergence within schools of attention to what he referred to as "manual training."

What Dewey draws attention to here are the close connections between school and society. As the two previous readings observed, society's system of education plays a vital role in society's survival, helping it make the adjustments and adaptations required of the times. Dewey and Dreeben both observe the important role played by schools in facilitating the shift from a household and neighborhood economy rooted in agriculture and small family enterprises to a factory-based economy rooted in mass production and urban living where most of the work occurred outside the home.

Dewey believed that the shift he observed regarding the new emphasis on manual training was a great innovation for the times, as schools had until very recently been dominated by what Dewey referred to as a medieval conception of learning (p. 102). What he meant by this is that the curriculum was almost entirely intellectual in orientation and quite removed from the reality of daily living. He heralded this shift to a curriculum that was more responsive to children's natural inclination to "make and do" (p. 103) as a way to make learning more meaningful: "The occupation supplies the child with a genuine motive; it gives him experience at first hand; it brings him into contact with realities" (p. 101).

Dewey believed that children learn best from experience and that the school had historically been too removed from real life—and thus difficult for most children. "The simple facts of the case are that in the great majority of human beings the distinctively intellectual interest is not dominant. They have the so-called practical impulse and disposition. In many of those in whom by nature intellectual interest is strong, social conditions prevent its adequate realization" (p. 103). For Dewey, the way to guarantee a good society would be to ". . . make each one of our schools an embryonic community life, active with types of occupations that reflect the life of the larger society, and permeated throughout with the spirit of art, history, and science" (p. 104).

The questions embedded in Dewey's propositions are still argued and examined to this day. What are your thoughts on these matters? Are schools today too removed from needed life skills? Do you believe that most people don't have a dominant interest in matters of the mind? Would children learn more if schools were more like natural communities, organized around the types of activities and problems found in the surrounding community? What did Dewey mean when he referred to social conditions preventing some children with the ability and motivation from pursuing the intellectual development afforded by schools?

Dewey's selection reminds us of the important connection functionalists draw between schooling and certain needs society has for its survival. Was Dewey arguing merely that schools should teach children more utilitarian skills, appropriate to the world of work? Perhaps Dewey is suggesting that by providing children with the opportunity to work as members of a community they will learn many of the attitudes and values required for success as workers and adult citizens. Perhaps Dewey, as Durkheim, was concerned with the importance of developing the child's "social being" and not just his/her individual intellectual capabilities. As Dewey states at the beginning of his essay, it is critical to look at the broader social dimension of school and not be restricted only to a focus on individual accomplishment. While important, individual achievement in the traditional school subjects is perhaps not the most important dimension of schooling. Or is it?

How does this "social being" get developed? Typically, it is not addressed in the curriculum as an explicit school subject like math or Spanish. The closest a school might come today would probably be a vocational class that teaches students to be medical assistants or clerical workers, for example. Some schools have group agricultural or home building projects. The fact is, the development of the "social" being is not a manifest part of the school curriculum. It is, rather, a product of what others have termed the "hidden curriculum," learning that is a latent function of participating in the regular academic curriculum as well as in the many extracurricular activities in most secondary schools.

Dreeben discusses four norms learned as a result of schooling. These include the norms of independence, achievement, universalism, and specificity. One answer to the question "What is learned in school?" is learning associated with the manifest curriculum—geography, writing, arithmetic, and assorted other facts and skills. Although functional to some degree in terms of preparation for adulthood and entry into the work force, such learning is almost exclusively what Durkheim would refer to as learning related to development of the individual being. Dewey would call this learning "accomplishments of the individual." Another answer to the question "What is learned in school?" is learning associated with the latent curriculum—the four norms observed by Dreeben. These norms are concerned primarily with the development of the "social being." To paraphrase Dreeben, these four norms are an outcome of *how* things are done in schools. They are not an explicit aspect of the curriculum. Nevertheless, the learning that occurs around these four norms is *functional* in helping children and adolescents develop the social and psychological orientations to succeed as workers and as adult citizens.

Dreeben provides numerous examples of how these four norms are learned as a result of student participation in both the academic curriculum and in extracurricular activities. Although not an explicit aspect of the goals and objectives of schooling, what students do in school—how schooling gets accomplished—has the effect of fostering the development of these norms. Although this has generally a positive effect on most students, Dreeben points out that this may not be the case for all. That is, "the conditions conducive to their development are also conducive to the creation of results widely regarded as undesirable" (p. 86). Dreeben offers these examples:

> . . . a sense of accomplishment and mastery, on the one hand, and a sense of incompetence and ineffectualness, on the other, both represent psychological consequences of continuously coping with tasks on an achievement basis. Similarly with independence: self-confidence and helplessness can each derive from a person's self-imposed obligation to work unaided and accept individual responsibility for his actions. Finally, willingness to acknowledge the rightness of categorical and specific treatment may indicate the capacity to adapt to a variety of social situations in which only a part of one's self is invested, or it may indicate a sense of personal alienation and isolation from human relationships. (p. 86)

So what is desirable? Dreeben makes a very strong case that these four norms are learned as a result of how schooling gets accomplished. For example, school bells ring to get students used to being on time and ready to work. That, in turn, prepares them to punch a time clock once they enter the world of work. Given the possibility that not just the more desirable consequences will result, should schools strive to avoid these norms and teach others? Could they? How? Why? What would replace them? These questions bring us to the third selected reading. In their examination of the importance of the idea of becoming and being a reflective teacher, Grant and Zeichner suggest that one of the most important things for a teacher to do is to think about one's teaching, the effects of schooling, and who is and isn't being served well by the school.

Grant and Zeichner urge teachers to be deliberate in choosing what kind of teacher they want to be. They argue for a model or image called the "reflective teacher." The main idea here is that as a teacher one develops the habit of reflection and engages in a critical examination of one's teaching, the school's curriculum, who is served and who isn't, and so forth. That is, teachers assume a moral obligation to think about their activities and effects as teachers and to consider the ramifications of the political, educational, and social contexts within which their teaching is embedded (p. 50).

They discuss three attitudes defined by Dewey that can help one be a reflective teacher. These include being open-minded, taking responsibility, and approaching the teaching task wholeheartedly. Being open-minded refers to the ability to genuinely consider that alternatives to existing school practices always exist, and that the current practice may or may not be the best practice given changing conditions. Responsibility refers to being aware of your actions as a teacher and being tuned-in to the effects of your actions on others. Are ditto sheets really the best instructional vehicle for a given lesson? If programs for gifted students are so effective, why not stimulate all children with appropriately challenging curricula? Is the gain for students of supplementing the regular text worth the time and energy required to locate other sources? Wholeheartedness refers to one's being dedicated and highly committed to serving all students and to giving each pupil your very best as a teacher. Some students are a delight, others are incorrigible, and some may have very severe learning disabilities. Do you give as much to each? Perhaps you give a little extra to some because you know that without the extra attention they just aren't going to make it! This is being wholehearted, and the sign of a reflective teacher.

Becoming a reflective teacher is not easy, but Grant and Zeichner include in their discussion a number of good ideas to help you develop your capacity to be reflective. Maybe you want to adopt another image besides being a reflective teacher. What would it look like? How would you defend your viewpoint? Remember the choice is yours, and the important thing is to think deliberately about what kind of teacher you want to be, and then to set a course of action for achieving your goal. As you move toward your ideal, keep in mind the critical importance of what happens in school to the continuing development and survival of the society. Given the emerging advances in technology and the increasing speed and globalization of communication, what should students learn in school? How will the school accomplish this? How will it help students become good citizens and workers? How will it help our society continue to adapt and survive as conditions in the world change?

THE SCHOOL AND SOCIAL PROGRESS

JOHN DEWEY

We are apt to look at the school from an individualistic standpoint, as something between teacher and pupil, or between teacher and parent. That which interests us most is naturally the progress made by the individual child of our acquaintance, his normal physical development, his advance in ability to read, write, and figure, his growth in the knowledge of geography and history, improvement in manners, habits of promptness, order, and industry—it is from such standards as these that we judge the work of the school. And rightly so. Yet the range of the outlook needs to be enlarged. What the best and wisest parent wants for his own child, that must the community want for all of its children. Any other ideal for our schools is narrow and unlovely; acted upon, it destroys our democracy. All that society has accomplished for itself is put, through the agency of the school, at the disposal of its future members. All its better thoughts of itself it hopes to realize through the new possibilities thus opened to its future self. Here individualism and socialism are at one. Only by being true to the full growth of all the individuals who make it up, can society by any chance be true to itself. And in the self-direction thus given, nothing counts as much as the school, for, as Horace Mann said, "Where anything is growing, one former is worth a thousand re-formers."

Whenever we have in mind the discussion of a new movement in education, it is especially necessary to take the broader, or social view. Otherwise, changes in the school institution and tradition will be looked at as the arbitrary inventions of particular teachers; at the worst transitory fads,

and at the best merely improvements in certain details—and this is the plane upon which it is too customary to consider school changes. It is as rational to conceive of the locomotive or the telegraph as personal devices. The modification going on in the method and curriculum of education is as much a product of the changed social situation, and as much an effort to meet the needs of the new society that is forming, as are changes in modes of industry and commerce.

It is to this, then, that I especially ask your attention: the effort to conceive what roughly may be termed the "New Education" in the light of larger changes in society. Can we connect this "New Education" with the general march of events? If we can, it will lose its isolated character, and will cease to be an affair which proceeds only from the over-ingenious minds of pedagogues dealing with particular pupils. It will appear as part and parcel of the whole social evolution, and, in its more general features at least, as inevitable. Let us then ask after the main aspects of the social movement; and afterwards turn to the school to find what witness it gives of effort to put itself in line. And since it is quite impossible to cover the whole ground, I shall for the most part confine myself to one typical thing in the modern school movement—that which passes under the name of manual training, hoping if the relation of that to changed social conditions appears, we shall be

---

Source: *"The School and Social Progress" by John Dewey was originally published as a pamphlet in 1899 by the University of Chicago Press. Material is in the public domain.*

ready to concede the point as well regarding other educational innovations.

I make no apology for not dwelling at length upon the social changes in question. Those I shall mention are writ so large that he who runs may read. The change that comes first to mind, the one that overshadows and even controls all others, is the industrial one—the application of science resulting in the great inventions that have utilized the forces of nature on a vast and inexpensive scale: the growth of a world-wide market as the object of production, of vast manufacturing centers to supply this market, of cheap and rapid means of communication and distribution between all its parts. Even as to its feebler beginnings, this change is not much more than a century old; in many of its most important aspects it falls within the short span of those now living. One can hardly believe there has been a revolution in all history so rapid, so extensive, so complete. Through it the face of the earth is making over, even as to its physical forms; political boundaries are wiped out and moved about, as if they were indeed only lines on a paper map; population is hurriedly gathered into cities from the ends of the earth; habits of living are altered with startling abruptness and thoroughness; the search for the truths of nature is infinitely stimulated and facilitated and their application to life made not only practicable, but commercially necessary. Even our moral and religious ideas and interests, the most conservative because the deepest-lying things in our nature, are profoundly affected. That this revolution should not affect education in other than formal and superficial fashion is inconceivable.

Back of the factory system lies the household and neighborhood system. Those of us who are here today need go back only one, two, or at most three generations, to find a time when the household was practically the center in which were carried on, or about which were clustered, all the typical forms of industrial occupation. The clothing worn was for the most part not only made in the house, but the members of the household were usually familiar with the shearing of the sheep, the carding and spinning of the wool, and the plying of the loom. Instead of pressing a but-

ton and flooding the house with electric light, the whole process of getting illumination was followed in its toilsome length, from the killing of the animal and the trying of fat, to the making of wicks and dipping of candles. The supply of flour, of lumber, of foods, of building materials, of household furniture, even of metal ware, of nails, hinges, hammers, etc., was in the immediate neighborhood, in shops which were constantly open to inspection and often centers of neighborhood congregation. The entire industrial process stood revealed, from the production on the farm of the raw materials, till the finished article was actually put to use. Not only this, but practically every member of the household had his own share in the work. The children, as they gained in strength and capacity, were gradually initiated into the mysteries of the several processes. It was a matter of immediate and personal concern, even to the point of actual participation.

We cannot overlook the factors of discipline and of character-building involved in this: training in habits of order and of industry, and in the idea of responsibility, of obligation to do something, to produce something, in the world. There was always something which really needed to be done, and a real necessity that each member of the household should do his own part faithfully and in coöperation with others. Personalities which became effective in action were bred and tested in the medium of action. Again, we cannot overlook the importance for educational purposes of the close and intimate acquaintance got with nature at first hand, with real things and materials, with the actual processes of their manipulation, and the knowledge of their social necessities and uses. In all this there was continual training of observation, of ingenuity, constructive imagination, of logical thought, and of the sense of reality acquired through first-hand contact with actualities. The educative forces of the domestic spinning and weaving, of the sawmill, the grist-mill, the copper shop, and the blacksmith forge, were continuously operative.

No number of object-lessons, got up *as* object-lessons for the sake of giving information, can afford even the shadow of a substitute for acquaintance with the plants and animals of the farm and garden, acquired through actual living among them and caring for them. No training of sense-organs in school, introduced for the sake of training, can begin to compete with the alertness and fullness of sense-life that comes through daily intimacy and interest in familiar occupations. Verbal memory can be trained in committing tasks, a certain discipline of the reasoning powers can be acquired through lessons in science and mathematics; but, after all, this is somewhat remote and shadowy compared with the training of attention and of judgment that is acquired in having to do things with a real motive behind and a real outcome ahead. At present, concentration of industry and division of labor have practically eliminated household and neighborhood occupations—at least for educational purposes. But it is useless to bemoan the departure of the good old days of children's modesty, reverence, and implicit obedience, if we expect merely by bemoaning and by exhortation to bring them back. It is radical conditions which have changed, and only an equally radical change in education suffices. We must recognize our compensations—the increase in toleration, in breadth of social judgment, the larger acquaintance with human nature, the sharpened alertness in reading signs of character and interpreting social situations, greater accuracy, of adaptation to differing personalities, contact with greater commercial activities. These considerations mean much to the city-bred child of today. Yet there is a real problem: how shall we retain these advantages, and yet introduce into the school something representing the other side of life—occupations which exact personal responsibilities and which train the child with relation to the physical realities of life?

When we turn to the school, we find that one of the most striking tendencies at present is toward the introduction of so-called manual training, shop-work, and the household arts—sewing and cooking.

This has not been done "on purpose," with a full consciousness that the school must now supply that factor of training formerly taken care of in the home, but rather by instinct, by experimenting and finding that such work takes a vital

hold of pupils and gives them something which was not to be got in any other way. Consciousness of its real import is still so weak that the work is often done in a half-hearted, confused, and unrelated way. The reasons assigned to justify it are painfully inadequate or sometimes even positively wrong.

If we were to cross-examine even those who are most favorably disposed to the introduction of this work into our school system, we should, I imagine, generally find the main reasons to be that such work engages the full spontaneous interest and attention of the children. It keeps them alert and active, instead of passive and receptive; it makes them more useful, more capable, and hence more inclined to be helpful at home; it prepares them to some extent for the practical duties of later life—the girls to be more efficient house managers, if not actually cooks and sempstresses; the boys (were our educational system only adequately rounded out into trade schools) for their future vocations. I do not underestimate the worth of these reasons. Of those indicated by the changed attitude of the children I shall indeed have something to say in my next talk, when speaking directly of the relationship of the school to the child. But the point of view is, upon the whole, unnecessarily narrow. We must conceive of work in wood and metal, of weaving, sewing, and cooking, as methods of life not as distinct studies.

We must conceive of them in their social significance, as types of the processes by which society keeps itself going, as agencies for bringing home to the child some of the primal necessities of community life, and as ways in which these needs have been met by the growing insight and ingenuity of man; in short, as instrumentalities through which the school itself shall be made a genuine form of active community life, instead of a place set apart in which to learn lessons.

A society is a number of people held together because they are working along common lines, in a common spirit, and with reference to common aims. The common needs and aims demand a growing interchange of thought and growing unity of sympathetic feeling. The radical reason that the present school cannot organize itself as a natural social unit is because just this element of common and productive activity is absent. Upon the playground, in game and sport, social organization takes place spontaneously and inevitably. There is something to do, some activity to be carried on, requiring natural divisions of labor, selection of leaders and followers, mutual coöperation and emulation. In the schoolroom the motive and the cement of social organization are alike wanting. Upon the ethical side, the tragic weakness of the present school is that it endeavors to prepare future members of the social order in a medium in which the conditions of the social spirit are eminently wanting.

The difference that appears when occupations are made the articulating centers of school life is not easy to describe in words; it is a difference in motive, of spirit and atmosphere. As one enters a busy kitchen in which a group of children are actively engaged in the preparation of food, the psychological difference, the change from more or less passive and inert recipiency and restraint to one of buoyant outgoing energy, is so obvious as fairly to strike one in the face. Indeed, to those whose image of the school is rigidly set the change is sure to give a shock. But the change in the social attitude is equally marked. The mere absorption of facts and truths is so exclusively individual an affair that it tends very naturally to pass into selfishness. There is no obvious social motive for the acquirement of mere learning, there is no clear social gain in success thereat. Indeed, almost the only measure for success is a competitive one, in the bad sense of that term—a comparison of results in the recitation or in the examination to see which child has succeeded in getting ahead of others in storing up, in accumulating the maximum of information. So thoroughly is this the prevalent atmosphere that for one child to help another in his task has become a school crime. Where the school work consists in simply learning lessons, mutual assistance, instead of being the most natural form of coöperation and association, becomes a clandestine effort to relieve one's neighbor of his proper duties. Where active work is going on all this is changed. Helping others, instead of being a form of charity which impover-

ishes the recipient, is simply an aid in setting free the powers and furthering the impulse of the one helped. A spirit of free communication, of interchange of ideas, suggestions, results, both successes and failures of previous experiences, becomes the dominating note of the recitation. So far as emulation enters in, it is in the comparison of individuals, not with regard to the quantity of information personally absorbed, but with reference to the quality of work done—the genuine community standard of value. In an informal but all the more pervasive way, the school life organizes itself on a social basis.

Within this organization is found the principle of school discipline or order. Of course, order is simply a thing which is relative to an end. If you have the end in view of forty or fifty children learning certain set lessons, to be recited to a teacher, your discipline must be devoted to securing that result. But if the end in view is the development of a spirit of social coöperation and community life, discipline must grow out of and be relative to this. There is little order of one sort where things are in process of construction; there is a certain disorder in any busy workshop; there is not silence; persons are not engaged in maintaining certain fixed physical postures; their arms are not folded; they are not holding their books thus and so. They are doing a variety of things, and there is the confusion, the bustle, that results from activity. But out of occupation, out of doing things that are to produce results, and out of doing these in a social and coöperative way, there is born a discipline of its own kind and type. Our whole conception of school discipline changes when we get this point of view. In critical moments we all realize that the only discipline that stands by us, the only training that becomes intuition, is that got through life itself. That we learn from experience, and from books or the sayings of others *only* as they are related to experience, are not mere phrases. But the school has been so set apart, so isolated from the ordinary conditions and motives of life, that the place where children are sent for discipline is the one place in the world where it is most difficult to get experience—the mother of all discipline worth the name. It is only where a narrow and fixed image of traditional school discipline dominates, that one is in any danger of overlooking that deeper and infinitely wider discipline that comes from having a part to do in constructive work, in contributing to a result which, social in spirit, is none the less obvious and tangible in form—and hence in a form with reference to which responsibility may be exacted and accurate judgment passed.

The great thing to keep in mind, then, regarding the introduction into the school of various forms of active occupation, is that through them the entire spirit of the school is renewed. It has a chance to affiliate itself with life, to become the child's habitat, where he learns through directed living; instead of being only a place to learn lessons having an abstract and remote reference to some possible living to be done in the future. It gets a chance to be a miniature community, an embryonic society. This is the fundamental fact, and from this arise continuous and orderly sources of instruction. Under the industrial *regime* described, the child, after all, shared in the work, not for the sake of the sharing, but for the sake of the product. The educational results secured were real, yet incidental and dependent. But in the school the typical occupations followed are freed from all economic stress. The aim is not the economic value of the products, but the development of social power and insight. It is this liberation from narrow utilities, this openness to the possibilities of the human spirit that makes these practical activities in the school allies of art and centers of science and history.

The unity of all the sciences is found in geography. The significance of geography is that it presents the earth as the enduring home of the occupations of man. The world without its relationship to human activity is less than a world. Human industry and achievement, apart from their roots in the earth, are not even a sentiment, hardly a name. The earth is the final source of all man's food. It is his continual shelter and protection, the raw material of all his activities, and the home to whose humanizing and idealizing all his achievement returns. It is the great field, the great mine, the great source of the energies of heat, light, and electricity; the great scene of ocean, stream, mountain, and plain, of which all our agriculture and mining and lumbering, all our manufacturing and distributing agencies, are but the partial elements and factors. It is through occupations determined by this environment that mankind has made its historical and political progress. It is through these occupations that the intellectual and emotional interpretation of nature has been developed. It is through what we do in and with the world that we read its meaning and measure its value.

In educational terms, this means that these occupations in the school shall not be mere practical devices or modes of routine employment, the gaining of better technical skill as cooks, seamstresses, or carpenters, but active centers of scientific insight into natural materials and processes, points of departure whence children shall be led out into a realization of the historic development of man. The actual significance of this can be told better through one illustration taken from actual school work than by general discourse.

There is nothing which strikes more oddly upon the average intelligent visitor than to see boys as well as girls of ten, twelve, and thirteen years of age engaged in sewing and weaving. If we look at this from the standpoint of preparation of the boys for sewing on buttons and making patches, we get a narrow and utilitarian conception—a basis that hardly justifies giving prominence to this sort of work in the school. But if we look at it from another side, we find that this work gives the point of departure from which the child can trace and follow the progress of mankind in history, getting an insight also into the materials used and the mechanical principles involved. In connection with these occupations, the historic development of man is recapitulated. For example, the children are first given the raw material—the flax, the cotton plant, the wool as it comes from the back of the sheep (if we could take them to the place where the sheep are sheared, so much the better). Then a study is made of these materials from the standpoint of their adaptation to the uses to which they may be put. For instance, a comparison of the cotton fiber with wool fiber is made. I did not know until the children told me, that the reason for the later development of the cotton industry as compared with the woolen is, that the cotton fiber is so very difficult to free by hand from the seeds. The children in one group worked thirty minutes freeing cotton fibers from the boll and seeds, and succeeded in getting out less than one ounce. They could easily believe that one person could only gin one pound a day by hand, and could understand why their ancestors wore woolen instead of cotton clothing. Among other things discovered as affecting their relative utilities, was the shortness of the cotton fiber as compared with that of wool, the former being one-tenth of an inch in length, while that of the latter is an inch in length; also that, the fibers of cotton are smooth and do not cling together, while the wool has a certain roughness which makes the fibers stick, thus assisting the spinning. The children worked this out for themselves with the actual material, aided by questions and suggestions from the teacher.

Then they followed the processes necessary for working the fibers up into cloth. They re-invented the first frame for carding the wool—a couple of boards with sharp pins in them for scratching it out. They re-devised the simplest process for spinning the wool—a pierced stone or some other weight through which the wool is passed, and which as it is twirled draws out the fiber; next the top, which was spun on the floor, while the children kept the wool in their hands until it was gradually drawn out and wound upon it. Then the children are introduced to the invention next in historic order, working it out experimentally, thus seeing its necessity, and tracing its effects, not only upon that particular industry, but upon modes of social life—in this way passing in review the entire process up to the present complete loom, and all that goes with the application of science in the use of our present available powers. I need not speak of the science involved in this—the study of the fibers, of geographical features, the conditions under which raw materials are grown, the great centers of manufacture and distribution, the physics involved in the machinery of production; nor, again, of the historical

side—the influence which these inventions have had upon humanity. You can concentrate the history of all mankind into the evolution of the flax, cotton, and wool fibers into clothing. I do not mean that this is the only, or the best, center. But it is true that certain very real and important avenues to the consideration of the history of the race are thus opened—that the mind is introduced to much more fundamental and controlling influences than usually appear in the political and chronological records that pass for history.

Now, what is true of this one instance of fibers used in fabrics (and, of course, I have only spoken of one or two elementary phases of that) is true in its measure of every material used in every occupation, and of the processes employed. The occupation supplies the child with a genuine motive; it gives him experience at first hand; it brings him into contact with realities. It does all this, but in addition it is liberalized throughout by translation into its historic values and scientific equivalencies. With the growth of the child's mind in power and knowledge it ceases to be a pleasant occupation merely, and becomes more and more a medium, an instrument, an organ—and is thereby transformed.

This, in turn, has its bearing upon the teaching of science. Under present conditions, all activity, to be successful, has to be directed somewhere and somehow by the scientific expert—it is a case of applied science. This connection should determine its place in education. It is not only that the occupations, the so-called manual or industrial work in the school, give the opportunity for the introduction of science which illuminates them, which makes them material, freighted with meaning, instead of being mere devices of hand and eye; but that the scientific insight thus gained becomes an indispensable instrument of free and active participation in modern social life. Plato somewhere speaks of the slave as one who in his actions does not express his own ideas, but those of some other man. It is our social problem now, even more urgent than in the time of Plato, that method, purpose, understanding, shall exist in the consciousness of the one who does the work, that his activity shall have meaning to himself.

When occupations in the school are conceived in this broad and generous way, I can only stand lost in wonder at the objections so often heard, that such occupations are out of place in the school because they are materialistic, utilitarian, or even menial in their tendency. It sometimes seems to me that those who make these objections must live in quite another world. The world in which most of us live is a world in which everyone has a calling and occupation, something to do. Some are managers and others are subordinates. But the great thing for one as for the other is that each shall have had the education which enables him to see within his daily work all there is in it of large and human significance. How many of the employed are today mere appendages to the machines which they operate! This may be due in part to the machine itself, or to the *régime* which lays so much stress upon the products of the machine; but it is certainly due in large part to the fact that the worker has had no opportunity to develop his imagination and his sympathetic insight as to the social and scientific values found in his work. At present, the impulses which lie at the basis of the industrial system are either practically neglected or positively distorted during the school period. Until the instincts of construction and production are systematically laid hold of in the years of childhood and youth, until they are trained in social directions, enriched by historical interpretation, controlled and illuminated by scientific methods, we certainly are in no position even to locate the source of our economic evils, much less to deal with them effectively.

If we go back a few centuries, we find a practical monopoly of learning. The term *possession* of learning was, indeed, a happy one. Learning was a class matter. This was a necessary result of social conditions. There were not in existence any means by which the multitude could possibly have access to intellectual resources. These were stored up and hidden away in manuscripts. Of these there were at best only a few, and it required long and toilsome preparation to be able to do anything with them. A high-priesthood of learning, which guarded the treasury of truth and which doled it out to the masses under severe re-

strictions, was the inevitable expression of these conditions. But, as a direct result of the industrial revolution of which we have been speaking, this has been changed. Printing was invented; it was made commercial. Books, magazines, papers were multiplied and cheapened. As a result of the locomotive and telegraph, frequent, rapid, and cheap intercommunication by mails and electricity was called into being. Travel has been rendered easy; freedom of movement, with its accompanying exchange of ideas, indefinitely facilitated. The result has been an intellectual revolution. Learning has been put into circulation. While there still is, and probably always will be, a particular class having the special business of inquiry in hand, a distinctively learned class is henceforth out of the question. It is an anachronism. Knowledge is no longer an immobile solid; it has been liquified. It is actively moving in all the currents of society itself.

It is easy to see that this revolution, as regards the materials of knowledge, carries with it a marked change in the attitude of the individual. Stimuli of an intellectual sort pour in upon us in all kinds of ways. The merely intellectual life, the life of scholarship and of learning, thus gets a very altered value. Academic and scholastic, instead of being titles of honor, are becoming terms of reproach.

But all this means a necessary change in the attitude of the school, one of which we are as yet far from realizing the full force. Our school methods, and to a very considerable extent our curriculum, are inherited from the period when learning and command of certain symbols, affording as they did the only access to learning, were all-important. The ideas of this period are still largely in control, even where the outward methods and studies have been changed. We sometimes hear the introduction of manual training, art and science into the elementary, and even the secondary schools, deprecated on the ground that they tend toward the production of specialists—that they detract from our present scheme of generous, liberal culture. The point of this objection would be ludicrous if it were not often so effective as to make it tragic. It is our present education which is highly specialized, one-sided and narrow. It is an education dominated almost entirely by the medieval conception of learning. It is something which appeals for the most part simply to the intellectual aspect of our natures, our desire to learn, to accumulate information, and to get control of the symbols of learning; not to our impulses and tendencies to make, to do, to create, to produce, whether in the form of utility or of art. The very fact that manual training, art and science are objected to as technical, as tending toward mere specialism, is of itself as good testimony as could be offered to the specialized aim which controls current education. Unless education had been virtually identified with the exclusively intellectual pursuits, with learning as such, all these materials and methods would be welcome, would be greeted with the utmost hospitality.

While training for the profession of learning is regarded as the type of culture, as a liberal education, that of a mechanic, a musician, a lawyer, a doctor, a farmer, a merchant, or a railroad manager is regarded as purely technical and professional. The result is that which we see about us everywhere—the division into "cultured" people and "workers," the separation of theory and practice. Hardly one per cent of the entire school population ever attains to what we call higher education; only five per cent to the grade of our high school; while much more than half leave on or before the completion of the fifth year of the elementary grade. The simple facts of the case are that in the great majority of human beings the distinctively intellectual interest is not dominant. They have the so-called practical impulse and disposition. In many of those in whom by nature intellectual interest is strong, social conditions prevent its adequate realization. Consequently by far the larger number of pupils leave school as soon as they have acquired the rudiments of learning, as soon as they have enough of the symbols of reading, writing, and calculating to be of practical use to them in getting a living. While our educational leaders are talking of culture, the development of personality, etc., as the end and aim of education, the great majority of those who pass under the tuition of the school regard it only as a narrowly practical tool with which to get bread and butter enough to eke out a restricted life. If we were to conceive our educational end and aim in a less exclusive way, if we were to introduce into educational processes the activities which appeal to those whose dominant interest is to do and to make, we should find the hold of the school upon its members to be more vital, more prolonged, containing more of culture.

But why should I make this labored presentation? The obvious fact is that our social life has undergone a thorough and radical change. If our education is to have any meaning for life, it must pass through an equally complete transformation. This transformation is not something to appear suddenly, to be executed in a day by conscious purpose. It is already in progress. Those modifications of our school system which often appear (even to those most actively concerned with them, to say nothing of their spectators) to be mere changes of detail, mere improvement within the school mechanism, are in reality signs and evidences of evolution. The introduction of active occupations, of nature study, of elementary science, of art, of history; the relegation of the merely symbolic and formal to a secondary position, the change in the moral school atmosphere, in the relation of pupils and teachers—of discipline; the introduction of more active, expressive, and self-directing factors—all these are not mere accidents, they are necessities of the larger social evolution. It remains but to organize all these factors, to appreciate them in their fullness of meaning, and to put the ideas and ideals involved into complete, uncompromising possession of our school system. To do this means to make each one of our schools an embryonic community life, active with types of occupations that reflect the life of the larger society, and permeated throughout with the spirit of art, history, and science. When the school introduces and trains each child of society into membership within such a little community, saturating him with the spirit of service, and providing him with the instruments of effective self-direction, we shall have the deepest and best guarantee of a larger society which is worthy, lovely, and harmonious.

The Contribution of Schooling to the Learning of Norms: Independence, Achievement, Universalism, and Specificity

ROBERT DREEBEN

Generally speaking . . . . a teacher must balance a concern with specific accomplishments with some concern for a state of well-being: he has to keep a relatively "happy" class which "learns." But a class is more than a collection of individuals. The teacher always has to manage children in groups. His acts towards individuals must somehow be interpreted either as expressions of general rules or of a particular circumstance. In the latter case he must draw the further line between legitimate special treatment and favoritism. He must teach the relegation of private needs as well as their occasional relevance.

Kaspar D. Naegele, "Clergymen, Teachers, and Psychiatrists: . . ."

In speaking of these four ideas as norms, I mean that individuals accept them as legitimate standards for governing their own conduct in the appropriate situations. Specifically, they accept the obligations to (1) act by themselves (unless collaborative effort is called for), and accept personal responsibility for their conduct and accountability for its consequences; (2) perform tasks actively and master the environment according to certain standards of excellence; and (3) acknowledge the rights of others to treat them as members of categories (4) on the basis of a few discrete characteristics rather than on the full constellation of them that represent the whole person. I treat these four norms because they are integral parts of public and occupational life in industrial societies, or institutional realms adjacent to the school.

In earlier parts of this book, I have discussed only the pre-adult phases of socialization, which occur in the family of orientation and in the school. In one sense, at least for men, full adult status requires occupational employment, and one of the outcomes of schooling is employability. The capacity to hold a job involves not only adequate physical capacities (in part the outcome of biological maturation), but also the appropriate intellectual and psychological skills to cope with the demands of work. The requirements of job-holding are multifarious; however, most occupations require, among other things, that individuals take personal responsibility for the completion and quality of their work and individual accountability for its shortcomings, and that they perform their tasks to the best of their ability.

Public life extends beyond occupational employment. Even though people work as members of occupational categories, and in association with others as clients, patients, customers, parishioners, students, and so on, they also have nonoc-cupational identities as voters, communicants, petitioners, depositors, applicants, and creditors (to name just a few), in which people are simi-larly classified according to one primary charac-teristic, irrespective of how they differ other-wise.

Goode observes:

The prime social characteristic of modern indus-trial enterprise is that the individual is ideally given a job on the basis of his ability to fulfill its de-mands, and that this achievement is evaluated uni-versalistically; the same standards apply to all who hold the same job.[1]

Industrially oriented societies tend to have occupational systems based on normative princi-ples different from those of kinship units. Many observers, recognizing that individuals must un-dergo psychological changes of considerable magnitude in order to make the transition from family of orientation to economic employment,[2] have noted (but at the same time understated) the contribution of schooling. Eisenstadt, for ex-ample, in an otherwise penetrating analysis of age-grouping, restricts his treatment of the school's contribution to that of ". . . adapting the psychological (and to some extent also physiolog-ical) learning potential of the child to the various skills and knowledges which must be acquired by him."[3] Eisenstadt's emphasis is too narrowly lim-ited to those cognitive outcomes of schooling re-lated to instrumental knowledge.

Furthermore, while stressing the transition between family and occupation, most writers have largely ignored the contribution of school-ing to the development of psychological capaci-ties necessary for participating in other (noneco-nomic) segments of society. It is my contention that the social experiences available to pupils in schools, by virtue of the nature and sequence of their structural arrangements, provide opportuni-ties for children to learn norms characteristic of several facets of adult public life, occupation being but one.

The social properties of schools are such that pupils, by coping with the sequence of classroom

tasks and situations, are more likely to learn the principles (i.e., social norms) of independence, achievement, universalism, and specificity than if they had remained full-time members of the household. Although I have spoken thus far only of the similarities and differences between the family and the school, the nature of that compari-son is largely determined by the character of pub-lic institutions, in particular the economy and the polity. Schools, that is to say, form one of several institutional linkages between the household and the public sphere of adult life, a linkage organized around stages of the life cycle in industrial soci-eties. There is substantial evidence that conduct in the family and conduct on the job are governed by contrasting normative principles. From this we can imply that if the education of children were carried on primarily within the jurisdiction of the family, the nature of experiences available in that setting would not provide conditions appropriate for acquiring those capacities that enable people to participate competently in the public realm.

It is not inevitable that schools should pro-vide such an institutional linkage, but the fact of the matter is that they do, even though there are other candidates for the job. Mass media, for ex-ample, might perform a comparable knowledge-dispensing function, and if their potentialities for effecting more profound psychological changes were plumbed, they might constitute an agency sufficiently potent to bring about changes in prin-ciples of conduct. The media have not yet proved up to the job, however, perhaps in part because children's early experiences in the family predis-pose them to be responsive to human agents, and the media do not provide such agents. In fact, much research on the impact of mass media points to the importance of human links in the chain from source to audience. Occupational ap-prenticeship might be an acceptable substitute for the schools; it has the human element and is directly related to occupational employment, one of the main locations of men's engagement in the public sphere of industrial society. Apprentice-ship, however, like the media, has its own liabili-ties, one of which is that it continues relation-ships of dependency (not of child on parent, but of worker on employer), and those relationships are often found to be incompatible with many of the institutional demands of public life. Since the media and apprenticeship arrangements do not exhaust the possibilities, and since I am not trying to demonstrate the inevitability of schools, the impact of schooling remains to be explained, because schools are what we have. I turn, then, to a discussion of how the experiences of schooling contribute to the acquisition of the four norms in question.

INDEPENDENCE

One answer to the question, "What is learned in school?" is that pupils learn to acknowledge that there are tasks they must do alone, and to do them that way. Along with this self-imposed obligation goes the idea that others have a legitimate right to expect such independent behavior under certain circumstances.[4] Independence has a widely acknowledged though not unequivocal meaning. In using it here I refer to a cluster of meanings: doing things on one's own, being self-reliant, accepting personal responsibility for one's behavior, acting self-sufficiently,[5] and handling tasks with which, *under different circumstances,* one can rightfully expect the help of others. The pupil, when in school, is separated from family members who have customarily provided help, support, and sustenance, persons on whom he has long been dependent.

A constellation of classroom characteristics, teacher actions, and pupil actions shape experiences in which the norm of independence is learned. In addition to the fact that school children are removed from persons with whom they have already formed strong relationships of dependency, the sheer size of a classroom assemblage limits each pupil's claim to personal contact with the teacher, and more so at the secondary levels than at the elementary. This numerical property of classrooms reduces pupils' opportunities for establishing new relationships of dependency with adults and for receiving help from them.

Parents expect their children to act independently in many situations, but teachers are more systematic in expecting pupils to adhere to standards of independence in performing academic tasks. There are at least two additional aspects of classroom operation that bear directly on learning the norm of independence: rules about cheating and formal testing. Let us consider cheating first. The word itself is condemnatory in its reference to illegal and immoral acts. Most commonly, attention turns to how much cheating occurs, who cheats, and why. But these questions, while of great importance elsewhere, are of no concern here. My interest is in a different problem: to what types of conduct is the pejorative "cheating" assigned?

In school, cheating pertains primarily to instructional activities and usually refers to acts in which two or more parties participate when the unaided action of only one is expected. Illegal or immoral acts such as stealing and vandalism, whether carried out by individuals or groups, are not considered cheating because they have no direct connection with the central academic core of school activities. Nor is joint participation categorically proscribed; joint effort is called cooperation or collusion depending on the teacher's prior definition of the task.

Cheating takes many forms, most of which involve collective effort. A parent and a child may collaborate to produce homework; two pupils can pool their wisdom (or ignorance, as the case may be) in the interest of passing an examination. In both cases the parties join deliberately, although deliberateness is not essential to the definition; one pupil can copy from another without the latter knowing. In the case of plagiarism, of course, the second party is not a person at all, but information compiled by another. The use of crib notes, perhaps a limiting case, involves no collusion; it consists, rather, of an illegitimate form of help. These are the main forms of school cheating, but there are many variations, routine to exotic. Thus actions called cheating are those closely tied to the instructional goals of the school and usually involve assisted performance when unaided performance is expected. As one observer put it: Pupils ". . . *must learn to distinguish between cooperating and cheating.*"[6]

The irony of cheating *in school* is that the same kinds of acts are considered morally acceptable and even commendable in other situations. It is praiseworthy for one friend to assist another in distress, or for a parent to help a child; and if one lacks the information to do a job, the resourceful thing is to look it up. In effect, many school activities called cheating are the customary forms of support and assistance in the family and among friends.

In one obvious sense, school rules against cheating are designed to establish the content of moral standards. In another sense, the school attaches the stigma of immorality to certain types of behavior for social as distinct from ethical reasons; namely, to change the character of prevailing social relationships in which children are involved. In the case of homework, the school, in effect, attempts to redefine the relationship between parents and children by proscribing one kind of parental support, which is not a problem in other circumstances. The teacher has no direct control over parents but tries to influence them at a distance by asking their adherence to a principle clothed in moral language whose violations are punishable. The line between legitimate parental support (encouraged when it takes the form of parents stressing the importance of school and urging their children to do well) and collusion is unclear, but by morally proscribing parental intervention beyond a certain point, the teacher attempts to limit the child's dependence on family members in doing his school work. In other words, he expects the pupil to work independently. The same argument applies to pupils and their friends; the teacher attempts to eliminate those parts of friendship that make it difficult or impossible for him to discover what a pupil can do on his own. In relationships with kin and friends, the customary sources of support in times of adversity, the school intervenes by restricting solidarity and, in the process, determines what the pupil can accomplish unaided. The pupil, for his part, discovers which of his actions

he is held accountable for individually within the confines of tasks set by the school.

This argument is indirectly supported by the comparison between schooling and the occupational employment for which school is intended as preparation. The question here is the sense in which school experience is preparatory. Usually workers are not restricted in seeking help on problems confronting them; on the contrary, many occupations provide resources specifically intended to be helpful: arrangements for consultation, libraries, access to more experienced colleagues, and so on. Only in rare situations are people expected not to enlist the aid of family and friends in matters pertaining to work where that aid is appropriate. In other words, activities on the job, directly analogous to school work, do not carry comparable restrictions. However, people in their occupational activities are required to accept individual responsibility and accountability for the performance of assigned and self-initiated tasks. To the extent that the school contributes to the development of independence, the preparation lies more in the development of a psychological disposition to act independently than to perform a certain range of tasks without help.

Second, as to testing, and particularly the use of achievement tests; most important for independence are the social conditions designed for the *administration* of tests, not their content or format. By and large, pupils are tested under more or less rigorously controlled conditions. At one end of the spectrum, formal standardized tests are administered most stringently; pupils are physically separated, and the testing room is patrolled by proctors whose job is to discover contraband and to guarantee that no communication occurs, these arrangements being designed so that each examination paper represents independent work. At the other end, some testing situations are more informal, less elaborately staged, although there is almost always some provision to ensure that each pupil's work represents the product of only his own efforts.

Testing represents an approach to establishing the norm of independence, which is different from the proscription against cheating even though both are designed to reduce the likelihood of joint effort. Whereas the rules against cheating are directed toward delineating the form of appropriate behavior, the restrictions built into the testing situation provide physical constraints intended to guarantee that teachers will receive samples of the work pupils do unassisted. Actually, unless they stipulate otherwise, teachers expect pupils to do most of their everyday work by themselves; daily assignments provide the opportunities for and practice in independent work. Tests, because they occur at less frequent intervals than ordinary assignments, cannot provide comparably frequent opportunities; by the elaborate trappings of their administration, particularly with college entrance exams, and the anxiety they provoke, they symbolize the magnitude of the stakes.

It may be objected that in emphasizing independence I have ignored cooperation, since an important item on the school agenda is the instruction of pupils in the skills of working with others. Teachers do assign work to groups and expect a collaborative product, and to this extent they require the subordination of individual to collective efforts, but judging the product according to collective standards is another question.

To evaluate the contribution of each member of a working team, the teacher must either judge the quality of each one's work, in effect relying on the standard of independence, or rate each contribution according to the quality of the total product. The latter procedure rests on the assumption that each member has contributed equally, an untenable assumption if one member has carried the rest or if a few members have carried a weak sister. That occurrences of this kind are usually considered "unfair" suggests the normative priority of independence and the simple fact of life in industrial societies; i.e., that institutions of higher learning and employers want to know how well each person can do and put constraints on the schools in order to find out. Thus, although the school provides opportunities for pupils to gain experience in cooperative situations, in the last analysis it is the individual assessment that counts.

ACHIEVEMENT

Pupils come to accept the premise that they should perform their tasks the best they can, and act accordingly. The concept of achievement, like independence, has several referents. It usually denotes activity and mastery, making an impact on the environment rather than fatalistically accepting it, and competing against some standard of excellence. Analytically, the concept should be distinguished from independence, since, among other differences, achievement criteria can apply to activities performed collectively.

Much of the recent literature treats achievement in the context of child-rearing within the family as if achievement motivation were primarily a product of parental behavior.[7] Even though there is reason to believe that early childhood experiences in the family do contribute to its development, classroom experiences also contribute through teachers' use of resources beyond those ordinarily at the command of family members.

Classrooms are organized around a set of core activities in which a teacher assigns tasks to pupils and evaluates and compares the quality of their work. In the course of time, pupils differentiate themselves according to how well they perform a variety of tasks, most of which require the use of symbolic skills. Achievement standards are not limited in applicability to the classroom nor is their content restricted to the cognitive areas. Schools afford opportunities for participation in a variety of extra-curricular activities, most conspicuously athletics, but also music, dramatics, and a bewildering array of club and small group activities serving individual interests and talents.

The direct relevance of classroom work in providing task experience judged by achievement criteria is almost self-evident; the experience is built into the assignment-performance-evaluation sequence of the work. Less evident, however, is the fact that these activities force pupils to cope with various degrees of success and failure, both of which can be psychologically problematic. Consistently successful performance requires that pupils deal with the consequences of their own excellence in a context of peer equality in nonacademic areas. For example, they confront the dilemma inherent in having surpassed their age-mates in some respects while depending on their friendship and support in others, particularly in out-of-school social activities. The classroom provides not only the achievement experience itself but by-products of it, taking the form of the dilemma just described.

Similarly, pupils whose work is consistently poor not only must participate in achievement activities leading to their failure, they must also experience living with that failure. They adopt various modes of coping with this, most of which center around maintaining personal self-respect in the face of continuing assaults upon it. Probably a minority succeed or fail consistently; a majority, most likely, do neither one consistently, but nonetheless worry about not doing well. Schooling, then, assures most pupils the experiences of both winning and losing, and to the extent that they gain some modicum of gratification from academic activities, it teaches them to approach their work in a frame of mind conducive to achievement. At the same time they learn how to cope, in a variety of ways and more or less well, with success and failure.

Failure is perhaps the more difficult condition with which to cope because it requires acknowledgement that the premise of achievement, to which failure itself can be attributed in part, is a legitimate principle by which to govern one's actions. Yet situations that constrain people to live with personal failure are endemic to industrial societies in which many facets of public life are based on achievement principles; political defeat and occupational non-promotion being two cases in point.

As suggested earlier, the school provides a broad range of experiences other than those restricted to the classroom and academic in nature; these experiences are also based on achievement criteria but differ in several important respects. Alternatives to academic performance give the pupil a chance to succeed in achievement-oriented activities even though he may not be able to do well in the classroom.

How these alternative activities differ from those of the classroom is as important as the fact that they do so differ, as evidenced by the case of athletics. Competitive sports resemble classroom activities in that both provide participants with the chance to demonstrate individual excellence. However, the former—and this is more true of team than individual sports—permit collective responsibility for defeat, whereas the latter by and large allow only individual responsibility for failure. That is to say, the chances of receiving personal gratification for success are at least as great in sports as in the classroom, while the assault on personal self-respect for failure is potentially less intense. Athletics should not be written off as a manifestation of mere adolescent nonintellectualism, as recent writers have treated it.[8] I do not suggest that athletics has an as yet undiscovered intellectual richness; rather that its contribution should not be viewed simply in terms of intellectuality. Wilkinson, in talking about athletics in the British public schools, makes a similar argument, not so much in terms of mitigating the psychological consequences of achievement for individuals as in striking a balance between competition and social cooperation:

> On the football field and on the river, the public school taught its boys to compete, not so much in personal contests, as in struggles between groups—between teams, houses, and schools. . . . They preserved middle-class morality and energy, but they adapted these to the needs of the public servant,[9] so important, according to Wilkinson, in establishing the ethic that private privilege meant public duty.

A similar contention holds for music and dramatics; both provide the potentiality for individual accomplishment and recognition without the persistent, systematic, and potentially corrosive evaluation typical of the classroom. Finally, in various club activities based on interest and talent, a pupil can do the things he is good at in the company of others who share an appreciation for them. In all these situations, either the rigors of competition and judgment characteristic of the classroom are mitigated, or the activity in question has its own built-in source of support and personal protection, not to the same extent as in the family, but more than is available in the crucible of the classroom.

The school provides a wider variety of achievement experiences than does the family, but it also has fewer resources for supporting and protecting pupils' self-respect in the face of failure. As pupils proceed through successive school levels, the rigors of achievement increase, at least for those who continue along the main academic line. Moreover, at the secondary levels the number of activities governed according to achievement principles increases as does the variety of these activities. As preparation for adult public life in which the application of these principles is widespread, schooling contributes to personal development in assuring that the majority of pupils not only will have performed tasks according to the achievement standard, but that they will have had experience in an expanding number of situations in which activities are organized according to it.

Unlike independence and achievement, universalism and specificity are not commonly regarded as good things. Parents and teachers admonish children to act independently and do their work well; few of them support the idea that people should willingly acknowledge their similarity to one another in specifically categorical terms while ignoring their obvious differences; that is, in a sense, denying their own individuality.

Ideologically, social critics have deplored the impersonal, ostensibly dehumanizing, aspects of categorization, a principle widely believed to lie at the heart of the problem of human alienation; the attachment of man to machine, the detachment of man from man. Often ignored, however, is the connection between this principle and the idea of fairness, or equity. Seen from this vantage point, categorization is widely regarded as a good thing, especially when contrasted to nepotism, favoritism, and arbitrariness. People resent the principle when they think they have a legitimate reason to receive special consideration, and when their individuality appears to vanish by being "processed." Yet when a newcomer breaks into a long queue of patiently waiting people instead of

proceeding to the end of the line, they usually condemn him for acting unfairly (for not following the standard rule for all newcomers to a line). They do *not* react by expressing any sense of their own alienation, since they accept the same categorical principle as binding on themselves. In other words, this is not the occasion to proclaim one's individuality, but to act like everybody else and be sure they do likewise. The contrasts between the two dualities (individuality and dehumanization, fairness and special privilege) are similarly predicated on the principles of universalism and specificity; people differ in their posture toward each duality according to ideological position, situation, and, more cynically, in their conception of self-interest.

The concepts of universalism and specificity have been formulated most comprehensively by Parsons, though only part of his formulation is directly germane to this discussion. As part of his concern with social systems, Parsons views universalism as one horn of a dilemma (the other being particularism) in role definition; under what circumstances does the occupant of one social position govern his actions by adopting one standard or another when dealing with the occupant of another social position? My concern, however, is not with a selection among alternative, conflicting standards, but with the conditions under which individuals learn to impose the standards of universalism and specificity on themselves and to act accordingly.

Defining the central theme of universalism raises problems because the term has been assigned a variety of meanings, not all of them clear.[10] The relevant distinction here is whether individuals are treated in terms of their membership in categories or as special cases. In one respect or another an individual can always be viewed as a member of one or more categories, universalistically; he is viewed particularistically if, considering his similarity to others in the same category, he still receives special treatment. As Blau puts it:

> An attribute is defined as a universalistic standard if persons, regardless of their own characteristics, direct a disproportionate number of their positive

(or negative) evaluations to others with a certain characteristic. An attribute is defined as a particularistic standard if persons tend to direct their positive (or, in special cases, negative) evaluations to others whose characteristics are like their own.[11]

The treatment of others does not become more particularistic as an increasing number of categories is taken into account. If age, sex, religion, ethnicity, and the like are considered, all examples of general categories, treatment is still categorical in nature because it is oriented to categorical similarities and not to what is special about the person. Thus, *"A man's orientation toward his family,"* according to Blau, *"is considered particularistic because it* singles out for special attention *the members of an ingroup, rather than persons with a certain attribute regardless of whether it makes them part of his ingroup or not."*[12]

The norm of specificity is easily confused with universalism despite its distinctiveness. It refers to the scope of one person's interest in another; to the obligation to confine one's interest to a narrow range of characteristics and concerns, or to extend them to include a broad range.[13] The notion of relevance is implicit; the characteristics and concerns that should be included within the range, whether broad or narrow, are those considered relevant in terms of the activities in which the persons in question are involved. Doctors and storekeepers, for example, differ in the scope of the interest they have in the persons seeking their services, but the content of their interests also varies according to the nature of the needs and desires of those persons.

It is my contention that what the school contributes to the acceptance by children of those norms that penetrate many areas of public life is critical, because children's pre-school experience in the family is weighted heavily on the side of special treatment and parental consideration of the whole child. To say that children learn the norm of universalism means that they come to accept being treated by others as members of categories (in addition to being treated as special cases, as in the family).

CATEGORIZATION

Schools provide a number of experiences that families cannot readily provide because of limitations in their social composition and structure. One such experience is the systematic establishment and demarcation of membership categories. First, by assigning all pupils in a classroom the same or similar tasks to perform, teachers in effect make them confront the same set of demands. Even if there are variations in task content, class members still confront the same teacher and the obligations he imposes. Second, parity of age creates a condition of homogeneity according to developmental stage, a rough equalization of pupil capacities making it possible for teachers to assign similar tasks. Third, through the process of yearly promotion from grade to grade, pupils cross the boundaries separating one age category from another. With successive boundary crossings comes the knowledge that each age-grade category is associated with a particular set of circumstances (e.g., teachers, difficulty of tasks, subject matter studied). Moreover, pupils learn the relationship between categories and how their present position relates to past and future positions by virtue of having experienced the transitions between them. In these three ways, the grade (more specifically the classroom within the grade) with its age-homogeneous membership and clearly demarcated boundaries provides a basis for categorical grouping that the family cannot readily duplicate. Most important, the experiences of membership in a group of age-equals and repeated boundary crossings makes it possible for pupils to acquire a relativity of perspective, a capacity to view their own circumstances from other vantage points that they themselves have occupied.[14]

Although each child holds membership in the category "children" at home, parents, in raising them, tend to take age differences into account and thereby accentuate the uniqueness of each child's circumstances, thus belying in some measure the categorical aspects of "childhood." However, even if the category "children" breaks into its age-related components within the family, it remains intact when children compare themselves with friends and neighbors of similar age. In typical situations of this kind, children inform their parents that friends of the same age have greater privileges or fewer responsibilities than they. Parents, if they cannot actually equalize the circumstances, often explain or justify the disparity by pointing to the special situation of the neighbor family; they have more money, fewer children, a bigger house. Whatever the reason, that is, parents point out the uniqueness of family circumstances and thereby emphasize the particularities of each child's situation. The school, in contrast, provides the requisite circumstances for making comparisons among pupils in categorical rather than particular terms.

Another school experience fostering the establishment of social categories is the re-equalization of pupils by means of the high school track system after they have differentiated themselves through academic achievement in the lower grades, a mechanism that minimizes the likelihood of teachers having to deal with special cases. Teachers with a variegated batch of pupils must adopt more individualized methods of instruction than those whose pupils are similar in their level of achievement. In so doing, they partially recreate a kinship-type of relationship with pupils, treating segments of the class differently according to differences in capacity, much as parents treat their children differently according to age-related capacities.

As far as level is concerned, the high school is a better place to acquire the principle of universalism than the lower school levels because pupils within each track, who are of roughly similar capacity, move from classroom to classroom, in each one receiving instruction in a different subject area by a different teacher. They discover that over a range of activities, they are treated alike and that relatively uniform demands and criteria of evaluation are applied to them. Thus they learn which differences in experience are subordinated to the principle of categorization. The elementary classroom, oriented more to instruction in different subjects by a single teacher, does not provide the necessary variations in persons and subjects

for a clear-cut demonstration of the categorical principle.

PERSONS AND POSITIONS

Although the idea of categorization is central to the norm of universalism, it has additional and derivative aspects. One is the crucial distinction, widely relevant in industrial societies, between the person and the social position he occupies. Individuals are often expected to treat one another according to their social position, rather than according to their individual identity. Schooling contributes to the capacity to make the distinction (and to the obligation to do so) by making it possible for pupils to discover that different individuals occupying a single social position often act in ways that are attached to the position rather than to the different persons filling it. Even though all members of a given classroom find themselves in the same circumstances (they are about equal in age and roughly resemble each other in social characteristics related to residence), they still differ in many respects: sex, race, religion, ethnicity, and physical characteristics being among the most obvious. Their situation, therefore, provides the experience of finding that common interests and shared circumstances are assigned a priority that submerges obvious personal differences. The same contention holds for adults. Male and female adults are found in both school and family settings; in school, pupils can discover that an increasingly large number of different adults of both sexes can occupy the same position, that of "teacher." This discovery is not as easily made in the family because it is not possible to determine definitively whether "parent" represents two positions, one occupied by a male, the other by a female, or a single position with two occupants differing in sex. Children are not left completely without clues in this matter since they do have other adult relatives who can be seen as distinct persons occupying the same position: aunts, uncles, grandparents, and the like. Yet even extended families do not provide the frequent and systematic comparisons characteristic of the schools. Schooling, in other words, enables pupils to distinguish between persons and the social positions they occupy (a capacity crucially important in both occupational and political life) by placing them in situations in which the membership of each position is varied in its composition and the similarities between persons in a single position are made evident.

SPECIFICITY

The school provides structural arrangements more conducive to the acquisition of the norm of specificity than does the family. First, since the number of persons and the ratio between adults and nonadults is much larger in classrooms than in the household, the school provides large social aggregates in which pupils can form many casual associations (in addition to their close friendships) in which they invest but a small portion of themselves. As both the size and heterogeneity of the student body increase at each successive level, the opportunities for these somewhat fragmented social contacts increase and diversify. The relative shallowness and transiency of these relationships increase the likelihood that pupils will have experiences in which the fullness of their individuality is *not* involved, as it tends to be in their relationships among kin and close friends.

Second, on leaving the elementary school and proceeding through the departmentalized secondary levels, pupils form associations with teachers who have a progressively narrowing and specialized interest in them. (This comes about both because of subject matter specialization itself and because the number of pupils each teacher faces in the course of a day grows larger.) Although it is true that children, as they grow older, tend to form more specific relationships with their parents (symptomatically, this trend manifests itself in adolescents' complaints of parental invasions of privacy), the resources of the school far exceed those of the family in providing the social basis for the establishment of relationships in which only narrow segments of personality are invested.

EQUITY

An additional facet of universalism is the principle of equity, or fairness (I use the terms interchangeably). When children compare their lot—their gains and losses, rewards and punishments, privileges and responsibilities—with that of others and express dissatisfaction about their own, they have begun to think in terms of equity; their punishments are too severe, chores too onerous, allowance too small compared to those of siblings and friends. Children's comparisons with siblings, who are almost always different in age, usually prompt parents to try to resolve the sensed inequities by equalizing age hypothetically. "If you were as young as he, you wouldn't have to shovel the walk either." "He is only a child and doesn't know any better." The pained questions to which these statements are replies are familiar enough.

Writers who have discussed problems of equity and inequity have usually done so in order to identify indicative expressions of them (e.g., indignation, dissatisfaction with job, joking relationships, disputes over payment, etc.) and to discover the conditions under which such expressions originate (e.g., status inconsistency, relative deprivation, frequency of supervision, etc.).[15] My concern here is not with these two questions, but with the nature of family and school experiences in which problems of equity and inequity are defined as such, and in which the underlying principles become established in children's minds.

Among children in a family, age is critical in determining what is fair and unfair.[16] In a sense, it is the clock by which we keep developmental time, changing constantly though not periodically. The gains and losses of life are inextricably tied to age; memory reminds us of what we once had, and the experiences of others inform us of our present standing and of what the future holds. The personal significance of age is heightened among young children because the younger they are, the more significant any given age difference between them. Thus the difference between a four-year old and an eight-year old is greater than that between a fourteen-year old and an

SOCIALIZATION AND PROGRESS

eighteen-year old because, on the average, there are greater developmental changes occurring during the earlier four year span than during the later one. When the circumstances of life change rapidly; when one is still in the process of learning what is one's due and what is due others; and when the younger children do not have to fight the battles that the older ones have already won, it is difficult to determine whether one is being treated fairly on any given occasion.

In the family, except for the sense of unity and similarity that comes from experience in a small, solitary group whose members are reciprocally affectionate and supportive, behavior *within* the setting is governed to a considerable extent by the unique personal characteristics of the members. Among children, as I have argued, age is one of the most important of these characteristics. Except in families with one child or multiple-birth children, age alone is sufficient to distinguish them, although it is certainly not the only distinguishing characteristic. Because of the developmental importance of age, it constitutes one basis according to which parents act toward their children and siblings act toward each other. There are, of course, occasions on which parents can and do treat their children as if they were alike, but where questions of responsibility, accountability, privilege, and the like are involved, the differences between children must be taken seriously. *In this sense,* and in the context of the earlier qualification about family unity, each child exists in his own set of circumstances and is treated accordingly. This statement does not deny that parents may in fact ignore the differences among their children. It does imply, though, that if they do so over the long run, there can be disruptive consequences for the children and for the family unit. As cases in point, there are well-known situations involving overdemandingness (treating children as if they were older), and overindulgence (treating them as if they were younger).

Questions of equity, always comparative, are tied to situations. As children grow older, their circumstances and those of siblings change. The basis on which they determine what is fair and

unfair also changes both absolutely and relatively. Because age is a unique personal attribute, and because there are unique constellations of events and personal characteristics associated with small age spans, there are always variables at the root of equity problems. Inequities among young children can only be set straight in the relatively short run because circumstances in the short run change steadily over time.

The contrast between age as a constant and as a variable in questions of equity is evidenced clearly in Homans' treatment of age: ". . . *one of the ways in which two men may be 'like' one another is in their investments [age being one]. Accordingly the more nearly one man is like another in age, the more apt he is to expect their net rewards to be equal and to display anger when his own are less.*"[17] In the context of this statement, age is the criterion for assessing the fairness of rewards as one man compares his gain with that of another.

In the context of the transition between childhood and adulthood, two children *within the same family* (unless they are twins) cannot easily settle a question of equity by referring to their ages (they may acknowledge that the older child is entitled to more, but not how much more) because they differ in age, because the meaning of age differences changes, and because there can be disagreement over the coefficient for converting age units into units of gain and loss. Such a conversion is unnecessary in the case described by Homans because the two men are alike in age.

The problem families have of settling equity questions attributable to age variations does not arise in school classrooms, since the age of class members is nearly constant. Teachers cannot treat all pupils identically, but they can use age similarity as a guide for assigning similar instructional tasks to all members of a class and to communicate, implicitly or explicitly, that they are all in the same boat.

Even without age differences, problems of fairness and unfairness do arise in classrooms, originating when pupils who are supposed to be treated similarly are not so treated. Grades, for example, according to the usual procedure, must be assigned according to the quality of work completed, and equivalent products should receive the same grade. Marking similar work differently, or unequal work the same, represents unfair grading. A similar principle holds for the punishment of offenses (the punishment should fit the crime, and similar forms of misbehavior should be treated alike[18]) and for the assignment of tasks and responsibilities according to difficulty and onerousness. But there are secondary considerations that enter the process of evaluating performance: how hard pupils work and how much they have improved. These criteria cannot readily replace quality of performance unless teachers, pupils, and parents are willing to acknowledge the justice of various anomalies (so defined, at least, within the scope of American values), as when pupils who do excellent work with little effort receive lower grades than pupils who produce mediocre work through feverish activity; or when pupils who do not pull their weight in a cooperative project receive the high grade assigned to the project.

As argued earlier, equity involves a comparative assessment of one's circumstances: gains and losses, rewards and punishments, rights and obligations, privileges and responsibilities. To determine whether the circumstances in a given situation are equitable, an individual must learn to make comparisons by which he can discover whose circumstances resemble his own and whose do not, who is treated like him and who is not; he must also discover the relationships between his circumstances and the way he is treated.

Schooling, then, through the structural properties of classrooms at each school level and the treatment of pupils by teachers, provides opportunities for making the comparisons relevant to defining questions of equity far more effectively than does the family. The process is similar to that (above described) of learning the norm of universalism in general. Both within the classroom and within each grade, age (and, to a lesser extent, other personal and social characteristics) provides a basis for discovering both similarities and differences in categorical terms. The existence of grade levels distinguished primarily by the demandingness of work and demarcated by the device of yearly promotion, and the progression of pupils through them year by year, make it possible for children to learn that, *within the context of the school,* certain qualities that determine their uniqueness as persons become subordinated to those specific characteristics in which they are alike. Thus, fourth and fifth graders, despite their individuality, are judged according to the specific criterion of achievement, and the content and difficulty of their assigned tasks are regulated according to developmental considerations symbolized by grade. The fourth grader, having completed the third grade, can grasp the idea that he belongs to a category of persons whose circumstances differ from those of persons belonging to another category.

Family relationships are not organized on a group basis, nor do they entail anything comparable to the systematic step-by-step progression of grades in which the boundaries between one category and another are clearly demarcated. Although a child knows the difference between family members and nonmembers, his experiences in a kinship setting do not allow him to distinguish clearly whether his circumstances are uniquely his own or are shared. In other words, these relationships are not structured in such a way as to form a basis for making the categorical comparisons basic to the universalistic norm. Moreover, since parents treat their children in terms of the full range of personal characteristics; that is, according to the norm of diffuseness rather than that of specificity, the family setting is conducive to the special rather than the categorical treatment of each child (since the boundaries of a category are more clearly delineated if one characteristic, not many, constitutes the basis of categorization).

A CONCEPTUAL CAVEAT

The argument of this volume rests on the assumption that schools, through their structural arrangements and the behavior patterns of teachers, provide pupils with certain experiences largely unavailable in other social settings, and that these experiences, by virtue of their peculiar characteristics, represent conditions conducive to the acquisition of norms. I have indicated how pupils learn the norms of independence, achievement, universalism, and specificity as outcomes of the schooling process. A critical point, however, is how the relationship between experience and outcome is formulated.

There is no guarantee that pupils will come to accept these four norms simply because these experiences are available, nor should one conclude that these experiences contribute to the learning of only the four discussed here; for example, the pupils may lack the necessary social and psychological support from sources outside the school or sufficient inner resources to cope with the demands of schooling. These are reasons external to the school situation and may be sufficient to preclude both the instructional and normative outcomes. However, forces inherent in the schooling process itself may be equally preclusive, since the same activities and sanctions from which some pupils derive the gratification and enhancement of self-respect necessary for both kinds of outcome may create experiences that threaten the self-respect of others. Potentialities for success *and* failure are inherent in tasks performed according to achievement criteria. Independence manifests itself as competence and autonomy in some, but as a heavy burden of responsibility and inadequacy in others. Universalistic treatment represents fairness for some, cold impersonality to others. Specificity may be seen as situational relevance or personal neglect.

Within industrial societies where norms applicable to public life differ markedly from those governing conduct among kin, schools provide a sequence of experiences in which individuals, during the early stages of personality development, acquire new principles of conduct in addition to those already accepted during childhood. For reasons earlier enumerated in detail, the family, as a social setting with its characteristic social arrangements, lacks the resources and the competence[19] to effect the psychological transition. This is not to say that only the school can produce the necessary changes, but of those institutions having some claim over the lives of children and adolescents (e.g., the family, child labor, occupational apprenticeship, tutoring, the church, the mass media[20]), only the schools provide adequate, though not always effective, task experiences and sanctions, and arrangements for the generalization and specification of normative principles throughout many spheres of public life.

It is conceivable, of course, that families (and those other institutions as well as some yet to be invented) can provide the experiences necessary for the acquisition of these norms; family life provides opportunities for achievement, for assuming individual responsibility, and for categorical and specific treatment. Yet the family is more likely than schools to provide experiences that also undermine the acquisition of these norms. Similarly, the impact of the experiences that schooling provides may prove insufficient and inappropriate for their acquisition, and even if they are acquired, their acceptance is not necessarily of equal or great importance in all segments of public life. One thing that makes schooling effective is the relevance of the school's contribution to subsequent participation in public institutions. Another is the relationship between structural arrangements and activities in determining whether one setting or another is more conducive to producing a given outcome, for if two or more activities interfere with each other, or if the situation is inappropriate to the performance of an activity, the desired outcome is unlikely to appear.

An Ideological Caveat

Although I have treated them as norms, independence and achievement have been regarded by many observers of the American scene as dominant cultural themes or values, general standards of what is desirable.[21] In view of this, it is important that the argument of this book not be taken as a defense of national values, although it should not surprise anyone that the normative commitments of individuals who have passed through American schools are generally (though not invariably) consistent with national values. The main purpose of this analysis is to present a formulation, hypothetical in nature, of how schooling contributes to the emergence of certain psychological outcomes, and not to provide an apology or justification for those outcomes on ideological grounds. I have avoided calling universalism and specificity cultural values even though both are norms, since few, if any, observers include them among the broad moral principles considered desirable in American life. Their exclusion from the list of values should further confirm the nonideological intent of this discussion.

Having the means to produce a desired result is not the same as an injunction to use them in producing it. Of the many considerations entering into the decision to employ available resources in creating even widely valued outcomes, the probable costs involved should give pause. For the norms in question here, whose desirability can be affirmed either on ideological grounds or in terms of their relevance to public life in an industrial society, conditions conducive to their development are also conducive to the creation of results widely regarded as undesirable. Thus, a sense of accomplishment and mastery, on the one hand, and a sense of incompetence and ineffectualness, on the other, both represent psychological consequences of continuously coping with tasks on an achievement basis. Similarly with independence: self-confidence and helplessness can each derive from a person's self-imposed obligation to work unaided and accept individual responsibility for his actions. Finally, willingness to acknowledge the rightness of categorical and specific treatment may indicate the capacity to adapt to a variety of social situations in which only a part of one's self is invested, or it may indicate a sense of personal alienation and isolation from human relationships.

From the viewpoint of ideological justification, the process of schooling is problematic in that outcomes morally desirable from one perspective are undesirable from another; and in the making of school policy the price to be paid must be a salient consideration in charting a course of action.

NOTES AND REFERENCES

1. William J. Goode, *World Revolution and Family Patterns*, p. 11, Free Press of Glencoe, New York (1963).

2. See, for example, Ruth Benedict, "Continuities and Discontinuities in Cultural Conditioning," in Clyde Kluckhohn, Henry A. Murray, and David M. Schneider (eds.), *Personality*, pp. 522–531, Alfred A. Knopf, New York (1953); Talcott Parsons, "The School Class as a Social System: Some of its Functions in American Society," *Harvard Educational Review* 29, No. 4, 297–318 (1959); and S. N. Eisenstadt, *From Generation to Generation*, pp. 115–185, Free Press, Glencoe, Ill. (1956).

3. S. N. Eisenstadt, *ibid.*, p. 164.

4. My emphasis here differs from Parsons' in that he views independence primarily as a personal resource: ". . . it may be said that the most important single predispositional factor with which the child enters the school is his level of *independence*," Talcott Parsons, *op. cit.*, p. 300. Although independence is very likely such a predisposition—whether it is the most important single one is debatable—it is part of the school's agenda to further the development of independence to a point beyond the level at which family resources become inadequate to do so.

5. Winterbottom, for example, lumps independence and mastery together; the indices she uses to measure them, however, involve ostensibly different phenomena in that the mastery items refer to tendencies toward activity rather than to independence. Marian R. Winterbottom, "The Relation of Need for Achievement to Learning Experiences in Independence and Mastery," in John T. Atkinson (ed.), *Motives in Fantasy, Action, and Society*, pp. 453–478, Van Nostrand, Princeton (1958). As a definitional guideline for this discussion, I have followed the usage of Bernard C. Rosen and Roy D'Andrade, "The Psychosocial Origins of Achievement Motivation," *Sociometry* 22, No. 3, 186 (1959) in their discussion of independence training; and of McClelland and his colleagues in a study of independence training, David C. McClelland, A. Rindlisbacher, and Richard DeCharms, "Religious and Other Sources of

Parental Attitudes toward Independence Training," in David C. McClelland (Ed.), *Studies in Motivation,* pp. 389-397, Appleton-Century-Crofts, New York (1955).

6. Kaspar D. Naegele, "Clergymen, Teachers, and Psychiatrists: A Study in Roles and Socialization," *Canadian Journal of Economics and Political Science* 22, No. 1, 53 (1956).

7. See, for example, Marian R. Winterbottom, *ibid.;* Bernard C. Rosen and Roy D'Andrade, *op. cit.,* pp. 185-218; and Fred L. Strodtbeck, "Family Interaction, Values, and Achievement," in David C. McClelland *et al., Talent and Society,* pp. 135-191, Van Nostrand, Princeton (1958).

8. For one attempt to treat athletics condescendingly as non-intellectualism, see James S. Coleman, *The Adolescent Society,* Free Press of Glencoe, New York (1961).

9. Rupert Wilkinson, *Gentlemanly Power,* p. 21, Oxford University Press, London (1964).

10. Although Parsons considers universalism-particularism to be a dichotomy, they are distinguished on at least two dimensions: cognitive and cathectic. "The primacy of cognitive values may be said to imply a *universalistic* standard, while that of appreciative values implies a *particularistic* standard. In the former case the standard is derived from the validity of a set of existential ideas, or the generality of a normative rule, in the latter from the particularity of the cathectic significance of an object or of the status of the object in a relational system." Talcott Parsons, *The Social System,* p. 62, Free Press, Glencoe, Ill. (1951).

11. Peter M. Blau, "Operationalizing a Conceptual Scheme: The Universalism-Particularism Pattern Variable," *American Sociological Review* 27, No. 2, 169 (1962). The permission of Peter M. Blau to quote from his paper is gratefully acknowledged.

12. Peter M. Blau, *ibid.,* p. 164; my emphasis.

13. In the case of specificity, ". . . the burden of proof rests on him who would suggest that ego has obligations vis-à-vis the object in question which transcend this specificity of relevance." Talcott Parsons, *The Social System,* p. 65. In the case of diffuseness, ". . . the burden of proof is on the side of the exclusion of an interest or mode of orientation as outside the range of obligations defined by the role-expectation." Parsons, *ibid.,* p. 66.

14. For a discussion of relativity of perspective, see Daniel Lerner, *The Passing of Traditional Society,* pp.

43-75, Free Press of Glencoe, Glencoe, Ill. (1958). See also Chapter 6, below.

15. For discussions of these problems, see George C. Homans, *Social Behavior: Its Elementary Forms,* pp. 235-251, Harcourt, Brace, and World, New York (1961); Elliott Jaques, *The Measurement of Responsibility,* pp. 32-60, Harvard University Press, Cambridge (1956); and Leonard R. Sayles, *Behavior of Industrial Work Groups,* pp. 41-118, John Wiley and Sons, New York (1963). One proposition relating expressions about inequity and its conditions is the following: "The past occasions in which a man's activities have been rewarded are apt to have been occasions in which other men, in some way like him, have been rewarded too. When others like him get their reward now, but he does not, he is apt to display emotional behavior." Homans, *ibid.,* pp. 73-74.

16. There are events in family life where the explanation that renders inequities fair lies not in age but in circumstances—"Your brother could stay home from school and watch television because he was sick (and you weren't)"—and in other personal characteristics beside age, such as sex—"It isn't safe for girls to walk home alone at that hour (but it's O.K. for your brother)."

17. George C. Homans, *ibid.,* p. 75.

18. Wheeler, in his investigation of Scandinavian prisons, cites the example of two men returned to prison following a joint escape; although they had committed the identical offense, one was judged to have escaped because of claustrophobic fears, the other because of persistent psychopathic tendencies. Their subsequent treatments differed according to medical criteria—open spaces for one, maximum security for the other—even though the separate treatments violated the dictum that the punishment should fit the crime; that is, same crime, same punishment. "Both among inmates who feel that their *sentences* are just and among those who feel they are unjust, the ones housed in preventive detention institutions [centers in which the nature of prison treatment is based in part on the personality characteristics of the offender] are less likely to have a sense of justice in the *treatment* they are receiving in the institution [than inmates held in custodial settings]." Stanton Wheeler, "Legal Justice and Mental Health in the Care and Treatment of Deviance," paper presented at the Meetings of the Ameri-

can Orthopsychiatric Association, San Francisco, April, 1966, p. 5.

19. For a discussion of competence as an organizational characteristic, see Philip Selznick, *Leadership in Administration,* pp. 38–56, Row, Peterson, Evanston, Ill. (1957).

20. Mary Engel, "Saturday's Children: A Study of Working Boys," Cambridge, Mass.; Harvard Graduate School of Education, Center for Research in Careers, Harvard Studies in Career Development No. 51, 1966; Carl I. Hovland, "Effects of the Mass Media of Communi-cation," in Gardner Lindzey (ed.), *Handbook of Social Psychology, II,* pp. 1062–1103, Addison-Wesley, Reading, Mass. (1954); Blanche Geer *et al.,* "Learning the Ropes: Situational Learning in Four Occupational Training Programs," in Irwin Deutscher and Elizabeth Thompson (eds.), *Among the People: Studies of the Urban Poor,* Basic Books, New York, in press.

21. For a general discussion of the concept of 'value' and of major American cultural themes, see Robin M. Williams, Jr., *American Society,* pp. 397–470, Alfred A. Knopf, New York (1960).

On Becoming a Reflective Teacher

CARL A. GRANT AND KENNETH M. ZEICHNER

*If teachers today are to initiate young people into an ethical existence, they them-
selves must attend more fully than they normally have to their own lives and its requirements; they have to break with the mechanical life, to overcome their own
submergence in the habitual, even in what they conceive to be virtuous, and to
ask the "why" with which all moral reasoning begins.[1]*

Maxine Greene, *Teacher as Stranger*

As you proceed with your professional education, you will continually be confronted with numerous choices about the kind of teacher to become. Recent literature in education has clearly shown that teachers differ substantially according to their goals and priorities and to the instructional and classroom management strategies that they employ. These differences among teachers have usually been portrayed as contrasting "types." For example, much has been written in recent years about the differences between teachers who are "open or traditional," "child-centered or subject-centered," "direct or indirect," and "humanistic or custodial." These dichotomies attempt to differentiate teachers who hold different views about what is important for children to learn, preferred instructional and management strategies, and types of curricular materials, and about the kinds of school and classroom organizational structures within which they want to work. The kind of teacher you wish to become, the stands you take on educational issues, and the knowledge and skills you need for putting your beliefs into action all represent decisions you as a prospective teacher need to make.

Over a hundred years of educational research has yet to discover the most effective instructional methods and school and classroom organizational structures for all students. This, together with the fact that "rules for practice" cannot now and probably never will be easily derived from either college coursework or practical school experience, makes your choices regarding these issues and the manner in which you determine them of great importance.

With regard to instructional strategies and methods, you will literally be bombarded in your courses and practicums with suggestions and advice regarding the numerous techniques and strategies that are now available for the instruction of children in the various content areas. For example, you will be taught various strategies for leading discussions, managing small groups, designing learning centers, administering diagnostic and evaluative procedures, and teaching concepts and skills.

Furthermore, in each of the content areas there are choices to be made about a general approach or orientation to instruction over and

---

Source: *"On Becoming a Reflective Teacher"* from Preparing
for Reflective Teaching, *copyright 1984 by Carl Grant and
Ken Zeichner. Reprinted by permission of the authors.*

above the choice of specific instructional techniques and procedures. You, ultimately, must make decisions about which approach or combination of approaches to employ amid competing claims by advocates that their approach offers the best solution to problems of instruction.

Undoubtedly, there is a great deal of debate in education today over how to go about teaching agreed upon content and skills and about the ways to manage classrooms and children. However, the question of *what* to teach, and to whom, precedes the question of *how* to teach. The selection of content to be taught to a particular group of children and of the types of instructional materials and resources to support this process are issues of great importance despite the fact that any school in which you are likely to work will have some set of policies. Although there are limits placed upon teachers regarding curricular content and materials, teachers usually have some latitude in the selection of specific content and materials within broad curricular guidelines.

For example, in the state of Wisconsin it is required that teachers teach the history of their state as part of the 4th grade social studies curriculum. Within these guidelines, individual teachers usually have some degree of choice about what to teach or emphasize about Wisconsin history and about what materials to use. This holds true in many curricular areas; even where schools have adopted particular instructional approaches and programs, such as in reading and math, teachers are still permitted some degree of personal discretion in the selection of content and materials.

You will also face a set of options about the kinds of school organizational structures in which you will work, and you will need to be aware that not all structures are compatible with all positions on issues of curriculum and instruction. At the elementary school level, for example, do you prefer to work in a self-contained classroom with one group of children or do you prefer to work closely with colleagues in a departmentalized context, such as is found in many individually guided education schools? Furthermore, you must begin to form positions about the kinds of school

and classroom structures that will support the kind of teaching you want to do.

In addition to these numerous choices and issues, there is another and more basic choice facing you. This choice concerns the way in which you go about formulating positions with regard to the issues mentioned above. To what degree will you consciously direct this process of decision making in pursuit of desired ends and in light of educational and ethical principles? On the other hand, to what degree will your decisions be mechanically directed by others; by impulse, tradition, and authority? An important distinction is made between being a reflective or an unreflective teacher, and it necessarily involves every prospective teacher no matter what your orientation and regardless of the specific position that you eventually adopt on the issues of curriculum and instruction.

You may be wondering what we mean by being a reflective teacher. In the early part of this century, John Dewey made an important distinction between human action that is reflective and that which is routine. Much of what Dewey had to say on this matter was directed specifically to teachers and prospective teachers, and his remarks remain very relevant for those in the process of becoming teachers in the 1980s. According to Dewey,[2] *routine action* is behavior that is guided by impulse, tradition, and authority. In any social setting, and the school is no exception, there exists a taken-for-granted definition of everyday reality in which problems, goals, and the means for their solution become defined in particular ways. As long as everyday life continues without major interruption, this reality is perceived to be unproblematic. Furthermore, this dominant world view is only one of the many views of reality that would theoretically be possible, and it serves as a barrier to recognizing and experimenting with alternative viewpoints.

Teachers who are unreflective about their work uncritically accept this everyday reality in schools and concentrate their efforts on finding the most effective and efficient means to achieve ends and to solve problems that have largely been defined for them by others. These teachers lose sight of the fact that their everyday reality is only one of many possible alternatives. They tend to forget the purposes and ends toward which they are working.

Dewey defines *reflective action*,[3] on the other hand, as behavior which involves active, persistent, and careful consideration of any belief or practice in light of the grounds that support it and the further consequences to which it leads. According to Dewey, reflection involves a way of meeting and responding to problems. Reflective teachers actively reflect upon their teaching and upon the educational, social and political contexts in which their teaching is embedded.

There are three attitudes that Dewey defines as prerequisites for reflective action.[4] First, *openmindedness* refers to an active desire to listen to more sides than one, to give full attention to alternate possibilities, and to recognize the possibility of error even in the beliefs that are dearest to us. Prospective teachers who are openminded are continually examining the rationales (educational or otherwise) that underlie what is taken to be natural and right and take pains to seek out conflicting evidence on issues of educational practice.

Second, an attitude of *responsibility* involves careful consideration of the consequences to which an action leads. Responsible student teachers ask themselves why they are doing what they are doing in the classroom in a way that transcends questions of immediate utility and in light of educational purposes of which they are aware. If all that is taught in schools were imparted through the formally sanctioned academic curriculum and if all of the consequences of teachers' actions could be anticipated in advance, the problem here would be much simpler than it is in actuality. However, there is a great deal of agreement among educators of various ideological persuasions that much of what children learn in school is imparted through the covert processes of the so called "hidden curriculum" and that many consequences of the actions of educators are unanticipated outcomes that often contradict formally stated educational goals. Given the powerful impact of the hidden curriculum on the actual outcomes of schooling and the frequently unanticipated consequences of our actions, re-

flection about the potential impact of our actions in the classroom is extremely important.

The third and final attitude of the reflective teacher is one of *wholeheartedness*. This refers to the fact that openmindedness and responsibility must be central components in the life of the reflective teacher and implies that prospective teachers who are reflective must take active control over their education as teachers. A great deal of research demonstrates that prospective teachers very quickly adopt beliefs and practices of those university and school instructors with whom they work. Many prospective teachers seem to become primarily concerned with meeting the oftentimes conflicting expectations of university professors and cooperating teachers, and with presenting a favorable image to them in the hope of securing favorable evaluations. This impression management is understandable and is a natural consequence of existing power relationships in teacher education, but the divided interest that results tends to divert students' attention from a critical analysis of their work and the context in which it is performed. If reflectiveness is to be part of the lives of prospective teachers, students will have to seek actively to be openminded and responsible or else the pressure of the taken-for-granted institutional realities will force them back into routine behavior.

Possession of these attitudes of openmindedness, responsibility, and wholeheartedness, together with a command of technical skills of inquiry (for example observation) and problem solving define for Dewey a teacher who is reflective. Reflection, according to Dewey,

> emancipates us from merely impulsive and routine activity . . . enables us to direct our actions with foresight and to plan according to ends in view of purposes of which we are aware. It enables us to know what we are about when we act.[5]

On the other hand, according to Dewey, to cultivate unreflective activity is "to further enslavement for it leaves the person at the mercy of appetite, sense and circumstance."[6]

Choosing between becoming a reflective teacher or an unreflective teacher is one of the most important decisions that you will have to make. The quality of all of your decisions regarding curriculum and instruction rests upon this choice.

You are probably saying to yourself, "Of course I want to be a reflective teacher, who wouldn't. But, you need to tell me more." The following sections of the paper discuss the three characteristics of reflective thinking in relation to classroom teaching, analyze whether reflective teaching is a realistic and/or desirable goal, and offer suggestions for how you can begin to become a reflective teacher.

FURTHER INSIGHT

We have pointed out that openmindedness, responsibility, and wholeheartedness are the characteristics of reflective thinking. Let us now discuss each characteristic in relation to classroom teaching.

OPENMINDEDNESS

When you begin to teach, both as a student teacher and as a licensed teacher, you will most likely be asked to accept teaching procedures and strategies that are already being used in that school or classroom. Will you accept these without question, or will you explore alternative ways of looking at existing teaching practices? For example, celebrating holidays like Thanksgiving and Columbus Day helps to affirm the prevailing historical accounts of these days as well as the customs and traditions associated with them. As a teacher, would you be willing to reevaluate what and how you teach about holidays if some of the students in your class hold a different point of view about them? Would you modify your teaching to take into account their views and beliefs? Being a reflective teacher means that you keep an open mind about the content, methods, and procedures used in your classroom. You constantly reevaluate their worth in relation to the students currently enrolled and to the circumstances. You not only ask why things are the way that they are, but also how they can be made better.

The reflective teacher understands that school practices are not accepted because they are clothed in tradition. If, for example, most of the boys but only a few of the girls are being assigned to Industrial Arts, you should inquire as to why this is happening. You could then begin to formulate teaching and counseling plans (for example, career opportunities, workshops) that would allow students regardless of gender to benefit from the training that is available in those courses.

RESPONSIBILITY

Teaching involves moral and responsible action. Teachers make moral choices when they make voluntary decisions to have students attain one educational objective instead of another. These decisions are conscious actions that result in certain consequences. These actions can be observed when teachers develop curriculum and choose instructional materials. For example, until recently a textbook company had two basal readers in its reading series. One basal reader was somewhat racially integrated and the other had all white characters. When teachers consciously chose one basal reader over the other or did not modify the all white reader to correct the racial bias, they made a decision that affected not only their students' racial attitudes and understanding about different groups of people, but also their attitudes about themselves. In other words, teachers can encourage ethnocentric attitudes as well as teach an unrealistic view of the world community beyond the school community by failing to provide knowledge about other groups.

As a reflective teacher you are aware of your actions and their consequences. You are aware that your teaching behavior should not be conditioned merely by the immediate utility of an action. For example, it may be much easier to have your students answer questions or work problems on conveniently prepared ditto sheets than to have them do small group projects or hold classroom debates. It may also be much easier if you use one textbook to teach a unit on the Mexican American War than if you use multiple textbooks and other historical documents that would represent both governments' points of view. But immediate utility cannot become the sole justification for your actions and cannot excuse you from the consequences of your actions. Your actions must have a definite and responsibly selected purpose. You have an obligation to consider their consequences in relation to the lives of the students you have accepted the responsibility to teach.

WHOLEHEARTEDNESS

A reflective teacher is not openminded and responsible merely when it is convenient. Openmindedness and responsibility are integral, vital dimensions of your teaching philosophy and behavior. For example, we have seen teachers publicly advocate a belief in integrating handicapped students into the regular class; however, when observing in their classrooms, we saw the handicapped students treated in isolation because the curriculum and the instructional strategies had not been modified to capitalize upon the students' strengths or to acknowledge the students' individual differences. The teachers often left handicapped students to sit in the outer boundaries of the classroom instead of changing the physical environment of the classroom—desk arrangements—to allow them to move about freely as other students would. As a reflective teacher, you do not hesitate or forget to fight for your beliefs and for a quality education for all.

The reflective teacher is dedicated and committed to teaching *all students,* not just certain students. Many of your peers say they want to teach because they love and enjoy working with kids. Are they *really* saying *any* and *all* kids, or are they saying kids that are just like them? The story of Mary Smith will help to illustrate our point. During a job interview with a rural school system, Mary Smith, a graduate from a large urban university, was composed and fluent in discussing teaching methods and curriculum. She also stressed her genuine love for and enjoyment of children and her desire to help them. Her "performance" was so compelling that she was invited to accept a teaching position. Mary Smith, we must point out, believed what she said in the interview and eagerly looked forward to her teaching assignment. Her assignment was to a six room rural school, where the majority of the students spoke with a heavy regional dialect that she had never before heard. The students' reading and mathematics achievement according to standardized tests was three to four years below grade level. Their behavior and attitudes toward school were different from what she had been accustomed to. They regarded the schools as boring and irrelevant to their life style and their future, and they demonstrated their disregard for the school and the teacher by disobeying many instructional and behavioral "requests." Mary tried diligently for three months to get the students to cooperate and follow her instructions. At the beginning of the fourth month, however, she resigned her position. In her letter of resignation she stated that "these kids are not ready to accept what I have been trained to give them. Therefore, I will seek teaching employment where the students want to learn."

There are many teachers like Mary Smith, but the reflective teacher is not one of them. The reflective teacher is wholehearted in accepting *all* students and is willing to learn about and affirm the uniqueness of each student for whom he or she accepts responsibility. If you are a reflective teacher, your teaching behavior is a manifestation of your teaching philosophy and you are unswerving in your desire to make certain that the two become one and the same.

IS REFLECTIVE TEACHING A REALISTIC AND/OR DESIRABLE GOAL?

Throughout this century many educators have argued that teachers need to be more reflective about their work. The argument is often made that schools and society are constantly changing and that teachers must be reflective in order to cope effectively with changing circumstances. By uncritically accepting what is customary and by engaging in fixed and patterned behaviors, teachers make it more unlikely that they will be able to change and grow as situations inevitably change. Furthermore, it is commonly accepted that no teacher education program, whatever its focus, can prepare teachers to work effectively in all kinds of classroom settings. Therefore, it becomes important for you to be reflective in order that you may intelligently apply the knowledge and skills gained in your formal preparation for teaching to situations that may be very different from those you experienced during your training.

At the same time many questions have been raised about whether reflective teaching is a realistic or even necessary goal to set before prospective teachers. The purpose of this section is to examine briefly three of the most common objections that have been raised about the goal of reflective teaching and to demonstrate how, despite these doubts, it is still possible and desirable for teachers to work toward a more reflective orientation to both their work and their workplace.

IS IT POSSIBLE TO TAKE THE TIME TO REFLECT?

Many have argued that the nature of teaching and the ecology of classrooms make reflective teaching unrealistic and even undesirable. For example, it is frequently pointed out that classrooms are fast-paced and unpredictable environments where teachers are often required to make spontaneous decisions in response to children's ongoing reactions to an instructional program. Phillip Jackson has estimated that teachers engage in approximately 1,000 interpersonal interactions on any given day and there is no way to describe life in the classroom as anything but extremely complex.[7]

Furthermore, institutional constraints such as high pupil-teacher ratios, the lack of released time for reflection, and pressures to cover a required curriculum with diverse groups of children who are compelled to come to school shape and limit the range of possible teacher actions. The point is made that teachers do not have the time to reflect given the necessity of quick action and the press of institutional demands. According to this view, intuitiveness (as opposed to reflectiveness) is an adaptive response and a natural consequence of

the fast-paced unpredictable nature of classroom life and is necessary for teachers to be able to negotiate classroom demands.

Phillip Jackson expresses serious doubts about whether teachers could even function at all in classrooms if they spent more time reflecting about the purposes and consequences of their work.

> If teachers sought a more thorough understanding of their world, insisted on greater rationality in their actions, were completely openminded in their consideration of pedagogical choices and profound in their view of the human condition, they might well receive greater applause from intellectuals, but it is doubtful that they would perform with greater efficiency in the classroom. On the contrary, it is quite possible that such paragons of virtue, if they could be found to exist, would actually have a deuce of a time coping in any sustained way with a class of third graders or a play yard full of nursery school tots.[8]

While classrooms are indeed fast-paced and complex environments, it does not automatically follow that reflective teaching is incompatible with this reality and that teachers by necessity must rely primarily upon intuition and unreflective actions. Several studies[9] have convincingly shown that the quality of teacher deliberations *outside* of the classroom (for example, during planning periods or team meetings) affects the quality of their future actions *within* the classroom. As Dewey points out, "To reflect is to look back on what has been done to extract the meanings which are the capital stock for dealing with further experience."[10] Reflection which is directed toward the improvement of classroom practice does not necessarily need to take place within the classroom to have an impact on classroom practice. Despite the fact that reflection as has been defined in this paper does not occur in many schools even when there has been time set aside for that purpose,[11] the possibility still exists.

Furthermore, the fast pace of classroom life does not preclude a certain amount of reflection within its boundaries. Those who have written about reflective teaching have never argued for "complete openness of mind." On the contrary, reflective teaching involves a balance between thought and action; a balance between the arrogance that blindly rejects what is commonly accepted as truth and the servility that blindly receives this "truth." There is clearly such a thing as too much thinking, as when a person finds it difficult to reach any definite conclusion and wanders helplessly among the multitude of choices presented by a situation, but to imply that reflection necessarily paralyzes one from action is to distort the true meaning of reflective teaching.

IS IT POSSIBLE TO ACT ON THE RESULTS OF REFLECTION?

Another objection that has frequently been raised is that even if teachers do reflect on the purposes and consequences of their actions, they are not able to act on the results of their inquiries if the desired course of action is in conflict with the dominant institutional norms of their school. According to this view, teachers are basically functionaries within a bureaucratic system; they have prescribed roles and responsibilities, and in order to survive in that system they must always give way to institutional demands. In other words, why bother with reflection if you always have to do what you are told to do anyway? Encouraging prospective teachers to reflect about their work is viewed as a hopeless endeavor, because whatever habits of reflectiveness are developed during preservice training will inevitably be "washed out" by inservice school experience as teachers are forced into standardized patterns of behavior and into conformity with bureaucratic norms of obedience and loyalty to those in authority. As Wayne Hoy and William Rees[12] point out, the forces of bureaucratic socialization in schools are strong and efficient.

As was mentioned earlier, there is little doubt that schools as institutions and the societal contexts in which they are embedded exert numerous pressures on teachers to conform to certain behavioral norms, to cover certain curricular content and to use particular methods of instruction and classroom management. However, while they are necessarily constrained by these institutional pressures and by their own individual biases and predispositions, teachers do to varying degrees play active roles in shaping their own occupational identities. If, for example, you were to survey the teachers within a given school, it would probably be fairly easy to identify a dominant "teacher culture" in that school, which defines a set of viewpoints about curriculum, instruction, classroom management and organization. Yet, at the same time, you will inevitably find differences and conflicts among teachers in that school in terms of their beliefs, their instructional methods, and the ways in which they have organized their classrooms. Not all teachers in a given school are alike, and the very existence of these differences within the same institutional conditions is evidence of the potential for teachers to act upon their beliefs even if they conflict with the dominant viewpoints in a given setting.

In reality, the habits of mind and pedagogical skills that you develop now in your formal education for teaching will not necessarily be "washed out" by school experience. The world of teaching necessarily involves a constant interplay between choice and constraint. No matter how prescribed the curriculum and whatever the degree of consensus over behavioral norms for teachers in the settings in which you will work, there will always be some degree of conflict over what is natural and right and some amount of space for you to act alone or with others to reshape the nature of the school in which you work. There are more than a few teachers who do not fit the bureaucratic mold that is frequently portrayed in educational literature, and there is potentially enough room for most teachers within their prescribed roles for some degree of reflection to take place.

IS IT NECESSARY TO REFLECT?

A third objection that has been raised about reflective teaching is that it is not necessary to be reflective in order to be an effective teacher. Advocates of this position point to the many highly regarded teachers in our schools who succeed without apparently reflecting on the purposes and consequences of their work. For example, Phillip Jackson studied fifty teachers who were identified by their principals and by general reputation as being outstanding teachers, and he concluded that these exemplars of educational practice approached their work in classrooms largely through intuition rather than through any process of rational analysis.

This conclusion has been confirmed by much of the recent research on teacher thinking[13] by studies of teacher-pupil interactions[14] and by Dan Lortie's[15] study of the "ethos" of the teaching profession. According to many education researchers, teachers for the most part, including good teachers, do not seem to be especially reflective or analytic about their work. On the contrary, a substantial number of teachers seem to accept uncritically what is currently fashionable. As a result, the position is often taken that it is unnecessary to be reflective because one can be a good teacher without being so.

There are several responses that one could make to this objection. First, there are numerous problems with the conclusions that many researchers have drawn about the predominance of intuitive behavior. Specifically, while it may be true that many teachers rely primarily on instinct and feeling while in the classroom, there is no basis for concluding that good teachers do not put a lot of thought into their work both before and after instruction. Many of these researchers have failed to study what teachers actually do in their classes and how they construct and justify specific activities. What actually goes on in the minds of good teachers—when it is studied—is still not well understood. Furthermore, there are some real problems with the view that university scholars are as a group more reflective than teachers, especially when these conclusions are drawn by those who identify themselves as being most reflective. In our view there is no convincing evidence that those in universities are any more or less likely as a group to be reflective or analytic about their work than teachers are.

Our own experience in talking with teachers has convinced us that the really good ones do reflect upon their work and that educational researchers have failed to capture much of what goes on in the minds of teachers. In fact, studies of attempted school reform provide some evidence that teachers *do* reflect. For example, those who have studied the processes of change in schools have generally concluded that teachers are very selective about what they will incorporate into their classrooms, and in our view this selectivity refutes the position that there is little thought and judgment underlying teachers' work.[16]

There is one further reason for rejecting the view that reflective teaching is not necessary. Scheffler clearly summarizes this view:

> Justification for reflection is not . . . simply a matter of minimal necessity. It is rather a matter of desirability, and a thing may be desirable, not because it is something that we could not do without, but because it transforms and enhances the quality of what we do and how we live.[17]

As Scheffler's statement points out, you may be able to get by, by putting little thought into your work, but if you want to strive to be the best teacher that you possibly can, then there is in reality no alternative to reflective teaching. Many teachers profess that they want their students to be thoughtful about the work that they do in school so that they will eventually develop an independence of mind that will enable them to be active participants in a democratic society. If we hold these goals for our children, the place to begin is with ourselves. If the schools of today were all that they could be, one could safely ignore our arguments. But if there is more that we can do to make our schools and our society more enriching, humane and just, then we need reflective teachers to play an integral role in this process.

HOW TO BEGIN

You may be asking, "How can I become reflective, especially given the fact that I haven't started teaching yet?" The suggestions that we will now offer will help you get started. Remember, becoming a reflective teacher is a continual process of growth.

Many educators have correctly pointed out that even before you enter a formal program of teacher preparation you have already been socialized to some extent by the twelve years or more you have spent as a student. You have spent literally thousands of hours assessing schools and classrooms and have by now internalized (largely unconsciously) conceptions of children, learning, the roles of teacher and student, curriculum, beliefs and assumptions concerning almost every issue related to schooling. From our point of view, a good place to begin the process of reflective teaching is to examine these numerous predispositions that you bring with you into formal preparation for teaching. Consciously or not, these will affect how you will perceive what will be presented to you in your teacher education program and how you will interpret your own and others' actions in the classroom.

It is important for you to begin to discriminate between beliefs and assumptions that rest upon tested evidence and those that do not, and to be cautious about putting confidence into beliefs that are not well justified. Some of our ideas have, in fact, been picked up from other people merely because they are widely accepted views, not because we have examined them carefully. Because of the nature of teaching, we may often be compelled to act without full confidence in a point of view or an approach to a problem. This is unavoidable. However, if we remain tentative about our beliefs, the possibility will remain that we may revise our thinking if future evidence warrants it. On the other hand, if we are dogmatic about our beliefs and refuse to entertain the possibility that we may be in error, the avenues for further growth are closed off. There are no greater errors that prospective teachers can make than those that stem from an unbending certainty in one's beliefs.

In *Dilemmas of Schooling,* Ann and Harold Berlak propose several specific steps for proceeding with a reflective analysis of the assumptions and beliefs regarding schooling that one brings into one's teacher preparation.[18] The first step is to begin to articulate your current beliefs regarding a host of specific issues and to examine the assumptions that underlie these beliefs. For example, what knowledge and skills should be taught to different groups of children? How much control should a teacher exert over children's learning and behavior? To what extent should teachers transmit a common core of values and beliefs to all children, and to what extent should the curriculum attend to the cultural knowledge and background experiences of children? The issues here are endless. The above examples are only intended as illustrations of the kinds of questions that can be considered.

The next step is to compare your own beliefs with the beliefs of others. It is important for you to seek actively to understand the beliefs of others (peers, instructors, friends) within your formal courses and, more generally, by reading, observing, and talking to others in both professional and nonprofessional settings. Prospective teachers who are sensitive to the tentative nature of their beliefs take pains to examine any issue from more than one perspective.

Once you have begun to identify the substance of your own beliefs and have become more conscious of alternatives that exist or could be created, it is important for you to do some thinking about the origins and consequences of these beliefs. For example, how has your own biographical history (for example, unique factors in your upbringing, your school experience as a pupil) affected the way in which you currently think about issues of schooling? Which of your current beliefs have you examined carefully through weighing and then rejecting alternative points of view, and which do you hold merely because they are widely accepted by those with whom you associate? Also, which of your current beliefs are the result of outside forces over which you have no control, and which beliefs are merely rationalizations masking an unwillingness to risk the difficulties and/or the possible displeasure of others that would result from their implementation?

Along with doing this analysis of the origin of your beliefs, you should begin to consider the possible consequences for yourself and others of holding particular beliefs. For example, what meanings (intended and unintended) are children likely to take from particular beliefs if they were actually implemented in the classroom? In considering the likely consequences of various courses of action it is important to consider more than the immediate utility of an action. The costs associated with what works in the short run to help you get through a lesson smoothly at times may outweigh the benefits to be gained.

Because of the intimate relationship that exists between the school and society, any consideration of the consequences of an educational action must inevitably take one beyond the boundaries of the classroom and even the school itself. There is no such thing as a neutral educational activity. Any action that one takes in the classroom is necessarily linked to the external economic, political and social order in either a primarily integrative or a creative fashion. Either a teaching activity serves to integrate children into the current social order or it provides children with the knowledge, attitudes or skills to deal critically and creatively with that reality in order to improve it. In any case, all teaching is embedded in an ideological background, and one cannot fully understand the significance or consequences of an activity unless one also considers that activity in light of the more general issues of social continuity and change.

For example, what are the likely consequences for the life chances of various groups of children if you present school knowledge as certain and objective to some groups of children and stress the tentativeness of knowledge to others? In other words, if you teach some students to accept what they are told and others to question and make their own decisions, how will this affect the social roles they hold later, and which group of children will you be preparing for which social roles? This example is cited to make the point that one can at least begin to identify the connections between everyday classroom practices and issues of social continuity and change. Because of the numerous forces acting upon children over a period of many years, we

can never be certain of the effect that any given course of action by one teacher has in the long run, but it is certain that, despite the complexity, linkages do exist. It is important at least to attempt to think about the consequences of our actions in a way that transcends questions of immediate utility.

Finally, once you have begun to think about the origins and consequences of the beliefs that you bring into your formal education, the issue of "craft" also needs to be considered. What knowledge and skills will you need to gain in order to implement successfully the kind of teaching that follows from your educational beliefs? If you as a prospective teacher are reflective, you do not passively absorb any and all of the skills and knowledge that others have decided are necessary for your education as a teacher. The craft knowledge and skills for teaching that you will gain during your formal preparation will originate from two major sources: your university instructors and supervisors, and the teachers and administrators with whom you will work during your practicum experiences in schools. If you are reflective about your own education for teaching, you will give some direction to the craft knowledge and skills that you learn in your training.

Within the university your socialization for teaching is much more than the learning of "appropriate" content and procedures for teaching. The knowledge and skills that will be communicated to you through your university courses are not neutral descriptions of how things are; in reality, they are *value governed selections* from a much larger universe of possibilities. Selections that reflect the educational ideologies of the instructors with whom you come into contact. Some things have been selected for your pursuance while other things have been deemphasized or even ignored. These selections reflect at least implicitly answers to normative questions about the nature of schooling, the appropriate roles for teachers and students, how to classify, arrange and evaluate educational knowledge, and how to think about educational problems and their solutions. But just as you will find diversity in the educational perspectives of a group of teachers in any given school, within any university program different university instructors will emphasize, deemphasize and ignore difficult points of view. As a result, it often becomes necessary for you to make decisions about the relevance of conflicting positions on an issue and to seek out information that supports views that may have been selected out by your instructors.

Therefore, if you want to give some direction to your education and to play an active role in shaping your own occupational identity, it becomes important for you to be constantly critical and reflective about that which is presented to you and that which has been omitted. That which is presented to you may or may not be the most appropriate craft knowledge and skill to help you get where you want to go. You need to filter all that is offered to you through your own set of priorities. At the same time, identify and use the instructors' stances about educational issues as alternatives that can help you develop your own beliefs. Generally, the same critical orientation that we have encouraged you to bring to bear upon your own prior experiences and beliefs should also be applied to that which is imparted to you by university instructors. Specifically, what are the origins and consequences of the viewpoints presented, and of the alternatives that are available or could be created?

Finally, one important part of your education for teaching will be the time you spend observing and working with teachers and administrators in school practicums. When you participate in a practicum you come into a setting (someone else's classroom) after certain patterns have been established and after certain ways of organizing time, space, instruction and so forth have become routine. Cooperating teachers, who make many of these decisions, will often not take the time to explain to you how and why these decisions have been made, partly because the routines are by then part of the taken-for-granted reality of their classrooms. Consequently, prospective teachers often fail to grasp how what they see came to be in the first place and are often incapable of creating certain structures on their own once they have their own classrooms. This is a serious lapse in an education student's learning because it is difficult to understand any setting adequately without understanding how it was produced. If you want to understand the settings in which you will work, you will need to question your teachers about the reasons underlying what exists and is presently taken for granted. The following questions illustrate the things you should seek to understand: Why is the school day organized as it is? Why is math taught every day but science taught only once per week? How and why was it decided to teach this particular unit on pollution? How are children placed into groups for reading and what opportunities exist for movement among groups? These regularities exist for particular reasons and it is up to you to seek an understanding of how what is, came to be.

You will also need to ask your cooperating teachers about the ways in which particular decisions are being made while you are there. Although many of the basic patterns of classrooms will be established before you arrive, others will still be developing. The basic problem here is for you to gain an understanding of the thought processes that underlie your cooperating teacher's current actions. Importantly, many researchers have discovered that unless education students initiate these kinds of discussions with their mentors, the logic behind classroom decisions is often missed by prospective teachers.[19] Experienced teachers may take many important factors for granted, and unless you actively probe for what underlies their behavior you will miss much of what is significant about the nature of teacher decision-making.

Seymour Sarason proposes that two basic questions be asked of any educational setting. One is what is the rationale underlying the setting? And the other is what is the universe of alternatives that could be considered?[20] We strongly feel that asking these questions is necessary in order for you to gain the maximum benefit from your practical experience in schools. If you choose not to follow our advice but to take a primarily passive role as a student teacher, your learning will be limited to that which you happen upon by chance. If you want to be a certain kind of teacher and to have a particular quality of impact on children, you will need to ensure that your education for teaching will help you get where you want to go and that where you want to go is worth the effort. As you gain more experience you may frequently change your mind about the kind of teacher you want to become, but taking an active part in your own professional preparation will at least give you some control over determining the direction in which you are headed.

We have attempted to alert you to some of the numerous issues that you will have to confront during the next few years of your education for teaching. We have argued that there is a fundamental choice for you to make: whether you will give some direction to your training or let others direct it for you. In doing so, we have argued that reflective teaching is both possible and desirable. If the teachers of tomorrow are to contribute to the revitalization and renewal of our schools, there is no alternative. However, as in all decisions, the final choice is up to you.

NOTES

1. Maxine Greene, *Teacher as Stranger* (Belmont, CA: Wadsworth Publishing Co., 1973), p. 46.

2. John Dewey, *How We Think: A Restatement of the Relation of Reflective Thinking to the Educative Process* (Chicago: Henry Regnery and Co., 1933).

3. *Ibid.*

4. *Ibid.*

5. *Ibid.*, p. 17.

6. *Ibid.*, p. 89.

7. Phillip Jackson, *Life in Classrooms* (New York: Holt, Rinehart and Winston, 1968).

8. *Ibid.*, p. 151.

9. For example, see John Eliott, "Developing Hypotheses about Classrooms From Teachers' Personal Constructs," *Interchange* 7:2 (1976-1977) 1-22.

10. Dewey, *How We Think,* p. 87.

11. Frequently, discussions that occur among teachers during planning sessions, team meetings, etc., focus almost entirely on procedural issues (for example, *How will we teach what has already been decided to teach?*) to the neglect of curricular questions, such as "What should we be teaching and why?" See Thomas Popkewitz, B. Robert Tabachnick, and Gary Wehlage, *The Myth of Educational Reform* (Madison: University of Wisconsin Press, 1982) for an example of how this occurs in exemplary "individually guided education" schools.

12. Wayne Hoy and William Rees, "The Bureaucratic Socialization of Student Teachers," *Journal of Teacher Education,* 28. (January–February, 1977) 23-26.

13. Christopher Clark and Robert Yinger, "Research on Teacher Thinking," *Curriculum Inquiry,* 7 (Winter, 1977): 279-304.

14. Jere Brophy and Thomas Good, *Teacher-Pupil Relationships: Causes and Consequences* (New York: Holt, Rinehart and Winston, 1974).

15. Dan Lortie, *School Teacher* (Chicago: University of Chicago Press, 1975).

16. John Goodlad and M. Frances Klein, *Behind the Classroom Door* (Washington, Ohio: Jones Publishers, 1970).

17. Israel Scheffler, "University Scholarship and the Education of Teachers," *Teachers College Record* 70 (October, 1968) 1-12.

18. Ann Berlak and Harold Berlak, *Dilemmas of Schooling* (London: Methuen, 1981).

19. B. Robert Tabachnick, Thomas Popkewitz, and Kenneth Zeichner, "Teacher Education and the Professional Perspectives of Student Teachers," *Interchange* 10:4 (1979-80) 12-29.

20. Seymour Sarason, *The Culture of the School and the Problem of Change* (Boston: Allyn and Bacon, 1971).

STUDY QUESTIONS FOR PART 3

1. If reflective teaching is a laudable goal, can teachers be taught to be reflective practitioners? What difference do you think this will make in the lives of children? Should an individual's disposition to be reflective be used as a teacher training admissions, school hiring, or promotion criterion? Why?

2. What is the relationship of Dewey's perspective on education to functionalism? What examples can you offer?

3. What are Dreeben's and Dewey's views of the role of schools in meeting the needs of an industrial society? Are these views relevant in a postindustrial information age? Why?

4. How do students who are home-schooled learn social norms? Is home-schooling in the state's or country's best interest? Why?

5. How are the ideas and issues in the readings for this section similar and different to those associated with the reforms being talked about or implemented in your state or in the whole country?

6. What is the difference between a reflective and a routine teacher? What are the pros and cons of each? If you aspire to be a reflective teacher, what do you anticipate will be the most difficult challenges of such an orientation? How would you respond to those?

7. How much control should a teacher exercise over a child's learning? Why?

8. What knowledge, skills, and values should be taught in our public schools and what methods of teaching should be used? Why should teaching occur this way?

9. How should learning in schools be assessed? Is some knowledge more valuable than other knowledge? What performance standards will apply, and who gets to decide? Explain your thinking in answering these questions.

PART

4

LEGITIMATION AND REPRODUCTION

The readings thus far have examined a number of important issues and have offered several useful concepts helpful in describing and understanding essential features of the U.S. system of universal and compulsory public education. These ideas include: education as cultural transmission; the function that education plays in society's survival; universal and compulsory public schooling as a primary means by which society maintains itself and adapts to the need to change; the contribution of education to the development of both the individual being and the social being; the Deweyan ideal of the public school as a living learning community reflective of the activities and problems of social life outside the school; and the latent, but highly important, function of the school in developing the needed societal norms of independence, achievement, universalism, and specificity.

Reflecting what is termed a functionalist perspective, the foregoing conception of the U.S. system of education is broadly accepted in society. Public schools are generally viewed as society's great leveler in striving to provide equal educational opportunities for children, regardless of gender, social class, race, language, or religion. Viewed also as important instruments of social, political, and economic policy, public schools in our country are judged both as major contributors to improving the economic and social well-being of our communities and, alternatively, as crippling our technological and industrial capacity to compete in the global economy.

Currently struggling to respond to major pressures to reform and restructure themselves to become more effective given important changes in the current economic and social environment, educators find themselves caught in the middle of a number of growing conflicts. These are reflected in the following questions:

- What should be the purpose(s) of public education?
- Should the school's curriculum be determined by professional educators, parents, or politicians?
- What is the relation of the school to the local community, the state, and the federal government, and who should set the performance standards for our schools?

These questions raise a multitude of issues for local school boards of education and state legislatures. In addition, this century will present continuing and new challenges as we come to terms with accelerating social and technological change; an increasingly more global economic community linked by instantaneous communication networks; an increasingly urban, heterogeneous, and multicultural school-age population; a burgeoning population of aging taxpayers without school-age children; a rapidly escalating disparity between rich and poor; and a shrinking middle class.

An alternative conception to the functionalist perspective is the conflict theorist interpretation of the educational system in a capitalist society such as ours. The three selections that follow provide an overview of this Marxian perspective on schooling and offer an example of one way public schools help maintain differences in social class as well as a sexually divided labor force (and the accompanying differentials in status, pay, and types of occupation—"men's work" and "women's work").

For conflict theorists, the ideas of hegemony and false consciousness are basic Marxian concepts used to explain how a person's understanding and awareness of class consciousness can be blocked to the point where she/he actually espouses the values of the dominant class, not recognizing one's lower status as a member of the subordinate class (Feinberg and Soltis, 1985, p. 49). For example, while most people believe that public schools exist to promote the pursuit of equality, conflict theorists argue to the contrary; they believe that the real purpose of the public school system is to reproduce and maintain the existing class structure in our society and to provide well-trained and disciplined workers for a labor force toiling to profit the owners of private enterprise (Bowles, 1972, p. 125).

Bowles examines this theme further, looking particularly at the connections between unequal education and reproduction of the social division of labor. His basic argument is that public schools in the United States have developed not to advance equality but to meet the needs of the rich to maintain political stability and to ensure the availability of a skilled labor force (p. 125). For Bowles, ". . . unequal education has its roots in the very class structure which it serves to legitimize and reproduce" (p. 125). In short, schools replicate social relations in the work force, thus socializing students to norms and role expectations similar to those of prospective employers: being a good subordinate, following directions, being on time, not questioning authority, and so on. Further, the schools set up the curriculum in a way that channels children into certain "tracks" based on their social class background: vocational schools and tracks on the one hand, and on the other the academic tracks for the college bound and "gifted." All of this is guided by the myth that because schooling was ostensibly equal and open to all, one's position in the social division of labor, in the class structure, was the natural result of one's own efforts and talents (p. 128). What Bowles thus illustrates is that the schooling process itself is inextricably linked to perpetuation and maintenance of the existing social class divisions.

In the next selection, by Jean Anyon, data provide vivid and compelling examples of the differences among schools serving children from different social class backgrounds, lending strong support to Bowles' thesis regarding the effects of schooling on reproducing and maintaining the existing social class structure in our society. In illustrating how schools contribute to the process of cultural reproduction, Anyon (1981) describes the messages about social class, place, and privilege that students internalize as a consequence of their participation in schools serving students from different social classes: those from *working class* backgrounds; those of the *middle class;* students of an *affluent-professional* class and those whose social class background is described as *executive-elite.*

Although there were similarities in the curriculum topics and materials in the fifth and second grades of the five elementary schools studied by Anyon, there was considerable social stratification of knowledge in the various school curricula as taught by the teachers in those schools. These differences were abundantly evident in the different understandings students held of *school knowledge* and its *meaning* for them. Differences also were quite evident regarding the perspectives teachers held of students and their capabilities.

The research results offered by Anyon, while limited in their scope and generalizability, offer provocative evidence that public schools contribute significantly to reproducing the existing class structure. The dominant class owns the means of production. U.S. values and beliefs promulgated by the schools are such that a false consciousness develops among the middle and lower classes, the working proletariat, which then serves to reinforce the existing class structure. This reinforcement rests on values and beliefs like education is the great equalizer; work hard and the system will reward your efforts; everyone has an equal chance to get ahead; people make it on their own achievements. Neither the students nor the teachers in the schools studied by Anyon appear to be aware of the significance of the connection between what gets taught in schools (values and attitudes as well as formal knowledge) and the reproduction of the existing class structure.

In the final selection for this section, Linda Valli describes how schools function to transmit culture. The instance she examines is the manner in which schools systematically reinforce gender-specific cultural patterns and relations found both in the home and in the workplace. She explores the experiences of young women in a cooperative office education program in which the students attended high school classes in the morning and then worked at office clerical jobs in the afternoons.

In illustrating how schools contribute to the process of cultural reproduction, in this case the perpetuation of a sexually divided labor force, she describes the messages given to the girls as they participate in the program. Messages from the school teacher and from superiors in the workplace about sexual appearance and sexual behavior encouraged the girls to use their gender identities in managing their self-presentation and appearance—a reinforcement of the idea of officeworker as sex object. Further, Valli observed that a second way in which the clerical worker's office role was linked to gender identity was "either through the equation of the work with women's work in the home or through the subordination of their role in the office to their role in the home" (Valli, 1983, p. 224).

Unequal Education and the Reproduction of the Social Division of Labor

SAMUEL BOWLES

The ideological defense of modern capitalist society rests heavily on the assertion that the equalizing effects of education can counter the disequalizing forces inherent in the free-market system. That educational systems in capitalist societies have been highly unequal is generally admitted and widely condemned. Yet educational inequalities are taken as passing phenomena, holdovers from an earlier, less enlightened era, which are rapidly being eliminated.

The record of educational history in the United States, and scrutiny of the present state of our colleges and schools, lend little support to this comforting optimism. Rather, the available data suggest an alternative interpretation. In what follows I argue (1) that schools have evolved in the United States not as part of a pursuit of equality, but rather to meet the needs of capitalist employers for a disciplined and skilled labor force, and to provide a mechanism for social control in the interests of political stability; (2) that as the economic importance of skilled and well-educated labor has grown, inequalities in the school system have become increasingly important in reproducing the class structure from one generation to the next; (3) that the U.S. school system is pervaded by class inequalities, which have shown little sign of diminishing over the last half century; and (4) that the evidently unequal control over school boards and other decision-making bodies in education does not provide a sufficient explanation of the persistence and pervasiveness of inequalities in the school system. Although the unequal distribution of political power serves to maintain inequalities in education, the origins of these inequalities are to be found outside the political sphere, in the class structure itself and in the class subcultures typical of capitalist societies. Thus, unequal education has its roots in the very class structure which it serves to legitimize and reproduce. Inequalities in education are part of the web of capitalist society, and are likely to persist as long as capitalism survives.

The Evolution of Capitalism and the Rise of Mass Education

In colonial America, and in most pre-capitalist societies of the past, the basic productive unit was the family. For the vast majority of male adults, work was self-directed, and was performed without direct supervision. Though constrained by poverty, ill health, the low level of technological development, and occasional interferences by the political authorities, a man had considerable leeway in choosing his working hours, what to produce, and how to produce it. While great inequalities in wealth, political power, and other aspects of status normally existed, differences in the degree of autonomy in work were relatively minor, particularly when compared with what was to come.

Transmitting the necessary productive skills to the children as they grew up proved to be a simple task, not because the work was devoid of

Source: *"Unequal Education and the Reproduction of the Social Division of Labor"* by Samuel Bowles *from* Schooling in a Corporate Society, *by Martin Carnoy, copyright 1972. Reprinted by permission of author.*

skill, but because the quite substantial skills required were virtually unchanging from generation to generation, and because the transition to the world of work did not require that the child adapt to a wholly new set of social relationships. The child learned the concrete skills and adapted to the social relations of production through learning by doing within the family. Preparation for life in the larger community was facilitated by the child's experience with the extended family, which shaded off without distinct boundaries, through uncles and fourth cousins, into the community. Children learned early how to deal with complex relationships among adults other than their parents, and children other than their brothers and sisters.[1]

Children were not required to learn a complex set of political principles or ideologies, as political participation was limited and political authority unchallenged, at least in normal times. The only major socializing institution outside the family was the church, which sought to inculcate the accepted spiritual values and attitudes. In addition, a small number of children learned craft skills outside the family, as apprentices. The role of schools tended to be narrowly vocational, restricted to preparation of children for a career in the church or the still inconsequential state bureaucracy.[2] The curriculum of the few universities reflected the aristocratic penchant for conspicuous intellectual consumption.[3]

The extension of capitalist production, and particularly the factory system, undermined the role of the family as the major unit of both socialization and production. Small peasant farmers were driven off the land or competed out of business. Cottage industry was destroyed. Ownership of the means of production became heavily concentrated in the hands of landlords and capitalists. Workers relinquished control over their labor in return for wages or salaries. Increasingly, production was carried on in large organizations in which a small management group directed the work activities of the entire labor force. The social relations of production—the authority structure, the prescribed types of behavior and response characteristic of the work place—became increasingly distinct from those of the family.

The divorce of the worker from control over production—from control over his own labor—is particularly important in understanding the role of schooling in capitalist societies. The resulting social division of labor—between controllers and controlled—is a crucial aspect of the class structure of capitalist societies, and will be seen to be an important barrier to the achievement of social-class equality in schooling.

Rapid economic change in the capitalist period led to frequent shifts of the occupational distribution of the labor force, and constant changes in the skill requirements for jobs. The productive skills of the father were no longer adequate for the needs of the son during his lifetime. Skill training within the family became increasingly inappropriate.

And the family itself was changing. Increased geographic mobility of labor and the necessity for children to work outside the family spelled the demise of the extended family and greatly weakened even the nuclear family.[4] Meanwhile, the authority of the church was questioned by the spread of secular rationalist thinking and the rise of powerful competing groups.

While undermining the main institutions of socialization, the development of the capitalist system created at the same time an environment—both social and intellectual—which would ultimately challenge the political order. Workers were thrown together in oppressive factories, and the isolation which had helped to maintain quiescence in earlier, widely dispersed peasant populations was broken down.[5] With an increasing number of families uprooted from the land, the workers' search for a living resulted in large-scale labor migrations. Transient, even foreign, elements came to constitute a major segment of the population, and began to pose seemingly insurmountable problems of assimilation, integration, and control.[6] Inequalities of wealth became more apparent, and were less easily justified and less readily accepted. The simple legitimizing ideologies of the earlier period—the divine right of kings and the divine origin of social rank, for example—fell under the capitalist attack on the royalty and the traditional landed interests. The general broadening of the electorate first sought by the capitalist class in the struggle against the entrenched interests of the pre-capitalist period—threatened soon to become an instrument for the growing power of the working class. Having risen to political power, the capitalist class sought a mechanism to ensure social control and political stability.[7]

An institutional crisis was at hand. The outcome, in virtually all capitalist countries, was the rise of mass education. In the United States, the many advantages of schooling as a socialization process were quickly perceived. The early proponents of the rapid expansion of schooling argued that education could perform many of the socialization functions that earlier had been centered in the family and to a lesser extent, in the church.[8] An ideal preparation for factory work was found in the social relations of the school, specifically, in its emphasis on discipline, punctuality, acceptance of authority outside the family, and individual accountability for one's work.[9] The social relations of the school would replicate the social relations of the work place, and thus help young people adapt to the social division of labor. Schools would further lead people to accept the authority of the state and its agents—the teachers—at a young age, in part by fostering the illusion of the benevolence of the government in its relations with citizens.[10] Moreover, because schooling would ostensibly be open to all, one's position in the social division of labor could be portrayed as the result not of birth, but of one's own efforts and talents.[11] And if the children's everyday experiences with the structure of schooling were insufficient to inculcate the correct views and attitudes, the curriculum itself would be made to embody the bourgeois ideology.[12] Where pre-capitalist social institutions, particularly the church, remained strong or threatened the capitalist hegemony, schools sometimes served as a modernizing counter-institution.[13]

The movement for public elementary and secondary education in the United States originated in the nineteenth century in states dominated by the burgeoning industrial capitalist class, most notably in Massachusetts. It spread rapidly to all parts of the country except the South.[14] In Massachusetts the extension of elementary education was in large measure a response to industrializa-

tion, and to the need for social control of the Irish and other non-Yankee workers recruited to work in the mills.[15] The fact that some working people's movements had demanded free instruction should not obscure the basically coercive nature of the extension of schooling. In many parts of the country, schools were literally imposed upon the workers.[16]

The evolution of the economy in the nineteenth century gave rise to new socialization needs and continued to spur the growth of education. Agriculture continued to lose ground to manufacturing; simple manufacturing gave way to production involving complex interrelated processes; an increasing fraction of the labor force was employed in producing services rather than goods. Employers in the most rapidly growing sectors of the economy began to require more than obedience and punctuality in their workers; a change in motivational outlook was required. The new structure of production provided little built-in motivation. There were fewer jobs such as farming and piece-rate work in manufacturing in which material reward was tied directly to effort. As work roles became more complicated and interrelated, the evaluation of the individual worker's performance became increasingly difficult. Employers began to look for workers who had internalized the production-related values of the firm's managers.

The continued expansion of education was pressed by many who saw schooling as a means of producing these new forms of motivation and discipline. Others, frightened by the growing labor militancy after the Civil War, found new urgency in the social-control arguments popular among the proponents of education in the antebellum period.

A system of class stratification developed within this rapidly expanding educational system. Children of the social elite normally attended private schools. Because working-class children tended to leave school early, the class composition of the public high schools was distinctly more elite than the public primary school.[17] And as a university education ceased to be merely training for teaching or the divinity and became important in gaining access to the pinnacles of the business world, upper-class families used their money and influence to get their children into the best universities, often at the expense of the children of less elite families.

Around the turn of the present century, large numbers of working-class and particularly immigrant children began attending high schools. At the same time, a system of class stratification developed within secondary education.[18] The older democratic ideology of the common school—that the same curriculum should be offered to all children—gave way to the "progressive" insistence that education should be tailored to the "needs of the child."[19] In the interests of providing an education relevant to the later life of the students, vocational schools and tracks were developed for the children of working families. The academic curriculum was preserved for those who would later have the opportunity to make use of book learning, either in college or in white-collar employment. This and other educational reforms of the progressive education movement reflected an implicit assumption of the immutability of the class structure.

The frankness with which students were channeled into curriculum tracks, on the basis of their social-class background, raised serious doubts concerning the "openness" of the social-class structure. The relation between social class and a child's chances of promotion or tracking assignments was disguised—though not mitigated much—by another "progressive" reform: "objective" educational testing. Particularly after World War I, the capitulation of the schools to business values and concepts of efficiency led to the increased use of intelligence and scholastic achievement testing as an ostensibly unbiased means of measuring the product of schooling and classifying students.[20] The complementary growth of the guidance counseling profession allowed much of the channeling to proceed from the students' own well-counseled choices, thus adding an apparent element of voluntarism to the system.

The legacy of the progressive education movement, like the earlier reforms of the mid-nineteenth century, was a strengthened system of class stratification within schooling which continues to play an important role in the reproduction and legitimation of the social division of labor.

The class stratification of education during this period had proceeded hand in hand with the stratification of the labor force. As large bureaucratic corporations and public agencies employed an increasing fraction of all workers, a complicated segmentation of the labor force evolved, reflecting the hierarchical structure of the social relations of production. A large middle group of employees developed, comprising clerical, sales, bookkeeping, and low-level supervisory workers.[21] People holding these occupations ordinarily had a modicum of control over their own work; in some cases they directed the work of others, while themselves under the direction of higher management. The social division of labor had become a finely articulated system of work relations dominated at the top by a small group with control over work processes and a high degree of personal autonomy in their work activities, and proceeding by finely differentiated stages down the chain of bureaucratic command to workers who labored more as extensions of the machinery than as autonomous human beings.

One's status, income, and personal autonomy came to depend in great measure on one's place in the work hierarchy. And in turn, positions in the social division of labor came to be associated with educational credentials reflecting the number of years of schooling and the quality of education received. The increasing importance of schooling as a mechanism for allocating children to positions in the class structure played a major part in legitimizing the structure itself.[22] But at the same time, it undermined the simple processes which in the past had preserved the position and privilege of the upper-class families from generation to generation. In short, it undermined the processes serving to reproduce the social division of labor.

In pre-capitalist societies, direct inheritance of occupational position is common. Even in the early capitalist economy, prior to the segmentation of the labor force on the basis of differential skills and education, the class structure was reproduced generation after generation simply through the inheritance of physical capital by the offspring of the capitalist class. Now that the social division of labor is differentiated by types of competence and educational credentials as well as by ownership of capital, the problem of inheritance is not nearly so simple. The crucial complication arises because education and skills are embedded in human beings; unlike physical capital, these assets cannot be passed on to one's children at death. In an advanced capitalist society in which education and skills play an important role in the hierarchy of production, then, the absence of confiscatory inheritance laws is not enough to reproduce the social division of labor from generation to generation. Skills and educational credentials must somehow be passed on within the family. It is a fundamental theme of this essay that schools play an important part in reproducing and legitimizing this modern form of class structure.

NOTES

Many of the ideas in this essay have been worked out jointly with Herbert Gintis and other members of the Harvard seminar of the Union for Radical Political Economics. I am grateful to them and to Janice Weiss and Christopher Jencks for their help.

1. This account draws upon two important historical studies: P. Aries, *Centuries of Childhood* (New York: Vantage, 1965) and B. Bailyn, *Education in the Forming of American Society* (Chapel Hill: University of North Carolina Press, 1960). Also illuminating are anthropological studies of education in contemporary pre-capitalist societies. See, for example, J. Kenyatta, *Facing Mount Kenya* (New York: Vintage Books, 1962) pp. 95–124. See also Edmund S. Morgan, *The Puritan Family Religion and Domestic Relations in Seventeenth Century New England* (New York: Harper and Row, 1966).

2. Aries, *Centuries of Childhood.* In a number of places, e.g., Scotland and Massachusetts, schools stressed literacy so as to make the Bible more widely accessible. See C. Cipolla, *Literacy and Economic Development* (Baltimore: Penguin Books, 1969) and Morgan, *Puritan Family*, chap. 4. Morgan quotes a Massachusetts law of 1647 which provided for the establishment of reading

schools because it was "one chief project of that old deluder, Satan, to keep men from knowledge of the Scriptures."

3. H.F. Kearney, *Scholars and Gentlemen: Universities and Society in Pre-Industrial Britain* (Ithaca, N.Y.: Cornell University Press, 1971).

4. See Bailyn, *Education in the Forming of American Society.* N. Smelser, *Social Change in the Industrial Revolution* (Chicago: University of Chicago Press, 1959).

5. F. Engels and K. Marx, *The Communist Manifesto* (London, England: G. Allen and Unwin, 1951); K. Marx, *The 18th Brumaire of Louis Bonaparte* (New York: International Publishers, 1935).

6. See, for example, S. Thernstrom, *Poverty and Progress: Social Mobility in a 19th Century City* (Cambridge: Harvard University Press, 1964).

7. B. Simon, *Studies in the History of Education, 1780–1870,* vol. I (London, England, Lawrence and Wishant, 1960).

8. Bailyn, *Education in the Forming of American Society.*

9. A manufacturer, writing to the Massachusetts State Board of Education from Lowell in 1841 commented

I have never considered mere knowledge . . . as the only advantage derived from a good Common School education. . . . (Workers with more education possess) a higher and better state of morals, are more orderly and respectful in their deportment, and more ready to comply with the wholesome and necessary regulations of an establishment. . . . In times of agitation, on account of some change in regulations or wages, I have always looked to the most intelligent, best educated and the most moral for support. The ignorant and uneducated I have generally found the most turbulent and troublesome, acting under the impulse of excited passion and jealousy.

Quoted in Michael B. Katz, *The Irony of Early School Reform* (Cambridge, Mass.: Harvard University Press, 1968), p. 88. See also David Isaac Bruck, "The Schools of Lowell, 1824–1861: A Case Study in the Origins of Modern Public Education in America" (Senior thesis, Harvard College, Department of Social Studies, April 1971).

10. In 1846 the annual report of the Lowell, Mass., School Committee concluded that universal education was "the surest safety against internal commotions" (*1846 School Committee Annual Report,* pp. 17–18). It seems more than coincidental that, in England, public support for elementary education—a concept which had been widely discussed and urged for at least half a century—was legislated almost immediately after the enfranchisement of the working class by the electoral reform of 1867. See Simon, *Studies in the History of Education, 1780-1870.* Mass public education in Rhode Island came quickly on the heels of an armed insurrection and a broadening of the franchise. See F. T. Carlton, *Economic Influences upon Educational Progress in the United States, 1820-1850* (New York: Teachers College Press, 1966).

11. Describing the expansion of education in the nineteenth century, Katz concludes:

A middle class attempt to secure advantage for their children as technological change heightened the importance of formal education assured the success and acceptance of universal elaborate graded school systems. The same result emerged from the fear of a growing, underschooled proletariat. Education substituted for deference as a source of social cement and social order in a society stratified by class rather than by rank (M. B. Katz, "From Voluntarism to Bureaucracy in U.S. Education," mimeograph, 1970).

12. An American economist, writing just prior to the "common school revival" had this to say:

Education universally extended throughout the community will tend to disabuse the working class of people in respect of a notion that has crept into the minds of our mechanics and is gradually prevailing, that manual labor is at present very inadequately rewarded, owing to combinations of the rich against the poor, that mere mental labor is comparatively worthless, the property or wealth ought not to be accumulated or transmitted, that to take interest on money let or profit on capital employed is unjust. . . . The mistaken and ignorant people who entertain these fallacies as truths will learn, when they have the opportunity of learning, that the institution of political society originated in the protection of property (Thomas Cooper, *Elements of Political Economy* [1828], quoted in Carlton, *Economic Influences upon Educational Progress in the United States, 1820-1850*, pp. 33-34).

Political economy was made a required subject in Massachusetts high schools in 1857, along with moral science and civic polity. Cooper's advice was widely but not universally followed elsewhere. Friedrich Engels, commenting on the tardy growth of mass education in early nineteenth-century England, remarked: "So shortsighted, so stupidly narrow-minded is the English bourgeoisie in its egotism, that it does not even take the trouble to impress upon the workers the morality of the day, which the bourgeoisie has patched together in its own interest for its own protection." (Engels, *The Condition of the Working Class in England* [Stanford, Calif,: Stanford University Press, 1968].)

13. See Thernstrom, *Poverty and Progress.* Marx said this about mid-nineteenth-century France:

The modern and the traditional consciousness of the French peasant contended for mastery . . . in the form of an incessant struggle between the schoolmasters and the priests. (Marx, *The 18th Brumaire of Louis Bonaparte*, p. 125).

14. Janice Weiss and I are currently studying the rapid expansion of southern elementary and secondary schooling which followed the demise of slavery and the establishment of capitalist economic institutions in the South.

15. Based on the preliminary results of a statistical analysis of education in nineteenth-century Massachusetts being conducted jointly with Alexander Field.

16. Katz, *Irony of Early School Reform* and "From Voluntarism to Bureaucracy in U.S. Education."

17. Katz, *Irony of Early School Reform.*

18. Sol Cohen describes this process in "The Industrial Education Movement, 1906-1917," *American Quarterly,* 20 no. 1 (Spring 1968); 95-110. Typical of the arguments then given for vocational education is the following, by the superintendent of schools in Cleveland:

It is obvious that the educational needs of children in a district where the streets are well paved and clean, where the homes are spacious and surrounded by lawns and trees, where the language of the child's playfellows is pure, and where life in general is permeated with the spirit and ideals of America, it is obvious that the educational needs of such a child are radically different from those of the child who lives in a foreign and tenement section. (William H. Elson and Frank P. Bachman. "Different Course for Elementary School," *Educational Review* 39 [April 1910] 361-63).

See also L. Cremin, *The Transformation of the School Progressivism in American Education, 1876-1957* (New York, Alfred A. Knopf, 1961), chap. 2, and David Cohen and Marvin Lazerson, "Education and the Industrial Order," mimeograph, 1970.

19. The superintendent of the Boston schools summed up the change in 1908:

Until very recently (the schools) have offered equal opportunity for all to receive *one kind* of education, but what will make them democratic is to provide opportunity for all to receive such education as will fit them *equally well* for their particular life work. (Boston, *Documents of the School Committee, 1908,* no. 7. p. 53, quoted in Cohen and Lazerson "Education and the Industrial Order")

20. R. Callahan, *Education and the Cult of Efficiency* (Chicago: University of Chicago Press, 1962), Cohen and Lazerson, "Education and the Industrial Order," and Cremin, *Transformation of the School.*

21. See M. Reich, "The Evolution of the U.S. Labor Force," in *The Capitalist System,* ed. R. Edwards, M. Reich, and T. Weisskopf (Englewood Cliffs, N.J., Prentice-Hall, Inc., 1971).

22. The role of school in legitimizing the class structure is spelled out in S. Bowles, "Contradictions in U.S. Higher Education," mimeograph, 1971.

SOCIAL CLASS AND SCHOOL KNOWLEDGE

JEAN ANYON

When Max Weber and Karl Marx suggested that there were identifiable and socially meaningful differences in the educational knowledge made available to literati and peasant, aristocrat and laborer, they were of course discussing earlier societies. Recent scholarship in political economy and sociology of knowledge has also argued, however, that in advanced industrial societies such as Canada and the U.S., where the class structure is relatively fluid, students of different social class backgrounds are still likely to be exposed to qualitatively different types of educational knowledge. Students from higher social class backgrounds may be exposed to legal, medical, or managerial knowledge, for example, while those of the working classes may be offered a more "practical" curriculum (e.g., clerical knowledge, vocational training) (Rosenbaum 1976; Karabel 1972; Bowles and Gintis 1976). It is said that such social class differences in secondary and postsecondary education are a conserving force in modern societies, an important aspect of the reproduction of unequal class structures (Karabel and Halsey 1977; Apple 1979; Young and Whitty 1977).

The present article examines data on school knowledge collected in a case study of five elementary schools in contrasting social class settings in two school districts in New Jersey. The data suggest, and the article will argue, that while there were similarities in curriculum topics and materials, there were also subtle as well as dramatic differences in the curriculum and the curriculum-in-use among the schools. The study reveals that even in an elementary school context, where there is a fairly "standardized" curriculum, social stratification of knowledge is possible. The differences that were identified among the schools suggest as well that rather than being simply conserving or "reproductive," school knowledge embodies contradictions that have profound implications for social change. The reproductive and nonreproductive possibilities of school knowledge involve theoretical implications of the data and will be delineated after the data have been presented.

METHODOLOGY

Data on the nature and distribution of school knowledge were gathered in an investigation of curriculum, pedagogy, and pupil evaluation practices in five elementary schools differentiated by social class.[1] The methods used to gather data were classroom observation; informal and formal interview of students, teachers, principals, and district administrative staff; and assessment of curriculum and other materials in each classroom and school. Classroom data to be reported here are

I would like to thank Michael Apple, Stewart Bird, Henry Giroux, Nancy King, James Scott, Roger Simon, Bob Tabachnick, Philip Wexler, and Geoff Whitty for their encouragement, critical comments, and editorial advice during various phases of the work involved in producing this article.

Source: *"Social Class and School Structure". In* Curriculum Inquiry *11:1 (1981) pp. 3–42. Reprinted by permission John Wiley & Sons, Inc.*

drawn primarily from the fifth and second grades in each school. All schools but one departmentalize at the fifth-grade level, and with the exception of the school that does not, where only one fifth-grade teacher agreed to be observed, in all schools two or three fifth-grade teachers and two second-grade teachers were observed and interviewed. All but one of the teachers in the study had taught for more than four years. The fifth grade in each school was observed by the investigator for ten three-hour periods, and the second grade was observed for two three-hour periods. Formal interviews were carried out during lunchtime, and before and after school. Data were gathered between September 15, 1978, and June 20, 1979.

For purposes of this study, social class is considered as a series of relationships to several aspects of the process in society by which goods, services, and culture are produced. That is, while one's occupational status and income level contribute to one's social class, they do not define it. Contributing as well are one's relationships to the system of ownership of physical and cultural capital, to the structure of authority at work and in society, and to the content and process of one's own work activity. For example, members of the capitalist class participate in ownership of the apparatus of production in society, while many middle-class and most working-class persons do not; capitalists and affluent professional persons have more access to decision-making power in work institutions and in society than do many middle-class and most working-class people; capitalist and professional work activity often involves more creativity, conceptualization, and autonomy than do the jobs of most middle-class and working-class people in, say, civil service (the bureaucracy) or industry. One's relationships to all three of these aspects of production (to the systems of ownership and authority, and to work itself) determine one's social class. All three relationships are necessary and no single one is sufficient for determining a relation to the process of production in society.[2]

The terminology defining social classes and differentiating the schools in this study is to be understood in a technical sense, as reflected in the process by which the sample of schools was selected. Thus, the schools in this study were differentiated not only by income level as an indicator of parent access to capital, but also by the kind of *work* that characterized the majority of parents in each school.

The first three schools were in a medium-size city district in northern New Jersey, and the final two were in a nearby New Jersey suburban district. In each of the three city schools, approximately 85% of the students were white. In the fourth school, 90% were white, and in the last school, all were white.

The first two schools are designated *working-class schools,* because the majority of the students' fathers (and approximately one-third of their mothers) were in unskilled or semiskilled occupations, with somewhat less than one-third of the fathers being skilled workers. Most family money incomes were at or below $12,000 during the period of the study, as were 38.6% of all U.S. families (U.S. Bureau of the Census 1979, p. 2, Table A). The third school is designated the *middle-class school,* although because of residence patterns the parents were a mixture of highly skilled, well-paid blue collar and white collar workers, as well as those with traditional middle-class occupations such as public school teachers, social workers, accountants, and middle-managers. There were also several local doctors and town merchants among the parents. Most family money incomes were between $13,000 and $25,000 during the period of the study, as were 38.9% of all U.S. families (U.S. Bureau of the Census 1979, p. 2, Table A).

The fourth school is designated the *affluent professional school,* because the bulk of the students' fathers were highly-paid doctors such as cardiologists; television or advertising executives; interior designers; or other affluent professionals. While there were a few families less affluent than the majority (e.g., the families of the superintendent of schools and of several professors at nearby universities, as well as several working-class families), there were also a few families who were more affluent. The majority of family money incomes were between $40,000 and $80,000 during the period of the study, as were approximately 7% of all U.S. families.[3]

The final school is called the *executive elite school*. The majority of pupils' fathers in this school were vice presidents or more advanced corporate executives in U.S.-based multinational corporations or financial firms on Wall Street. Most family money incomes were over $100,000 during the period of the study, as were less than 1% of U.S. families (see Smith and Franklin 1974).

SOCIAL CLASS AND SCHOOL KNOWLEDGE

There were several similarities in curriculum among the schools in this study. (Indeed, all schools were subject to the same state requirements.) All schools used the same math textbook and series throughout the elementary grades (*Mathematics Around Us,* Scott Foresman, 1978). In language arts, both district courses of study included punctuation, sentence types and structure, grammar, and some writing exercises. In all fifth grades there was at least one box of an individualized reading program available; all classes had a basal reading series available, and two of the five schools (middle-class and executive elite) had the same basal reading series available in several grades of the school (*The Holt Basic Reading System,* Holt, Rinehart and Winston, 1977).

The schools did, however, use different social studies and science textbooks and materials, but there were several curriculum similarities among them. For example, all social studies books exhibited what I have called elsewhere "key ideas" in United States social studies content (Anyon 1979a): a positive and overtly stated valuing of American political democracy and freedom, American "progress," industry, and technology (see also Fox and Hess 1972; FitzGerald 1979; and Anyon 1978, 1979b). The natural science textbooks and program materials in both districts were similar in that they emphasized empirical investigation as the basis of scientific understanding, the use by students of processes of observation and experimentation, and "the scientific method."

Despite curriculum similarities, there were substantial differences in knowledge among the schools. The following sections of this article present and discuss data on these differences. Data from each social setting include significant information on the school, the teachers, and the community; what school personnel said, in interviews, about school knowledge; evidence from the curriculum and the curriculum-in-use in several content areas (e.g., math, science, social studies); and what students expressed concerning school knowledge and its meaning for them. A dominant theme emerged in each social setting, and these are also presented and briefly discussed.

WORKING-CLASS SCHOOLS

On the streets surrounding each school are small wooden frame houses. Many have small front porches and most date from the first decade of this century. The streets are clean, but there are no trees on the streets near either school. A railroad track separates the neighborhoods of each school from the rest of the town. One of the schools was constructed in 1912, the other in 1919. No additions have been built onto either school, but there are two trailers (for the second grades) in one asphalt playground. The rooms in the schools are sparsely furnished. There are no clocks in any of the classrooms. The halls and rooms are clean. The school population is heterogeneous as to white ethnic group composition, and there are small but growing Hispanic and black populations. Neither principal knows the history of his or her school building.

Approximately one-third of the teachers in each school were born in the city and lived there, but most are from "uptown," a different section. Most graduated from local state teachers colleges and were young; many were single. There were more male teachers in the working-class schools than in the other schools of this study.

One male teacher characterized his school as a "tough" school and said he had been nervous when they told him he would be teaching there. He said he felt better after the principal had told him, "Just do your best. If they learn to add and subtract, that's a bonus. If not, don't worry about it." A second-grade teacher stated to me that she did not mind teaching in this school because it was "easy," compared to many other schools. She said that she would not want to teach in the district's school for the "gifted and talented." "You have to work too hard. I have a friend who teaches there and she goes in early every *day*. She's always doing something special." Another second-grade teacher said that the children in her school were getting "dumber" as the years went by. She also said, "I would *never* teach in the suburbs. The parents there think their kids are God's gift. Although, some parents *here* are beginning to think they have rights, too." One day a fifth-grade teacher brought into the teachers' room a box of cards labeled "Diacritic Reading." A sixth-grade teacher looked at the box, laughed, and said, "Are you kidding? *I* can hardly read that!" The face of the woman who had brought the box reddened, and she turned the box over so that the title was not visible.

WHAT SCHOOL PERSONNEL SAID ABOUT SCHOOL KNOWLEDGE

I asked the two fifth- and two second-grade teachers in each school what knowledge was most appropriate for the children in their classes. Most spoke of school knowledge in terms of facts and simple skills. One fifth-grade teacher said, for example, "What these children need is the basics." When I asked her what the basics were, she said, "The three Rs— simple skills." When I asked why, she responded, "They're lazy. I hate to categorize them, but they're lazy." Another fifth-grade teacher said, "Take social studies. History is a fact-oriented subject. But I really don't do much. I do map skills, though. It's practical—it's good for measuring and it's math." A fifth-grade teacher in the other school said she did social studies by putting notes on the board which the children then copied. I asked why she did that, and she said, "Because the children in this school don't *know* anything about the U.S., so you can't teach them much." The male fifth-grade teacher in this school said, "You can't teach these kids anything. Their parents don't take care about them, and they're not interested." A second-grade teacher when asked what was important knowledge for her students said, "Well, we keep them *busy*."

EVIDENCE FROM THE CURRICULUM AND THE CURRICULUM-IN-USE

Mathematical knowledge was often restricted to the procedures or steps to be followed in order to add, subtract, multiply, or divide. All schools in the district use the same math text. It has numerous pages which are explicitly intended as departures from the mechanics of such skills as adding and substracting. These pages call for mathematical reasoning, inference, pattern identification, or ratio setup, for example. One of the fifth-grade teachers called these pages "the thinking pages" and said she "rarely" uses them. "They're too hard." She concentrates, she said, "on the basics." That is, "how you multiply and divide." The fifth-grade math teacher in the other working-class school said, "These pages are for creativity—they're the extras." She uses them "sometimes."

A common feature of classroom mathematics in both working-class schools was that a large portion of what the children were asked to carry out procedures, the purposes of which were often unexplained, and which were seemingly unconnected to thought processes or decision making of their own. An example of this type of instruction was when one of the fifth-grade teachers led the children through a series of steps to make a one-inch grid on their papers without telling them that they were making a one-inch grid or that it would be used to study scale. She said, "Take your ruler. Put it across the top. Make a mark at every number. Then move your ruler down the bottom. Now, put it across the bottom. Now make a mark on top of every number. Now draw a line from . . ." At this point, one student said that she had a faster way to do it and the teacher said, "No, you don't; you don't even know what I'm making yet. Do it this way, or it's wrong." After the students had made the lines up and down and across the page, the teacher said she wanted them to make a figure by connecting some dots, measure the figure, using the scale of one inch equals one mile, and then cut it out. After she had led them through these steps, she said, "Don't cut until I check it."

Teachers in each school in the district are given a choice of the social studies text they want to use. The texts chosen by the fifth-grade teachers in the working-class schools contained less information, fewer inquiry or independent research activities, and more of an emphasis on social studies knowledge as facts to be remembered than the texts used in any other school of this study. In one of the working-class schools the fifth-grade teachers chose *The American Nation: Adventure in Freedom* (Follet 1975). This text is "designed for educationally deficient secondary school students" (teachers guide, p. 3). It is written on a sixth-to-seventh-grade level. It was intended for "low ability students . . . who often exhibit environmental deficiencies . . . and social and emotional problems" (teachers guide, p. 3). A striking characteristic of the textbook is the paucity of information. The book is intended as a year's work; it is divided into 16 "lessons." There are one to four paragraphs of history in each lesson, a vocabulary drill, and a review and skills exercise in each to check "recall and retention." The teachers guide explains the sparsity of information by saying that an important criterion of teaching materials for "educationally deficient students" is that "[e]xtraneous subject matter and excessive details should be eliminated in order to present subjects and concepts that are important and also within the[ir] comprehension range . . ." (p. 39). The teachers guide also states that "It ought to be said at the outset that students with educational deficiencies are not always able to succeed in an inquiry lesson that places great demands on them" (p. 20). Rather, "The students feel secure in doing routine tasks" (p. 8). "You should follow fairly regular patterns from day to day so that the students do not become confused or distracted" (p. 8). The students should be "conditioned" to make "organized responses" (p. 11). The students should be "trained in the techniques of assembling information . . ." (p. 16). "Tests should seek to determine the students' retention of factual matter and their reading and comprehension" (p. 23).[4]

The textbook chosen by the fifth-grade teachers in the other working-class school is *Your Country and Mine* (1969 edition) in Ginn's Tiegs Adams series. This textbook is not explicitly designed for any particular type of student. It is not an inquiry text; it is fact oriented. Two of three evaluative activities at the end of each chapter are "Do you know?" (asking for facts in 84% of the cases), and "See if you remember" (asking for recall—filling in the blanks or matching). A third activity involved, in approximately 60% of the cases, reading a map.

The social studies knowledge in these schools was the least "honest" about U.S. society. There was less mention of potentially controversial topics than in other series in other schools. Both texts refer to the economic system as a "free enterprise" system. There are five paragraphs on minority and women's rights and history in one text and ten in the other. (As we will see, this is considerably less than discussions of these topics in books used in other schools in this study.) As in most U.S. history texts, however, (Anyon 1979b; FitzGerald 1979) there is contained in both texts the history of powerful groups—political parties and leaders, military systems, business, technology, industry. There is little information on the working class in either book—four pages in one book and two in the other discuss labor history. Neither text attempts to identify interests workers have in common, nor discusses the situations of economic and social conflict in which workers exist.

Social studies instruction commonly involved carrying out tasks such as copying teacher's notes, answering textbook questions, or coloring and assembling paper cutouts. For example, in the school where the second book was available, the fifth-grade teacher had purchased a supplemental booklet from Instructo entitled *The Fabulous Fifty States*. Each day she put information from the booklet in outline form on the board and the children copied it. The type of information did not vary: the name of the state, its abbreviation, state capital, nickname of the state, its main products, main business, and a "fabulous fact" (e.g., "Idaho grew 27 billion potatoes in one year. That's enough potatoes for each man, woman, and. . ."). As the children finished copying the sentences, the teacher erased them and wrote more. Children would occasionally go to the front of the classroom and pull down the wall map in order to locate the states they were studying, and the teacher did not dissuade them. But I never saw her refer to the map; nor did I hear her make other than perfunctory remarks concerning the information the children were copying. Occasionally, the children colored in a ditto (also from an Instructo booklet) and cut it out to make a stand-up figure of some sort (representing, for example, a man roping a cow in the Southwest). The teacher referred to these cutouts as social studies projects.

There were occasions when the teachers did seem to make attempts to go beyond simple facts and skills and to transmit more elaborate conceptual knowledge. Science instruction was often such a case, and the male fifth-grade teacher's use of the science textbook (*STEM*, Addison-Wesley, 1977) was in large measure such a symbolic gesture. He assigned the text, did demonstrations and "experiments," but, he said, "I don't do the tests [provided by the manual]. It's too depressing. They never get it, and they'll never *use* it!"

WHAT STUDENTS SAID ABOUT KNOWLEDGE   To get some impression of what the children thought about school knowledge, I interviewed ten students in the fifth grade in each working-class school (and twenty fifth-grade children in each of the other schools). After discussing with them what they did in school, I asked each child to tell me what knowledge is (not school knowledge, just knowledge in the general sense). Most children in the working-class schools had some difficulty interpreting my question. Many asked, "What?" or "What do you mean?" It seemed that my question was not meaningful to them. I said, "What do you think of when I say the word 'knowledge?' " They gave the following answers: "To know stuff?" "The skills to do the work." "A chance to make a better world?" "Skills." "Ability—you have ability to do things." "Doing pages in our books and things." "Worksheets." "The three Rs . . . Miss [P] said if we don't have the three Rs, we can't do anything. . . . Say if you work in a store you gotta add up prices." "You gain facts, like." "He knows his stuff." Two children said, "How to do math. Mr. [T] likes math." "You answer questions." "To remember things?" Six children said they did not know.

I then asked them, "Where does knowledge come from?" Six said, [It comes from] "teachers." Other answers were, "Books." "The Board of Ed." "Scientists." "Dictionary." "Your mind?" "Your personality?" "From learning." Seven said they did not know. I asked if they could *make* knowledge, and if so, how. After some discussion of what I meant, in which I said, "Can you make it, or is it already made?" "Could you make it yourself or could somebody else?" "What would you have to do to make knowledge?" fifteen children said no (you can't make knowledge). One girl said, "No, because the Board of Ed makes knowledge." I asked her how, and she said, "Oh, just by listening to stuff." Four said they did not know. One child said, "Yes, you can make knowledge." When I asked how, he said, "You have to act normal. Don't put on your radio."

It should be noted that during discussions of school knowledge not a single child in either working-class school used words such as "think," or "thinking." Most spoke in terms of behaviors or skills, and only one mentioned the word "mind." About half the children appeared uncomfortable during the interview, even though they knew me and were quite friendly in the playground and in class. Many twisted, blushed, and seemed tense and anxious. Most of their answers were short, and they did not elaborate without prodding, and often not even then. They, more than the children in any other school, seemed to be trying to guess what it was I wanted them to say rather than to reflect on their own experience.

During my interviews with the children, I also asked them if they thought they would go to college. All but three of the children in these working-class schools said no, they didn't think they would. Two said that they might not have the money, and 11 said their grades wouldn't be good enough. I asked what they wanted to be when they grew up, and then if they could "be anything they wanted"—if, for example, they could "get any type of job" they wanted. Sixteen said no. The reasons they gave were that they weren't "smart enough," or they "didn't have the skills," or "if it's hard I couldn't do it." Three children mentioned there might not be enough jobs. It should be noted that most responses to these last questions suggest that many of these children already "know" that what it take to get ahead is being smart, and that they themselves are not smart.

RESISTANCE AS A DOMINANT THEME   A dominant theme that emerged in these two schools was student *resistance*. Although some amount of resistance appeared in every school in this study, in the working-class schools it was a dominant characteristic of student-teacher interaction. In the fifth grades there was both active and passive resistance to teachers' attempts to impose the curriculum. Active sabotage sometimes took place: someone put a bug in one student's desk; boys fell out of their chairs; they misplaced books, or forgot them; they engaged in minor theft from each other; sometimes they rudely interrupted the teacher. When I asked the children during interviews why they did these things they said, "To get the teacher mad"; "Because he don't teach us nothin'"; "They give us too many punishments." When I asked them what the teachers *should* do, they said, "Teach us some more"; "Take us alone and help us"; "Help us learn."

The children also engaged in a good deal of resistance that was more passive. They often resisted by withholding their enthusiasm or attention on occasions when the teacher attempted to do something special. For example, on one of my visits a teacher had found something she said was "nice" and "different"; it was a cartoon filmstrip on punctuation. The children, however, watched apathetically and did not respond enthusiastically or with thanks. The teacher then berated them for not "thanking" her and gave them a worksheet on punctuation to do.

Passive resistance can also be seen on some occasions when the children do not respond to the teacher's questions. For example, they sit just staring at the board or the teacher while the teacher tries to get them to say the answer, any answer. On one such occasion, the teacher shouted sarcastically across the room to me, "Just *look* at the motivation on their faces." On occasions when teachers finally explode with impatience because nobody "knows" the answer, one can see fleeting smiles flicker across some of the students' faces: they are pleased to see the teacher get angry, upset.

The teachers often complain that the students "don't care" about anything. For example, one morning before the school day began, several teachers were discussing recent vandalism in the school. It seems that the last several years had seen a sharp rise in expressions of disregard for school property. Fires had been set during the summer in the second-grade trailers, and windows in the school had recently been broken. Several teachers said they were sure the vandals were the fifth and sixth graders. A teacher remarked on how little these students cared about the school. Another teacher turned to me and said, "You know, a lot of them don't care about anything. And some don't care about America, either. Last year the sixth grade refused to sing patriotic songs at [their] graduation. They said, 'What did America do for me?' Well, I know they're wrong. I lived overseas for a while [as a military wife]."

It seems to be the case that what counts as school knowledge in these two working-class schools is not knowledge as concepts, cognitions, information or ideas about society, language, math, or history, connected by conceptual principles or understandings of some sort. Rather, it seems that what constitutes school knowledge here is (1) fragmented *facts,* isolated from context and connection to each other or to wider bodies of meaning, or to activity or biography of the students; and (2) knowledge of "practical" rule-governed *behaviors*—procedures by which the students carry out tasks that are largely mechanical. Sustained conceptual or "academic" knowledge has only occasional, symbolic presence here.

MIDDLE-CLASS SCHOOL

The streets in the neighborhood of this school are lined with trees. The homes are larger than in the working-class sections. Most are built of brick, have full front porches, lawns in front and back, many of which have flowers. The school building has a yard in front and on two sides, and is enclosed by several large trees. Their is an asphalt playground in back. The school building is larger than either of the working-class schools and is built of a light-colored stone. The floors are polished wood. The "old wing" of the school was built in 1888. The "new wing" was constructed in 1924. On the wall in the front hall hangs a plaque with the likeness of Horace Mann and a quote from him: "Knowledge is a possession of which man cannot be robbed."

Approximately one-third of the teachers in the school grew up in the neighborhoods of this and two other nearby schools. Many graduated from a local state teachers college, and a good portion of them now live in the neighborhood of the school. Some are married to other teachers or accountants, one is married to a policeman, another to a nurse, and several to managers of local businesses. Several teachers recently bought their own homes in the neighborhood and just had their first child. Conversations in the teachers' room often revolved around homes, children, television programs, diets, and the fact that "It" was coming (state-ordered desegregation of the city's schools). This school, in contrast to the two working-class schools, has considerable activity surrounding school events such as games of the school's basketball team. (Each school in the district has a team.) One of the fifth-grade teachers I observed was very involved in arranging the activities of the team and its cheerleaders, and raffles, hot dog, and cake sales to augment available funds.

The ethnic background and history of the school are of recent interest to a group of parents and to the principal. Several parents suggested the idea of doing a history of the school, and the principal contacted a "local university historian" to do oral histories of the school. She spoke enthusiastically about the project.

WHAT SCHOOL PERSONNEL SAID ABOUT SCHOOL KNOWLEDGE   When I asked teachers what knowledge was appropriate for their students, most of them directly or indirectly referred to what was in the books they were using. One teacher said, "What they need for high school and maybe college." She nodded at the social studies textbook and said, "It's a little hard for them. It's on a sixth-grade level. But my goal is understanding. I try to help them understand what

they read. I think that's more important than the skills, although they're important, too. But if they don't understand what they read, they won't know anything." The language arts teacher said, "You could say knowledge is what they need for daily life." This teacher suggested the major role the textbook played in her instruction. After she had given a homework assignment a child asked, "Is it in the book?" The teacher said, "Of *course* it's in the book. Did I ever give you anything that's *not* in the book?" "No," said the child. (The English textbook she used is the 1969 edition of *Language for Everyday Life.*) A second-grade teacher said, "The most important thing is comprehension, even in math. I explain, and if they don't understand, they go to the board."

Part of the attitude that knowledge is what is in textbooks seems to be the feeling that knowledge is made by experts and consists of standard rules and "content." This content is perceived as more important or legitimate than what one discovers or attempts to define for oneself. In a second-grade lesson on pluralization, for example, the teacher explained a page in the spelling workbook that had rules for forming plurals.

T: Remember, more than one mouse is called mice. Remember what we said the other day: it's an irregular noun. I'm glad you gave me that one [that example] so you won't use the wrong one.

S: Everybody was going to say that one. (pause) It wouldn't *sound* right if you said mouses.

T: Yes, (pause) but who can give me a better reason [than how it sounds]? Remember what it's called? Remember what we said the other day?

The teacher told me she was trying to elicit the rule that mouse is an irregular noun. She said that the rule is "more important" than the "guess" of the boy for whom it was mice because mouses sounds wrong.[5]

EVIDENCE FROM THE CURRICULUM AND THE CURRICULUM-IN-USE   In this school I observed more flexibility regarding procedures in math than in the working-class schools. For example, there is sometimes a choice: one may do two-digit division the long way or the short way, and there are some math problems that can be done "in one's head." Moreover, in contrast to the teacher's explanations in the working-class schools, when this teacher explained how to do math or what to do next, there was usually a recognition that a cognitive process of some sort was involved: rather than simply lead the children through a series of steps, she usually gave several ways to do a problem, and then said, "I want to make sure you understand what you're doing." She often asked a child to say how he "did" a problem.

Social studies knowledge in this school was more "conceptual" than in the working-class schools in that there was less emphasis on retention of facts and development of simple "skills" and more emphasis on children's *understanding* of the generalizations and other content of the books. The social studies textbook chosen for use in the school is *Let Freedom Ring* (1977), an American history text that is part of Silver Burdett's "discipline centered" social studies series. One purpose of the text is to introduce fundamental concepts from the various disciplines of the social sciences. The authors say, "The curriculum must identify the basic social science concepts and generalizations that are to be developed" (teachers guide, p. 4). At least two "understandings" in either anthropolgy, economics, history, geography, or political science are listed in the teachers guide for each chapter in the text, and a "unifying generalization" is stated for each chapter.

The following are eight of the 36 understandings listed as *economics* understandings in the (entire) text: "Andrew Carnegie was only one of the many men who went from 'rags to riches' in the age of industrialization." "Industrialization requires not only workers but also people who are willing to invest their surplus capital." "Stockholders are the real owners of a company that is operated by a board of directors who acts in the stockholders' name." "Workers organized into unions to protect their interests." "The slum is visible evidence of a city's inability to solve its problems." "Minority group members often suffer from at least three conditions—social exclusion, economic oppression, political powerlessness—in their relationship

with the majority." "To prevent further expansion of communism in western Europe the United States created the Marshall Plan" (teachers guide, pp. 12-24). It should be noted that these basic "understandings" are not particularly analytical of U.S. society, or of the economic system; indeed, one could argue that some of them are not *about* the economy (e.g., the first and last).

The textbook itself contains repeated statements about the value of reform, such as the need for continued improvement in providing civil rights for minorities. In addition, there is an emphasis throughout on cultural pluralism and the value of ethnicity: Indeed, of nine units, one entire unit, "Investigating Cultural Plurality," focuses on pluralism and on various ethnic groups in U.S. society. Its chapter titles are "Immigrants to the United States," "What is an American?" "Civil Rights for all Americans."

Each chapter in the text is followed by activities called "Finding the Facts," "Using the Facts," and "Using the Main Idea." The last one is intended to provide opportunities for creative activities and independent research. It asks the child to "extend the unifying understanding of the chapter" (teachers guide, p. 9). An example is the following: "Using the knowledge you have gotten here, you and your classmates prepare a series of news broadcasts, informing your listeners about each of the developments listed below (the Boston Massacre, the Battle at Lexington and Concord . . .")." (p. 158).

Social studies activity commonly involved reading the text and listening to the teacher's explanations, answering the teacher's questions or those in the text, and occasionally doing a report (e.g., "getting information" on an Indian tribe). Classroom activity rarely involved sustained inquiry into a topic. The fifth-grade social studies teacher said she did not use the text's "Using the Main Idea" activities very often. She said she didn't have time. She said that she has "enough to do to get them to understand the generalizations." "They read it [the text], I explain, and sometimes I give them a quiz." The following are examples of her classroom use of the textbook and a filmstrip that the school bought to accompany the section on American Indian tribes. The teacher introduces the filmstrip by saying, "When you do your report, include any information on your tribe that you see here." After several frames, a student comments, "They [the Indians] look Chinese." The teacher says, "They're from Eurasia, aren't they, so?" Later, the teacher says, "When this tribe died, they _____ (notes undecipherable)." A child asks, "Why did they do that?" The teacher says, "This is the way they wanted to do it." Several days later, when the class is viewing another filmstrip, the teacher reads a frame about the Incas: "There were rich people, nobles, chiefs, and slaves." (To herself, she says, "Now how am I going to explain this?") To the class she then says, "The rich happen to be the chiefs," and she continues reading. Later, a child asks, regarding an Indian tribe, "Why did they kill the bison?" The teacher answers, "I don't know. They had to live. [pause] You eat *hamburgers,* don't you?"

Several days later, reading the text on the Puritan culture the teacher says, "The word was 'economic.' What does that refer to?" A child looks at the page then says, "To make a better living?" The teacher also glances at the page, and says, "Yes, making money."

WHAT STUDENTS SAID ABOUT KNOWLEDGE   When I asked the children what knowledge was, seventeen gave me the following responses: "To remember." "You go to a museum." "You learn facts and history." "You study about your ancestors." "To study things we need to know." "It's smartness." "It means you're intelligent." "Remembering." "Knowledge is something you learn." "To know things." "Doing your work in school." "When you study." "It's how you learn in school, what you learn." "Knowing the answers to stuff," "Brains," "Being smart." "It's studying. What you do is store facts in your head like cold storage until you need it later for a test, or your job." Three children said they didn't know what knowledge was; perhaps they did not understand my question.

When I asked where knowledge comes from, I got the following answers: Two said, "From the teacher." "From the old times." "From old books." "From scientists." Two said, "From libraries." Three students said, "From encyclopedias." Three children said, "From books." "From my mother—she tells me what to do." "From movies or TV?" "From Sesame Street." "Knowledge comes from everywhere." "From Latin?" "You hear other people talk with the big words." It should be noted that these responses have to do mostly with knowledge being "out there," existing in books and libraries, not resulting from one's own activity.

When I asked the children in the middle-class school if they or someone else could make knowledge, nine said no and eleven said yes. The children who said yes gave responses like the following (when I asked them how knowledge would or could be made): Three said, "I'd look it up." (After one of these responses, I asked, "Are you making knowledge when you do a report?" The child said, "No, it's giving yourself knowledge, but not making it. We can't make knowledge, someone has already *made* it!") "You can make knowledge by listening and doing what you're told." Two said, "I'd go to the library." "By doing extra credit." It should be noted that these responses do not suggest a particularly active relationship to the production of knowledge; rather, knowledge is "given" and not made by themselves. Only two boys gave responses that indicated a more active approach to creation of knowledge. One said, "I'd go around and study things. Different countries." The other said, "I'd invent something."

"POSSIBILITY" AS A DOMINANT THEME   What emerged as a dominant theme in this school was the sense of *possibility.* While I saw in all schools bulletin boards or lesson plans announcing observance of national holidays such as Columbus Day and Lincoln's Birthday, there was, in the middle-class school, an increased amount of this kind of holiday and patriotic activity, more than in any other school in this study. There were more auditorium plays of a patriotic flavor put on by classes than in any other school (an example was the fifth-grade play, *An All-American Thank You*). The second grades open the day with what is an unusually patriotic introduction to the pledge of allegiance: "We will now pay homage and respect to the flag of our country." Education in particular seems to be accepted as important, indeed vital, to one's ability to get a job or enter college. There was the feeling that if one works *hard* in school (and in life), one will go far. A prominent attitude expressed by the children in interviews and elsewhere was anxiety about tests and grades. All but two said that yes, they were going to go to college, although they did not know where they would go. This sense of possibility also emerged in the children's answers when I asked them if they could be anything that they wanted to be when they grew up; most students (14 of 20) said yes. When I asked what it would depend on, I got the following types of answers: "It depends on how smart you are." "If your grades are good enough." "It's marks—you have to go to college." "Everything is by education." Three of the four who said they might *not* be able to be anything they wanted said it was because "I wouldn't know enough"; "My marks might not be good enough"; and "I wouldn't go to college."

It seems to be the case that knowledge in this school is more conceptual than in the working-class schools in that it is less a matter of facts and skills and more a matter of traditional bodies of "content." It is, in this sense, understanding and information from socially approved sources. It is also, as Horace Mann said, a possession. Information, facts, and dates can be accumulated and exchanged for good grades and college or a job. Knowledge here, however, is not usually connected to biographies or exploratory activities of the learners, and is thus divorced from processes of personal discovery (as indeed it is in the working-class schools as well). There is, however, in this school, the sense of possibility: school knowledge has real value, if one has "enough" of it.

AFFLUENT PROFESSIONAL SCHOOL

This school in a nearby suburb is surrounded by tall pine trees. Behind it are swings, a playground area, and beyond that two large grassy playing fields. The main building was built in 1911; it has a ranch-style modern wing constructed 15 years ago. The homes along the streets vary in size. Some are set back from the street, with large lawns and long driveways; these are the larger ones and have up to 25 rooms (by count from the street). Others are smaller, with smaller grounds. Inside the school are glass showcases in each hall, with displays of trophies, modern sculpture, children's art work, and, in one, old musical instruments. There are large, overstuffed couches in several corners of the building, in which children often sit and read, or work. The bulletin boards are crowded with children's pictures, charts and writings, and are bright and attractive. Each of the rooms between kindergarten and third grade has a rug in the front. The principal said he wanted his school to have "a family atmosphere," where "we know and nurture every child."

According to several of the teachers, this principal is the only one in the district who "stands up" to the superintendent or the Board of Education. (During the period of the study he resigned—temporarily, as it turned out—because the superintendent denied tenure to a teacher he had recommended highly.) A majority of the teachers in the school are from middle-class or upper-middle-class backgrounds; most are from various parts of the state. All but three are female; most of these are married to professionals or men in business; for example, one fifth-grade teacher was married to a stockbroker, another to a lawyer; one second-grade teacher was married to an "accountant with an M.A. in business," the other to a psychologist.

WHAT SCHOOL PERSONNEL SAID ABOUT SCHOOL KNOWLEDGE   Most of the personnel I interviewed in this school referred to school knowledge as involving either individual discovery and creativity, "important ideas," or personal activity on the part of the student (as in the use of science or math equipment).

In response to my question of what knowledge is most appropriate for her students, one of the two fifth-grade teachers said, "My goal is to have the children learn from experience. I want them to think for themselves." She also expressed the wish that they "try to make sense of their experience."

I asked the other fifth-grade teacher (who did not agree to be observed) what was most important in social studies education (her specialty). She told me, "It's learning to think. I use questioning techniques [to get them to think]." The principal said that the students should not just "regurgitate" facts, but should "immerse themselves in ideas." He said that "creativity and personal development" are important goals for the children in his school.

EVIDENCE FROM THE CURRICULUM AND THE CURRICULUM-IN-USE   Mathematical knowledge is supposed to come from discovery and direct experience. Activities I observed in the teaching of math included the use of geoboards, making and producing an 8-mm film on the metric system, measuring perimeters of their own drawings and generating questions for others to answer about the drawings, collecting data in surveys, and carrying out other empirical investigations with objects such as cubes and scales. The teacher says she does "all" the pages in the math book which concern mathematical patterns. She told me the publisher has supplemental dittoes for those pages, and she does "a lot of those."

Scientific knowledge in her class is also intended to result from children's experience and attempts to discover for themselves. All fourth, fifth, and sixth grades use the Elementary Science Study (ESS) where typical problems in the fifth grade ask the children to experiment in their own ways with materials such as aluminum and copper and glass rods in order to discover properties of the materials (e.g., which one heats the fastest).[6] The teacher said the value of the ESS approach to science is that they can "think about what they do." She said, "It gives them a hands-on experience so they can make sense of it. It doesn't matter whether it [what they find] is right or wrong, I bring them together and there's value in discussing their ideas."

In the fifth grade I observed, the teacher often responded to children's questions of "I don't get this," or "How should I do this?" or "What does this mean?" with "*You* decide"; "What do you *think*?" or "Test it to see if it's right"; "Does that make *sense*?" and "You can figure that out for yourself."

The teacher engages the children in creative writing at least once a day. Many children appear interested in these projects, and the teacher reported that some of them write on their own. A black child, one of three students in the class from working-class families, told me that he keeps a journal and writes a "magazine" on the weekend. Another boy, reading a C. S. Lewis book, said, when I asked him how he liked it, "It's very good, but he writes poorly; he uses too many 'ands.'" When the teacher asked the class to decide how to reassemble on cards and punctuate a short story called "Wally the Watermelon," several children said, as the activity began, "Oh, good." "This is fun." One boy said, "Ooh, can't we *change* it [the story] just a little?"

Although knowledge, thus, is intended as resulting from personal activity, thought, and creativity, there are multiple constraints on this. The teacher, for example, often asks for the "right answer" especially in math, where "right answers" are part of the system of manipulating numbers. And in science and math, one's work must fit empirical reality (e.g., one must measure accurately, and one's answers must lie in the accuracy of the fit between one's own measurements and the physically observable reality—what is measured). Moreover, in this class one must have one's science and math "data" "verified" by a peer before it is handed in.

Another type of constraint appears in the published reading programs for individualized instruction which form the basis of reading programs above fourth grade in this school (and in the executive elite school). A boxed set of each of the following programs was available and used consistently in the fifth grade that I observed: EDL *Listen and Think* series; SRA *Power Builder;* SRA *Reading Laboratory; Reading for Concepts; The Yearling.*[7] While most of these reading programs do attempt to engage the children in conceptual thinking of one sort or another (i.e., analyzing stories, reading for main ideas) all of them are highly systematized and there are almost always "right answers." These answers have been decided on by the designers of the program, and not by the children. Indeed, a problem that a fifth-grade teacher reported to me was that some of the children would write answers to the questions on the basis of what they *thought*, without going back to look at the story. She said she had to remind them often to "look back."

The social studies series used in this school (and in the executive elite school) is Allyn and Bacon's *Concepts and Inquiry Program*. It emphasizes what it calls "higher concept" learning. Unlike the series in the working-class and middle-class schools, it discusses at length such topics as social class, the power of dominant ideas, and "competing world views." The district fifth-grade curriculum is intended to cover ancient civilization (e.g., Sumer, ancient Greece and Rome) and Latin America. This fifth grade spent eight of ten months on Sumer and ancient civilization. The teachers guides to the series emphasize repeatedly that "conceptual learning should never degenerate into rote memorization followed by boring, parrotlike regurgitation of facts" (*Ancient Civilization*, p. 3). This guide lists 30 "performance objectives" for fourth- and fifth-grade social studies. Although called "performance" objectives, almost all are conceptual rather than behavioral.

The following are typical performance objectives for the fourth and fifth grades: "To understand the roles of savings, capital, trade, education, skilled labor, skilled managers, and cultural factors (religious beliefs, attitudes toward change) in the process of economic development." "To understand the power of controlling ideas." "To understand that the controlling ideas of Western culture came largely from two preceding cultures: The Judaic and Greco-Roman." "To know what is meant by the two world views of Western civilization and to perceive their implications." "To distinguish a mixed economy from a totalitarian system and to identify the United States as a nation with a mixed economy and the Soviet Union as a nation with a totalitarian system." "Given a description of class structure and interclass tension, to explain the idea of class struggle or class war as in the Roman Republic (teachers guide, pp. 8–12).

Classroom social studies in the fifth grade that I observed involved some discussion of the text, but the teacher's emphasis was on artistic, graphic, dramatic, and written elucidation of cultural artifacts and ideas of Sumarians and Ancient Greeks. The teacher said she used the books "basically as a resource." She has the children "read it, and outline it," and uses it as a guide for inquiry activities and

discussion. But, she said, most of her ideas for craft activities come from other sources. The class baked clay cuneiform replicas, wrote stories and plays, and created murals on the division of labor in ancient societies. Such activities were supported and facilitated when several families took their children to see the Tutankhamen exhibit and when one boy who had seen a different version of this exhibit in Paris brought in catalogues so the class could compare the two exhibits.

The teacher said she spends a lot of time discussing current events, "because they're so opinionated anyway, and they love it." Each table of four desks had a "News Captain" who assigns the topic for the week, and whose job is to bring in examples from the news. The children often write "editorials," and there were news clipping posted on labor strife, inflation, a nuclear power plant accident, and solar power.

During one discussion I observed, the teacher explained that some people think nuclear power is dangerous. Then she said, regarding the use of coal:

T: Yes. It pollutes. It's a vicious cycle, and nobody knows what the solution is. We do know we need alternative sources of energy. What would happen if we *had* no energy? [And then they got into a discussion of what life would be like "if we had no energy"— i.e., no coal, oil, or electricity.]

I asked the teacher later about her view of discussing controversial issues, noting that she had indeed shied away from a discussion of potential social responsibility and alleged suppression of harmful news by the nuclear industry. She said yes. I asked her why. She paused, then said, "One year I had the superintendent's son, the mayor's son, and the daughter of the president of the Board of Education in my room—all at one time! I *really* had to watch what I said. That was quite a year." She then indicated that she did not want to discuss the matter further.

WHAT STUDENTS SAID ABOUT KNOWLEDGE   When asked about what knowledge is, the children gave the following responses: "The way you think. Yes, the way you think." "Ideas and, um, smart people can find a lot of problems. They can think about them and they can realize them [sic]. When there is something wrong, they can realize what's wrong with it." "You think up ideas and then find things wrong with those ideas." "I don't know." "Being smart." "Knowing a lot of subjects." "It's when you know something— you can be a great scientist." "When you know something really well. It's . . . you'll never forget it; you got it down pact in your mind [sic]." "A way of learning, of finding out things." "Figuring out stuff." "Brains—I just think of Albert Einstein." "I forgot." "How smart you are—a brain." "Thinking." Three said, "What you know." "What you think about, what you learn in school." Two said they weren't sure.

It is interesting to note that many of their answers involved use of the word "think" or involved some type of personal activity having to do with things or ideas. It should also be noted that of the children in any school the children in this school had the least trouble with my questions. I reasoned that they were more relaxed (I interviewed them sitting on a comfortable couch) and perhaps they were most used to questions for which they were supposed to "figure things out," and to which there was not necessarily one right answer.

I asked them, "Where does knowledge come from?" and got the following responses: "People and computers." "Your head." "People—what they do." "Something you learn." "From your brain; if you don't know about it at the start and you don't understand, but if you really work hard at it you will." "Your brain, you make it up in your brain." (Two other children also said that "their brains did the work.") "From reading and learning." "From going places." Four children said, "From reading." "When you learn in school." "You learn it in schools and college and high school." "Anybody, if they're willing to really learn something, can really go far in that subject—be a scientist, study craters. You could study ancient times or be a geologist." (Three said they didn't know.)

When I asked, "Can you make knowledge?" sixteen children said yes; only four said no. They said that making knowledge involved the following: "Work hard, doing your best." "Albert Einstein studied very hard, and the first time he flunked out of college, but then he studied very hard and made it to the top." "You can make knowledge if you invent something." "If I were making knowledge, I'd take it step by step." "If you discover something." "I'd think of something to discover, then I'd make it." "I guess you could make some, but you have to be willing to learn and work hard." (I asked this child, "Does knowledge come from inside or outside?" He said, "A little of each. If you're especially good at it, it comes from inside, but if you're not, it comes from outside . . . like Jonathan. I watch him. He has the ability to do great in math, but he doesn't *think*. He knows more science than anybody, but you wouldn't know it." I asked another child if knowledge comes from inside or outside, and he said, "If you're smart, it comes from inside, but if you're not and you're not organized, the teacher *tells* you what to do.") "You can go explore for new things." "Yes, I guess, you could get stuff and work around with it. You could find a different way to add math and you would be making knowledge." "I'd probably think, and try things, like mixing colors." It should be noted that many of these answers reveal a rather active approach to the acquisition, if not creation, of knowledge.

NARCISSISM AS A DOMINANT THEME   A dominant theme in this school was what I call *narcissism,* or extreme individualism. This emerges, for example, in the emphasis in the classroom on thinking for oneself, on externalizing, in creative projects of all sorts, what is internal in the attempts to individualize instruction, in the personal discovery intended by the science and math programs, and in the principal's and teachers' stated emphasis on personal development and creativity as important goals of education. The emphasis on individual expression was apparent in the play put on by the sixth grade. It was written by several girls in the class and it was extremely funny. To quote from my observation notes:

It's an original play written by some girls in 6A. It amazed me. It's upper-middle-class individualism at its utmost. They're really hamming it up, enjoying it, and it's really very clever and funny. It parodies silly girls who flirt with boys and act "cute," but who do not act intelligently. It is about an Orange King and a Pink Queen who order the children ("peasants") around without telling them why, and who have great power to give the peasants tasks. The peasants were told to go and look for something. But they weren't told what it is they're supposed to be looking for. The problem is solved when a girl decides that they will kill the king and queen, who "would die of hate anyway." Several roles were reversed, with boys playing girls' roles and girls playing boys' roles. As I'm sitting by the fifth-grade teacher watching and laughing, she says, "It'd be even funnier if you *knew* them. Each one has *such* a personality." During lunch in the teachers' room the teacher whose class it was said, "Yes, [it was good]. But, you know, you're always limited when they [the children] write the script."

In addition to the stress in this school on individual development and expression, there was a stress on (or minor theme of) what I will call "humanitarianism" or "liberal ideals." The principal closes the morning intercom announcement each day with "do something nice for someone today." There is a "Good Deed Box" in the office and a certificate distributed on Fridays for a child who has done the nicest thing for "somebody who needs something nice." As in the executive elite school, there are clothing and food drives "for the poor." The social studies series attempts to be honest about society, recognizing, as it does, social classes, controlling ideas, and class conflict. It is also the most "liberal": Because of the recognition of social conflict, for example, there appear to be good reasons for social struggle, labor unions, and civil rights legislation. There is an entire fourth-grade textbook devoted to discussion of (and entitled) *Prejudice and Discrimination.*

Almost half of the children (8 of 20) expressed, in interviews, an attitude of antagonism to "the rich." In each case I had asked the children whether they thought they would be poor, middle class, or rich when they grew up. After they answered, eight volunteered comments such as "Rich people are greedy," and "spoiled." "They get everything they want; I know a kid who gets a new ten-speed bike every two years!" Rich children are "snobby." The girl who said that pointed out another in the hall who "comes to school with her chauffeur," and who "wears little muffs." Another student later pointed out a boy who is "so rich he thinks he can get away with anything! He has two *elevators* in his house!" One girl whose father and mother are both doctors said, "I wouldn't *want* to be rich. You don't have to work then, and I *like* to work."

Many of these children of affluent professionals are not at all sure they can be anything they want when they grow up, and their futures seem less than certain to them. Only half of them thought they could be anything they wanted, although all but one were sure they were going to college. Almost all wanted to go to a "good college." They all told me that to be anything you want "You really have to try hard" and "You have to go to the right college." One boy said, "It's luck. You need so much luck, it's incredible." Several spoke of wanting to meet their "potential." Two boys said they wanted to be "known," and spoke of how much hard work that would take. (For example, "You come in and ask the teacher for help even if you don't need it.") A black working-class boy said that what you will be depends on "your marks and if you go to college." He thought he probably *wouldn't* go to college, he wouldn't have the money; "and I'm *broke,* now!" he said.

It seems to be the case that knowledge in the affluent professional school is not only conceptual but is open to discovery, construction, and meaning making; it is not always given. Knowledge is often concepts and ideas that are to be used to make sense, and that thus have personal value. Although knowledge may result from personal creativity and independent thinking, there are constraints and directives on what count as answers. Knowledge has individualistic goals, but it also may be a resource for social good. It is analytical and more realistic about society than knowledge in the middle-class and working-class schools. The children are also getting a good dose of two dominant social ideologies: that the system itself will be made more humane by expressions of concern for the less fortunate, and that individuals, not groups, make history.

EXECUTIVE ELITE SCHOOL

The school is a handsome Colonial-style building, with a large white portico on the front. It was originally built in 1929; an addition was added in 1949; a second in 1956, and a new library in 1972. The school sits back from the street on a broad lawn with several bushes and trees in front of it. The door has shiny brass trim, as do the principal's office and the teachers' lounge. Each classroom has polished oak cabinets with cut-glass doors. The windows of the classrooms sparkle. There is an asphalt play area in back, and beyond that two large grassy playing fields and a running track. The principal is involved, with some of the parents, in building a "tire playground." Most of the homes along the streets near the school are large estates, partially hidden by foliage and long driveways.

A recent state order to integrate the town's schools led to a Board of Education plan to bus students from a school which had the majority of the town's blacks and low-income whites. Some of the students were to be bused to the executive elite school. The plan was dropped after parents at the executive elite school threatened to pull their children out of the school and put them in private schools. As of this writing, all elementary schools in the town will be integrated except the executive elite school: there will be no busing; the school that is predominantly black and low income will be closed, and its students will walk to other schools (the closest is over a mile away). There will be no black or low-income children in the executive elite school. One of the teachers I was observing offered her reason for the parents' actions. She said, "It was class, not race. They [the parents in this school] didn't want any low-income kids here. They didn't want the discipline problems. And they didn't want the [achievement] scores lowered, to hold back their kids. I taught over there once," she said, referring to the

school that would be closed, "and you can't teach them *anything!* They're flying all over the room. And their parents don't care about education. One father, he was a plumber, he said, 'well, if being a plumber is good enough for me, it's good enough for my son. What does he have to go to college for?'"[8]

Many of the teachers in the executive elite school are from middle- and upper-middle-class backgrounds. One older teacher spoke of her first year teaching, saying she loved it so much that she never even cashed her paychecks, just threw them in her drawer (she had been living with her parents). All the teachers are female except for the gym teacher. Most are married to professionals or to men in business (e.g., to a doctor, an insurance executive).

All teachers with whom I spoke regarded their students as of higher social status than themselves. One teacher contrasted the part of town she lived in with this one, saying she lived in a section like that of the [affluent professional] school which is "more mixed." Another teacher said, "These people are the successful ones. They know who they are; there is a class structure in this society and these people are at the top. And they know what they want for their kids. And some of them know where they came from—the ones who worked their way up." Another teacher said, "It's in their genes. They're handsome, you should see the fathers. They even *look* like executives!" A third-grade teacher said, "They're the successful ones. And some got that way through marriage." Said a first-grade teacher, "They're at the top, and they have breeding." "Breeding?" I asked. "It's a way of talking, dressing, even the mothers are well educated," she responded. "And they run the town!"

WHAT SCHOOL PERSONNEL SAID ABOUT SCHOOL KNOWLEDGE   When I asked the two fifth-grade and two-second grade teachers in this school what knowledge was important for their students, most referred to intellectual processes such as reasoning and problem solving. One said, "They'll go to the best schools, and we have to prepare them." Another said, "It's not just academics; they need to learn to think. They will have important jobs, and they need to be able to think things through." When I asked a second-grade teacher who I was observing what was appropriate knowledge for her students, she said, "They need to learn the basics, we're going back to that now." "The basics?" I asked. "Yes, to think and write properly." Referring to science, a fifth-grade teacher said, "I try to get them to create an environment where they can solve problems—they manipulate variables and solve a problem."

The superintendent of schools, who has an Ed.D. from Harvard University, is attempting to institute a "Philosophy for Children Program" in the school, the purpose of which would be "to teach children to think and reason correctly, and to come up with valid conclusions."[9] The fifth-grade teachers in this school said they have been instructed by the superintendent to develop an "Olympics of the Mind"—a competition of "open-ended questions" for which there are no "set answers." (This would accompany the Field Olympics held by the fifth grades [in this and the affluent professional school] at the end of the year, at the end of their study of ancient Greece. The Field Olympics during this particular year included chariot races, a torch-lighting ceremony written by several children, and the culminating races to year-long competition in gym class track and field. Gold and silver medals were awarded.)

EVIDENCE FROM THE CURRICULUM AND THE CURRICULUM-IN-USE The fifth-grade teacher who teaches math said that her goal in this subject is the development of mathematical reasoning. She said the "demands" of "getting through the curriculum" do not leave her time to have the children "explore" with manipulables such as geoboards. She said she also tries to teach math as a "decision-making process." For example, presenting a new type of division problem to her class, she asks, "What's the *first* decision you'd make if presented with this kind of example? What is the first thing you'd *think*, Craig?" Craig says, "To find my first partial quotient." She responds, "Yes, that would be your first decision. How would you do that?" Craig explains, and then

she says, "OK, we'll see how that works for you." She usually asks the children to explain why their answers are right or wrong, to explain how they know or how they found out an answer. She often says to her classes, "If you think logically [or rationally] about it, you can figure it out." Indeed, in every math class observed, she asked her class questions which required them to manipulate hypothetical variables to solve the problem.

Science is another subject in which intellectual process such as reasoning was stressed. The principal said that all teachers in the school are "required" to use a science program. The fifth- and sixth-grade teachers used the ESS. According to the principal, the rest of the teachers in the school use Science—A Process Approach (SAPA). SAPA was designed to present instruction that is "intellectually stimulating and scientifically authentic." It focuses on the processes involved in scientific reasoning, and there is a "progressive intellectual development with each process category." The children are expected to learn such things as how to infer internal mechanisms of plants, how to make and verify hypotheses about animal behavior, and how to perform experiments on the actions of gases.[10] A second-grade teacher I observed said she likes the program because "it's integrated and organized. And it tells you exactly what to do."

While this school used the same social studies series as the affluent professional school, social studies instruction in the classes I observed here was more academically (rigorously) organized than in the affluent professional school, followed more closely the discussion questions posed by the text, and involved a large amount of independent library research but very little creative or artistic project work. The fifth-grade social studies teacher said she based her instruction on discussion questions in the text and district study guides, and on activities provided by ten "individual study packets."

The fifth-grade social studies guide for the district was written by the former fifth-grade teacher in this school and the district social studies specialist. The former social studies teacher in this school also wrote the individual study packets of research and writing activities for the fifth-grade topics. (These were not available in the affluent professional school.) The district guide to the fifth-grade units on ancient Greece and Rome states the rationale for the course of study: "By an increased awareness of past problems and the human conditions which cause these problems, maybe we can prevent what Arnold Toynbee has pointed out, 'Nineteen of twenty-one civilizations have died from within and not by conquest from without. There were no bands playing and flags waving when these civilizations decayed. It happened slowly, in the quiet and the dark when no one was aware'" (p. 2). The guide takes many of its questions and activities from the Allyn and Bacon series.

Social studies knowledge was more sophisticated, complex, and analytical than in other schools. The social studies teacher I observed said she tried to have the children tackle the "important concepts." The following are examples of questions from the children's text that I heard discussed in class: "Greek comedies often poked fun at popular leaders. Would this be possible in a society that was not free? Can you think of any bad effects this might have? Any good effects?" "Look up the word imperialism,' What are some good and bad effects of imperialism?" (p. 41) "Were the Athenians wrong in condemning Socrates for his beliefs? Would you expect a person to be put to death for their ideas in a democracy? Explain" (p. 51). "There were two main classes in the early Roman republic. There were the noble, wealthy *Patricians.* There were the common people, or *plebs.* Would you expect these classes to get into quarrels?. . . Find out about the struggle between plebs and patricians in 494 B.C. The plebs went "on strike." What rights and protections did they get as a result?" (p. 80)

Social studies knowledge in this school also involved an explicit recognition of social class in ancient history. For example, the text identified, and the students discussed, what the text calls a "ruling class" in ancient society. In every chapter but two in the text on Greek and Roman civilization, there is the heading "Classes in Society" (with relevant concepts identified). Questions I heard discussed in the classroom included "What

class conflicts occurred?" (*Greek and Roman Civilization,* p. 74) and "How was class structure affected by changes in property ownership after the Punic Wars?" (p. 74).

Not only textbooks but the individual study packets as well included an explicit recognition of social class. There were two fifth-grade packets for independent study of Latin America. One was on geography, and the other was called "Class and Culture." Sample questions follow: "Pretend you are a member of the upper class or lower class of Latin America. Write your "life story." Include the history of the group you are in. Where were you born? What were your ancestors and parents like? Will you always belong to this social class? What is your day-to-day life like?"

Scattered throughout the teachers guide are references to other social classes, for instance, "the lower classes," "the common classes." For example, "Rule by the ignorant and easily swayed lower classes led to grave errors in judgment like the Syracusan expedition" (teachers guide, *Greek and Roman Civilization,* p.55). "Whatever his political views, Pericles was no imitator of the 'common man.' It was precisely this restraint, control and rationality that made Pericles a valuable leader. Witness the conditions after his death, when 'common men' became leaders of Athens: the rationality, direction, and sensible restraint that had characterized policy in Pericles' day suddenly evaporated, leaving a splintered, chaotic, and impulsive Assembly in charge of formulating policy" (teachers guide, *Greek and Roman Civilization,* p. 39). [Interestingly, however, while the series is quite explicit about classes in ancient Greece and Rome (and Sumer), and a sixth-grade text called *The Challenge of Change* is quite explicit about the social class divisions in European history ("upper classes" were "the gentry, nobles, bishops"; the "middle classes" were "the Bourgoisie [sic] or merchants, tradesmen, yeoman farmers, lawyers, doctors and clergymen" and the "lower classes were small farmers, laborers, the poor") (p. 29), the textbook series does not discuss class in this fashion in the American history textbook it provides for fourth grade, and there is no division there of U.S. society into social classes.]

While classroom social studies knowledge tends to be *analytical,* neither text nor most social studies discussions were *critical* of the social class structure or distribution of wealth and power; rather, they gave it high value and a "naturalness," or "timelessness," going back, indeed, to ancient Greece. There were occasions, however, in the classroom of the fifth-grade teacher who teaches math, science, and health but not social studies, when class discussions were "almost" critical; that is, the teacher often asked the children *why* things were done or happened in a certain way, when that way appeared to be *irrational.* For example, after showing the class a film on the making of a Morton's "cream" pie almost entirely with chemicals, she asked, "Why do companies put chemicals in food when the natural ingredients are available?" The following excerpt of a discussion in this teacher's class provides a further example of her attempt to have her class give critical thought to a social problem. Strikes of newspaper workers, sanitationmen and truckers had been in the news. The children had just read for homework a story in their *Scholastic News* about a teachers' strike.[11]

T: OK, suppose I'm the manager and you ask me, and I won't give you a raise. Then what do you do? David?

S: Strikes are *not* a good idea: the public is always affected. Students don't learn if teachers strike.

S: Companies don't make profits if workers strike.

T: I'm asking you questions to help you think this through, I'm not saying I'm not agreeing with you.

S: It goes both ways. Take the newspaper strike. A worker may have a family he or she has to support, but without newspapers, we don't know, as David said.

T: But what if you really feel . . .

S: (cuts off the teacher) If you really feel strongly, you should.

S: No. The students were hurt by the strike of the teachers. (He begins a monologue about how the teachers shouldn't strike because it

hurts the public. The teacher finally calls on another student.)

S: Workers say, "I think I deserve a raise for building really good cars." But the managers are against strikes. They say, "Workers only work eight hours and I work twelve. Why *shouldn't* I get more?"

T: A lot of you are concerned about the public. But suppose you have a boss who really takes advantage of you. What then?

S: *I'd* probably try to find another job. I wouldn't stay with that creep!

T: I want you to think about this. We won't have time to discuss it; I'm the boss.

S: You're always the boss. (Laughter, teacher smiles).

T: I say, "Strike and I'll fire you. I don't need you. . . . I'm going to buy a machine!" Think about that. (They get up for lunch.)

Discussions like this one and indications that such discussions may go on in other rooms (e.g., intricate bulletin board displays of designs for home heating with solar power; school clothing and food drives; stories written about families who are poor and black; and district-run affirmative action and sexism awareness workshops for teachers) indicate that the school may play a politically liberalizing role in the children's upbringing. For example, the discussion the teacher and students had about strikes seems to have made some impression on them. During the discussion only one child came out in favor of strikes. One said to me on the playground at lunch, "Mrs. [B] was for strikes, but we weren't." Several weeks later when I was interviewing the children I asked all interviewees if they thought strikes were right or wrong. Only two children said strikes were wrong; three children said yes, strikes are right; and all the rest but one (14) said "It depends." The children who said it depended gave responses like the following: "They're right *and* wrong; it depends on how you do it. The union figured out a way to make picket lines legal, and that's wrong. But you can't fire all the people; you won't be good in the public eye and your product will go down. Then you'd go bankrupt and have to close the company for a while." "Well, it depends; it's OK if it's really gone too far, but the *idea* doesn't hit me too well. It's just a public disturbance." "They're right and wrong. Mrs. [B] said people *should* strike to get enough money. And most people in the class didn't agree with her. My parents said maybe the company can't give the workers more, and they should try to talk it out."[12]

WHAT STUDENTS SAID ABOUT KNOWLEDGE   When I asked them what knowledge was, the children in this executive elite school gave the following answers: "Knowing certain things." "You have to really figure it out." "Thinking." "Knowing something that not too many people know; deep down, that's your knowledge. You have your opinion and then you know inside for sure, but the other person's never heard it before." "What you're *expected* to know." "What you're supposed to know." "It's being able to know and answer questions." One child said, "It depends on how you use it [the word]. There are two kinds of knowing: information knowing and wise knowing. Information knowledge, that's what you learn in school. Wise knowing is moral knowing, it's maturity. You learn that in life. . . ." "It's information that you've gotten, like in school." "It's like knowing what something is when the teacher is explaining," "It's—you know what it is you understand—that's knowledge: *Understanding!*" (He smiled; he was quite pleased.) "Questions that you try to answer after the teacher has given you an idea. Some questions have only one right answer and some have more than one right answer, like in social studies." (She smiled.) (I asked her to give me an example of a question with more than one right answer. She said, "What did the Athenians do wrong? What mistakes did the great leader Pericles make?") "You have to be able to figure out things sensibly. A mouse wouldn't just walk from here to there; he would only do it for cheese. You don't do things just for the exercise!" "Knowledge is really the confidence that you *got* knowledge." "Knowing more than anybody." "Being the best." Three others said, "Knowing things." "When someone asks you a question you can answer it without any trouble—like I've been answering yours—only thinking for a minute."

The answers of the children in this school seem to speak less to creativity or thinking independently or making "sense," as did the answers given by many affluent professional children. Rather, these children spoke to the need to know *existing* knowledge and to do well, to understand, explain, and answer correctly (and quickly). The answers of many of these children were, without prodding on my part, longer than those of most others in other schools, and some were conceptually more sophisticated. Most of these children were quite tense during the interviews. They listened closely, tried to answer precisely and quickly, and were somewhat stiff, very formal and polite. (Each, when getting up, very carefully pushed his or her chair under the desk in the science room where we had been sitting. Most, as they left the room, said very politely, "Thank you.") One boy came back after lunch to change his answer to the question, "What is knowledge?"

When I asked where knowledge comes from, more than half (13 of 20) said, "from past experience" or from "tradition," or "other people." Only three mentioned that knowledge comes from one's brain or what one does. Several answers that call forth tradition were "How are you using that [the word knowledge]?" I say, "information knowing." He says, "Well, actually it began long ago—as accidents. Like fire, supposedly the Greeks . . . Somebody learned it, say, two pebbles and two stones, that's four. They figured it out, and now it's been passed down and everybody knows it, or most people."

When I asked, "Can you make knowledge?" ten said yes, nine said no, and one said, "That's a ridiculous question!" When I asked, "How could you make knowledge?" five said, "Learning—when other people teach you." "If you find something." "If I do an experiment in school I can find out if something is true or false." "If you invented something." "If you wanted to figure something out—whether if no one knew that two plus two is four, you could go out and figure it out." The rest said, "It depends." For example, "It depends. You could learn *some* stuff by yourself, but you could never learn to *talk* by yourself. Yes, that's a good example." "Not really," said one girl, "you can make computers, and they make knowledge. But you can get it, or have it, and put it in something." These children, as compared to the affluent professional children, took a somewhat more passive attitude toward the creation of knowledge. For many, it comes from tradition, it is "out there," in what is known and expected of you, and you must learn it and know it.

One boy, who said he wants to be "a well-known lawyer like my father," told me, "You don't know you're the best until you've beaten the best." Seventeen of the 20 children said, without hesitation, yes they could be whatever they wanted when they grew up. Most (14), however, did not have any clear idea of what they wanted to be. They spoke of how good they were at soccer, skiing, swimming ("better than most kids my age," said one boy). Another said, "I'm interested in so *many* things that I can make something good out of anything." One boy said, "I could be the president if I wanted, but that doesn't turn me on." A girl offered that she could be the president's wife if she wanted, and then she said, "But I'm not *that* smart" (she was one of three children in the class whose IQ was above 140). When I asked what being anything they wanted to be would depend on, they said, "It depends on how hard you try," "on having self-confidence," and "on going to the right school." The schools they mentioned were (in declining order of number of times mentioned): Harvard, Yale, Princeton, Notre Dame, Lehigh, Columbia, "Harvard graduate school for business," and "MIT graduate school in science."

EXCELLENCE AS A DOMINANT THEME
Where resistance appeared as a dominant theme in the working-class schools, "possibility" in the middle-class school, and narcissism in the affluent professional school, what emerged in the executive elite school was a theme of excellence—the necessity of preparation for being the best, for top-quality performance. This does not allow for narcissistic coddling, but demands a great deal of "toeing the line," and self-discipline. (This is not to imply that all the children had such self-discipline, for, indeed, there was a competing subculture in the fifth grade, to be discussed in a

following paragraph. What it does imply, however, is that the exhortation to top-quality performance was a dominant theme in the school and in student-teacher interactions.)[13] For example, the academic pace was much brisker here than in any other school. The teachers often told the children that they alone were responsible for themselves, for "keeping up," and for their work. This was the only school in the study in which the children were required to be doing school-work *before* the late bell rang to start the day. The principal, referring to his teachers, said, "We have no laggards in this school." He issued numerous memos regarding "quality instruction," "making use of every moment," and the importance of high student achievement scores. In April a fifth-grade teacher said to me, "The teachers are panicked. There's so much of the curriculum to get through before the end of the year." Many children in the school, it appeared to me, were more intense in competition and performance than most children in other schools. Indeed, some of them defined school knowledge in terms of their ability to perform well, for example, to answer my questions.

There was a small subculture that runs counter to this theme. There was a group in the fifth grade (and sixth grade as well, according to the principal) who made a great show of being "cool," being "hip," "not trying too hard," wearing work overalls, carrying "hair picks," hand-slapping each other, and trying to use street talk in the classroom. This group exhibited a bit of cynicism in social studies classes about patriotism, as well. For example, during a discussion of the ancient Greeks in which the class was comparing the Greek polis with the U.S. republic, the teacher mentioned the patriotism and pride that the Athenians had had in their city. One girl then said, "I'm not patriotic anymore." The teacher glanced at me, with a half-smile and a raised brow, and then asked the girl why she wasn't patriotic. The girl began telling how "ticked off" her second-grade class had got when they wrote a letter to President Ford telling him that he had won their mock election. "We copied the letters over and over to make them perfect," she said. "And he only answered one person!" The teacher then said,

"Hmm, how *do* we show patriotism?" One child said, "We don't." Another said, "Voting?" A third, "Enlisting in the army?" Another, "We come to *school!*" Someone responded, "But that's a law!" The teacher said, "Let's take a vote. Who is more patriotic—the Greeks . . . or us?" All the children voted for the Greeks. A girl said, "We don't *have* much patriotism. We don't force anyone to do *any*thing." The teacher went on to another topic.

The data suggest that knowledge in this executive elite school is academic, intellectual, and rigorous. There is an attempt to teach more, and more difficult, concepts than in any other school. Knowledge results not from personal activity or attempts to make sense, but from following rules of good thought, from rationality and reasoning. In many cases, knowledge involves understanding the internal structure of things: the logic by which systems of numbers, words, or ideas are arranged and may be rearranged. There is a sense and a practice that the rationality of logic and math is the model of correct and ethical thinking, and living. Intimately connected to what counts as knowledge for most children in this school is the perceived pressure to perform, to excel, to get into the "best" schools. Although highly privileged, many of these children are working very hard to keep what they have.

CONCLUSION AND IMPLICATIONS

I would conclude that despite similarities in some curriculum topics and materials, there are profound differences in the curriculum and the curriculum-in-use in the sample of schools in this study. What counts as knowledge in the schools differs along dimensions of structure and content. The differences have been identified and discussed briefly in the foregoing sections; now they will be assessed for social and theoretical implications. The assessment will focus on reproductive and nonreproductive aspects of knowledge in each social-class setting. "Reproductive" will refer to aspects of school knowledge that contribute directly to the legitimation and perpetuation of ideologies, practices, and privileges constitutive

of present economic and political structures. "Nonreproductive" knowledge is that which facilitates fundamental transformation of ideologies and practices on the basis of which objects, services, and ideas (and other cultural products) are produced, owned, distributed, and publicly evaluated. The present definition of social change as fundamental transformation transcends the goals of, but does not deny the importance of, humanitarian efforts and practices in institutions such as the school. As we shall see, however, the genesis of truly transformative activity is in the contradictions within and between social settings.

In the working class schools there are two aspects of school knowledge that are reproductive. First, and quite simply, students in these schools were not taught their own history—the history of the American working class and its situation of conflict with powerful business and political groups, e.g., its long history of dissent and struggle for economic dignity. Nor were these students taught to value the interests which they share with others who will be workers. What little social information they were exposed to appears to provide little or no conceptual or critical understanding of the world or of their situation in the world. Indeed, not knowing the history of their own group—its dissent and conflict—may produce a social amnesia or "forgetting" (Jacoby, 1975). Such "forgetting" by the working class has quietistic implications in the social arena and potentially reproductive consequences.

A second reproductive aspect of school knowledge in these working-class schools was the emphasis in curriculum and in classrooms on mechanical behaviors, as opposed to sustained conception. This is important to a reproduction of the division of labor at work and in society between those who plan and manage (e.g., technical professionals, executives) and the increasing percentage of the work force whose jobs entail primarily carrying out the policies, plans, and regulations of others. These working-class children were not offered what for them woud be *cultural capital*—knowledge and skill at manipulating ideas and symbols in their own interest, e.g., historical knowledge and analysis that legitimates their dissent and furthers their own class in society and in social transformation.

These aspects of school knowledge in the working-class schools contribute to the reproduction of a group in society who may be without marketable knowledge; a reserve group of workers whose very existence, whose availability for hire, for example, when employed workers strike, serves to keep wages down and the work force disciplined. A reserve group is, of course, essential to capitalism because lower wages permit profit accumulation, which is necessary to the viability of firms, banks, state budgets and other bank-finance budgets of, one could argue, the entire system.

On the other hand, however, there is a major contradiction in school knowledge in these working-class schools, and from this may emerge a situation that is potentially socially transformative. Teacher control of students is a high priority in these schools, as in other schools. What the teachers attempted, in these two working-class schools, however, was *physical* control. There was little attempt to win the hearts and minds of these students. Now, our own era in history is one in which social control is achieved primarily through the dominant ideology and the perceived lack of ideological alternatives. But the working-class children in the schools studied here were taught very little of the ideology that is central to stable reproduction of the U.S. system, e.g., traditional bodies of knowledge that include the ideologies of an alleged lack of social alternatives to capitalist organization, patriotism and nationalism, faith in one's own chance of "making it big," and belief that the economy and polity are indeed designed in the interests of the average man and woman. In some cases, children in this study gave evidence that they had already rejected the ideologies of patriotism and of equal chances for themselves.

The absence of traditional bodies of knowledge and ideology may make these children vulnerable to alternative ideas; the children may be more open to ideas that support fundamental social change. Indeed, some of the children were already engaged in struggle against what was to them an exploitative group—the school teachers and administrators. They were struggling against the imposition of a foreign curriculum. They had "seen through" that system. The children's struggle, however, was destructive to themselves. Really *useful* knowledge for these students, e.g., honest "citizenship" education, would authenticate students' own meanings and give them skills to identify and analyze their own social class and to transform a situation that some already perceive is not in their own interest.

A social and theoretical implication of the education of the working-class students in this study, then, is that while a reserve pool of marginally employed workers is perhaps assured by modern schooling, ideological hegemony is not. Ideological hegemony is, rather, extremely tenuous, and the working class may be less ideologically secured than some other social groups. What is important is to make available to working-class students the cultural and ideological tools to begin to transform perspicacity into power.[14]

In the middle-class school, the children I observed were not taught the history of workers or of dissent, nor were they instructed to unify around common interests they will have as wage earners in a system in which many middle-class jobs are becoming increasingly like industrial and clerical jobs—mechanical and rote (for example, computer, technical, and social work; other service jobs; perhaps teaching; nursing and other formerly professional jobs). There were, however, distinguishing characteristics of knowledge in this middle-class school that are important primarily because of the social-class location of the families. For example, the notion of knowledge as originating in external and externally approved sources, as generated and validated by experts, may yield a passive stance before ideas and ideology and before the creation or legitimation of new ideas. This, of course, has implications of intellectual passivity, and ideological quietude. Moreover, school knowledge in the middle-class school was highly commodified. The reification of ideas and knowledge into given facts and "generalizations" that exist separately from one's biography or discovery contributes to the commodification of knowledge. It is true that knowledge in the working-class schools was reified as well. However, in order to be a commodity, a product must have some value in the marketplace and must be perceived as having some value, or no one would "buy" it. That is, it must have an exchange value. Traditional conceptual or academic knowledge in the working-class schools is not perceived by many teachers or students as having exchange value in the marketplace, or workplace, of working-class jobs. Therefore, it does not have commodity status. In the social class position of the present middle-class school, however, the teachers and students perceive the knowledge to have market value: there is a perceived chance that if one can accumulate facts, information and "generalizations," one can exchange them for college entrance or for a white-collar (perhaps even professional) job. But as is true of all commodities, when one exchanges an object, one gives up its use for oneself. Furthermore, a commodity is useful only in an exchangeable, objectified form. Forms in which knowledge is useful for reflection, critical thought, or making sense do not generate as much value in the competition for college entrance and the majority of U.S. jobs.

Commodification of knowledge in the middle-class school is reproductive in part because it helps to legitimate and reproduce the ideology of production for consumption, for example, production of knowledge and other cultural products for the market rather than for personal use or for social transformation. (An actively consuming public is, of course, a material necessity in a capitalist system, and thus legitimation of the ideology of consumption—of production *for* consumption—has direct economic reproductive consequences as well.)

There is a second aspect of knowledge in the middle-class school that is reproductive. This is also a part of the apparent acceptance or belief in the possibility of success for oneself. It is a social fact of major importance that the U.S. middle class is a group whose recent history has shown rapidly decreasing economic stability for individual families. There is, thus, material reason for the reification of knowledge into accumulatable form and for the anxiety which the children manifest concerning tests, college, and jobs. For example, the amount of attention one must pay to "getting

ahead" not only leaves little interest or time for critical attention, but it also actively fosters and strengthens belief in the ideologies of upward mobility and success. For example, "If I do not believe that there is a chance for me, and that I can succeed, why should I try so hard? Why go along?" I must *believe* in order to work hard; and to work hard increases the personal (psychological) necessity of my belief. So, the perception of social possibilities for the middle class hinted at in this study and the ideologized and reified school knowledge found in their schooling contribute not only to some of them "getting ahead," but to the production of a class with perhaps the highest degree of mystification and ideological internalization. This, of course, is reproductive.

There is, however, a potentially nonreproductive contradiction to be foreseen regarding school knowledge and the lives of these children. Many of those whose schooling and families have promised them a high reward for working hard and doing well will actually *not* succeed in the job market. This situation, after years of schooling in ideology and promises, may serve to generate cynicism or, more constructively, a critical view of the system. Also, the fact that many of these students will go to college may expose them to alternative ideas. They may be exposed to authors and professors who present alternative views and critical assessments of the social order. From this new knowledge and social perspective, they may, perhaps, be moved to utilize their own curiosity, to begin to use knowledge to question what is. Such questioning is a beginning of any socially transformative activity.

In the affluent professional school there are several aspects of school knowledge that are reproductive. First, the children are taught what is, for most of them, their own history—the history of the wealthy classes. They are taught that the power of their own group is legitimate. They are, as well, taught ways of expressing and using such ideas—that ideology—in their own interests. They are being provided with cultural capital. Indeed, the fact that the knowledge of their own group is socially prestigious knowledge enhances the exchange value of their knowledge as capital. Moreover, because many affluent professional jobs (doctor, lawyer, professor, scientist) still require conception and creativity and independent thought, many of the children in this school will be in the privileged position of having the *use* value of their knowledge (for personal creativity, for example) be at the same time its *exchange* value (for example, they will get paid for doing creative, conceptual work).

A second aspect of school knowledge that is reproductive here is its nascent empiricism (by empiricism I refer to the emphasis in adult science on basing knowledge on experience and on appearances, on observable data this experience produces.) As the basis for knowledge or explanations, empiricism is socially reproductive when it provides a framework for allegedly independent thought. Empiricism uses characteristics of observable data and characteristics of the observed relationships between data for its explanations; empiricism eschews explanations and analyses which are based on transcendent and nonempirical knowledge (see Bernstein 1978). This mode of inquiry thus uses categories and explanations that are confined to what already exists, to what can be observed. This mitigates against challenges to the necessity or naturalness of these categories and of what exists. School science programs and math manipulables make a small contribution, then, to the legitimation of empiricism as a way of seeking and testing knowledge, and to the acceptance of what is, as opposed to what could be. The programs are, in this case, a potential invisible boundary of the social thought of these children.

Accompanying the nascent empiricism in this affluent professional school is the emphasis on individual development as a primary goal of education (as opposed, for example, to the development of the priority of collective goals). A priority on personal expression, personal "meaning making" and the "construction of reality" mitigates against collectivistic values and meanings and solutions; it is thereby reproductive of values important to an individualistic, privately owned, and competitive economy.

Finally, the emphasis in the curriculum and classrooms on active use of concepts and ideas by students, as opposed to a stress on mechanics or rote behaviors, facilitates the perpetuation of an unequal division of labor in U.S. society, where some (these children?) will plan and others (working-class and middle-class children?) will have jobs that entail carrying out the plans.

There are, however, basic contradictions apparent in the school knowledge of these affluent professional children. In these conflicts one can see powerful implications for social transformation. For example, the contradiction between attempting as a student, and making sense as an adult, presumably later in one's professional creative labors, in a society where many things do *not* make sense and are irrational is a conflict which may generate political radicalism. Such a conflict may lead to intellectuals who are highly critical of the system and who attempt to persuade others by disseminating their own views. Or, it may lead to political activism, to overt attempts to take physical action against perceived political and economic irrationalities, as, for example, the students in Students for a Democratic Society (SDS)—a radical, anti-Vietnam War group—a majority of whom were from affluent professional families. Indeed, as Alvin Gouldner points out (1979), almost all leaders of social revolutions in the modern era have come from families of comparatively high standing in their society who were exposed to large amounts of cultural capital (e.g., Marx, Engels, the majority of the early Bolsheviks, Mao Tse-tung, Chou En-Lai, Ho Chi Minh, and Fidel Castro).

It is probably true that the conflict inherent in attempting to make sense in a world that is in many ways irrational is present for all children in all schools and social classes. What makes the conflict a potentially powerful force in the affluent professional school, however, is first the social-class position of these children, their cultural capital, and future access to information, power, and further cultural capital afforded to them by their social position. A second factor important here is the nature of their schooling. These children were told, and encouraged, more than the children in any other school to be creative, to think for themselves, and to make sense. It is indeed because of such encouragement to the young that the increasingly ideological notions of freedom and democracy can be turned back upon the economically and politically powerful and made into truly transformative demands.

Another contradiction to the school knowledge of these children that is nonreproductive is the contradiction between the value placed on creativity and personal decision making, and the systematic, increasingly rationalized nature of school and professional work in U.S. society. This conflict, already apparent in the use of science and reading programs in this school, is a contradiction that suggests possible later conflicts between the use and exchange values of knowledge in adult work, for example, between one's own creativity and the increasing rationalization and control of professional work by technology, bureaucratic trends, and centralization. It also suggests class conflict between affluent professionals, with their own interests and skills and relative power in the bureaucracy on one hand, and the capitalists, who are their "bosses" and who hold the purse strings, on the other. Conflict between the educated classes and the ruling class has long been a source of movement for social transformation. Indeed, as Gouldner (1979) reminds us, it has been this class—the educated, the intellectuals—who have, to date, taken control in periods of revolutionary upheaval, e.g., in the early Soviet Union and China. It is, then, important to provide the children of the affluent professional class with school knowledge that is not just conceptual, analytical, and expressive, but that is also critical and collective. Such knowledge would foster responsiveness not only to the needs of individual "meaning making" and development, but to the development of a wider social collectivity that, not coincidentally, would affirm the needs of the working and middle classes as well.

The executive elite school offers cultural capital to its children, whose families as a class have the major portion of available physical capital in society. These children are taught the history of "ruling" groups, and that rule by the wealthy and aristocratic is rational and natural, going back, for example, to the Ancient Greeks. Such knowledge is, for them, symbolic capital. They are provided

with other kinds of symbolic capital as well—practice in manipulating socially prestigious language and concepts in systematic ways. They are told the importance of controlling ideas and given some insight into controlling ideas in their own (Western) culture. The fact that the culture of their social class is the dominant and most prestigious one enhances the exchange value or "worth" of their knowledge in the marketplace.

Some of these children had a fair amount of class consciousness, if this is defined as knowledge of themselves as part of a group in society and in history, and an appreciation of their own group's interests as opposing the interests of other groups in society (e.g., plebs, strikers). While class consciousness among the working classes is likely to be nonreproductive, such a consciousness among the capitalist class is, of course, likely to increase their efforts to win conflicts, to conserve culture, and to maintain their social position, e.g., to prevent what Toynbee said was the "decay of civilization from within."

School knowledge in the executive elite school was the most "honest" about society, U.S. social problems, and social irrationalities. It was sometimes expressive of liberal concerns, as well. Indeed, it came the closest to being socially critical. The children were given analytical and unsentimental insight into the system. Whereas, for example, middle-class children might see a pluralism of equal or competing ethnic cultures, the children of the executive elite might perceive social class and economic conflict. Thus, these children may be less ideologically mystified than, for example, the middle-class students. The executive elite students—in different and more socially profitable ways than the working-class students—may see more clearly through the rhetoric of nationalism and equal opportunity to the raw facts of class and class conflict.

There is a potential contradiction here in the "clarity" of understanding the system that may, in the particular context of the social-class position of these children, have transformative possibilities. This is the contradiction for them between the use and exchange values in their knowledge: the contradiction between using knowledge for pleasure and enjoying one's class privilege, for example, and the exchange value of knowledge when it must be used to maintain that privilege. Two particular characteristics that empower this contradiction for these children (because the contradiction does appear in weaker forms in other schools) are, first, that extreme pressure is necessary, and excruciating struggle is demanded in a capitalist political democracy to actually maintain one's position of economic power and privilege. To grow up in the modern capitalist class is not only to enjoy travel, luxury, good schools, and financial wealth; it is also to have to maintain power in the face of others competing with you, within an irrational economic system that is increasingly difficult to predict, manage, and control—not only in the U.S. but in a rebellious Third World, as well. To be the "best," one must continually "beat the best." This is severe pressure. Second, to be a powerful capitalist, one must cause suffering and actually exploit others. Indeed, one's wealth and power are possible only because there are others (e.g., a reserve "pool" of workers) who do not have power and resource. These two "facts of life" of "being a capitalist" mean that if one is not ideologically secured, one may reject these demands. In contrapuntal fashion, the pressures, the irrationalities, and the exploitative characteristics of one's role in the system may one day cause the system to be perceived as the enemy—to be destroyed, rather than exploited. One thinks, as examples, of ruling class "children" who have rejected their privileges for radical politics and who have attempted to destroy members of their own class (the Baader-Meinhoff Group in Germany, the Red Brigades in Italy, or, indeed, the Weathermen in the U.S.). While such efforts at social transformation are violent and irrational and are not condoned, they must be acknowledged as nonreproductive in intent.

By situating school knowledge in its particular social location, we can see how it may contribute to contradictory social processes of conservation and transformation. We see the schools reproducing the tensions and conflicts of the larger society. It becomes apparent as well that an examination of only one social site may blur the distinctions and subtleties that a comparative study illuminates. That is, a social phenomenon may differ by social class; and indeed similar (or the same) phenomena may have different meanings in different social contexts.

This study has suggested, as well, that there are class conflicts in educational knowledge and its distribution. We can see class conflict in the struggle to impose the knowledge of powerful groups on the working class and in student resistance to this class-based curriculum. We can see class conflict in the contradictions within and between school knowledge and its economic and personal values, and in attempts to impose liberal public attitudes on children of the rich.

Class conflict in education is thus not dormant, nor a relic of an earlier era; nor is the outcome yet determined. No class is certain of victory, and ideological hegemony is not secure. Those who would struggle against ideological hegemony must not confuse working-class powerlessness with apathy, middle-class ideology with its inevitability, or ruling-class power and cultural capital with superior strength or intelligence. Just as blacks were not the happy-go-lucky fellows of former stereotypes, so the working class is not dull or acquiescent, and the rich are not complacent or secure. Indeed, perhaps the most important implication of the present study is that for those of us who are working to transform society, there is much to do, at all levels, in education.

NOTES

1. The study was funded by two grants from Rutgers University Research Council, whose generous support is hereby acknowledged.

2. For further discussion of social class in these terms, see Anyon (1980).

3. This figure is an estimate. According to the Bureau of the Census, only 2.6% of families in the United States had money incomes of $50,000 or over in 1977 (U.S. Bureau of the Census 1979, Table A p. 2). For figures on income at these higher levels, see Smith and Franklin (1974).

4. One might assume from the social studies text chosen by these teachers that their students were some-

what retarded. In fact, the mean IQ of the fifth-grade children for whom the book was chosen was 102; the mean IQ of the fifth graders in the other working-class school was 104 (CBT, McGraw Hill, Short Form). [Mean IQ in the middle-class school fifth grades was 105; in the affluent professional, 117; and in the executive elite, 120 (Otis-Lennun).] (Seven fifth graders in the working-class fifth grades combined had IQs that indicated above-average intelligence: 129, 139, 125, 133, 126, 130, 128. One other boy had tested in the second grade as having an IQ of 140; on the fifth grade test his score was 120.)

It is my opinion (contradicted after completion of the study by the two teachers to whom I offered it) that the reasons for choosing this book were first, its assumption of low ability in the students, and second, the fact that this assumption provides a rationale that makes teaching as work much easier: If the students cannot *do* anything but vocabulary drill and skill work, then we, as teachers, do not have to *plan* anything else. The teachers said they chose the book because it was "easy," and stressed "skills the children need."

5. The value attached to socially approved sources of knowledge was apparent in the reactions of school personnel to my presence in this school. The fifth-grade teachers I observed here acted as if I, as a university professor, was an expert who had the correct answers regarding child development, curriculum, and discipline. This can be contrasted with the attitude of other teachers in other schools. For example, both fifth- and second-grade teachers in the working-class schools let me know (albeit, subtly) that I, as a non-practitioner, "couldn't tell *them* anything!" Teachers in the affluent and executive elite schools had a different attitude. They were receptive to me as a researcher, but they had district "experts" and their own ideas regarding teaching methods. The principal said that all their in-service workshops were done by "nationally known people." The fifth-grade teachers in the middle-class school, on the other hand, asked me lots of questions about what is best in reading, classroom management, and the like. Their tone of voice suggested to me that they wanted and expected me to know what they should do. (The questioning stopped, of course, as I declined to answer, and as I began to make clear to them that I was not there in an advisory capacity.)

6. Stated goals of the *Elementary Science Study* are to encourage children to use science materials to find answers to their own questions in their own ways. The emphasis is not on the teaching of a series of science concepts or on the creation of scientific prodigies, but on relatively unstructured experiences that emphasize "active involvement, freedom to pursue one's own interests, imagination and individuality." The materials are aimed at "developing self-directing, autonomous and self-actualizing individuals." See accounts by Hal (1972) and also Educational Development Center (1971).

In some second- and third-grade classrooms I noticed *Science—A Process Approach* (SAPA) materials on shelves. Five of the eight teachers in k–3 said that they didn't use these materials, that they did science "on their own," or "informally"; the other three reported that they did use the SAPA materials.

7. Reading in the working-class and middle-class schools was not individualized at any level [they did, however, use a *programmed* reading series (Sullivan Programmed Readers) in the early grades]. None of the boxed reading programs mentioned as used in the affluent professional school was in any of the working-class or middle-class schools except for SRA. An SRA kit was available in all classrooms I visited. The teachers in the working-class schools said they did not use it. A teacher in one of the working-class schools said she didn't use it "because the kids cheat." In the middle-class school, one teacher used her SRA *Power Builder* and another skills kit from SRA that she got because she lied, by telling the state "comped" person that she had more students eligible than she did. She says she has the kids use the kits once a week because "it's fun, and they like it"; also, "so I don't miss any skills." I asked four other teachers in the fourth and fifth grades in the middle-class school, and they said they did not use their SRAs; one teacher stated, "It's too much trouble."

8. My request to include in this study (i.e., in 1978–1979) the school that had the majority of the town's blacks and most of the low-income whites was denied by the Board of Education.

9. See Hugh Munby's (1979) critique of the program which appeared in *Curriculum Inquiry* 9:3.

10. The quote and descriptions are taken from Mayor's (1972) account. See also American Association for the Advancement of Science (1972).

11. An interesting contrast here is that during the same week, in one working-class fifth grade I saw copies of *My Weekly Reader* in several children's desks. On the cover were striking truck drivers, and the lead story asked. "Do workers have the right to strike?" (The article suggested that they did.) I asked the teacher if he had used that issue with his class and he said, "No, some of them did the puzzle, but they just throw it away."

12. During interviews of children in other schools I asked if they knew what strikes were (practically all did) and if they thought strikes were right or wrong. In the working-class schools 13 of 20 said yes, strikes were right ("people have the right to strike"); five said "strikes are wrong"; two said "sometimes they're right." In the middle-class school seven said strikes were right; eight said strikes were wrong; and three said, "sometimes." In the affluent professional school two said strikes were "OK" and "Yes, they're all right"; eight said strikes were wrong, and nine said, "It depends."

13. It is at this point that I would make sure that it is understood that I do not intend the themes reported in the schools to be monolithic; no theme purports to include every child. There were subcultures or groups in all of the schools (e.g., there were children in the working-class schools who did not resist, and children in the middle-class school who did resist and who were cynical about their "possibilities.") It is not possible here, however, to include all data and all interpretations. I must choose what is most representative, or what appears to be significant for some other reason. The subculture in the executive elite school appears to me to have significance because it was so strong and yet involved a clear minority of children.

14. It is interesting to note (as information that supports my interpretation of a "perspicacious" working class) that several academic surveys in the 1960s (reported in Zinn 1980) showed that in 1964 (before students and intellectuals had discovered the Vietnam War) and throughout the war, Americans with only a grade-school education were much stronger for withdrawal from the war than Americans with a college education. Zinn argues that "the regular polls, based on samplings, underestimated the opposition to the war among lower-class people" (p. 482). Just as the earliest anti-Vietnam protests came out of the Civil Rights movement as blacks began being drafted, so opposition was stronger earlier in working-class com-

munities as young men from these communities were drafted.

REFERENCES

AMERICAN ASSOCIATION FOR THE ADVANCEMENT OF SCIENCE. *Science—a process approach: Purposes, accomplishements, expectations.* (AAAS Miscellaneous Publication no. 67-12, September 1967). Lexington, Mass.: American Association for the Advancement of Science, 1972.

ANYON, JEAN. "Elementary social studies textbooks and legitimating knowledge." *Theory and Research in Social Education* 6, no. 3 (September 1978): 40–55.

———. "Education, social 'structure' and the power of individuals." *Theory and Research in Social Education* 7, no. 1 (Spring 1979): 49–60. (a)

———. "Ideology and United States history textbooks." *Harvard Educational Review* 49, no. 3 (August 1979): 361–386. (b)

———. "Social class and the hidden curriculum of work." *Journal of Education* 162, no. 1 (Winter 1980): 67–92.

———. "Schools as agencies of social legitimation." *Journal of Curriculum Theorizing,* to appear.

APPLE, MICHAEL. *Ideology and curriculum.* Boston: Routledge and Kegan Paul, 1979.

BERNSTEIN, RICHARD. *The restructuring of social and political theory.* Philadelphia: University of Pennsylvania Press, 1978.

BOWLES, SAMUEL, and GINTIS, HERBERT. *Schooling in capitalist America: Educational reform and the contradictions of economic life.* New York: Basic Books, 1976.

EDUCATIONAL DEVELOPMENT CENTER. *A working guide to the elementary science study.* Newton, Mass.: Educational Development Center, 1971.

FITZGERALD, FRANCES. *America revised.* Boston: Little, Brown, 1979.

FOX, THOMAS, and HESS, ROBERT. *An analysis of social conflict in social studies textbooks.* Final Report, Project no. II-116. Washington, D.C.: United States Department of Health, Education and Welfare, 1972.

GIROUX, HENRY. "Schooling and the culture of positivism: Notes on the 'death' of history." *Educational Theory,* to appear.

GOULDNER, ALVIN. *The future of intellectuals and the rise of the new class.* New York: Seabury Press, 1979.

HAL, CHRISTOPHER. "Elementary science study." In *The eighth report of the National Clearinghouse on Science and Mathematics Curricular Development,* edited by David Lockard. Baltimore, Md.: University of Maryland, 1972.

JACOBY, RUSSELL. *Social amnesia.* Boston: Beacon Press, 1975.

KARABEL, JEROME. "Community colleges and social stratification." *Harvard Educational Review* 42. no. 4 (November 1972): 521–562.

————, and HALSEY, A.H. *Power and ideology in education.* New York: Oxford University Press. 1977.

MAYOR, JOHN. "Science—a process approach." In *The eighth report of the National Clearinghouse on Science and Mathematics Curricular Development,* edited by David Lockard. Baltimore, Md.: University of Maryland, 1972.

MUNBY, HUGH. "Philosophy for children: An example of curriculum review and criticism." *Curriculum Inquiry* 9, no. 3 (Fall 1979): 229–249.

ROSENBAUM, JAMES. *Making inequality: The hidden curriculum of high school tracking.* New York: Wiley, 1976.

SMITH, JAMES, and FRANKLIN, STEPHAN. "The concentration of personal wealth, 1922–1969." *American Economic Review* 64, no. 4 (May 1974): 162–167.

UNITED STATES BUREAU OF THE CENSUS. "Money income in 1977 of families and persons in the United States." In *Current population reports,* Series P-60, no. 118. Washington, D.C.: United States Government Printing Office, 1979

YOUNG, MICHAEL, and WHITTY, GEOFF. *Society, state and schooling.* Sussex, England: Falmer Press, 1977.

ZINN, HOWARD. A people's history of the United States. New York: Harper and Row, 1980.

Becoming Clerical Workers: Business Education and the Culture of Femininity

LINDA VALLI

The purpose of this chapter is to map out the relation between the ideological messages of a high-school office education program regarding appropriate sex roles and gendered subjectivity, and the cultural orientations of a group of primarily working-class girls.[1] The chapter delineates the ways in which the young women acquire a basically feminine work identity, the role of the school program in strengthening that identity, and the manner in which educational practices can reinforce or contribute to the reproduction of a sexually divided labor force, in which men and women not only fill different occupations, but have different relations to wage and domestic labor as well.[2]

Since boys generally select themselves out of vocational preparation for office work before their high-school years, I was not able to study the gender-based occupational selection process.[3] I focus exclusively on the production and reproduction of gender-related meanings, behaviors, and orientations that make up the world of the office worker.

Although this chapter falls into the broad category of the study of socialization processes, I attempt to avoid a basic flaw of that approach. I do not presume that the messages that are taught or transmitted to students are the ones that are received or accepted. This assumption creates a model of the world that is far more static than reality, and produces agents who are passive recipients of their own "internalized structures." Following the models of Willis and McRobbie, I reject this concept of socialization, replacing it with a notion of cultural orientations that implies involvement by individuals and groups in the ongoing creation of their own identities, in a way that is neither mechanistic nor wholly voluntaristic, but is rooted in their social and economic pasts and in their perceived futures.[4]

Three general relations to cultural reproduction processes seem possible: acceptance, negotiation, and resistance.[5] Although it is difficult to predict which relationship will be chosen, certain factors appear to structure the choices. Acceptance of specific aspects of culture (in this situation, gender-related work aspects) tends to occur when these messages are congruent with the past and the perceived future, and when no alternatives are perceived. Negotiation and resistance, both of which imply rejection of the cultural messages and practices, occur when there is an element of incongruity, when the culture is experienced as imposed, when it does not fit with a sense of self. Negotiation will be the chosen course of action when the individual or group perceives some element of control or power over the situation, and when the struggle seems worth the effort. Resistance is chosen when, from the participants' point of view, there is no room to negotiate. In this particular context, overt resistance can take such varied forms as saying no to a directive given by a boss or teacher, entering into argumentation, or quitting a job. Covert or hidden resistance is the chosen course of action when the person or group involved is unwilling to bear the

---

Source: *"Becoming Clerical Workers: Business Education and the Culture of Femininity" by Linda Valli from* Ideology and Schooling, *edited by Michael Apple and Lois Weis, copyright 1983. Reprinted by permission of Temple University Press.*

consequences of overt resistance, consequences such as being fired. Hidden resistance looks like passive acceptance only to the outsider.

As the details of this ethnographic study suggest, the ideological messages the students received were fairly congruent with the gender-specific patterns and relations they had become accustomed to both in their homes and at school. Their primary mode of behavior, therefore, was to accept, almost to fall naturally and spontaneously into, a sexual division of labor and the subordinate roles for women it implies. In the process of elaborating their lives at work, the students utilized a fairly conventional culture of femininity that identified them not as raw labor power, but as sex objects, on the one hand, and as office wives and mothers, on the other. In so doing, they partially realized (in the dual sense of created and were aware of) their double subordination, in domestic labor and in wage labor. But because this awareness was only partial, and because they saw no alternative, they tended to fantasize an ideal future in which they worked part time and stayed home part time, regardless of the fact that this solution would only strengthen their subordination, keeping them dependent on a male provider and condemning them to low-level positions in the job market.[6]

This chapter develops by giving a brief account of the methodology employed in the study, and descriptions of the cooperative office education program, the teacher, and the students upon which it is based. The main part of the chapter is devoted to an account of those parts of the program that emphasized a work identity that was gender specific, the ways in which the students dealt with those messages, and the implications of those practices.

METHODOLOGY

The analysis presented here is based on an ethnographic study of a cooperative office education program, a vocational program in which senior high students go to school part time and work part time in an office. This methodology was selected because I was interested in analyzing the processes of cultural transmission. I focused on a group of senior high-school students who were being prepared for office work because I was primarily concerned with women's acquisition of a work identity. Since office occupations employ the largest single group of the female labor force, and since many of the areas are currently expanding, office education was the compelling choice for this study.

The data were collected during the 1980-81 school year. The site was a comprehensive, urban high school, which I will call Woodrow High, in a Midwestern city. I was present at Woodrow from September through June on approximately half the school days, scattered throughout the year. Three related techniques were used to collect the data: participant observation in the school and at work (fourteen sites in all); formal and informal interviewing, throughout the year, of significant subjects (for example, teachers, students, supervisors, alumnae and coworkers); and analysis of curricular materials and other related documents. These techniques allowed me to study the transmission of ideological messages and to understand why students accepted, negotiated, or resisted attempts to socialize them in certain ways.

In addition to sixteen students, I interviewed seventeen alumnae: ten from the previous graduating class and seven from the years 1972 to 1979. My goal was threefold: to obtain more information on family backgrounds and influences, since I had no direct contact with parents; to collect reflective accounts of their decision to take, and their experiences within, cooperative office education; and to obtain information on work life and perspectives after high school. I anticipated that these accounts would both confirm and elaborate upon the information I was gathering from my work within the school, and this expectation was realized.

THE PROGRAM

Cooperative education is a specific form of vocational education, that, unlike most educational programs, which take place primarily within school buildings, alternates work experience with school experience. Students receive help in finding career-related jobs and are to receive on-the-job, as well as classroom, training. The implicit rationale of the program is that the work site is a valuable source of learning and should be utilized as an educational tool. The stated expectation is that cooperative education will help students identify their career objectives, that this identification will lead to appropriate training in attitudes, skills, and knowledge, and that the training will lead to careers. These careers are then supposed to create a better community, a community that will "experience a productive growth of its citizens, schools and businesses."

The cooperative office education program at Woodrow High was organized in a fairly typical manner. During their senior year, students who selected the program attended classes in the morning and worked for three to four and a half hours in the afternoon. They received both one school credit and pay for their work. Both students and teacher believed that at least two credits should be given for work. In their behavior and in their conversations with me, work was a far more salient aspect of the cooperative experience than what went on in the classroom.

Students were supposed to carry three morning classes in addition to the "related" office education class, which was specifically designed to relate to their afternoon work experience. This class was scheduled to meet five times a week for forty minutes each day. Students would often miss class, excused or not, but would report for work that afternoon. Four times a year, the teacher (referred to here as Mrs. Shapiro) met with each supervisor for a student evaluation session. Within a day or two, Mrs. Shapiro would then meet with each student in her private office to discuss the evaluation.

While a full analysis of cultural reproduction mechanisms would have to take all aspects of the curriculum into consideration, it should be apparent from the above description that in this particular context too much attention to the formal corpus of knowledge would distort rather than illuminate the ideological messages actually conveyed and received. The fact is that although most of the formal syllabus was organized around the teaching of particular skills (for example,

how to reconcile a checkbook, how to fill out tax forms, how to type using a dictaphone, how to proofread), in actual practice little class time was devoted to concentrated work in these areas, and the development of these skills was not the primary concern of either the teacher or the students. During interviews with the teacher, the students, and the graduates, the same refrain was consistently repeated.

> I don't attempt to teach much in the class because, unlike the other city high schools, we have a junior prerequisite. I'm also less demanding in this class than in my others because the students and I spend a long time together. I'm more relaxed in here because I want to build up personal relationships. I see myself as more in a counselor's role.
> —Mrs. Shapiro

> The hour in school seemed wasted. We didn't discuss problems at work and what we were doing. That's what I thought it would be like—saying what problems we had at work and discussing what we could do about them.
> —Kathryn '80

> I don't think I'd want the class part again. I don't think it taught that much. I don't think there needs to be a class part. It doesn't help that much in the jobs most of us are in. I don't see the point of having it.
> —Dorothy '81

> My parents thought I was skipping when I got home early. They didn't believe she was letting us out, or that there was nothing to do.
> —Jane '80

My contention is that the absence of a rigid syllabus created a gap, a space that was filled with incidental teaching and learning. The absence of an overt curriculum created a situation in which the messages students received from casual comments, relationships, school and work structures and practices were stronger than they would otherwise have been.

THE TEACHER

Mrs. Shapiro had been directing the program at Woodrow High for twelve years. She perceived herself and introduced herself as a feminist, as a person who believed in and worked toward women's equality with men, particularly in the business world. Having had parents who encouraged her to succeed just as much as they encouraged her brothers, Mrs. Shapiro belonged to numerous professional and women's organizations, and had a life history that was very much career oriented. She was married, the mother of two, and, at the time of the study, a recent grandmother.

Mrs. Shapiro was quite verbal about her feminism. On the bulletin board in her office was the saying "All discrimination against all women must be removed" and Erica Jong's poem "Woman Enough." When the principal distributed the faculty roster, she confronted him over the asterisks placed after the names of married women. A new roster was distributed the next day with the asterisks removed. During class time, she told the students she considered the term "Gentlemen" to be an inappropriate salutation since the unknown addressees could be women and, during a filing unit, she told the class that the formulation "Mrs. John Smith" was incorrect, that a woman always kept her own first name.

Because of Mrs. Shapiro's feminist orientation, this case study should be one of the strongest in testing the school's role in the reproduction of a culture of femininity in the labor force and the reinforcement of traditional, sex-typed work orientations. Since gender-related occupational training definitely and explicitly occurred in this situation, I infer that it also occurs in a large percentage of other office education programs in secondary schools across the country.

THE STUDENTS

Although an elite subdivision is within its catchment area and it draws its students from a wide range of social class backgrounds, Woodrow High is located in the industrial part of town and is basically considered a working-class high school. The seniors who elected cooperative office education did not seem any different from their female counterparts who did not. A few were unusually wealthy; a few were unusually bright. One of the

graduates I interviewed was the valedictorian of her class. She went on to take the two-year Executive Secretary course at the community college. Some of the students went on to four-year universities, but the vast majority stayed in office work, occasionally supplementing their preparation with community college or on-the-job training.

Many of the students had mothers, and sometimes older sisters, who had worked in offices. This work was often done on a part-time basis, or had been returned to once families had been raised. Mothers who did not work in offices tended to be employed as sales clerks or cafeteria workers. The fathers of the students, on the other hand, generally had histories of full-time manual labor or civil-service work; most of them were loading-dock workers, mechanics, truck drivers, factory workers, or building custodians. A few students had fathers who were mail carriers or police officers; one father was a high-school teacher, and one was listed as an industrial engineer although he had never been to college.

The division of labor in the home as well as at the workplace basically followed the traditional sexual patterns. Although, for example, three students mentioned fathers who cooked for the family, in no instance did the activity flow out of a basic role identity. In one case, the mother had suffered a mental breakdown and had been institutionalized. The father, thereafter, assumed the role of housekeeper. In another instance, the father started sharing the responsibility for cooking with his high-school daughters after his wife had died. In the third instance, the father had been retired for some time because of disability. Gourmet cooking had become a hobby for him.

The usual pattern, however, was the mother-as-homemaker. Not even a working mother and retired father guaranteed that the father would partake in routine housekeeping chores. In these cases, the running of the vacuum cleaner once a week seemed to vindicate the father, in his own eyes at least.

But the fact that students came from homes with a traditional division of labor did not necessarily mean that these practices were automatically internalized. Some of the students had older sisters whose marriages did not follow the traditional pattern of their parents, others took child-development or other classes in school that raised the possibility of other marital patterns. One student, for instance, who tenaciously clung to a strict sexual division of wage labor ideology, arguing that "men are stronger than women and that's just the way it should be," simultaneously argued that men should help with everything in the house, although her own father did not, because that was the way her mother said it should be and that was what her brother-in-law did.

The reverse situation also obtained: some students envisioned a world in which women had better jobs than men without it being harmful to business or to personal relationships, and yet believed in the dominance of the man in the home. As one graduate put it,

> I like men paying for my food and opening doors for me. All this stuff about keeping your own name and being equal to your husband, I don't go for.
> —Jane '80

To a few of the students, there seemed to be a fairly clear distinction between gender relations in wage labor and those in personal relations and domestic labor; they saw no need for congruence between the two.

Such were the sex-role orientations with which the students began the cooperative office education program. Because of these orientations, the students were predisposed to accept a work world that men and women related to in naturally different manners. Their job training and work experiences reaffirmed this basic sexual division of labor ideology.

THE OFFICE WORKER AS SEX OBJECT

Messages about sexual appearance and sexual behavior were integral elements of the students' office education training both at school and in the workplace. On the level of appearance and self-presentation, the young women were encouraged to emphasize and use their gender identities. But on the level of practice, when it came to actual behavior, they were warned to control their sexuality. The subtle message was that they would be blamed if sexual improprieties occurred at work.

In terms of their mode of self-presentation, students were informed in numerous ways of how important it was to cultivate a feminine, even provocative, appearance if they were serious about getting a job and being promoted once they had a job. Early in the school year, for instance, a woman from a job placement center spoke to the students about interviewing, stressing the importance of their appearance:

> Look professional. Your best source for that is *Glamour* magazine. It regularly runs sections for the professional woman: her image, what to wear, how to get a job. Dress like you already have the job, like you would to find a boyfriend. That's a good parallel. You have to attract someone.

Later that week, Mrs. Shapiro re-emphasized how important it was for the students to sell themselves at an interview. In encouraging them to listen calmly and collect their thoughts before they answered a question in order to organize their ideas and speak intelligently she used the phrase, "just like the finalists in the Miss America contest."

This association of job with sexual attraction was graphically depicted throughout the year by an advertisement on a classroom bulletin board. Although the overt purpose of the bulletin board display was to show examples of new office machines and technology, in so doing, it also presented a certain image of women office workers. The most striking example was the advertisement for Dictaphone's Dual Display Word Processor. In an attempt to encourage readers (presumably male managers) to purchase Dictaphone's new equipment, the creator of this advertisement cleverly equated obsolete office equipment with the Stone Age and used a photograph of a young attractive woman clad only in a leopard skin to demonstrate the point. Because this picture was displayed without comment in a business classroom of a public school, it seems that an unspoken approval or legitimation of the image was necessarily conveyed.

The issue of appearance was also regularly discussed during Mrs. Shapiro's evaluation sessions with supervisors. Appearance, was, in fact, one of the criteria on the formal student-trainee evaluation report, which included such items as quality and quantity of work, attitude, attendance, reliability. On the evaluation sheet, appearance was defined in a sex-neutral way as "neatness and personal care, appropriateness to the job." But in conversation Mrs. Shapiro often added a gender-specific element:

> You might do her a favor. She's a pretty girl. She could do a lot with herself and I don't think she's doing it. A lot of women in businesses are making appearance an important part of their day. She could capitalize on that. She puts herself together very nicely. She was wearing some very sexy shoes the other day.

While not forbidden, clogs and slacks, particularly those cut like men's, which were the fashion at the time, were frowned upon. One supervisor talked about how her student-trainee had a figure for skirts, not slacks, how slacks put twenty pounds on her, and how you could see the look of disgust on the older men's faces when young women came to work dressed casually. Appearance, she said, was a definite factor in promotability, even for a woman who was extremely capable.

The accuracy of this perception was born out in the students' experiences with job placement. One student's difficulties in finding a job best highlight the employment obstacles some women are faced with. By the end of their first two weeks in the cooperative program all the students in the class had found jobs, except one. This student, Dorothy, stood out from the rest of the class in that she was overweight and, while always neat, dressed in old, inexpensive jeans, blouses, and shoes. Not until the end of the second month of school did Dorothy find a job. Unlike the other students, who all found afternoon jobs, Dorothy was hired for an evening shift in an assembly-line type department of a large insurance company with no public contact.

Mrs. Shapiro explained to me during those initial weeks that she was not able to place Dorothy very fast because her business background was slim and her appearance poor. In fact, however, Dorothy had more business background than many of the students in the class, had the third highest senior class rank among the cooperative office education students, and had taken a more rigorous academic program than the two students who were ranked ahead of her. In an eleventh grade standardized test, Dorothy had placed in the 99th percentile for math computation and in the 90th for math concepts. She was one of the fastest, most accurate typists in the class, and was the only student who took classroom work home to finish. The other students were apparently quick to perceive her capabilities, for they often went to her for help on their own work. It became clear that her mode of self-presentation was the only reason she was experiencing difficulty in finding a job.

One of the places to which Dorothy applied was a small bookstore, where she was turned down in favor of Cynthia, a tall, slender model-type. I was told later in the year by a graduate (a nice-looking, but plain, honor roll student who had also been rejected for the job in favor of a more attractive but less capable student) that the man in charge of hiring at the bookstore had a "penchant" for a certain type of female employee—blond and well built. Nor did this appear to be an isolated example. Mrs. Shapiro told the class that a bank employer called one day a few years back to complain that she was not sending him very pretty girls.

These examples indicate that there is not only a dual labor market, in which men and women fill different occupational categories, but that there is also a dual market within women's work. Apparently, not only are women primarily relegated to lower-level jobs, but certain types of women are excluded from the best of even these jobs.

Cultivation of a feminine appearance is only one aspect of the situation that women must deal with, for they must learn not only how to cultivate their femininity, but how to control it as well. Sheila Rowbotham makes this point in *Woman's Consciousness, Man's World*, when she says that a certain "contained sexuality" is required as part of the office worker's job.[7] Both

Mrs. Shapiro and the students seemed to understand this requirement.

During a classroom discussion of a magazine article on the topic of sexual harassment this issue of "contained sexuality" arose. Mrs. Shapiro stressed the importance of an appropriate degree and type of sexual conduct on the job. While on the other occasions she had been subtly encouraging the students to present themselves with a certain amount of "sexiness," on this particular day she highlighted the importance of knowing what the limits should be if they wanted to avoid detrimental consequences. She told them they would be asking for abuse if they were too timid to control the situation or if they wore attire that was too skimpy, giving signals that they wanted to be noticed. She cautioned them to be aware of what they were communicating through their dress and bodies, indicating an awareness that their sexuality was not only something they could use to gain job benefits but was also something that could be used against them.

In order to make the most of opportunities on the job, then, young workers apparently have to be skilled not only in running typewriters and photocopiers, but in monitoring their sexuality and sexual lives as well. But in case workers do not internalize the "proper" sexual code, companies often have either formal or informal policies about social and sexual relations.

One personnel department, for example, discouraged employees from dating each other. If two employees married, one had to quit the job; that was official company policy. (The one who quit was generally the woman, of course, since she typically had the lower-paying job.)

Eleanor, a 1980 graduate, told the story of a bachelorette party for female employees held at a local bar. As part of the entertainment, a young male employee clad in bikini underwear and bow leapt out of a gift box during the course of the evening. He ended up quitting his job shortly thereafter because of the treatment he was receiving from his supervisor because of the incident, treatment that included a demotion.

Needless to say, students and employees did not always appreciate or accept attempts to control their sexual identities and practices. One student, for instance, explicitly rejected the "image of the secretary" that was conveyed to her. As she put it,

> Mrs. Shapiro had this obsession with secretaries looking gorgeous. Getting up at 5:00 in the morning to do their hair and nails. She taught us a lot about appearance, eye contact, interviews, dressing up. I thought that was good, but you don't have to put on all that make-up. Cleanliness is the important thing.
> —Jane '80

Most students, however, did not verbalize any opposition to suggestions that were made about their appearance. But in their nonverbal behavior, in the manner in which they actually dressed for work, there were indications that they, like many office workers, were not passively accepting imposed standards, but were negotiating and creating their own style. This style combined the popular men's cut slacks with open toed, spiked, "sexy" shoes. It was a definite blend of a unisex work look with a feminine social look, and appeared to be an attempt to control the issue of appearance while still emphasizing sexuality.

Resistance to company definition and control of their identities as women workers was also exemplified in a widely distributed cartoon graphic. The graphic simply added two words and a visual to the universal phone memo that is the staple of the secretary's office life. The originally staid and official memo thus read, "While you were out fucking off . . ." and displayed a naked boss "making it" with an extremely buxom nude woman. The term "fucking off" here obviously connotes both sexual intercourse and screwing around, having fun, wasting time, using company time for personal pleasure. It thus attacks both the sexual and the work identity of the boss, projecting onto him the demeaning identity women office workers feel is at times attributed to them.

But all in all, most of the students seemed to internalize definitions of themselves as women workers that took into account traditional notions of feminine appearance. Many of the reasons they could or could not imagine themselves doing certain jobs hinged on physical criteria.

> I would never be a mechanic. You get messy. I really like to fly and travel and I like to meet new people, but you have to have a lot of qualifications to be a stewardess. You have to be tall and skinny. They want you to be really perfect.
> —Kris '81

> I'm not into all that liberated stuff. I still want to be pampered. I don't want muscles or to get dirty.
> —Debbie '80

> I thought of being an airline stewardess, but I weighed too much. You have to only weigh 120 or something.
> —Jennifer '80

> I can't imagine myself getting my hands all gooey, being sweaty and dirty all the time.
> —Tanya '80

> I wouldn't want to work in a garage—to be a mechanic. I wouldn't want to come home greasy.
> —Priscilla '79

So, although there was some disagreement, resistance, and negotiation about the exact amount and type of "femininity" women office workers should cultivate and display, there was basic agreement on a more fundamental level. In general, a gender-specific, feminine appearance that could be contrasted to a masculine appearance was accepted and adopted.

This internalization of a gender-specific identity, an identity defined in many ways in relation to men, was strikingly evident in graffiti written on a sign posted on one of the company's bulletin boards. The sign announced "Fun and games" at a Women's Christmas Party. The graffiti responded, "How can we have fun without men?" and "Who are we going to play games with?" While obviously acting to reject what they perceived to be the company's attempt to control their social and sexual lives, the women, at one and the same time, affirmed and reinforced their dependence on men. They could not visualize an identity, or even an activity, for themselves apart from a relation to men. What they appear to object to is not their subordination to men, but to interference

from the company in the way they acted out that identity.

THE OFFICE WORKER AS WIFE AND MOTHER

A second way in which office work roles were linked to the students' gender identity was through an association of office work with domestic labor, either through the equation of the work with women's work in the home or through the subordination of their role in the office to their role in the home.

The observation has often been made that the role of women in the office parallels their role in the home: picking up after men; doing the daily, repetitive, tedious housekeeping tasks; and keeping men's lives organized and undisturbed, so they can concentrate on their important work. Quoting a 1935 *Fortune* magazine article, Margery Davies claims that male bosses preferred women over "pushy young men" as office workers because, as *Fortune* stated, women "are capable of making the office a more pleasant, peaceful, and homelike place."[8] Taking on this kind of work, which has changed little in half a century, deepens women's wage labor identity as secondary and peripheral, for it patterns a gendered subjectivity already deeply etched into their day-to-day existence.

The objective structuring of these asymmetrical roles, of male leading roles and female serving roles, was already so much taken for granted in the students' lives that they were unable to even perceive it. One young graduate told me that during high school "everyone wants to be a cheerleader." She naturally presumed that in this context I would know "everyone" meant "every girl," so that she did not have to make it explicit. In much the same way, the students took the sexual division of labor they found in their offices for granted. During an interview of a graduate who had worked in the same department of the same large corporation for almost two years, I asked her to mention the types of jobs that were filled by men, by women, or by both men and women. After reflecting for a few moments, she said,

All of the big bosses are men. I've never noticed that before, but that's the way it is. And all the secretaries are females . . . and all the key punch operators are ladies. I've never thought of that before.
—Eleanor '80

At another workplace, a student made daily mail runs, picking up and delivering mail to every office in the building. On the desk of each employee was a name plate. The typical nameplate for a female employee read, "Beth," "Jo," "Susie," or "Pat." The typical male employee's nameplate was "Mr. Mott," "Mr. Gleeson," or "Mr. J. L. Stone." When I brought the distinction to the student's attention it was again apparent it was something she had never really noticed; she said almost in passing,

> I don't think there is anything behind the difference. I think it's just a matter of preference.
> —Donna '81

The relation of the woman office worker's status to that of the male worker was objectified in the structure of the workplace as well as in how the workers were addressed. Men often had offices that were private or closed off, in contrast to the public work areas of the women.[9] Even if women had their own desks, they were generally grouped together in a large, open space. About eight or nine of the places at which students worked were fairly large bureaucracies housed on more than one building level. Inevitably, when this was the case, status differentials were structured into the floor on which one's office was located. So, when referring to bosses, workers would naturally employ expressions like,

> I don't know if there are any ladies up there—up at the very top.
> —Dorothy '81
>   One of the big bosses who sits upstairs is over him.
> —Eleanor '80

These linguistic expressions reinforce notions of superiority and inferiority that are so naturally linked with the English concepts of up/down, high/low, over/under, and top/bottom.

While the students often watched upper-level, male employees taking work home, having their work lives spill over into their home lives, so to speak, they usually saw the converse in the lives of the women with whom they worked. These women often worked only part-time so that they could see their children off to school in the mornings and be home before the school day ended. They often brought in candy or cookies to sell for their children's scout troop or hung homemade skeletons they had constructed in their role as den mother. Sometimes they had to take a temporary maternity leave or had to quit work altogether because they were no longer able to juggle working and child care, even though the family needed the money. One of the students vividly recalled how her mother was fired from her clerical job years before because she and her siblings kept walking over to her office (located just blocks from their home) to visit, ask questions, or get permissions.

In many ways, then, the identity of women office workers seems to be closely linked with their identity and work in the home. This was underscored for the students at the Appreciation Banquet given by the class in honor of their supervisors. The two main speeches were given by the teacher and by a retiring supervisor, Mrs. Carter, who was held in high esteem by coworkers, the teacher, and the numerous students whom she had supervised over the years. In both speeches, reference was made to the woman worker as mother. Mrs. Carter told the group:

> My first family was all raised and scattered around the country. I thought my parenting days were over. Then, six years ago, I began a second family. And in six years I've had forty-two offspring.

Mrs. Shapiro's speech was filled primarily with appreciative remarks to those at the banquet who had contributed to the success of the program. A special note of thanks was addressed to Mrs. Carter.

> They gained so much from being in your office. You became the mother at work that I was in school.

It is difficult to imagine male supervisors or teachers so naturally using paternal imagery in speaking about their work relationship to male apprentices.

Mrs. Shapiro also underscored her own identity as mother by knitting baby clothes during class time and used traditional notions about sex-appropriate behavior by advising the students not to express "emotionalism" if they wanted to rise up the corporate ladder, and not to shout, since "it's not ladylike." One of their texts warned them not to "chit-chat" during the workday, since it wasted their employer's dollars.

Another teaching aid, a filmstrip, similarly reinforced traditional notions of the sexual division of labor. Titled "Telephone Impressions," the filmstrip was geared to teaching students good phone techniques: courtesy, clear speaking, and promptness. Mrs. Shapiro made a point of telling the class that although the filmstrip was excellent at demonstrating good phone usage, the school system could not purchase it, because it was sexist. All the examples of the wrong way to answer the phone, she elaborated, were delivered by a male voice; all the correct examples were delivered by a female voice. Therefore, the filmstrip had an antimale bias. It should have portrayed mistakes being made equally by the man and the woman.

It appeared to me, however, that there was a deeper, more subtle sexism at work in the filmstrip. The incorrect phone manner was not just a male voice, it was an authoritative, busy, important-sounding male voice, one that was irritated that it had to be bothered by answering the phone. The female voice, on the other hand, sounded trained for the job: that was her proper work and the task for which she was perfectly suited. Far from being antimale, the filmstrip reinforced the age-old notion that men have more important things to do than answer the phone. Since women are not doing anything of value, they are the ones who should be constantly interrupted to screen and direct messages.

At some of the workplaces women workers were beginning to resist this traditional telephone role, requesting the installation of a decentralized phone system where each person would have to take his or her own messages. Mrs. Carter was one supervisor who was adamant about this. Shortly after she was hired as an executive secretary, she told her boss to take the phones away or she would leave the job. She resented the burden of answering her boss's phone, claiming that if women were relieved of that kind of task they would be freer to do "the administrative work that men won't let women do." Office workers were also starting to resist the secretary's traditional task of serving coffee. Maureen, for example, was startled when a boss asked if she had offered coffee to the men who had arrived for a business meeting. She responded in surprise, "No, was I supposed to?" Her boss replied, "You bet you are, and do it with a smile, too." Maureen characterized this attitude as chauvinistic, but when she checked with other office workers and was told it was appropriate for her to be asked to do that task, she was reluctant to say anything because she feared it would turn people against her, and affect the way she felt about working there. So, even though she thought she would "raise a ruckus" if she were an older worker, employed full time, and if the practice were habitual, because of her structural relationship to the job she ended up complying with the direction.

But, all in all, just as the students partially accept sexuality as a criterion of themselves as office workers, so do they tend to accept being defined as man's helper, as his office wife. Some students saw this as a natural division of labor, some as a social division, and some seemed unable to distinguish between the two.

Office work is mostly for women because it's typing and a lot of guys don't like to type. Filing and receptionist, that's more for girls too, because that's secretary work and girls are secretaries, you know.
—Kris '81

I guess there aren't any boys in the class because the role of secretary has almost always been all women. Probably because it's traditional for the man to be the boss.
—Katrina '81

Women shouldn't do construction work. Men are stronger and that's just the way it should be. Secretary jobs are probably for women mostly. That's just the way things are.
—Terri '81

Boys don't take the class because boys aren't secretaries. They're more into manual labor. That's just today's society. Men don't sit and push pencils. Being a secretary is a girl's job.
—Marion '80

A guy should be the boss. I can't see a lady telling a guy what to do. He'd probably be bigger than her. . . . I'm not used to a lady boss. I mean, you don't see it on television. There a man is always the boss. And that's just the way I think it should be. Sure, there could be a lady doing Robert's job, but that wouldn't be right.
—Cynthia '81

What "is" often became equated with what "should be" and, surprisingly enough, as late as 1981 many of these eighteen- to twenty-year-olds had not seriously considered alternatives. In fact, the ideology of the sexual division of labor remained so strong that many of the students continued to advance arguments that their everyday experiences clearly contradicted (for example, seeing men who pushed pencils, having women as bosses).

When students elaborated on the reasons why men did not or should not do women's work and why women did not or should not do men's work, a striking contrast could be heard. Generally using euphemistic language, they explained that men who ventured into what was traditionally regarded as women's work would be considered homosexual.

I guess there weren't any boys in the class because they have the idea that it's for secretaries and they think boys aren't secretaries. I guess they think a lot of people might get the wrong idea.
—Jessica '80

I really can't picture a man doing a woman's job. My uncle is a nurse, but he's like this [she made a limp-wristed gesture]. That's why it would be hard for guys to have a woman's job. Because it's considered delicate and people might think they're gay.
—Debbie '80

Guys aren't cheerleaders because they think it's too faggy.
—Kathryn '80

I guess guys don't take something like the cooperative office class because they don't think it's

right for them. They think they'd be laughed at—wow, what a weirdo!
—Cynthia '81

It's only in big cities that guys are secretaries; because they're able to get lost or hide more there.
—Doris '81

Doris went on to confirm my interpretation of her statement; if men did office work it meant they were gay; and if they were gay they would naturally want to hide their identity.

On the other hand, the young women who thought that the sexual division of labor should be maintained explained that women who were after men's jobs were trying to be like men or trying to prove their (mistaken) equality.

I don't think ladies should be police or firemen either. They're just trying to show the guys they can do it and have the ability.
—Priscilla '79

On "Real People" they showed two women who were working on the docks doing loading. I'm sure they needed the job, but I think they were also proving a point.
—Debbie '80

I think jobs like construction and firefighters should go to men. Some women are trying to prove they're as equal as men, but the jobs should go to the guy.
—Cynthia '81

According to these students, then, when men do women's work, they are denying or rejecting their masculinity, their natural claim to superiority. They are becoming effeminate. When women try to do men's work, they are not accepting their natural limitations and subordination, but are trying to be as good as men, when in fact they are not.

Just as most of these students had a hard time imagining men and women doing the same wage labor jobs, so too did they find it hard to imagine men and women filling the same domestic labor roles. For them, the notion of women's work automatically meant the primary role in domestic labor. In one way or another, they made it clear that men were the primary breadwinners and they, the women, the primary homemakers and childcarers.

If I were to marry, I would still want to work part time. Otherwise I'd get bored. But I wouldn't want to work full time if my husband were bringing in a good income. There's a lot to do already with housekeeping and kids.
—Jane '80

I can't imagine not working unless I had kids. Then I might stay home until they were in school. But then I'd be bored. The perfect situation would be to work half time.
—Charlotte '77

If I had kids I would sit around the house with them. I wouldn't work. You can tell kids who have been raised by a baby sitter. I don't know if I would let John stay home with them or not. It's not what guys are supposed to do.
—Anne '80

I don't know many guys who would stay home with the kids. It's always been that it's the woman that stays home—because they're the gentle sex. Or that's what I've been told. It's just always been that way.
—Katrina '81

I would like not to be working sometimes. It's hard to come home every evening and just start to do what every housewife has to do. And I'm the one who always has to get the baby off to the sitter.
—Connie '77

I do resent having to have worked all these years, full time, while my kids were little. But there's no way I could have afforded not to. If I were able to find a part time job now, though, I would take it. In fact, I'm looking.
—Mary '71

While they might have been able to imagine themselves having full-time, interesting, or important careers when they were younger or if they were to stay single, the central force directing the students' and graduates' sense of a work identity was the expectation of eventual marriage and family. Interview material from two of the young women illustrates this underlying dynamic.

Kathryn, a 1980 graduate and an accounting student at a major university, was the most career-minded of the students I interviewed. In discussing her future she said,

I want to be independent for my own satisfaction, so I can prove to myself that I can do it, so no one has to take care of me.

She went on, however, to explain that only if she remained single would she ever attempt to be a CPA, an auditor, or the president of a credit union. That type of work, she said, was too stressful to allow other responsibilities as well. Since she definitely wanted a family, she would probably never hold those jobs, but said she would instead look for an accountant's job at a small business or credit union, which would be a good job and offer a good salary "for a woman."

Mary Jo, one of the high-school students, told much the same story from a different perspective. Reflecting on her youthful fantasies rather than her projected future, she explained how she had wanted to be an archeologist when she was in the eighth grade, how she loved to watch accounts of "digs" in various parts of the world. But even at fourteen years of age, she knew that was not practical. She knew that she had to get on with her life: to settle down, get a job, prepare for marriage and a family. So she planned to go to the community college after high school for a degree as an accountant clerk. When I asked why she had decided on a two-year rather than a four-year degree, she responded.

Why should I waste my time in school? I'd rather get going right away and get it over with.

Mary Jo said she had the old-fashioned ambition of raising a couple of children and working part time.

CONCLUSION

Experiencing office work as either secondary to or synonymous with a sexual/home/family identity further marginalized these students' work identities. The culture of femininity associated with office work made it easier for them to be less attached to their work and their workplace than men, who stay in paid employment because they must live up to a masculine ideology of male-as-provider. Women's identities tend to be much less intrinsically linked to wage labor than are men's.

The beliefs the young women had about themselves being inferior workers were, thus, re-inforced by the ideological messages in the class-room and at the work site, and by their structured experiences as office workers and became even more taken for granted as part of their everyday existence. While in some minimal ways the women may have rejected the ideology of male supremacy, at a more fundamental and persistent level, they affirmed it. They conceded legitimacy to the dominance of men in a way that appeared spontaneous and natural. By denying wage labor primacy over domestic labor, they inadvertently consented to and confirmed their own subordina-tion, preparing themselves "for both unskilled, low-paid work and unpaid domestic service."[10]

The women used a culture of femininity to re-sist the impositions of wage labor, not just because work was boring and tedious—as it often is, too, for working-class men—but because it created a double work load. So they refused identities as full-time and serious workers; they resisted being sub-sumed into, and consumed by, capital. But this re-sistance did not change their primary relationships. Ultimately, the women prepared themselves to be-come part-time producers and part-time con-sumers, remaining subordinate to men in the work-place and dependent on them in the home. In this way, office women recreate their own subordinate culture, a culture they have learned to use and ben-efit from, since they see no way to change the ma-terial conditions from which it arises.

REFERENCES

1. I would like to thank Michael Olneck, Michael Apple, and Vandra Masemann for their comments on the draft of this article.

2. An underlying assumption of this article is that while an advanced capitalist economy does not need a sexual division of labor in any absolute sense, a reserve labor force is used to control workers and keep wages down, and is drawn upon in times of economic expan-sion. In a society where patriarchal practices and ide-ologies prevail, where it is seen as natural and right that men are the primary breadwinners and women the child-raisers and husband-supporters, the logical group to be that reserve wage labor is women. They can move in and out of the wage labor force with the least distur-bance and least strain to the economy because they can be absorbed into the family where, for working class mothers at least, domestic labor is generally a full time job anyway. For detailed discussions see Annette Kuhn and AnnMarie Wolpe, eds., *Feminism and Material-ism: Women and Modes of Production* (London: Rout-ledge and Kegan Paul, 1978); and Michelle Barrett, *Women's Oppression Today: Problems in Marxist Feminist Analysis* (London: Verso Editions, 1980).

3. "Selected themselves" is the correct formulation here, since Title IX guidelines explicitly forbid sex-seg-regated programs in public schools and since there was some evidence of affirmative action attempts to recruit males to the cooperative office education program, at the success rate of two boys in thirteen years. Unfortu-nately, the term conveys an individual-voluntaristic con-notation I do not wish to imply. The weight of cultural pressures on adolescents to choose traditional sex-typed classes is formidable. Generally, they do not even need the type of discouragement reported to have oc-curred at Woodrow High School in the form of a male counselor asking a hockey player, "What the hell do you want to take a second year of typing for?" For other accounts of the ways in which schools help orient girls and boys to occupations on the basis of gender, see Ju-dith Stacey, Susan Bereaud, and Joan Daniels, eds., *And Jill Came Tumbling After: Sexism in American Educa-tion* (New York: Dell, 1974); Rosemary Deem, ed., *Schooling for Women's Work* (London: Routledge and Kegan Paul, 1980); and Nancy Frazier and Myra Sadker, *Sexism in School and Society* (New York: Harper & Row, 1973).

4. See Paul E. Willis, *Learning to Labour: How Working Class Kids Get Working Class Jobs* (Farnbor-ough: Saxon House, 1977), and Angela McRobbie, "Working Class Girls and the Culture of Femininity," in *Women Take Issue: Aspects of Women's Subordina-tion*, ed. Women's Studies Group, Centre for Contempo-rary Cultural Studies (London: Hutchinson, 1978), pp. 96–108.

5. Similar formulations can be found in Stuart Hall and Tony Jefferson, eds., *Resistance through Rituals:*

Youth Subcultures in Post-War Britain (London: Hutchinson & Co., 1975) and by Jean Anyon, "Accommodation and Resistance in Gender and Gender Development," a paper presented at the Ontario Institute for Studies in Education Conference on the *Political Economy of Gender* (Toronto, Ontario, October 30, 1981) and to be published in *Gender, Class and Education,* Len Barton, ed. (Sussex: Falmer Press, 1982).

6. This conclusion is also drawn by Madeleine MacDonald in "Cultural Reproduction: The Pedagogy of Sexuality," *Screen Education,* no. 32/33 (Autumn/Winter 1979–80): 141-53.

7. Sheila Rowbotham, *Woman's Consciousness, Man's World* (Middlesex: Penguin Books, 1973), p. 89.

8. Margery Davies, "Woman's Place is at the Typewriter: The Feminization of the Clerical Labor Force," in *Capitalist Patriarchy and the Case for Socialist Feminism,* ed. Zillah R. Eisenstein (New York: Monthly Review Press, 1979), p. 257.

9. Although this is a basic authority relation that would probably exist irrespective of gender, because gender and authority are strongly correlated in offices, hierarchical authority structures necessarily structure gender relations.

10. MacDonald, "Cultural Reproduction," p. 152.

STUDY QUESTIONS FOR PART 4

1. What does the selection by Anyon reveal about universal norms and who controls them?
2. How do schools, education, and teachers socialize students? Is that good or bad?
3. While Valli's work is a bit dated now, is the feminine work identity she describes still operating today? Give evidence that it is or is not.
4. Drawing on the selection by Anyon, what examples can you find of legitimation and reproduction of society by schools?
5. Do public schools really equalize educational opportunities for all students? Explain your answer.
6. What does social class have to do with schooling?
7. Do the schools benefit some groups at the expense of others? Explain.
8. Functionalists would say that schools perform an appropriate and useful sorting job in our society. Agree or disagree and explain your reasoning.
9. What connection(s) are there between schooling and achievement of the "American dream"? Explain your reasoning.
10. How will policies like "school choice" and "charter schools" mitigate or improve the equality of educational opportunity in the United States?

PART
5

SCHOOL LIFE

The two reading selections to follow provide vivid descriptions of life in schools and include a discussion of the challenges of education in a multicultural society. While they certainly do not represent every school or classroom, the conditions and practices pictured here provoke several critical questions:

- From a student's viewpoint, what does happen in school, or in the classroom, that helps/hinders learning?
- What differences do the assumptions and expectations of teachers make for children's opportunity to learn and succeed in school?
- Should teachers and schools attempt to serve all children equally, assuming this is possible?
- What assumptions and stereotypes do teachers hold about poor children or children of color that hinder student learning?
- How might these challenges for teachers differ between elementary, middle/junior, and high schools?

The ethnographies in this section show how influential the teacher is and how a teacher's expectations and social inequities are imposed on children. They illustrate how teachers operate with one set of rules and expectations while students often operate with different ones. Knowledge is highly subjective. Important power relations are reflected in the teachers' pedagogical practices and in the school curriculum.

The first reading vividly describes the consequences for children of teachers' expectations for their academic performance. Rist's study of kindergarten, first-grade, and second-grade children in a poor, urban school confirms earlier investigations about what has been termed the "self-fulfilling prophecy" of teacher expectations. The results of Rist's study also explain in part Coleman's (1966) earlier observations, which showed that academic achievement was related to student social class and that the gap between the academic performance of poor students increased the longer those students remained in school (Rist, 1970, p. 441).

Both Rist's and Coleman's studies suggest that one of the major effects of schooling in the United States is the perpetuation of a social class structure that relegates low-income children to a future that simply mirrors the social and economic inequality of their childhood. Although schools may espouse equal opportunity for all, and although a majority of U.S. citizens may continue to believe that a major purpose of public schools is to enable those with ability to achieve and succeed in our society despite the obstacles of poor beginnings, the evidence offered by Rist suggests that children's social class and ethnic backgrounds will in large measure determine their success in school.

A major contribution of Rist's study is that it shows us how this happens. Although these results have been known for more than 25 years, many schools and teachers continue practices very similar to those observed by Rist. What is especially alarming is that the kindergarten teacher observed by Rist made judgements about the academic potential of the children in her class by the eighth day of school, *using criteria that have absolutely nothing to do with academic ability or performance!* The teacher appeared to use four criteria to make this judgment:

- the child's physical appearance (quality and quantity of clothes, body odor, blackness of their skin [all children were African American, as was the teacher and the rest of the school's teachers and children], and the condition of their hair)
- their interactive behavior with each other and with the teacher
- their use of language (Standard American English or "school language" versus Black dialect)
- a set of indicators about the children's social and family conditions, suggestive of their general social status and known to the teacher prior to her decisions about their academic potential.

The teacher's decisions about the children's academic potential were reflected in the permanent seating plan she implemented on the eighth day of school. Those children she felt would be "fast learners" she seated at Table 1, closest to her. Those children who didn't appear to satisfy her image of the "ideal" student were seated further away, at Tables 2 and 3. In short, the teacher ascribed highest status to those she deemed to be fast learners, giving this group preferential treatment and essentially directing all of her attention to its members. Rist's ethnography describes in detail these actions by the teacher, and their unfortunate short- and long-term consequences for the children at the other tables. He observed a parallel set of actions by teachers in the first and second grades.

Not only were the patterns similar, but once placed in a slow group the children had no opportunity to move to a higher level, despite their real ability to do so. Similarly, children who were placed in the fast group in kindergarten were subsequently placed in the equivalent group in both the first and second grades. In terms of the self-fulfilling prophecy, those expected to do well did so, and those whom teachers deemed to be slow learners performed at the expected slow level. Teacher expectations for student performance make a difference! As you read the article by Rist, give special thought to your own image of the "ideal" student. How will this affect the way you respond to students? If a teacher doesn't consider it possible to successfully reach all of the students in a class, should the teacher focus primarily on the children most likely to succeed in school? Why? What does the Rist study say about the function of schooling in U.S. society?

The second selection, by Lisa Delpit, explores the challenges for teachers of education in a multicultural society. The racial, social class, and linguistic differences among children in our communities create tremendous challenges for schoolteachers. The cultural clash between students and school presents teachers with the necessity of being especially sensitive and responsive to a number of important factors that influence student success in school: differences in discourse styles, differences in interaction patterns and physicality of children, the influence of gender mix on the propensity (or reluctance) to exhibit academic prowess, and other culturally grounded orientations on the part of children. Her discussion notes the effects of stereotyping by teachers and how this can result in a child not receiving the appropriate instruction. For example, Delpit discusses the " . . . widespread belief that Asian-American children are the 'perfect' students, that they will do well regardless of the academic setting in which they are placed" (p. 170). She points out how this has resulted in many teachers overlooking the needs of the majority of Asian-American students. Ignorance of community norms, stereotypes about certain ethnic or class groups, and the "labeling" of children are examined as practices among teachers that hurt children and diminish teachers as professional educators. The reading offers many specific examples of what teachers—black, white, and "other"—can do to be respectful of the cultural differences among poor children and children of color, noting that rather than expecting "less" of these children, teachers can serve them well by holding appropriately high expectations and teaching in a culturally responsive manner.

As you read these selections, consider your own experience in school. How was it similar and different? Why? How does breaking the school day into segmented and disconnected blocks of 50-minute periods help or hinder learning and teaching? What is your image of the "ideal" student? What will you do with students who don't fit your image? What can teachers do with students who aren't interested in what schools have to offer? What cultural patterns does life in school reinforce? What cultural patterns do teachers frequently fail to recognize?

STUDENT SOCIAL CLASS AND TEACHER EXPECTATIONS: THE SELF-FULFILLING PROPHECY IN GHETTO EDUCATION

RAY C. RIST

Many studies have shown that academic achievement is highly correlated with social class. Few, however, have attempted to explain exactly *how* the school helps to reinforce the class structure of the society. In this article, Dr. Rist reports the results of an observational study of one class of ghetto children during their kindergarten, first-, and second-grade years. He shows how the kindergarten teacher placed the children in reading groups that reflected the social class composition of the class and how these groups persisted throughout the first several years of elementary school. The way in which the teacher behaved toward the different groups became an important influence on the children's achievement. Dr. Rist concludes by examining the relationship between the "caste" system of the classroom and the class system of the larger society.

A dominant aspect of the American ethos is that education is both a necessary and a desirable experience for all children. To that end, compulsory attendance at some type of educational institution is required of all youth until somewhere in the middle teens. Thus on any weekday during the school year, one can expect slightly over 35,000,000 young persons to be distributed among nearly 1,100,000 classrooms throughout the nation (Jackson, 1968).

There is nothing either new or startling in the statement that there exist gross variations in the educational experience of the children involved. The scope of analysis one utilizes in examining these educational variations will reveal different variables of importance. There appear to be at least three levels at which analysis is warranted. The first is a macro-analysis of structural relationships where governmental regulations, federal, state, and local tax support, and the presence or absence of organized political and religious pressure all affect the classroom experience. At this level, study of the policies and politics of the Board of Education within the community is also relevant. The milieu of a particular school appears to be the second area of analysis in which one may examine facilities, pupil-teacher ratios, racial and cultural composition of the faculty and students, community and parental involvement, faculty relationships, the role of the principal, supportive services such as medical care, speech therapy, and library facilities—all of which may have a direct impact on the quality as well as the quantity of education a child receives.

Analysis of an individual classroom and the activities and interactions of a specific group of children with a single teacher is the third level at which there may be profitable analysis of the variations in the educational experience. Such micro-analysis

---

Source: *Rist, Ray C., "Student Social Class and Teacher Expectations: The Self-Fulfilling Prophecy in Ghetto Education,"* Harvard Educational Review, *40:3, pp. 411–451. Copyright Fall 1970 by the President and Fellows of Harvard College.*

could seek to examine the social organization of the class, the development of norms governing interpersonal behavior, and the variety of roles that both the teacher and students assume. It is on this third level—that of the individual classroom—that this study will focus. Teacher-student relationships and the dynamics of interaction between the teacher and students are far from uniform. For any child within the classroom, variations in the experience of success or failure, praise or ridicule, freedom or control, creativity or docility, comprehension or mystification may ultimately have significance far beyond the boundaries of the classroom situation (Henry, 1955, 1959, 1963).

It is the purpose of this paper to explore what is generally regarded as a crucial aspect of the classroom experience for the children involved—the process whereby expectations and social interactions give rise to the social organization of the class. There occurs within the classroom a social process whereby, out of a large group of children and an adult unknown to one another prior to the beginning of the school year, there emerge patterns of behavior, expectations of performance, and a mutually accepted stratification system delineating those doing well from those doing poorly. Of particular concern will be the relation of the teacher's expectations of potential academic performance to the social status of the student. Emphasis will be placed on the initial presuppositions of the teacher regarding the intellectual ability of certain groups of children and their consequences for the children's socialization into the school system. A major goal of this analysis is to ascertain the importance of the initial expectations of the teacher in relation to the child's chances for success or failure within the public school system. (For previous studies of the significance of student social status to variations in educational experience, cf. Becker, 1952; Hollingshead, 1949; Lynd, 1937; Warner, et al., 1944).

Increasingly, with the concern over intellectual growth of children and the long and close association that children experience with a series of teachers, attention is centering on the role of the teacher within the classroom (Sigel, 1969). A long series of studies have been conducted to

determine what effects on children a teacher's values, beliefs, attitudes, and, most crucial to this analysis, a teacher's expectations may have. Asbell (1963), Becker (1952), Clark (1963), Gibson (1965), Harlem Youth Opportunities Unlimited (1964), Katz (1964), Kvaraceus (1965), MacKinnon (1962), Riessman (1962, 1965), Rose (1956), Rosenthal and Jacobson (1968), and Wilson (1963) have all noted that the teacher's expectations of a pupil's academic performance may, in fact, have a strong influence on the actual performance of that pupil. These authors have sought to validate a type of educational self-fulfilling prophecy: if the teacher expects high performance, she receives it, and vice versa. A major criticism that can be directed at much of the research is that although the studies may establish that a teacher has differential expectations and that these influence performance for various pupils, they have not elucidated either the basis upon which such differential expectations are formed or how they are directly manifested within the classroom milieu. It is a goal of this paper to provide an analysis both of the factors that are critical in the teacher's development of expectations for various groups of her pupils and of the process by which such expectations influence the classroom experience for the teacher and the students.

The basic position to be presented in this paper is that the development of expectations by the kindergarten teacher as to the differential academic potential and capability of any student was significantly determined by a series of subjectively interpreted attributes and characteristics of that student. The argument may be succinctly stated in five propositions. First, the kindergarten teacher possessed a roughly constructed "ideal type" as to what characteristics were necessary for any given student to achieve "success" both in the public school and in the larger society. These characteristics appeared to be, in significant part, related to social class criteria. Secondly, upon first meeting her students at the beginning of the school year, subjective evaluations were made of the students as to possession or absence of the desired traits necessary for anticipated "success." On the basis of the evaluation, the class was divided into groups expected to succeed (termed by the teacher "fast learners") and those anticipated to fail (termed "slow learners"). Third, differential treatment was accorded to the two groups in the classroom, with the group designated as "fast learners" receiving the majority of the teaching time, reward-directed behavior, and attention from the teacher. Those designated as "slow learners" were taught infrequently, subjected to more frequent control-oriented behavior, and received little if any supportive behavior from the teacher. Fourth, the interactional patterns between the teacher and the various groups in her class became rigidified, taking on caste-like characteristics, during the course of the school year, with the gap in completion of academic material between the two groups widening as the school year progressed. Fifth, a similar process occurred in later years of schooling, but the teachers no longer relied on subjectively interpreted data as the basis for ascertaining differences in students. Rather, they were able to utilize a variety of informational sources related to past performance as the basis for classroom grouping.

Though the position to be argued in this paper is based on a longitudinal study spanning two and one-half years with a single group of black children, additional studies suggest that the grouping of children both between and within classrooms is a rather prevalent situation within American elementary classrooms. In a report released in 1961 by the National Education Association related to data collected during the 1958–1959 school year, an estimated 77.6% of urban school districts (cities with a population above 2500) indicated that they practiced between-classroom ability grouping in the elementary grades. In a national survey of elementary schools, Austin and Morrison (1963) found that "more than 80% reported that they 'always' or 'often' use readiness tests for pre-reading evaluation [in first grade]." These findings would suggest that within-classroom grouping may be an even more prevalent condition than between-classroom grouping. In evaluating data related to grouping within American elementary classrooms, Smith (1971, in press) concludes, "Thus group assignment on the

basis of measured 'ability' or 'readiness' is an accepted and widespread practice."

Two grouping studies which bear particular mention are those by Borg (1964) and Goldberg, Passow, and Justman (1966). Lawrence (1969) summarizes the importance of these two studies as "the two most carefully designed and controlled studies done concerning ability grouping during the elementary years. . . ." Two school districts in Utah, adjacent to one another and closely comparable in size, served as the setting for the study conducted by Borg. One of the two districts employed random grouping of students, providing all students with "enrichment," while the second school district adopted a group system with acceleration mechanisms present which sought to adapt curricular materials to ability level and also to enable varying rates of presentation of materials. In summarizing Borg's finding, Lawrence states:

> In general, Borg concluded that the grouping patterns had no consistent, general effects on achievement at any level. . . . Ability grouping may have motivated bright pupils to realize their achievement potential more fully, but it seemed to have little effect on the slow or average pupils. (p. 1)

The second study by Goldberg, Passow, and Justman was conducted in the New York City Public Schools and represents the most comprehensive study to date on elementary school grouping. The findings in general show results similar to those of Borg indicating that narrowing the ability range within a classroom on some basis of academic potential will in itself do little to produce positive academic change. The most significant finding of the study is that "variability in achievement from classroom to classroom was generally greater than the variability resulting from grouping pattern or pupil ability" (Lawrence, 1969). Thus one may tentatively conclude that teacher differences were at least as crucial to academic performance as were the effects of pupil ability or methods of classroom grouping. The study, however, fails to investigate within-class grouping.

Related to the issue of within-class variability are the findings of the Coleman Report (1966) which have shown achievement highly correlated with individual social class. The strong correlation present in the first grade does not decrease during the elementary years, demonstrating, in a sense, that the schools are not able effectively to close the achievement gap initially resulting from student social class (pp. 290–325). What variation the Coleman Report does find in achievement in the elementary years results largely from within—rather than between—school variation. Given that the report demonstrates that important differences in achievement do not arise from variations in facilities, curriculum, or staff, it concludes:

> One implication stands out above all: That schools bring little influence to bear on a child's achievement that is independent of his background and general social context; and that this very lack of independent effect means that the inequalities imposed on children by their home, neighborhood, and peer environment are carried along to become the inequalities with which they confront adult life at the end of school. For equality of educational opportunity through the schools must imply a strong effect of schools that is independent of the child's immediate social environment, and that strong independent effect is not present in American schools. (p. 325)

It is the goal of this study to describe the manner in which such "inequalities imposed on children" become manifest within an urban ghetto school and the resultant differential educational experience for children from dissimilar social-class backgrounds.

METHODOLOGY

Data for this study were collected by means of twice weekly one and one-half hour observations of a single group of black children in an urban ghetto school who began kindergarten in September of 1967. Formal observations were conducted throughout the year while the children were in kindergarten and again in 1969 when these same children were in the first half of their second-grade year. The children were also visited informally four times in the classroom during their first-grade year.[1] The difference between the formal and informal observations consisted in the fact that during formal visits, a continuous handwritten account was taken of classroom interaction and activity as it occurred. Smith and Geoffrey (1968) have labeled this method of classroom observation "microethnography." The informal observations did not include the taking of notes during the classroom visit, but comments were written after the visit. Additionally, a series of interviews were conducted with both the kindergarten and the second-grade teachers. No mechanical devices were utilized to record classroom activities or interviews.

I believe it is methodologically necessary, at this point, to clarify what benefits can be derived from the detailed analysis of a single group of children. The single most apparent weakness of the vast majority of studies of urban education is that they lack any longitudinal perspective. The complexities of the interactional processes which evolve over time within classrooms cannot be discerned with a single two- or three-hour observational period. Secondly, education is a *social process* that cannot be reduced to variations in IQ scores over a period of time. At best, IQ scores merely give indications of potential, not of process. Third, I do not believe that this school and the classrooms within it are atypical from others in urban black neighborhoods (cf. both the popular literature on urban schools: Kohl, 1967; and Kozol, 1967; as well as the academic literature: Eddy, 1967; Fuchs, 1969; Leacock, 1969; and Moore, 1967). The school in which this study occurred was selected by the District Superintendent as one of five available to the research team. All five schools were visited during the course of the study and detailed observations were conducted in four of them. The principal at the school reported upon in this study commented that I was very fortunate in coming to his school since his staff (and kindergarten teacher in particular) were equal to "any in the city." Finally, the utilization of longitudinal study as a research method in a ghetto school will

---

[1] *The author, due to a teaching appointment out of the city, was unable to conduct formal observations of the children during their first-grade year.*

enhance the possibilities of gaining further insight into mechanisms of adaptation utilized by black youth to what appears to be a basically white, middle-class, value-oriented institution.

THE SCHOOL

The particular school which the children attend was built in the early part of the 1960s. It has classes from kindergarten through the eighth grade and a single special education class. The enrollment fluctuates near the 900 level while the teaching staff consists of twenty-six teachers, in addition to a librarian, two physical education instructors, the principal, and an assistant principal. There are also at the school, on a part time basis, a speech therapist, social worker, nurse, and doctor, all employed by the Board of Education. All administrators, teachers, staff, and pupils are black. (The author is caucasian.) The school is located in a blighted urban area that has 98% black population within its census district. Within the school itself, nearly 500 of the 900 pupils (55%) come from families supported by funds from Aid to Dependent Children, a form of public welfare.

THE KINDERGARTEN CLASS

Prior to the beginning of the school year, the teacher possessed several different kinds of information regarding the children that she would have in her class. The first was the pre-registration form completed by 13 mothers of children who would be in the kindergarten class. On this form, the teacher was supplied with the name of the child, his age, the name of his parents, his home address, his phone number, and whether he had had any pre-school experience. The second source of information for the teacher was supplied two days before the beginning of school by the school social worker who provided a tentative list of all children enrolled in the kindergarten class who lived in homes that received public welfare funds.

The third source of information on the child was gained as a result of the initial interview with the mother and child during the registration period, either in the few days prior to the beginning

of school or else during the first days of school. In this interview, a major concern was the gathering of medical information about the child as well as the ascertaining of any specific parental concern related to the child. This latter information was noted on the "Behavioral Questionnaire" where the mother was to indicate her concern, if any, on 28 different items. Such items as thumb-sucking, bed-wetting, loss of bowel control, lying, stealing, fighting, and laziness were included on this questionnaire.

The fourth source of information available to the teacher concerning the children in her class was both her own experiences with older siblings, and those of other teachers in the building related to behavior and academic performance of children in the same family. A rather strong informal norm had developed among teachers in the school such that pertinent information, especially that related to discipline matters, was to be passed on to the next teacher of the student. The teachers' lounge became the location in which they would discuss the performance of individual children as well as make comments concerning the parents and their interests in the student and the school. Frequently, during the first days of the school year, there were admonitions to a specific teacher to "watch out" for a child believed by a teacher to be a "trouble-maker." Teachers would also relate techniques of controlling the behavior of a student who had been disruptive in the class. Thus a variety of information concerning students in the school was shared, whether that information regarded academic performance, behavior in class, or the relation of the home to the school.

It should be noted that not one of these four sources of information to the teacher was related directly to the academic potential of the incoming kindergarten child. Rather, they concerned various types of social information revealing such facts as the financial status of certain families, medical care of the child, presence or absence of a telephone in the home, as well as the structure of the family in which the child lived, *i.e.,* number of siblings, whether the child lived with both, one, or neither of his natural parents.

THE TEACHER'S STIMULUS

When the kindergarten teacher made the permanent seating assignments on the eighth day of school, not only had she the above four sources of information concerning the children, but she had also had time to observe them within the classroom setting. Thus the behavior, degree and type of verbalization, dress, mannerisms, physical appearance, and performance on the early tasks assigned during class were available to her as she began to form opinions concerning the capabilities and potential of the various children. That such evaluation of the children by the teacher was beginning, I believe, there is little doubt. Within a few days, only a certain group of children were continually being called on to lead the class in the Pledge of Allegiance, read the weather calendar each day, come to the front for "show and tell" periods, take messages to the office, count the number of children present in the class, pass out materials for class projects, be in charge of equipment on the playground, and lead the class to the bathroom, library, or on a school tour. This one group of children, that continually were physically close to the teacher and had a high degree of verbal interaction with her, she placed at Table 1.

As one progressed from Table 1 to Table 2 and Table 3, there was an increasing dissimilarity between each group of children at the different tables on at least four major criteria. The first criterion appeared to be the physical appearance of the child. While the children at Table 1 were all dressed in clean clothes that were relatively new and pressed, most of the children at Table 2, and with only one exception at Table 3, were all quite poorly dressed. The clothes were old and often quite dirty. The children at Tables 2 and 3 also had a noticeably different quality and quantity of clothes to wear, especially during the winter months. Whereas the children at Table 1 would come on cold days with heavy coats and sweaters, the children at the other two tables often wore very thin spring coats and summer clothes. The single child at Table 3 who came to school quite nicely dressed came from a home in which the mother was receiving welfare funds, but was supplied with clothing for the children by the families of her brother and sister.

An additional aspect of the physical appearance of the children related to their body odor. While none of the children at Table 1 came to class with an odor of urine on them, there were two children at Table 2 and five children at Table 3 who frequently had such an odor. There was not a clear distinction among the children at the various tables as to the degree of "blackness" of their skin, but there were more children at the third table with very dark skin (five in all) than there were at the first table (three). There was also a noticeable distinction among the various groups of children as to the condition of their hair. While the three boys at Table 1 all had short hair cuts and the six girls at the same table had their hair "processed" and combed, the number of children with either matted or unprocessed hair increased at Table 2 (two boys and three girls) and eight of the children at Table 3 (four boys and four girls). None of the children in the kindergarten class wore their hair in the style of a "natural."

A second major criterion which appeared to differentiate the children at the various tables was their interactional behavior, both among themselves and with the teacher. The several children who began to develop as leaders within the class by giving directions to other members, initiating the division of the class into teams on the playground, and seeking to speak for the class to the teacher ("We want to color now"), all were placed by the teacher at Table 1. This same group of children displayed considerable ease in their interaction with her. Whereas the children at Tables 2 and 3 would often linger on the periphery of groups surrounding the teacher, the children at Table 1 most often crowded close to her.

The use of language within the classroom appeared to be the third major differentiation among the children. While the children placed at the first table were quite verbal with the teacher, the children placed at the remaining two tables spoke much less frequently with her. The children placed at the first table also displayed a greater use of Standard American English within the classroom. Whereas the children placed at the last

TABLE 1

Distribution of Socio-Economic Status Factors by Seating Arrangement at the Three Tables in the Kindergarten Classroom

FACTORS	SEATING ARRANGEMENT*		
	TABLE 1	TABLE 2	TABLE 3
Income			
1) Families on welfare	0	2	4
2) Families with father employed	6	3	2
3) Families with mother employed	5	5	5
4) Families with both parents employed	5	3	2
5) Total family income below $3,000./yr**	0	4	7
6) Total family income above $12,000./yr**	4	0	0
Education			
1) Father ever grade school	6	3	2
2) Father ever high school	5	2	1
3) Father ever college	1	0	0
4) Mother ever grade school	9	10	8
5) Mother ever high school	7	6	5
6) Mother ever college	4	0	0
7) Children with pre-school experience	1	1	0
Family Size			
1) Families with one child	3	1	0
2) Families with six or more children	2	6	7
3) Average number of siblings in family	3–4	5–6	6–7
4) Families with both parents present	6	3	2

*There are nine children at Table 1, eleven at Table 2, and ten children at Table 3.
**Estimated from stated occupation.

two tables most often responded to the teacher in black dialect, the children at the first table did so very infrequently. In other words, the children at the first table were much more adept at the use of "school language" than were those at the other tables. The teacher utilized Standard American English in the classroom and one group of children were able to respond in a like manner. The frequency of a "no response" to a question from the teacher was recorded at a ratio of nearly three to one for the children at the last two tables as op-posed to Table 1. When questions were asked, the children who were placed at the first table most often gave a response.

The final apparent criterion by which the children at the first table were quite noticeably different from those at the other tables consisted of a series of social factors which were known to the teacher prior to her seating the children. Though it is not known to what degree she utilized this particular criterion when she assigned seats, it does contribute to developing a clear profile of the children at the various tables. Table 1 gives a summary of the distribution of the children at the three tables on a series of variables related to social and family conditions. Such variables may be considered to give indication of the relative status of the children within the room, based on the income, education, and size of the family. (For a discussion of why these three variables of income, education, and family size may be considered as significant indicators of social status, cf. Frazier, 1962; Freeman, *et al.*, 1959; Gebhard, *et al.*, 1958; Kahl, 1957; Notestein, 1953; Reissman, 1959; Rose, 1956; Simpson and Yinger, 1958.)

Believing, as I do, that the teacher did not randomly assign the children to the various tables, it is then necessary to indicate the basis for the seating arrangement. I would contend that the teacher developed, utilizing some combination of the four criteria outlined above, a series of expectations about the potential performance of each child and then grouped the children according to perceived similarities in expected performance. The teacher herself informed me that the first table consisted of her "fast learners" while those at the last two tables "had no idea of what was going on in the classroom." What becomes crucial in this discussion is to ascertain the basis upon which the teacher developed her criterion of "fast learner" since there had been no formal testing of the children as to their academic potential or capacity for cognitive development. She made evaluative judgments of the expected capacities of the children to perform academic tasks after eight days of school.

Certain criteria became indicative of expected success and others became indicative of expected failure. Those children who closely fit the teacher's "ideal type" of the successful child were chosen for seats at Table 1. Those children that had the least "goodness of fit" with her ideal type were placed at the third table. The criteria upon which a teacher would construct her ideal type of the successful student would rest in her perception of certain attributes in the child that she believed would make for success. To understand what the teacher considered as "success," one would have to examine her perception of the larger society and whom in that larger society she perceived as successful. Thus, in the terms of Merton (1957), one may ask which was the "normative reference group" for Mrs. Caplow that she perceived as being successful.[2] I believe that the reference group utilized by Mrs. Caplow to determine what constituted success was a mixed black-white, well-educated middle class. Those attributes most desired by educated members of the middle class became the basis for her evaluation of the children. Those who possessed these particular characteristics were expected to succeed while those who did not could be expected not to succeed. Highly prized middle-class status for the child in the classroom was attained by demonstrating ease of interaction among adults; high degree of verbalization in Standard American English; the ability to become a leader; a neat and clean appearance; coming from a family that is educated, employed, living together, and interested in the child; and the ability to participate well as a member of a group.

The kindergarten teacher appeared to have been raised in a home where the above values were emphasized as important. Her mother was a college graduate, as were her brother and sisters. The family lived in the same neighborhood for many years, and the father held a responsible position with a public utility company in the city. The family was devoutly religious and those of the family still in the city attend the same church. She and other members of her family were active in a number of civil rights organizations in the city. Thus, it appears that the kindergarten teacher's "normative reference group" coincided quite closely with those groups in which she did participate and belong. There was little discrepancy between the normative values of the mixed black-white educated middle-class and the values of the groups in which she held membership. The attributes indicative of "success" among those of the educated middle class had been attained by the teacher. She

---

[2] *The names of all staff and students are pseudonyms. Names are provided to indicate that the discussion relates to living persons, and not to fictional characters developed by the author.*

was a college graduate, held positions of respect and responsibility in the black community, lived in a comfortable middle-class section of the city in a well-furnished and spacious home, together with her husband earned over $20,000 per year, was active in a number of community organizations, and had parents, brother, and sisters similar in education, income, and occupational positions.

The teacher ascribed high status to a certain group of children within the class who fit her perception of the criteria necessary to be among the "fast learners" at Table 1. With her reference group orientation as to what constitute the qualities essential for "success," she responded favorably to those children who possessed such necessary attributes. Her resultant preferential treatment of a select group of children appeared to be derived from her belief that certain behavioral and cultural characteristics are more crucial to learning in school than are others. In a similar manner, those children who appeared not to possess the criteria essential for success were ascribed low status and described as "failures" by the teacher. They were relegated to positions at Tables 2 and 3. The placement of the children then appeared to result from their possessing or lacking the certain desired cultural characteristics perceived as important by the teacher.

The organization of the kindergarten classroom according to the expectation of success or failure after the eighth day of school became the basis for the differential treatment of the children for the remainder of the school year. From the day that the class was assigned permanent seats, the activities in the classroom were perceivably different from previously. The fundamental division of the class into those expected to learn and those expected not to permeated the teacher's orientation to the class.

The teacher's rationalization for narrowing her attention to selected students was that the majority of the remainder of the class (in her words) "just had no idea of what was going on in the classroom." Her reliance on the few students of ascribed high social status reached such proportions that on occasion, the teacher would use one of these students as an exemplar that the remainder of the class would do well to emulate.

(It is Fire Prevention Week and the teacher is trying to have the children say so. The children make a number of incorrect responses, a few of which follow:) Jim, who had raised his hand, in answer to the question, "Do you know what week it is?" says, "October." The teacher says "No, that's the name of the month. Jane, do you know what special week this is?" and Jane responds, "It cold outside." Teacher says, "No, that is not it either. I guess I will have to call on Pamela. Pamela, come here and stand by me and tell the rest of the boys and girls what special week this is." Pamela leaves her chair, comes and stands by the teacher, turns and faces the rest of the class. The teacher puts her arm around Pamela, and Pamela says, "It fire week." The teacher responds, "Well Pamela, that is close. Actually it is Fire Prevention Week."

On another occasion, the Friday after Halloween, the teacher informed the class that she would allow time for all the students to come to the front of the class and tell of their experiences. She, in reality, called on six students, five of whom sat at Table 1 and the sixth at Table 2. Not only on this occasion, but on others, the teacher focused her attention on the experiences of the higher status students.[3]

(The students are involved in acting out a skit arranged by the teacher on how a family should come together to eat the evening meal.) The students acting the roles of mother, father, and daughter are all from Table 1. The boy playing the son is from Table 2. At the small dinner table set up in the center of the classroom, the four children are supposed to be sharing with each other what they had done during the day—the father at work, the mother at home, and the two children at school. The Table 2 boy makes few comments. (In real life he has no father and his mother is supported by ADC funds.) The teacher comments, "I think that we are going to have to let Milt (Table 1) be the new son. Sam, why don't you go and sit down.

---

[3] *Through the remainder of the paper, reference to "high" or "low" status students refers to status ascribed to the student by the teacher. Her ascription appeared to be based on perceptions of valued behavioral and cultural characteristics present or absent in any individual student.*

Milt, you seem to be one who would know what a son is supposed to do at the dinner table. You come and take Sam's place."

In this instance, the lower-status student was penalized, not only for failing to have verbalized middle-class table talk, but more fundamentally, for lacking middle-class experiences. He had no actual father to whom he could speak at the dinner table, yet he was expected to speak fluently with an imaginary one.

Though the blackboard was long enough to extend parallel to all three tables, the teacher wrote such assignments as arithmetic problems and drew all illustrations on the board in front of the students at Table 1. A rather poignant example of the penalty the children at Table 3 had to pay was that they often could not see the board material.

> Lilly stands up out of her seat. Mrs. Caplow asks Lilly what she wants. Lilly makes no verbal response to the question. Mrs. Caplow then says rather firmly to Lilly, "Sit down." Lilly does. However, Lilly sits down sideways in the chair (so she is still facing the teacher). Mrs. Caplow instructs Lilly to put her feet under the table. This Lilly does. Now she is facing directly away from the teacher and the blackboard where the teacher is demonstrating to the students how to print the letter, "O."

The realization of the self-fulfilling prophecy within the classroom was in its final stages by late May of the kindergarten year. Lack of communication with the teacher, lack of involvement in the class activities, and infrequent instruction all characterized the situation of the children at Tables 2 and 3. During one observational period of an hour in May, not a single act of communication was directed towards any child at either Table 2 or 3 by the teacher except for twice commanding "sit down." The teacher devoted her attention to teaching those children at Table 1. Attempts by the children at Tables 2 and 3 to elicit the attention of the teacher were much fewer than earlier in the school year.

In June, after school had ended for the year, the teacher was asked to comment on the children in her class. Of the children at the first table, she noted:

> I guess the best way to describe it is that very few children in my class are exceptional. I guess you could notice this just from the way the children were seated this year. Those at Table 1 gave consistently the most responses throughout the year and seemed most interested and aware of what was going on in the classroom.

Of those children at the remaining two tables, the teacher commented:

> It seems to me that some of the children at Table 2 and most all the children at Table 3 at times seem to have no idea of what is going on in the classroom and were off in another world all by themselves. It just appears that some can do it and some cannot. I don't think that it is the teacher that affects those that cannot do it, but some are just basically low achievers.

THE STUDENTS' RESPONSE

The students in the kindergarten classroom did not sit passively, internalizing the behavior the teacher directed towards them. Rather, they responded to the stimuli of the teacher, both in internal differentiations within the class itself and also in their response to the teacher. The type of response a student made was highly dependent upon whether he sat at Table 1 or at one of the two other tables. The single classroom of black students did not respond as a homogenous unit to the teacher-inspired social organization of the room.

For the high-status students at Table 1, the response to the track system of the teacher appeared to be at least three-fold. One such response was the directing of ridicule and belittlement towards those children at Tables 2 and 3. At no point during the entire school year was a child from Table 2 or 3 ever observed directing such remarks at the children at Table 1.

> Mrs. Caplow says, "Raise your hand if you want me to call on you. I won't call on anyone who calls out." She then says, "All right, now who knows that numeral? What is it, Tony?" Tony makes no verbal response but rather walks to the front of the classroom and stands by Mrs. Caplow. Gregory calls out, "He don't know. He scared." Then Ann

calls out, "It sixteen, stupid." (Tony sits at Table 3, Gregory and Ann sit at Table 1.)

Jim starts to say out loud that he is smarter than Tom. He repeats it over and over again, "I smarter than you. I smarter than you." (Jim sits at Table 1, Tom at Table 3.)

Milt came over to the observer and told him to look at Lilly's shoes. I asked him why I should and he replied, "Because they so ragged and dirty." (Milt is at Table 1, Lilly at Table 3.)

When I asked Lilly what it was that she was drawing, she replied, "A parachute." Gregory interrupted and said, "She can't draw nothin'."

The problems of those children who were of lower status were compounded, for not only had the teacher indicated her low esteem of them, but their peers had also turned against them. The implications for the future schooling of a child who lacks the desired status credentials in a classroom where the teacher places high value on middle-class "success" values and mannerisms are tragic.

It must not be assumed, however, that though the children at Tables 2 and 3 did not participate in classroom activities and were systematically ignored by the teacher, they did not learn. I contend that in fact they did learn, but in a fundamentally different way from the way in which the high-status children at Table 1 learned. The children at Tables 2 and 3 who were unable to interact with the teacher began to develop patterns of interaction among themselves whereby they would discuss the material that the teacher was presenting to the children at Table 1. Thus I have termed their method of grasping the material "secondary learning" to imply that knowledge was not gained in direct interaction with the teacher, but through the mediation of peers and also through listening to the teacher though she was not speaking to them. That the children were grasping, in part, the material presented in the classroom, was indicated to me in home visits when the children who sat at Table 3 would relate material specifically taught by the teacher to the children at Table 1. *It is not as though the children at Tables 2 and 3 were ignorant of what was being taught in the class, but rather that the patterns of classroom interaction estab-*

lished by the teacher inhibited the low-status children from verbalizing what knowledge they had accumulated. Thus, from the teacher's terms of reference, those who could not discuss must not know. Her expectations continued to be fulfilled, for though the low-status children had accumulated knowledge, they did not have the opportunity to verbalize it and, consequently, the teacher could not know what they had learned. Children at Tables 2 and 3 had learned material presented in the kindergarten class, but would continue to be defined by the teacher as children who could not or would not learn.

A second response of the higher-status students to the differential behavior of the teacher towards them was to seek solidarity and closeness with the teacher and urge Table 2 and 3 children to comply with her wishes.

The teacher is out of the room. Pamela says to the class, "We all should clean up before the teacher comes." Shortly thereafter the teacher has still not returned and Pamela begins to supervise other children in the class. She says to one girl from Table 3, "Girl, leave that piano alone." The child plays only a short time longer and then leaves.

The teacher has instructed the students to go and take off their coats since they have come in from the playground. Milt says, "Ok y'al, let's go take off our clothes."

At this time Jim says to the teacher, "Mrs. Caplow, they pretty flowers on your desk." Mrs. Caplow responded, "Yes, Jim, those flowers are roses, but we will not have roses much longer. The roses will die and rest until spring because it is getting so cold outside."

When the teacher tells the students to come from their desks and form a semi-circle around her, Gregory scoots up very close to Mrs. Caplow and is practically sitting in her lap.

Gregory has come into the room late. He takes off his coat and goes to the coat room to hang it up. He comes back and sits down in the very front of the group and is now closest to the teacher.

The higher-status students in the class perceived the lower status and esteem the teacher ascribed to those children at Tables 2 and 3. Not only would the Table 1 students attempt to control and ridicule the Table 2 and 3 students, but they also perceived and verbalized that they, the Table 1 students, were better students and were receiving differential treatment from the teacher.

> The children are rehearsing a play, Little Red Riding Hood. Pamela tells the observer, "The teacher gave me the best part." The teacher overheard this comment, smiled, and made no verbal response.
>
> The children are preparing to go on a field trip to a local dairy. The teacher has designated Gregory as the "sheriff" for the trip. Mrs. Caplow stated that for the field trip today Gregory would be the sheriff. Mrs. Caplow simply watched as Gregory would walk up to a student and push him back into line saying, "Boy, stand where you suppose to." Several times he went up to students from Table 3 and showed them the badge that the teacher had given to him and said, "Teacher made me sheriff."

The children seated at the first table were internalizing the attitudes and behavior of the teacher towards those at the remaining two tables. That is, as the teacher responded from her reference group orientation as to which type of children were most likely to succeed and which type most likely to fail, she behaved towards the two groups of children in a significantly different manner. The children from Table 1 were also learning through emulating the teacher how to behave towards other black children who came from low-income and poorly educated homes. The teacher, who came from a well-educated and middle-income family, and the children from Table 1 who came from a background similar to the teacher's, came to respond to the children from poor and uneducated homes in a strikingly similar manner.

The lower-status students in the classroom from Tables 2 and 3 responded in significantly different ways to the stimuli of the teacher. The two major responses of the Table 2 and 3 students were withdrawal and verbal and physical ingroup hostility.

The withdrawal of some of the lower-status students as a response to the ridicule of their peers and the isolation from the teacher occasionally took the form of physical withdrawal, but most often it was psychological.

> Betty, a very poorly dressed child, had gone outside and hidden behind the door. . . . Mrs. Caplow sees Betty leave and goes outside to bring her back, says in an authoritative and irritated voice, "Betty, come here right now." When the child returns, Mrs. Caplow seizes her by the right arm, brings her over to the group, and pushes her down to the floor. Betty begins to cry. . . . The teacher now shows the group a large posterboard with a picture of a white child going to school.
>
> The teacher is demonstrating how to mount leaves between two pieces of wax paper. Betty leaves the group and goes back to her seat and begins to color.
>
> The teacher is instructing the children in how they can make a "spooky thing" for Hallowe'en. James turns away from the teacher and puts his head on his desk. Mrs. Caplow looks at James and says, "James, sit up and look here."
>
> The children are supposed to make United Nations flags. They have been told that they do not have to make exact replicas of the teacher's flag. They have before them the materials to make the flags. Lilly and James are the only children who have not yet started to work on their flags. Presently, James has his head under his desk and Lilly simply sits and watches the other children. Now they are both staring into space. . . . (5 minutes later) Lilly and James have not yet started, while several other children have already finished. . . . A minute later, with the teacher telling the children to begin to clean up their scraps, Lilly is still staring into space.
>
> The teacher has the children seated on the floor in front of her asking them questions about a story that she had read to them. The teacher says, "June, your back is turned. I want to see your face." (The child had turned completely around and was facing away from the group.)
>
> The teacher told the students to come from their seats and form a semi-circle on the floor in front of her. The girls all sit very close to the piano where the teacher is seated. The boys sit a good distance back away from the girls and away from the teacher. Lilly finishes her work at her desk and

comes and sits at the rear of the group of girls, but she is actually in the middle of the open space separating the boys and the girls. She speaks to no one and simply sits staring off.

The verbal and physical hostility that the children at Tables 2 and 3 began to act out among themselves in many ways mirrored what the Table 1 students and the teacher were also saying about them. There are numerous instances in the observations of the children at Tables 2 and 3 calling one another "stupid," "dummy," or "dumb dumb." Racial overtones were noted on two occasions when one boy called another a "nigger," and on another occasion when a girl called a boy an "almond head." Threats of beating, "whoppins," and even spitting on a child were also recorded among those at Tables 2 and 3. Also at Table 2, two instances were observed in which a single child hoarded all the supplies for the whole table. Similar manifestations of hostility were not observed among those children at the first table. The single incident of strong anger or hostility by one child at Table 1 against another child at the same table occurred when one accused the other of copying from his paper. The second denied it and an argument ensued.

In the organization of hostility within the classroom, there may be at least the tentative basis for the rejection of a popular "folk myth" of American society, which is that children are inherently cruel to one another and that this tendency towards cruelty must be socialized into socially acceptable channels. The evidence from this classroom would indicate that much of the cruelty displayed was a result of the social organization of the class. Those children at Tables 2 and 3 who displayed cruelty appeared to have learned from the teacher that it was acceptable to act in an aggressive manner towards those from low-income and poorly educated backgrounds. Their cruelty was not diffuse, but rather focused on a specific group—the other poor children. Likewise, the incidence of such behavior increased over time. The children at Tables 2 and 3 did not begin the school year ridiculing and belittling each other. This social process began to emerge with the outline of the social organization the teacher imposed upon the class. The children from the first table were also apparently socialized into a pattern of behavior in which they perceived that they could direct hostility and aggression towards those at Tables 2 and 3, but not towards one another. The children in the class learned who was vulnerable to hostility and who was not through the actions of the teacher. She established the patterns of differential behavior which the class adopted.

FIRST GRADE

Though Mrs. Caplow had anticipated that only twelve of the children from the kindergarten class would attend the first grade in the same school, eighteen of the children were assigned during the summer to the first-grade classroom in the main building. The remaining children either were assigned to a new school a few blocks north, or were assigned to a branch school designed to handle the overflow from the main building, or had moved away. Mrs. Logan, the first-grade teacher, had had more than twenty years of teaching experience in the city public school system, and every school in which she had taught was more than 90 percent black. During the 1968–1969 school year, four informal visits were made to the classroom of Mrs. Logan. No visits were made to either the branch school or the new school to visit children from the kindergarten class who had left their original school. During my visits to the first-grade room, I kept only brief notes of the short conversations that I had with Mrs. Logan; I did not conduct formal observations of the activities of the children in the class.

During the first-grade school year, there were thirty-three children in the classroom. In addition to the eighteen from the kindergarten class, there were nine children repeating the first grade and also six children new to the school. Of the eighteen children who came from the kindergarten class to the first grade in the main building, seven were from the previous year's Table 1, six from Table 2, and five from Table 3.

In the first-grade classroom, Mrs. Logan also divided the children into three groups. Those children whom she placed at "Table A" had all been Table 1 students in kindergarten. No student who had sat at Table 2 or 3 in kindergarten was placed at Table A in the first grade. Instead, all the students from Tables 2 and 3—with one exception—were placed together at "Table B." At the third table which Mrs. Logan called "Table C," she placed the nine children repeating the grade plus Betty who had sat at Table 3 in the kindergarten class. Of the six new students, two were placed at Table A and four at Table C. Thus the totals for the three tables were nine students at Table A, ten at Table B, and fourteen at Table C.

The seating arrangement that began in the kindergarten as a result of the teacher's definition of which children possessed or lacked the perceived necessary characteristics for success in the public school system emerged in the first grade as a caste phenomenon in which there was absolutely no mobility upward. That is, of those children whom Mrs. Caplow had perceived as potential "failures" and thus seated at either Table 2 or 3 in the kindergarten, not one was assigned to the table of the "fast learners" in the first grade.

The initial label given to the children by the kindergarten teacher had been reinforced in her interaction with those students throughout the school year. When the children were ready to pass into the first grade, their ascribed labels from the teacher as either successes or failures assumed objective dimensions. The first-grade teacher no longer had to rely on merely the presence or absence of certain behavioral and attitudinal characteristics to ascertain who would do well and who would do poorly in the class. Objective records of the "readiness" material completed by the children during the kindergarten year were available to her. Thus, upon the basis of what material the various tables in kindergarten had completed, Mrs. Logan could form her first-grade tables for reading and arithmetic.

The kindergarten teacher's disproportionate allocation of her teaching time resulted in the Table 1 students' having completed more material at the end of the school year than the remainder of the class. As a result, the Table 1 group

from kindergarten remained intact in the first grade, as they were the only students prepared for the first-grade reading material. Those children from Tables 2 and 3 had not yet completed all the material from kindergarten and had to spend the first weeks of the first-grade school year finishing kindergarten level lessons. The criteria established by the school system as to what constituted the completion of the necessary readiness material to begin first-grade lessons ensured that the Table 2 and 3 students could not be placed at Table A. The only children who had completed the material were those from Table 1, defined by the kindergarten teacher as successful students and whom she then taught most often because the remainder of the class "had no idea what was going on."

It would be somewhat misleading, however, to indicate that there was absolutely no mobility for any of the students between the seating assignments in kindergarten and those in the first grade. All of the students save one who had been seated at Table 3 during the kindergarten year were moved "up" to Table B in the first grade. The majority of Table C students were those having to repeat the grade level. As a tentative explanation of Mrs. Logan's rationale for the development of the Table C seating assignments, she may have assumed that within her class there existed one group of students who possessed so very little of the perceived behavioral patterns and attitudes necessary for success that they had to be kept separate from the remainder of the class. (Table C was placed by itself on the opposite side of the room from Tables A and B.) The Table C students were spoken of by the first-grade teacher in a manner reminiscent of the way in which Mrs. Caplow spoke of the Table 3 students the previous year.

Students who were placed at Table A appeared to be perceived by Mrs. Logan as students who not only possessed the criteria necessary for future success, both in the public school system and in the larger society, but who also had proven themselves capable in academic work. These students appeared to possess the characteristics considered most essential for "middle-class" success by the teacher. Though students at Table B lacked many of the "qualities" and characteristics of the Table A students, they were not perceived as lacking them to the same extent as those placed at Table C.

A basic tenet in explaining Mrs. Logan's seating arrangement is, of course, that she shared a similar reference group and set of values as to what constituted "success" with Mrs. Caplow in the kindergarten class. Both women were well educated, were employed in a professional occupation, lived in middle-income neighborhoods, were active in a number of charitable and civil rights organizations, and expressed strong religious convictions and moral standards. Both were educated in the city teacher's college and had also attained graduate degrees. Their backgrounds as well as the manner in which they described the various groups of students in their classes would indicate that they shared a similar reference group and set of expectations as to what constituted the indices of the "successful" student.

SECOND GRADE

Of the original thirty students in kindergarten and eighteen in first grade, ten students were assigned to the only second-grade class in the main building. Of the eight original kindergarten students who did not come to the second grade from the first, three were repeating first grade while the remainder had moved. The teacher in the second grade also divided the class into three groups, though she did not give them number or letter designations. Rather, she called the first group the "Tigers." The middle groups she labeled the "Cardinals," while the second-grade repeaters plus several new children assigned to the third table were designated by the teacher as "Clowns."[4]

In the second-grade seating scheme, no student from the first grade who had not sat at Table

A was moved "up" to the Tigers at the beginning of second grade. All those students who in first grade had been at Table B or Table C and returned to the second grade were placed in the Cardinal group. The Clowns consisted of six second-grade repeaters plus three students who were new to the class. Of the ten original kindergarten students who came from the first grade, six were Tigers and four were Cardinals. Table 2 illustrates that the distribution of social economic factors from the kindergarten year remained essentially unchanged in the second grade.

By the time the children came to the second grade, their seating arrangement appeared to be based not on the teacher's expectations of how the child might perform, but rather on the basis of past performance of the child. Available to the teacher when she formulated the seating groups were grade sheets from both kindergarten and first grade, IQ scores from kindergarten, listing of parental occupations for approximately half of the class, reading scores from a test given to all students at the end of first grade, evaluations from the speech teacher and also the informal evaluations from both the kindergarten and first-grade teacher.

The single most important data utilized by the teacher in devising seating groups were the reading scores indicating the performance of the students at the end of the first grade. The second-grade teacher indicated that she attempted to divide the groups primarily on the basis of these scores. The Tigers were designated as the highest reading group and the Cardinals the middle. The Clowns were assigned a first-grade reading level, though they were, for the most part, repeaters from the previous year in second grade. The caste character of the reading groups became clear as the year progressed, in that all three groups were reading in different books and it was school policy that no child could go on to a new book until the previous one had been completed. Thus there was no way for the child, should he have demonstrated competence at a higher reading level, to advance, since he had to continue at the pace of the rest of his reading group. The teacher never allowed individual reading in order that a child might finish a

[4] *The names were not given to the groups until the third week of school, though the seating arrangement was established on the third day.*

TABLE 2

Distribution of Socio-Economic Status Factors by Seating Arrangement in the Three Reading Groups in the Second-Grade Classroom

FACTORS	SEATING ARRANGEMENT*		
	TIGERS	CARDINALS	CLOWNS
Income			
1) Families on welfare	2	4	7
2) Families with father employed	8	5	1
3) Families with mother employed	7	11	6
4) Families with both parents employed	7	5	1
5) Total family income below $3,000./yr**	1	5	8
6) Total family income above $12,000./yr**	4	0	0
Education			
1) Father ever grade school	8	6	1
2) Father ever high school	7	4	0
3) Father ever college	0	0	0
4) Mother ever grade school	12	13	9
5) Mother ever high school	9	7	4
6) Mother ever college	3	0	0
7) Children with pre-school experience	1	0	0
Family Size			
1) Families with one child	2	0	1
2) Families with six or more children	3	8	5
3) Average number of sibling in family	3-4	6-7	7-8
4) Families with both parents present	8	6	1

*There are twelve children in the Tiger group, fourteen children in the Cardinal group, and nine children in the Clown group.
**Estimated from stated occupation.

book on his own and move ahead. *No matter how well a child in the lower reading groups might have read, he was destined to remain in the same reading group. This is, in a sense, another manifestation of the self-fulfilling prophecy in that a "slow learner" had no option but to continue to be a slow learner, regardless of performance or potential.* Initial expectations of the kindergarten teacher two years earlier as to the ability of the child resulted in placement in a reading group, whether high or low, from which there appeared to be no escape. The child's journey through the early grades of school at one reading level and in one social grouping appeared to be pre-ordained from the eighth day of kindergarten.

The expectations of the kindergarten teacher appeared to be fulfilled by late spring. Her description of the academic performance of the children in June had a strong "goodness of fit" with her stated expectations from the previous September. For the first- and second-grade teacher alike, there was no need to rely on intuitive expectations as to what the performance of the child would be. They were in the position of being able to base future expectations upon past performance. At this point, the relevance of the self-fulfilling prophecy again is evident, for the very criteria by which the first- and second-grade teachers established their three reading groups were those manifestations of performance most affected by the previous experience of the child. That is, which reading books were completed, the amount of arithmetic and reading readiness material that had been completed, and the mastery of basic printing skills all became the significant criteria established by the Board of Education to determine the level at which the child would begin the first grade. A similar process of standard evaluation by past performance on criteria established by the Board appears to have been the basis for the arrangement of reading groups within the second grade. Thus, again, the initial patterns of expectations and her acting upon them appeared to place the kindergarten teacher in the position of establishing the parameters of the educational experience for the various children in her class. The parameters, most clearly defined by the seating arrangement at the various tables, remained intact through both the first and second grades.

The phenomenon of teacher expectation based upon a variety of social status criteria did not appear to be limited to the kindergarten teacher alone. When the second-grade teacher was asked to evaluate the children in her class by reading group, she responded in terms reminiscent of the kindergarten teacher. Though such a proposition would be tenuous at best, the high degree of similarity in the responses of both the kindergarten and second-grade teacher suggests that there may be among the teachers in the school a common set of criteria as to what constitutes the successful and promising student. If such is the case, then the particular individual who happens to occupy the role of kindergarten teacher is less crucial. For if the expectations of all staff within the school are highly similar, then with little difficulty there could be an interchange of teachers among the grades with little or no noticeable effect upon the performance of the various groups of students. If all teachers have similar expectations as to which types of students

perform well and which types perform poorly, the categories established by the kindergarten teacher could be expected to reflect rather closely the manner in which other teachers would also have grouped the class.

As the indication of the high degree of similarity between the manner in which the kindergarten teacher described the three tables and the manner in which the second-grade teacher discussed the "Tigers, Cardinals, and Clowns," excerpts of an interview with the second-grade teacher are presented, where she stated her opinions of the three groups.

Concerning the Tigers:

Q: Mrs. Benson, how would you describe the Tigers in terms of their learning ability and academic performance?

R: Well, they are my fastest group. They are very smart.

Q: Mrs. Benson, how would you describe the Tigers in terms of discipline matters?

R: Well, the Tigers are very talkative. Susan, Pamela, and Ruth, they are always running their mouths constantly, but they get their work done first. I don't have much trouble with them.

Q: Mrs. Benson, what value do you think the Tigers hold for an education?

R: They all feel an education is important and most of them have goals in life as to what they want to be. They mostly want to go to college.

The same questions were asked of the teacher concerning the Cardinals.

Q: Mrs. Benson, how would you describe the Cardinals in terms of learning ability and academic performance?

R: They are slow to finish their work . . . but they get finished. You know, a lot of them, though, don't care to come to school too much. Rema, Gary, and Toby are absent quite a bit. The Tigers are never absent.

Q: Mrs. Benson, how would you describe the Cardinals in terms of discipline matters?

R: Not too bad. Since they work so slow they don't have time to talk. They are not like the

Tigers who finish in a hurry and then just sit and talk with each other.

Q: Mrs. Benson, what value do you think the Cardinals hold for an education?

R: Well, I don't think they have as much interest in education as do the Tigers, but you know it is hard to say. Most will like to come to school, but the parents will keep them from coming. They either have to baby sit, or the clothes are dirty. These are the excuses the parents often give. But I guess most of the Cardinals want to go on and finish and go on to college. A lot of them have ambitions when they grow up. It's mostly the parents' fault that they are not at the school more often.

In the kindergarten class, the teacher appeared to perceive the major ability gap to lie between the students at Table 1 and those at Table 2. That is, those at Tables 2 and 3 were perceived as more similar in potential than were those at Tables 1 and 2. This was not the case in the second-grade classroom. The teacher appeared to perceive the major distinction in ability as lying between the Cardinals and the Clowns. Thus she saw the Tigers and the Cardinals as much closer in performance and potential than the Cardinals and the Clowns. The teacher's responses to the questions concerning the Clowns lends credence to this interpretation.

Q: Mrs. Benson, how would you describe the Clowns in terms of learning ability and academic performance?

R: Well, they are really slow. You know most of them are still doing first-grade work.

Q: Mrs. Benson, how would you describe the Clowns in terms of discipline matters?

R: They are very playful. They like to play a lot. They are not very neat. They like to talk a lot and play a lot. When I read to them, boy, do they have a good time. You know, the Tigers and the Cardinals will sit quietly and listen when I read to them, but the Clowns, they are always so restless. They always want to stand up. When we read, it is really something else. You know—Diane and Pat especially like to stand up. All these children, too, are very aggressive.

Q: Mrs. Benson, what value do you think the Clowns hold for an education?

R: I don't think very much. I don't think education means much to them at this stage. I know it doesn't mean anything to Randy and George. To most of the kids, I don't think it really matters at this stage.

FURTHER NOTES ON THE SECOND GRADE: REWARD AND PUNISHMENT

Throughout the length of the study in the school, it was evident that both the kindergarten and second-grade teachers were teaching the groups within their classes in a dissimilar manner. Variations were evident, for example, in the amount of time the teachers spent teaching the different groups, in the manner in which certain groups were granted privileges which were denied to others, and in the teacher's proximity to the different groups. Two additional considerations related to the teacher's use of reward and punishment.

Though variations were evident from naturalistic observations in the kindergarten, a systematic evaluation was not attempted of the degree to which such differential behavior was a significant aspect of the classroom interactional patterns. When observations were being conducted in the second grade, it appeared that there was on the part of Mrs. Benson a differentiation of reward and punishment similar to that displayed by Mrs. Caplow. In order to examine more closely the degree to which variations were present over time, three observational periods were totally devoted to the tabulation of each of the individual behavioral units directed by the teacher towards the children. Each observational period was three and one-half hours in length, lasting from 8:30 A.M. to 12:00 noon. The dates of the observations were the Fridays at the end of eight, twelve, and sixteen weeks of school—October 24, November 21, and December 19, 1969, respectively.

A mechanism for evaluating the varieties of teacher behavior was developed. Behavior on the part of the teacher was tabulated as a "behavioral unit" when there was clearly directed towards an individual child some manner of communication, whether it be verbal, non-verbal, or physical contact. When, within the interaction of the teacher and the student, there occurred more than one type of behavior, *i.e.,* the teacher spoke to the child and touched him, a count was made of both variations. The following is a list of the nine variations in teacher behavior that were tabulated within the second-grade classroom. Several examples are also included with each of the alternatives displayed by the teacher within the class.

1. Verbal Supportive—"That's a very good job." "You are such a lovely girl." "My, but your work is so neat."
2. Verbal Neutral—"Laura and Tom, let's open our books to page 34." "May, your pencil is on the floor." "Hal, do you have milk money today?"
3. Verbal Control—"Lou, sit on that chair and shut up." "Curt, get up off that floor." "Mary and Laura, quit your talking."
4. Non-verbal Supportive—Teacher nods her head at Rose. Teacher smiles at Liza. Teacher claps when Laura completes her problem at the board.
5. Non-verbal Neutral—Teacher indicates with her arms that she wants Lilly and Shirley to move farther apart in the circle. Teacher motions to Joe and Tom that they should try to snap their fingers to stay in beat with the music.
6. Non-verbal Control—Teacher frowns at Lena. Teacher shakes a finger at Amy to quit tapping her pencil. Teacher motions with hand for Rose not to come to her desk.
7. Physical Contact Supportive—Teacher hugs Laura. Teacher places her arm around Mary as she talks to her. Teacher holds Trish's hand as she takes out a splinter.
8. Physical Contact Neutral—Teacher touches head of Nick as she walks past. Teacher leads Rema to new place on the circle.
9. Physical Contact Control—Teacher strikes Lou with stick. Teacher pushes Curt down in his chair. Teacher pushes Hal and Doug to the floor.

Table 3 which follows is presented with all forms of control, supportive, and neutral behavior grouped together within each of the three observational periods. As a methodological precaution, since the categorization of the various types of behavior was decided as the interaction occurred and there was no cross-validation check by another observer, all behavior was placed in the appropriate neutral category which could not be clearly distinguished as belonging to one of the established supportive or control categories. This may explain the large percentage of neutral behavior tabulated in each of the three observational periods.

The picture of the second-grade teacher, Mrs. Benson, that emerges from analysis of these data is of one who distributes rewards quite sparingly and equally, but who utilizes somewhere between two and five times as much control-oriented behavior with the Clowns as with the Tigers. Alternatively, whereas with the Tigers the combination of neutral and supportive behavior never dropped below 93 percent of the total behavior directed towards them by the teacher in the three periods, the lowest figure for the Cardinals was 86 percent and for the Clowns was 73 percent. It may be assumed that neutral and supportive behavior would be conducive to learning while punishment or control-oriented behavior would not. Thus for the Tigers, the learning situation was one with only infrequent units of control, while for the Clowns, control behavior constituted one-fourth of all behavior directed towards them on at least one occasion.

Research related to leadership structure and task performance in voluntary organizations has given strong indications that within an authoritarian setting there occurs a significant decrease in performance on assigned tasks that does not occur with those in a non-authoritative setting (Kelly and Thibaut, 1954; Lewin, Lippitt, and White, 1939). Further investigations have generally confirmed these findings.

Of particular interest within the classroom are the findings of Adams (1945), Anderson (1946), Anderson, *et al.* (1946), Preston and Heintz (1949), and Robbins (1952). Their findings may be generalized to state that children within an au-

Variations in Teacher-Directed Behavior for Three Second-Grade Reading Groups During Three Observational Periods Within a Single Classroom

VARIATIONS IN TEACHER-DIRECTED BEHAVIOR

ITEM	CONTROL	SUPPORTIVE	NEUTRAL
Observational period #1*			
Tigers	5%–(6)**	7%–(8)	87%–(95)
Cardinals	10%–(7)	8%–(5)	82%–(58)
Clowns	27%–(27)	6%–(6)	67%–(67)
Observational Period #2			
Tigers	7%–(14)	8%–(16)	85%–(170)
Cardinals	7%–(13)	8%–(16)	85%–(157)
Clowns	14%–(44)	6%–(15)	80%–(180)
Observational Period #3			
Tigers	7%–(15)	6%–(13)	86%–(171)
Cardinals	14%–(20)	10%–(14)	85%–(108)
Clowns	15%–(36)	7%–(16)	78%–(188)

*Forty-eight (48) minutes of unequal teacher access (due to one group of children's being out of the room) was eliminated from the analysis.
**Value within the parentheses indicates total number of units of behavior within that category.

thoritarian classroom display a decrease in both learning retention and performance, while those within the democratic classroom do not. In extrapolating these findings to the second-grade classroom of Mrs. Benson, one cannot say that she was continually "authoritarian" as opposed to "democratic" with her students, but that with one group of students there occurred more control-oriented behavior than with other groups. The group which was the recipient of this control-oriented behavior was that group which she had defined as "slow and disinterested." On at least one occasion Mrs. Benson utilized nearly five times the amount of control-oriented behavior with the Clowns as with her perceived high-interest and high-ability group, the Tigers. For the Clowns, who were most isolated from the teacher and received the least amount of her teaching time, the results noted

above would indicate that the substantial control-oriented behavior directed towards them would compound their difficulty in experiencing significant learning and cognitive growth.

Here discussion of the self-fulfilling prophecy is relevant: given the extent to which the teacher utilized control-oriented behavior with the Clowns, data from the leadership and performance studies would indicate that it would be more difficult for that group to experience a positive learning situation. The question remains unanswered, though, as to whether the behavior of uninterested students necessitated the teacher's resorting to extensive use of control-oriented behavior, or whether that to the extent to which the teacher utilized control-oriented behavior, the students responded with uninterest. If the prior experience of the Clowns was in any way similar to that of the students in kindergarten at Table 3 and Table C in the first grade, I am inclined to opt for the latter proposition.

A very serious and, I believe, justifiable consequence of this assumption of student uninterest related to the frequency of the teachers' control-oriented behavior is that the teachers themselves contribute significantly to the creation of the "slow learners" within their classrooms. Over time, this may help to account for the phenomenon noted in the Coleman Report (1966) that the gap between the academic performance of the disadvantaged students and the national norms increased the longer the students remained in the school system. During one of the three and one-half hour observational periods in the second grade, the percentage of control-oriented behavior oriented toward the entire class was about 8 percent. Of the behavior directed toward the Clowns, however, 27 percent was control-oriented behavior—more than three times the amount of control-oriented behavior directed to the class as a whole. Deutsch (1968), in a random sampling of New York City Public School classrooms of the fifth through eighth grades, noted that the teachers utilized between 50 and 80 percent of class time in discipline and organization. Unfortunately, he fails to specify the two individual percentages and thus it is unknown whether the classrooms were dominated by either discipline or organization as opposed to their combination. If it is the case, and Deutsch's findings appear to lend indirect support, that the higher the grade level, the greater the discipline and control-oriented behavior by the teacher, some of the unexplained aspects of the "regress phenomenon" may be unlocked.

On another level of analysis, the teacher's use of control-oriented behavior is directly related to the expectations of the ability and willingness of "slow learners" to learn the material she teaches. That is, if the student is uninterested in what goes on in the classroom, he is more apt to engage in activities that the teacher perceives as disruptive. Activities such as talking out loud, coloring when the teacher has not said it to be permissible, attempting to leave the room, calling other students' attention to activities occurring on the street,

making comments to the teacher not pertinent to the lesson, dropping books, falling out of the chair, and commenting on how the student cannot wait for recess, all prompt the teacher to employ control-oriented behavior toward that student. The interactional pattern between the uninterested student and the teacher literally becomes a "vicious circle" in which control-oriented behavior is followed by further manifestations of uninterest, followed by further control behavior and so on. The stronger the reciprocity of this pattern of interaction, the greater one may anticipate the strengthening of the teacher's expectation of the "slow learner" as being either unable or unwilling to learn.

THE CASTE SYSTEM FALTERS

A major objective of this study has been to document the manner in which there emerges within the early grades a stratification system, based both on teacher expectations related to behavioral and attitudinal characteristics of the child and also on a variety of socio-economic status factors related to the background of the child. As noted, when the child begins to move through the grades, the variable of past performance becomes a crucial index of the position of the child within the different classes. The formulation of the system of stratification of the children into various reading groups appears to gain a caste-like character over time in that there was no observed movement into the highest reading group once it had been initially established at the beginning of the kindergarten school year. Likewise, there was no movement out of the highest reading group. There was movement between the second and third reading groups, in that those at the lowest reading table one year are combined with the middle group for a following year, due to the presence of a group of students repeating the grade.

Though formal observations in the second-grade class of Mrs. Benson ended in December of 1969, periodic informal visits to the class continued throughout the remainder of the school year. The organization of the class remained stable save for one notable exception. For the first time during observations in either kindergarten, first or second grade, there had been a reassignment of two students from the highest reading group to the middle reading group. Two students from the Tiger group were moved during the third week of January, 1970 from the Tiger group to the Cardinal group. Two Cardinal group students were assigned to replace those in the Tiger group. Mrs. Benson was asked the reason for the move and she explained that neither of the two former Tiger group students "could keep a clean desk." She noted that both of the students constantly had paper and crayons on the floor beside their desks. She stated that the Tigers "are a very clean group" and the two could no longer remain with the highest reading group because they were "not neat." The two Cardinals who were moved into the Tiger reading group were both described as "extremely neat with their desk and floor."

POOR KIDS AND PUBLIC SCHOOLS

It has been a major goal of this paper to demonstrate the impact of teacher expectations, based upon a series of subjectively interpreted social criteria, on both the anticipated academic potential and subsequent differential treatment accorded to those students perceived as having dissimilar social status. For the kindergarten teacher, expectations as to what type of child may be anticipated as a "fast learner" appear to be grounded in her reference group of a mixed white-black educated middle class. That is, students within her classroom who displayed those attributes which a number of studies have indicated are highly desired in children by middle-class educated adults as being necessary for future success were selected by her as possessing the potential to be a "fast learner." On the other hand, those children who did not possess the desired qualities were defined by the teacher as "slow learners." None of the criteria upon which the teacher appeared to base her evaluation of the children were directly related to measurable aspects of academic potential. Given that the I.Q.

test was administered to the children in the last week of their kindergarten year, the results could not have been of any benefit to the teacher as she established patterns of organization within the class.[5] The I.Q. scores may have been significant factors for the first- and second-grade teachers, but I assume that consideration of past performance was the major determinant for the seating arrangements which they established.[6]

For the first-grade teacher, Mrs. Logan, and the second-grade teacher, Mrs. Benson, the process of dividing the class into various reading groups, apparently on the basis of past performance, maintained the original patterns of differential treatment and expectations established in the kindergarten class. Those initially defined as "fast learners" by the kindergarten teacher in subsequent years continued to have that position in the first group, regardless of the label or name given to it.

It was evident throughout the length of the study that the teachers made clear the distinctions

_____

[5] The results of the I.Q. Test for the kindergarten class indicated that, though there were no statistically significant differences among the children at the three tables, the scores were skewed slightly higher for the children at Table 1. There were, however, children at Tables 2 and 3 who did score higher than several students at Table 1. The highest score came from a student at Table 1 (124) while the lowest came from a student at Table 3 (78). There appear to be at least three alternative explanations for the slightly higher scores by students at Table 1. First, the scores may represent the result of differential treatment in the classroom by Mrs. Caplow, thus contributing to the validation of the self-fulfilling prophecy. That is, the teacher by the predominance of teacher time spent with the Table 1 students, better prepared the students to do well on the examination than was the case for those students who received less teaching time. Secondly, the tests themselves may have reflected strong biases towards the knowledge and experience of middle-class children. Thus, students from higher-status families at Table 1 could be expected to perform better than did the low-status students from Table 3. The test resulted not in a "value free" measure of cognitive capacity, but in an index of family background. Third, of course, would be the fact that the children at the first table did possess a higher degree of academic potential than those at the other tables, and the teacher was intuitively able to discern these differences. This third alternative, however, is least susceptible to empirical verification.

[6] When the second-grade teacher was questioned as to what significance she placed in the results of I.Q. tests, she replied that "They merely confirm what I already know about the student."

they perceived between the children who were defined as fast learners and those defined as slow learners. It would not appear incorrect to state that within the classroom there was established by the various teachers a clear system of segregation between the two established groups of children. In the one group were all the children who appeared clean and interested, sought interactions with adults, displayed leadership within the class, and came from homes which displayed various status criteria valued in the middle class. In the other were children who were dirty, smelled of urine, did not actively participate in class, spoke a linguistic dialect other than that spoken by the teacher and students at Table 1, did not display leadership behavior, and came from poor homes often supported by public welfare. I would contend that within the system of segregation established by the teachers, the group perceived as slow learners were ascribed a caste position that sought to keep them apart from the other students.

The placement of the children within the various classrooms into different reading groups was ostensibly done on the promise of future performance in the kindergarten and on differentials of past performance in later grades. However, the placement may rather have been done from purely irrational reasons that had nothing to do with academic performance. The utilization of academic criteria may have served as the rationalization for a more fundamental process occurring with the class whereby the teacher served as the agent of the larger society to ensure that proper "social distance" was maintained between the various strata of the society as represented by the children.

Within the context of this analysis there appear to be at least two interactional processes that may be identified as having occurred simultaneously within the kindergarten classroom. The first was the relation of the teacher to the students placed at Table 1. The process appeared to occur in at least four stages. The initial stage involved the kindergarten teacher's developing expectations regarding certain students as possessing a series of characteristics that she considered essential for future academic "success." Second, the teacher reinforced through her mechanisms

of "positive" differential behavior those characteristics of the children that she considered important and desirable.

Third, the children responded with more of the behavior that initially gained them the attention and support of the teacher. Perceiving that verbalization, for example, was a quality that the teacher appeared to admire, the Table 1 children increased their level of verbalization throughout the school year. Fourth, the cycle was complete as the teacher focused even more specifically on the children at Table 1 who continued to manifest the behavior she desired. A positive interactional scheme arose whereby initial behavioral patterns of the student were reinforced into apparent permanent behavioral patterns, once he had received support and differential treatment from the teacher.

Within this framework, the actual academic potential of the students was not objectively measured prior to the kindergarten teacher's evaluation of expected performance. The students may be assumed to have had mixed potential. However, the common positive treatment accorded to all within the group by the teacher may have served as the necessary catalyst for the self-fulfilling prophecy whereby those expected to do well did so.

A concurrent behavioral process appeared to occur between the teacher and those students placed at Tables 2 and 3. The student came into the class possessing a series of behavioral and attitudinal characteristics that within the frame of reference of the teacher were perceived as indicative of "failure." Second, through mechanisms of reinforcement of her initial expectations as to the future performance of the student, it was made evident that he was not perceived as similar or equal to those at the table of fast learners. In the third stage, the student responded to both the definition and actual treatment given to him by the teacher which emphasized his characteristics of being an educational "failure." Given the high degree of control-oriented behavior directed toward the "slower" learner, the lack of verbal interaction and encouragement, the disproportionally small amount of teaching time given to him, and the ridicule and hostility, the child withdrew from class participation. The fourth stage was the cyclical repetition of behavioral and attitudinal characteristics that led to the initial labeling as an educational failure.

As with those perceived as having high probability of future success, the academic potential of the failure group was not objectively determined prior to evaluation by the kindergarten teacher. This group also may be assumed to have come into the class with mixed potential. Some within the group may have had the capacity to perform academic tasks quite well, while others perhaps did not. Yet the reinforcement by the teacher of the characteristics in the children that she had perceived as leading to academic failure may, in fact, have created the very conditions of student failure. With the "negative" treatment accorded to the perceived failure group, the teacher's definition of the situation may have ensured its emergence. What the teacher perceived in the children may have served as the catalyst for a series of interactions, with the result that the child came to act out within the class the very expectations defined for him by the teacher.

As an alternative explanation, however, the teacher may have developed the system of caste segregation within the classroom, not because the groups of children were so dissimilar they had to be handled in an entirely different manner, but because they were, in fact, so very close to one another. The teacher may have believed quite strongly that the ghetto community inhibited the development of middle-class success models. Thus, it was her duty to "save" at least one group of children from the "streets." Those children had to be kept separate who could have had a "bad" influence on the children who appeared to have a chance to "make it" in the middle class of the larger society. Within this framework, the teacher's actions may be understood not only as an attempt to keep the slow learners away from those fast learners, but to ensure that the fast learners would not be so influenced that they themselves become enticed with the "streets" and lose their apparent opportunity for future middle-class status.

In addition to the formal separation of the groups within the classroom, there was also the persistence of mechanisms utilized by the teacher to socialize the children in the high reading group with feelings of aversion, revulsion, and rejection towards those of the lower reading groups. Through ridicule, belittlement, physical punishment, and merely ignoring them, the teacher was continually giving clues to those in the high reading group as to how one with high status and a high probability of future success treats those of low status and low probability of future success. To maintain within the larger society the caste aspects of the position of the poor *vis à vis* the remainder of the society, there has to occur the transmission from one generation to another the attitudes and values necessary to legitimate and continue such a form of social organization.

Given the extreme intercomplexity of the organizational structure of this society, the institutions that both create and sustain social organization can neither be held singularly responsible for perpetuating the inequalities nor for eradicating them (cf. Leacock, 1969). The public school system, I believe, is justifiably responsible for contributing to the present structure of the society, but the responsibility is not its alone. The picture that emerges from this study is that the school strongly shares in the complicity of maintaining the organizational perpetuation of poverty and unequal opportunity. This, of course, is in contrast to the formal doctrine of education in this country to ameliorate rather than aggravate the conditions of the poor.

The teachers' reliance on a mixed black-white educated middle class for their normative reference group appeared to contain assumptions of superiority over those of lower class and status positions. For they and those members of their reference group, comfortable affluence, education, community participation, and possession of professional status may have afforded a rather stable view of the social order. The treatment of those from lower socio-economic backgrounds within the classrooms by the teachers may have indicated that the values highly esteemed by them were not open to members of the lower groups. Thus the lower groups were in numerous ways informed of their lower status and were socialized for a role of lower self expectations and also for respect and deference towards those of higher status. The social distance between the groups within the classrooms was manifested in its extreme form by the maintenance of patterns of caste segregation whereby those of lower positions were not allowed to become a part of the peer group at the highest level. The value system of the teachers appeared to necessitate that a certain group be ostracized due to "unworthiness" or inherent inferiority. The very beliefs which legitimated exclusion were maintained among those of the higher social group which then contributed to the continuation of the pattern of social organization itself.

It has not been a contention of this study that the teachers observed could not or would not teach their students. They did, I believe, teach quite well. But the high quality teaching was not made equally accessible to all students in the class. For the students of high socio-economic background who were perceived by the teachers as possessing desirable behavioral and attitudinal characteristics, the classroom experience was one where the teachers displayed interest in them, spent a large proportion of teaching time with them, directed little control-oriented behavior towards them, held them as models for the remainder of the class and continually reinforced statements that they were "special" students. Hypothetically, if the classrooms observed had contained only those students perceived by the teachers as having a desirable social status and a high probability of future success outside the confines of the ghetto community, the teachers could be assumed to have continued to teach well, and under these circumstance, to the entire class.

Though the analysis has focused on the early years of schooling for a single group of black children attending a ghetto school, the implications are far-reaching for those situations where there are children from different status backgrounds within the same classroom. When a teacher bases her expectations of performance on the social status of the student and assumes that the higher the social status, the higher the potential of the child, those children of low social status suffer a stigmatization outside of their own choice or will. Yet there is a greater tragedy than being labeled

as a slow learner, and that is being treated as one. The differential amounts of control-oriented behavior, the lack of interaction with the teacher, the ridicule from one's peers, and the caste aspects of being placed in lower reading groups all have implications for the future life style and value of education for the child.

Though it may be argued from the above that the solution to the existence of differential treatment for students is the establishment of schools catering to only a single segment of the population, I regard this as being antithetical to the goals of education—if one views the ultimate value of an education as providing insights and experience with thoughts and persons different from oneself. The thrust of the educational experience should be towards diversity, not homogeneity. It may be utopian to suggest that education should seek to encompass as wide a variety of individuals as possible within the same setting, but it is no mean goal to pursue.

The success of an educational institution and any individual teacher should not be measured by the treatment of the high-achieving students, but rather by the treatment of those not achieving. As is the case with a chain, ultimate value is based on the weakest member. So long as the lower-status students are treated differently in both quality and quantity of education, there will exist an imperative for change.

It should be apparent, of course, that if one desires this society to retain its present social class configuration and the disproportional access to wealth, power, social and economic mobility, medical care, and choice of life styles, one should not disturb the methods of education as presented in this study. This contention is made because what develops as "caste" within the classrooms appears to emerge in the larger society as "class." The low-income children segregated as a caste of "unclean and intellectually inferior" persons may very well be those who in their adult years become the car washers, dishwashers, welfare recipients, and participants in numerous other un- or underemployed roles within this society. The question may quite honestly be asked, "Given the treatment of low-income children from the beginning of their kindergarten experience, for what class strata are they being prepared other than that of the lower class?" It appears that the public school system not only mirrors the configurations of the larger society, but also significantly contributes to maintaining them. Thus the system of public education in reality perpetuates what it is ideologically committed to eradicate—class barriers which result in inequality in the social and economic life of the citizenry.

REFERENCES

Adams, R. G. "The Behavior of Pupils in Democratic and Autocratic Social Climates." Abstracts of Dissertations, Stanford University, 1945.

Anderson, H. *Studies in Teachers' Classroom Personalities.* Stanford: Stanford University Press, 1946.

Anderson, H.; Brewer, J.; and Reed, M. "Studies of Teachers' Classroom Personalities, III. Follow-up Studies of the Effects of Dominative and Integrative Contacts on Children's Behavior." *Applied Psychology Monograph.* Stanford: Stanford University Press, 1946.

Asbell, B. "Not Like Other Children." *Redbook,* 65 (October, 1963), pp. 114-118.

Austin, Mary C. and Morrison, Coleman. *The First R; The Harvard Report on Reading in Elementary Schools,* New York: Macmillan, 1963.

Becker, H. S. "Social Class Variation in Teacher-Pupil Relationship." *Journal of Educational Sociology,* 1952, 25, 451-465.

Borg, W. "Ability Grouping in the Public Schools." Cooperative Research Project 557. Salt Lake City: Utah State University, 1964.

Clark, K. B. "Educational Stimulation of Racially Disadvantaged Children." *Education in Depressed Areas.* Edited by A.H. Passow, New York: Columbia University Press, 1963.

Coleman, J. S., *et al. Equality of Educational Opportunity.* Washington, D.C.: United States Government Printing Office, 1966.

Deutsch, M. "Minority Groups and Class Status as Related to Social and Personality Factors in Scholastic Achievement." *The Disadvantaged Child.* Edited by M. Deutsch, *et al.* New York: Basic Books, 1967.

Eddy, E. *Walk the White Line.* Garden City, N.Y.: Doubleday, 1967.

Frazier, E. F. *Black Bourgeoisie.* New York: The Free Press, 1957.

Freeman, R.; Whelpton, P.; and Campbell, A. *Family Planning, Sterility and Population Growth.* New York: McGraw-Hill, 1959.

Fuchs, E. *Teachers Talk.* Garden City, N.Y.: Doubleday, 1967.

Gebhard, P.; Pomeroy, W.; Martin, C.; and Christenson, C. *Pregnancy, Birth and Abortion.* New York: Harper & Row, 1958.

Gibson, G. "Aptitude Tests." *Science,* 1965, *149,* 583.

Goldberg, M.; Passow, A.; and Justman, J. *The Effects of Ability Grouping.* New York: Teachers College Press, Columbia University, 1966.

Harlem Youth Opportunities Unlimited. *Youth in the Ghetto.* New York: HARYOU, 1964.

Henry, J. "Docility, or Giving the Teacher What She Wants." *Journal of Social Issues,* 1955, *11,* 2.

———, "The Problem of Spontaneity, Initiative and Creativity in Suburban Classrooms." *American Journal of Orthopsychiatry,* 1959, *29,* 1.

———, "Golden Rule Days: American Schoolrooms." *Culture Against Man,* New York: Random House, 1963.

Hollingshead, A. *Elmtown's Youth.* New York: John Wiley & Sons, 1949.

Jackson, P. *Life in Classrooms.* New York: Holt, Rinehart & Winston, 1968.

Kahl, J. A. *The American Class Structure.* New York: Holt, Rinehart & Winston, 1957.

Katz, I. "Review of Evidence Relating to Effects of Desegregation on Intellectual Performance of Negroes." *American Psychologist,* 1964, *19,* 381-399.

Kelly, H. and Thibaut, J. "Experimental Studies of Group Problem Solving and Process." *Handbook of Social Psychology,* Vol. 2. Edited by G. Lindzey, Reading, Mass.: Addison-Wesley, 1954.

Kohl, H. *36 Children.* New York: New American Library, 1967.

Kozol, J. *Death at an Early Age.* Boston: Houghton Mifflin, 1967.

Kvaraceus, W.C. "Disadvantaged Children and Youth: Programs of Promise or Pretense?" Burlingame: California Teachers Association, 1965. (Mimeographed.)

Lawrence, S. "Ability Grouping." Unpublished manuscript prepared for Center for Educational Policy Research, Harvard Graduate School of Education, Cambridge, Mass., 1969.

Leacock, E. *Teaching and Learning in City Schools.* New York: Basic Books, 1969.

Lewin, K.; Lippitt, R.; and White, R. "Patterns of Aggressive Behavior in Experimentally Created Social Climates." *Journal of Social Psychology,* 1939, *10,* 271-299.

Lynd, H. and Lynd, R. *Middletown in Transition.* New York: Harcourt, Brace & World, 1937.

MacKinnon, D. W. "The Nature and Nurture of Creative Talent." *American Psychologist,* 1962, *17,* 484-495.

Merton, R. K. *Social Theory and Social Structure.* Revised and Enlarged. New York: The Free Press, 1957.

Moore, A. *Realities of the Urban Classroom.* Garden City, N.Y.: Doubleday, 1967.

Notestein, F. "Class Differences in Fertility." *Class, Status and Power.* Edited by R. Bendix and S. Lipset. New York: The Free Press, 1953.

Preston, M. and Heintz, R. "Effects of Participatory Versus Supervisory Leadership on Group Judgment." *Journal of Abnormal Social Psychology,* 1949, *44,* 345-355.

Reissman, F. *The Culturally Deprived Child.* New York: Harper and Row, 1962.

———, "Teachers of the Poor: A Five Point Program." Burlingame: California Teachers Association, 1965. (Mimeographed.)

Reissman, L. *Class in American Society.* New York: The Free Press, 1959.

Robbins, F. "The Impact of Social Climate upon a College Class." *School Review,* 1952, *60,* 275-284.

Rose, A. *The Negro in America.* Boston: Beacon Press, 1956.

Rosenthal, R. and Jacobson, Lenore. *Pygmalion in the Classroom.* New York: Holt, Rinehart & Winston, 1968.

Sigel, I. "The Piagetian System and the World of Education." *Studies in Cognitive Development.* Edited by D. Elkind and J. Flavell, New York: Oxford University Press, 1969.

Simpson, G. and Yinger, J. M. *Racial and Cultural Minorities.* New York: Harper and Row, 1958.

Smith, L. and Geoffrey, W. *The Complexities of an Urban Classroom.* New York: Holt, Rinehart & Winston, 1968.

Smith, M. "Equality of Educational Opportunity: The Basic Findings Reconsidered." *On Equality of Educational Opportunity.* Edited by F. Mosteller and D. P. Moynihan. New York: Random House, 1971 (In Press).

Warner, W. L.; Havighurst, R.; and Loeb, M. *Who Shall Be Educated?* New York: Harper and Row, 1944.

Wilson, A. B. "Social Stratification and Academic Achievement." *Education in Depressed Areas.* Edited by A. H. Passow. New York: Teachers College Press, Columbia University, 1963.

Education in a Multicultural Society: Our Future's Greatest Challenge

LISA DELPIT

———————

In any discussion of education and culture, it is important to remember that children are individuals and cannot be made to fit into any preconceived mold of how they are "supposed" to act. The question is not necessarily how to create the perfect "culturally matched" learning situation for each ethnic group, but rather how to recognize when there is a problem for a particular child and how to seek its cause in the most broadly conceived fashion. Knowledge about culture is but one tool that educators may make use of when devising solutions for a school's difficulty in educating diverse children.

THE CULTURAL CLASH BETWEEN STUDENTS AND SCHOOL

The clash between school culture and home culture is actualized in at least two ways. When a significant difference exists between the students' culture and the school's culture, teachers can easily misread students' aptitudes, intent, or abilities as a result of the difference in styles of language use and interactional patterns. Secondly, when such cultural differences exist, teachers may utilize styles of instruction and/or discipline that are at odds with community norms. A few examples: A twelve-year-old friend tells me that there are three kinds of teachers in his middle school: the black teachers, none of whom are afraid of black kids; the white teachers, a few of whom are not afraid of black kids; and the largest group of white teachers, who are *all* afraid of black kids. It is this last group that, according to my young informant, consistently has the most difficulty with teaching and whose students have the most difficulty with learning.

I would like to suggest that some of the problems may certainly be as this young man relates. Yet, from my work with teachers in many set-tings, I have come to believe that a major portion of the problem may also rest with how these three groups of teachers interact and use language with their students. These differences in discourse styles relate to certain ethnic and class groups. For instance, many African-American teachers are likely to give directives to a group of unruly students in a direct and explicit fashion, for example, "I don't want to hear it. Sit down, be quiet, and finish your work NOW!" Not only is this directive explicit, but with it the teacher also displays a high degree of personal power in the classroom. By contrast, many middle-class European-American teachers are likely to say something like, "Would you like to sit down now and finish your paper?", making use of an indirect command and downplaying the display of power. Partly because the first instance is likely to be more like the statements many African-American children hear at home, and partly because the second statement sounds to

———————

many of these youngsters like the words of some-one who is fearful (and thus less deserving of re-spect), African-American children are more likely to obey the first explicit directive and ignore the second implied directive.

The discussion of this issue is complex, but, in brief, many of the difficulties teachers en-counter with children who are different in back-ground from themselves are related to this under-lying attitudinal difference in the appropriate display of explicitness and personal power in the classroom.

If teachers are to teach effectively, recogni-tion of the importance of student perception of teacher intent is critical. Problems arising from culturally different interactional styles seem to disproportionately affect African-American boys, who, as a result of cultural influences, exhibit a high degree of physicality and desire for interac-tion. This can be expressed both positively and negatively, as hugging and other shows of affec-tion or as hitting and other displays of displeas-ure. Either expression is likely to receive negative sanction in the classroom setting.

Researcher Harry Morgan documents in a 1990 study what most of us who have worked with African-American children have learned intu-itively: that African-American children, more than white, and boys more than girls, initiate interac-tions with peers in the classroom in performing assigned tasks. Morgan concludes that a classroom that allows for greater movement and interaction will better facilitate the learning and social styles of African-American boys, while one that disal-lows such activity will unduly penalize them. This, I believe, is one of the reasons that there re-cently has been such a movement toward devel-oping schools specifically for African-American males. Black boys *are* unduly penalized in our reg-ular classrooms. They *are* disproportionately as-signed to special education. They do not have to be, and would not be, if our teachers were taught how to redesign classrooms so that the styles of African-American boys are accommodated.

I would like to share with you an example of a student's ability being misread as a result of a mismatch between the student's and teacher's cultural use of language. Second-grader Marti was reading a story she had written that began, "Once upon a time, there was an old lady, and this old lady ain't had *no* sense." The teacher interrupted her, "Marti, that sounds like the beginning of a wonderful story, but could you tell me how you would say it in Standard English?" Marti put her hand on her hip, raised her voice and said, "But this old lady ain't had *no* sense!" Marti's teacher probably did not understand that the child was actually exhibiting a very sophisticated sense of language. Although she clearly knew the Standard English form, she chose a so-called nonstandard form for emphasis, just as world-class writers Charles Chesnutt, Alice Walker, Paul Laurence Dunbar, and Zora Neale Hurston have done for years. Of course, there is no standardized test presently on the market that can discern that level of sophistication. Marti's misuse of Standard English would simply be assessed as a "mistake." Thus, differences in cultural language patterns make inappropriate assessments commonplace.

Another example of assessment difficulties arising from differences in culture can be found in the Latino community. Frequently, Latino girls find it difficult to speak out or exhibit academic prowess in a gender-mixed setting. They will often defer to boys, displaying their knowledge only when in the company of other girls. Most teachers, unaware of this tendency, are likely to insist that all groups be gender-mixed, thus de-pressing the exhibition of ability by the Latino girls in the class.

A final example involves Native Americans. In many Native American communities there is a prohibition against speaking for someone else. So strong is this prohibition that to the question, "Does your son like moose?", an adult Native American man responded to what should have been asked instead: "*I* like moose." The conse-quence of this cultural interactional pattern may have contributed to the findings in Charlotte Basham's study of a group of Native American college students' writing. The students appeared unable to write summaries and, even when ex-plicitly told not to, continued to write their opin-ions of various works rather than summaries of the authors' words. Basham concludes that the prohibition against speaking for others may have caused these students considerable difficulty in trying to capture in their own words the ideas of another. Because they had been taught to always speak for themselves, they found doing so much more comfortable and culturally compatible.

STEREOTYPING

There is a widespread belief that Asian-American children are the "perfect" students, that they will do well regardless of the academic setting in which they are placed. This stereotype has led to a negative backlash in which the academic needs of the majority of Asian-American students are overlooked. I recall one five-year-old Asian-American girl in a Montessori kindergarten class. Cathy was dutifully going about the task assigned to her, that of placing a number of objects next to various numerals printed on a cloth. She appeared to be thoroughly engaged, attending totally to the task at hand, and never disturbing anyone near her. Meanwhile, the teacher's attention was devoted to the children who demanded her presence in one form or another or to those she believed would have difficulty with the task assigned them. Small, quiet Cathy fit neither category. At the end of work time, no one had come to see what Cathy had done, and Cathy neatly put away her work. Her behavior and attention to task had been exemplary. The only problem was that at the end of the session no numeral had the correct number of objects next to it. The teacher later told me that Cathy, like Asian-American students she had taught previously, was one of the best students in the class. Yet, in this case, a child's culturally influenced, nondisruptive classroom behavior, along with the teacher's stereotype of "good Asian students," led to her not receiving appropriate instruction.

Another example of stereotyping involved African-American girls. Research has been conducted in classroom settings which shows that African-American girls are rewarded for nurturing behavior while white girls are rewarded for academic behavior. Though it is likely true that many African-American girls are excellent nurturers, having played with or helped to care for younger siblings or cousins, they are penalized by the nurturing "mammy" stereotype when they are not given the same encouragement as white girls toward academic endeavors.

Another example of stereotyping concerns Native American children. Many researchers and classroom teachers have described the "nonverbal Indian child." What is often missed in these descriptions is that these children are as verbal and eager to share their knowledge as any others, but they need appropriate contexts—such as small groups—in which to talk. When asked inappropriate questions or called on to talk before the entire class, many Native American children will refuse to answer, or will answer in as few words as possible. Thus, teachers sometimes refrain from calling on Native American students to avoid causing them discomfort, and these children subsequently miss the opportunity to discuss or display their knowledge of the subject matter.

A primary source of stereotyping is often the teacher education program itself. It is in these programs that teachers learn that poor students and students of color should be expected to achieve less than their "mainstream" counterparts.

CHILD-DEFICIT ASSUMPTIONS THAT LEAD TO TEACHING LESS INSTEAD OF MORE

We say we believe that all children can learn, but few of us really believe it. Teacher education usually focuses on research that links failure and socioeconomic status, failure and cultural difference, and failure and single-parent households. It is hard to believe that these children can possibly be successful after their teachers have been so thoroughly exposed to so much negative indoctrination. When teachers receive that kind of education, there is a tendency to assume deficits in students rather than to locate and teach to strengths. To counter this tendency, educators must have knowledge of children's lives outside of school so as to recognize their strengths.

One of my former students is a case in point. Howard was in first grade when everyone thought that he would need to be placed in special education classes. Among his other academic problems, he seemed totally unable to do even the simplest mathematics worksheets. During the unit on money, determining the value of nickels and dimes seemed hopelessly beyond him. I agreed with the general assessment of him until I got to know something about his life outside of school. Howard was seven years old. He had a younger sister who was four and afflicted with cerebral palsy. His mother was suffering from a drug problem and was unable to adequately care for the children, so Howard was the main caretaker in the family. Each morning, he would get his sister up, dressed, and off to school. He also did the family laundry and much of the shopping. To do both those tasks, he had become expert at counting money and knowing when or if the local grocer was overcharging. Still, he was unable to complete what appeared to his teachers to be a simple worksheet. Without teachers having knowledge of his abilities outside of school he was destined to be labeled mentally incompetent.

This story also exposes how curriculum content is typically presented. Children who may be gifted in real-life settings are often at a loss when asked to exhibit knowledge solely through decontextualized paper-and-pencil exercises. I have often pondered that if we taught African-American children how to dance in school, by the time they had finished the first five workbooks on the topic, we would have a generation of remedial dancers!

If we do not have some knowledge of children's lives outside of the realms of paper-and-pencil work, and even outside of their classrooms, then we cannot know their strengths. Not knowing students' strengths leads to our "teaching down" to children from communities that are culturally different from that of the teachers in the school. Because teachers do not want to tax what they believe to be these students' lower abilities, they end up teaching less when, in actuality, these students need *more* of what school has to offer. This is not a new concept. In 1933

Carter G. Woodson discussed the problem in *The Mis-Education of the Negro:*

> The teaching of arithmetic in the fifth grade in a backward county in Mississippi should mean one thing in the Negro school and a decidedly different thing in the white school. The Negro children, as a rule, come from the homes of tenants and peons who have to migrate annually from plantation to plantation, looking for light which they have never seen. The children from the homes of white planters and merchants live permanently in the midst of calculation, family budgets, and the like, which enable them sometimes to learn more by contact than the Negro can acquire in school. Instead of teaching such Negro children less arithmetic, they should be taught much more of it than white children.

Teaching less rather than teaching more can happen in several ways. Those who utilize "skills-based" approaches can teach less by focusing solely on isolated, decontextualized bits. Such instruction becomes boring and meaningless when not placed in any meaningful context. When instruction allows no opportunity for children to use their minds to create and interpret texts, then children will only focus on low-level thinking and their school-based intellect will atrophy. Skills-oriented approaches that feature heavy doses of readiness activities also contribute to the "teaching less" phenomenon. Children are typically assigned to these activities as a result of low scores on some standardized test. However, they end up spending so much time matching circles and triangles that no one ever introduces them to actually learning how to read. Should anyone doubt it, I can guarantee you that no amount of matching circles and triangles ever taught anyone how to read. Worse, these activities take time away from real kinds of involvement in literacy such as listening to and seeing the words in real books.

Teaching less can also occur with those who favor "holistic" or "child-centered" approaches. While I believe that there is much of value in whole language and process writing approaches, some teachers seem almost to be using these methodologies as excuses for not teaching. I am reminded of a colleague who visited a classroom in California designed around the state-mandated whole language approach. My colleague witnessed one child in a peer reading group who clearly could not read. When she later asked the teacher about this child, the teacher responded that it was "OK" that this fourth-grader could not read, because he would understand the content via the subsequent discussion. While it is great that the child would have the opportunity to learn through a discussion, it is devastating that no one was providing him with what he also needed—explicit instruction in learning how to read.

In some "process writing" classrooms, teachers unfamiliar with the language abilities of African-American children are led to believe that these students have no fluency with language. They therefore allow them to remain in the first stages of the writing process, producing first draft after first draft, with no attention to editing or completing final products. They allow African-American students to remain at the level of developing fluency because these teachers do not understand the language competence their students already possess. The key here is not the kind of instruction but the attitude underlying it. When teachers do not understand the potential of the students they teach, they will underteach them no matter what the methodology.

IGNORANCE OF COMMUNITY NORMS

Many school systems have attempted to institute "parent training" programs for poor parents and parents of color. While the intentions of these programs are good, they can only be truly useful when educators understand the realities with which such parents must contend and why they do what they do. Often, middle-class school professionals are appalled by what they see of poor parents, and most do not have the training or the ability to see past surface behaviors to the meanings behind parents' actions.

In a preschool I have often visited, four-year-old David's young mother once came to his class to provide a birthday party for her son. I happened to hear the conversation of the teachers that afternoon. They said she came to school in a "bum costume" yelling, "Let's party!" and running around the room. She had presents for all the children and a cake she or someone else had baked for the occasion. The teachers were horrified. They said they could smell alcohol on her breath, that the children went wild, and that they attempted to get the children out to recess as quickly as possible.

From an earlier conversation, I happened to know that this woman cares deeply for her son and his welfare. She is even saving money to put him in private school—a major sacrifice for her—when he enters kindergarten. David's teachers, however, were not able to see that, despite her possible inappropriateness, his mother had actually spent a great deal of effort and care in putting together this party for her son. She also probably felt the need to bolster her courage a bit with a drink in order to face fifteen four-year-olds and keep them entertained. We must find ways for professionals to understand the different ways in which parents can show their concern for their children.

Another example of a cultural barrier between teacher understandings and parental understanding occurred at a predominantly Latino school in Boston. Even though the teachers continually asked them not to, the parents, primarily mothers, kept bringing their first graders into their classroom before the school day officially began. The teachers wanted all children to remain on the playground with a teacher's aide, and they also wanted all parents to vacate the school yard as soon as possible while the teacher readied the classrooms for the beginning of the day. When the parents continued to ignore the request, the teachers began locking the school doors. Pretty soon feelings escalated to the point of yelling matches, and the parents even approached the school board.

What the teachers in this instance did not understand was that the parents viewed six-year-olds as still being babies and in need of their mother's or their surrogate mother's (the teacher's) attention. To the parents, leaving children outside without one of their "mothers" present was tantamount to child abuse and exhibited a most callous disregard for the children's welfare. The situation did not have to have become so highly charged. All that was needed was some knowledge about the parents and community of the children they were teaching, and the teachers could have resolved the problem easily—perhaps by stationing one of the first-grade teachers outside in the mornings, or by inviting one of the parents to remain on the school grounds before the teachers called the children in to class.

INVISIBILITY

Whether we are immediately aware of it or not, the United States is surely composed of a plethora of perspectives. I am reminded of this every time I think of my friend Martha, a Native American teacher. Martha told me how tired she got of being asked about her plans for Thanksgiving by people who seemed to take no note that her perspective on the holiday might be a bit different than their own. One year, in her frustration, she told me that when the next questioner asked, "What are you doing for Thanksgiving?", she answered, "I plan to spend the day saying, 'You're welcome!'"

If we plan to survive as a species on this planet we must certainly create multicultural curricula that educate our children to the differing perspectives of our diverse population. In part, the problems we see exhibited in school by African-American children and children of other oppressed minorities can be traced to this lack of a curriculum in which they can find represented the intellectual achievements of people who look like themselves. Were that not the case, these children would not talk about doing well in school as "acting white." Our children of color need to see the brilliance of their legacy, too.

Even with well-intentioned educators, not only our children's legacies but our children themselves can become invisible. Many of the teachers we ed-

ucate, and indeed their teacher educators, believe that to acknowledge a child's color is to insult him or her. In her book *White Teacher,* Vivian Paley openly discusses the problems inherent in the statement that I have heard many teachers—well-intentioned teachers—utter, "I don't see color, I only see children." What message does this statement send? That there is something wrong with being black or brown, that it should *not* be noticed? I would like to suggest that if one does not see color, then one does not really see children. Children made "invisible" in this manner become hard-pressed to see themselves worthy of notice.

ADDRESSING THE PROBLEMS OF EDUCATING POOR AND CULTURALLY DIVERSE CHILDREN

To begin with, our prospective teachers are exposed to descriptions of failure rather than models of success. We expose student teachers to an education that relies upon name calling and labelling ("disadvantaged," "at-risk," "learning disabled," "the underclass") to explain its failures, and calls upon research study after research study to inform teachers that school achievement is intimately and inevitably linked with socioeconomic status. Teacher candidates are told that "culturally different" children are mismatched to the school setting and therefore cannot be expected to achieve as well as white, middle-class children. They are told that children of poverty are developmentally slower than other children.

Seldom, however, do we make available to our teacher initiates the many success stories about educating poor children and children of color: those institutions like the Nairobi Day-School in East Palo Alto, California, which produced children from poor African-American communities who scored three grade levels above the national average. Nor do we make sure that they learn about those teachers who are quietly going about the job of producing excellence in educating poor and culturally diverse students: teachers like Marva Collins of Chicago, Illinois, who has educated many African-American students considered uneducable by public schools; Jaime Escalante, who has consistently taught hundreds of Latino high school students who live in the poorest *barrios* of East Los Angeles to test their way into advanced-placement calculus classes; and many other successful unsung heroes and heroines who are seldom visible in teacher education classrooms.

Interestingly, even when such teaching comes to our consciousness, it is most often not by way of educational research but via the popular media. We educators do not typically research and document this "power pedagogy" (as Asa Hilliard calls it), but continue to provide, at worst, autopsies of failure and, at best, studies in minimalist achievement. In other words, we teach teachers rationales for failure, not visions of success. Is there any wonder that those who are products of such teacher education (from classroom teachers to principals to central office staff) water down the curriculum for diverse students instead of challenging them with more, as Woodson says, of what school has to offer?

A second reason problems occur for our culturally diverse students is that we have created in most schools institutions of isolation. We foster the notion that students are clients of "professional" educators who are met in the "office" of the classroom where their deficiencies are remediated and their intellectual "illnesses" healed. Nowhere do we foster inquiry into who our students really are or encourage teachers to develop links to the often rich home lives of students, yet teachers cannot hope to begin to understand who sits before them unless they can connect with the families and communities from which their students come. To do that, it is vital that teachers and teacher educators explore their own beliefs and attitudes about non-white and non-middle-class people. Many teachers—black, white, and "other"— harbor unexamined prejudices about people from ethnic groups or classes different from their own. This is partly because teachers have been so conditioned by the larger society's negative stereotypes of certain ethnic groups, and partly because they are never given the opportunity to learn to value the experiences of other groups.

I propose that a part of teacher education include bringing parents and community members into the university classroom to tell prospective teachers (and their teacher educators) what their concerns about education are, what they feel schools are doing well or poorly for their children, and how they would like to see schooling changed. I would also like to see teacher initiates and their educators go out to community gatherings to acquire such firsthand knowledge. It is unreasonable to expect that teachers will automatically value the knowledge that parents and community members bring to the education of diverse children if valuing such knowledge has not been modelled for them by those from whom they learn to teach.

Following a speech I made at a conference a few years ago, I have been corresponding with a very insightful teacher who works at a prestigious university lab school. The school is staffed by a solely European-American faculty, but seeks to maintain racial and cultural balance among the student body. They find, however, that they continue to lose black students, especially boys. The teacher, named Richard, wrote to me that the school often has problems, both behavioral and academic, with African-American boys. When called to the school to discuss these problems, these children's parents typically say that they do not understand, that their children are fine at home. The school personnel interpret these statements as indications of the parents' "being defensive," and presume that the children are as difficult at home as at school, but that the parents do not want to admit it.

When Richard asked for some suggestions, my first recommendation was that the school should work hard to develop a multicultural staff. Of course, that solution would take a while, even if the school was committed to it. My next and actually most important suggestion was that the school needed to learn to view its African-American parents as a resource and not as a problem. When problems arise with particular African-American children, the school should get the parents of these children involved in helping to point out what the school might do better.

Richard wrote back to me:

The change though that has made me happiest so far about my own work is that I have taken your advice and I am asking black parents about stuff I never would have brought up before. . . . We do a lot of journal writing, and with the 6- to 8-year-olds I teach, encourage them to draw as well as write, to see the journal as a form of expression. I was having a conference with the mother of one black boy. . . . We looked at his journal and saw that he was doing beautiful intricate drawings, but that he rarely got more than a few words down on the page. I talked to his mother about how we were trying to encourage C. to do the writing first, but that he liked to draw.

During the conversation I started to see this as something like what you were talking about, and I asked C.'s mom how she would handle this at home. I only asked her about how she herself might deal with this, but she said, "In black families, we would just tell him write the words first." I passed that information on to C.'s reading teacher, and we both talked to him and told him he had to get the words down first. Suddenly he began making one- and two-page entries into his journal.

While this is pleasing in and of itself, it is an important lesson to us in terms of equity. C. is now getting equal access to the curriculum because he is using the journal for the reasons we intended it. All we needed was a culturally appropriate way to tell him how to do it.

I am not suggesting that excellent teachers of diverse students *must* be of their students' ethnicity. I have seen too many excellent European-American teachers of African-American students, and too many poor African-American teachers of African-American students to come to such an illogical conclusion. I do believe, however, that we should strive to make our teaching force diverse, for teachers who share the ethnic and cultural backgrounds of our increasingly diverse student bodies may serve, along with parents and other community members, to provide insights that might otherwise remain hidden.

The third problem I believe we must overcome is the narrow and essentially Eurocentric curriculum we provide for our teachers. At the university level, teachers are not being educated with the broad strokes necessary to prepare them properly for the twenty-first century. We who are concerned about teachers and teaching must insist that our teachers become knowledgeable of the liberal arts, but we must also work like the dickens to change liberal arts courses so that they do not continue to reflect only, as feminist scholar Peggy McIntosh says, "the public lives of white Western men." These new courses must not only teach what white Westerners have to say about diverse cultures, they must also share what the writers and thinkers of diverse cultures have to say about themselves, their history, music, art, literature, politics, and so forth.

If we know the intellectual legacies of our students, we will gain insight into how to teach them. Stephanie Terry, a first-grade teacher I have recently interviewed, breathes the heritage of her students into the curriculum. Stephanie teaches in an economically strapped community in inner-city Baltimore, Maryland, in a school with a 100 percent African-American enrollment. She begins each year with the study of Africa, describing Africa's relationship to the United States, its history, resources, and so forth. As her students learn each new aspect of the regular citywide curriculum, Stephanie connects this knowledge to aspects of their African ancestry; while covering a unit about libraries she tells them about the world's first libraries, which were established in Africa. A unit on health presents her with the opportunity to tell her students about the African doctors of antiquity who wrote the first texts on medicine. Stephanie does not replace the current curriculum; rather, she expands it. She also teaches about the contributions of Asian-Americans, Native Americans, and Latinos as she broadens her students' minds and spirits. All of Stephanie's students learn to read by the end of the school year. They also learn to love themselves, love their history, and love learning.

Stephanie could not teach her children the pride of their ancestry and could not connect it to the material they learn today were it not for her extraordinarily broad knowledge of the liberal arts. However, she told me that she did not acquire this knowledge in her formal education, but worked, read, and studied on her own to make such knowledge a part of her pedagogy.

Teachers must not merely take courses that tell them how to treat their students as multicultural clients, in other words, those that tell them how to identify differences in interactional or communicative strategies and remediate appropriately. They must also learn about the brilliance the students bring with them "in their blood." Until they appreciate the wonders of the cultures represented before them—and they cannot do that without extensive study most appropriately begun in college-level courses—they cannot appreciate the potential of those who sit before them, nor can they begin to link their students' histories and worlds to the subject matter they present in the classroom.

If we are to successfully educate all of our children, we must work to remove the blinders built of stereotypes, monocultural instructional methodologies, ignorance, social distance, biased research, and racism. We must work to destroy those blinders so that it is possible to really see, to really know the students we must teach. Yes, if we are to be successful at educating diverse children, we must accomplish the Herculean feat of developing this clear-sightedness, for in the words of a wonderful Native Alaskan educator: "In order to teach you, I must know you." I pray for all of us the strength to teach our children what they must learn, and the humility and wisdom to learn from them so that we might better teach.

STUDY QUESTIONS FOR PART 5

1. Given that teacher expectations and social interactions are strong forces within classrooms, what are the ways that they can have positive consequences for students? What are some examples where these forces might diminish a child's success in the classroom?

2. Even though many school drop-outs usually do not physically "leave" until high school, the seeds for that destiny seem to be planted much earlier. What can teachers do to reduce the number of children inclined to leave school?

3. The first teacher in the Rist article believed it was going to be very tough for her students to "make it" because of their ethnicity and poverty. Because she felt as an individual that she couldn't help all of her children succeed, she decided to focus on the students with the most potential and pump them up by building their skills and self-esteem. In her view, rather than giving just a little bit to everyone, she gave a lot to a few. She felt she was simply trying to give every advantage to the best of the group in the hopes that these few could make it and return one day as teachers, social workers, doctors, lawyers, and so forth to help in the community. Is this a defensible position for a teacher? Why? Was she a reflective teacher? What would Lisa Delpit say about this attitude?

4. How would a functionalist explain the scenario described by Rist? What would Lisa Delpit say about what Rist described? How would a conflict theorist explain the scenario described by Rist?

5. If the teacher in the school described by Rist had followed the principles advocated by Delpit, how might things have been different for the children? What might have been some differences in the teacher's orientation to students?

6. What changes in our expectations for the role of teachers might enable teachers to more adequately serve the diverse range of learners in contemporary classrooms? What changes in our expectations for the role of students might enable teachers to more adequately serve more students?

7. Should the ideas espoused by Delpit be applied in a school serving primarily middle-class white children? Why? How? In a school like this, what are teachers' responsibilities as educators in a multicultural society?

8. The tools available to students and teachers have changed considerably over the last decade, and the emerging advances in electronic technology promise even greater possibilities than have heretofore been imaginable. In what ways might teaching and learning be enhanced by these new tools; and in what ways might these new tools change the roles of students and teachers?

PART 6

EDUCATION AND SOCIETAL INEQUALITY: RACE, GENDER, CLASS, AND ETHNICITY

It is tempting to think in this day and age, given our nation's resources and everything we've learned about effective schooling, that the harmful practices of the past have by now been "fixed" in education. That is, that sufficient federal and state laws have been enacted and public awareness has been raised to the level where schools are truly equitable places in which all students can learn.

This, unfortunately, is not the case. Despite the tremendous strides that have been made since the inception of a system of free public schooling in this country some 100 years ago, much remains to be done. The readings selected for this section prompt these questions:

- Do Americans want equity in schools; if so, why?
- Given the reality of limited resources to support public education, what aspects of schooling would you be willing to forego to achieve educational equity, and why?
- In what ways are some children privileged over others in public schools, and why is this differentiation tolerated in a society espousing democratic ideals?

Our communities and hence our schools are becoming more and more heterogeneous, and these conditions severely complicate the challenges for classroom teachers. The growing cultural diversity in our nation's schools and the increasingly broad band of ability levels among the children attending school make the teacher's job ever more complicated, and this is particularly so in the face of dwindling resources and public support for education.

As you will recall from the readings in Part 1, we looked at the connections between education and cultural transmission and the impact of schools on shaping and sustaining such values as humanitarianism, equality, and the effort and optimism associated with productivity and problem-solving. One of the beliefs we hold most dear is that a good part of what it means to be American is that each individual has an equal opportunity to get ahead, to make the most of his or her abilities.

Related to this central value of equality is the belief in *equal educational opportunity,* that is, that every member of society has an equal chance to receive an appropriate education. However, as Spring reminds us in the next reading, many groups of U.S. citizens have historically been denied the opportunity to attend public schools, and even when the legal right to attend has been won, the education received often is of poor quality, or at least inadequate to enable recipients to compete on a level playing field with members of more advantaged groups.

The reading by Joel Spring chronicles the struggles many groups in U.S. society have experienced in securing basic civil rights for their members, in particular the right to equality of educational opportunity. The obstacles to equal educational opportunity affect many different social groups and come in many different forms. Although we might initially think of the historical disenfrachisement of African Americans and their struggle for civil rights and equality of educational opportunity, many other groups have had similar struggles. These include Native Americans; Hispanic Americans; Asian Americans; Americans with physical, mental, and emotional disabilities; young girls and women; and many children from families who do not speak English in their homes or communities. Beyond these groups, and unfortunately the largest and most rapidly expanding groups, are the urban and rural poor. While federal and state laws now for the most part provide special opportunities for members of these groups, the available resources are inadequate to serve their needs. As schools and classrooms become increasingly diverse in terms of the ability range and cultural complexity of the groupings of children served in the public schools, teachers and communities face unprecedented challenges to be responsive and to provide an education suited to the economic, social, and political challenges that children face in the world today, as they enter the workplace and take on the responsibilities of adulthood and citizenship in a democratic society.

While basic access to educational opportunity is now available to the great majority of U.S. citizens, the educations received are by no means equal for many reasons beyond the limitations of resources to support public education. Among these are unequal treatment *within* schools, for boys and girls, for poor and middle-class children, for white and people of color, and for native and nonnative English speakers. Teachers' and administrators' prejudices, school textbooks and other aspects of the curriculum, and local community values all influence the quality, extent, and nature of the education provided in public schools. Although there are many good examples of public schools that demonstrably meet these challenges head-on and do their very best to provide equitable educations to all who enter their doors, we should not be deluded into thinking this is typical practice. It is not; it is *still* the exception in many schools and communities.

An emergent strategy intended to respond to some of these conditions in our schools is *multicultural education.* As discussed so compellingly by James Banks in the second selection, strategies of multicultural education hold much promise for the reform of public education and the achievement of educational equality for children with diverse racial, ethnic, and social-class backgrounds. Multicultural education is a way to assist students to gain the attitudes needed to work and live successfully in an increasingly diverse society. To accomplish this goal, educators themselves need to be able to implement a curriculum that is multicultural. What does this mean?

The selection by Banks offers teachers a framework for understanding the complexity of this task and as a guide to their efforts to achieve educational equality for the students in their classrooms. Banks (1995) discusses five dimensions of multicultural education: (1) content integration, (2) knowledge construction, (3) prejudice reduction, (4) equity pedagogy, and (5) empowering school culture. It is through the integration and interrelationship among all five of these dimensions that the goal of multicultural education is reached. It is important to recognize that this conception of multicultural education goes far beyond the 1960's ideas of integrating diverse racial, gender, and cultural perspectives within the school's curriculum. While such curricular improvements continue to be important and necessary, they are by themselves not sufficient.

Multicultural education is important no matter where one teaches, be it in urban, rural, inner-city, suburban, homogeneous, or racially mixed schools. And, multicultural education is important no matter what the students' age or grade level. Quality multicultural education that makes a difference in the lives of children goes far beyond celebrating ethnic or religious holidays, or merely adding a story about an important person of color, or a woman, to the school's curriculum. To be significant, the curriculum (in *all* its manifestations, including what is studied, how children are taught, and how children interrelate) must change so that students experience themselves, others, and their world from *different* perspectives. With a truly multicultural perspective, students can develop the capacity to understand and challenge broader societal issues and help to ameliorate them. Gaining a multicultural perspective will enable children to more fully live their lives and participate in their communities. The demographic picture in our society, and throughout the world, is rapidly approaching the point at which diversity, not homogeneity, is the norm. Children not only need to understand and work toward the amelioration of social ills related to the inequitable treatment of those traditionally disenfranchised by society, they need as well to be comfortable with and appreciative of the importance and value of differences among people.

While educators struggle to overcome their prejudices and strive to implement effective instructional practices, states and local communities continue to debate how public schools are funded. As Ward so aptly illustrates in the third reading in this section, public school finances can have a tremendous impact on the quality of education. The quality and amount of education our children receive depends heavily on the level of one's family's social strata, and on the community in which one lives (Ward, 1992, p. 242).

Most public schools are funded through local property taxes, and thus the amounts available to support education vary substantially between wealthy and poor communities. Although there have been numerous efforts to redress the inequities caused by the nature of funding for education, the "politics of privilege and exclusion" (Ward, 1992, p. 246) and the historically rooted belief by communities in local control of education have hampered initiatives to equalize funding across school communities.

Ward suggests a number of policies and strategies states could adopt that would end these disparities in funding. Without such efforts, U.S. public schools will, as they have historically, tend to reproduce and maintain many of the inequalities evident in society. As discussed earlier in Part 4, without measures such as those proposed by Ward, schools will reproduce and continue to legitimize the current inequities in U.S. society. Although public schools are but one ingredient in a very complex web of influences on children, they undoubtedly are a critical ingredient and one well within our grasp to affect. We currently spend on average about $5,000 annually per child to support public schools. The average cost to incarcerate a person for one year exceeds $25,000 and is increasing.

Perhaps the biggest challenge we face is helping the public understand the benefits and the opportunities of a system of public education that truly yields an equally well-educated citizenry. Schooling and democracy are critically intertwined, and the nature and quality of schooling bear directly on the capacity of citizens to govern themselves well and to preserve the traditions of a democratic society.

EQUALITY OF EDUCATIONAL OPPORTUNITY

JOEL SPRING

Equality of educational opportunity means that everyone has an equal chance to receive an education. When defined as an equal chance to attend publicly supported schools, equal educational opportunity is primarily a legal issue. In this context, the provision of equal educational opportunity can be defined solely on the grounds of justice: If government provides a service like education, all classes of citizens should have equal access to that service.

Still, legal equality of opportunity to attend public schools does not guarantee an equal education. Public schools can be structured to deny equal educational opportunity. This is illustrated by events in Selma, Alabama, in the early 1990s. During the 1950s and 1960s, Selma was a center of violent civil rights protests demanding equal voting rights and integrated education. As a result, by the time of the school protests of 1990, legislation guaranteed African-American children equal educational opportunity to attend publicly supported schools. However, this right of attendance was undermined by a system of tracking students into different curricula. The dispute in 1990 centered on the racial distribution in advanced-placement and college preparatory courses offered in Selma's public high school.

Selma, like many other communities in the South, separates races within the public schools by placing them in different curriculum tracks, such as college preparatory and advanced placement. The racial bias underlying the placement of students in such tracks is evident in Selma's high school. In Selma 90 percent of all white students were placed in college preparatory and advanced-placement tracks, while only 3 percent of all African-American students were placed in those tracks. According to Phyllis McClure, an education specialist with the Legal Defense and Education Fund of the National Association for the Advancement of Colored People (NAACP), this form of racial segregation through tracking is common throughout southern states.

When Dr. Norward Roussell, Selma's first African-American school superintendent, tried to correct this racial imbalance by increasing the percentage of African-American students in college preparatory and advanced-placement tracks to 10 percent, he was notified by the white-dominated school board that he was being dismissed. Dr. Roussell stated that the school system was violating students' rights by tracking them primarily based on teachers' recommendations. "Of course, as you might imagine, most of the students in the bottom levels were black," he said in an interview in the February 21, 1990, issue of Education Week, "although many had standardized-test scores as high as or higher than those in the upper level." It required a school boycott by African-American students before he was reinstated. White parents reacted with threats to remove their children from the public schools and send them to private institutions.

Therefore, equality of educational opportunity requires more than just an equal chance to attend a

Source: *"Equality of Educational Opportunity" from* American Education, 9E, *by Joel Spring copyright 2000. Reprinted by permission of McGraw-Hill, Inc.*

publicly supported school. It also requires equal treatment within schools. Inequality of treatment in school can be a result of other factors as well. For many years handicapped students were denied equal access to an education because of the lack of provisions to fit their special needs. Entry into buildings and movement between floors were difficult for many handicapped students because they could not negotiate stairs, and neither ramps for wheelchairs nor elevators were provided. Equal educational opportunity for handicapped people has meant making physical changes in buildings.

Besides providing equal treatment in placement in curricular tracks and physical access to buildings, equality of educational opportunity requires positive recognition of the gender, race, and ethnic background of the student. Equality of educational opportunity has little meaning if students gain equal access to an education and then are taught they are inferior.

Inequality of treatment can occur in very subtle ways. This is particularly evident in the history of discrimination against women in education. For instance, while doing research on the history of education during World War II, Felecia Briscoe encountered a reproduction of a poster of which the National Education Association had distributed 50,000 copies in 1944 as part of its "teacher-recruiting and morale-building campaign." Titled "The Teacher," the poster depicts a female teacher and an elementary-school-age boy and girl standing around a world globe. The little girl is wearing a neat dress and her hair is perfectly groomed. She is staring passively at the globe with a blank expression on her face, and her empty arms dangle beside her. The teacher is seated between the two children. Her head is turned away from the girl and she gazes with approval at the boy. The boy clutches a book in one hand and points to a place on the globe with the other. Unlike the girl, his hair is rumpled and his face is animated. The poster clearly conveys an impression that males are active learners and intellectually superior to females, whereas girls are passive and intellectually dull.

Equality of educational opportunity can be denied also to children from homes where English is not the spoken language, when no special provision for this language problem is made by the schools. Courts have ruled that children who do not fully comprehend the language of the school are being denied equal access to instruction. Equality of educational opportunity in this situation means that the schools must provide special help for children with non-English-speaking backgrounds.

In summary, the idea of equal educational opportunity covers a broad spectrum of educational issues including an equal chance to attend public supported schools, educational practices within schools, the content of the curriculum and textbooks, and recognition of the cultural and language background of the student. All of these issues are highlighted by the long history of racism in public schooling. Traditionally, racism played a major role in the denial of an equal chance to attend public school for African-Americans, Native Americans, Mexican-Americans, and Asians. Today, problems of racism still affect efforts to provide equal educational opportunity. However, issues of race are entangled with issues of social class.

RACE AND SOCIAL CLASS

Does race or social class determine equal educational opportunity? Take the case of African-American Professor Cornell West. While a professor of theology at Princeton University, West, after lecturing on Plato's *Republic,* drove into New York City for a photo session for his new book. Driving, as he described it, an expensive car and planning to have dinner at an expensive restaurant, West felt the burden of the race line when stepping onto the streets of Manhattan. After parking his car, West tried to hail a taxicab to take him to the photo session. In a simmering rage, West watched taxi after taxi stop for white people while ignoring him. After an hour, a cab finally stopped for him. A similar experience occurred to David Dinkins, the former mayor of New York City. The first black mayor of the city watched as taxis responded to whites while ignoring him. Even the former leader of the city could not escape its racist temperament.

No matter how high a person's status or income, racism is still a problem. However, social class remains important. Opportunities are quite different for an African-American growing up in an upper-class household as compared with an African-American or white child growing up in poverty. Social class lines are as sharply drawn in the black community as they are in the white community. Therefore, it is important to consider social class as it intersects with race. White poverty is as detrimental to life chances as black poverty. Table 1 compares the share of aggregate household incomes by social class and race. Social class is identified, as described in Chapter 4, by rankings of 20 percent (upper, top 20%; upper-middle, next 20%; middle, next 20%; lower-middle, next 20%; lower, bottom 20%).

As indicated in Table 1, wealth is as disproportionately distributed in the African-American and Hispanic communities as in the white community. The upper class in the white community commands about the same percentage (49.1) of total white income as the upper class of the African-American and Hispanic communities, 48.7 percent and 49.5 percent, respectively. Indeed, the lower class of each racial grouping shares similar small percentages of the total income of their race—white, 3.8 percent; African-American, 3.2 percent; Hispanic, 3.6 percent.

Although social class is highlighted by the income distribution within each racial group, race is still a factor in the overall distribution of income in

the United States. Table 2 indicates these racial differences according to household median income and per capita income. According to Table 2, white household incomes and per capita incomes are significantly above those of African-Americans and Hispanics with white median household income at $38,972 as compared with African-Americans ($25,050) and Hispanics ($26,626).

Race is also reflected in poverty rates. However, it is again important to remember that social class remains a factor within each racial group. Poverty in Table 3 is defined as a family of four with an annual income of $16,400 or less and a family of three with an annual income of $12,802 or less.

In actual numbers, according to Table 3, whites are the largest group (24.4 million) living in poverty as compared with 9.1 million African-Americans and 8.3 million Hispanics. In fact, the number of whites living in poverty is much larger than the combined numbers of African-Americans and Hispanics living in poverty (24.4 million whites compared with a combined total of 17.4 million for African-Americans and Hispanics). On the other hand, the actual percentages of African-Americans (26.5%) and Hispanics (27.1%) is more than double that of whites (11%).

Therefore, both race and social class must be considered in the provision of equal educational opportunity. An African-American child living in an upper-class family will probably have greater educational opportunities than a white child living in

TABLE 1

Share of Aggregate Income by Social Class and Race, 1997

SOCIAL CLASS	WHITE (%)	AFRICAN-AMERICAN (%)	HISPANIC (%)
Upper	49.1	48.7	49.5
Upper-Middle	23	24.5	23.1
Middle	15	15.1	14.9
Lower-Middle	9.1	8.5	8.9
Lower	3.8	3.2	3.6

Source: U.S. Bureau of the Census, "Money Income in the United States: 1997," http://www.census.gov/.

TABLE 2

Median Household and per Capita Income by Race, 1997

RACE	MEDIAN INCOME PER HOUSEHOLD	PER CAPITA INCOME
White	$38,972	20,425
African-American	25,050	12,351
Hispanic	26,626	10,773

Source: U.S. Census Bureau, "Poverty Rate Down, Household Income Up—Both Return to 1989 Prerecession Levels," http://www.census.gov/.

poverty. On the other hand, an African-American child might feel the disadvantage of race regarding educational opportunities in comparison to a white child from the same social class. In addition, the African-American child has a greater probability of being born into poverty than a white child.

THE ECONOMICS OF RACISM

What is the economic value of being white instead of African-American? Andrew Hacker, along with his white students, determined that being white was worth a million dollars a year. In *Two Nations: Black and White, Separate, Hostile, Unequal,* Hacker describes presenting his students with a fictional account of a white person being visited by representatives of an unnamed institution. The white person is informed that a terrible mistake was made and that he should have been born black. Consequently, the person was now going to be given a black skin and facial features but his memory and ideas would remain the same. Since this was a mistake, the person would be offered financial compensation for being made black. The white students were then asked to name what they felt should be the compensation for becoming black. Their answer was $1 million yearly.

The economic value of race might be determined by comparing income based on educational attainment. In Chapter 4, I demonstrated the close relationship between educational attainment and income. What happens when race is introduced as a factor? Table 4 presents the answer.

TABLE 3

Percentage Living in Poverty and Numbers by Race, 1997

RACE	PERCENTAGE LIVING IN POVERTY (%)	NUMBERS LIVING IN POVERTY (MILLIONS)
White	11	24.4
African-American	26.5	9.1
Hispanic	27.1	8.3

Source: U.S. Census Bureau, "Poverty Rate Down, Household Income Up—Both Return to 1989 Prerecession Levels," http://www.census.gov/.

So the economic value of being white, as suggested by Table 4, could range from 20 to 23 percent when comparing educational attainment. On the average, black men earned 21.8 percent *less* than white men when they had the same level of education. For instance, an African-American male without a high school education earned on the average 20.3 percent less than a white man without a high school education. An African-American male with more than five years of college earned 22.9 percent less than a white man with a similar education.

DEFINING RACISM

Racism means prejudice plus power. The preceding differences in income based on educational attainment highlight this definition of racism. Racism refers to acts of oppression of one racial group toward another. One form of oppression is economic exploitation.

This definition of racism distinguishes between simple feelings of hostility and prejudice toward another racial group and the ability to turn those feelings into some form of oppression. For instance, black people might have prejudicial feelings toward white people, but they have little opportunity to express those prejudicial feelings in some form of economic or political oppression of white people. On the other hand, prejudicial feelings that white people might have toward blacks can turn into racism when they become the basis for discrimination in education, housing, and the job market. Within this framework, racism becomes the act of social, political, and economic oppression of another group.

When discussions of racism occur in my multicultural education classes, white students complain of a sense of hostility from black students and, consequently, accuse black students of racism. Black students respond that their feelings represent prejudice and not racism because they lack the power to discriminate against whites. The troubling aspect of this response is the implication that if these black students had the power, they would be racist. One black student pointed out that there are situations where blacks can commit racist acts against whites. The black student used the example of the killings of white passengers by a black man on a commuter railroad several years ago. The evidence seemed to indicate that the killer was motivated by extreme hatred of whites that the newspapers labeled "black rage." This was a racist act, the black student argued, because the gun represented power.

Racism is often thought of as "whites" oppressing "people of color." Of course, there are many problems with this definition. If one parent is black and another white, are their children considered black or white? Can one white-skinned child of this

TABLE 4

African-American Male Income Compared with White Male Income by Educational Attainment, 1990

EDUCATIONAL ATTAINMENT OF AFRICAN-WHITE MALE (%)	PERCENTAGE DIFFERENCE OF AFRICAN-AMERICAN MALE INCOME COMPARED WITH AMERICAN AND WHITE MALES
Less than high school diploma	−20.3
High school diploma	−23.6
Four years of college	−20.9
Five years of college	−22.9

Source: Adapted from Andrew Hacker, *Two Nations: Black and White, Separate, Hostile, Unequal.* New York: Charles Scribner's Son,. 1992.

marriage be considered white while one dark-skinned child is considered black? Jake Lamar recalls how the confusion over skin color sparked the development of his racial consciousness at the age of 3. Jake was sitting at the kitchen table when his Uncle Frank commented "about how obnoxious white people were." Jake responded, "But Mommy's white." His uncle replied that his mother was not white but was "just light-skinned." Jake then said that he thought his father, brother, and himself were black while his sister and mother were white. His mother then explained that they had many white ancestors that caused the variation in skin color, but they were still "all Negroes." Thinking back on this incident, Jake Lamar reflected, "Black and white then meant something beyond pigmentation . . . so my first encounter with racial awareness was at once enlightening and confusing, and shot through with ambiguity."

The complicated issue of identifying race is reflected in Table 5. Table 5 presents the racial composition of a 1992 sophomore class and its dropout rate. In composing this table, the National Center for Educational Statistics used the racial classifications of White, Asian/Pacific Islander, Hispanic, Black, and Native American.

But what do these racial classifications mean? Many residents of the United States have a mixed racial ancestry. For instance, how do you classify a person with ancestors who were European, African, and Native American? How do you classify an immigrant from Mexico whose parents are Native American? Most immigrants from Central and South America are descendants from Europeans, Africans, and Native Americans. One woman (from Central America) in my class had an Asian father and a Mayan Indian mother. Is she Hispanic, Asian, or Native American? A resolution is to create a separate category called multiracial. Many U.S. citizens who now identify themselves as whites also have Native American ancestors. Should they continue to be classified as white or should they be considered multiracial?

With the problem of racial classification in mind, you should consider the differences in dropout rates presented in Table 5. Admittedly, a student may drop out of high school for a variety of reasons. One can assume that a major factor is a student's attitude toward school. The high dropout rate of 18.2 percent among Native Americans reflects a historical pattern where Native Americans identify school as the institution of the conqueror. Are the high dropout rates, in comparison with whites (4.3%), of Hispanic (10.9%) and black (7.6%) youth a reflection of institutional racism? The high dropout rate of 10.9 per-

TABLE 5

Demographic Characteristics and Dropout Rates; Tenth Grade, 1992

	DEMOGRAPHIC CHARACTERISTICS	DROPOUT RATE
Total	100%	5.6%
White, non-Hispanic	71.7	4.3
Asian/Pacific Islander	4	4.6
Hispanic	10.7	10.9
Black, non-Hispanic	12.5	7.6
Native American	1.1	18.2
Below poverty level	13	10.9
Intact family	69.6	4.2

Source: This table was adapted from National Center for Education Statistics, "Dropout Rates in the United States: 1994," http://www.ed.gov/NCES.

cent for students from families living below the poverty line suggests that poverty is a factor. Is poverty a more important factor than race for dropouts? Interestingly, the type of family structure has little relationship to dropping out.

Keeping in mind the complexities of racial classification and the importance of social class, certain generalities can be made about the racial attitudes of whites at the end of the twentieth century. In *Prejudice and Racism*, social psychologist James Jones summarizes the racial attitudes of some whites.

■ Whites feel more negatively toward blacks than Hispanics, Asians, and legal and illegal immigrants.

■ Whites perceive blacks as lazy, violent, and less intelligent than Hispanics, Asians, and legal and illegal immigrants.

■ Whites believe blacks are receiving more attention from government than they deserve.

■ Whites believe blacks are too demanding in their struggle for equal rights.

■ High levels of antiblack racism are correlated with white attitudes that police and the death penalty make streets safe, and with opposition to assistance to the poor.

■ Antiblack and anti-Hispanic racism correlated with whites' opposition to open immigration and multilingualism.

THE CHANGING COLOR OF THE UNITED STATES

The changing complexion of the U.S. population highlights the importance of overcoming racism and prejudice in providing equal educational opportunity. White-antiblack racism has traditionally been the focus of concern. However, with Native American and Mexican-American activism, and immigration, other forms of prejudice and racism play a role in providing equal educational opportunity. Some African-Americans have hostile attitudes toward immigrants as they compete for jobs. Some Asian immigrants arrive with racist feelings about African-Americans. Native Americans are demand-

ing restoration of traditional rights and lands. All of these factors complicate efforts at providing equal educational opportunity.

In 1998, the changing racial/ethnic composition of the U.S. population and resulting educational issues were underscored by the Advisory Board for the President's Initiative on Race in *One America in the 21st Century: Forging a New Future*. The Advisory Board's report presented the following projections and facts:

■ By the year 2050, about 50 percent of the U.S. population will be composed of Asians, non-Hispanic blacks, Hispanics, and American Indians.

■ By the year 2005, Hispanics, who may be of any race, are projected to be the largest minority group in the United States.

■ As of 1997, 61 percent of the Asian population and 38 percent of the Hispanic population were foreign-born. In contrast, only 8 percent of whites, 6 percent of blacks, and 6 percent of American Indians were foreign-born.

Educational issues regarding this changing population are directly related to residential patterns and educational attainment of immigrants. Of fundamental importance for the future funding of public schools and the provision of equal educational opportunity is the fact that most African-Americans, Asians, and Hispanics are living in central cities. According to the Advisory Board for the President's Initiative on Race:

■ Blacks, Asians, and Hispanics are more likely to live in central cities of metropolitan areas than are non-Hispanic whites or American Indians.

■ A large percentage of non-Hispanic whites and Asians live in suburbs. The fraction living in suburbs has increased since 1970.

In addition, immigrant populations bring with them a variety of educational backgrounds. The Advisory Board emphasized the following:

■ On the average, Asian immigrants are highly educated and have high incomes.

■ Hispanic immigrants, along with immigrants from some Asian countries, have relatively low average levels of educational attainment and income.

Overall, the picture presented by the Advisory Board is a growing gap between the educational advantages of the suburbs and the educational problems of the central cities with changes in the population. These problems are related to the intersection of social class and race.

RACE, SOCIAL CLASS, AND EQUAL EDUCATIONAL OPPORTUNITIES

The Advisory Board for the President's Initiative on Race recognized that the problem of equal educational opportunity involves the intersection of poverty and race. Wealthy African-Americans, whites, Asians, and Hispanics can choose to live in school districts with adequate and exceptional public schools. In the words of the Advisory Board, "Our concern is that educational opportunities and public services are being restricted to those who live disproportionately in areas of concentrated poverty." The Advisory Board identified the following conditions in areas of concentrated poverty:

■ Schools with low expectations and standards
■ Substandard and crumbling school facilities
■ Inadequate public transportation
■ Poorly financed social services

In addition, the Advisory Board found that students from low-income families were less likely to have access to such educational opportunities and resources as:

■ Preschool programs
■ High-quality teachers
■ Challenging curriculums
■ High standards
■ Up-to-date technology
■ Modern facilities

In the context of the changing U.S. population and existing educational problems, the Advisory Board recommended the following to achieve equal educational opportunity:

ADVISORY BOARD FOR THE PRESIDENT'S INITIATIVE ON RACE RECOMMENDATIONS FOR EQUAL EDUCATIONAL OPPORTUNITY

1. *Enhance early childhood learning.* Data indicate that racial disparities persist in terms of early childhood learning. For example, 1996 data show that 89 percent of white children ages 3 to 5 were read to three or more times per week compared with 74 percent of black children and 62 percent of Hispanic children . . . efforts could include providing training and services for parents . . . and expanding support for such programs as Head Start, Early Head Start, and Even Start.

2. *Strengthen teacher preparation and equity.* High-quality teachers are too scarce a resource, especially in high-poverty, high-minority communities . . . [action] could include creating incentives to both attract top students to teaching and encourage certified teachers to teach in under-served communities.

3. *Promote school construction.* It is estimated that building and renovating our public schools to adequately serve all students will cost more than $100 billion.

4. *Promote movement from K–12 to higher education.* Efforts must be taken to ensure equal opportunity in higher education and to strengthen the pipeline from K–12 through higher education. Such efforts should include support for partnerships between colleges and K–12 schools that increase expectations by exposing students to future educational opportunities . . . efforts could include increasing the availability of advanced-placement courses in high-poverty, high-minority school districts and providing financial support, such as loans or grants, for college test preparation courses.

5. *Promote the benefits of diversity in K–12 and higher education.* Diversity can promote many benefits that accrue to all students and society, including: improve teaching and learning by providing a range of perspectives that enrich the learning environment; strengthen students' critical-thinking skills by challenging their ex-

isting perspectives . . . improve students' preparation for employment . . . and foster the advancement of knowledge by spurring study in new areas of concern.

6. *Provide education and skills training to overcome increasing income inequality that negatively affects lower-skilled and less-educated immigrants.* The high rates of Hispanic high school dropouts suggest . . . there is a clear need for continued English-language training to ensure that limited-English-proficient students can perform and compete in the educational system.

7. *Implement the comprehensive American Indian and Alaska Native education policy.* To meet the particular needs of American Indian and Alaska Native students, we urge . . . improving and expanding educational opportunities.

In summary, the recommendations for equality of educational opportunity include early childhood education, high-quality teachers in schools serving low-income families, school construction, equal access to higher education, diversity in the classroom, and adequate English instruction for children from non-English-speaking homes.

TEACHING ABOUT RACISM

The Advisory Board for the President's Initiative on Race was primarily concerned about the intersection of poverty and racial differences. It did not deal directly with the role that schools can play in reducing racism through classroom instruction. A variety of approaches to teaching about racism are available. One excellent book is Beverly Tatum's *Why Are All the Black Kids Sitting Together in the Cafeteria?: A Psychologist Explains the Development of Racial Identity.* As Tatum points out, discussions of race often make white students feel guilty and their guilt can quickly turn into hostility and resentment. Educator and African-American activist Beverly Tatum worries about the loss of white allies in the struggle against racism and the hostility she feels from white college students when teaching about racism. Reflecting on her teaching experiences, she writes, "White students . . . often struggle with strong feelings of guilt

when they become aware of the pervasiveness of racism. . . . These feelings are uncomfortable and can lead white students to resist learning about race and racism." Part of the problem, she argues, is that seeing oneself as the oppressor creates a negative self-image, which results in a withdrawal from a discussion of the problem. What needs to be done, she maintains, is to counter the guilt by giving white students a positive self-image of whites fighting against racism. In other words, a self-image of whites being allies with blacks in the struggle against racism.

A popular antiracist curricula for preschool children is the National Association for the Education of Young Children's Anti-Bias Curriculum: Tools for Empowering Young Children. This curriculum and related methods of instruction are designed to reduce prejudice among young children regarding race, language, gender, and physical ability differences. The premise of the method is that at an early age children become aware of the connection between power and skin color, language, and physical disabilities. Cited as examples are a 2 1/2-year-old Asian child who refuses to hold the hand of a black classmate because "It's dirty" and a 4-year-old boy who takes over the driving of a pretended bus because "Girls can't be bus drivers."

According to the Anti-Bias Curriculum, research findings show that young children classify differences between people and they are influenced by bias toward others. By the age of 2, children are aware of gender differences and begin to apply color names to skin colors. Between ages 3 and 5, children try to figure out who they are by examining the differences in gender and skin color. By 4 or 5 years old, children engage in socially determined gender roles and they give racial reasons for the selection of friends. Based on these research findings, the advocates of the curriculum believe that prejudice can be reduced if there is conscious intervention to curb the development of biased concepts and activities.

Another antiracist education program is the Teaching Tolerance Project that began after a group of teenage skinheads attacked and beat to death an Ethiopian man on a street in Portland,

Oregon, in 1988. After this incident, members of the Southern Poverty Law Center decided it was time to do something about teaching tolerance. Dedicated to pursuing legal issues involving racial incidents and denial of civil rights, the Law Center sued, for the man's family, the two men who were responsible for teaching violent racism to the Portland skinheads. These two teachers, Tom Metzger, the head of the White Aryan Resistance, and his son, became symbols of racist teachings in the United States. In a broad sense, the Teaching Tolerance Project is designed to provide information about teaching methods and materials that will counter the type of racist teachings represented by Metzger and his son.

Similar to the Anti-Bias Curriculum, the Teaching Tolerance Project primarily defines racism as a function of psychological attitudes, in contrast to an emphasis on racism as a function of economic exploitation. On the inside cover of its magazine, *Teaching Tolerance,* tolerance is defined as "the capacity for or the practice of recognizing and respecting the beliefs or practices of others." Within the context of this definition, the project members "primarily celebrate and recognize the beliefs and practices of racial and ethnic groups such as African-Americans, Latinos, and Asian-Americans."

The primary purpose of the Teaching Tolerance Project is to provide resources and materials to schools to promote "interracial and intercultural understanding between whites and nonwhites." Although this is the primary focus of the project, there have been decisions to include material dealing with cultural tolerance, homelessness, and poverty. The Teaching Tolerance Project is only one of many educational attempts to end racism in the United States. The end of racism is essential for the full provision of equality of opportunity and equality of educational opportunity in U.S. society.

THE LEGAL REQUIREMENTS FOR EQUAL EDUCATIONAL OPPORTUNITY

There are legal justifications for the demand that schools provide equal educational opportunity.

The historic case is the 1954 Supreme Court school desegregation case *Brown v. Board of Education of Topeka,* which gave legal meaning to the idea that segregated education means unequal education. Until 1954, segregated schools in the United States operated under a ruling given by the Supreme Court in 1895, *Plessy v. Ferguson,* that segregation did not create a badge of inferiority if segregated facilities were equal and the law was reasonable. The decision in both cases centered around the meaning of the Fourteenth Amendment to the Constitution. This amendment was ratified in 1868, shortly after the close of the Civil War. One of its purposes was to extend the basic guarantees of the Bill of Rights into the areas of state and local government. The most important and controversial section of the Fourteenth Amendment states: "No State shall make or enforce any law which shall abridge the privileges or immunities of citizens . . . nor . . . deprive any person of life, liberty, or property, without due process of law; nor deny to any person within its jurisdiction the equal protection of the laws."

The 1895 decision, *Plessy v. Ferguson,* involved Homer Plessy, who was one-eighth African-American and seven-eighths white. He was arrested for refusing to ride in the colored coach of a train, as required by Louisiana state law. The Supreme Court's decision in this case that segregated facilities could exist if they were equal, became known as the "separate but equal" doctrine.

The 1954 desegregation decision, *Brown v. Board of Education of Topeka,* overturned the "separate but equal" doctrine by arguing, from the findings of social science, that segregated education was inherently unequal. This meant that even if school facilities, teachers, equipment, and all other physical conditions were equal between two racially segregated schools, the two schools would still be unequal because of the fact of racial segregation.

In 1964 Congress took a significant step toward speeding up school desegregation by passing the important Civil Rights Act. About school desegregation, Title VI of the 1964 Civil Rights Act was most important because it provided a means for the federal government to force school desegregation. In its final form, Title VI required the mandatory withholding of federal funds from institutions that practiced racial discrimination. Title VI states that no person, because of race, color, or national origin, could be excluded from or denied the benefits of any program receiving federal financial assistance. It required all federal agencies to establish guidelines to implement this policy. Refusal by institutions or projects to follow these guidelines was to result in the "termination of or refusal to grant or to continue assistance under such program or activity."

Title VI of the 1964 Civil Rights Act was important for two reasons. First, it established a major precedent for federal control of American public schools, by making explicit that the control of money would be one method used by the federal government to shape local school policies. (This aspect of the law will be discussed in more detail in Chapter 9.) Second, it turned the federal Office of Education into a policing agency with the responsibility of determining whether or not school systems were segregated and, if they were, of doing something about the segregated conditions.

One result of Title VI was to speed up the process of school desegregation in the South, particularly after the passage of federal legislation in 1965 that increased the amount of money available to local schools from the federal government. In the late 1960s southern school districts rapidly began to submit school desegregation plans to the Office of Education.

In the North, prosecution of inequality in educational opportunity as it related to school segregation required a different approach from that used in the South. In the South, school segregation existed by legislative acts that required separation of the races. There were no specific laws requiring separation of the races in the North. But even without specific laws, racial segregation existed. Therefore, it was necessary for individuals bringing complaints against northern school districts to prove that the existing patterns of racial segregation were the result of purposeful action by the school district. It had to be proved that school officials intended racial segregation to be a result of their educational policies.

The conditions required to prove segregation were explicitly outlined in 1974, in the Sixth Circuit Court of Appeals case *Oliver v. Michigan State Board of Education.* The court stated, "A presumption of segregative purpose arises when plaintiffs establish that the natural, probable and foreseeable result of public officials' action or inaction was an increase or perpetuation of public school segregation." This did not mean that individual motives or prejudices were to be investigated, but that the overall pattern of school actions had to be shown to increase racial segregation; that is, in the language of the court: "the question whether a purposeful pattern of segregation has manifested itself over time, despite the fact that individual official actions, considered alone, may not have been taken for segregative purposes."

INTEGRATION: MAGNET SCHOOLS AND CHOICE

As school desegregation proceeded across the country it caused a fundamental change in the organization of school curricula, with the introduction of magnet, or alternative, schools. Magnet, or alternative, schools are designed to provide an attractive program that will have wide appeal throughout a school district. Theoretically, magnet schools will attract enough students from all racial backgrounds to achieve integrated schools. For instance, a school district might establish a school for creative and performing arts that would attract students of all races from all areas of the district. If one criterion in selecting students is the maintenance of racial balance, then that school becomes a means of achieving integration.

The great attraction of magnet schools, and a major reason they are widely supported, is that they provide a means of voluntary desegregation. Also, they are supported because it is believed they will reduce the flight of middle-class and white families from school districts undergoing desegregation. It is hoped that by providing unique and attractive programs, school districts will stabilize their populations as voluntary desegregation takes place.

The concept of magnet schools also received support from the federal government, which aided in their rapid adoption by school districts. The 1976 amendments to the Emergency School Aid Act (ESAA) provided financial support specifically for magnet school programs. In addition, President Ronald Reagan's administration in 1984 used magnet-school plans as its method of achieving out-of-court settlements of desegregation cases.

Some school districts developed elaborate plans for magnet schools. In Houston, Texas, magnet schools were established ranging from the Petro-Chemical Careers Institute to the High School for Law Enforcement and Criminal Justice. In most school districts, magnet schools are introduced by first offering a program in creative and performing arts. For example, both Philadelphia and Cincinnati established a School of Creative and Performing Arts as their early magnet-school offering. In Philadelphia, school-desegregation plans resulted in schools offering programs that range from the study of foreign affairs to community-based education. Often, special programs already in existence, particularly for academic excellence and vocational training, were classified as magnet schools.

By the 1990s, the magnet-school movement was incorporated into the concept of "choice" in education. Conservative and Republican political leaders in the 1980s argued that public schools would improve if they were forced to compete for students. A free marketplace idea of quality through competition was introduced into education. If schools were unable to attract students in a school district, they would either have to improve or close their doors.

THE FAILURE OF DESEGREGATION

Although the civil rights struggle held out the hope for greater equality of educational opportunity for many groups that were traditionally oppressed in American society, its actual results regarding desegregation have been rather dismal. On the positive side, there no longer exist state laws requiring school segregation. On the negative side, segregated schools continue to exist around the country. In 1992, the following figures (see Table 6) were reported regarding the percentage of African-Americans and Hispanics attending segregated schools. As Table 6 indicates, Illinois, New York, Michigan, New Jersey, California, and Texas now lead the nation in segregation.

Although actual segregation of students by race is increasing in some areas, the courts are beginning to rule that some school systems are now "legally" desegregated. In 1994, federal judges declared school systems in Savannah, Georgia, and Dallas, Texas, to be legally desegregated. These decisions ended court supervision of the school systems. To accomplish desegregation, the Savannah school system spent $57 million since 1988, which, in part, was spent on creating twenty-two magnet schools. The Dallas school system spent $20 million on a "supermagnet" school to house six existing magnet high schools. While "legal" segregation has ended in some school systems, many schools are experiencing second-generation segregation.

SECOND-GENERATION SEGREGATION

Second-generation segregation refers to forms of racial segregation that are a result of school practices such as tracking, ability grouping, and the misplacement of students in special education classes. Unlike segregation that existed by state laws in the South before the 1954 *Brown* decision, second-generation forms of segregation can occur in schools with balanced racial populations. In schools with balanced racial populations, students can be segregated by, for instance, placing all white students in one academic track and all African-American or Hispanic students in another track.

Occasionally, second-generation segregation is not accidental, but the result of conscious school policies. The situation in Selma, Alabama, in 1990 is a perfect example of consciously planned second-generation segregation. The boycott of Selma schools was prompted by the school board's attempt to fire the African-American superintendent who tried to increase the percentage of African-

TABLE 6

Segregation of African-Americans and Hispanics by State (Percentage Attending Schools with 50 to 100% Minority Population)

AFRICAN-AMERICANS	(%)	HISPANICS	(%)
Illinois	88.8	New York	86.1
New York	85.7	Illinois	85.0
Michigan	84.6	Texas	84.3
New Jersey	79.6	New Jersey	84.1
California	78.7	California	79.1
Maryland	76.1	Rhode Island	77.8
Wisconsin	75.3	New Mexico	74.4
Texas	67.9	Connecticut	72.4
Pennsylvania	67.5	Pennsylvania	66.9
Connecticut	65.9	Arizona	56.9

Source: This table was adapted from Kern DeWitt, "The Nation's Schools Learn a 4th R: Resegregation," *New York Times* (19 January 1992): E5.

American students in the upper-ability tracks of the high school from 3 to 10 percent. The obvious purpose of the tracking system was to segregate white from African-American students. This segregation paralleled the economic segregation existing in the community.

The continuing economic segregation in Selma is highlighted in an interview with Professor William Bernard of the University of Alabama, conducted by Ronald Smothers for the *New York Times.* Bernard describes what he considers to be the "dual view of great change and no change." In this case, "the great change" is the appearance of African-Americans on the city councils and school boards of the South and the "no change" is the continuation of a segregated social order and white domination of economic power. Professor Bernard provides the following description of the economic order of the South:

Like Sinclair Lewis's "Main Street," there is a group of real estate, banking and other professional people who are the power in town, and much of the way people live is more affected by the decision of the banker than of the City Council. You don't

have black bankers, but neither do you have white bankers from the wrong side of the tracks.

In reporter Smothers's interviews, African-Americans refer to the "white elite" and whites refer to the "blue bloods" who controlled the town's economy and political system. Aspiring African-American businesspeople spoke of their inability to get loans to start new businesses because of the economic elite working behind the scenes. Obviously, new African-American businesses would compete with existing white businesses. This white power elite controls Selma's city council, which includes four African-Americans among nine members. In Selma, the school board is appointed by the city council and includes five African-Americans among eleven members. Thus, the city council and school board reflect Professor Bernard's statement about the "dual view of great change and no change." The great change is the presence of African-Americans on the city council and school board, and the no change is the continuing economic power of a white elite.

Also, tracking in the Selma high school reflects the "dual view of great change and no change."

The great change is the integration of the school building and the 3 percent of African-Americans placed in the high-ability tracks with 90 percent of the white students. The no change is the racial segregation that continues with the tracking system. The segregation resulting from the tracking systems reflects the economic differences in the community. Tracking is a method of closing the door to equal economic opportunity for African-Americans in Selma.

Nationally, most studies examine the process of great change and no change as integration of schools results in segregation within schools. One collection of studies can be found in Ray Rist's *Desegregated Schools: Appraisals of an American Experiment.* The studies describe the subtle forms of segregation that began to occur as white and African-American students were placed in integrated schools for the first time. For instance, in one recently integrated school, African-American students were suspended for committing the same offenses for which white students received only a reprimand. A teacher in the school complained that, unlike African-American students, when white students were sent to the principal's office, they were immediately sent back to class. In this school, equal opportunity to attend the school did not result in equal treatment within the school.

Unequal treatment of different races within the same school is one problem in integrated schools; the establishment of racial boundaries among students creates another. One study in the Rist book describes how racial boundaries were established in a high school in Memphis, Tennessee, after the students of an all-African-American school were integrated with the students of an all-white school. Here, white students maintained control over most student activities. Activities in which African-American students began to participate after integration were athletics and cheerleading. When this occurred, the status of these activities was denigrated by white students. On the other hand, whites could maintain control of the student government, ROTC, school clubs, and the staff of the yearbook.

This division of control among student activities reflected the rigid social boundaries that existed in the high school between the two groups. Individuals who crossed these social boundaries had to adapt to the social customs of those on the other side. For instance, African-American students changed their style of dress and social conduct to be accepted by white students. African-American students who crossed racial lines by making such changes found themselves accused by other African-American students of "acting white" and were subsequently rejected by "unchanged" African-American students. The same was true of white students who crossed racial boundaries.

The racial boundaries that continue to exist in high schools after integration reflects the racial barriers that continue in the larger society. The social life of a school often reflects the social world outside the school. Integration of a school system can help ensure equality of educational opportunity, but it cannot break down society's racial barriers. Although schools attempt to deal with this problem, its solution requires a general transformation of racial relationships in the larger society.

SEGREGATION AND POLITICAL POWER

Two important books—Kenneth Meier, Joseph Stewart, Jr., and Robert England's, *Race, Class, and Education: The Politics of Second-Generation Discrimination,* and Kenneth Meier and Joseph Stewart, Jr.'s, *The Politics of Hispanic Education*—focus on the relationship between political involvement and second-generation segregation. The two books are concerned with political organizations that promote segregative practices in schools and deny certain groups equality of educational opportunity. In addition, they link segregative practices with student achievement. They consider student achievement to be dependent on equal access to educational opportunities.

The main conclusion of these authors' studies is that segregative practices in schools are reduced by the presence on boards of education and in educational bureaucracies of representatives from affected groups such as Hispanics and African-Americans. Therefore, their suggested reforms focus on ways to increase representation from dominated groups.

In their research, they found that schools still practice segregation through academic grouping, such as placement in special education classes, ability grouping, curriculum tracking, and segregated bilingual education. In addition, the researchers found that discipline is applied in different ways to different ethnic and racial groups. For instance, Hispanic and African-American students might be suspended or expelled from school at different rates than white students. Finally, they concluded that these segregative practices affect high school graduation rates.

About Hispanic-Americans, they conclude that the larger the number of Hispanic representatives in an educational system, the less chance of second-generation segregation. In their study, representation includes boards of education, educational bureaucracies, and teachers. In other words, there will be less second-generation segregation if there are more Hispanics on boards of education, and working as school administrators and teachers.

In addition, Meier and Stewart found an interrelationship between representation on boards of education and representation in the bureaucracy and teaching ranks. The higher representation of Hispanics on boards of education, the higher representation of Hispanics in the school administration. In other words, Hispanic representation on boards of education creates a greater-than-normal possibility that the board will choose Hispanic administrators. In turn, they found, the higher the representation of Hispanics in the bureaucracy, the higher the number of Hispanic teachers.

These findings suggest a chain reaction. Hispanics are elected to the board of education and they select more Hispanic administrators, who in turn select more Hispanic teachers, which results in a decline in second-generation segregation and greater equality of educational opportunity. Specially, the authors found that greater Hispanic representation is associated with proportionately fewer Hispanic students in special education classes and larger numbers of Hispanic students in gifted programs. Also, higher rates of Hispanic representation are related to less disparity in dis-

cipline. And finally, a higher representation of Hispanics is related to a higher proportion of Hispanics graduating from high school.

Policy recommendations follow logically from these conclusions. Of course, Meier and Stewart recommend greater representation of minority populations on school boards. They recommend greater federal scrutiny of second-generation forms of discrimination and that school districts hire more Hispanic administrators and teachers. They recommend the elimination of most academic grouping.

Finally, the most important message in their research is that political power is the key to having a school system serve a group's educational interests. And for Hispanics, African-Americans, and Native Americans, this political power is essential to ending forms of inequality of educational opportunity. Just as African-Americans in the South had to organize to stop segregation, other groups must exercise political muscle to stop second-generation forms of segregation.

NATIVE AMERICANS

Although African-Americans are at the forefront of the struggle for equal educational opportunity, Native Americans, Mexican-Americans, and Asian-Americans joined the civil rights movement with complaints that government schools were destroying their cultures and languages, and that they were subject to segregation. In particular, Native Americans wanted to gain control of the education of their children and restore their cultural heritage and languages to the curriculum. The demand for self-determination by Native Americans received consideration in government decisions after the election of John F. Kennedy in 1960. The Kennedy administration advocated Indian participation in decisions regarding federal policies. Kennedy's secretary of interior, Stewart Udall, appointed a Task Force on Indian Affairs that, in its 1961 report, recommended that Native Americans be given full citizenship and self-sufficiency.

A result of the drive for self-determination was the creation of the Rough Rock Demonstration School in 1966. Established on a Navajo reservation in Arizona, the school was a joint effort of the Office of Economic Opportunity and the Bureau of Indian Affairs. One major goal of the demonstration school was for Navajo parents to control the education of their children and to participate in all aspects of their schooling.

Besides tribal control, one important feature of the Rough Rock Demonstration School was the attempt to preserve the Navajo language and culture. In contrast to the attempts to destroy Native cultures and languages that took place in the nineteenth and early twentieth centuries, the goal of learning both Navajo and English was presented for preparing children to live in both cultures.

The struggle for self-determination was aided by the development of a pan-Indian movement in the United States. The pan-Indian movement was based on the assumption that Native American tribes shared a common set of values and interests. Pan-Indian organizations, such as the American Indian Movement (AIM) and the Indians of All Tribes, led demonstrations demanding self-determination. In 1969, members of the Indians of All Tribes seized Alcatraz Island in San Francisco Bay calling attention to the plight of Native Americans and demanding that the island, which Indians had originally sold to the federal government for $24 worth of beads, be made an Indian cultural and education center. In 1972, AIM organized a march on Washington, D.C., called the Trail of Broken Treaties. Members of the march seized the Bureau of Indian Affairs and hung a large sign at its entrance declaring it the American Indian Embassy.

It was in this climate of civil rights activism and political support for Indian self-determination that the U.S. Senate Committee on Labor and Public Welfare issued in 1969 the report *Indian Education: A National Tragedy—A National Challenge*. The report opened with a statement condemning previous educational policies of the federal government: "A careful review of the historical literature reveals that the dominant policy of the Federal Government toward the American Indian has been one of forced assimilation . . . [because of] a desire to divest the Indian of his land."

After a lengthy review of the failure of past educational policies, the report's first recommendation was for "maximum participation and control by Indians in establishing Indian education programs." In its second recommendation, the report called for maximum Indian participation in the development of educational programs in federal schools and local public schools. These educational programs were to include early childhood education, vocational education, work-study, and adult literacy education.

The congressional debates resulting from the report eventually culminated in the passage of the Indian Education Act in 1972. The declared policy of the legislation was to provide financial assistance to local schools to develop programs to meet the "special" educational needs of Native American students. In addition, the legislation created a federal "Office of Indian Education."

In 1974, the Bureau of Indian Affairs issued a set of procedures for protecting student rights and due process. In contrast to the brutal and dictatorial treatment of Indian students in the boarding schools of the late nineteenth and early twentieth centuries, each Indian student was extended the right "to make his or her own decisions where applicable." And, in striking contrast to earlier deculturalization policies, Indian students were granted "the right to freedom of religion and culture."

The most important piece of legislation supporting self-determination was the 1975 Indian Self-Determination and Education Assistance Act, which gave tribes the power to contract with the federal government to run their own education and health programs. The legislation opened with the declaration that it was "an Act to provide maximum Indian participation in the Government and education of Indian people; to provide for the full participation of Indian tribes in programs and services conducted by the federal government. . . ."

The Indian Self-Determination and Education Assistance Act strengthened Indian participation in the control of education programs. The legislation provided that a local school district receiving funds for the education of Indian students that did not have a school board composed of mostly Indians had to establish a separate local committee composed of parents of Indian students in the school. This committee was given the authority over any Indian education programs contracted with the federal government.

The principles embodied in the Indian Self-Determination and Education Assistance Act of 1975 were expanded upon in 1988 with the passage of the Tribally Controlled Schools Act. Besides the right to operate schools under a federal contract as provided in the 1975 legislation, the Tribally Controlled Schools Act provided for outright grants to tribes to support the operation of their own schools.

On August 6, 1998, President Bill Clinton issued an Executive Order for American Indian and Alaska Native Education directing a comprehensive and coordinated federal effort to improve academic performance and reduce dropout rates among Native Americans. The Executive Order emphasized that this effort would be consistent with "tribal traditions and cultures." President Clinton identified six major goals:

1. Improving reading and mathematics
2. Increasing high school completion and postsecondary attendance rates
3. Reducing poverty and substance abuse
4. Creating strong, safe, and drug-free school environments
5. Improving science education
6. Expanding educational technology

In addition, the Executive Order requested a writing of a comprehensive federal Indian education policy by the year 2000. Included in this policy would be a consideration of the role of native languages and cultures in the development of educational strategies.

MEXICAN-AMERICANS

Similar to African-Americans, Mexican-Americans experienced many years of segregation in schools throughout the Southwest and attempted to redress their grievances through the courts. In Ontario, California, in 1945, Mexican-American parents demanded that the school board grant all requests for transfer out of segregated Mexican

schools. When the board refused this request, Gonzalo Mendez and William Guzman sued for violation of the Fourteenth Amendment to the Constitution. The school board responded to this suit by claiming that segregation was not based on race or national origins but on the necessity of providing special instruction. In other words, the school district justified segregation on the basis that Mexican-American children required special instruction because they came from homes where Spanish was the spoken language.

In 1946 a U.S. District Court ruled in *Mendez et al. v. Westminster School District of Orange County* that the only possible argument for segregation was the special educational needs of Mexican-American children. These needs involved the issue of learning English. Completely reversing the educational justification for segregation, the judge argued that "evidence clearly shows that Spanish-speaking children are retarded in learning English by lack of exposure to its use by segregation." Therefore, the court ruled segregation was illegal because it was not required by state law and because there was no valid educational justification for segregation.

Heartened by the *Mendez* decision, the League of United Latin American Citizens (LULAC), the Mexican-American equivalent of the NAACP, forged ahead in its legal attack on segregation in Texas. With support from LULAC, a group of parents in 1948 sued the Bastrop Independent School District, charging that local school authorities had no legal right to segregate children of Mexican descent and that segregation was solely because the children were of Mexican descent. In *Delgado v. Bastrop Independent School District,* the court ruled that segregating Mexican-American children was illegal and discriminatory. The ruling required that the local school district end all segregation. The court did give local school districts the right to separate some children in the first grade, only if scientific tests showed that they needed special instruction in English and the separation took place on the same campus.

Overall, LULAC was pleased with the decision. The one point they were dissatisfied with was the provision for the separation of children in the first grade. This allowed local schools to practice what was referred to in the latter part of the twentieth century as second-generation segregation. As discussed, second-generation segregation refers to the practice of using educational justifications for segregating children within a single school building. In fact, many local Texas school districts did use the proviso for that purpose.

Although the *Mendez* and *Delgado* decisions did hold out the promise of ending segregation of Mexican-Americans, local school districts used many tactics to avoid integration, including manipulation of school district lines, choice plans, and different forms of second-generation segregation. For instance, the California State Department of Education reported in 1966 that 57 percent of the children with Spanish surnames were still attending schools that were predominantly Mexican-American. In 1973, a civil rights activist, John Caughey, estimated that two-thirds of the Mexican-American children in Los Angeles attended segregated schools. In *All Deliberate Speed: Segregation and Exclusion in California Schools, 1855–1975,* Charles Wollenberg estimates that in California by 1973 more Mexican and Mexican-American children attended segregated schools than in 1947.

In 1970, Mexican-Americans were officially recognized by the federal courts as an identifiable dominated group in the public schools in a Mexican-American Legal Defense and Education Fund (MALDEF) case, *Cisernos v. Corpus Christi Independent School District.* A central issue in the case was whether or not the 1954 school desegregation decision could be applied to Mexican-Americans. The original *Brown* decision dealt specifically with African-Americans who were segregated by state and local laws. In his final decision, Judge Owen Cox ruled that blacks and Mexican-Americans were segregated in the Corpus Christi school system and that Mexican-Americans were an identifiable dominated group because of their language, culture, religion, and Spanish surnames.

Despite years of struggle, many Mexican-Americans still feel their demands for equality of educational opportunity have not been met. In the fall of 1994, the Latino Education Coalition in Denver, Colorado, threatened to call a student strike if the school district did not hire more bilingual education teachers (see Chapter 6), involve Latino parents in policy decisions, and increase the number of Latino students going on to college. The threat was reminiscent of 1969, when three thousand Latino students went on strike against the Denver school district because of high dropout rates, low academic achievement, and the district's failure to be sensitive to cultural differences. It would appear that only steady political pressure can ensure equality of educational opportunity.

ASIAN-AMERICANS

Also suffering a history of discrimination in U.S. schools, Asian-Americans are often viewed by others as the model minority group. And, until the publication of Ronald Takaki's *Strangers from a Different Shore: A History of Asian-Americans,* Asian-Americans were usually invisible in standard U.S. history texts.

Ironically, the stereotype of a model minority student has caused many educators to overlook the educational problems encountered by many Asian-American students in U.S. schools. Part of the problem is the tendency for non-Asians to lump all Asian-Americans together. In fact, Asian-Americans represent a broad spectrum of different cultures and nations including, as Valerie Ooka Pang indicates in her article "Asian-American Children: A Diverse Population," "Cambodian, Chinese, East Indian, Filipino, Guamian, Hawaiian, Hmong, Indonesian, Japanese, Korean, Laotian, Samoan, and Vietnamese . . . [and] smaller Asian-American groups within the category of all other Asians." According to U.S. Census classification there are sixteen of these smaller Asian-American groups.

The diversity of Asian-Americans also reflects a wide range of adjustment to conditions in the United States. Most non-Asians think of Asian-Americans as successful entrepreneurs and professionals who were model students while in school and quickly moved up the economic ladder after graduation. In fact, a report issued in 1994 by the Asian Pacific American Public Institute and the Asian-American Center suggests that many Asian-Americans face a difficult economic life in the United States. For instance, according to the report, while 8 percent of households nationally received public assistance in 1991, 77 percent of Cambodian and Laotian households in California received public assistance. The report states that Cambodians, Vietnamese, and Laotians have the highest rate of welfare dependency of any racial or ethnic group in the United States. For all Asian-Americans the per capita income in 1990 was $10,500, which was less than the $12,000 per capita income for non-Hispanic whites. Or, another way of viewing the economic differences in the Asian-American community, according to the report, is to consider that for every Asian-American family earning more than $75,000, there is an Asian-American family earning less than $10,000 a year. Although a third of Asian-Americans have college degrees, 23 percent of those Asian-Americans over the age of 25 have less than a high school diploma. A quarter of all families in Chinatown in New York City are living below the poverty line.

While economic figures highlight the plight of many Asian-Americans, history points out the educational discrimination encountered by Asian-American students. In *All Deliberate Speed*, Charles Wollenberg tells the story of the denial of equal educational opportunity to Asian-Americans in California schools. With cries of "yellow peril" coming from the European-American population, the state superintendent of public instruction in California, William Welcher, pointed out in 1884 that the state constitution called Chinese "dangerous to the well-being of the state" and, therefore, argued that San Francisco did not have "to undergo the expense of educating such people." Denied a public education for his daughter, Joseph Tape, an Americanized Chinese, challenged the decision in court. Judge Maguire of the municipal court ruled that since the daughter, Mamie, was an American citizen she could not be denied equal educational opportunity according to the Fourteenth Amendment to the U.S. Constitution. In addition, Judge Maguire argued that it was unjust to tax Chinese for the support of a school system that excluded Chinese children. State superintendent Welcher reacted angrily to the decision, declaring it a "terrible disaster" and asked, "Shall we abandon the education of our children to provide that of the Chinese who are thrusting themselves upon us?"

In reaction to the court decision, the California State Assembly passed legislation allowing school districts to establish segregated schools for "Mongolians." This legislation empowered the San Francisco Board of Education to establish a segregated school for Asians. The courts affirmed this action in 1902, when Wong Him challenged the requirement of attending a segregated institution. Eventually, pressure from the Chinese-American community brought an end to segregation. In 1921, Chinese-American educator Mary Bo-Tze Lee challenged the segregation policy by showing that Chinese students scored as well as white students on IQ tests. As the Chinese population dispersed through the city, traditionally white schools were forced to open their doors to Chinese students. A study in 1947 found that formal school segregation had ended but that the original segregated Commodore Stockton school was still 100 percent Chinese.

Asian-American students are currently discriminated against because of the stereotype of "model minority" student. Asian-American students with educational problems are often neglected because teachers assume they will do well in school. On the other hand, many non-Asian educators resent the achievement of some Asian-Americans. In 1987, *Time* magazine called Asian-Americans the "new whiz kids." *Time* reported that Asian-Americans comprised 25 percent of the entering class at the University of California at Berkeley, 21 percent at the California Institute of Technology, 20 percent at the Massachusetts Institute of Technology, and 14 percent at Harvard. *Time* magazine also reported in 1987 that because of quota systems many qualified Asian-Americans were being refused admission to major universities.

The largest number of complaints centered on the admission policies of the University of

California at Berkeley. *Time* quotes the cochairperson of the Asian-American Task Force on University Admissions, Alameda County Superior Court Judge Ken Kawaichi, as stating that university administrators envision a campus that "is mostly white, mostly upper-class with limited numbers of African-Americans, Hispanics and Asians. One day they looked around and said, 'My goodness, look at this campus. What are all these Asian people doing here?' Then they started tinkering with the system."

The political actions taken by Asian-Americans, Mexican-Americans, and Native Americans to gain equal educational opportunity highlight the recent research findings that second-generation segregation can be reduced by the exercise of effective political power. As an earlier section suggests, there is evidence of a relationship among decreasing second-generation segregation, the election of Hispanics and African-Americans to school boards, and the hiring of Hispanics and African-Americans as teachers and school administrators. These findings are applicable to situations of segregation encountered by Native Americans and Asian-Americans.

THE RECENT STRUGGLE FOR EQUAL EDUCATION FOR WOMEN

Equal educational opportunity for women was high on the agenda of the National Organization for Women (NOW) when it organized in 1966. The founding document of the organization declared, "There is no civil rights movement to speak for women as there has been for Negroes and other victims of discrimination. The National Organization for Women must therefore begin to speak." In the NOW's founding document, education is called "the key to effective participation in today's economy . . . [and public schools should educate woman] to her full potential of human ability."

During its first years of activism, NOW focused on the following:

■ Eliminating discriminatory quotas against women in college and professional school admissions

■ Urging parents, counselors, and teachers to encourage women to pursue higher education and professional education
■ Eliminating discriminatory practices against women in the awarding of fellowships and loans
■ Investigating the problem of female school dropouts

NOW's activities and that of other women's organizations turned to legal action with the passage of Title IX of the 1972 Higher Education Act. Title IX provided for sexual equality in employment in educational institutions and for sexual equality in educational programs. The legislation applied to all educational institutions, including preschool, elementary and secondary schools, vocational and professional schools, and public and private undergraduate and graduate institutions. A 1983 U.S. Supreme Court decision, *Grove City College v. Bell,* restricted Title IX in its application to specific educational programs within institutions. In the 1987 Civil Rights Restoration Act, Congress overturned the Court's decision and amended Title IX to include all activities of an educational institution receiving federal aid.

Armed with Title IX, NOW and other women's organizations placed pressure on local school systems and colleges to ensure equal treatment of women in vocational education, athletic programs, textbooks and the curriculum, testing, and college admissions. Following is a brief chronological list of achievements in providing equality of educational opportunity for women:

■ 1972 Legal action against school systems with segregated courses in home economics and industrial arts
■ 1974 With backing from NOW, more than 1,000 women's studies departments are created on college campuses
■ 1975 Federal regulations to end sex discrimination in athletics
■ 1976 Lawsuits regarding female participation in athletics and gender-biased hiring in school administration
■ 1976 Educational Equity Act authorizes Office of Education to prepare "non-sexist

curricula and non-discriminatory vocational and career counseling, sports education, and other programs designed to achieve equity for all students regardless of sex"

- 1983 Last all-male school in Ivy League, Columbia University, becomes coeducational
- 1986 FairTest organized to counter sex bias in high-stakes tests
- 1996 Virginia Military Institute and the Citadel become coeducational

By 1996, NOW and other women's organizations could claim the following accomplishments:

- The number of female medical school graduates increased from 8.4 percent in 1969 to 34.5 percent in 1990.
- The percentage of doctoral and professional degrees awarded women increased from 14.4 Percent in 1971 to 36.8 percent in 1991.
- Most discrimination in vocational programs ended.
- Female participation in high school athletics increased from 7 percent in 1972 to 37 percent in 1992 and in college athletics from 15.6 percent in 1972 to 34.8 percent in 1993.

SEXISM AND EDUCATION

In *Failing at Fairness: How America's Schools Cheat Girls,* Myra and David Sadker summarize current research on educational discrimination against girls. One surprising result of their research and analysis of other data was that girls are equal to or ahead of boys in most measures of academic achievement and psychological health during the early years of schooling, but by the end of high school and college, girls have fallen behind boys on these measurements. On entrance examinations to college, girls score lower than boys, particularly in science and mathematics. Boys receive more state and national scholarships. Women score lower than men on all entrance examinations to professional schools.

An explanation for the decline in test scores is that girls suffer a greater decline than boys in self-esteem from elementary school to high school. (Of course, an important general question about the following statistics is why both boys and girls decline in feelings of self-esteem.) As a measure of self-esteem, the Sadkers rely on responses to the statement, "I'm happy the way I am." The Sadkers report that in elementary school 60 percent of girls and 67 percent of boys responded positively to the statement. By high school these positive responses declined to 29 percent for girls and 46 percent for boys. In other words, the decline in self-esteem for girls was thirty-one percentage points as compared with twenty-one percentage points for boys. Why is there less self-esteem and a greater decline in self-esteem among girls as compared with boys?

To get an answer to the question, the Sadkers asked students how their lives would be different if they suddenly were transformed into members of the opposite sex. Overall, girls responded with feelings that it wouldn't be so bad and that it would open up opportunities to participate in sports and politics. In addition, girls felt they would have more freedom and respect. Regarding self-esteem, girls expressed little regret about the consequences of the sex change. In contrast, boys expressed horror at the idea, and many said they would commit suicide. They saw themselves becoming second-class citizens, being denied access to athletics and outdoor activities, and being racked with physical problems. Concerning self-esteem, and in contrast to girls, boys expressed nothing but regret about the consequences of the sex change.

Contributing to the lack of self-esteem among girls, the Sadkers argue, are modes of classroom interaction, the representation of women in textbooks and other educational materials, and the discriminatory content of standardized tests. In one of their workshops with classroom teachers, the Sadkers illustrate classroom sex bias by asking four of the participants—two men and two women—to act like students in a middle-school social studies classroom. The lesson is about the American Revolution and it begins with an examination of homework. Acting as the teacher, David Sadker perfunctorily tells one woman that two of her answers are wrong and comments to the group on the neatness of the other woman's homework. He tells one man that two of his answers are wrong and, unlike his response to the woman with wrong answers, he urges the man to try harder and suggests ways of improving his answers. David then states to the other man that he failed to do his homework assignment. In contrast to the woman with the neat paper, this man illustrates what the Sadkers call the "bad boy role."

David Sadker then continues the lesson by discussing battles and leaders. All of the Revolutionary leaders are, of course, male. During the lesson he calls on the males twenty times each while only calling on one woman twice and completely ignoring the other woman. The one woman called on misses her question because she is given only half a second to respond. When questioning the men, David Sadker spends time giving hints and probing. At the end of this demonstration lesson, the Sadkers report, one woman commented that she felt like she was back in school. She often had the right answer but was never called on by the teacher.

What this workshop demonstration illustrates, based on the Sadkers' findings on classroom interaction, is that boys receive more and better instruction. Boys are more often called on by the teacher and boys interact more with the teacher than girls. In a typical classroom situation, if both boys and girls have their hands raised to answer a question, the teacher is most likely to call on a boy. A teacher will spend more time responding to a boy's question than to a girl's question. In other words, girls do not receive equal educational opportunity in the classroom.

In addition, women are not so well represented as men in textbooks. The Sadkers found in 1989 elementary school language arts textbooks that there were from two to three times as many pictures of men as women. In one elementary history text, they found four times as many pictures of men as women. In one 1992 world history textbook, of 631 pages they found only 7 pages related to women. Two of those pages were devoted to a fifth-grade female student who made a peace trip to the Soviet Union.

It is most likely that the treatment received by girls in the classroom and in textbooks contributes to their low self-esteem and to their decline, as compared with boys, in performance on standardized tests from elementary school to high school. It seems logical that if less instructional time is spent with girls than boys, that boys would more rapidly advance academically. In addition, without equal representation in textbooks, girls might value themselves less and have less incentive to achieve. Instructional time and representation in textbooks contribute to the glass ceiling of the classroom.

The lowering of self-esteem and content bias may contribute to the significant gender gap in scores on standardized college entrance examinations and entrance examinations to professional schools. For instance, on the widely used Scholastic Aptitude Test (SAT) males score fifty points higher on the math section and up to twelve points higher on the verbal section. It is important to understand that discrimination in standardized testing involves the denial of economic rewards. These economic rewards are scholarships and career opportunities.

The content bias and economic value of standardized tests were recognized in a 1989 ruling by a federal judge in New York. The judge ruled that the awarding of New York State scholarships using the SAT discriminated against female students. The case was brought to court by the Girls Clubs of America and the National Organization for Women. The court argued that the scholarships were to be awarded based on academic achievement in high school and that the SAT was not constructed to test achievement but to determine college performance. The court's decision states, "The evidence is clear that females score significantly below males on the SAT while they do equally or slightly better in high schools."

In this court case, academic achievement was defined according to grades received in high school courses. Interestingly, the Sadkers argue that this apparent paradox between girls' high grades and low standardized-test scores is a result of grade inflation. This grade inflation results from female passivity and their willingness to follow classroom rules. Often, teachers formally and informally incorporate evaluations of student behavior in their academic grading practices. For girls, good behavior can result in good grades.

But the issue of grade inflation still doesn't solve the puzzle of lower performance by girls on tests like the SAT. The Sadkers suggest that one possible reason for the differences in scores between males and females is that the content of standardized tests is biased. Boys are more familiar with organized sports, financial issues, science, wars, and dates. Consequently, test items referring to these areas tend to favor boys. As an example, the Sadkers describe a gifted high school girl who lost her concentration on the Preliminary SAT when she encountered an analogy question comparing a "football and a gridiron." The analogy baffled her because she had little knowledge of football.

One possible solution to teacher bias in classroom interaction, the Sadkers suggest, is to have an observer code classroom interaction so that the teacher becomes aware of any possible bias. If teachers are unconsciously favoring boys, then this observation provides the opportunity for them to change their behavior. One teacher told the Sadkers that she distributed two chips to all students. When students want to comment or ask a question, they have to give up one chip. Before the class is over, all students must use their two chips. This guarantees equal participation of all students and ensures that classroom interaction is not dominated by only a few students. In addition, the Sadkers recommend that teachers consciously search for books portraying strong female characters in a variety of occupational and social roles. They point to the work of the National Women's History Project, which since the 1970s has published materials emphasizing women's roles in history. In addition, the Sadkers recommend the use of workshops to heighten teachers' awareness of their own possible sexist behavior and to understand how to find nonsexist educational material for the classroom.

Another possible solution is single-sex education. This would eliminate the problem of female students having to compete with male students for teachers' attention. In classrooms of only girls, teachers would not tend to push girls aside and focus their instructional efforts on boys. In an all-girls school or classroom, female students might receive the equal educational opportunity denied to them in a coed classroom.

Writing in favor of girls' schools, Susan Estrich, professor of law and political science at the University of Southern California, notes that 60 percent of the National Merit Scholarship finalists are boys. Echoing the Sadkers' findings, she reports from a 1992 study of the American Association of University Women, "that even though girls get better grades (except in math), they get less from schools." While she does not dismiss efforts to equalize opportunities for girls in coed schools, she argues that currently single-sex education is working. For instance, in all-girls schools 80 percent of girls take four years of math and science, whereas in coed schools the average is two years of math and science. In Fortune 1000 companies, one-third of the female board members are graduates of women's colleges even though graduates of women's colleges represent only 4 percent of all female college graduates. In addition, graduates of women's colleges earn 43 percent of the math and 50 percent of engineering doctorates earned by all women, and they outnumber all other females in *Who's Who*.

Estrich does see the possibility of offering single-sex classes within a coed institution. She cites the example of the Illinois Math and Science Academy, which experimented with a girls-only calculus-based physics class. Instead of sitting meekly at their desks while boys command all the attention, girls are actively asking and answering questions. In an all-girls algebra class in Ventura, California, the teacher reports spending time building self-confidence along with teaching math. For Estrich, at least at this point in time, all-girls schools are a means for ending sexism in education.

Of course, for an all-girls school or classroom to overcome the problems of sexism completely it would require the maintenance of the same educational expectations as there are for boys and the use of textbooks and other educational materials that provide strong female role models. As I discussed previously in this chapter, one of the problems with segregated female education in the nineteenth century was the belief that women did not have the physical and mental stamina to undergo the same academic demands as men. Consequently, to avoid sexism, there should be no watering down of the curriculum in female schools and classrooms. In addition, sex-segregated education would have to avoid the pitfalls of tracking women into a sex-segregated labor market. One of the problems in the development of the high school in the early twentieth century was that it tended to track women into certain occupations. For an all-girls school or classroom to avoid this form of discrimination, there would have to be an emphasis on opening up all career opportunities for women.

There are many critics of proposals for all-female schools. One University of Michigan researcher, Valerie Lee, found that many all-girls classrooms still contained high levels of sexist behavior on the part of the teacher. In one case, a history teacher assigned a research paper and told students that she would provide "major hand-holding" to help the students. Lee argued that the offer of major hand-holding would not occur in a boy's school. In addition, she found "male bashing" taking place in some all-female schools.

In addition, Lee found boys in all-male schools engaging in serious sexist comments about women. In other words, all-female schools do not do anything about the sexist attitudes of men. In fact, all-male schools might reinforce male sexist behavior. For instance, in a 1994 court case involving a suit by Shannon Faulkner to gain entrance to the all-male military college, The Citadel, one of the witnesses, a 1991 graduate of the school, reported that the word *woman* was used on campus in a derogatory manner "every day, every minute, every hour [it was] a part of the life there."

Therefore, there is the possibility that single-sex education might result in greater academic achievement for girls while doing nothing about sexist attitudes among men. The academic gains made by women might mean little in a world dominated by sexist males. Also, the courts may not approve of single-sex public schools, because of a decision regarding all-boys African-

American schools in Detroit. The court argued that the all-boys schools were a violation of the 1954 *Brown* decision that declared as unconstitutional "separate but equal" schools that were racially segregated. In the Detroit case, separate but equal all-boys schools were declared unconstitutional.

In 1998, the American Association of University Women (AAUW) released a follow-up report to its earlier charges that public schools were "shortchanging" girls. The new study found that the number of girls enrolled in algebra, trigonometry, precalculus, and calculus was growing at a faster rate than boys. Probably the most impressive statistic was that the differences between boys and girls was the smallest in the world on international tests in math and science.

However, the report found that technology, particularly computer technology, is emerging as the new "boys' club." The report found that girls have less exposure to computers inside and outside of school and that girls feel less confident about using computers. The gap between boys and girls in computer knowledge and use increases from grades 8 to 11. Only 17 percent of students taking the College Board's Advanced Placement test in computer science were women.

In reference to the technological gap between males and females, Janice Weinman, the executive director of the Washington-based AAUW said, "This is becoming the new club [computer technology] from which girls are feeling disenfranchised. Consequently, girls are not going to be appropriately prepared for the technology era of the new 21st century."

However, there are areas where girls outperform boys. More girls than boys are enrolled in advanced English, foreign language, and arts courses. In addition, girls outscore boys by wide margins on reading and writing tests in middle and elementary grades.

Education Week reporter Debra Viadero provides the following summary of other findings in the AAUW study:

- In school-to-work programs, which combine challenging academics with vocational training, girls still tend to cluster in traditional female occupations.

- Although girls are taking more advanced-placement courses and getting better grades than boys, their scores on those exams still tend to be lower.
- On large-scale exams, such as the National Assessment of Educational Progress, the top scorers in math and science still tend to be boys.

STUDENTS WITH SPECIAL NEEDS

By the 1960s, the civil rights movement encompassed students with special needs, including students with physical handicaps; special mental, emotional, and behavioral needs; and hearing and visual impairments. Within the context of equality of educational opportunity, students with special needs could only participate equally in schools with other students if they received some form of special help. Since the nineteenth century many of the needs of these students have been neglected by local and state school authorities because of the expense of special facilities and teachers.

The political movement for federal legislation to aid students with special needs followed a path similar to the rest of the civil rights movement. First, finding themselves unable to change educational institutions by pressuring local and state governments, organized groups interested in improving educational opportunities for students with special needs turned to the courts. This was the path taken in the late 1960s by the Pennsylvania Association for Retarded Children (PARC). PARC was one of many associations organized in the 1950s to aid citizens with special needs. These organizations were concerned with state laws that excluded children with special needs from educational institutions because they were considered uneducable and untrainable. State organizations like PARC and the National Association for Retarded Children campaigned to eliminate these laws and to demonstrate the educability of all children. But, as the civil rights movement discovered throughout the century, local and state officials

were resistant to change and relief had to be sought from the judicial system.

In *Pennsylvania Association for Retarded Children (PARC) v. Commonwealth of Pennsylvania,* a case that was as important for the rights of children with special needs as the *Brown* decision was for African-Americans, PARC objected to conditions in the Pennhurst State School and Hospital. In framing the case, lawyers for PARC focused on the legal right to an education for children with special needs. PARC, working with the major federal lobbyist for children with special needs, the Council for Exceptional Children (CEC), overwhelmed the court with evidence on the educability of children with special needs. The state withdrew its case, and the court enjoined the state from excluding children with special needs from a public education and required that every child be allowed access to an education. Publicity about the PARC case prompted other lobbying groups to file thirty-six cases against different state governments. The CEC prepared model legislation and lobbied for its passage at the state and federal levels.

In 1975, Congress passed Public Law 94–142 (Education for All Handicapped Children Act) that guaranteed equal educational opportunity for all children with special needs. One of the issues confronting Congress during the debates over the legislation was that of increased federal control over local school systems. One way that Congress decided to resolve this issue was to require that an individual education plan (IEP) be written for each student with special needs. This avoided direct federal control by requiring that each student's IEP be developed at the local level. IEPs are now a standard part of education programs for children with special needs. Public Law 94–142 requires that an IEP be developed for each child jointly by the local educational agency and the child's parents or guardians. This gives the child or the parents the right to negotiate with the local school system about the type of services to be delivered.

INCLUSION

Another concern regarding the education of children with special needs is their isolation from other students and lack of access to the educational opportunities of a regular classroom. Federal legislation called for placing students in the "least restrictive environment." The result was the practice of mainstreaming. The basic idea of mainstreaming is that students with special needs will spend part of their day in a special education classroom and part of the day in regular classrooms. Obviously, this arrangement requires the classroom teacher to have some knowledge of the requirements of students with special needs. Working together, special education teachers and regular classroom teachers plan the mainstreaming of students with special needs into regular classrooms.

Many parents of students with special needs and many special education professionals felt that mainstreaming did not go far enough in providing a "least restrictive environment." They demanded full inclusion. Full inclusion is different from mainstreaming because students with special needs spend all their time in a regular classroom. The basic argument for full inclusion is that even with mainstreaming, students with special needs spend a majority of their time segregated from regular students. Similar to any form of segregation, the isolation of children with special needs often deprives them of contact with other students and denies them access to equipment found in regular classrooms, such as scientific equipment, audiovisual aids, classroom libraries, and computers. Full inclusion, it is believed, will improve the educational achievement and social development of children with special needs.

In 1990, advocates of full inclusion received federal support with the passage of the Americans with Disabilities Act. This historic legislation bans all forms of discrimination against the disabled. The Americans with Disabilities Act played an important role in the 1992 court decision, *Oberti v. Board of Education of the Borough of Clementon School District*, which involved an 8-year-old, Rafael Oberti, classified as educable mentally retarded. U.S. District Court Judge John F. Gerry argued that the Americans with Disabilities Act requires that people with disabilities be given equal access to services provided by any

agency receiving federal money, including public schools. Judge Gerry decided that Rafael Oberti could manage in a regular classroom with special aides and a special curriculum. In his decision, Judge Gerry wrote, "Inclusion is a right, not a privilege for a select few."

In 1992, the National Association of State Boards of Education gave its support to the idea of full inclusion with the issuance of its report, *Winners All: A Call for Inclusive Schools.* The report calls for a fundamental shift in the provision of services for students with special needs. As the report envisions the full-inclusion process, rather than teaching in a separate classroom, special-education teachers would provide their services in regular classrooms by team-teaching with the regular teacher or providing other support.

The idea of inclusion is resisted by some parents who believe that separate special education classrooms provide important benefits for their children. For instance, twenty parents of children with special needs attending the Vaughn Occupational High School in Chicago carried signs at the board of education meeting on September 7, 1994, reading "The board's inclusion is exclusion." The parents were protesting the board's decision to send their children to neighborhood schools for inclusion in regular classrooms. Traditionally, Vaughn provided vocational training for students with special needs. The students would hold low-level jobs at McDonald's, an airline food service company, and a glass-installation business.

The board's action regarding the Vaughn students was the result of a 1992 complaint by the Illinois state board that Vaughn students were not spending time with nondisabled peers. The state board threatened to remove all federal and state funds from the school district if the students were not included in regular classrooms. Martha Luna complained about the decision because it denied her 15-year-old son, Tony, vocational training to meet his needs. Ms. Luna stated, "I know Tony won't go to college so I don't expect that, just for him to learn everyday living and work skills."

TEACHERS RESIST THE CALL FOR INCLUSION

Why do some surveys find that over 70 percent of practicing teachers object to including students with special needs in their classrooms? The West Virginia Federation of Teachers released a survey of 1,121 teachers showing that 87 percent did not believe that inclusion helped general education students and 78 percent did not believe that inclusion helped students with special needs. A survey of teachers in Howard County, Maryland, reports that 64 percent of middle-school teachers believe "that inclusion detracts from their ability to fully serve the needs of the general student population." Also, only 21 percent believed inclusion benefited children with special needs. The complaints about inclusion are occurring as the proportion of disabled students receiving their education in regular classrooms increases. For instance, in 1991 32.8 percent of disabled students were receiving their educations in regular classrooms. By 1995, the figure rose to 44.5 percent.

The preceding figures indicate the complications in implementing inclusion programs. The following is a list of objections by teachers to inclusion programs:

- Disabled students are moved into regular classrooms without any support services.
- Experienced teachers have never received training in teaching students with special needs or in teaching in an inclusive classroom.
- School districts implementing inclusion policies do not provide adequate training for general education teachers.
- Education schools do not provide prospective teachers with a basic knowledge of learning disabilities or situations they are likely to confront in inclusive classrooms.
- General education teachers are often excluded from the individualized education plan (IEP) team.
- Parents of nondisabled students worry that their children's education will be compromised in inclusive classrooms.

The preceding list of issues contains its own solutions, which include (1) more education and training for experienced and future teachers, (2) adequate support services for teachers in inclusive classrooms, (3) teacher participation on the individual planning team, and (4) education of parents about inclusive classrooms. Model full-inclusion schools and teacher education programs do exist that address the preceding issues. Teachers and administrators at the Zachery Taylor Elementary School, a suburban Washington, D.C., community, operate a model full-inclusion school that they believe is improving the academic and social performance of disabled students and has made other students more caring and tolerant. Syracuse University, in response to the problem of inadequately prepared teachers, instructs general education and special education teachers together. At the end of four years, both groups receive dual certification. In answer to worried parents of students in general education, John McDonnell, chair of the special education department at the University of Utah, states, "There really has been no effect on the educational progress of kids without disabilities by including kids with disabilities at the classroom level."

The Education for All Handicapped Children Act, IEP, mainstreaming, the Americans with Disabilities Act, and full inclusion highlight the extent to which the civil rights movement reached out to include concerns for equal educational opportunity for all children, including children with special needs. It is a matter of justice that if all citizens are taxed to support schools, then all citizens should have an equal opportunity to attend school and benefit from an education.

CONCLUSION

Unequal educational opportunities continue to plague American schools. Even though the civil rights movement was able to overturn laws requiring school segregation, racial segregation between schools and second-generation segregation in schools continue to be problems. Differences between school districts in expenditures per student tend to increase the effects of segregation.

Many Hispanic, African-American, and Native American students attend schools where per student expenditures are considerably below those of elite suburban and private schools. These reduced expenditures contribute to unequal educational opportunity that, in turn, affects a student's ability to compete in the labor market.

It is possible, according to the discussion of the labor market in Chapter 4, that unequal school expenditures, segregation, and second-generation segregation will result in the vast majority of Hispanics, African-Americans, and Native Americans being confined to boring and tedious jobs in routine production services and in-person services. Of course, large numbers of low-income whites will also fill the ranks of these occupations. If education remains the key to advancement to high-paying and interesting work, and if present inequalities and forms of segregation continue, then it is possible that the children of routine production and in-person services workers will be trapped in the occupations of their parents. If the promise of America is that hard work will lead to social mobility, then these conditions might foretell the end of the American Dream.

EXERCISES

1. Have students write a short paper on their own experiences with segregated schools. For instance, students should consider whether or not they attended schools that were primarily one-race schools. Often, white students will say to me that they never experienced segregation because they lived in a community that was all white. I immediately ask if this isn't a form of segregation. On the other hand, African-American, Native American, and Hispanic students identify their attendance at schools composed of mainly one race as segregation. The reason for the difference, as I perceive it, is that white students benefit from segregation and therefore never spend much time thinking about segregation, while African-Americans, Native Americans, and Hispanics do not benefit from segregation and therefore

are more aware of its existence. Therefore, in writing this paper, students should explore the reasons for segregation or the lack of segregation in the schools they attended. Also, students should consider whether their education was improved or harmed by attendance at an integrated or segregated school. In addition, students should consider whether students attending schools in surrounding districts were harmed by segregation or integration.

2. Students should write a paper on their experiences with second-generation segregation. Similar to the previous exercise, I frequently encounter white students who never experienced second-generation segregation because they attended a school that was all white. If a student attended a one-race school, then he or she should be asked to interview a student who attended an integrated school and report that student's experience with second-generation segregation.

3. Divide students into small groups. Have each group write a lesson plan for teaching sixth-grade students about discrimination against girls in the classroom. Have each group present this lesson to the class.

4. Divide students into small groups. Have each group write a short skit on the development of an individual education plan (IEP). Have these skits presented in class. This exercise will require students to do research on the educational needs of children with special needs and the concerns of parents of children with special needs.

SUGGESTED READINGS AND WORKS CITED IN CHAPTER

Ballantine, Jeanne. *The Sociology of Education.* Englewood Cliffs, NJ: Prentice-Hall, 1983. Chapter 4 is devoted to a discussion of sexism in education.

Borman, Kathryn M., and Joel Spring. *Schools in Central Cities.* White Plains, NY: Longman, 1984. Chapter 6 analyzes the impact of desegregation on the curriculum.

Committee on Labor and Public Welfare, U.S. Senate 91st Congress, 1st Session. *Indian Education: A*

National Tragedy—A National Challenge. Washington, D.C.: U.S. Government Printing Office, 1969. This is the report that set the stage for recent efforts in Indian education.

DeWitt, Karen. "The Nation's Schools Learn a 4th R: Resegregation." *New York Times* (19 January 1992): E5. This article provides statistics on the degree of segregation in the United States.

Dunn, Ashley. "Southeast Asians Highly Dependent on Welfare in U.S." *New York Times* (19 May 1994): 1, 23. This article summarizes a report of the Asian Pacific American Public Policy Institute and the Asian-American Studies Center on the economic conditions of Asian-Americans.

Estrich, Susan. "For Girls' Schools and Women's Colleges, Separate Is Better." *New York Times Magazine* (22 May, 1994): 39. Estrich argues against coeducation.

"Feminist Chronicles." http://www.now.org. NOW's official account of its struggle for equal opportunity and equal educational opportunity for women.

Hacker, Andrew. *Two Nations: Black and White, Separate, Hostile, Unequal.* New York: Charles Scribner's Son, 1992. A study of racial divisions in the United States.

Heller, Carol, and Joseph Hawkins. "Teaching Tolerance: Notes from the Front Line." *Teachers College Record* (Spring 1994): 1–30. A history and description of the Teaching Tolerance project.

Holmes, Steven. "Quality of Life Is Up for Many Blacks, Data Say." *New York Times* (18 November 1996): 1, B10. Article reports the findings of the Joint Center for Political and Economic Studies on the economic improvements in the black community in the 1990s.

Kluger, Richard. *Simple Justice.* New York: Random House, 1975. A good history of *Brown v. Board of Education* and the struggle for equality.

Krsycke, Cindy. "Efforts Fail to Advance Women's Jobs: 'Glass Ceiling' Intact Despite New Benefits." *Compuserve Executive News Service Washington Post* (20 February 1990). This article summarizes studies of difficulties encountered by women in trying to climb the corporate ladder.

Lamar, Jake. *Bourgeois Blues: An American Memoir.* New York: Plume Books, 1992. An autobiography dealing with the racism encountered by an upper-middle-class African-American.

Levine, Daniel, and Robert Havighurst. *Society and Education.* 6th ed. Boston: Allyn and Bacon, 1984. Chapter 18 is devoted to women in education.

Manegold, Catherine. "Save the Males' Becomes Battle Cry in Citadel's Defense Against Woman." *New York Times* (25 May 1994): A4. Story of female student's struggle to enter an all-boys school.

Meier, Kenneth, and Joseph Stewart, Jr. *The Politics of Hispanic Education.* Albany: State University of New York Press, 1991. This is an important study of the relationship between second-generation segregation and Hispanic political power.

Meier, Kenneth, Joseph Stewart, Jr., and Robert England. *Race, Class, and Education: The Politics of Second-Generation Discrimination.* Madison: University of Wisconsin Press, 1989. This book studies the politics of second-generation segregation.

"Mid- and Low-Income Minorities in Decline on College Rolls." *New York Times* (15 January 1990): A13. This article reports on a study by the American Council of Education on the decline in minority college attendance.

National Center for Education Statistics. "Dropout Rates in the United States: 1994," http://www.ed.gov/NCES. Provides demographic and dropout rates by racial classification.

"National Organization for Women's 1966 Statement of Purpose" (Adopted at the Organizing Conference in Washington, D.C., October 29, 1966), http://www.now.org. This historic document establishes the foundation for the participation of women in the civil rights movement.

Neal, David, and David Kirp. "The Allure of Legalization Reconsidered: The Case of Special Education." In David Kirp and Donald Jensen, eds., *School Days, Rule Days: The Legalization and Regulation of Education.* Philadelphia: Falmer Press, 1986. This is an important study of the evolution of court cases and laws affecting students with special needs.

"Opening Doors in Education," http://www.feminist.org. Lists the educational accomplishments of the women's movement.

O'Reilly, Patricia, and Kathryn Borman. "Sexism in Education: Documented Biases, Destructive Practices and Some Hope for the Future." *Theory into Practice,* 23, no. 2 (Spring 1984). A good summary of information on institutional sexism in education.

Orfield, Gary. *The Reconstruction of Southern Education: The Schools and the 1964 Civil Rights Act.* New York: Wiley-Interscience, 1969. A study of the desegregation of southern schools following the passage of the 1964 Civil Rights Act.

Pang, Valerie Ooka. "Asian-American Children: A Diverse Population." *The Educational Forum* (Fall 1990): 49–66. This is a good discussion of diversity in the Asian-American population in the United States.

Prucha, Francis Paul. *Documents of United States Indian Policy.* Lincoln: University of Nebraska Press, 1990. This volume contains reprints of all the important laws, court cases, and reports affecting Indian education.

Reyhner, Jon, and Jeanne Eder. *A History of Indian Education.* Billings: Eastern Montana College Press, 1989. This book provides a history of Indian education to present times. It discusses Native American civil rights actions and recent legislation.

Rist, Ray. *Desegregated Schools: Appraisals of an American Experiment.* New York: Academic Press, 1979. This book provides many examples of second-generation segregation.

Rossell, Christine. "Magnet Schools As a Desegregation Tool." *Urban Education,* 14, no. 3 (October 1979). A study of the role of magnet schools in desegregation plans.

Sack, Joetta. "Side by Side." *Education Week* (25 March 1998), http://www.edweek.org. An extensive article on the objections, problems, and solutions for creation of inclusive schools and classrooms.

San Miguel, Jr., Guadalupe. *"Let All of Them Take Heed": Mexican-Americans and the Campaign for Educational Equality in Texas, 1910–1981.* Austin: University of Texas Press, 1987. This is a good history of the events and court cases surrounding efforts by Mexican-Americans to end segregation.

Schmidt, Peter. "Outlook Is Bleak for Many Blacks Study Concludes." *Education Week* (2 August 1989): 1, 29. Summary of report by the National Research Council titled, *A Common Destiny: Blacks and American Society.*

Schnaiberg, Lynn. "Chicago Flap Shows Limits of 'Inclusion,' Critics Say." *Education Week* (5 October 1994): 1, 12. Article describes parent protest about inclusion in Chicago.

Sims, Calvin. "The Overlooked." *New York Times* (18 February 1990). Article reports on studies of the decline in minority college attendance.

———. "Frustrated Hispanics Call for School Boycott in Denver." *Education Week* (21 September 1994): 3. A report on the threatened Latino student strike in Denver.

Smothers, Ronald. "In Pupil 'Tracks,' Many See a Means of Resegregation." *New York Times* (18 February 1990): E5. A report on how the use of tracking as a means of second-generation segregation caused a school boycott in Selma, Alabama.

———. "In School Conflict, Selma Discovers Old Racial Tensions Are Unresolved." *New York Times* (20 February 1990): A12. A report of student boycotts caused by second-generation segregation.

Smylie, Mark. "Reducing Racial Isolation in Large School Districts: The Comparative Effectiveness of Mandatory and Voluntary Strategies." *Urban Education,* 17, no. 4 (January 1983). A good analysis of the different types of school desegregation plans.

Snider, William. "Schools Are Reopened in Selma amid Continuing Racial Tension." *Education Week* (21 February 1990): 1, 14. A report of the school boycott and second-generation segregation in Selma, Alabama.

Takaki, Ronald. *Strangers from a Different Shore: A History of Asian-Americans.* New York: Penguin Books, 1989. An excellent history of Asian-Americans.

Tatum, Beverly Daniel. "Teaching White Students about Racism: The Search for White Allies and the Restoration of Hope." Paper presented at the American Educational Research Association Annual Meeting, April 5, 1994. Discussion of methods of creating positive antiracist models for white students.

Viadero, Debra. "'Full Inclusion' of Disabled in Regular Classes Favored." *Education Week* (30 September 1992): 11. This is a report on the court case, *Oberti v. Board of Education of the Borough of Clementon School District,* involving full inclusion.

———. "NASBE Endorses 'Full Inclusion' of Disabled Students." *Education Week* (4 November 1992): 1, 30. This article discusses the report supporting full inclusion of students with special needs. The report, *Winners All: A Call for Inclusive Schools,* was issued by the National Association for State Boards of Education.

———. "Some Progress, But Gaps Remain." *Education Week* (14 October 1998), http://www.edweek.org. Article summarizes American Association of University Women's 1998 report on inequities faced by girls in public schools.

———. "Va. Hamlet at Forefront of 'Full Inclusion' Movement for Disabled." *Education Week* (18 November 1992): 1, 14. This article describes the implementation of a full-inclusion plan in a community in Virginia.

Walsh, Mark. "Judge Finds Bias in Scholarships." *Education Week* (15 February 1989): 1, 20. This article describes the court ruling that found the awarding of scholarships using test scores to be biased against female students.

West, Cornell. *Race Matters,* New York: Vintage Books, 1994. A set of essays emphasizing the continuing importance of race in social relationships in U.S. society.

West, Peter. "Interior Dept. Sets 4 Objectives for Indian Education: Tribal Leaders Asked to Help Shape Goals." *Education Week* (21 February 1990): 1, 22. A report on some of the plans for the education of Native Americans.

Wilkerson, Isabel. "Des Moines Acts to Halt White Flight After State Allows Choice of Schools." *New York Times* (16 December 1992): B9. This article briefly describes choice plans instituted by states and focuses on the issue of choice plans resulting in white flight from urban areas.

Wilson, William J. *The Declining Significance of Race: Blacks and Changing American Institutions.* Chicago: University of Chicago Press, 1979. This book argues that social class is a more important factor than race in determining equality of opportunity among African-Americans.

Wollenberg, Charles. *All Deliberate Speed: Segregation and Exclusion in California Schools, 1855–1975.* Berkeley: University of California Press, 1976. This is a good history of segregation in California. It includes a discussion of the important court decision regarding Mexican-Americans, *Mendez et al. v. Westminster School District of Orange County,* and of the segregation of Asian-Americans.

Multicultural Education: Historical Development, Dimensions, and Practice

JAMES A. BANKS

The heated discourse on multicultural education, especially in the popular press and among non-specialists (Gray, 1991; Leo, 1990; Schlesinger, 1991), often obscures the theory, research, and developing consensus among multicultural education specialists about the nature, aims, and scope of the field. Gay (1992), as well as J. A. Banks (1993c), has noted the high level of consensus about aims and scope in the literature written by multicultural education theorists. Gay, however, points out that there is a tremendous gap between theory and practice in the field. In her view, theory development has outpaced development in practice, and a wide gap exists between the two.

Gibson (1976) reviewed the multicultural education literature and identified five approaches. She noted how the approaches differ and how they overlap and interrelate. In their review of the literature, published 11 years later, Sleeter and Grant (1987) also identified five approaches to multicultural education, four of which differ from Gibson's categories. Sleeter and Grant noted the lack of consensus in the field and concluded that a focus on the education of people of color is the only common element among the many different definitions of multicultural education. Although there are many different approaches, statements of aims, and definitions of multicultural education, an examination of the recent literature written by specialists in the field indicates that there is a high level of consensus about its aims and goals (J. A. Banks, 1993c: Bennett, 1990; Nieto, 1992; Parekh, 1986; Sleeter & Grant, 1988; Suzuki, 1984).

A major goal of multicultural education, as stated by specialists in the field, is to reform the school and other educational institutions so that students from diverse racial, ethnic, and social-class groups will experience educational equality. Another important goal of multicultural education—revealed in this literature—is to give male and female students an equal chance to experience educational success and mobility (Klein, 1985; Sadker & Sadker, 1982). Multicultural education theorists are increasingly interested in how the interaction of race, class, and gender influences education (J. A. Banks, 1993c; Grant & Sleeter, 1986; Sleeter, 1991). However, the emphasis that different theorists give to each of these variables varies considerably.

Although there is an emerging consensus about the aims and scope of multicultural education (J. A. Banks, 1992), the variety of typologies, conceptual schemes, and perspectives within the field reflects its emergent status and the fact that complete agreement about its aims and boundaries has not been attained (Baker, 1983; J. A. Banks, 1994; Bennett, 1990; Garcia, 1991; Gollnick & Chinn, 1990). Because of its forensic and polarized nature, the current acrimonious debate about the extent to which the histories and cultures of women and people of color should be incorporated into the study of Western civilization in the nation's schools, colleges, and universities has complicated the quest for sound definitions and clear disciplinary boundaries within the field (Asante, 1991; Asante & Ravitch, 1991; Ravitch, 1990; Schlesinger, 1990).

GOALS AND SCOPE

There is general agreement among most scholars and researchers that, for multicultural education to be implemented successfully, institutional changes must be made, including changes in the curriculum; the teaching materials; teaching and learning styles; the attitudes, perceptions, and behaviors of teachers and administrators; and the goals, norms, and culture of the school (J. A. Banks, 1992; Bennett, 1990; Sleeter & Grant, 1988). However, many school and university practitioners have a limited conception of multicultural education, viewing it primarily as curriculum reform that involves only changing or restructuring the curriculum to include content about ethnic groups, women, and other cultural groups. This conception of multicultural education is widespread because curriculum reform was the main focus when the movement first emerged in the 1960s and 1970s (Blassingame, 1972; Ford, 1973), and because the multiculturalism discourse in the popular media has focused on curriculum reform and largely ignored other dimensions and components of multicultural education (Gray, 1991; Leo, 1990; Schlesinger, 1990, 1991).

If multicultural education is to become better understood and implemented in ways more consistent with theory, its various dimensions must be more clearly described, conceptualized, and researched. Multicultural education is conceptualized in this review as a field that consists of the five dimensions formulated by J. A. Banks (1991a, 1992). The dimensions are based on his research, observations, and work in the field from the late 1960s (J. A. Banks, 1970) through 1991 (J. A. Banks, 1992). Because of the limited scope of this review, no attempt is made to review the research comprehensively in each of the five dimensions.

Rather, a selected group of studies in each of the dimensions is reviewed. Race, ethnicity, class, gender, and exceptionality—and their interaction—are each important factors in multicultural education. Since it is not possible within one review to examine each of the variables in sufficient depth, this review focuses on racial and ethnic groups.

THE DIMENSIONS OF MULTICULTURAL EDUCATION

The dimensions of multicultural education used to conceptualize, organize, and select the literature for review in this chapter are (a) content integration, (b) the knowledge construction process, (c) prejudice reduction, (d) an equity pedagogy, and (e) an empowering school culture and social structure. Each of the dimensions is defined and illustrated, and a brief overview of each major section of the chapter is presented. The interrelationship of the five dimensions is discussed later.

CONTENT INTEGRATION

Content integration deals with the extent to which teachers use examples, data, and information from a variety of cultures and groups to illustrate key concepts, principles, generalizations, and theories in their subject area or discipline. In many school districts, as well as in popular writings, multicultural education is viewed only or primarily as content integration. This widespread belief that content integration constitutes the whole of multicultural education might be the factor that causes many teachers of subjects such as mathematics and science to view multicultural education as an endeavor primarily for social studies and language arts teachers.

The historical development of content integration movements is discussed, beginning with the historical work of George Washington Williams (1882–1883), usually considered the first African American historian in the United States (Franklin, 1985). The early ethnic studies movement, which began with Williams, continued quietly until the ethnic studies movement of the 1960s and 1970s. The rise and fall of the intergroup education movement is also described in this section.

KNOWLEDGE CONSTRUCTION

The knowledge construction process describes the procedures by which social, behavioral, and natural scientists create knowledge, and the manner in which the implicit cultural assumptions, frames of reference, perspectives, and biases within a discipline influence the ways that knowledge is constructed within it (Berger & Luckman, 1966; Gould, 1981; Harding, 1991; Kuhn, 1970). When the knowledge construction process is implemented in the classroom, teachers help students to understand how knowledge is created and how it is influenced by the racial, ethnic, and social-class positions of individuals and groups.

This section describes how the dominant paradigms about ethnic groups that were established by mainstream social scientists were challenged by revisionist social scientists in the 1960s and 1970s; many of these revisionists were scholars of color (Acuña, 1972; Blassingame, 1972; Ladner, 1973), whereas others were not (Daniels, 1988; Genovese, 1972; Levine, 1977). Literature that illustrates how paradigm shifts are taking place and identifies models that can be used to teach students to understand the knowledge construction process is also described in this section.

PREJUDICE REDUCTION

The prejudice reduction dimension of multicultural education describes the characteristics of children's racial attitudes and suggests strategies that can be used to help students develop more democratic attitudes and values. Researchers have been investigating the characteristics of children's racial attitudes since the 1920s (Lasker, 1929). Since the intergroup education movement of the 1940s and 1950s (Miel with Kiester, 1967; Trager & Yarrow, 1952), a number of investigators have designed interventions to help students to develop more positive racial attitudes and values. This section briefly reviews selected studies on the characteristics of children's racial attitudes, and studies that describe the results of interventions designed to help students to acquire more democratic racial attitudes (J. A. Banks, 1991b).

EQUITY PEDAGOGY

An equity pedagogy exists when teachers use techniques and methods that facilitate the academic achievement of students from diverse racial, ethnic, and social-class groups. This section consists of a review of selected studies of approaches, theories, and interventions that are designed to help students who are members of low-status population groups to increase their academic achievement (Delpit, 1988; Ogbu, 1990; Shade, 1989).

The literature reviewed in this section is discussed within a historical context. The kinds of theories that have been constructed to help teachers develop more effective strategies for use with students of color and low-income students have varied throughout time. In the early 1960s the cultural deprivation paradigm was developed (Bloom, Davis, & Hess, 1965; Davis, 1948/1962; Riessman, 1962). The cultural difference theory emerged in the 1970s and challenged the cultural deprivationists (Baratz & Baratz, 1970; Ginsburg, 1972; Ramírez & Castañeda, 1974). Today the "at-risk" conception has emerged, which is akin to the cultural deprivation paradigm (Cuban, 1989; Richardson, Casanova, Placier, & Guilfoyle, 1989).

EMPOWERING SCHOOL CULTURE

The concept of an empowering school culture and social structure is used in this chapter to describe the process of restructuring the culture and organization of the school so that students from diverse racial, ethnic, and social-class groups will experience educational equality and cultural empowerment (Cummins, 1986). Creating an empowering school culture for students of color and low-income students involves restructuring the culture and organization of the school.

Among the variables that need to be examined in order to create a school culture that empowers students from diverse ethnic and cultural groups are grouping practices (Braddock, 1990; Oakes, 1985), labeling practices (Mercer, 1989), the social climate of the school, and staff expectations for student achievement (Brookover, Beady, Flood, Schweitzer, & Wisenbaker, 1979). This section reviews literature that focuses on institutionalized factors of the school culture and environment that need to be reformed in order to increase the academic achievement and emotional growth of students from diverse ethnic, racial, and social-class groups.

LIMITATIONS AND INTERRELATIONSHIPS OF THE DIMENSIONS

The dimensions typology is an ideal-type conception in the Weberian sense. It approximates but does not describe reality in its total complexity. Like all classification schemas, it has both strengths and limitations. Typologies are helpful conceptual tools because they provide a way to organize and make sense of complex and disparate data and observations. However, their categories are interrelated and overlapping, not mutually exclusive. Typologies are rarely able to encompass the total universe of existing or future cases. Consequently, some cases can be described only by using several of the categories.

The dimensions typology provides a useful framework for categorizing and interpreting the extensive and disparate literature on diversity and education. The five dimensions are conceptually distinct but highly interrelated. Content integration, for example, describes any approach that is used to integrate content about racial and cultural groups into the curriculum. The knowledge construction process describes a method by which teachers help students to understand how knowledge is created, and how it reflects the experiences of various ethnic and cultural groups.

Content integration is a necessary but not sufficient condition for the knowledge construction process (i.e., content integration can take place without the knowledge construction process). Teachers can, for example, insert into the curriculum content about Mexican Americans without helping students to view the content from Mexican American perspectives. However, the knowledge construction process cannot be included in the curriculum without content integration first taking place.

Some of the publications examined for this review crossed several of the categories. Cooperative learning techniques, for example, can help students to increase their academic achievement, as well as to develop more positive racial attitudes. Consequently, some cooperative learning studies can be categorized as both equity pedagogy and prejudice reduction strategies (Aronson & Bridgeman, 1979; Slavin, 1985).

Criteria for selecting studies in each of the five dimensions included the extent to which the study or publication (a) is a prototype of the particular dimension being discussed; (b) has been influential in the field, as determined by the extent to which it is cited and has contributed to the theoretical and empirical growth of the field; and (c) has promise, in the author's judgment, of contributing to the future development of theory, research, and practice in multicultural education.

CONTENT INTEGRATION

The literature on content integration focuses on what information should be included in the curriculum, how it should be integrated into the existing curriculum, and where it should be located within the curriculum (i.e., whether it should be taught within separate courses or as part of the core curriculum). Another important issue discussed in this literature concerns who should be the audience for ethnic content (i.e., whether it should be for all students or primarily for students of color).

An exhaustive body of literature describes the various debates, discussions, and curricula that have focused on the integration of content about ethnic groups and women into school, college, and university curricula (J. A. Banks, 1991c; Butler

& Walter, 1991; Lauter, 1991). The scope of this section is limited primarily to a description of the literature that focuses on the integration of content about racial and ethnic groups into the curriculum. The literature that describes the effects of curricular materials on students' racial and ethnic attitudes is reviewed in the section that discusses the prejudice reduction dimension.

THE NEED FOR A HISTORICAL PERSPECTIVE

It is important to view the movements by ethnic groups to integrate school, college, and university curricula with ethnic content from a historical perspective (see Table 1). A historical perspective is necessary to provide a context for understanding the contemporary developments and discourse in multicultural education and to restructure schools, colleges, and universities to reflect multicultural issues and concerns. Contemporary reformers need to understand, for example, why the intergroup education movement of the 1940s and 1950s ultimately failed (Cook, 1947; Taba & Wilson, 1946) and why early ethnic studies leaders such as Woodson (1919/1968), DuBois (1935), Wesley (1935), and Franklin (1947), and their successors, were able to continue the early ethnic studies movement quietly with publications, research, and teaching from the turn of the century to the 1960s, when the new ethnic studies movement began.

At least a partial explanation is that the early ethnic studies movement was sustained by ethnic self-help organizations such as the Association for the Study of Negro Life and History (ASNLH; now the Association for the Study of Afro-American Life and History) and The Associated Publishers—two organizations cofounded and headed by Woodson. The Associated Publishers published many important and seminal works by and about African American scholars such as Woodson (1919/1968), Wesley (1935), and Bond (1939). African American schools and colleges were the major consumers of Black scholarship during the first decades of the 20th century. Ethnic community support might be essential for sustaining in-

terest in ethnic studies and multicultural concerns over the long haul. Further investigations are needed to determine the different fates of the early ethnic studies and intergroup education movements.

African Americans led the movement that pushed for the integration of ethnic content into the curriculum during the 1960s and 1970s. Consequently, it is appropriate to provide a brief historical discussion of the movement to integrate the curriculum with ethnic content, using African Americans as a case study.

THE EARLY ETHNIC STUDIES MOVEMENT

The Black studies movement that emerged in the 1960s and 1970s has historical roots in the early national period (Brooks, 1990; White, 1973; Woodson, 1919/1968). It is more directly linked to the work in ethnic studies research and the development of teaching materials by African American scholars such as G. W. Williams (1882–1883), Woodson and Wesley (1922) and DuBois (1935, 1973). Scholars such as G. W. Williams, Wesley, Woodson, and DuBois created knowledge about African Americans that could be integrated into the school and college curriculum. Educators such as Woodson and Wesley (1922) worked during the early decades of the 20th century to integrate the school and college curriculum with content about African Americans.

Brooks (1990) discusses the early history of schools for African American children. He points out that from slavery to today, Black education has been characterized by desegregation in the colonial and early national periods, a push for segregation in the early 1800s, a movement toward desegregation during the 1950s and 1960s, and another swing toward segregation today.

The first public schools that were organized in Massachusetts and Virginia in the 1640s were desegregated (Brooks, 1990; White, 1973; Woodson, 1919/1968). However, because of the discrimination they experienced in these schools, African Americans took the leadership in establishing separate schools for their children. When the city of Boston refused to fund separate schools for African

TABLE 1

Landmark Events and Publications in the Historical Development of Ethnic Studies and Multicultural Education

YEAR(S)	EVENT/PUBLICATION
1882–1883	*History of the Negro Race in America* by George Washington Williams
1896	*The Suppression of the African Slave Trade to the United States of America* 1638–1870 by W. E. B. DuBois
1899	*The Philadelphia Negro* by W. E. B. DuBois
1915	The Association for the Study of Negro Life and History is founded in Chicago
1916	*The Journal of Negro History* begins publication
1921	The Associated Publishers is established
1922	*The Negro in Our History* by Carter G. Woodson and Charles C. Wesley
1929	*Race Attitudes in Children* by Bruno Lasker
1930	*Mexican Immigration to the United States* by Manuel Gamio
1933	*The Mis-Education of the Negro* by Carter G. Woodson
1936	Eugene Horowitz's study of young children's attitudes toward the Negro
1937	*The Negro History Bulletin*, designed for schools, begins publication
1939	*Negro Education in Alabama: A Study in Cotton and Steel* by Horace Mann Bond; first reported study by Kenneth B. and Mamie P. Clark on young children's racial attitudes
1941	*Deep South: A Social Anthropological Study of Caste and Class* by Allison Davis, Burleigh B. Gardner, and Mary R. Gardner
1944	*An American Dilemma: The Negro Problem and Modern Democracy* by Gunnar Myrdal with Richard Sterner and Arnold Rose
1945	*Democratic Human Relations: Promising Practices in Intergroup and Intercultural Education in the Social Studies,* 16th yearbook of the National Council for the Social Studies, edited by Hilda Taba and William Van Til; *Black Metropolis: A Study of Negro Life in Northern City* by St. Clair Drake and Horace R. Cayton
1947	A review of research on intergroup education is published in the *Review of Educational Research* by Lloyd A. Cook; first edition of *From Slavery to Freedom: A History of Negro Americans* by John Hope Franklin
1950	*College Programs in Intergroup Relations* by Lloyd A. Cook; *The Authoritarian Personality* by. T. W. Adorno et al.
1951	*Intergroup Relations in Teacher Education* by Lloyd A. Cook

TABLE 1

Landmark Events and Publications in the Historical Development of Ethnic Studies and Multicultural Education — *(Continued)*

YEAR(S)	EVENT/PUBLICATION
1952	*Intergroup Education in Public Schools* by Hilda Taba, Elizabeth H. Brady, and John T. Robinson; *They learn What They Live: Prejudice in Young Children* by Helen G. Trager and Marian R. Yarrow; *Race Awareness in Young Children* by Mary Ellen Goodman
1954	*The Nature of Prejudice* by Gordon W. Allport
1962	*Social-Class Influences Upon Learning* by Allison Davis
1965	*Compensatory Education for Cultural Deprivation* by Benjamin S. Bloom, Allison Davis, and Robert Hess
1966	*Equality of Educational Opportunity* by James Coleman et al.
1972	*Inequality: A Reassessment of the Effect of Family and Schooling in America* by Christopher Jencks et al.
1973	*No One Model American* (American Association of Colleges for Teacher Education); *Teaching Ethnic Studies: Concepts and Strategies,* National Council for the Social Studies 43rd yearbook, edited by James A. Banks
1974	*Cultural Democracy, Bicognitive Development, and Education* by Manuel Ramirez and Alfredo Castañeda: *The Next Generation: An Ethnography of Education in an Urban Neighborhood* by John U. Ogbu; *Students' Right to Their Own Language,* a position statement by the National Council of Teachers of English
1975	*Adolescent Prejudice* by Charles Y. Glock, Robert Wuthnow, Jane A. Piliavin, and Metta Spencer, sponsored by the Anti-Defamation League of B'nai B'rith
1976	*Curriculum Guidelines for Multiethnic Education,* a position statement issued by the National Council for the Social Studies; *Race, Color, and the Young Child* by John E. Williams and J. Kenneth Morland—a synthesis of research conducted in the late 1960s and 1970s on young children's racial attitudes
1977	*Multicultural Education: Commitments, Issues and Applications,* edited by Carl A. Grant, published by the Association for Supervision and Curriculum Development; *Pluralism and the American Teacher: Issues and Case Studies,* edited by Frank H. Klassen and Donna M. Gollnick, published by the American Association of Colleges for Teacher Education; *Pluralism in a Democratic Society,* edited by Melvin M. Tumin and Walter Plotch, sponsored by the Anti-Defamation League of B'nai B'rith; *Standards for the Accreditation of Teacher Education,*

TABLE 1

TABLE 1

Landmark Events and Publications in the Historical Development
of Ethnic Studies and Multicultural Education — *(Continued)*

YEAR(S)	EVENT/PUBLICATION
	issued by the National Council for the Accreditation of Teacher Education, includes a requirement for multicultural education in teacher education programs
1983	*Ways with Words: Language, Life, and Work in Communities and Classrooms* by Shirley Brice Heath
1985	*Beginnings: The Social and Affective Development of Black Children,* edited by Margaret B. Spencer, Geraldine K. Brookins, and Walter R. Allen
1988	*The Education of Blacks in the South,* 1860–1935 by James D. Anderson
1989	*A Common Destiny: Blacks and American Society,* edited by Gerald D. James and Robin M. Williams, Jr., National Research Council report
1991	*Shades of Black: Diversity in African-American Identity* by William E. Cross, Jr.

American children in 1800, the Black community set up its own schools and hired the teachers. In 1818 the city of Boston started funding separate schools for African American children. The first schools established for African Americans in the South after the Civil War were segregated by laws formulated by White legislators.

Separate schools for African Americans proved to be a mixed blessing, especially in the southern states and later in northern cities. In the South, African American schools were separate and unequal in terms of expenditures per pupil, the salaries of teachers and administrators, and the quality and newness of textbooks and other teaching materials (Anderson, 1988; Bond, 1939).

Although separate Black public schools in the South had African American teachers and administrators, their school boards, curricula, and textbooks were White controlled and dominated. Consequently, integration of the curriculum with content about African Americans was problematic. In his influential book *The Mis-Education of the Negro,* Woodson (1933) stated that schools and colleges were miseducating African Americans because they were being taught about European civilization but not about the great African civilizations and cultures of their own people. He described what he felt were the harmful effects of neglecting Black history and civilization on the thinking and self-esteem of African American youth.

From 1920 until his death in 1950, Woodson probably did more than any other individual to promote the study and teaching of African American history in the nation's schools and colleges. He spent most of his career writing histories, editing journals, and building ASNLH. Woodson taught high school in Washington, D.C., from 1909 to 1918, and received his doctorate in history from Harvard in 1912. He was one of the founders of ASNLH and established the *Journal of Negro History* in 1916. In 1921 he established The Associated Publishers, a subsidiary of ASNLH, which published a score of histories about African

Americans, many of them written by Woodson and his historian colleagues.

Woodson's books were widely used in African American high schools and colleges. He started Negro History Week (now National Afro-American History Month) in 1926 to promote the study and teaching of African American history in the elementary and secondary schools. In 1937 he started publishing the *Negro History Bulletin* to provide historical materials for use by elementary and secondary school teachers. Other early African American scholars, such as G. W. Williams (1882–1883), DuBois (1935), Wesley (1935), Quarles (1953), and Logan (1954), played key roles in constructing the knowledge needed to develop teaching materials for the schools and colleges. However, none of these scholars were as directly involved as Woodson in promoting the inclusion of content about African Americans into the curriculum of the nation's schools and colleges.

THE INTERGROUP EDUCATION MOVEMENT

The intergroup education movement, although not a direct link to the work of early African American scholars such as Woodson, Wesley, DuBois, and Logan, is an important precedent to the ethnic studies movement that emerged in the 1960s and 1970s. The intergroup education movement is linked to the work of these scholars because content about religious, national, and racial groups was one of the variables it used to reduce prejudice and discrimination (Cook & Cook, 1954; Trager & Yarrow, 1952). It is linked to the contemporary multicultural education movement because it shared many of the goals of today's multicultural education movement and experienced many of the same problems (Taba & Wilson, 1946; J. A. Banks, 1994).

The social forces that gave rise to the intergroup education movement grew out of the consequences of World War II. The demands of the war created job opportunities in the North and the West that were not available in the South. Consequently, many African Americans, Mexican Americans, and Whites living in rural areas migrated to northern and western cities to find jobs

in war-related industries. Ethnic and racial tension developed as Anglos and Mexican Americans in western cities and African Americans and Whites in northern cities competed for jobs and housing. These tensions resulted in a series of racial incidents and riots that stunned the nation.

Intergroup education emerged as an educational response to the racial and ethnic tension in the nation (Taba, Brady, & Robinson, 1952). One of its major goals was to help reduce prejudice and create interracial understanding among students from diverse national, religious, and racial groups (Cook & Cook, 1954; Taba & Wilson, 1946). Several national organizations, such as the Progressive Education Association (Locke & Stern, 1942), the National Council for the Social Studies (NCSS) (Taba & Van Til, 1945), and the American Council on Education (Cook, 1950), sponsored projects, activities, and publications in intergroup education. Projects and activities were developed for both elementary and secondary schools (Taba et al., 1952), as well as for teachers colleges (Cook, 1951).

Many of the intergroup education publications, like multicultural education publications today, were practical sources that described ways to set up an intergroup relations center (Clinchy, 1949), identified objectives and methods for schools (Vickery & Cole, 1943), described curricula and units for schools (Taba, 1950, 1951, 1952), and described intergroup education programs and projects in colleges and universities (Cook, 1951). Some of these publications were based on intergroup theories developed by social scientists such as Louis Wirth (1928) and Gordon W. Allport (1954).

Some of the nation's leading social scientists and philosophers participated in the development of theoretical ideas about the reduction of interracial tensions during the intergroup education era. Wirth, the University of Chicago sociologist, and Allport, the Harvard social psychologist, contributed chapters to a book edited by Lloyd A. Cook (1952), a leading intergroup educator. Wirth's paper was titled "Freedom, Power and Values in Our Present Crisis"; Allport's was called "Resolving Intergroup Tension: An Appraisal of Methods."

Alain Locke, the African American philosopher of Howard University, coedited a background book on intergroup education for the Progressive Education Association (Locke & Stern, 1942). This comprehensive book on race and culture consists of reprinted articles by some of the leading social scientists of the day, including Ruth Benedict, Franz Boas, John Dollard, E. Franklin Frazier, Melville J. Herskovits, Otto Klineberg, Ralph Linton, and Margaret Mead.

Allison Davis, the noted African American anthropologist at the University of Chicago and coauthor of *Deep South: A Social Anthropological Study of Caste and Class,* a classic study of an old southern city (Davis, Gardner, & Gardner, 1941), wrote a chapter for NCSS's 16th yearbook. The chapter is titled "Some Basic Concepts in the Education of Ethnic and Lower-Class Groups." Davis urged social studies teachers to teach students "a devotion to democratic values, and group disapproval of injustice, oppression, and exploitation" (Taba & Van Til, 1945, p. 278). He also believed that teachers should teach social action: "Teach the underprivileged child to learn to help organize and improve his community" (p. 279). The fact that scholars of the stature of Davis and Locke contributed to books on intergroup education sponsored by educational organizations indicated that some of the leading social science scholars of the 1940s believed that they should become involved in a major social problem facing the nation and the schools.

Several landmark studies in race relations were published during the intergroup education era. Jewish organizations, such as the American Jewish Committee and the Anti-Defamation League of B'nai B'rith, sponsored several of these studies. One important factor that contributed to the rise of the intergroup education movement was anti-Semitism in Western nations which reached its peak in Germany during World War II. Jewish organizations were especially interested in taking actions and sponsoring research that would ease racial tension and conflict. They were poignantly aware of the destructive power of ethnic hate (Wyman, 1984).

In 1950 *The Authoritarian Personality* (Adorno, Frenkel, Brunswik, Levinson, & Sanford, 1950) was published. In this landmark study the authors identify the personality factors that contribute to the formation of prejudice. Although they overemphasize personality-factor explanations of prejudice and give insufficient attention to structural factors, their study remains an important one.

Allport's seminal study, *The Nature of Prejudice,* was published in 1954. In this book Allport formulates his influential principles about ways to create effective intergroup interactions. He states that effective contact situations must be characterized by equal-status, cooperative rather than competitive interactions, and by shared goals. Positive interracial contact must also be sanctioned by authorities. Allport's principles are highly influential in social science research today and provide an important theoretical base for the work of researchers such as Cohen (1972), Aronson and Bridgeman (1979), and Slavin (1985).

Important theoretical and research work related to children's racial attitudes was also completed during the intergroup education period. The Anti-Defamation League of B'nai B'rith sponsored a major study by Goodman that was published in 1952. This study provided evidence that supported earlier findings by researchers such as E. L. Horowitz (1936), R. E. Horowitz (1939), and a series of studies by Kenneth B. and Mamie P. Clark (1939a, 1939b, 1940, 1947). These studies established the postulate that preschool children have racial awareness and attitudes that mirror those of adults.

Intergroup educators wanted to help students to develop more democratic racial attitudes and values (Cook, 1947; Taba & Wilson, 1946). Investigations designed to determine the effects of curricular interventions on students' racial attitudes were an important part of the intergroup education movement. Significant intervention studies conducted during this period include those by Trager and Yarrow (1952) and by Hayes and Conklin (1953). Most of these studies support the postulate that multicultural lessons, activities, and teaching materials, when used within a democratic classroom atmosphere and implemented for a sufficiently long period, help students to develop more democratic racial attitudes and values. Studies both prior to and during this period established that children internalize the adult attitudes that are institutionalized within the structures and institutions of society (Clark & Clark, 1947; Goodman, 1952; E. L. Horowitz, 1936).

Important textbooks and reports published during the intergroup education era include those by Locke and Stern (1942), Cook (1950), Taba et al. (1952), and Cook and Cook (1954), which reveal that intergroup educators emphasized democratic living and interracial cooperation within mainstream American society. The ethnic studies movements that both preceded and followed the intergroup education movement emphasized ethnic attachment, pride, and empowerment. The focus in intergroup education was on intercultural interactions within a shared, common culture (Cook, 1947; Taba & Wilson, 1946).

THE EARLY ETHNIC STUDIES AND INTERGROUP EDUCATION MOVEMENTS COMPARED

Woodson (1933) and DuBois (1973) were concerned that African Americans develop knowledge of Black history and culture, and a commitment to the empowerment and enhancement of the African American community. This was in contrast to the emphasis in intergroup education, which promoted a weak form of diversity and the notion that "we are different but the same."

The Sleeter and Grant (1987) typology consists of five categories: (a) teaching the culturally different, (b) human relations, (c) single-group studies, (d) multicultural education, and (e) education that is multicultural and social reconstructionist. Most of the literature and guides that were produced during the intergroup education era can be categorized as human relations. In this approach, according to Sleeter and Grant (1987), multicultural education is "a way to help students of different backgrounds communicate, get along better with each other, and feel good about themselves" (p. 426).

Like the human relations books and materials examined by Sleeter and Grant that were published in the 1970s and 1980s, intergroup education materials devote little attention to issues and problems such as institutionalized racism, power, and structural inequality. However, unlike most of the human relations materials examined by Sleeter and Grant, some of the materials published during the intergroup education period are based on theories developed by psychologists and social psychologists (Taba, 1950, 1951; Taba & Wilson, 1946).

The intergroup education publications and projects emphasized interracial harmony and human relations. The early ethnic studies advocates endorsed ethnic empowerment and what Sleeter and Grant call "single group studies." Thus, the aims and goals of the intergroup education and ethnic studies movements were quite different. The ethnic studies movement emphasized the histories and cultures of specific ethnic groups (single-group studies). Taba and Wilson (1946) identified the following focuses in intergroup education: concepts and understandings about groups and relations, sensitivity and goodwill, objective thinking, and experiences in democratic procedures.

The racial backgrounds and cultural experiences of the leaders of the two ethnic studies movements and those of the leaders of the intergroup education movement were factors that influenced the goals, aims, and nature of these movements. Most of the influential leaders of the early ethnic studies movement in the United States and the one that emerged in the 1960s and 1970s were people of color. Most of the leaders of the intergroup education movement were White liberal educators and social scientists who functioned and worked within mainstream colleges, universities, and other institutions and organizations. Hilda Taba (who taught at the University of Chicago and directed the Intergroup Education in Cooperating Schools Project for the American Council on Education) and Lloyd A. Cook (who taught at Wayne State University and directed the College Programs in Intergroup Relations project) were the most prolific and noted intergroup education leaders.

The different cultural experiences, perceptions, and values of the leaders of the ethnic studies and intergroup education movements significantly influenced their perceptions of the goals of citizenship education and the role of ethnic content in instruction. Ethnic studies scholars and educators probably endorsed a more pluralistic view of citizenship education than did intergroup educators because they worked and functioned primarily outside mainstream institutions and believed that parallel ethnic institutions were essential for the survival and development of ethnic groups in the United States. The experiences of most intergroup educators in mainstream institutions influenced their view that assimilation into mainstream culture and its institutions was the most appropriate way to resolve ethnic tensions.

The history of the early ethnic studies and intergroup education movements and an analysis of current curriculum reform efforts reveal that movements related to the integration of ethnic content into the curriculum move cyclically from a single-group to an intergroup focus. The fact that single-group studies movements continue to emerge within a society with a democratic ethos suggests that the United States has not dealt successfully with the American dilemma related to race that Myrdal (with Sterner & Rose, 1944) identified nearly 50 years ago.

THE ETHNIC STUDIES MOVEMENT OF THE 1960s AND 1970s

A prominent vision within the intergroup education ideology was interracial harmony and desegregation. Another name for the movement was *intercultural education*. Intergroup education emerged when the nation was sharply segregated along racial lines and was beginning its efforts to create a desegregated society. The early goal of the civil rights movement of the 1960s was racial desegregation. However, by the late 1960s many African Americans had grown impatient with the pace of desegregation. Imbued with racial pride, they called for Black power, separatism, and Black studies in the schools and colleges that would contribute to the empowerment and advancement of African Americans (Carmichael & Hamilton, 1967).

When the civil rights movement began, the intergroup education movement had quietly died without a requiem. The separatist ideology that emerged during the 1970s was antithetical to the intergroup education vision. The America envisioned by most intergroup educators was a nation in which ethnic and racial differences were minimized and all people were treated fairly and lived in harmony.

During the late 1960s and early 1970s, sometimes in strident voices, African Americans, frustrated with deferred and shattered dreams, demanded community control of their schools, African American teachers and administrators, and the infusion of Black history into the curriculum. At the university level, frequent demands included Black studies programs and courses, heritage rooms or houses, and Black professors and administrators. During this period there was little demand for the infusion of ethnic content into the core or mainstream curriculum—that demand would not emerge until the 1980s and 1990s. Rather, the demand was primarily for separate courses and programs (Blassingame, 1971; Ford, 1973; Robinson, Foster, & Ogilvie, 1969).

As schools, colleges, and universities began to respond to the demand by African Americans for curriculum changes, other ethnic groups of color that felt victimized by institutionalized discrimination in the United States began to demand similar programs. These groups included Mexican Americans, Puerto Ricans, American Indians, and Asian Americans. A rich array of books, programs, curricula, and other materials that focused on the histories and cultures of ethnic groups of color was edited, written, or reprinted between the late 1960s and the early 1970s.

One major development during this period was the reprinting of books and research studies that had been written during the early and more silent period of ethnic studies. A few of these publications had remained in print for many years, and had been best-sellers at all-Black colleges; such books included John Hope Franklin's popular history, *From Slavery to Freedom*, first published in 1947, and *The Souls of Black Folk* by W. E. B. DuBois, first published in 1953.

However, more frequent was the reprinting of long-neglected works that had been produced during the earlier period of ethnic studies. George Washington William's *History of the Negro Race in America* (1882–1883) was reissued by Arno Press in 1968. Important earlier works on Hispanics reprinted during this period included Carey McWilliams's *North from Mexico: The Spanish-Speaking People of the United States* (1949), which provides an informative overview of Hispanic groups in the United States, and Manuel Gamio's *Mexican Immigration to the United States* (1930), a well-researched description of the first wave of Mexican immigrants to the United States. Two important earlier works on Filipino Americans were also reissued during this period: *Filipino Immigration to the Continental United States and Hawaii,* by Bruno Lasker (1931), and *Brothers Under the Skin,* by Carey McWilliams (1943).

More significant than the older books that were kept in print or reissued was the new crop of publications that focused primarily on the struggles and experiences of particular ethnic groups. The emphasis in many of these publications was on ways that ethnic groups of color had been victimized by institutionalized racism and discrimination in the United States. The quality and meticulousness of research of this rash of books varied widely. However, they all provided perspectives that gave Americans new ways to view the history and culture of the United States. Many of them became required reading in ethnic studies courses and degree programs. Among the significant books of this genre are *Japanese Americans* by Harry H. L. Kitano (1969); *The Story of the Chinese in America* by Betty Lee Sung (1967); *Occupied America: The Chicano's Struggle Toward Liberation* by Rudy Acuña (1972); *Custer Died for Your Sins: An Indian Manifesto* by Vine Deloria, Jr. (1969); and *The Rise of the Unmeltable Ethnics* by Michael Novak (1971), a highly rhetorical and ringing plea for justice for White ethnic groups such as Poles, Italians, Greeks, and Slavs.

THE EVOLUTION OF MULTICULTURAL EDUCATION

The intergroup education movement is an important antecedent of the current multicultural education movement but is not an actual root of it. The current multicultural education movement is directly linked to the early ethnic studies movement initiated by scholars such as G. W. Williams (1882–1883) and continued by individuals such as DuBois (1935), Woodson (1919/1968), Bond (1939), and Wesley (1935). The major architects of the multicultural education movement were cogently influenced by African American scholarship and ethnic studies related to other ethnic minority groups in the United States.

Baker (1977), J. A. Banks (1973), Gay (1971), and Grant (1973, 1978) have each played significant roles in the formulation and development of multicultural education in the United States. Each of these scholars was heavily influenced by the early work of African American scholars and the African American ethnic studies movement. They were working in ethnic studies prior to participating in the formation of multicultural education. Other scholars who have helped to fashion multicultural education since its inception, and were also influenced by the African American ethnic studies movement, include James B. Boyer (1974), Asa Hilliard III (1974), and Barbara A. Sizemore (1972).

Scholars who are specialists on other ethnic groups, such as Carlos E. Cortés (1973; Mexican Americans), Jack D. Forbes (1973: American Indians), Sonia Nieto (1986; Puerto Ricans), and Derald W. Sue (1981; Asian Americans), also played early and significant roles in the evolution of multicultural education.

The first phase of multicultural education emerged when educators who had interests and specializations in the history and culture of ethnic minority groups initiated individual and institutional actions to incorporate the concepts, information, and theories from ethnic studies into the school and teacher-education curricula. Consequently, the first phase of multicultural education was ethnic studies.

A second phase of multicultural education emerged when educators interested in ethnic studies began to realize that inserting ethnic studies content into the school and teacher-education curricula was necessary but not sufficient to bring about school reform that would respond to the unique needs of ethnic minority students and help all students to develop more democratic racial and ethnic attitudes. Multiethnic education was the second phase of multicultural education. Its aim was to bring about structural and systemic changes in the total school that were designed to increase educational equality.

A third phase of multicultural education emerged when other groups who viewed themselves as victims of the society and the schools, such as women and people with disabilities, demanded the incorporation of their histories, cultures, and voices into the curricula and structure of the schools, colleges, and universities. The current, or fourth, phase of multicultural education consists of the development of theory, research, and practice that interrelate variables connected to race, class, and gender (J. A. Banks & Banks, 1993; Grant & Sleeter, 1986). It is important to note that each of the phases of multicultural education continues to exist today. However, the later phases tend to be more prominent than the earlier ones, at least in the theoretical literature, if not in practice.

During the 1970s a number of professional organizations, such as the American Association of Colleges for Teacher Education (AACTE), the National Council of Teachers of English (NCTE), and NCSS, issued position statements and publications that encouraged schools to integrate the curriculum with content and understandings about ethnic groups. In 1973 AACTE published its brief and widely quoted statement, *No One Model American.* That same year, the NCSS 43rd yearbook was titled *Teaching Ethnic Studies: Concepts and Strategies* (J. A. Banks, 1973). The following year, NCTE (1974) issued *Students' Right to Their Own Language.* An early landmark conference on multicultural education through competency-based teacher education was sponsored by AACTE in 1974 (Hunter, 1974). In 1976 NCSS published

Curriculum Guidelines for Multiethnic Education (J. A. Banks, Cortés, Gay, Garcia, & Ochoa, 1976). This publication was revised and reissued in 1992 with a title change to "Curriculum Guidelines for Multicultural Education" (NCSS Task Force, 1992).

Several landmark developments in the emergence of multicultural education occurred in 1977. The Association for Supervision and Curriculum Development (ASCD) published a book on multicultural education (Grant, 1977). That same year, AACTE published *Pluralism and the American Teacher; Issues and Case Studies* (Klassen & Gollnick, 1977). This book resulted from its conference series on the topic that was supported by a grant from the U.S. Office of Education. Using the grant funds, AACTE established the Ethnic Heritage Center for Teacher Education, its unit that sponsored the conferences and the book. One of the most influential developments during the early emergence of multicultural education was the issuance of *Standards for the Accreditation of Teacher Education* by the National Council for Accreditation of Teacher Education (NCATE) in 1977. These standards required all of its member teacher-education institutions, which comprised about 80% of the teacher-education programs in the United States, to implement components, courses, and programs in multicultural education. The standards were later issued in revised form (NCATE, 1987).

Many professional associations, school districts, and state departments of education published guidelines and teacher's guides to help school districts integrate content about ethnic groups into the elementary and high school curriculum. The United Federation of Teachers published *Puerto Rican History and Culture: A Study Guide and Curriculum Outline* (Aran, Arthur, Colon, & Goldenberg, 1973). This curriculum guide, like most materials produced by professional organizations, school districts, and commercial publishers during this period, focused on a single ethnic group. Publications and materials that focused on more than one ethnic group were developed later. One of the first publications to recommend a multiethnic approach to the study of ethnic groups was the NCSS 1973 yearbook (J. A. Banks, 1973). The guides and books published during this period varied in quality. Many were produced quickly, but others provided teachers with sound and thoughtful guidelines for integrating their curricula with ethnic content.

RESEARCH DEVELOPMENTS SINCE THE 1960s

A rich array of research in the social sciences, humanities, and education focusing on people of color has been published since 1960. Much of this research challenges existing interpretations, paradigms, assumptions, and methodologies and provides pertinent data on long-neglected topics (Gates, 1988; King & Mitchell, 1990; Slaughter, 1988). The three decades between 1960 and 1990 were probably the most productive research period in ethnic studies in the nation's history. St. Claire Drake (1987, 1990), shortly before his death, completed a massive two-volume anthropological study, *Black Folk Here and There.* Bernal's (1987, 1991) comprehensive two-volume work, *Black Athena: The Afroasiatic Roots of Classical Civilization,* challenges existing historical interpretations about the debt that ancient Greece owes to Africa, and supports earlier works by African and African American scholars such as Diop (1974) and Van Sertima (1988). Many of the insights from this new scholarship are being incorporated into the school, college, and university curriculum.

THE KNOWLEDGE CONSTRUCTION PROCESS

The ethnic studies research and literature published during the 1960s and 1970s (Acuña, 1972), like the ethnic studies scholarship in the early decades of the century (DuBois, 1935; Woodson, 1919/1968), challenged some of the major paradigms, canons, and perspectives established within mainstream scholarship (Blea, 1988; Gordon, 1985; Gordon, Miller & Rollock, 1990; Ladner, 1973). Ethnic studies scholarship also challenges

some of the key assumptions of mainstream Western empiricism (J. A. Banks, 1993b; Gordon & Meroe, 1991).

The construction of descriptions and interpretations of the settlement of the West (Turner, 1894/1989) and of slavery (Phillips, 1918) are two examples of how people of color have been described and conceptualized in mainstream U.S. history and social science. Frederick Jackson Turner (1894/1989) constructed a view of the settlement of European Americans in the West that has cogently influenced the treatment and interpretation of the West in school, college, and university textbooks (Sleeter & Grant, 1991). Turner described the land occupied by the Indians as an empty wilderness to which the Europeans brought civilization. He also argued that the wilderness in the West, which required individualism for survival, was the main source of American democracy. Although revisionist historians have described the limitations of Turner's theory, its influence on the curricula of the nation's elementary and high schools, and on textbooks, is still powerful.

The treatment and interpretation of slavery within mainstream U.S. scholarship provide another revealing example of how ethnic groups of color have been depicted in such scholarship. Ulrich B. Phillips's interpretation of slavery remained dominant from the time his book was published in 1918 to the 1950s, 1960s, and 1970s, when the established slavery paradigm was revised by a new generation of historians (Blassingame, 1972; Genovese, 1972; Stampp, 1956). Phillips's interpretation of slavery, which is essentially an apology for southern slaveholders, was one of the major sources for the conception of slaves as happy, contented, and loyal to their masters that dominated textbooks in the 1950s and 1960s (J. A. Banks, 1969).

The description of the settlement of Europeans in the western United States and the treatment of slavery in U.S. scholarship from the turn of the century to the 1950s indicate the extent to which knowledge reflects ideology, human interests, values, and perspectives (Habermas, 1971). Yet a basic assumption of Western empiricism is that knowledge is objective and neutral and that its principles are universal (Kaplan 1964). Multicultural scholars (Acuña, 1972; Hilliard, Payton-Stewart, & Williams, 1990; King & Mitchell, 1990)—like critical theorists such as Habermas (1971) and Giroux (1983) and feminist postmodernists such as Farganis (1986), Code (1991), and Harding (1991)—reject these assumptions about the nature of knowledge.

Multicultural scholars maintain that knowledge reflects the social, cultural, and power positions of people within society, and that it is valid only when it "comes from an acknowledgment of the knower's specific position in any context, one always defined by gender, class, and other variables" (Tetreault, 1993, p. 142). Multicultural and feminist theorists maintain that knowledge is both subjective and objective and that its subjective components need to be clearly identified (Code, 1991; Hooks, 1990; King & Mitchell, 1990). Multicultural theorists also contend that by claiming that their knowledge is objective and neutral, mainstream scholars are able to present their particularistic interests and ideologies as the universal concerns of the nation-state (Asante, 1991; Hilliard et al., 1990). According to Gordon and Meroe (1991):

> We often wonder if the socially adapted human being, who happens to be a scholar, is truly capable of discarding her or his individual frame of reference when it comes to the study of a subject to which she or he has chosen to commit her or his life's work. This is a precarious and dangerous situation because too many times "objectivity" has served as a mask for the political agenda of the status quo, thus marginalizing and labeling the concerns of less empowered groups as "special interests." (p. 28)

A number of conceptualizations have been developed by multicultural and feminist theorists that are designed to help teachers acquire the information and skills needed to teach students how knowledge is constructed, how to identify the writer's purposes and point of view, and how to formulate their own interpretations of reality.

Four approaches used to integrate ethnic content into the elementary and high school curriculum and to teach students about ethnic groups were conceptualized by J. A. Banks (1993a): *contributions, additive, transformation* and *social action* (see Figure 1). The contributions approach focused on heroes and heroines, holidays, and discrete cultural elements. When using the additive approach, teachers append ethnic content, themes, and perspectives to the curriculum without changing its basic structure. In the transformation approach, which is designed to help students learn how knowledge is constructed, the structure of the curriculum is changed to enable students to view concepts, issues, events, and themes from the perspectives of various ethnic and cultural groups. In the social action approach, which is an extension of the transformation approach, students make decisions on important social issues and take action to help solve them.

Tetreault (1993) describes a model for teaching content about women that is also designed to help students understand the nature of knowledge and how it is constructed. In the curriculum model, the teacher moves from a male-defined curriculum to one that is gender balanced. The phases are as follows: contributions curriculum, bifocal curriculum, women's curriculum, and gender-balanced curriculum. In the contributions curriculum, a male framework is used to insert women into the curriculum; the world is viewed through the eyes of women and men in the bifocal curriculum; subjects of primary importance to women are investigated in the women's curriculum; and the gender-balanced curriculum investigates topics and concepts that are important to women but also consider how women and men relate to each other.

PREJUDICE REDUCTION

The prejudice reduction dimension of multicultural education is designed to help students develop more democratic attitudes, values, and behaviors (Gabelko & Michaelis, 1981; Lynch, 1987). Researchers and educators who are concerned

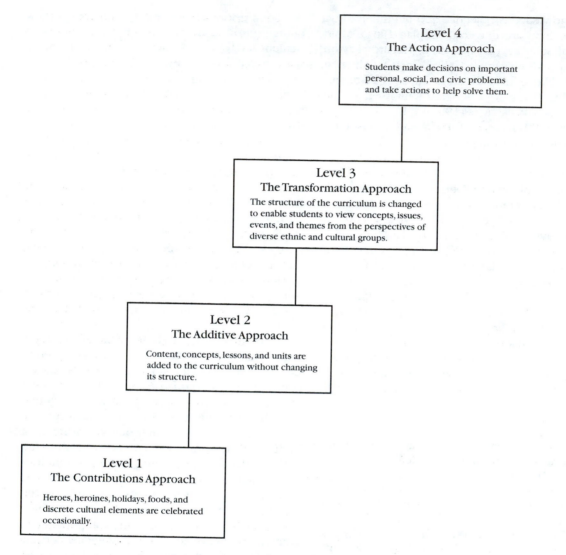

FIGURE 1 Approaches to Multicultural Curriculum Reform

about helping students develop more democratic attitudes and behaviors have devoted much of their attention to investigating how children develop racial awareness, preferences, and identification (Clark, 1963; Katz, 1976; Milner, 1983; Phinney & Rotheram, 1987). This discussion is divided into two sections: (a) the nature of children's racial attitudes and identities and (b) the modification of students' racial attitudes.

THE NATURE OF CHILDREN'S RACIAL ATTITUDES

A common belief among elementary school teachers is that young children have little awareness of racial differences and hold positive attitudes toward both African Americans and Whites. Many teachers with whom I have worked have told me that because young children are unaware of racial differences, talking about race to them will merely create racial problems that do not exist. This common observation by teachers is inconsistent with reality and research.

During a period of nearly 50 years, researchers have established that young children are aware of racial differences by the age of three (Phinney & Rotheram, 1987; Ramsey, 1987) and have internalized attitudes toward African Americans and Whites that are established in the wider society. They tend to prefer white (pinkish-colored) stimulus objects, such as dolls and pictures, to brown dolls and pictures, and to describe white (pinkish) objects and people more positively than brown ones.

Early studies by Lasker (1929) and Minard (1931) indicate that young children are aware of racial differences and that children's racial attitudes are formed early in life. Studies by E. L. Horowitz (1936) and R. E. Horowitz (1939) indicate that both African American and White nursery school children are aware of racial differences and show a statistically significant preference for Whites. The Horowitzes interpreted their findings to mean that the African American children in their studies evidenced self-rejection when they showed a White bias in their responses to stimulus objects and pictures.

In a series of pioneering studies conducted between 1939 and 1950, Kenneth B. and Mamie P. Clark confirmed the findings of the Horowitzes and gave considerable support to the self-rejection paradigm first formulated by the latter (Cross, 1991). The Clarks are usually credited with originating the self-rejection paradigm; however, Cross states that the Horowitzes, and not the Clarks, created the paradigm. Nevertheless, the famous Clark studies gave the self-rejection paradigm its widest visibility and credibility.

In the series of studies conducted by the Clarks, African American nursery school children were the subjects; the stimuli were brown and white (pinkish) dolls. The Clarks studied racial awareness, preference, and identification (Clark & Clark, 1939a, 1939b, 1940, 1947, 1950). They concluded that the children in their studies had accurate knowledge of racial differences, some-times made incorrect racial self-identifications, and often expressed a preference for white. The Clarks concluded that many of the African American children in their studies evidenced self-rejection.

The self-rejection paradigm associated with the Clarks has had a cogent influence on research and the interpretation of research on children's racial attitudes and self-esteem for nearly a half century. A series of significant and influential studies during the 1950s, 1960s, and 1970s confirmed the early findings by the Horowitzes and the Clarks (Morland, 1966; Porter, 1971; Radke & Trager, 1950; J. E. Williams & Morland, 1976)—that young children are aware of racial differences and that both African American and White children tend to evidence a white bias.

The self-rejection paradigm has been strongly challenged during the last decade on both methodological and interpretative grounds (W. C. Banks, 1976; Cross, 1991; Spencer, 1987). During the 1980s and 1990s, Spencer (1982, 1985, 1987) and Cross (1985, 1991) developed concepts and theories and conducted research that challenge the interpretation that the Horowitzes and the Clarks used to explain their findings. They have made a useful distinction between *personal* and *group* identity and have reinterpreted the early findings, as well as their own research findings, within this new paradigm.

An important group of studies by Spencer (1982, 1985, 1987) indicates that young African American children can distinguish their personal and group identities. They can express high self-esteem and a white bias at the same time. She formulates a cognitive theory to explain these findings: African American children often make white bias choices because they have learned from the wider society (a cognitive process) to make these choices, not because they reject themselves or have low self-concepts. In other words, the children are choosing the "right" answer when asked to select the white or colored stimulus. Research by J. A. Banks (1984) supports the postulate that African American children make choices related to race that indicate that personal and group identity are distinguished. Cross (1991) also provides strong theoretical and empirical evidence to support this conceptual distinction.

THE MODIFICATION OF CHILDREN'S RACIAL ATTITUDES

Studies designed to modify children's racial attitudes have been conducted at least since the 1940s (Agnes, 1947; Jackson, 1944). However, the literature that describes the characteristics of children's racial attitudes is much richer than the modification literature. In two comprehensive reviews of the modification literature, J. A. Banks (1991b, 1993d) identifies four types of modification studies: (a) curricular intervention studies, (b) reinforcement studies, (c) perceptual differentiation studies, and (d) cooperative learning studies.

Curricular studies are the earliest type of intervention studies; they date back to the intergroup education period of the 1940s. In their studies, Agnes (1974) and Jackson (1944) concluded that reading materials about African Americans helped students develop more positive racial attitudes. However, most of the early studies have serious methodological problems. One of the most well-designed and significant studies of the intergroup education period was conducted by Trager and Yarrow (1952). They found that a democratic curriculum had a positive effect on the racial attitudes of both students and teachers. Hayes and Conklin (1953), with an experimental treatment that took place over a two-year period, also found that an intercultural curriculum had a positive effect on the racial attitudes of students. However, the description of the intervention is imprecise.

Studies of the effects of units, courses, and curriculum materials have also been conducted by Fisher (1965), Leslie and Leslie (1972), Yawkey (1973), Lessing and Clarke (1976), Litcher and Johnson (1969), Litcher, Johnson, and Ryan (1973), and Shirley (1988). Most of these studies provide evidence for the postulate that curricular materials and interventions can have a positive effect on the racial attitudes of students. However, the studies by Lessing and Clarke and Litcher et al. had no measurable effects on the racial attitudes of students.

In an important study, Litcher and Johnson (1969) found that multiethnic readers had a positive effect on the racial attitudes of second-grade White students. However, when they replicated this study using photographs rather than readers (Litcher et al., 1973), no significant effects were attained. The investigators believe that the shorter duration of the latter study (one month compared with four) and the different ethnic compositions of the cities in which the studies were conducted may explain the conflicting findings in the two studies. In summarizing the effects of curriculum intervention studies, J. A. Banks (1991b) concludes:

> The studies . . . indicate that curriculum intervention can help students to develop more positive racial attitudes but . . . the effects of such interventions are likely not to be consistent. . . . The inconsistencies may be due in part to the use of different measures to assess attitude change and because the duration of the interventions has varied widely. The duration of the intervention has rarely been varied to determine the effects. (p. 464)

J. E. Williams and his colleagues have conducted a series of reinforcement studies with young children since the 1960s (J. E. Williams & Edwards, 1969; J. E. Williams & Morland, 1976). These experiments are designed to reduce white bias in young children. In the typical design of these experiments, the children are given pictures of black and white animals or objects and are reinforced for choosing the black objects or animals and for describing them positively. When they choose the white objects or animals, they receive negative reinforcement or no reinforcement. Williams and his colleagues (J. E. Williams, Best, Wood, & Filler, 1973; J. E. Williams & Edwards, 1969) have found that these types of interventions reduce white bias in children and that the children's responses are generalized from objects and animals to people. Laboratory reinforcement studies by other researchers have generally confirmed the findings by Williams and his colleagues (Hohn, 1973; Parish & Fleetwood, 1975; Parish, Shirazi, & Lambert, 1976).

Katz and her colleagues have conducted a series of studies that have examined the perceptual components of the racial attitudes of young children. In one study she confirmed her predictions that young children can more easily differentiate the faces of in-group members than the faces of out-group members and that if young children are taught to differentiate the faces of out-groups, prejudice is reduced (Katz, 1973). She and Zalk (Katz & Zalk, 1978) examined the effects of four different interventions on the racial attitudes of second- and fifth-grade White students: (a) perceptual differentiation of minority group faces, (b) increased positive racial contact, (c) vicarious interracial contact, and (d) reinforcement of the color black. Each of the interventions reduced prejudice. However, the most powerful interventions were vicarious contact and perceptual differentiation.

Most of the research on cooperative learning has been conducted since the 1970s. Cooperative learning studies tend to support the postulate that cooperative learning situations, if based on the principles formulated by Allport (1954), can increase the academic achievement of minority students and help all students to develop more positive racial attitudes and cross-racial friendships (Aronson & Bridgeman, 1979; Cohen, 1972; Slavin, 1979, 1985). Cohen emphasizes the importance of providing students with experiences that will prepare them for equal-status interactions prior to assigning group tasks to students from different races. Her research indicates that if this is not done, both minority and White students will expect the White students to dominate the group situation. She calls this phenomenon *interracial interaction disability* and has demonstrated that pregroup treatment activities can enable African American students to experience equal status in group situations with Whites (Cohen, 1972; Cohen & Roper, 1972).

EQUITY PEDAGOGY

When the civil rights movement began in the 1960s, much attention was focused on poverty in the United States. In *The Other America,* Michael Harrington (1962) stirred the nation's conscience about the plight of poor people. Educational concepts and theories developed that reflected the national concern for low-income citizens and were designed to help teachers and other educators to develop teaching techniques and strategies that would improve the academic achievement of low-income students.

THE CULTURAL DEPRIVATION PARADIGM

The educational theories, concepts, and research developed during the early 1960s reflected the dominant ideologies of the time, as well as the concepts and theories used in the social sciences to explain the behavior and values of low-income populations. Social scientists developed the *culture of poverty* concept to describe the experiences of low-income populations (Lewis, 1965). In education, this concept became known as *cultural deprivation* or *the disadvantaged.* Cultural deprivation became the dominant paradigm that guided the formulation of programs and pedagogies for low-income populations during the 1960s (Bereiter & Engelmann, 1966; Bloom et al., 1965; Crow, Murray, & Smythe, 1966; Riessman, 1962).

A paradigm can be defined as a system of explanations that guides policy and action (Kuhn, 1970). When a paradigm becomes established and dominates public discourse, it becomes difficult for other systems of explanations to emerge or to become institutionalized. When one paradigm replaces another, Kuhn states, a scientific revolution takes place. However, in education and the social sciences, rarely does one paradigm replace another. More typically, new paradigms compete with established ones and they coexist. Particular paradigms have been dominant at various times in the history of the education of low-income populations since the 1960s, but the educational landscape is usually characterized by competing paradigms and explanations.

A paradigm is not only a system of explanations, it is also a perspective on reality that reflects the experiences, perceptions, and values of its creators (Code, 1991; Harding, 1991). The cultural deprivation theorists, unlike the geneticists (Herrn-stein, 1971; Jensen, 1969), believe that low-income students can attain high levels of academic achievement, but that socialization experiences in their homes and communities do not enable them to attain the knowledge, skills, and attitudes that middle-class children acquire and that are essential for academic success.

Cultural deprivation theorists consequently believe that the major focus of educational reform must be to change the students by enhancing their early socialization experiences. Cultural deprivation and disadvantaged theorists believe that the school must help low-income students to overcome the deficits that result from their early family and community experiences. The focus on the deficits of low-income children often prevents cultural deprivation theorists from seeing their strengths. The emphasis on the students' deficits also does not allow the deprivationists to consider seriously structural changes that are needed in schools.

When it emerged, the cultural deprivation paradigm was the most enlightened and liberal theory of the day about educating low-income populations. Some of the nation's most eminent and committed social scientists contributed to its formulation. Allison Davis did pioneering work on the education of low-income students (Davis, 1948/1962). Davis was one of the organizers of the landmark Research Conference on Education and Cultural Deprivation, held at the University of Chicago in June 1964. Some of the nation's most eminent educators and social scientists participated in this conference, including Anne Anastasi, Basil Bernstein, Benjamin Bloom, Martin Deutsch, Erik Erikson, Edmund W. Gordon, Robert Havighurst, and Thomas Pettigrew. In the book based on the conference, Bloom et al. (1965) defined *culturally deprived* children:

> We refer to this group as culturally disadvantaged or deprived because we believe the roots of their problem may in large part be traced to their experiences in homes which do not transmit the cultural patterns necessary for the types of learning characteristic of the schools and the larger society. (p. 4)

The book was highly influential among educational leaders.

Another influential book resulted from a conference held two years earlier at Teachers College, Columbia University, led by A. Harry Passow (1963), who edited *Education in Depressed Areas.* Like the Chicago conference, the Teachers College conference included papers by some of the nation's leading social scientists and educators, including David P. Ausubel, Kenneth B. Clark, and Robert J. Havighurst.

Probably the most influential book published for teachers was *The Culturally Deprived Child* by Frank Riessman (1962), which was used widely in teacher-preparation and in-service programs. He told teachers to respect low-income students and pointed out that he thought *culturally deprived* was an inappropriate term but was using it because it was popular. He wrote: "The term 'culturally deprived' refers to those aspects of middle-class culture—such as education, books, formal language—from which these groups have not benefited" (p. 3). Implicit in this statement is the assumption that a student must be middle class to have a culture.

THE CULTURAL DIFFERENCE THEORISTS

When the 1970s began, a new group of scholars strongly challenged the explanations and values that underlie the cultural deprivation paradigm. Some of the critics of the cultural deprivationists used powerful language in their critiques (Baratz & Baratz, 1970; Ryan, 1971). Head Start preschool programs were funded generously during the war on poverty of the 1960s. The most popular educational models used in these programs were based on the cultural deprivation paradigm. One of the most commercially successful of these programs was marketed as Distar, and was popularized by Bereiter and Engelmann (1966). In a highly influential article published in the *Harvard Educational Review,* Baratz and Baratz argued that many of these programs and models were an expression of institutional racism. Ryan stated that middle-class professionals were blaming the poor, who were victims.

The critics of the cultural deprivationists constructed a different explanation for the school failure of low-income students. They contend that these students are not having academic success because they experience serious cultural conflicts in school. The students have rich cultures and values, but the schools have a culture that conflicts seriously with the cultures of students from low-income and ethnic minority groups (Hale-Benson, 1982; Shade, 1982).

In developing their concepts and theories about the rich cultures of low-income students and students of color, the cultural difference theorists make far more use of ethnic culture than do cultural deprivationists (Ramírez & Castañeda, 1974). The cultural deprivationists focus on social class and the culture of poverty and tend to ignore ethnic culture as a variable. The cultural difference theorists emphasize ethnic culture and devote little attention to class. Ignoring the ethnic cultures of students has evoked much of the criticism of the cultural deprivationists. The lack of attention to social class is problematic in the cultural difference literature (J. A. Banks, 1988). Cultural difference theorists have developed lists of cultural characteristics designed to help teachers build on the cultural strengths of ethnic students (Hale-Benson, 1982; Ramírez & Castañeda, 1974). However, the lists become problematic when teachers interpret them as static characteristics that apply to all members of the ethnic group (Cox & Ramírez, 1981).

The most influential work related to the cultural difference paradigm deals with learning styles, teaching styles, and language (Heath, 1983). In their seminal book. Ramírez and Castañeda (1974) delineate two major types of learning styles, *field independent* and *field sensitive*. They describe theoretical and empirical evidence to support the postulate that traditional Mexican American students tend to be more field sensitive in their learning styles than Anglo students. The school, however, most often uses a field-independent teaching style. Consequently, Mexican American students tend not to achieve as well as Anglo students. Ramírez and Castañeda state that the school should help all students, including Mexican American and Anglo students, to become bicognitive in their learning styles.

Theories similar to the one described by Ramírez and Castañeda have also been formulated by Hale-Benson (1982) and Shade (1982, 1989). Hale-Benson (1987), for example, states that the African American child, more than the Anglo child, tends to he "highly affective, expresses herself or himself through considerable body language . . . [and] seeks to be people oriented" (p. 123). Shade (1982), in a comprehensive review article, summarizes an extensive body of research that supports the cultural learning style concept. In a study by Damico (1985), African American children took more photographs of people and Anglo children took more photographs of objects, thus confirming her hypothesis that African American students are more people oriented than object oriented and that Anglo children are more object oriented.

Kleinfeld (1975, 1979) has spent much of her career researching the characteristics of effective teachers of Native American students. She has become skeptical of the learning-style concept and its usefulness in instruction. After they reviewed the few studies of the educational effects of adapting instruction to Native American learning styles, Kleinfeld and Nelson (1991) concluded that "virtually no research has succeeded in demonstrating that instruction adapted to Native Americans' visual learning style results in greater learning" (p. 273). The few weak studies reviewed by Kleinfeld and Nelson do not constitute a sufficient reason to abandon the learning-style paradigm. However, the paradigm is a contentious one. Both its advocates and its critics are strongly committed to their positions.

The controversy about learning-style theory and research is difficult to resolve. J. A. Banks (1988) examined the research literature on learning style to determine the extent to which learning style is a variable related to class and ethnicity. He concluded that the issue is a complex one, and that class mobility mediates but does not eliminate the effects of ethnic culture on the learning characteristics of Mexican American and African American students.

Some researchers believe that the best way to understand the learning characteristics of students of color is to observe and describe them in ethnographic studies, rather than classifying them into several brief categories. These researchers believe that thick descriptions of the learning and cultural characteristics of ethnic minority students are needed to guide educational practice. Influential ethnographic studies of the cultural characteristics of students of color have been conducted by researchers such as Ogbu (1974), Heath (1983), and Philips (1983).

Since the 1960s, cultural difference theorists have done rich and pioneering theoretical and empirical work on the language characteristics of ethnic minority students. Prior to the 1960s, most teachers considered the version of English spoken by most low-income African Americans as an abnormal form of standard English. Within the last three decades, linguists have produced a rich body of literature that documents that Black English (Ebonics) is a legitimate communication system that has its own rules and logic (Heath, 1983; Labov, 1969; Smitherman, 1977; F. Williams, 1970). Spanish-speaking children in schools of the Southwest were prohibited from speaking their first language for many decades. However, research in recent decades has revealed that it is important for the school to recognize and make use of children's first languages (Ovando & Collier, 1985).

THE REBIRTH OF THE CULTURAL DEPRIVATION PARADIGM

The history of the ethnic studies and intergroup education movements indicates that ideas related to these movements reemerge cyclically. We can observe a similar phenomenon in cultural deprivation. The cultural difference paradigm dominated discourse about the education of ethnic groups throughout much of the late 1970s and the early 1980s. However, since the late 1980s the cultural deprivation/disadvantaged conception has been exhumed and given new life in the form of the novel concept "at-risk" (Richardson et al., 1989; Slavin, Karweit, &

Madden, 1989). Like cultural deprivation, the definition of at-risk is imprecise. The term is used to refer to students who are different in many ways (Cuban, 1989).

One of the reasons that at-risk is becoming popular is that it has become a funding category for state and federal educational agencies. When a term becomes a funding category, it does not need to be defined precisely to attain wide usage and popularity. One reason that at-risk is politically popular is that it can be used to refer to any population of youth experiencing problems in school. Consequently, every interest group can see itself in the term. Although the term is problematic, as Cuban (1989) points out in a thoughtful article, it is increasingly used among both researchers and practitioners (Richardson et al., 1989; Slavin et al., 1989). The term *disadvantaged* has also reemerged from the 1960s. Disadvantaged children are the subject of an informative book by Natriello, McDill, and Pallas (1990).

AN EMPOWERING SCHOOL CULTURE AND SOCIAL STRUCTURE

The four dimensions of multicultural education discussed above—content integration, the knowledge construction process, prejudice reduction, and an equity pedagogy—each deal with an aspect of a cultural or social system: the school. However, the school can also be conceptualized as one social system that is larger than its interrelated parts (e.g., its formal and informal curriculum, teaching materials, counseling programs, and teaching strategies). When conceptualized as a social system, the school is viewed as an institution that "includes a social structure of interrelated statuses and roles and the functioning of that structure in terms of patterns of actions and interactions" (Theodorson & Theodorson, 1969, p. 395). The school can also be conceptualized as a cultural system (Bullivant, 1987) with a specific set of values, norms, ethos, and shared meanings.

A number of school reformers have used a systems approach to reform the school in order to increase the academic achievement of low-income students and students of color. There are a number of advantages to approaching school reform from a holistic perspective. To implement any reform successfully in a school, such as effective prejudice reduction teaching, changes are required in a number of other school variables. Teachers, for example, need more knowledge and need to examine their racial and ethnic attitudes; consequently, they need more time as well as a variety of instructional materials. Many school reform efforts fail because the roles, norms, and ethos of the school do not change in ways that will make the institutionalization of the reforms possible.

The effective school reformers constitute one group of change agents that has approached school reform from a systems perspective. This movement emerged as a reaction to the work of Coleman et al. (1966) and Jencks et al. (1972); their studies indicate that the major factor influencing student academic achievement is the social-class composition of the students and the school. Many educators interpreted the research by Coleman et al. and Jencks et al. to mean that the school can do little to increase the academic achievement of low-income students.

Brookover (Brookover & Erickson, 1975) developed a social psychological theory of learning that states that students internalize the conceptions of themselves that are institutionalized within the ethos and structures of the school. Related to Merton's (1968) self-fulfilling prophecy, Brookover's theory states that student academic achievement will increase if the adults within the school have high expectations for students, clearly identify the skills they wish them to learn, and teach those skills to them.

Research by Brookover and his colleagues (Brookover et al., 1979; Brookover & Lezotte, 1979) indicates that schools populated by low-income students within the same school district vary greatly in student achievement levels. Consequently, Brookover attributes the differences to variations in a school's social structure. He calls the schools in low-income areas that have high academic achievement *improving* schools. Other

researchers, such as Edmonds (1986) and Lezotte (1993), call them *effective* schools.

Brookover and his colleagues (Brookover et al., 1979; Brookover & Lezotte, 1979) have identified the characteristics that differentiate effective from ineffective schools. Staff in effective or improving schools emphasize the importance of basic skills and believe that all students can master them. Principals are assertive instructional leaders and disciplinarians and assume responsibility for the evaluation of the achievement of basic skills objectives. Staff members accept the concept of accountability, and parents initiate more contact than in nonimproving schools.

Edmonds (1986), who was a leading advocate of effective schools as an antidote to the doom that often haunts inner-city schools, identified characteristics of effective schools similar to those formulated by Brookover and his colleagues. Rutter, Maughan, Mortimore, Ouston, and Smith (1979) studied 12 secondary schools in an urban section of London. They concluded that some schools were much better than others in promoting the academic and social success of their students. Effective schools researchers have conducted a large number of studies that provide support for their major postulates (see Chapter 29 of this *Handbook*). However, some educators have a number of concerns about the effective schools movement, including the use of standardized tests as the major device to ascertain academic achievement (Bliss, Firestone, & Richards, 1991; Cuban, 1983; Purkey & Smith, 1982).

Comer (1988) has developed a structural intervention model that involves changes in the social psychological climate of the school. The teachers, principals, and other school professionals make collaborative decisions about the school. Parents also participate in the decision-making process. Comer's data indicate that this approach has been successful in increasing the academic achievement of low-income, inner-city students. He started the program in New Haven, Connecticut, that is now being implemented in a number of other U.S. cities using private foundation support.

IMPLICATIONS FOR RESEARCH AND PRACTICE

RESEARCH

The historical development of multicultural education needs to be more fully described. Careful historical descriptions and analyses will help the field to identify its links to the past, gain deeper insights into the problems and promises of multicultural education today, and plan more effectively for the future. Studies are needed to determine the details of the teaching of African American history in the schools and colleges from the turn of the century to the 1960s. Studies are also needed to determine the extent to which the intergroup education movement intersected with the ethnic studies tradition initiated by George Washington Williams in 1882 and continued by his successors until the new ethnic studies movement began in the 1960s. The role of African American institutions, such as churches, schools, sororities, fraternities, and women's clubs (Hine, Brown, & Terborg-Penn, 1993), in promoting the study and teaching of African American history also needs to be researched (Dabney, 1934).

The broad outlines of the early ethnic studies movement related to African Americans have been described here. Studies are needed that will reveal the extent to which scholarship and teaching sources about other ethnic groups, such as American Indians and Mexican Americans, were developed from the turn of the century to the 1960s and 1970s.

A comprehensive history of the intergroup education movement is needed. We also need to determine the extent to which intergroup education practices became institutionalized within the typical school. The publications reviewed for this chapter indicate that intergroup education was often implemented as special projects within schools that were leaders in their cities or districts. Many of the nation's schools were tightly segregated when the movement arose and died, especially in the South. The geographical regions in which intergroup education project schools were located, as well as the types of

schools, are important variables that need to be investigated.

Other major issues that warrant investigation are: (a) the reasons why the movement had failed by the time the new ethnic studies movement emerged in the 1960s, and (b) why its leaders, such as Hilda Taba, Lloyd A. Cook, and William Van Til, did little work in intergroup education after the mid-1950s. Seemingly, intergroup education was not a lifetime commitment for its eminent leaders. In the 1960s Taba became a leading expert and researcher in social studies education. However, in her posthumously published book, coauthored with Deborah Elkins (Taba & Elkins, 1966), *Teaching Strategies for the Culturally Disadvantaged*, Taba incorporated concepts and strategies from the intergroup education project that she directed in the 1940s, funded by the National Conference of Christians and Jews and sponsored by the American Council on Education. Intergroup education concepts and aims also had a significant influence on her famous social studies curriculum (Taba, 1967). This curriculum focuses on thinking, knowledge, attitudes, feelings, and values, as well as on academic and social skills. These components are similar to the aims that Taba stated for intergroup education in an article she coauthored with Harold W. Wilson (Taba & Wilson, 1946).

Empirical studies need to be undertaken of each of the five dimensions of multicultural education described in this chapter. Content integration studies, using both interview and ethnographic techniques, should describe the approaches that teachers use to integrate their curricula with ethnic content, the problems they face, and how they resolve them. The major barriers that teachers face when trying to make their curricula multicultural also need to be identified.

The knowledge construction process is a fruitful topic for empirical research. Most of the work related to this concept is theoretical and philosophical (J. A. Banks, 1993c; Code, 1991; Gordon, 1985; Harding, 1991). This concept can be investigated by interventions that present students with documents describing different perspectives on the same historical event, such as the Japanese American internment, the westward movement, and Indian removal. Studies could be made of teacher questions and student responses when discussing the conflicting accounts.

Studies that describe students' racial attitudes and intervention studies designed to modify them need to be conducted. A literature search using ERIC, PsychLit, and Sociofile revealed that few intervention studies related to children's racial attitudes have been conducted since 1980. Most of the studies related to children's racial attitudes reviewed here were conducted before 1980. Since 1980 there has been little support for research in race relations; consequently, there are few studies. Perhaps multicultural researchers could implement small-scale observational studies funded by civil rights organizations. Jewish civil rights organizations funded a number of important studies during the intergroup education era.

Research related to effective teaching strategies for low-income students and students of color (equity pedagogy) needs to examine the complex interaction of race, class, and gender, as well as other variables such as region and generation (Grant & Sleeter, 1986). The rising number of outspoken African American conservatives, such as Carter (1991), Sowell (1984), Steele (1990), and Wortham (1981), should help both the research and wider community understand the enormous diversity within the African American community. Conservative Mexican American writers, such as Rodriguez (1982) and Chavez (1991), reveal the ideological and cultural diversity within the Mexican American community.

Since the 1960s, diversity within U.S. ethnic minority groups has increased greatly, as a significant number of African Americans, Mexican Americans, and Puerto Ricans have joined the middle class and the exodus to the suburbs (Wilson, 1987). White flight has become middle-class flight. A sharp class schism has developed within ethnic minority communities (Wilson, 1987). Consequently, research on people of color—especially studies on learning styles and their cultural characteristics—that does not examine class as an important variable is not likely to result in findings that are helpful and generalizable.

PRACTICE

The most important implication of this research review is that multicultural education must be conceptualized and implemented broadly if it is to bring about meaningful changes in schools, colleges, and universities. Several serious problems result when multicultural education is conceptualized only or primarily as content integration. Teachers in subjects such as mathematics and science perceive multicultural education, when it is conceptualized only as content integration, as appropriate for social studies and language arts teachers but not for them.

When multicultural education is narrowly conceptualized, it is often confined to activities for special days and occasions, such as Martin Luther King's birthday and Cinco de Mayo. It may also be viewed as a special unit, an additional book by an African American or a Mexican American writer, or a few additional lessons. The knowledge construction dimension of multicultural education is an essential one. Using this concept, content about ethnic groups is not merely added to the curriculum. Rather, the curriculum is reconceptualized to help students understand how knowledge is constructed and how it reflects human interests, ideology, and the experiences of the people who create it. Students themselves also create interpretations. They begin to understand why it is essential to look at the nation's experience from diverse ethnic and cultural perspectives to comprehend fully its past and present.

The research reviewed in this chapter indicates that children come to school with misconceptions about outside ethnic groups and with a white bias. However, it also indicates that students' racial attitudes can be modified and made more democratic and that the racial attitudes of young children are much more easily modified than the attitudes of older students and adults (Katz, 1976). Consequently, it suggests that if we are to help students acquire the attitudes needed to survive in a multicultural and diverse world, we must start early. Beginning in kindergarten, educators need to implement a well-conceptualized and sequential curriculum that is multicultural.

A school experience that is multicultural includes content, examples, and realistic images of diverse racial and ethnic groups. Cooperative learning activities in which students from diverse groups work to attain shared goals is also a feature of the school, as well as simulated images of ethnic groups that present them in positive and realistic ways. Also essential within such a school are adults who model the attitudes and behaviors they are trying to teach. Actions speak much louder than words.

Jane Elliott (as described in Peters, 1987) has attained fame for a simulated lesson she taught on discrimination that is described in the award-winning documentary *The Eye of the Storm.* One day Elliott discriminated against blue-eyed children; the next day brown-eyed children experienced the sting of bigotry. In 1984, 11 of her former third graders returned to Riceville, Iowa, for a reunion with their teacher. This event is described in another documentary, *A Class Divided,* in which the students describe the power of a classroom experience that had taken place 14 years earlier.

Elliott, who taught third grade in an all-White Iowa town, was moved to act because of the racial hate she observed in the nation. Racial incidents are on the rise throughout the United States (Altbach & Lomotey, 1941). The research reviewed in this chapter, and in two previous reviews. (J. A. Banks, 1991b, 1993b), can help empower educators to act to help create a more democratic and caring society. Jane Elliott acted and made a difference; she is a cogent example for us all.

REFERENCES

Acuña, R. (1972). *Occupied America: The Chicano's struggle toward liberation.* San Francisco: Canfield Press.

Adorno, T. W., Frenkel-Brunswik, E., Levinson, D. J., & Sansford, R. N. (1950). *The authoritarian personality.* New York: Norton.

Agnes, M. (1947). Influences of reading on the racial attitudes of adolescent girls. *Catholic Educational Review, 45,* 415–420.

Allport, G. W. (1954). *The nature of prejudice.* Cambridge, MA: Addison-Wesley.

Altbach, P. G., & Lomotey, K. (Eds.). (1991). *The racial crisis in American higher education.* Albany: State University of New York Press.

American Association of Colleges for Teacher Education. (1973). *No one model American.* Washington, DC: Author.

Anderson, J. D. (1988). *The education of Blacks in the South, 1860–1935.* Chapel Hill: University of North Carolina Press.

Aran, K. Arthur, H., Colon, R., & Goldenberg, H. (1973). *Puerto Rican history and culture. A study guide and curriculum outline.* New York: United Federation of Teachers.

Aronson, E., & Bridgeman, D. (1979). Jigsaw groups and the desegregated classroom: In pursuit of common goals. *Personality and Social Psychology Bulletin, 5,* 438–446.

Asante, M. K. (1991). The Afrocentric idea in education. *Journal of Negro Education, 60,* 170–180.

Asante, M. K., & Ravitch, D. (1991). Multiculturalism: An exchange. *The American Scholar, 60,* 267–276.

Baker, G. (1977). Multicultural education: Two preservice approaches. *Journal of Teacher Education, 28,* 31–33.

Baker, G. (1983). *Planning and organizing for multicultural instruction.* Menlo Park, CA: Addison-Wesley.

Banks, J. A. (1969). A content analysis of the Black American in textbooks. *Social Education, 33,* 954–957, 963.

Banks, J. A. (1970). *Teaching the Black experience: Methods and materials.* Belmont, CA: Fearon.

Banks, J. A. (Ed.). (1973). *Teaching ethnic studies: Concepts and strategies* (43rd yearbook). Washington, DC: National Council for the Social Studies.

Banks, J. A (1984). Black youths in predominantly White suburbs: An exploratory study of their attitudes and self-concepts. *Journal of Negro Education, 53,* 3–17.

Banks, J. A (1988). Ethnicity, class, cognitive, and motivational styles: Research and teaching implications. *Journal of Negro Education, 57,* 452–466.

Banks, J. A. (1991a). The dimensions of multicultural education. *Multicultural Leader, 4*, 5-6.

Banks, J. A. (1991b). Multicultural education: Its effects on students' ethnic and gender role attitudes. In J. P. Shaver (Ed.), *Handbook of research on social studies teaching and learning* (pp. 459-469). New York: Macmillan.

Banks, J. A. (1991c). *Teaching strategies for ethnic studies* (5th ed.). Boston: Allyn and Bacon.

Banks, J. A. (1992). Multicultural education: Approaches, developments, and dimensions. In J. Lynch, C. Modgil, & S. Modgil (Eds.), *Cultural diversity and the schools, Vol. 1, Education for cultural diversity: Convergence and divergence* (pp. 83-94). London: The Falmer Press.

Banks, J. A. (1993a). Approaches to multicultural curriculum reform. In J. A. Banks & C. A. M. Banks (Eds.), *Multicultural education: Issues and perspectives* (2nd ed., pp. 195-214). Boston: Allyn and Bacon.

Banks, J. A. (1993b). The canon debate, knowledge construction, and multicultural education. *Educational Researcher, 22*(5), 4-14.

Banks, J. A. (1993c). Multicultural education: Characteristics and goals. In J. A. Banks & C. A. M. Banks (Eds.), *Multicultural education: Issues and perspectives* (2nd ed., pp. 3-28). Boston: Allyn and Bacon.

Banks, J. A. (1993d). Multicultural education for young children: Racial and ethnic attitudes and their modification. In B. Spodek (Ed.), *Handbook of research on the education of young children* (pp. 236-250). New York Macmillan.

Banks, J. A. (1994). *Multiethnic education: Theory and practice* (3rd ed.). Boston: Allyn and Bacon.

Banks, J. A., & Banks, C. A. M. (Eds.). (1993). *Multicultural education: Issues and perspectives* (2nd ed.). Boston: Allyn and Bacon.

Banks, J. A., Cortés, C. E., Gay, G., Garcia, R. L., & Ochoa, A. S. (1976). *Curriculum guidelines for multiethnic education.* Washington, DC: National Council for the Social Studies.

Banks, W. C. (1976). White preference in Blacks: A paradigm in search of a phenomenon. *Psychological Bulletin, 83*, 1170-1186.

Baratz, S. S., & Baratz, J. C. (1970). Early childhood intervention: The social science base of institutional racism. *Harvard Educational Review, 40*, 29-50.

Bennett, C. I. (1990). *Comprehensive multicultural education* (2nd ed.). Boston: Allyn and Bacon.

Bereiter, C., & Engelmann, S. (1966). *Teaching disadvantaged children in the preschool.* Englewood Cliffs, NJ: Prentice-Hall.

Berger, P. L., & Luckman, T. (1966). *The social construction of knowledge: A treatise in the sociology of knowledge.* Garden City, NY: Doubleday.

Bernal, M. (1987, 1991). *Black Athena: The Afroasiatic roots of classical civilization* (Vols. 1 & 2). New Brunswick, NJ: Rutgers University Press.

Blassingame. J. W. (Ed.). (1971). *New perspectives in Black studies.* Urbana: University of Illinois Press.

Blassingame. J. W. (1972). *The slave community: Plantation life in the antebellum South.* New York: Oxford University Press.

Blea, I. I. (1988). *Toward a Chicano social science.* New York: Preager.

Bliss, J. R., Firestone, W. A., & Richards, C. E. (Eds.). (1991). *Rethinking effective schools: Research and practice.* Englewood Cliffs, NJ: Prentice-Hall.

Bloom, B. S., Davis, A., & Hess, R. (1965). *Compensatory education for cultural deprivation.* New York: Holt.

Bond, H. M. (1939). *Negro education in Alabama: A study in cotton and steel.* Washington, DC: The Associated Publishers.

Boyer, J. B. (1974). Needed: Curriculum diversity for the urban economically disadvantaged. *Educational Leadership, 31*, 624-626.

Braddock, J. H., II (1990). Tracking the middle grades: National patterns of grouping for instruction. *Phi Delta Kappan, 71*, 445-449.

Brookover, W. B., Beady, C., Flood, P., Schweitzer, J., & Wisenbaker, J. (1979). *School social systems and student achievement: Schools can make a difference.* New York: Praeger.

Brookover, W. B., & Erickson, E. (1975). *Sociology of education.* Homewood, IL: Dorsey.

Brookover, W. B., & Lezotte, L. W. (1979). *Changes in school characteristics coincident with changes in student achievement.* East Lansing: Institute for Research on Teaching, College of Education, Michigan State University.

Brooks, R. L. (1990). *Rethinking the American race problem.* Berkeley: University of California Press.

Bullivant, B. M. (1987). *The ethnic encounter in the secondary school.* New York: The Falmer Press.

Butler, J. E., & Walter, J. C. (Eds.). (1991). *Transforming the curriculum: Ethnic studies and women's studies.* Albany: State University of New York Press.

Carmichael, S., & Hamilton, C. V. (1967). *Black power: The politics of liberation in America.* New York: Vintage.

Carter, S. L. (1991). *Reflections of an affirmative action baby.* New York: Basic Books.

Chavez, L. (1991). *Out of the barrio: Toward a new politics of Hispanic assimilation.* New York: Basic Books.

Clark, K. B. (1963). *Prejudice and your child.* Boston: Beacon Press.

Clark, K. B., & Clark, M. P. (1939a). The development of consciousness of self and the emergence of racial identification in Negro preschool children. *Journal of Social Psychology, 10,* 591-599.

Clark, K. B., & Clark, M. P. (1939b). Segregation as a factor in the racial identification of Negro preschool children. *Journal of Experimental Education, 8,* 161-163.

Clark, K. B., & Clark, M. P. (1940). Skin color as a factor in racial identification and preference in Negro children. *Journal of Negro Education, 19,* 341-358.

Clark, K. B., & Clark, M. P. (1947). Racial identification and preference in Negro children. In T. M. Newcomb & E. L. Hartley (Eds.), *Readings in social psychology* (pp. 169-178). New York: Holt, Rinehart & Winston.

Clark, K. B., & Clark, M. P. (1950). Emotional factors in racial identification and preference of Negro children. *Journal of Negro Education, 19,* 341-350.

Clinchy, E. R. (1949). *Intergroup relations centers.* New York: Farrar, Straus & Company.

Code, L. (1991). *What can she know? Feminist theory and the construction of knowledge.* Ithaca, NY: Cornell University Press.

Cohen, E. G. (1972). Interracial interaction disability. *Human Relations, 25,* 9-24.

Cohen, E. G., & Roper, S. S. (1972). Modification of interracial interaction disability: An application of status characteristics theory. *American Sociological Review, 37,* 643-657.

Coleman, J. S., Campbell, E.G., Hobson, C. J., McPartland, J., Mood, A. M., Weinfeld. F. D., & York, R. L. (1966). *Equality of educational opportunity.* Washington, DC: U.S. Government Printing Office.

Cormer, J. P. (1988). Educating poor minority children. *Scientific American, 259,* 42-48.

Cook, L. A. (1947). Intergroup education. *Review of Educational Research, 17,* 267-278.

Cook, L. A. (1950). *College programs in intergroup relations.* Washington, DC: American Council on Education.

Cook, L. A. (1951). *Intergroup relations in teacher education: An analytical study of intergroup education in colleges and schools in the United States: Functions, current expressions, and improvements.* Washington, DC: American Council on Education.

Cook, L. A. (Ed.). (1952). *Toward better human relations.* Detroit: Wayne State University Press.

Cook, L., & Cook, E. (1954). *Intergroup education.* New York: McGraw-Hill.

Cortés, C. E. (1973). Teaching the Chicano experience. In J. A. Banks (Ed.), *Teaching ethnic studies: Concepts and strategies* (pp. 181-199). Washington, DC: National Council for the Social Studies.

Cox, B. G., & Ramírez, M., III (1981). Cognitive styles: Implications for teaching ethnic studies. In J. A. Banks (Ed.), *Education for the 80s: Multiethnic education* (pp. 61-71). Washington, DC: National Education Association.

Cross, W. E., Jr. (1985). Black identity: Rediscovering the distinction between personal identity and reference group orientation. In M. B. Spencer, G. K. Brookins, & W. R. Allen (Eds.), *Beginnings: The social and affective development of Black children* (pp. 155-171). Hillsdale, NJ: Erlbaum.

Cross, W. E., Jr., (1991). *Shades of Black: Diversity in African American identity.* Philadelphia: Temple University Press.

Crow, L. D., Murray, W. I., & Smythe, H. H. (1966). *Educating the culturally disadvantaged child: Principles and programs.* New York: David McKay.

Cuban, L. (1983). Effective schools: A friendly but cautionary note. *Phi Delta Kappan, 64,* 695-696.

Cuban, L. (1989). The "at risk" label and the problem of urban school reform. *Phi Delta Kappan, 70,* 780-801.

Cummins, J. (1986). Empowering minority students: A framework for intervention. *Harvard Educational Review, 56,* 18-36.

Dabney, T. L. (1934). The study of the Negro. *Journal of Negro History, 19,* 266-307.

Damico, S. B. (1985). The two worlds of school: Differences in the photographs of Black and White adolescents. *The Urban Review, 17,* 210–222.

Daniels, R. (1988). *Asian America: Chinese and Japanese in the United States since 1850.* Seattle: University of Washington Press.

Davis, A. (1962). *Social-class influences upon learning.* Cambridge, MA: Harvard University Press. (Original work published 1948)

Davis, A., Gardner, B. B., & Gardner, M. R. (1941). *Deep South: A social anthropological study of caste and class.* Chicago: University of Chicago Press.

Deloria, V., Jr. (1969). *Custer died for your sins: An Indian manifesto.* New York: Avon.

Delpit, L. D. (1988). The silenced dialogue: Power and pedagogy in educating other people's children. *Harvard Educational Review, 58,* 280–298.

Diop, C. A. (1974). *The African origin of civilization: Myth or reality.* New York: Lawrence Hill.

Drake, St. C. (1987, 1990). *Black folk here and there* (Vols. 1 & 2). Los Angeles: University of California, Center for Afro-American Studies.

DuBois, W. E. B. (1935). *Black reconstruction.* New York: Harcourt, Brace.

DuBois, W. E. B. (1953). *The souls of Black folk.* New York: The Blue Heron Press.

DuBois, W. E. B. (1973). *The education of Black people: Ten critiques, 1906–1960.* New York: Monthly Review Press.

Edmonds, R. (1986). Characteristics of effective schools. In U. Neisser (Ed.), *The school achievement of minority children* (pp. 93–104). Hillsdale, NJ: Erlbaum.

Farganis, S. (1986). *The social construction of the feminine character.* Totowa, NJ: Rowman and Littlefield.

Fisher, F. (1965). *The influence of reading and discussion on the attitudes of fifth graders toward American Indians.* Unpublished doctoral dissertation, University of California, Berkeley.

Forbes, J. D. (1973). Teaching Native American values and cultures. In J. A. Banks (Ed.), *Teaching ethnic studies: Concepts and strategies* (pp. 201–225). Washington, DC: National Council for the Social Studies.

Ford, N. A. (1973). *Black studies: Threat-or-challenge.* Port Washington, NY: Kennikat Press.

Franklin, J. H. (1947). *From slavery to freedom: A history of Negro Americans.* New York: Knopf.

Franklin, J. H. (1985). *George Washington Williams: A biography.* Chicago: University of Chicago Press.

Gabelko, N. H., & Michaelis, J. U. (1981). *Reducing adolescent prejudice: A handbook.* New York: Teachers College Press.

Gamio, M. (1930). *Mexican immigration to the United States. A study of human migration and adjustment.* Chicago: University of Chicago Press.

Garcia, R. L. (1991). *Teaching in a pluralistic society: Concepts, models, strategies* (2nd ed.). New York: HarperCollins.

Gates, H. L., Jr. (1988). *The signifying monkey: A theory of African-American literary criticism.* New York: Oxford University Press.

Gay, G. (1971). Ethnic minority studies: How widespread? How successful? *Educational Leadership, 29,* 108–112.

Gay, G. (1992). The state of multicultural education in the United States. In K. Adam-Moodley (Ed.), *Education in plural societies: International perspectives* (pp. 47–66). Calgary, Alberta, Canada: Detselig.

Genovese, E. D. (1972). *Roll, Jordon, roll: The world the slaves made.* New York: Pantheon Books.

Gibson, M. A. (1976). Approaches to multicultural education in the United States: Some concepts and assumptions. *Anthropology and Education Quarterly, 7,* 7–18.

Ginsburg, H. (1972). *The myth of the deprived child: Poor children's intellect and education.* Englewood Cliffs, NJ: Prentice-Hall.

Giroux, H. A. (1983). *Theory and resistance in education.* South Hadley, MA: Bergin and Garvey.

Gollnick, D. M., & Chinn, P. C. (1990). *Multicultural education in a pluralistic society* (3rd ed.). Columbus, OH: Merrill.

Goodman, M. A. (1952). *Race awareness in young children.* New York: Collier.

Gordon, E. W. (1985). Social science knowledge production and the Afro-American experience. *Journal of Negro Education, 54,* 117–133.

Gordon, E. W., & Meroe, A. S. (1991). Common destinies—Continuing dilemmas. *Psychological Science, 2,* 23–30.

Gordon, E. W., Miller, M., & Rollock, D. (1990). Coping with communicentric bias in knowledge production in the social sciences. *Educational Researcher, 19,* 14–19.

Gould, S. J. (1981). *The mismeasure of man.* New York: Norton.

Grant, C. A. (1973). Black studies materials do make a difference. *Journal of Educational Research, 66,* 400–404.

Grant, C. A. (Ed.). (1977). *Multicultural education: Commitments, issues, and applications.* Washington, DC: Association for Supervision and Curriculum Development.

Grant, C. A. (1978). Education that is multicultural: Isn't that what we mean? *Journal of Teacher Education, 29,* 45–48.

Grant, C. A., & Sleeter, C. E. (1986). Race, class, and gender in education research: An argument for integrative analysis. *Review of Educational Research, 56,* 195–211.

Gray, P. (1991, July 8). Whose America? *Time,* pp. 12–17.

Habermas, J. (1971). *Knowledge and human interests.* Boston: Beacon Press.

Hale-Benson, J. (1982). *Black children: Their roots, culture and learning styles* (Rev. ed.). Baltimore: Johns Hopkins University Press.

Hale-Benson, J. (1987). Black children: Their roots, culture, and learning styles. In J. B. McCracken (Ed.), *Reducing stress in young children's lives* (pp. 122–129). Washington, DC: National Association for the Education of Young Children.

Harding, S. (1991). *Whose science? Whose knowledge? Thinking from women's lives.* Ithaca, NY: Cornell University Press.

Harrington, M. (1962). *The other America.* New York: Macmillan.

Hayes, M. L., & Conklin, M. E. (1953). Intergroup attitudes and experimental change. *Journal of Experimental Education, 22,* 19–36.

Heath, S. B. (1983). *Ways with words: Language, life, and work in communities and classrooms.* New York: Cambridge University Press.

Herrnstein, R. J. (1971). *I.Q. in the meritocracy.* Boston: Little, Brown.

Hilliard, A. G., III (1974). Restructuring teacher education for multicultural imperatives. In W. A. Hunter (Ed.), *Multicultural education through competency-based teacher education* (pp. 40–55). Washington,

DC: American Association of Colleges for Teacher Education.

Hilliard, A. G., III, Payton-Stewart, L., & Williams, L. O. (Eds.). (1990). *Infusion of African and African American content in the school curriculum.* Morristown, NJ: Aaron Press.

Hine, D. C., Brown, E. B., & Terborg-Penn, R. (Eds.). (1993). *Black women in America: An historical encyclopedia.* Brooklyn, NY: Carlson.

Hohn, R. L. (1973). Perceptual training and its effect on racial preference of kindergarten children. *Psychological Reports, 32,* 435–441.

hooks, b. (1990). *Yearning: Race, gender, and cultural politics.* Boston: South End Press.

Horowitz, E. L. (1936). The development of attitude toward the Negro. In *Archives of Psychology* (No. 104). New York: Columbia University.

Horowitz, R. E. (1939). Racial aspects of self-identification in nursery school children. *Journal of Psychology, 7,* 91–99.

Hunter, W. A. (Ed.). (1974). *Multicultural education through competency-based teacher education.* Washington, DC: American Association of Colleges for Teacher Education.

Jackson, E. P. (1944). Effects of reading upon the attitudes toward the Negro race. *The Library Quarterly, 14,* 47–54.

Jencks, C., Smith, M., Acland, H., Bane, M. J., Cohen, D., Gintis, H., Heyns, B., & Michelson, S. (1972). *Inequality: A reassessment of the effect of family and schooling in America.* New York: Basic Books.

Jensen, A. R. (1969). How much can we boost IQ and scholastic achievement? *Harvard Educational Review, 39,* 1–123.

Kaplan, A. (1964). *The conduct of inquiry: Methodology for behavioral science.* San Francisco: Chandler.

Katz, P. A. (1973). Perception of racial cues in preschool children: A new look. *Developmental Psychology, 8,* 295–299.

Katz, P. A. (Ed.). (1976). *Towards the elimination of racism.* New York: Pergamon.

Katz, P. A., & Zalk, S. R. (1978). Modification of children's racial attitudes. *Developmental Psychology, 14,* 447–461.

King, J. A., & Mitchell, C. A. (1990). *Black mothers to sons: Juxtaposing African American literature with social practice.* New York: Peter Lang.

Kitano, H. H. L. (1969). *Japanese Americans: The evolution of a subculture.* Englewood Cliffs, NJ: Prentice-Hall.

Klassen, F. H., & Gollnick, D. M. (Eds.). (1977). *Pluralism and the American teacher: Issues and case studies.* Washington, DC: Ethnic Heritage Center for Teacher Education of the American Association of Colleges for Teacher Education.

Klein, S. S. (Ed.). (1985). *Handbook for achieving sex equity through education.* Baltimore: Johns Hopkins University Press.

Kleinfeld, J. (1975). Effective teachers of Eskimo and Indian students. *School Review, 83,* 301-344.

Kleinfeld, J. (1979). *Eskimo children on the Andrearsky.* New York: Praeger.

Kleinfeld, J., & Nelson, P. (1991). Adapting instruction to Native Americans' learning styles: An iconoclastic view. *Journal of Cross-Cultural Psychology, 22,* 273-282.

Kuhn, T. S. (1970). *The structure of scientific revolutions* (2nd ed., enlarged). Chicago: University of Chicago Press.

Labov, W. (1969). *The study of nonstandard English.* Urbana, IL: National Council of Teachers of English.

Ladner, J. A. (Ed.). (1973). *The death of White sociology.* New York: Vintage Books.

Lasker, B. (1929). *Race attitudes in children.* New York: Holt, Rinehart & Winston.

Lasker, B. (1931). *Filipino immigration to the continental United States and Hawaii.* Chicago: University of Chicago Press.

Lauter, P. (1991). *Canons and contexts.* New York: Oxford University Press.

Leo, L. (1990, November 12). A fringe history of the world. *U.S. News and World Report,* pp. 25-26.

Leslie, L. L., & Leslie, J. W. (1972). The effects of a student centered special curriculum upon the racial attitudes of sixth graders. *Journal of Experimental Education, 41,* 63-67.

Lessing, E. E., & Clarke, C. (1976). An attempt to reduce ethnic prejudice and assess its correlates. *Educational Research Quarterly, 1,* 3-16.

Levine, L. W. (1977). *Black culture and Black consciousness: Afro-American folk thought from slavery to freedom.* New York: Oxford University Press.

Lewis, O. (1965). *La vida: A Puerto Rican family in the culture of poverty—San Juan and New York.* New York: Random House.

Lezotte, L. W. (1993). Effective schools: A framework for increasing student achievement. In J. A. Banks & C. A. M. Banks (Eds.), *Multicultural education: Issues and perspectives* (2nd ed., pp. 303-316). Boston: Allyn and Bacon.

Litcher, J. H., & Johnson, D. W. (1969). Changes in attitudes toward Negroes of White elementary school students after use of multiethnic readers. *Journal of Educational Psychology, 60,* 148-152.

Litcher, J. H., Johnson, D. W., & Ryan, F. L. (1973). Use of pictures of multiethnic interaction to change attitudes of White elementary school students toward Blacks. *Psychological Reports, 33,* 367-372.

Locke, A., & Stern, B. J. (Eds.). (1942). *When people meet: A study in race and culture contacts.* New York: Progressive Education Association.

Logan, R. W. (1954). *The betrayal of the Negro.* New York: Collier.

Lynch, J. (1987). *Prejudice reduction and the schools.* New York: Nichols.

McWilliams, C. (1943). *Brothers under the skin.* Boston: Little, Brown.

McWilliams, C. (1949). *North from Mexico: The Spanish-speaking people of the United States.* Philadelphia: Lippincott.

Mercer, J. R. (1989). Alternative paradigms for assessment in a pluralistic society. In J. A. Banks & C. A. Banks (Eds.), *Multicultural education: Issues and perspectives* (pp. 289-304). Boston: Allyn and Bacon.

Merton, R. K. (1968). *Social theory and social structure.* New York: The Free Press.

Miel, A., with Kiester, E., Jr. (1967). *The short-changed children of suburbia: What schools don't teach about human differences and what can be done about it.* New York: The American Jewish Committee.

Milner, D. (1983). *Children and race.* Beverly Hills, CA: Sage.

Minard, R. D. (1931). *Race attitudes of Iowa children.* Iowa City: University of Iowa.

Morland, J. K. (1966). A comparison of race awareness in northern and southern children. *American Journal of Orthopsychiatry, 36,* 22-31.

Myrdal, G., with the assistance of Sterner, R., & Rose, A. (1944). *An American dilemma: The Negro problem and modern democracy.* New York: Harper & Row.

National Council for the Accreditation of Teacher Education. (1977). *Standards for the accreditation of teacher education.* Washington, DC: Author.

National Council for the Accreditation of Teacher Education. (1987). *NCATE standards, procedures, and policies for the accreditation of professional education units.* Washington, DC: Author.

National Council for the Social Studies Task Force on Ethnic Studies. (1992). Curriculum guidelines for multicultural education. *Social Education, 56,* 274–294.

National Council of Teachers of English. (1974). *Students' right to their own language.* Urbana, IL: Author.

Natriello, G., McDill, E. L., & Pallas, A. M. (1990). *Schooling disadvantaged children: Racing against catastrophe.* New York: Teachers College Press.

Nieto, S. (1986). Excellence and equity. The case for bilingual education. *Bulletin of the Council on Interracial Books for Children, 17,* 3–4.

Nieto, S. (1992). *Affirming diversity. The sociopolitical context of multicultural education.* New York: Longman.

Novak, M. (1971). *The rise of the unmeltable ethnics.* New York: Macmillan.

Oakes, J. (1985). *Keeping track: How schools structure inequality.* New Haven, CT: Yale University Press.

Ogbu, J. U. (1974). *The next generation: An ethnography of education in an urban neighborhood.* New York: Academic Press.

Ogbu, J. U. (1990). Overcoming racial barriers to equal access. In J. I. Goodlad & P. Keating (Eds.). *Access to knowledge: An agenda for our nation's schools* (pp. 59–89). New York: The College Board.

Ovando, J., & Collier, V. P. (1985). *Bilingual and ESL classrooms: Teaching in multicultural contexts.* New York: McGraw-Hill.

Parekh, B. (1986). The concept of multicultural education. In S. Modgil, G. Verma, K. Mallick, & C. Modgil (Eds.), *Multicultural education: The interminable debate* (pp. 19–31). Philadelphia: The Falmer Press.

Parish, T. S., & Fleetwood, R. S. (1975). Amount of conditioning and subsequent change in racial attitudes of children. *Perceptual and Motor Skills, 43,* 907–912.

Parish, T. S., Shirazi, A., & Lambert, F. (1976). Conditioning away prejudicial attitudes in children. *Perceptual and Motor Skills, 43,* 907–912.

Passow, A. H. (Ed.). (1963). *Education in depressed areas.* New York: Teachers College Press.

Peters, W. (1987). *A class divided: Then and now* (Expanded ed.). New Haven, CT: Yale University Press.

Philips, S. U. (1983). *The invisible culture: Communication in classroom and community on the Warm Springs Indian reservation.* New York: Longman.

Phillips, U. B. (1918). *American Negro slavery.* New York: D. Appleton & Company.

Phinney, J. S., & Rotheram, M. J. (Eds.). (1987). *Children's ethnic socialization: Pluralism and development.* Beverly Hills, CA: Sage.

Porter, J. D. R. (1971). *Black child, White child: The development of racial attitudes.* Cambridge, MA: Harvard University Press.

Purkey, S. C., & Smith, M. S. (1982). Too soon to cheer? Synthesis of research on effective schools. *Educational Leadership, 40,* 64–69.

Quarles, B. (1953). *The Negro in the Civil War.* New York: Da Capo Press.

Radke, M. J., & Trager, H. G. (1950). Children's perceptions of the social roles of Negroes and Whites. *Journal of Psychology, 29,* 3–33.

Ramírez, M., & Castañeda, A. (1974). *Cultural democracy, bicognitive development, and education.* New York: Academic Press.

Ramsey, P. G. (1987). Young children's thinking about ethnic differences. In J. S. Phinney & M. J. Rotheram (Eds.), *Children's ethnic socialization: Pluralism and development* (pp. 56–72). Beverly Hills, CA: Sage.

Ravitch, D. (1990). Diversity and democracy: Multicultural education in America. *American Educator, 14,* 16–48.

Richardson, V., Casanova, U., Placier, P., & Guilfoyle, K. (1989). *School children at risk.* New York: The Falmer Press.

Riessman, F. (1962). *The culturally deprived child.* New York: Harper & Row.

Robinson, A. L., Foster, C. C., & Ogilvie, D. H. (Eds.). (1969). *Black studies in the university.* New York: Bantam.

Rodriguez, R. (1982). *Hunger of memory: The education of Richard Rodriguez: An autobiography.* Boston: David R. Godine.

Rutter, M., Maughan, B., Mortimore, P., Ouston, I., & Smith, A. (1979). *Fifteen thousand hours: Secondary schools and their effects on children.* Cambridge, MA: Harvard University Press.

Ryan, W. (1971). *Blaming the victim.* New York: Vintage.

Sadker, M. P., & Sadker, D. M. (1982). *Sex equity handbook for schools.* New York: Longman.

Schlesinger, A., Jr. (1990, Summer). When ethnic studies are un-American. *Social Studies Review: A Bulletin of the American Textbook Council,* pp. 11-13.

Schlesinger, A., Jr. (1991). *The disuniting of America: Reflections on a multicultural society.* Knoxville, TN: Whittle Direct Books.

Shade, B. J. (1982). Afro-American cognitive style: A variable in school success? *Review of Educational Research, 52,* 219-244.

Shade, B. J. (Ed.). (1989). *Culture, style and the educative process.* Springfield, IL: Charles C. Thomas.

Shirley, O. L. B. (1988). *The impact of multicultural education on self-concept, racial attitude and student achievement of Black and White fifth and sixth graders.* Unpublished doctoral dissertation, University of Mississippi, University, MS.

Sizemore, B. A. (1972). Social science and education for a Black identity. In J. A. Banks & J. D. Grambs (Eds.), *Black self-concept: Implications for education and social science* (pp. 141-170). New York: McGraw-Hill.

Slaughter, D. T. (Ed.). (1988). *Black children and poverty: A developmental perspective.* San Francisco: Jossey-Bass.

Slavin, R. E. (1979). Effects of biracial learning teams on cross-racial friendships. *Journal of Educational Psychology, 71,* 381-387.

Slavin, R. E. (1985). Cooperative learning: Applying contact theory in desegregated schools. *Journal of Social Issues, 41,* 45-62.

Slavin, R. E., Karweit, N. L., & Madden, N. A. (1989). *Effective programs for students at risk.* Boston: Allyn and Bacon.

Sleeter, C. E. (Ed.). (1991). *Empowerment through multicultural education.* Albany: State University of New York Press.

Sleeter, C. E., & Grant, C. A. (1987). An analysis of multicultural education in the United States. *Harvard Educational Review, 7,* 421-444.

Sleeter, C. E., & Grant, C. A. (1988). *Making choices for multicultural education: Five approaches to race, class and gender.* Columbus, OH: Merrill.

Sleeter, C. E., & Grant, C. A. (1991). Race, class, gender, and disability in current textbooks. In M. W. Apple & L. K. Christian-Smith (Eds.), *The politics of the textbook* (pp. 78-110). New York: Routledge.

Smitherman, G. (1977). *Talking and testifying: The language of Black America.* Boston: Houghton Mifflin.

Sowell, T. (1984). *Civil rights: Rhetoric or reality?* New York: William Morrow.

Spencer, M. B. (1982). Personal and group identity of Black children: An alternative synthesis: *Genetic Psychology Monographs, 106,* 59-84.

Spencer, M. B. (1985). Cultural cognition and social cognition as identity correlates of Black children's personal-social development. In M. B. Spencer, G. K. Brookins, & W. R. Allen (Eds.), *Beginnings: The social and affective development of Black children* (pp. 215-234). Hillsdale, NJ: Erlbaum.

Spencer, M. B. (1987). Black children's ethnic identity formation: Risk and resilience of caste-like minorities. In J. S. Phinney & M. J. Rotheram (Eds.), *Children's ethnic socialization: Pluralism and development* (pp. 103-116). Beverly Hills, CA: Sage.

Stampp, K. M. (1956). *The peculiar institution: Slavery in the antebellum South.* New York: Vintage.

Steele, S. (1990). *The content of our character: A new vision of race in America.* New York: St. Martin's Press.

Sue, D. W. (Ed.). (1981). *Counseling the culturally different: Theory and practice.* New York: Wiley.

Sung, B. L. (1967). *The story of the Chinese in America.* New York: Macmillan.

Suzuki, B. H. (1984). Curriculum transformation for multicultural education. *Education and Urban Society, 16,* 294-322.

Taba, H. (1950). *With a focus on human relations: A story of the eighth grade.* Washington, DC: American Council on Education.

Taba, H. (1951). *Diagnosing human relations needs.* Washington, DC: American Council on Education.

Taba, H. (1952). *Curriculum in intergroup relations: Case studies in instruction.* Washington, DC: American Council on Education.

Taba, H. (1967). *Teacher's handbook for elementary social studies.* Palo Alto, CA: Addison-Wesley.

Taba, H., Brady, E. H., & Robinson, J. T. (1952). *Intergroup education in public schools.* Washington, DC: American Council on Education.

Taba, H., & Elkins, D. (1966). *Teaching strategies for the culturally disadvantaged.* Chicago: Rand McNally.

Taba, H., & Van Til, W. (Eds.). (1945). *Democratic human relations* (16th yearbook). Washington, DC: National Council for the Social Studies.

Taba, H., & Wilson, H. (1946). Intergroup education through the school curriculum. *Annals of the American Academy of Political and Social Science, 244,* 19-25.

Tetreault, M. K. (1993). Classrooms for diversity: Rethinking curriculum and pedagogy. In J. A. Banks & C. A. M. Banks (Eds.), *Multicultural education: Issues and perspectives* (2nd ed., pp. 129-148). Boston: Allyn and Bacon.

Theodorson, G. A., & Theodorson, A. G. (1969). *A modern dictionary of sociology.* New York: Barnes & Noble.

Trager, H. G., & Yarrow, M. R. (1952). *They learn what they live: Prejudice in young children.* New York: Harper & Brothers.

Turner, F. J. (1989). The significance of the frontier in American history. In C. A. Milner II (Ed.), *Major problems in the history of the American West* (pp. 2-34). Lexington, MA: D. C. Heath. (Original work published 1894)

Van Sertima, I. (Ed.). (1988). *Great Black leaders: Ancient and modern.* New Brunswick, NJ: Rutgers University, Africana Studies Department.

Vickery, W. E., & Cole, S. G. (1943). *Intercultural education in American schools: Proposed objectives and methods.* New York: Harper & Brothers.

Wesley, C. H. (1935). *Richard Allen: Apostle of freedom.* Washington, DC: The Associated Publishers.

White, A. O. (1973). The Black leadership class and education in antebellum Boston. *Journal of Negro Education, 42,* 505-515.

Williams, F. (Ed.). (1970). *Language and poverty: Perspectives on a theme.* Chicago: Markham Publishing Company.

Williams, G. W. (1882-1883). *History of the Negro race in America from 1619 to 1880: Negroes as slaves, as soldiers, and as citizens* (2 vols.). New York: G. P. Putnam's Sons.

Williams, J. E., Best, D. L., Wood, F. B., & Filler, I. W. (1973). Changes in the connotations of racial concepts and color names: 1963-1970. *Psychological Reports, 33,* 983-996.

Williams, J. E., & Edwards, C. D. (1969). An exploratory study of the modification of color and racial concept attitudes in preschool children. *Child Development, 40,* 737-750.

Williams, J. E., & Morland, J. K. (1976). *Race, color, and the young child.* Chapel Hill: University of North Carolina Press.

Wilson, W. J. (1987). *The truly disadvantaged: The inner city, the underclass, and public policy.* Chicago: University of Chicago Press.

Wirth, L. (1928). *The ghetto.* Chicago: University of Chicago Press.

Woodson, C. G. (1933). *The mis-education of the Negro.* Washington, DC: The Associated Publishers.

Woodson, C. G. (1968). *The education of the Negro prior to 1861.* New York: Arno Press, (Original work published 1919)

Woodson, C. G., & Wesley, C. H. (1922). *The Negro in our history.* Washington, DC: The Associated Publishers.

Wortham, A. (1981). *The other side of racism: A philosophical study of Black race consciousness.* Columbus: Ohio State University Press.

Wyman, D. S. (1984). *The abandonment of the Jews: America and the Holocaust, 1941-1945.* New York: Pantheon.

Yawkey, T. D. (1973). Attitudes toward Black Americans held by rural and urban White early childhood subjects based upon multi-ethnic social studies materials. *Journal of Negro Education, 42,* 164-169.

Schools and the Struggle for Democracy: Themes for School Finance Policy

JAMES GORDON WARD

. . . U.S. schools are becoming more racially and culturally diverse. Another way of saying this is that the differences among children are increasing, raising issues of pedagogy, community building, and financing as well as issues relating to governance and political support. Many of these differences relate to different experiences prior to formal schooling. U.S. public schools will see more children whose home language is not English, more children who were not born or whose parents were not born in the United States, more children who were born and are growing up in poverty, and more children who have home lives that differ significantly from the traditional American dream. Many of these children will live and go to school in communities that are geographically and socially isolated from "middle-class America." Poverty and culturally diverse populations are not evenly spread across the landscape and tend to be concentrated in urban enclaves as well as in certain self-contained suburban and rural communities.

At the same time, economic and political power in the United States is more and more concentrated in an elite that has seceded from the rest of society in much of their daily lives (Reich, 1991). This elite is well educated, affluent, and not likely to live near those different from themselves. This elite uses private transportation to travel between a home in an urban high-rise building, trendy town house, or lush suburban community to a secure and opulent office building in the city center or suburban office park, rarely seeing the rest of the world along the way. Class and race have a lot to do with the cultural differences that exist in the United States, and these factors all have a major impact on education and school finance. The quality of schooling received and the amount of money spent on that schooling differ greatly depending on where one lives and in what social strata one's parents reside. This has provided an enduring dilemma for public school finance specialists and for public policymakers, and demographic changes are likely to worsen the situation. What is emerging is a situation where, more than ever before in the history of our nation, the acquisition of economic and political power is dependent on access to high-quality education. As a scarce resource, high-quality education is carefully allocated, and it is no accident that those who have economic and political power allocate it to their own children, either through private schools or excellent public schools, and the rest of society makes do with the leftovers. Demographic trends in the United States set the stage for a situation where economic and political power will be held by a maturing, affluent middle class who will tend to live in the suburbs, while the greatest educational needs will be among poor and often minority children in the inner city or in rural ghettoes. Will the former pay higher taxes to properly educate the latter?

Source: *"Schools and the Struggle for Democracy: Themes for School Finance Policy" by James G. Ward from* Who Pays for Student Diversity? Population Changes and Educational Policy, *edited by James G. Ward and Patricia Anthony. Copyright 1992 by American Education Finance Association. Reprinted by permission of Corwin Press, Inc.*

SCHOOLS AND DEMOCRACY

This question raises the question of what schools are likely to be like as organizations. Greenfield (1984, p. 145) has written that "organizations are manifestations of culture and we may understand them with only so much ease or difficulty as we can understand the culture in which they are embedded." Recent social and economic analysis has indicated that the rich are getting richer and the poor are getting poorer in the United States, and the implication is that two distinctly different cultures can be associated with the affluent and the needy in this country (Phillips, 1990; Reich, 1991). Reich (1991) argues that the affluent are part of a global culture, based on information and the ability to engage in symbolic analysis. Those performing routine production services or in-person services are less mobile, have fewer life opportunities, and earn much less money. This social analysis would suggest that these two different cultures will produce two different kinds of school organizations, which will in turn produce educational experiences that will vary greatly in nature and quality through the process of cultural reproduction (Bowles & Gintis, 1989).

The nature and quality of schooling not only are important for economic reasons, such as career preparation, but are politically important as well. The political aspects of education may have been stated best by Cremin (1990, p. 85) when he wrote that "education has always served political functions insofar as it affects, or at least is believed or intended to affect, the future character of the community and the state." Giroux and McLaren (1989, p. xxi) remind us that "American schooling becomes a vital sphere for extending civil rights, fighting for cultural justice, and developing new forms of democratic public life within a life-affirming public culture." These issues suggest the development of a community with common cultural values and argue for an approach to public schooling that prepares children for living through common experiences. Values form the basis for public policy decisions about schooling and for school finance policy decisions (Guthrie, Garms, & Pierce, 1988; Ward, 1987). It is funda-

mental to a democracy that public institutions will represent democratic values. Gutman (1987, p. 14) argues that

> a democratic theory of education recognizes the importance of empowering citizens to make educational policy and also of constraining their choices among policies in accordance with these principles—of nonrepression and nondiscrimination—that preserve the intellectual and social foundations of democratic deliberations.

The issue of nondiscrimination must be raised concerning the differing nature and quality of education among different schools and school districts. When different cultures produce different school organizations that support very different kinds of educational services, questions of discrimination arise because of the economic, social, and political consequences of those educational services. This is the essence of the issue of student equity in school finance. The question is not fundamentally one of finance, however, but one of governance and control. Gutman (1987, p. 16) goes on to say that "the central question posed by democratic education is: Who should have authority to shape the education of future citizens?"

THE CONTROL AND FINANCING OF SCHOOLS

The traditional view of public education in the United States is that it is the responsibility of the states but is delivered through local agencies under state supervision. Therefore the systems of governance and finance for U.S. public schools have been mixed state-local systems. This very fact has produced much discontent, because different individuals and groups have had different views on what the relative responsibilities of each party should be in differing circumstances. Much of this has had to do with differences in values and interests. This poses a dilemma, which has been described as follows:

> Education for citizenship and self-government . . . affirmatively obligates the state to provide all citizens with the quality and character of education

appropriate for participation in political and community affairs. The state must provide an education that conforms to the level of participation self-governing communities expect from the citizenry. (Hubsch, 1989, p. 99)

The precise nature of the dilemma concerns what constitutes a community for purposes of self-governing. The implication in much of the school governance and school finance literature is that the community is a local community, such as a city, town, or village and its hinterlands. This is embodied in the traditional idea of local control, which has had a long and healthy life in public education in the United States. While not predicting its demise, Alexander (1990) makes a powerful argument that local control is a powerful mechanism for fostering discrimination and perpetuating privilege in public schooling. What then might constitute the proper community?

In his classic work, Morrison (1930) argues that the state is the community. After careful and exhaustive analysis of the history and functions of the U.S. public school system, he concluded that

the several states themselves are the appropriate fiscal and administrative units in the support and conduct of the citizenship school which has long been held to be the cornerstone of our policy as a self-governing State. (Morrison, 1930, p. 214)

To the extent that the affluent and the less than affluent live in the same state, although not in the same local community, by regarding the self-governing community as the state, we can move toward removing some of the repression and discrimination that may now exist in public schooling. If the "quality and character" of education is determined at the state level, and that quality and character are assured for all children, then progress is being made. The critical issues become the definition of the quality and character of public education and the enforcement of that definition across school districts. Local community control, just as parental or family control, will undermine attempts to ensure a high level of quality and character for all children. Local communities will lose much of their ability to be enclaves for the protection of privilege or as places

to which the "successful have seceded" from the rest of society (Reich, 1991).

POLICY MECHANISMS FOR ATTAINING EQUALITY OF OPPORTUNITY

Following the early intellectual leadership of Cubberley (1905), school finance policymakers have used state equalization formulas as one mechanism for providing some standardization of education quality among communities. There is a broad literature in this area, and there is no need to examine it here. State equalization formulas, however, have generally failed to accomplish their purposes for two reasons: They are seldom funded at a high enough level by the state to be effective, and they continue to allow local communities discretion in setting local property tax rates for school purposes. The politics of privilege and exclusion prevent either of these from being changed. Affluent local school districts can support a high level of education without a great deal of assistance from the state. Any increase in state taxes to assure this level of education for all children in the state would produce a heavy tax burden on the residents of these affluent districts with the economic benefit flowing to other districts in the state. Affluent communities also want no restrictions on their tax levying ability because they fear that state controls may reduce their ability to maintain their position of privilege. In many states, the growing political power of suburban legislators, representing areas where most of the affluent districts are located, prevent any resolution of this problem.

Another policy mechanism that has been used to address this problem is petition to the courts for redress for alleged discrimination or failure to provide quality education. This approach has had varying popularity with particularly heavy periods of judicial activity in the early 1970s and since 1989 (Thro, 1990). While there is ample evidence that such legal suits have altered state school finance formulas in states where the plaintiffs have been successful in court, the evidence is much less clear on whether there have been any significant gains in overall funding levels as a result of school finance reform suits, and there is scant evidence that the quality and character of the education of children of the poor have been significantly improved (Salmon & Alexander, 1990; Ward, 1990).

Outside of the realm of school finance policy, a variety of policy interventions have been attempted to solve the problem through attempts at the alleviation of poverty, income distribution, and local community economic development. Williams (1989) has documented the extreme difficulties inherent in indigenous neighborhood organizing for urban school reform, while Wilson (1987) has analyzed the persistence of urban poverty and the difficulties of maintaining high-quality social institutions and services in the midst of urban decay. The problems of rural poverty and maintaining viable social institutions under conditions of rural decline have been well established by Davidson (1990). Finally, the classic work of Ogbu (1978) has discussed the issues of race and education and documented the caste-like rigidity of race-based barriers to educational and economic success. The politics of redistribution have also met with little success in alleviating urban poverty and the low quality of social services in declining urban areas (Peterson, 1981). These all call into question the effectiveness of various social policy interventions in moving our society toward quality education for all children.

What can be some avenues for freeing U.S. public schools from being antidemocratic instruments of social reproduction that support the perpetuation of privilege among our political and economic elite and fail to properly serve many of our children?

SOME THEMES FOR POLICY RESEARCH AND DEVELOPMENT

I do not propose that I have the answer to the question I just posed, but I do want to suggest some areas for the redirection of our current policy research and development activities in educa-

tion finance and governance that I think will move us toward answering the question.

The connections between educational outcomes and results and spending and governance patterns need additional exploration. The weak link in much of the educational research and in the factual base for school finance reform cases is the relationship among governance systems, expenditures per pupil, and educational outcomes. Traditional production function studies are limited methodologically and present few useful outcomes. Their error factors are too large to be of any explanatory value. Many of the school finance reform lawsuit complaints claim a direct relationship between spending per pupil and educational results, but upon careful scrutiny, they fail to prove the case. We need more studies that show the relationship between the way schools are organized and the way they are financed and the results they produce. Outcome variables are needed to make these studies useful; process variables are of much less value. If commentators like Reich and Phillips are correct, we should be able to discern the relationship between the dollars spent on education and the qualitative outcomes of that education.

We need to rethink the state's role in specifying educational outcomes and results for local schools. While states have constitutional responsibility for public education, they allow tremendous latitude in what they permit local school districts to do in the name of curriculum and instructional programs. As a result, the quality of education varies greatly across districts according to patterns described in this chapter. We need to give greater consideration to state standards and state expectations without constraining local districts in their ability to innovate and experiment. Accountability measures need to focus on outcomes and results rather than processes.

The federal role in education also needs reexamination. If some consistency of quality and character of education within states is important, then a similar degree of consistency among states is also a critical issue. The traditional federal role of funding programs for special needs students will require expansion. States do not have the fiscal resources, in many cases, to provide sufficient funding for programs for those with special needs. In a global economy, based on information and symbolic analysis, there is sufficient national interest in high-quality educational services for all children to justify a much larger federal role in education.

We need to rethink the program content and curriculum of our public schools. Some schools offer the kind of curriculum that allows students to succeed in an information-based society; many do not. One of the problems of local control is that the preferences of many communities do not include the quality and character of education that is needed for success in contemporary society. While parents have a responsibility to do what is best for their children, they should not have the right to intellectually handicap their children for life. In these instances, the responsibility of the state should take precedence over the rights of the parents. Local control is often a stalking-horse for educational mediocrity.

We need to institute systems of full-state funding and statewide school systems to protect the rights of all children. The current state-local system of public schools fails many children. Only a system where the state assumes responsibility for the quality and character of education for all children will ensure equal educational opportunities. It has been known for more than 60 years that current systems of school finance and school governance are inadequate to the task, but we are not willing to change. Until we are willing to do so, little if any progress will be made.

We need to engage in a public dialogue about why all these innovations are necessary. We cannot underestimate the power of public discourse in convincing the citizens of our states that major systemic changes need to take place to ensure the equal educational opportunity for all children for the future of our society. Public conversations can be a powerful device to arrive at social consensus.

All of these ideas require additional research and development work. They should help set the research agenda for school finance specialists for the next decade or so. We have a moral imperative to make sure that they do.

REFERENCES

Alexander, K. (1990). Equitable financing, local control, and self-interest. In J. K. Underwood & D. A. Verstegen (Eds.), *The impacts of litigation and legislation on public school finance: Adequacy, equity, and excellence* (pp. 293–309). New York: Harper & Row.

Bowles, S., & Gintis, H. (1989). Can there be a liberal philosophy of education in a democratic society? In H. A. Giroux & P. McLaren (Eds.), *Critical pedagogy, the state, and cultural struggle* (pp. 24–31). Albany: State University of New York Press.

Cremin, L. A. (1990). *Popular education and its discontents.* New York: Harper & Row.

Cubberley, E. P. (1905). *School funds and their apportionment.* New York: Columbia University, Teachers College.

Davidson, O. G. (1990). *Broken heartland: The rise of America's rural ghetto.* New York: Free Press.

Giroux, H. A., & McLaren, P. (1989). Introduction: Schooling, cultural politics, and the struggle for democracy. In H. A. Giroux & P. McLaren (Eds.), *Critical pedagogy, the state, and cultural struggle* (pp. xi–xxxv). Albany: State University of New York Press.

Greenfield, T. B. (1984). Leaders and schools: Willfulness and nonnatural order in organizations. In T. J. Sergiovanni & J. E. Corbally (Eds.), *Leadership and organizational culture* (pp. 142–169). Urbana: University of Illinois Press.

Guthrie, J. W., Garms, W. I., & Pierce, L. C. (1988). *School finance and education policy: Financing educational efficiency, equality, and choice.* Englewood Cliffs, NJ: Prentice-Hall.

Gutman, A. (1987). *Democratic education.* Princeton, NJ: Princeton University Press.

Hubsch, A. W. (1989). Education and self-government: The right to education under state constitutional law. *Journal of Law and Education, 18,* 93–140.

Morrison, H. C. (1930). *School revenue.* Chicago: University of Chicago Press.

Ogbu, J. U. (1978). *Minority education and caste: The American system in cross-cultural perspective.* New York: Academic Press.

Peterson, P. E. (1981). *City limits.* Chicago: University of Chicago Press.

Phillips, K. (1990). *The politics of rich and poor.* New York: Random House.

Reich, R. B. (1991). *The work of nations: Preparing ourselves for 21st-century capitalism.* New York: Knopf.

Salmon, R. G., & Alexander, M. D. (1990). State legislative responses. In J. K. Underwood & D. A. Verstegen (Eds.), *The impacts of litigation and legislation on public school finance: Adequacy, equity, and excellence* (pp. 249–271). New York: Harper & Row.

Thro, W. F. (1990). The third wave: The impact of the Montana, Kentucky, and Texas decisions on the future of public school finance reform litigation. *Journal of Law and Education, 19,* 219–250.

Ward, J. G. (1987). An inquiry into the normative foundations of American public school finance. *Journal of Education Finance, 12,* 463–477.

Ward, J. G. (1990). Implementation and monitoring of judicial mandates: An interpretive analysis. In J. K. Underwood & D. A. Verstegen (Eds.), *The impacts of litigation and legislation on public school finance: Adequacy, equity, and excellence* (pp. 225–248). New York: Harper & Row.

Williams, M. R. (1989). *Neighborhood organizing for urban school reform.* New York: Teachers College Press.

Wilson, W. J. (1987). *The truly disadvantaged: The inner city, the underclass, and public policy.* Chicago: University of Chicago Press.

STUDY QUESTIONS FOR PART 6

1. Does equal access to education produce equal results for students? Why?

2. Have changes in the law produced "real" changes in opportunities for those who have historically not been advantaged by education (ethnic minorities, poor people, women, linguistic minorities, and the physically challenged)? Explain your reasoning.

3. What are some of the reasons to adopt a multicultural perspective in your teaching? What does this mean?

4. Within your academic specialty (literature, mathematics, science, music, etc.) can you talk about five famous women and five famous ethnic minorities who have contributed to your discipline? If this is hard, why is that? What can you do in the classroom to be more inclusive of diversity within the curriculum?

5. If laws, rules, and policies are not making sufficient positive changes in the lives of students, what needs to be done to make improvements? How can individual teachers help?

6. Some argue that multicultural education will fragment and Balkanize our society. What is the gist of this argument and how would a teacher supportive of multicultural education respond to those charges?

7. Who deserves to receive schooling in our society? Why?

8. What knowledge (whose?), skills, values, etc. should be taught in public schools? What are your reasons?

9. Cooperative learning strategies are effective and appropriate within certain parameters. What is cheating?

10. Some would argue that the U.S. mind is being systematically closed to the heritage of the United States; that some groups are being systematically disparaged while others are being applauded. Whose legends and stories should be remembered and celebrated in schools?

11. What might be some reasons to fund education for the children of undocumented immigrants?

TRANSFORMATIONAL
EDUCATORS

The readings in the first six parts of this book provide a frame of reference for help-ing both the novice and the experienced teacher understand the milieu within which teaching occurs and how various elements of the system interact and influence the work of teaching in complex and multiple ways. The next set of readings offer ex-amples of the ways in which teachers themselves come to grips with these realities in positive and transformative ways.

The phrase *transformational educators* reflects a major challenge facing our na-tion's educators in the twenty-first century. Needed changes in public schools will not happen merely with the passage of time. Change requires deliberate and thought-ful effort and a strong commitment to stay the course. The selections chosen to con-clude this book reflect the hope that resides in the accomplishments of every good teacher—that children develop as a result of their schooling experience the knowl-edge, skills, attributes, and attitudes needed to make their way successfully in the world and to contribute fully as responsible citizens and adults to their families and communities. Transformational teachers facilitate such progress through helping children broaden their horizons and aspirations and by being genuinely responsive to their full range of needs as students. Transformational educators are reflective and re-sponsive—cognizant not only of the implications their students' backgrounds hold for them as teachers but attuned as well to the world for which the children in their charge must be prepared.

Educators who bring about positive change and empower their students aren't all approaching their teaching and learning in the same way. There is no single magi-cal template for success as a teacher. Social context, teacher personality, knowledge, experience, and student characteristics are just a few among the many variables that play a role in determining how one teaches and what students learn. Passion and a penchant for activism, in their teaching and in other facets of their lives as well, are qualities that distinguish many transformative educators. They not only strive to be responsive to their students but work as well for social justice beyond their class-rooms. In many ways, such teachers model for their students, through their activism, their visions of what responsible adulthood and citizenship might mean. Examples of such activism is represented in the efforts of teachers, administrators, and students speaking out and writing to their local newspapers to oppose ending the funding for bilingual education or affirmative action legislation.

The selection by Bigelow offers a good example of what is possible as a transformative educator. Although the efforts Bigelow describes do not always work out exactly as anticipated or perhaps as desired, Bigelow and his colleague Linda Christensen put into practice their vision of what it means to be a critical and transformative educator. In constructing the classroom and the curriculum experienced by their students, Bigelow and Christensen give careful consideration not only to what "facts" to offer up to students for their consideration and reflection but concern themselves as well with being responsive in their teaching to the social class backgrounds and experiences of their students. An important aspect of their vision of themselves as teachers is that through their teaching they are able to engage their students in a transformative dialogue—one that empowers students to view and experience their worlds in new ways and to understand that it *is* within the students' capability to act on their world and to change it.

Rose, in his vignettes of transformational educators working in many different school and community contexts, offers vivid examples of teaching that makes a difference! Whether it is in the inner city of Los Angeles or Baltimore, the practically abandoned coal-mining town of Wheelwright, Kentucky, or rural and isolated Polaris, Montana, teachers are finding powerful ways to connect with children and to make their experience in schools truly transformative. This does not happen by accident. It occurs as a result of teacher planning that considers the child, the classroom as a social group, and the specific knowledge and skills to be learned as well as the broader values and attitudes being developed through the school's curriculum. What Rose's observations capture is an essential fact of transformative teaching—there are many ways to succeed in helping children grow and develop—and what works depends in large measure on a teacher's motivation and ability to be *responsive* to the needs and the potential of the children in their charge. Again, this is not an accident—nor does it happen when teachers treat all children as if they were the same. The teachers described by Rose are inspiring and a tribute to what is possible in public education.

Finally, what are the basics of culturally relevant teaching? What does it look like? Throughout this book are many references to examples of teaching practices that do not serve the culturally different child well, be it a difference of culture related to ethnicity, race, religion, language, sexuality, or social class. Gloria Ladson-Billings offers useful guidance to those who aspire to teach in a manner that is transformative—who empower students through their teaching, and who see teaching as an art and themselves as artists (Ladson-Billings, 1994, p. 42). As she takes us on a journey through the classrooms she visited, we gain a rich awareness of what teachers can do (or fail to do) to teach in a culturally relevant way. Why is this important? Culturally responsive teaching is a way to assist students to realize their true potential, to help them gain the attitudes needed to live in a culturally diverse society, and to more fully develop through their schooling experience the attitudes, skills, and dispositions they will need to lead successful and fulfilling lives as adults contributing to their communities and families. Ladson-Billings offers specific strategies to teachers aspiring to teach in transformative and culturally relevant ways.

INSIDE THE CLASSROOM: SOCIAL VISION AND CRITICAL PEDAGOGY

WILLIAM BIGELOW

Bigelow, a secondary school teacher in Portland, Oregon, believes that public schooling in the United States serves social and economic class interests very unequally, and that one justifiable response for the educator is to help equip students to understand and critique the society in which they live. This article portrays students and teachers engaging in the kind of structured dialogue that Bigelow says is essential to the critical pedagogy he employs.

There is a quotation from Paulo Freire that I like; he writes that teachers should attempt to "live part of their dreams within their educational space."[1] The implication is that teaching should be partisan. I agree. As a teacher I want to be an agent of transformation, with my classroom as a center of equality and democracy—an ongoing, if small, critique of the repressive social relations of the larger society. That does not mean holding a plebiscite on every homework assignment, or pretending I do not have any expertise, but I hope my classroom can become part of a protracted argument for the viability of a critical and participatory democracy.

I think this vision of teaching flies in the face of what has been and continues to be the primary function of public schooling in the United States: to reproduce a class society, where the benefits and sufferings are shared incredibly unequally. As much as possible I refuse to play my part in that process. This is easier said than done. How *can* classroom teachers move decisively away from a model of teaching that merely reproduces and legitimates inequality? I think Freire is on the right track when he calls for a "dialogical education."[2] To me, this is not just a plea for more classroom conversation. In my construction, a dialogical classroom means inviting students to critique the larger society through sharing their lives. As a teacher I help students locate their experiences socially; I involve students in probing the social factors that make and limit who they are and I try to help them reflect on who they *could* be.

STUDENTS' LIVES AS CLASSROOM TEXT

In my Literature in U.S. History course, which I co-teach in Portland, Oregon, with Linda Christensen, we use historical concepts as points of departure to explore themes in students' lives and then, in turn, use students' lives to explore history and our society today. Earlier this year, for instance, we studied the Cherokee Indian Removal through role play. Students portrayed the Indians, plantation owners, bankers, and the Andrew Jackson administration and saw the forces

Source: *"Inside the Classroom: Social Visions and Critical Pedagogy" from* Foundational Studies in Teacher Education: A Reexamination, *by Steven Tozier, Thomas Anderson, and Bonnie Armbruster (Eds.) copyright 1990. Reprinted by permission of Teachers College Press, Columbia University.*

that combined to push the Cherokees west of the Mississippi against their will. Following a discussion of how and why this happened, Linda and I asked students to write about a time when they had their rights violated. We asked students to write from inside these experiences and to recapture how they felt and what, if anything, they did about the injustice.

Seated in a circle, students shared their stories with one another in a "read-around" format. (To fracture the student/teacher dichotomy a bit, Linda and I also complete each assignment and take our turns reading.) Before we began, we suggested they listen for what we call the "collective text"—the group portrait that emerges from the read-around.[3] Specifically, we asked them to take notes on the kinds of rights people felt they possessed; what action they took after having their rights violated; and whatever other generalizations they could draw from the collective text. Here are a few examples: Rachel wrote on wetting her pants because a teacher would not let her go to the bathroom; Christie, on a lecherous teacher at a middle school; Rebecca, on a teacher who enclosed her in a solitary confinement cell; Gina, who is black, on a theater worker not believing that her mother, who is white, actually was her mother; Maryanne, on being sexually harassed while walking to school and her subsequent mistreatment by the school administration when she reported the incident; Clayton, on the dean's treatment when Clayton wore an anarchy symbol on his jacket; Bobby, on convenience store clerks who watched him more closely because he is black. Those are fewer than a quarter of the stories we heard.

To help students study this social text more carefully, we asked them to review their notes from the read-around and write about their discoveries. We then spent over a class period interpreting our experiences. Almost half the instances of rights violations took place in school. Christy said, "I thought about the school thing. The real point [of school] is to learn one concept: to be trained and obedient. That's what high school is. A diploma says this person came every day, sat in their seat. It's like going to dog school." A number of people, myself included, expressed surprise that so many of the stories involved sexual harassment. To most of the students with experiences of harassment, it had always seemed a very private oppression, but hearing how common this kind of abuse is allowed the young women to feel a new connection among themselves—and they said so. A number of white students were surprised at the varieties of subtle racism black students experienced.

We talked about the character of students' resistance to rights violations. From the collective text we saw that most people did not resist at all. What little resistance occurred was individual; there was not a single instance of collective resistance. Christie complained to a counselor, Rebecca told her mother, many complained to friends. This provoked a discussion about what in their lives and, in particular, in the school system encouraged looking for individual solutions to problems that are shared collectively. They identified competition for grades and for positions in sought-after classes as factors. They also criticized the fake democracy of student government for discouraging activism. No one shared a single experience of schools' encouraging groups of students to confront injustice. Moreover, students also listed ways—from advertising messages to television sitcoms—through which people are conditioned by the larger society to think in terms of individual problems requiring individual solutions.

The stories students wrote were moving, sometimes poetic, and later opportunities to rewrite allowed us to help sharpen their writing skills, but we wanted to do more than just encourage students to stage a literary show-and-tell. Our larger objective was to find social meaning in individual experience—to push students to use their stories as windows not only on their lives, but on society.

There were other objectives. We hoped that through building a collective text, our students—particularly working-class and minority students—would discover that their lives are important sources of learning, no less important than the lives of the generals and presidents, the Rockefellers and Carnegies, who inhabit their textbooks. One function of the school curriculum is to celebrate the culture of the dominant and to ignore or scorn the culture of subordinate groups. The personal writing, collective texts, and discussion circles in Linda's and my classes are an attempt to challenge students not to accept these judgments. We wanted students to grasp that they can *create* knowledge, not simply absorb it from higher authorities.[4]

All of this sounds a little neater than what actually occurs in a classroom. Some students rebel at taking their own lives seriously. A student in one of my classes said to me recently, "Why do we have to do all this personal stuff? Can't you just give us a book of a worksheet and leave us alone?" Another student says regularly, "This isn't an English class, ya know." Part of this resistance may come from not wanting to resurface or expose painful experiences; part may come from not feeling capable as writers; but I think the biggest factor is that they simply do not feel that their lives have anything *important* to teach them. Their lives are just their lives. Abraham Lincoln and Hitler are important. Students have internalized self-contempt from years of official neglect and denigration of their culture. When for example, African-American or working-class history *is* taught it is generally as hero worship: extolling the accomplishments of a Martin Luther King, Jr., or a John L. Lewis, while ignoring the social movements that made their work possible. The message given is that great people make change, individual high school students do not. So it is not surprising that some students wonder what in the world they have to learn from each other's stories.

Apart from drawing on students' own lives as sources of knowledge and insight, an alternative curriculum also needs to focus on the struggle of oppressed groups for social justice. In my history classes, for example, we study Shay's Rebellion, the abolition movement, and alliances between blacks and poor whites during Reconstruction. In one lesson, students role-play Industrial Workers of the World organizers in the 1912 Lawrence, Massachusetts, textile strike as they try to overcome divisions between men and women and between workers speaking over a dozen different languages.

STUDYING THE HIDDEN CURRICULUM

In my experience as a teacher, whether students write about inequality, resistance, or collective work, school is *the* most prominent setting. Therefore, in our effort to have the curriculum respond to students' real concerns, we enlist them as social researchers, investigating their own school lives. My co-teacher and I began one unit by reading an excerpt from the novel *Radcliffe*, by David Storey.[5] In the selection, a young boy, Leonard Radcliffe, arrives at a predominately working-class British school. The teacher prods Leonard, who is from an aristocratic background, to become her reluctant know-it-all—the better to reveal to others their own ignorance. The explicit curriculum appears to concern urban geography: "Why are roofs pointed and not flat like in the Bible?" the teacher asks. She humiliates a working-class youth, Victor, by demanding that he stand and listen to her harangue: "Well, come on then, Victor. Let us all hear." As he stands mute and helpless, she chides: "Perhaps there's no reason for Victor to think at all. We already know where he's going to end up, don't we?" She points to the factory chimneys outside. "There are places waiting for him out there already." No one says a word. She finally calls on little Leonard to give the correct answer, which he does.

Students in our class readily see that these British schoolchildren are learning much more than why roofs are pointed. They are being drilled to accept their lot at the bottom of a hierarchy with a boss on top. The teacher's successful effort to humiliate Victor, while the others sit watching, undercuts any sense the students might have of their power to act in solidarity with one another. A peer is left hanging in the wind and they do nothing about it. The teacher's tacit alliance with Leonard and her abuse of Victor legitimate class inequalities outside the classroom.[6]

We use this excerpt and the follow-up discussion as a preparatory exercise for students to research the curriculum—both explicit and "hidden"[7]—at their own school (Jefferson High School). The student body is mostly African-

American and predominately working class. Linda and I assign students to observe their classes as if they were attending for the first time. We ask them to notice the design of the classroom, the teaching methodology, the class content, and the grading procedures. In their logs, we ask them to reflect on the character of thinking demanded and the classroom relationships: Does the teacher promote questioning and critique or obedience and conformity? What kind of knowledge and understandings are valued in the class? What relationships between students are encouraged?

In her log, Elan focused on sexism in the hidden curriculum:

> In both biology and government, I noticed that not only do boys get more complete explanations to questions, they get asked more questions by the teacher than girls do. In government, even though our teacher is a feminist, boys are asked to define a word or to list the different parts of the legislative branch more often than the girls are. . . . I sat in on an advanced sophomore English class that was doing research in the library. The teacher, a male, was teaching the boys how to find research on their topic, while he was finding the research himself for the girls. Now, I know chivalry isn't dead, but we are competent of finding a book.

Linda and I were pleased as we watched students begin to gain a critical distance from their own schooling experiences. Unfortunately, Elan did not speculate much on the social outcomes of the unequal treatment she encountered, or on what it is in society that produces this kind of teaching. She did offer the observation that "boys are given much more freedom in the classroom than girls, and therefore the boys are used to getting power before the girls."

Here is an excerpt from Connie's log:

> It always amazed me how teachers automatically assume that where you sit will determine your grade. It's funny how you can get an A in a class you don't even understand. As long as you follow the rules and play the game, you seem to get by. . . . On this particular day we happen to be taking a test on chapters 16 and 17. I've always liked classes such as algebra that you didn't have

to think. You're given the facts, shown how to do it, and you do it. No questions, no theories, it's the solid, correct way to do it.

We asked students to reflect on who in our society they thought benefited from the methods of education to which they were subjected. Connie wrote:

> I think that not only is it the teacher, but more importantly, it's the system. They purposely teach you using the "boring method." Just accept what they tell you, learn it and go on, no questions asked. It seems to me that the rich, powerful people benefit from it, because we don't want to think, we're kept ignorant, keeping them rich.

Connie's hunch that her classes benefit the rich and powerful is obviously incomplete, but it does put her on the road to understanding that the degrading character of her education is not simply accidental. She is positioned to explore the myriad ways schooling is shaped by the imperatives of a capitalist economy. Instead of being just more of the "boring method," as Connie puts it, this social and historical study would be a personal search for her, rooted in her desire to understand the nature of her *own* school experience.

In class, students struggled through a several-page excerpt from *Schooling in Capitalist America* by Samuel Bowles and Herbert Gintis. They read the Bowles and Gintis assertion that

> major aspects of educational organization replicate the relationships of dominance and subordinancy in the economic sphere. The correspondence between the social relation of schooling and work accounts for the ability of the educational system to produce an amenable and fragmented labor force. The experience of schooling, and not merely the content of formal learning, is central to this process.[8]

If they are right, we should expect to find different hidden curricula at schools enrolling students of different social classes. We wanted our students to test this notion for themselves.[9] A friend who teaches at a suburban high school south of Portland, serving a relatively wealthy community, enlisted volunteers in her classes to host our students for a day. My students logged comparisons of Jefferson and the elite school, which I will call Ridgewood. Trisa wrote:

> Now, we're both supposed to be publicly funded, equally funded, but not so. At Jefferson, the average class size is 20-25 students, at Ridgewood—15. Jefferson's cafeteria food is half-cooked, stale and processed. Ridgewood—fresh food, wide variety, and no mile-long lines to wait in. Students are allowed to eat anywhere in the building as well as outside, and wear hats and listen to walkmen [both rule violations at Jefferson].

About teachers' attitudes at Ridgewood, Trisa noted: "Someone said, 'We don't ask if you're going to college, but what college are you going to.'"

In general, I was disappointed that students' observations tended to be more on atmosphere than on classroom dynamics. Still, what they noticed seemed to confirm the fact that their own school, serving a black and working-class community, was a much more rule-governed, closely supervised environment. The experience added evidence to the Bowles and Gintis contention that my students were being trained to occupy lower positions in an occupational hierarchy.

Students were excited by this sociological detective work, but intuitively they were uneasy with the determinism of Bowles and Gintis's correspondence theory. It was not enough to discover that the relations of schooling mirrored the relations of work. They demanded to know exactly who designed a curriculum that taught them subservience. Was there a committee somewhere, sitting around plotting to keep them poor and passive? "We're always saying 'they' want us to do this, and 'they' want us to do that," one student said angrily. "Who is this 'they'?" Students wanted villains with faces and we were urging that they find systemic explanations.

Omar's anger exploded after one discussion. He picked up his desk and threw it against the wall, yelling: "How much more of this shit do I have to put up with?" "This shit" was his entire educational experience, and while the outburst was not directed at our class in particular—thank heavens—we understood our culpability in his frustration.

We had made two important and related errors in our teaching. Implicitly, our search had encouraged students to see themselves as victims—powerless little cogs in a machine daily reproducing the inequities of the larger society. Though the correspondence theory was an analytical framework with a greater power to interpret their school lives than any other they had encountered, ultimately it was a model suggesting endless oppression and hopelessness. If schooling is always responsive to the needs of capitalism, then what point did our search have? Our observations seemed merely to underscore students' powerlessness.

I think the major problem was that although our class did discuss resistance by students, it was anecdotal and unsystematic, thereby depriving students of the opportunity to question their own roles in maintaining the status quo. The effect of this omission, entirely unintentional on our part, was to deny students the chance to see schools as sites of struggle and social change—places where they could have a role in determining the character of their own education. Unwittingly, the realizations students were drawing from our study of schools fueled a world view rooted in cynicism; they might learn about the nature and causes for their subordination, but they could have no role in resisting it.

THE "ORGANIC GOODIE SIMULATION"

Still stinging from my own pedagogical carelessness, I have made efforts this year to draw students into a dialogue about the dynamics of power and resistance. One of the most effective means to carry on this dialogue is metaphorically, through role play and simulation.[10]

In one exercise, called the "Organic Goodie Simulation," I create a three-tiered society. Half the students are workers, half are unemployed,[11] and I am the third tier—the owner of a machine that produces organic goodies. I tell students that we will be in this classroom for the rest of our lives and that the machine produces the only sustenance. Workers can buy adequate goodies with their wages, but the unemployed will slowly starve to death on their meager dole of welfare-goodies. Everything proceeds smoothly until I begin to drive wages down by offering jobs to the unemployed at slightly less than what the workers earn. It is an auction, with jobs going to the lowest bidder. Eventually, all classes organize some kind of opposition, and usually try to take away my machine. One year, a group of students arrested me, took me to a jail in the corner of the room, put a squirt gun to my head, and threatened to "kill" me if I said another word. This year, before students took over the machine, I backed off, called a meeting to which only my workers were invited, raised their wages, and stressed to them how important it was that we stick together to resist the jealous unemployed people who wanted to drag all of us into the welfare hole they are in. Some workers defected to the unemployed, some vigorously defended my right to manage the machine, but most bought my plea that we had to talk it all out and reach unanimous agreement before any changes could be made. For an hour and a half they argued among themselves, egged on by me, without taking any effective action.

The simulation provided a common metaphor from which students could examine firsthand what we had not adequately addressed the previous year: To what extent are we complicit in our own oppression? Before we began our follow-up discussion, I asked students to write on who or what was to blame for the conflict and disruption of the previous day. In the discussion some students singled me out as the culprit. Stefani said, "I thought Bill was evil. I didn't know what he wanted." Rebecca concurred: "I don't agree with people who say Bill was not the root of the problem. Bill was management, and he made workers feel insecure that the unemployed were trying to take their jobs." Others agreed with Rebecca that it was a divisive structure that had been created, but saw how their own responses to that structure perpetuated the divisions and poverty. Christie said: "We were so divided that nothing got decided. It kept going back and forth. Our discour-

agement was the root of the problem." A number of people saw how their own attitudes kept them from acting decisively. Mira said: "I think that there was this large fear: We have to follow the law. And Sonia kept saying we weren't supposed to take over the machine. But if the law and property hurt people why should we go along with it?" Gina said: "I think Bill looked like the problem, but underneath it all was us. Look at when Bill hired unemployed and fired some workers. I was doin' it too. We can say it's a role play, but you have to look at how everything ended up feeling and learn something about ourselves, about how we handled it."

From our discussion students could see that their make-believe misery was indeed caused by the structure of the society: The number of jobs was held at an artificially low level, and workers and unemployed were pitted against each other for scarce goodies. As the owner I tried every trick I knew to drive wedges between workers and the unemployed, to encourage loyalty in my workers, and to promote uncertainty and bickering among the unemployed. However, by analyzing the experience, students could see that the system worked only because they let it work—they were much more than victims of my greed; they were my accomplices.

I should hasten to add—and emphasize—that it is not inherently empowering to understand one's own complicity in oppression. I think it is a start, because this understanding suggests that we can do something about it. A critical pedagogy, however, needs to do much more: It should highlight times, past and present, when people built alliances to challenge injustice. Students also need to encounter individuals and organizations active in working for a more egalitarian society, and students need to be encouraged to see themselves as capable of joining together with others, in and out of school, to make needed changes. I think that all of these are mandatory components of the curriculum. The danger of students' becoming terribly cynical as they come to understand the enormity of injustice in this society and in the world is just too great. They have to know that it is possible—

even joyous, if I dare say so—to work toward a more humane society.

TEACHERS AND TEACHER EDUCATORS AS POLITICAL AGENTS

At the outset I said that all teaching should be partisan. In fact, I think that all teaching *is* partisan. Whether or not we want to be, all teachers are political agents because we help shape students' understandings of the larger society. That is why it is so important for teachers to be clear about our social visions. Toward what kind of society are we aiming? Unless teachers answer this question with clarity we are reduced to performing as technicians, unwittingly participating in a political project but with no comprehension of its objectives or consequences. Hence teachers who claim "no politics" are inherently authoritarian because their pedagogical choices act on students, but students are denied a structured opportunity to critique or act on their teachers' choices. Nor are students equipped to reflect on the effectiveness of whatever resistance they may put up.

For a number of reasons, I do not think that our classrooms can ever be exact models of the kind of participatory democracy we would like to have characterize the larger society. If teachers' only power were to grade students, that would be sufficient to sabotage classroom democracy. However, as I have suggested, classrooms can offer students experiences and understandings that counter, and critique, the lack of democracy in the rest of their lives. In the character of student interactions the classroom can offer a glimpse of certain features of an egalitarian society. We can begin to encourage students to learn the analytic and strategic skills to help bring this new society into existence. As I indicated, by creating a collective text of student experience we can offer students practice in understanding personal problems in their social contexts. Instead of resorting to consumption, despair, or other forms of self-abuse, they can ask why these circumstances exist and what can they do about it. In

this limited arena, students can begin to become the subjects of their lives.

When Steve Tozer of the University of Illinois asked me to prepare this article, he said I should discuss the implications of my classroom practice for people in social foundations of education programs. First, I would urge you who are teacher educators to model the participatory and exploratory pedagogy that you hope your students will employ as classroom teachers. Teachers-to-be should interrogate their own educational experiences as a basis for understanding the relationship between school and society. They need to be members of a dialogical community in which they can experience themselves as subjects and can learn the validity of critical pedagogy by doing it. If the primary aim of social foundations of education coursework is to equip teachers-to-be to understand and critically evaluate the origins of school content and processes in social context, then the foundations classroom should be a place for students to discuss how their own experiences as students are grounded in the larger society, with its assumptions, its inequities, its limits and possibilities.

As you know, a teacher's first job in a public school can be frightening. That fear mixed with the conservative pressures of the institution can overwhelm the liberatory inclinations of a new teacher. Having *experienced,* and not merely having read about, an alternative pedagogy can help new teachers preserve their democratic ideals. Part of this, I think, means inviting your students to join you in critiquing *your* pedagogy. You need to be a model of rigorous self-evaluation.

The kind of teaching I have been describing is demanding. The beginning teacher may be tempted to respond, "Sure, sure, I'll try all that when I've been in the classroom five or six years and when I've got a file cabinet full of lessons." I think you should encourage new teachers to overcome their isolation by linking up with colleagues to reflect on teaching problems and to share pedagogical aims and successes. I participated in a support group like this my first year as a teacher and our meetings helped maintain my courage and morale. After a long hiatus, two years ago I joined another group that meets bi-weekly to talk about everything from educational theory to confrontations with administrators to union organizing.[12] In groups such as this your students can come to see themselves as creators and evaluators of curriculum and not simply as executors of corporate- or administrative-packaged lesson plans.

It is also in groups like this that teachers can come to see themselves as activists in a broader struggle for social justice. The fact is that education will not be *the* engine of social change. No matter how successful we are as critical teachers in the classroom, our students' ability to use and extend the analytic skills they have acquired depends on the character of the society that confronts them. Until the economic system requires workers who are critical, cooperative, and deeply democratic, teachers' classroom efforts amount to a kind of low-intensity pedagogical war. Unfortunately it is easy to cut ourselves off from outside movements for social change—and this is especially true for new teachers. As critical teachers, however, we depend on these movements to provide our students with living proof that fundamental change is both possible and desirable. It seems to me you cannot emphasize too strongly how teachers' attempts to teach humane and democratic values in the classroom should not be isolated from the social context in which schooling occurs.

In closing, let me return to Freire's encouragement that we live part of our dreams within our educational space. Teachers-to-be should not be ashamed or frightened of taking sides in favor of democracy and social justice. I hope *your* students learn to speak to *their* students in the language of possibility and hope and not of conformity and "realism." In sum, your students ought to learn that teaching is, in the best sense of the term, a subversive activity—and to be proud of it.

NOTES

1. Paulo Freire and Donaldo Macedo, *Literacy: Reading the Word and the World* (South Hadley, Mass.: Bergin and Garvey, 1987), p. 127.

2. See especially Ira Shor and Paulo Freire, *A Pedagogy for Liberation* (South Hadley, Mass.: Bergin and Garvey, 1983.)

3. See Linda Christensen, "Writing the Word and the World," *English Journal* 78, no. 2 (February 1989): 14–18.

4. See William Bigelow and Norman Diamond, *The Power in Our Hands: A Curriculum on the History of Work and Workers in the United States* (New York: Monthly Review Press, 1988), pp. 15–23.

5. David Storey, *Radcliffe* (New York: Avon, 1963), pp. 9–12. I am grateful to Doug Sherman for alerting me to this excerpt.

6. While most students are critical of the teacher, they should always be allowed an independent judgment. Recently, a boy in one of my classes who is severely hard of hearing defended the teacher's actions. He argued that because the students laughed at Leonard when he first entered the class they deserved whatever humiliation the teacher could dish out. He said the offending students ought to be taught not to make fun of people who are different.

7. See Henry Giroux, *Theory and Resistance in Education: A Pedagogy for the Opposition* (South Hadley, Mass.: Bergin and Garvey, 1983). See especially Chapter 2, "Schooling and the Politics of the Hidden Curriculum," pp. 42–71. Giroux defines the hidden curriculum as "those unstated norms, values, and beliefs embedded in and transmitted to students through the underlying rules that structure the routines and social relationships in school and classroom life" and points out that the objective of critical theory is not merely to describe aspects of the hidden curriculum, but to analyze how it "functions to provide differential forms of schooling to different classes of students" (p. 47).

8. Samuel Bowles and Herbert Gintis, *Schooling in Capitalist America* (New York: Basic Books, 1976), p. 125.

9. See Jean Anyon, "Social Class and the Hidden Curriculum of Work," *Journal of Education* 162 (Winter 1980): 67–92, for a more systematic comparison of hidden curricula in schools serving students of different social classes.

10. There is an implication in many of the theoretical discussions defining critical pedagogy that the proper role of the teacher is to initiate group reflec-

tion on students' outside-of-class experiences. Critics consistently neglect to suggest that the teacher can also be an initiator of powerful in-class experiences, which can then serve as objects of student analysis.

11. Bigelow and Diamond, *The Power in Our Hands,* pp. 27-30 and pp. 92-94. See also Mike Messner, "Bubblegum and Surplus Value," *The Insurgent Sociologist* 6, no. 4 (Summer 1976): 51-56.

12. My study group gave valuable feedback on this article. Thanks to Linda Christensen, Jeff Edmundson, Tom McKenna, Karen Miller, Michele Miller, Doug Sherman, and Kent Spring.

POSSIBLE LIVES

MIKE ROSE

LOS ANGELES AND THE LA BASIN

It was three in the afternoon in Room 56, and Yvonne Divans Hutchinson had just kicked off her shoes and was stretching out, spent, releasing the day. She began reflecting on her long local history.

"I grew up here, over in the projects, and went to school in the neighborhood, went to this school, in fact. And I can remember some teachers saying awful things to us. I remember one in particular who told us that we should be glad he came to Watts, because no one wanted to teach here. We were always confronted with attitudes like that. Well, I took umbrage at that comment. I had wanted to be a teacher for as long as I could remember, and on that day, I decided that not only was I going to be a teacher, but I was going to teach at *this* school because we needed teachers who *believed* in us."

She was about eight when her parents moved to Los Angeles from Arkansas and settled in Exposition Park, an area close to the LA Coliseum. She remembers a rooming house, her sister and brother and her sleeping in one bed. And she remembers her mother's excitement when they were finally able to move into the projects called Imperial Courts: "We're going to have a house all our own!" That was in 1954. Yvonne remembers roller-skating around the neighborhood, over to the library on Grandee. She recalls walking to school along the tracks of the Red Car, playing in the courtyard of the Watts Towers, going to the Largo Theater for thirty-five cents. She entered Edwin Markham Junior High School when it opened and was in the first graduating class, in

1958. She returned to teach in 1966 and has been there ever since.

"I've been a mentor teacher and the department chair, and I've had teachers tell me, 'This class can't think; they can't do the work; I can't find anything they can do.' And I'm astounded. You can look at a child and see that brightness, that eagerness. People who come to the classroom with preconceived notions about the kids don't give them a chance. It angers me and saddens me."

Room 56 was brick and dry wall, painted light mustard, some water stains along the baseboards. A long sign over one of the blackboards read: NOTHING IS MORE IMPORTANT THAN YOUR EDUCATION. A life-sized cut-out of Bill Cosby on the back door said the same thing. A table in the back of the class was filled with autobiographies, stood upright on display: Ernesto Galarza's *Barrio Boy*, Dick Gregory's *Nigger*, *The Autobiography of Malcolm X*, Elie Wiesel's *Night*, Russell Baker's *Growing Up*. Along the chalk tray of the blackboard was a range of novels and stories, many of them autobiographical in content: Amy Tan's *The Kitchen God's Wife*, Maya Angelou's *I Know Why the Caged Bird Sings*, John Knowles's *A Separate Peace*, Sandra Cisnero's *The House on Mango Street*. One of the themes in the district guidelines for ninth grade is "understanding ourselves," and

Source: *"Los Angeles and the LA Basin (14-23); Baltimore, Maryland (112-116); Berea and Wheelwright, Kentucky (265-69); Polaris and Missoula, Montana (339-342)" from* Possible Lives: The Promise of Public Education in America *by Mike Rose copyright 1995. Reprinted by permission Houghton Mifflin Company.*

Yvonne had selected books that, for the most part, reflected the backgrounds of her students.

"I had a young Hispanic man tell me last year that he couldn't carry books because he was a homeboy—he didn't want to be a schoolboy. A lot of boys want to be cool, so they'll put their books in their lockers when they go to class. A lot of African-American boys will carry Pee-Chee folders because they can roll them up and put them in their coat pockets or jam them down the back of their pants. So I give notice on the first day of school that for my class you have to have a notebook that can't be folded up. A lot of our kids, the boys especially, identify with the streets; they want to be cool. They don't want to look like nerds. But I like to tell them [laughs], 'The nerds shall inherit the Earth!' [pause] It *is* serious, though. The whole idea of being identified as a tough guy yet also doing well in school is a real dilemma for young Black men—in this neighborhood especially. We have people who are scholarly types, and when they leave the school, they go to the projects and have to prove themselves. It's really difficult."

All around the classroom, student writing and student art was on display. To the right of Yvonne's desk was Mariah Legans's drawing of four very different women, sort of middle-school Cubist in style, colorful, striking: an oblong face, a full, round face, blue spiked hair, tight black hair, tiny eyes, big eyes, a smile, a frown, a nose ring. "We are all individuals," she had written under it. "We don't look alike, we don't dress the same way, but we are all humans living on the same earth. So we need to learn to get along and respect each other."

On the bulletin board by the door was a cluster of four-by-six index cards, arrayed against orange, yellow, and blue art paper. These were done in class, responses to the books the students were reading. Yvonne had asked them to select a passage that grabbed them, draw it as best they could in pencil or pen, and comment on it.

Yardenna Aaron rendered a moment from the early pages of Malcolm X's autobiography:

The scene depicted is when the police took Mrs. Little to the hospital to see and identify her dead husband. She was very hysterical. My drawing represents my idea and Malcolm's about her. The atmosphere when she entered the room containing the dead bodies. I think the policemen were laughing when she saw her husband. I believe that having no compassion in a case like this is a sin. The police were probably happy that he was killed because he was a strong man and taught Negroes about themselves.

Evonne Santiago had this to say about page 45 of *The House on Mango Street:*

This nun has made Esperanza embarrassed of where she lived. This reminds me of myself. I always hated where I lived (in New Jersey) because everyone in my Catholic school had beautiful houses and my house was in a bad neighborhood and had rats and roaches.

Alejandra Mendoza, who was still mastering written English, wrote about a scene in Elie Wiesel's *Night:*

My drawing represents the German throwing the kids up in the air and killing them with a machine gun. The reason the German killed them is because the kids are Jewish. It reminds me of LA because every day there's a kid dying by violence.

Yvonne continued. "Teachers will say either 'We can't lower our standards' or 'This poor child is reading below grade level, so I'll need a third- or fourth-grade book.' But what you need to do is find a way to make that eighth-grade book *accessible.* You have to respect the child . . . I used to give a speech to new teachers in which I began by enumerating all the adjectives used to describe our kids: *slow, poor, impoverished, deprived, oppressed.* We get so busy looking at children in terms of labels that we fail to look for the *potential*—and to demand that kids live up to that potential. I tell these teachers, 'Do not think that because a child cannot read a text, he cannot read *you.*' Children can tell right off those people who believe in them and those who patronize them. They can tell once they come into the room—as if there's a smell in the air—they can tell right away if this teacher means business or if this teacher is, as they say, *jive.* They rise to whatever expectations are set. They rise or fail to rise. And when they rise, they can sometimes rise to great heights."

And so it was in this room on that day that Michallene Hooper read a draft of a profile of her friend Jennifer:

"Nothing is more important than my education," declared Jennifer Rene McKnight, ninth-grader of Markham Intermediate School, who thinks very highly of her education. She plans on getting a scholarship for college and becoming a worker in the medical field. . . . This tall, slim, dark-skinned 14-year-old was born and raised in Los Angeles and has always been for helping her fellow Los Angelenos and influencing them to do the same. . . . Once while she was [stranded in the rain] a boy of her age with an umbrella offered to walk her home. "And after that," explained Jennifer, "I have never doubted the abilities of my neighbors. There's no telling what these good people are capable of or are going to do."

And it was in this room that the class held what Yvonne called a Quaker reading of Maya Angelou's inaugural poem, "On the Pulse of Morning." Each student selected some lines that spoke to him or her and read them, in sequence, into a tape recorder, creating a class reading, a new rendering:

Across the wall of the world,
A River sings a beautiful song. It says
Come, rest here by my side . . .

So say the Asian, the Hispanic, the Jew
The African, the Native American, the
   Sioux . . .

I, the Rock, I, the River, I, the Tree
I am yours—your passages have been paid.

And it was in this room that Evonne Santiago—the girl who, in reading *The House on Mango Street,* recalled her old house in New Jersey—it was Evonne who explained to the class what she thought Maya Angelou's poem meant:

She tells us our faults so we can see what to do with our country, she's telling us how to make it a better country . . .

The rock means strength. And the river—you know how a river goes through the land and

picks up different water, well, that's like different cultures. And the tree is America—that can grow big and strong . . .

She's asking all these people—the Asian, the Hispanic, the African American—she's asking them to come under the tree, to let their dream grow. And she writes it for the inauguration because the president, he has to lead the country, he has great influence. If we grow today, we will be strong tomorrow . . .

And all day long in the room, in every class—just as she did every day here in this room—Yvonne Divans Hutchinson demonstrated, encouraged, celebrated, and guided students through an active and critical reading process that undercut the common perception that reading simply involved the decoding of words, that print had single, basic meanings that students had to decipher quietly and store away. She had students write in a "Reading Journal" a dialogue between themselves and the author of whatever book they were currently reading, "agreeing, disagreeing, sympathizing, questioning—engaging the *ideas* in the pages." Before distributing an essay on courage, she asked her students to talk about a movie or television show in which people acted courageously, and from those examples try to explain what courage meant—all this to raise to critical consciousness their own definitions of courage. She had been involved in the development of a new statewide proficiency exam—one that encourages students to offer interpretations of texts—and she handed out a draft of the scoring guide and urged her students to analyze it. And Mariah Legans, whose Cubist plea for tolerance decorated the wall behind Yvonne's desk, said that "when they say *literal* they mean that you just write down what you got from the reading, but when they say *thoughtful* they mean you put some interpretation in it." And Michallene Hooper, the author of the personality profile, explained that when they ask for *implications,* they're referring to those times "when you read something, and it won't just come right out and say what it meant, but kind of suggests it." And from there the class began to discuss what it meant to read critically.

And in this room, at the end of the day, Rahsaan Thorpe took a moment to look at his paper that Yvonne had on yet another display, a response to a quotation about the value of interracial friendships. It began:

I recall from ages 8 to 12, I was in close relation to other races. I grew up in a house-apartment, and during my time living there many neighbors came and went. Until one Christmas Eve a family moved in next door to me. The next morning I looked outside and there was a [Salvadoran] boy sitting alone playing. I saw him and decided to make conversation, and ever since that day, we have been friends . . .

And from there, Rahsaan and the others went out to 104 Street or to Compton Avenue, some leaving for surrounding communities, some walking home, holding their words clean and tight.

Directly east of Watts, about four miles, across turf boundaries kids from Watts rarely used to cross, lies Bell, a city of 34,000, another of the blue-collar communities that had grown with the development of LA's once robust industry. I came the long way, driving south out of downtown, picking up the Long Beach Freeway, passing over expansive freight yards, dark factories, storage tanks, and tract houses. Huge power grids ran alongside the freeway; graffiti were on the railroad bridges and the exit signs; and, to the west, the dry LA River. I took the off ramp at Florence Avenue, headed west, passing over the river, and in a few minutes saw a small brick wall displaying the raised metal outline of a bell. Welcome to Bell. The smog was thick, the air still and hot. Bell High School sits in the middle of the southern residential edge of the city. I found a parking space under the full trees on Flora Avenue between two customized Toyotas— lowered, miniature mag wheels, many layers of maroon, lustrous. LA car culture. A tricked-out VW Beetle drove by, tinted windows, boom box throbbing, and took a sharp turn into a gated driveway. A kid ran from within the school yard and scrambled, hand over hand, up the chain links, half rolling, half vaulting over the top, leaping down to the pavement. He got into the VW, and it sped off.

Not too far inside that gate Ed Murphy and Larry Stone were teaching their classes in video production, using the old drama room that Ed, over the years, had converted into a studio. Both men were English teachers who have developed their expertise by trial and error. Ed started twenty-two years ago with Super-8 technology and, through donations, grants, and personal expense, has built a classy video production facility; Larry joined in about five years ago as the student demand for the courses continued to grow. Now the students' one-minute public service announcements (about smoking, drugs, rape, gangs) and their video essays (usually three- to four-minute arrangements of images set to popular or original music) regularly win local and state contests. Students enroll in the classes now because they hear so much about them in the school yard. Herbert Aparicio, a senior who has contributed original music to a number of videos, said this: "I started seeing these big changes in my friends. They were starting to get more responsible. These guys! A big change—real quick. I thought, 'What's the big deal here?' So I went to Mr. Murphy and said, 'Do you need help with music?' And he said, 'Yeah, sure.' And I said, 'Well, I'd love to try.'"

Central to Ed's success, and to Larry Stone's, is the fact that they have fostered a culture of achievement, one that includes both college-bound students and students who are sleepwalking through the rest of the curriculum. Ed begins each term with technical instruction—how to use the camera, basic shots, fundamentals of script writing—and uses as illustration videos from his growing library of student work. He then divides the class into groups and turns them loose to develop and execute their projects. From that point until the end of the term, most of his instruction takes place through individual and small group conferences. So, on any given day, you would find Ed up at his desk going over a script with a student while other students were coming in and out with video equipment, or working on scripts at the computer terminals, or surveying the video encyclopedia for just the right images, or whirring through footage at the editing machines. There would be a constant but shifting blend of voices—

English, Spanish, street talk, laughter—the beeps and tones of electronic equipment, scuffles behind the stage where scripts were being rehearsed, and music—Metallica, Doctor Dre, Chicano rapper Kid Frost—as students tried to synchronize images with a lyric and a beat.

Driving it all is a demand for quality and originality—generated by the collective student work, both past and present. So student projects get shown in "premieres" and are celebrated continually. During the first of my visits, Ed premiered two recently completed videos. In the first, a sixty-second instructional video, a soft-spoken, bespectacled boy named Frank had dubbed a lesson on amphibians onto a clip from a Teenage Mutant Ninja Turtles cartoon. To match the new dialogue with the cavorting turtles, Frank had worked and reworked his script, finding different ways to phrase things, running the tape over and over again—more than twenty times, Mr. Murphy said—to create the right fit between word and image. So when Raphael turns to Donatello, nose to nose, he asks "Did you know there are many kinds of amphibians?" And when the four muscle-bound mutants dive into water, they are asked by a fifth character if they found amphibians there. Finally, as the cartoon closes, the turtles turn to the screen and in farewell say, "So remember, dudes, when you think amphibious, think land and water."

The second video, a video essay, done by two girls in Larry Stone's class was entitled "Civil Wars" (after the Guns 'n' Roses song "Civil War"), and it took Melanie Alvarenga and Leonor Martinez two months to produce. A visitor from a public television station said it was one of the most professional pieces of student work he had ever seen. The video opened with the scene from *Cool Hand Luke* where Strother Martin knocks Paul Newman into a ditch and, looking down at him, says, "What we have here is failure to communicate." Then "Civil War" fades in and the screen delivers a series of images of battlefields, candlelight vigils, cross burnings, hooded Klansmen, mourners, demagogic speeches, the Vietnam War Memorial, hospital corridors lined with bodies, an autopsy—all paced to the urgent

rhythm of the song, the images moving in slow motion or staccato or real time, their shift each to the other enhanced by computer graphics: wipes and fades and a frame folding into a box and tumbling out of sight. The words Bosnia, El Salvador, Kuwait, Vietnam flash in red across the screen; at the end we freeze on If This Was Our Past; Let's Not Make It Our Future.

"It's really powerful," Helen Salcedo said as she walked over to an editing machine. "We don't get a chance in other classes to show our work like this. I like watching other people's stuff. You can make comparisons with what you're doing, and you can learn that way."

Leticia Lopez sat at another editing machine trying to tighten her video essay on rape. "I learned a lot about rape doing this," she explained. "Other students have done videos on rape, but I wanted to do one from a woman's perspective. I wanted it to be different. I didn't want to do a video that was violent; I think that's tasteless. I wanted to get my message across in a different way, so I have the camera follow this young lady through her day—there are no explicit scenes—and at the end the camera zooms in on a pamphlet about rape that's sitting on her coffee table. Would you like to see it?"

Ed had gone across the room to check on Jesse Barrios, who was leaning over a table, looking at a script, tapping his pencil, running his free hand through his orange hair; he wore a nose ring and an oversized jean jacket that smelled of tobacco. He was stuck. Using footage shot by another student, he was trying to create a documentary on a local artist. As he viewed the film, and then viewed it again, he became interested in the painter's involvement with her Mexican heritage. He wanted to do more with that, and was trying to figure out how he could use his film in this new thematic context. And how he could make it interesting. "I don't want it to be just a talking head. Maybe background music—something Latin—maybe fresh angles, maybe computer graphics . . . I don't know. I might have to go back and shoot again, but I'd like to see if I can do something with what I have." As one of seven children, Ed would later tell me,

Jesse had to work just about full-time, so he often had to do a lot with a little. "He never liked school," Ed explained, "never thought of himself as someone who could do much. But now he's beginning to see he has potential, and he's tying some hopes to this work."

After Jesse, I spent time with Juan Jauregui and Frank Santos.

Juan was the most prolific of Ed's students, producing eight public service announcements. He had a distinctive style, and his topics were disturbing: AIDS from shared needles, gang violence, death from smoking, alcohol, and drugs. And his images came at you quickly, sharply, but rhythmic, skillfully timed: gangsters, guns, cocaine; hooded chess players, fingers splayed, caressing a rook, a bishop; car grills and tires, chain link and concrete; graveyards; lost, anguished faces. Harsh, but flowing somehow through eerie music or driving guitar or rap.

Frank's style, on the other hand, was playful, celebratory. He came to the United States four years ago from Mexico, took courses in English as a second language, and moved into the standard curriculum as an LEP (limited English proficiency) student. He still spoke an unsure English, but, Ed said, was "probably the most technically adept student" he had ever had. "He learned it all so quickly, and now he virtually lives here; morning, lunch, he's just here." I saw two of Frank's projects. In the first, young and old Mexicans dance in a local club to Banda Machos's "Casimira": cowboy hats, bandannas, women in jeans and ruffled dresses; the images up close, receding, modulated to the catchy syncopation and back beat of this music, called *banda*. In his manipulation of the images, Frank conveyed the joy of the dance that accompanies *banda, la quebradita* or "the little break": elbows pumping, shoulders dipping, a young woman, chin up, lips pursed, flashing her eyes at the camera, while around the dance a multicolored frame shimmers—*¡Orale!* (all right!), *¡Arre!* (giddy-up!)—with bright encouragement. The second was a brief animated French lesson, in which a boy lies on his bed while his mother berates him for not doing his homework. "If you do not do your homework *(Si tu ne fais ton devoir),*" she says, "you are not going to find a job *(tu ne vas pas trouvé de job).*" The boy remains immobile, grumpy: *"Je ne désire pas trouvé de job!"*—I don't want to find a job! The futile exchange continues—you won't be able to get married (so what?), have a family (so?)—until Mom adds the clincher: then you must not fall in love and can't kiss the girls. *Ooh la la,* the cartoon boy says, springing from bed and doing a half-dance to his desk. "I can't talk to you anymore, because I have homework to do!"

And at the end of the day, I got a chance to sit and talk with Melanie and Leonor, who made "Civil Wars." Melanie was from El Salvador, Leonor from Colombia, both seniors who had met in tenth-grade geometry and who had collaborated on two other videos. They had spent two months on "Civil Wars," trying to get it right, despairing, coming back again. They were good friends, close, effective partners, and they occasionally completed each other's sentences:

> There were times when we felt like quitting. And it wasn't until Mr. Stone pushed us—he said, "Girls, you have to do this." And we were procrastinating. We got so tired looking for the *right* shots. I mean, *shots*—we had plenty of them. But looking for the right one, well . . . then Mr. Stone would say, "It'll work out, I believe in you." We don't like to do simple work. We like to get into what we're doing. Quality work is what we like—that's what we're all about.

Melanie had applied to college, wanting to major in film, Leonor was a single mother who had to stay close to home and make an immediate, practical choice: she would most likely go to nearby East Los Angeles Community College and train to be a physician's assistant. A number of Ed and Larry's students lived with limits. (Seventy-five percent of the students at Bell were from families categorized as "low income.") Some of these young people had had their sights set on college for a while, but a number were not in the college track at all—weren't oriented that way, weren't interested, had, in all kinds of ways, been scared or barred from it. The video classes provided one of the few opportunities for such a range of students to work together and see what each could do. And it was often the student who was less successful by traditional standards who excelled. Some visitors might find a class like Ed Murphy's too unstructured, too loud; might worry, too, about the focus of so much student work on drugs, gangs, violence. And Ed has tried to get his students to reflect critically on this focus—does it inadvertently feed stereotypes about communities like Bell?—but with little result. What seemed undeniable, though, was that the students were engaged, had a sense of importance, worked within a tradition of recognized student achievement, and gave expression to deeply held concerns. Melanie lost her father in the Salvadoran civil war and saw people killed in front of her house. And as a secondary result of the work, some students who had never imagined themselves in college began to see possibilities. It was not uncommon for Ed and Larry's students to gear themselves up for the local community college or for California State University at Los Angeles, just back up the Long Beach Freeway, four miles northeast.

BALTIMORE, MARYLAND

The Author's Chair might have come from an inexpensive set of kitchen furniture, if it weren't so small—housekeeping drilled and pressed in miniature. Steel tubing, blue-green speckled plastic seat and back rest. A sign, curled at the edges, was taped across the top: Author's Chair. At least once a week, each student in Stephanie's class had the opportunity to sit in it and read something he or she had written, the rest of the class listening and responding. The students looked forward to the readings, letting out a moan when, for some reason, a scheduled session had to be canceled, or an athletic "*yesssss*"—hitting that *s* with brio—when Mrs. Terry announced that it was time for the authors to come forward.

Jamika's trip to the Author's Chair was typical. Jamika's parents were devout Jehovah's Witnesses, so it was not uncommon for Jamika to write on religious themes. She was small and serious and had the full cheeks that relatives yearn to

pinch. Just before Jamika started to read, she inched forward on the chair so that her feet were steady on the ground:

> Saturday and Sunday I went to a Assembly. I ate breakfast in the Assembly's cafeteria. They gave me a chicken sandwich. I took my food home. When I was in the Assembly in the Auditorium I took off my shoes because my mother said I could. Lots of Brothers gave lots of talks. People got on the stage.

When she finished, she looked over the top of her paper, anticipating questions. "That was a good story," said Shaquente. "Thank you," replied Jamika, glancing at Mrs. Terry and smiling. "You gave a lot of details," said Leon from the back, standing up to be heard. "Thank you," Jamika said again. "Why did you take your sandwich home?" asked Frank, alert to the advent of lunch. "Because I wasn't hungry," explained Jamika. "Well, uh, maybe you could say that, too," he offered. "If you decide to say something more about your sandwich"—Mrs. Terry tapped her lip with her index finger, as if in thought—"where would you put it?" "I could put it where I say 'I took my food home,'" answered Jamika. "I could say, 'I took my food home because I wasn't hungry.'" "OK," replied her teacher. "Think about it."

Kenneth was next, shooting his hand up in the air, waving it, pressing his cheek against his arm. "Wa . . . what did the people do on the stage?" Stephanie waited a moment, then added that she was curious about that, too. Jamika set the paper on her lap. "They talked about the ministry, and they told stories from the scripture and . . ."—a pause here, looking at Mrs. Terry again—"and that's what I remember." "Well, Jamika," said Mrs. Terry, "I think your readers would like to know that," and leaned over to provide a quick assist to Jamika, who was fishing a pencil out of the pocket of her dress.

When Stephanie first introduced me to the children some days earlier, she told them I was a teacher and an author. "We're going to have an author staying with us for a while." "Ooooo, Miss Terry," Dondi offered, waving his hand, "we're authors too!" You couldn't be in Stephanie Terry's classroom for long before the children walked up to you, their dog-eared journals folded back, asking whether you'd like to hear a story. They saw themselves as writers. And, thanks to Mrs. Terry's feedback and the experience of the Author's Chair, a number of them were becoming reflective about their prose. Ciera came up to me—hair in cornrows, pretty, a little coy—and read me a description of her rings: "I have four rings. One has a whitish stone. One has a red stone. One is gold, one silver." She finished and looked up. I complimented her, and she said "Thank you," but then she paused, puts her lips, and said, "I think I need more ideas, huh?" "Like what else?" I asked. Again a pause. "Maybe how I *got* the rings?" "Now that's a good idea," I said. She turned on her heel and ran off, still holding her paper in both hands. Six or seven minutes later and she came back, a big smile on her face. "OK," she said, "this is better." She read her original description and then her new sentences: "My mother got me the rings. She got two at Kmart and two at Sears."

Not too long ago, it was assumed that children couldn't learn to write until they had learned to read. It was—and in many classrooms still is—assumed that a critical awareness of one's writing and the impulse to revise should not be expected or encouraged until the later elementary grades. And in many settings it is assumed that the most effective language arts curriculum for poor kids, inner city or rural or immigrant, is one that starts with the alphabet, phonics, and lists of simple words, presented in sequence, learned through drills and packaged games, and builds slowly toward the reading of primer prose. Stephanie Terry's classroom challenged those assumptions.

Writing and reading were taught as related processes and were developed space. Children did receive instruction in letter recognition and principles of phonics, both from Stephanie and from the school's reading teacher, Carol Hicks. Carol was, by her own description, "a traditionalist," who worked with Stephanie in her classroom and, together with Stephanie, planned supplemental instruction for those children "who may fall through the cracks." But while the students were learning about letter-sound correspondences, they were also learning to brainstorm, consider an audience, reflect on their writing, add detail, and revise. The development of these complex processes was not put on hold until more discrete language skills were perfected. So Ciera spelled "stone" as *ston* and "Sears" as *Sers,* and Jamika, who was the most proficient speller in the class, wrote *Sauterday* and *cafetereia* and *chiken.* Errors like these would gradually disappear as Ciera and Jamika read more and wrote more, as Stephanie and Carol gave them feedback on their work, as they received more direct instruction—from Stephanie, from Carol, from an aide—in phonics and spelling. Meanwhile, they were using language in full, rich ways to tell the stories they wanted to tell.

"It's all part of it," Stephanie had said to me. "Everything contributes to the writing. The animals, the books, the music, the things on the wall, the African themes and images—it all feeds into their journals. And the activities. They need lots of opportunities to talk, to hear good books, to ask questions, to share experiences with classmates, to help each other, to read the things they've written." So any given reading at the Author's Chair may grow from a number of sources, all part of the classroom environment.

There were, of course, the books. Each day, Stephanie read at least one book to the class: fairy tale or folktale, a story about children, biography, history, an account of other cultures, an explanation of the biology or ecology of the creatures living along the wall of the classroom. In any given month, then, the children might hear a tale set in the African rain forest, a linguistic romp by Dr. Seuss, an explanation of the Navajo cosmology, information on the newt or hermit crab, the life of Harriet Tubman or Rosa Parks, a story about a magic fish or a spirited girl or a trickster spider. A wide range of genres.

The children could check out any of the books overnight. In the front of the room, taped to the blackboard, was a long sign-out sheet, and at the end of each day, those children who wanted a book would line up and write in the title and their initials. This usually went surprisingly fast; the kids were used to the procedure. When they came in the next morning, they would, along with hanging their coats and other routines, put a check by their name and indicate, in one of three columns, whether the book was "easy," "just right," or "a challenge." Stephanie could thereby tell a lot at a glance. And the children had the chance to be with books. Reading them for a first or second or third time, or just looking at the illustrations—words and pictures feeding their imagination.

There was music. Some was instrumental—drums, harps, guitars, and birdsong to accompany that rain forest tale, for example. But most involved language play and storytelling: Taj Mahal's "Shake Sugaree," Sweet Honey in the Rock's "All for Freedom," "Yoruba Children's Tales," and a collection called "Peace Is the World Smiling." Picking up on the lyrics of the peace songs, Kenneth started one of his entries with "My Earth give us Love and Peace. You got to love the Earth just like you love your friends."

There were the creatures and all the print surrounding them. Words referring to their anatomies—*claw, antenna, gill*—to their habitats and birth cycles—which the children had observed—words about how to care for them ("In our room, we feed praying mantis nymphs apple bits"), and words on the ecological functions they served: "aquatic snails keep our aquarium clean." The language, for the most part, came from the children themselves—with a spelling assist from Mrs. Terry. (It was not uncommon to see children leave their desks to copy from the walls the correct spelling of a difficult word.) And there was all that talk, "science talk," the language of close observation that led to the creation of the children's own explanatory texts.

Another kind of generative talk was the daily recounting of the children's experience: fishing expeditions, trips to the zoo, church services, birthday parties, visits to relatives, neighborhood journeys with "best, very best" friends. These accounts were taken seriously as contributions to the linguistic environment. Children's oral stories were celebrated, analyzed, incorporated into discussions of written stories, and considered for

further elaboration. And occasionally one student's story would find its way into another student's composing.

If the books and animals and the rest provided a multilayered content for the children's writing, the journals themselves offered the occasion to learn about the process. Each month, Stephanie passed out home-made stapled booklets filled with lined paper. The children wrote every day, sometimes on an assigned topic, more often on a topic of their choosing—but not infrequently with some kind of guiding principle that arose from other classroom work. If, for example, Stephanie had read a book that was especially rich in description, she might ask the children to try to "add lots of detail" to their own writing. And as Stephanie or an aide circulated around the room, they would give on-the-spot instruction in spelling or encourage a student to be a little more descriptive or point out an unhelpful repetition. All of this, of course, set the stage for revision.

Such work was done on the fly, but once or twice a week Stephanie drew from everything she saw to present a more formal demonstration of the composing process. Resting on an easel in the front of the room, right by the blackboard, was a three-foot-high version of a journal. On the front was Stephanie's self-portrait in crayon, braids twisting into the air. *Mrs. Terry's Journal,* it said across the top. With felt pen in hand, she would model how to get started and how to revise, and would provide opportunity for children to apply their editing skills. "Last week I went to the Baltimore Aquarium," she might say in mock consternation, "but, uh, but I don't know what to say about it." And the children would jump in: "Did you go alone?" "What fish did you see first?" "Did you have fun?" These were the kinds of questions they heard when they were in the Author's Chair. Then Stephanie would start writing, making many simple errors—"on sunday i wnt to the aquarium"—and a chorus of her students would happily edit her writing: "Miss Terry, you need to start with a capital." "Miss Terry, there's a *e* between the *w* and the *n*." "Miss Terry, oooh, you didn't put a period at the end." As she proceeded, she repeated herself or put sentences out of logical sequence, and that would lead to discussion of broader revisions—as would a question like: "What else would you as a reader like to know about my trip?" With time, these questions and operations, and an awareness of the linguistic contexts that give rise to them, would gradually work their way into the children's composing process.

The journals encouraged another kind of work. At the table close to the door, Romarise leaned over and asked Kevin how to spell *night*. Kevin thought for a moment, then wrote *n-i-g-b-t* across the top of his page. A few minutes later, Kevin turned to Shereese. "Hey, Shereese, do you know how to spell *Friday?*" Shereese ticked off the letters, and Kevin wrote it out and thanked her. At another table Rachel had gotten up with her journal in her hand and was guiding Shaquente toward the comfortable section of rug end pillows by the piano. They settled in, and Rachel read to Shaquente her thoughts on the biography of Sojourner Truth that had been capturing her interest for the past week or so. Stephanie encouraged her students to work with one another: to write about each other's experiences, to help with spelling and punctuation, to share stories and elicit peer reactions. Individual writing, in her eyes, was enhanced by a community of writers.

It was all this that made possible Ciera's and Jamika's and Romarise's performances at the Author's Chair.

BEREA AND WHEELWRIGHT, KENTUCKY

The curriculum Bud and Delores developed—or, more accurately, were developing, for it was very much in process—required a degree of intellectual self-sufficiency that was traditionally not the norm in many Kentucky classrooms, especially those in poorer districts. This active, problem-solving orientation was central to the Kentucky Education Reform Act, or KERA, as everyone called it, and it drove Bud and Delores's experimental course of study. There were three fundamental components of this curriculum, and during my visit I would get

to see the students engage in all three, both effectively and with complications.

There was the American Studies component, an attempt to cross disciplinary lines—fusing social studies and English—to encourage students to think and write about historical and social issues in a more original and creative way than is usually done in the standard curriculum. The general theme Bud and Delores chose for this component was "The Struggle for Freedom," and, over the year, this theme would be further broken out into units on which students would spend four to five weeks. Bud and Delores posed the first unit, "The American Revolution," but the remainder would be determined jointly by the teachers and their students. (They would, for example, eventually work on the civil rights movement and the passing of the cold war.) Students worked in groups on topics related to these units—what were the reasons behind the desire for colonial independence, who were the great civil rights leaders before Martin Luther King, Jr.—deciding, with Bud and Delores's help, how to research a topic, how best to present it, and how to divide labor and schedule time to carry out the work.

The second component emerged from the Kentucky Telecommunications Project. Here, the students, again in groups, were to develop, over the entire year, a community-based project; it was this ongoing project that would provide the foundation for their communication with the students in Lexington, Louisville, Covington, and Paducah. As it would turn out, Bud and Delores's students would develop a recycling project, establish a tutoring service for the students at the elementary school, survey the needs of the local senior citizens, and explore the question: Is there a future in Wheelwright? Such endeavors would require that they use writing in a number of ways, for a number of purposes: field notes, rough, preliminary reports, letters to county, state, and federal agencies (the recycling group, for example, would write to the EPA), letters to the editor, position papers, and so on. The teachers' hope was that the projects would stimulate the development of both a local community of writers—groups of students at Wheelwright using writing around shared concerns—and a community that extended beyond the boundaries of Floyd County. And such broader community-building, in fact, did begin once the students mastered the technology: those students working on the recycling project would ask the students at other sites about recycling efforts in their neighborhoods, and those pondering the future of Wheelwright would gather unemployment statistics from across the commonwealth. Students would do work that was rich in local meaning even as they sought assistance and audience well beyond the local.

The third component involved the development, by each student, of a portfolio of writing reflecting a range of genres: personal narrative, book review, critical analysis, story, poem, and so on. The writing, for the most part, would come from the American Studies curriculum or the Telecommunications Project, and though there would be due dates for the papers, the students could, as their skills improved, revise them throughout the year or substitute a new piece of a particular genre for an old one.

During the week of my visit, the students were working on an editorial for their portfolios and, in groups, researching an issue related to the struggle for freedom in the American Revolution. They had not yet determined their projects for the Telecommunications Project, but were hard at work on their video introducing Wheelwright and were learning the ways and means of electronic mail and FAX machines in the Computer Lab.

After Sherry, Mary Rose, Terry, and the others had presented their video storyboard to the class, Bud and Delores broke the students into groups to pursue their work on the American Revolution. They had been at this for a little over a week and, predictably, were having some trouble striking out on their own. "Remember," Bud told them once they had reconfigured into clusters of four and five, "there are some basic questions you want to keep asking yourselves. What were the economic conditions in the colonies and in England? What were the differences in the colonies themselves—economic differences, political differences, differences in geography? What were

the motives driving some Colonists to break away? Can you relate to any of those motives? Put yourselves in their shoes. And how about the Loyalists? Why did they resist revolution? See if you can put yourselves in their shoes, too."

Over the course of my stay, I would come to know two groups. One was trying to compile information on specific Revolutionary War figures—what led each of them to take extraordinary action. The other was struggling to find a way to convey to the class what it felt like to be a Loyalist in the colonies. "You don't want to just stand in front of the class and read a paper," Mr. Reynolds had said. "Make it lively." Bud and Delores had been coaching the groups, sitting with them and playing out options, making suggestions, recommending sources, retrieving materials from places beyond the school's library, which was terribly outdated and understocked. But the students still had to plan and execute academic work in a way that was unfamiliar to them.

There were some things they could do well. Some were pretty resourceful at scouting around for materials. One girl had gone to Morehead State College, three counties away, and checked out from the library a set of slides of posters and broadsides decrying the Stamp Act and the Quartering Act and the other British actions that sparked Colonial outrage. These created a big stir in her group. Most students, from what I could tell, were also willing to help each other out. There were religious and social traditions in eastern Kentucky that probably set the stage for mutual assistance, and Bud and Delores's students took to collaboration. A student in one of the groups had photocopied some pages from a history book and, as she was reading a passage from them to her colleagues, she came across the name Roger Sherman. "Who was he?" she asked. No one knew—nor did I—so she turned to another group and asked them. And a girl in that group said she knew how to find out real quick, went over to the bookcase by the door, and ran her finger through the index of an old edition of Samuel Eliot Morrison's *The History of the American Republic*. "Here," she said coming back with the book open. "He was one of the guys who signed the Constitution," and she handed the book to her classmate.

But, overall, this curriculum was proving to be a significant challenge for them. And for Bud and Delores as well.

For some time, Bud had run a pretty open classroom, rich with student projects—that was what had attracted Janet Fortune to him in the first place. And since the mid-1980s, Delores, along with Carol Stumbo—the creator of the Telecommunications Project—had been supervising a student-produced magazine called *Mantrip,* a compilation of interviews with local people about the economic, cultural, and political history of the region. These teachers believed in the capacities of their students for independent work and also had an experimental bent. But so much was new here: the cross-disciplinary American Studies curriculum; the eschewing of textbook instruction—with very limited materials to put in its place; the number of unknowns in the Telecommunications Project; the first-time use of the portfolio method for compiling and evaluating student writing; the pressures and expectations of the new school-reform legislation. As I got to know Bud and Delores, I became convinced that Carol—on leave herself to help the local schools implement the state's reforms—had recommended them quite deliberately for this experiment. Bud was tapped because of his willingness to try new things, his pedagogical restlessness. He had a high tolerance for ambiguity, could throw himself into the middle of things and ride them out. And Carol knew that he was in desperate need of something fresh. Delores was chosen because she was rock solid, had roots here that went back generations, had taught kids and their kids—yet, as well, possessed a streak of antitraditionalism, valued her students tremendously, and liked to set them loose. Yet, like their students, the teachers were setting forth on new terrain, and they were bound to misstep. How much or how little should they guide the students? What degree of structure was paradoxically necessary to foster self-sufficiency? With so much new going on, some blunders would be inevitable, and how in God's name were successful teachers supposed to get used to failure—and then pick up the pieces, recalibrate, and start again? Was this *really* the way Delores wanted to end a fine career? Between them, Bud and Delores had spent over fifty years in the classroom, and they were launching into a curriculum more complex and uncertain than anything in their experience.

POLARIS AND MISSOULA, MONTANA

Ten o'clock, and it was time for a snack and recess. Michele and Andy took turns supervising the children during these breaks, and on this day Andy watched over them while Michele checked their "dictionaries," the lists of words they had misspelled in their writing. She was particularly concerned about James, handsome, laconic James, whom they were trying to prepare for ninth grade at the high school in Dillon. "He has the intelligence," she said to me, rubbing her temple, "but he just hasn't done the work he's capable of doing." She opened his folder, running her finger down a list of words: *historical, museum, process.* Earlier in the month, in quick script in his journal, he had written lyrically about a trip to nearby Black Mountain:

> All I hear is the gentle whisper of the creek and the wind blowing through the willows . . . I see a beautiful green valley and creeks and a big mountain with a little snow on it. The sun is hidden behind a cloud. I see baby horses, baby elk and baby antelope . . . curious about life and how God made the earth. I feel a crisp and cool mountain breeze; then the sun pokes out and warms everything up. Touching each and every soul. I love this earth.

There were many sides to this boy. And much promise. Michele closed his folder, turned and looked out the window.

Melissa stayed inside to practice her piano, and the empty classroom and the library—where Michele was fretting over James—filled with a hesitant but melodic rendition of "Pony Ride." Melissa guided herself with a whispered *one-two-three, one-two-three-four,* the keys yielding an almost muted tinkle, like the sound of an old recording, *one-two-three*, played in this room so many times before, Melissa beginning again.

On the top shelf of the library, above *Huckleberry Finn, Wind in the Willows,* and the like, was a pile of old documents and record books. At various times during my stay I would page through them, uncovering a copy of the original petition from Polaris to the county superintendent of public schools announcing that "[m]oney has been raised by public subscription for the purpose of building a schoolhouse." I found the dusty forms that guided the governance and management of a school on the frontier, announcing that "the Public Free Schools of the State shall be open to all children and youths between the ages of six and twenty-one years." I read the minutes of board meetings: a resolution to "levy extra 3 mill tax to cover debt;" a contract sent to a Miss Emma Bartels, who, the board determined; "was best qualified to teach," a vote "to ask people of the district to furnish wood for the year as we're short of funds." I found various school census reports and teacher's reports dating back to 1894, some attached to others with straight pins, the paper rusted slightly at the point of piercing. They recorded enrollment, attendance, visits by trustees and parents, number of books in the library (forty-two in 1919), teachers' salaries [$85 per month in 1919), whether Arbor Day was observed "in accordance with the law," and whether instruction was given on "the effects of alcoholic drinks and narcotics" and on "the prevention of communicable diseases." I found, as well, student registries, written in the neat and ornate hand of various district clerks. As I turned the pages, the same names appeared year after year—Tash, Harrison, Marchesseau—the children seeming to grow up before me as I ran my finger down the lists of names, the names of the families migrating from Canada, from the Midwest, from Kentucky, who settled this valley. Those names were now represented on the school board that hired Andy, now appeared on the Polaris School registry. How many sat at that piano? Listening to Melissa play "Pony Ride," I wondered about the harsh journey, the solitude, and the powerful sense of continuity that some in the Grasshopper Valley must feel.

And outside, the class ran an energetic game of tag while the snow fell in gently manic flurries, flowing sideways, kicking up, up, down, riding the erratic breeze.

Ten-twenty. Erica, Russell, Tyler, Heather, and James, the seventh- and eighth-graders, crammed themselves around the small table in the library, preparing for another phase of Montana Studies. This was the delivery of basic geographical, historical, and civic facts about the state, the story the state tells itself about itself and expects its students to know. Andy gave it his own twist, however. Knowing that once these young people begin high school, they would have to be able to take efficient notes, he decided to simulate for them the academic lecture. The transition to town high schools was a big concern for rural educators, and it was that concern Andy was playing out here.

He reviewed some basic note-taking techniques and explained the setting the students could expect in the typical science or history or social studies classroom. Then, using the materials provided to rural teachers by the county, he surveyed the official Montana symbols: bitterroot, the state flower; ponderosa pine, the state tree; black spotted cutthroat trout, the state fish; grizzly bear, the state animal. The basic geography of Montana: the western mountains and the continental divide—directing the flow of rivers to opposite sides of the Rockies—and the vast eastern plains, part of the Great Plains. And Montana's primary sources of revenue: agriculture, ranching, mining, tourism. Then came a quick historical sketch: from the indigenous peoples, to the French explorers and trappers, to the Louisiana Purchase, to the gold and silver rush (Polaris figured here), to the Indian wars, to copper. Montana was organized as a territory in 1864 and became a state in 1889. Its motto: *Oro y plata,* gold and silver.

When he finished, Andy walked around the table, asking to see people's notes, pointing out different methods—Heather's outline format, Russell's list—and making suggestions for improvement. He paid special attention to James who, come fall, would be facing the real thing. Because of the possibility of stretching beyond grade level and because of the presence of older role models, Andy believed that the multigrade classroom was a stimulating place for younger students, but he worried that it was not as rich for the older ones. James. Was he doing all he could do for James?

Michele thought Rossy was "incredible in math" and wanted to "keep pushing her." So while Andy lectured on Montana Studies, and the younger children worked independently in the larger room, Michele slid in alongside Rossy with a sheet of new math problems. She had copied these from a more advanced textbook and wanted to see how Rossy would do with them.

Though the school board was able to buy into the co-op that provided itinerant teachers for some enrichment and certain special needs—like the speech therapist for Colt—a district with one school and fifteen kids clearly cannot mount a gifted-and-talented program or hire a special education resource teacher. Rural children miss out on some of the services that are a part of urban schooling, historically, that has been one of the arguments for consolidation. But it is also true that, in the hands of good teachers, the small multigrade classroom gives rise to the possibility of dealing with special needs directly and within the flow of daily instruction. There would be multiple opportunities for Rossy to work beyond the confines of her mathematics textbook.

Difficulties can be addressed in similar fashion. Andy told me about one of the girls who, during the previous two years of schooling, displayed the kinds of problems with reading that could have gotten her diagnosed as learning disabled. By the time Andy arrived at Polaris, she was doing better but was still reading below grade level. So he worked out a plan with her parents whereby she continued to read the books her peers were reading, but received extra help in the classroom, and read at least a half-hour a night under her parents' supervision. And Andy saw her patents frequently, after school, at local events, so there was a steady exchange of information. "Little schools should not try to act like big schools," Claudette said to me on our way to Polaris. "They need to take advantage of their smallness." "This classroom is a full-inclusion classroom," Andy quipped when I quoted Claudette to him. "It has to be."

When I was getting out of Claudette's car in the school yard that morning, I noticed some plastic ribbons tied to the pussy willows growing along Farlin Creek, a pink flutter among the thin, dense branches. It turned out that these were identifying markers that Andy's students had tied around the clusters of buds they were studying.

Eleven o'clock and time for science. Andy tried as much as possible to make his curriculum "continuous with experiences outside school." The class had been keeping a naturalist's journal, a detailed account of the growth of a bud on the willows, and, on this day, Andy wanted them to go out and make further observations. The naturalist's journal has a long and venerable history, and the way Andy used it, it involved close observation, description, drawing, and notions of scale and context.

The students had to note day, time, weather, direction of wind, and, using all their senses, had to write a narrative account: "smell the buds and the ground; listen and look for birds or other wildlife; feel the bark or the buds." As well, they were to attempt scale drawings of the bud and its surrounding leaves and branches. The younger students needed help with this, but they were able to approximate most of the tasks.

On this day, I stayed with Tyler. He had watched his bud grow from 1/2 cm to 2 1/2 cm, into the silky flower that gives the pussy willow its name. "This is a harsh place," Andy told him. "How has the willow adapted to it?" Tyler measured the bud, recorded the weather, checked the wind, a gentle breeze from the northeast, and sketched what he would need to complete his scale drawing. Andy had asked why the willow grows in this dense, clustered way, rather than, say, long and snaky up a phone pole. Tyler assumed that the plant was able to protect itself and make the most of available water. When he finally completed his series of observations and sketches, he would be required to draw a map of the surrounding area and the location of the plant within it, and, using his data, write a paragraph on the way the willow has adapted to the type of land and climate in which it lives. "Tyler's fished in creeks like that for years," Andy later told me. "I just wanted him to take a little closer look, maybe a little different look, at what he already knows."

Eleven-thirty and time for silent reading. Clarissa, Dustin, Tyler, and Reba sat on the couch. Erica was deep in pillows alongside the piano. James and Leo sat at opposite sides of one of the tables by the windows, bending over their books, their heads in alignment, a foot apart. Rossy, Heather, and Charlie sat at separate tables. Russell and Stephen slid down against the back wall by the restrooms, their feet, big in high-top athletic shoes, sticking out into the room from under the corkboard partition. Occasionally a thump and rustle would send Michelle back there to investigate. ("Boys, I've had enough!") Andy was in the library with Colt, working on that story about the adaptation of the antelope. Most of the children were reading mysteries or horror stories—*The Curse of the Mummy's Tomb, The Headless Cupid*—though Heather was leaning back in her chair with *To Kill a Mockingbird,* and James was engrossed in his favorite author, Louis L'Amour.

The books were of the children's own choosing, though Andy required that they keep a journal in which they responded to one of a list of questions: "What is the setting?" "Why did the author include minor characters?" "Why do you think the book ended as it did?" And so on. Toward the end of the half-hour period—or at some other time in the day when people were working independently—students would be pulling out notebooks and steno pads and writing about their reading.

Reading is, of course, central to the elementary school curriculum, and Andy found multiple ways for students to use it and enjoy it. He had Colt dictate texts that became his reader. He encouraged students to consult the library's reference books on projects ranging from the Montana Studies map to the adaptation-habitat assignment to the dimensions and characteristics of objects appearing in their artwork. (For example, I saw Rossy retrieve for Melissa a book on bats for one of her drawings.) He had teams of children select a poem, decide

how it should be read, and read it aloud to the class—Edgar Allan Poe to Shel Silverstein. He was vigilant for the quick lesson, like the time he zeroed in on the lyric sheet to "America the Beautiful"—sung so often, so mechanically—asking the class the meaning of "amber waves of grain" and "purple mountain majesties," and asking someone to please look up "grace" in the dictionary, leading to a discussion of the phrase "shed His grace on thee." And he usually read a story or part of a novel to the class just for fun before or after lunch or at the end of the day. Once when I was in the library with Erica helping her revise a story, I could hear him reading from *Scary Stories* in a Peter Lorre voice.

Twelve noon. Lunch. Those who brought mini-pizzas or containers of cooked food lined up in front of the microwave; the others unwrapped sandwiches, opened bags of chips, peeled oranges and bananas. Since there were no vending or ice machines here, most children brought their lunches in small portable coolers, the modern version of the lunch pail. Lunch was a quick affair, a little chatter inflected with sports and mainstream popular culture—Heather and Tyler talking to each other in the voice of Pauly Shore. It was not long before someone yelled, "Last one out is *it,*" and there was a scramble for jackets and the door. Andy followed outside holding at chest-level a Tupperware container of left-over spaghetti, scooping a forkful toward his open mouth.

Andy Bayliss was thirty-four, five-eleven, thin, brown hair, boyish. He grew up in Marshall, Missouri, went to grade school and high school there, worked for a few years after graduation. When his parents moved to Oregon, he enrolled at Southern Oregon State College, where he took a bachelor of science degree in geography and biology. He worked six years as a biology technician for the Forest Service—"running around streams, counting fish"—and, during the winters, was a ski instructor. He used his athletic skill as a passport, and skied in the Italian Alps, in Argentina and Chile, and in Alaska. He was in his early thirties when he began to think that the work he was doing "had no effect on the flow of events," and wondered about teaching as a way to make a difference, to help young people "develop informed opinions and think for themselves." So he enrolled in a teacher-education program at the University of Alaska Southeast at Juneau and did his student teaching in Anchorage. He became intrigued by the possibilities of the multigrade classroom, and craved a place where he could settle in and ski and canoe and hike. So he followed a path that began somewhere back in the recesses of the Republic, following hundreds of thousands before him, mostly women, mostly young, often inexperienced, working under term-to-term contracts, staying half a year, a year, maybe two or three, living at home, if local, or boarding, often in tight quarters (bathing, as one woman put it, "with a teacup and handkerchief"), or, as time progressed and conditions improved, living in a teacherage like Andy's. It was, for many, lonely work, and, for women especially, terribly underpaid. Much has changed for teachers in small rural districts, but it is still common for them to be employed, as Andy was, from year to year, with minimal possibility for tenure, and they still got paid less than their larger-district counterparts. In Montana some country teachers are paid in the $11,000-to-$13,000 range. Andy's starting salary, and this was somewhere close to average in rural Montana, was $15,500. But add the teacherage. And the multigrade experience. And the landscape. From the front door of the school, Andy showed me the slopes he skied when the snow was fresh.

It did, however, get lonely. Andy's weekdays, of course, were filled with activity, and on weekend days, weather permitting, he was out on the land. Occasionally after school there were board meetings or other civic events, but for the most part evenings were solitary. Hospitable as the residents of the Grasshopper Valley were, they were spread out, and for someone like Andy, who came to Polaris without a family, there was minimal opportunity for companionship. As for having a woman visitor to the teacherage, well, that would be, to the community's way of thinking, a delicate proposition. There were definite strictures on behavior. Andy felt the isolation in another way. Like all new teachers, even ones with

a feel for the classroom, Andy was wrestling with the question of authority. How to "be myself" yet do something about the bickering, and how to pull in those students who had a tendency to withdraw or rebel. At heart, he was trying to figure out how to *be* in his classroom, and he had to come to an answer pretty much on his own. There was an experienced and talented teacher named Linda Hicks at a small school in Glen who had befriended Andy, and she provided good counsel, but Glen was on the other side of the Pioneer mountain range, on the eastern edge of the county, so it was difficult to meet with her—particularly during school hours, when Andy could watch her teach. Laments about such isolation, both social and professional, are scattered through the letters and diaries of rural teachers; Andy's questions and conflicts echo across the history of the one-room school.

But for now, Andy was *it*, standing in the middle of the dirt driveway, the children on either side of him. One, then another tried to sprint around him to get to the other side. Dustin or Reba or Russell, his long legs pumping, would take off, running through the grass, jutting hips forward or to the side to elude Andy's tag. And Andy, with a big grin and a grunt of exertion, accelerated across the dirt, the grass, down an incline by the propane tank, striding out, catching the curve of a shoulder with his fingertips.

Twelve-thirty-five, and the students were settling back into the classroom. In a packet of materials provided by the county, Andy found a role-playing activity that caught his fancy. It was a council between Nez Perce leader Chief Joseph and General Oliver Otis Howard, who had traveled west to force the Nez Perce onto a reservation. (This figured in Montana history for, in their subsequent attempts to elude containment, the Nez Perce would travel across southwestern Montana—engaging the U.S. Army in a bloody battle at Big Hole, about 60 miles from Polaris—and up the middle of the state, through the plains toward Canada.) In addition to the general and Chief Joseph, there were roles for eight other students—from a Nez Perce warrior to a railroad executive to a rancher—so, with a little doctoring, adding a few warriors and aides, Andy was able to fit the assignment to his class.

The curricular materials gave paragraph-long descriptions of each character, but Andy felt they didn't offer an adequate account of the history surrounding the council, nor did they convey Chief Joseph's eloquence on the injustice of the government's treatment of the Nez Perce. So he found a brief history in the school's library and read it by way of introduction. "As I read this," he said, "be thinking of the role you might want to play." "This'll be interesting," I heard Heather whisper to Erica. When he asked the students to choose roles, to his relief there were no major disputes. Only James chose not to participate. Andy had the class spend about ten minutes working up their roles, and he and Michele moved among them, asking questions, providing direction.

The event itself lasted about twenty minutes. Andy had rearranged the tables into a square, and the children seemed to get carried away with the drama. The younger children had to lean into things to be heard, but they made themselves known. Some children, both younger and older, tended to follow the descriptions in the materials, the line of argument, the phrasing, but some truly assumed the role and generated passionate language and real exchange.

Erica played an Indian warrior, one of the younger Nez Perce who could no longer tolerate the dislocation and slaughter of his people. She argued fiercely, articulately, the role seeming to touch some personal understanding of injustice. Taking on Tyler, who chose the role of a rancher, and Stephen, who played General Howard, she proclaimed in various retorts: "I'm a warrior . . . The more land we give you, the more you want

. . . You ask us to move to a reservation Why don't *your* people move to a reservation? . . . There are White men killing Indians, but it is only against the law when an Indian kills a White."

Heather was the other vocal spokesperson for the Nez Perce, assuming the role of Chief Joseph, gaining from Andy's reading a sense of the chief's eloquence, trying to match it as she played off Erica's spirited defense. "How can we make peace?" she asked toward the end of the council, "when you kill our people and our livestock? You say you need protection, but you would not need protection if Whites weren't killing our women and children. This land is our father and mother, and it is being taken from us."

And fifth-grader Stephen, who wasn't particularly engaged by school and made that known in his daily interactions with Andy, took on the role of General Howard with vigor. Stephen had Russell roll up and tape the right arm of his jean jacket—the general had lost an arm in the Civil War—and using his left fist as a gavel, called the council to order. In line with the historical account, he played the general as insistent and uncompromising—"I give you three days to make a decision to move"—and as an impatient emissary dead-set on a resolution favorable to the U.S. government. During one of Heather's impassioned declarations, he stood up and interrupted: "I say we should have peace here. Let's get to the point."

When Stephen called the council to a close, Andy directed the class to think about what they had heard and to ask themselves what might have gone differently and how that would have affected the course of history. They would write on this later in the week.

SEEING COLOR, SEEING CULTURE

GLORIA LADSON-BILLINGS

In second grade my classmates and I all read from the same Dick and Jane basal reader. I was chastised more than once for reading ahead. But during that year I was also chosen to attend a special reading class. Unlike today's remedial reading classes, that class was reserved for accelerated readers. We were a select group of about five or six students and we went to reading class each day for about thirty to forty minutes. There we read "real" books, not basal textbooks, about faraway places and interesting people.

Our teacher was Mrs. Gray, a tall, elegant African American woman who seemed to love children and the idea that she could expose them to new experiences. One Saturday just before Christmas break Mrs. Gray took the class downtown on the subway train to see the dancing fountains and the Christmas display at John Wanamaker's, Philadelphia's landmark department store. I had been in Wanamaker's many times to shop with my mother, but this was the first time I could remember being taken for the express purpose of being entertained. "Now remember," admonished Mrs. Gray, "when we get downtown people will be looking at us. If you misbehave they're not going to say, look at those bad children. They're going to say look at those bad colored children!" She did not have to tell us twice. We knew that we were held to a higher standard than other people. We knew that people would stare at us and that the stares would come because of our skin color. Despite the "burden of blackness," it was a magical visit. I felt special. I felt important. I felt smart!

THE BASICS OF CULTURALLY RELEVANT TEACHING

In this chapter I discuss the ways that the teachers in my study see themselves, their students, and their students' parents. With each vignette I attempt to introduce the teachers individually and to share information about them—by way of interview comments and classroom observations—that illustrates their culturally relevant practices. Rather than attempt to show how all of the teachers demonstrate culturally relevant teaching in all of its aspects, I have selected examples that I believe are most illustrative of each aspect.

First, let us begin with a look at the many teachers who are reluctant to acknowledge racial differences or grapple with these and other differences in the classroom.

In her book *White Teacher*, Paley suggested that teachers must take care not to ignore color.[1] When she moved to an integrated private school, an African American parent confronted her with the "knowledge" that her children were black and knew they were black, and she wanted that difference to be recognized as a comfortable and natural one. Delpit's review of Paley's book points to this as the beginning of "the journey toward acknowledging and valuing differences."[2]

Source: *"Seeing Color, Seeing Culture"* from The Dreamkeepers: Successful Teachers of African American Children, *by Gloria Ladson-Billings copyright 1994. Reprinted by permission of Jossey-Bass, Inc.*

My own experiences with white teachers, both preservice and veteran, indicate that many are uncomfortable acknowledging any student differences and particularly racial differences. Thus some teachers make such statements as "I don't really see color, I just see children" or "I don't care if they're red, green, or polka dot, I just treat them all like children." However, these attempts at color-blindness mask a "dysconscious racism," an "uncritical habit of mind that justifies inequity and exploitation by accepting the existing order of things as given."[3] This is not to suggest that these teachers are racist in the conventional sense. They do not consciously deprive or punish African American children on the basis of their race, but at the same time they are not unconscious of the ways in which some children are privileged and others are disadvantaged in the classroom. Their "dysconsciousness" comes into play when they fail to challenge the status quo, when they accept the given as the inevitable.

In an earlier study that illustrated this kind of behavior, preservice teachers were asked to explain the economic, social, and educational disparities that exist between white and African American children.[4] Presented with data on African American and white children's life chances, the students were asked three questions: How can you explain these disparities? What are some differing ideological explanations for these disparities? What can schools do about these disparities?

The students' responses to the first question provide some telling insights. Most cited the fact that African Americans had been enslaved as the explanation for their present economic, social, and educational conditions. A few students suggested that African Americans' failure to gain equal opportunities in the society explained the disparities. Only one student offered racism as an explanation.

The belief of the majority of the students— that African Americans' enslavement more than a hundred years ago explains today's disparities— suggests that they could not envision how conditions could be otherwise. The enslavement of African Americans is a part of history. Thus, according to this view, the past alone determines the future of a people. A more fundamental problem with this point of view in the classroom context is the following: If a teacher looks out at a classroom and sees the sons and daughters of slaves, how does that vision translate into her expectations for educational excellence? How can teachers who see African American students as mere descendants of slaves be expected to inspire them to educational, economic, and social levels that may even exceed their own?

The usual antidote for this persistent view of African American children is for the viewer to pretend that he or she does not see the color that once forced their ancestors into slavery. Thus the teacher claims to be color-blind. However, such claims cannot be valid. Given the significance of race and color in American society, it is impossible to believe that a classroom teacher does not notice the race and ethnicity of the children she is teaching. Further, by claiming not to notice, the teacher is saying that she is dismissing one of the most salient features of the child's identity and that she does not account for it in her curricular planning and instruction. Saying we are aware of students' race and ethnic background is not the same as saying we treat students inequitably. The passion for equality in the American ethos has many teachers (and others) equating equality with sameness. An example may further clarify this point.

In a classroom of thirty children a teacher has one student who is visually impaired, one who is wheelchair-bound, one who has limited English proficiency, and one who is intellectually gifted. If the teacher presents identical work in identical ways to all of the students, is she dealing equitably or inequitably with the children? The visually impaired student cannot read the small print on an assignment, the wheelchair-bound student cannot do push-ups in gym, the foreign-language student cannot give an oral report in English, and the intellectually gifted student learns nothing by spelling words she mastered several years ago.

The notion of equity as sameness only makes sense when all students *are* exactly the same. But even within the nuclear family children born from the same parents are not exactly the same. Different children have different needs and addressing those different needs is the best way to deal with them equitably. The same is true in the classroom. If teachers pretend not to see students' racial and ethnic differences, they really do not see the students at all and are limited in their ability to meet their educational needs.

TEACHERS WITH CULTURALLY RELEVANT PRACTICES HAVE HIGH SELF-ESTEEM AND A HIGH REGARD FOR OTHERS

Although my neighborhood was predominately African American, a few white families lived there. Most attended Catholic schools. It made sense to us; they were Catholic. One of the neighborhood white boys went to a private boarding school. His father had died, and this made him eligible for a private school for orphan boys (I guess a mother's presence did not count in those days). The school he attended did not accept African American boys. (Many years later that school would become a battleground in the civil rights struggle in our city.) Only one white family, which consisted of seventeen children, sent their kids to my elementary school. They were extremely poor and often showed up unclean and unkempt. Everyone in the school community knew them and some felt a pang of sympathy for them, for as poor as we all were, we knew we were not quite as poor as they were.

But they seemed to take some comfort in the fact that although they were extremely poor at least they were not black. Every fight these children ever had came as a result of their calling one of the African American children "nigger." We had to wonder who or what they thought we were. And what did that make them, since they were resigned to spending six hours of every school day with us?

One dimension of culturally relevant teaching is the teachers' perceptions of themselves and others. Too often teachers have a poor opinion of themselves and their profession. In contrast, teachers who practice culturally relevant

TABLE 3.1

Conceptions of Self and Others.

CULTURALLY RELEVANT	ASSIMILATIONIST
Teacher sees herself as an artist, teaching as an art.	Teacher sees herself as technician, teaching as a technical task.
Teacher see herself as part of the community and teaching as giving something back to the community, encourages students to do the same.	Teacher sees herself as an individual who may or may not be a part of the community; she encourages achievement as a means to escape community.
Teacher believes all students can succeed.	Teacher believes failure is inevitable for some.
Teacher helps students make connections between their community, national, and global identities.	Teacher homogenizes students into one "American" identity.
Teacher sees teaching as "pulling knowledge out"—like "mining."	Teacher sees teaching as "putting knowledge into"—like "banking."

methods not only see themselves as professionals but also strongly identify with teaching. I begin my individual profiles of the teachers in my study with one who exemplifies this quality.

Pauline Dupree is an African American woman who lives in the more affluent white community that borders the district where my study was carried out. She attends an African American Baptist church that many of the students and parents in the district attend. To some she appears reserved and humorless but during my two years of study, I found her to be serious and sophisticated. She describes herself as a no-nonsense, no-frills teacher.

Dupree is a slender, attractive African American woman. She is always impeccably dressed in a style that reminds one of a corporate executive. Her outfits always are coordinated; she seems to have a different pair of shoes for each. During our first interview she said that the girls in her class sometimes peek around the classroom door in the morning to see what she is wearing. When one of her students asked why she was always "so dressed up," Dupree replied that she dressed the way she did because she was coming to work and she worked with very important people, so she wanted to look good.

Dupree's classroom reflects her penchant for neatness. As the saying goes, there is a place for everything and everything is in its place. Despite the fact that her class is housed in one of the school's smaller portable classrooms, she has found a way to utilize the space efficiently and avoid a sense of clutter. Stepping from the boisterous playground into her classroom is like stepping into another world. The students are well behaved and orderly—much like Pauline Dupree herself.

During our interview Dupree commented that she was somewhat dismayed at some of the young white teachers who had come to work in the district. "They come in here dressed like people going to scrub somebody's kitchen. I mean what kind of message do you send the children when you don't care enough to put on clean, pressed clothes?"

Mrs. Harris, my third-grade teacher, was quite a sharp dresser. She wore beautiful high-heeled shoes. Sometimes she switched to flats in the afternoon if her feet got tired, but every morning began with the click, click, click of her high heels as she greeted us up and down the rows. I wanted to dress the way Mrs. Harris did. I didn't want to wear old-lady comforters like Mrs. Benn's and I certainly didn't want to wear worn-out loafers like those of my first-grade teacher, Miss Schwartz. I wanted to wear beautiful, shiny, high-heeled shoes like Mrs. Harris's. That was the way a teacher should look, I thought.

Dupree's thinking about the importance of personal appearance is supported by Foster.[5] In Foster's memoirs of his years as a high school teacher in New York City, he cites several examples of students' recollections of teachers who dressed poorly. Foster suggests that in minority communities attention to personal appearance and presentation are extremely important. He describes jailed civil rights protestors who urged their lawyers to change from their blue jeans to conservative suits and to trim their long hair into more conservative haircuts so that they would look more like the prosecutor and the judge. Foster also suggests that the worst dressed teachers are white male secondary-school teachers. He believes that their feelings about the low status of teachers contribute to poor self-esteem that translates into little or no regard for how they dress.

This is clearly not the case for Pauline Dupree. She cares very much about the way she dresses. This suggests that she also cares about the people she works with and about her profession. Being a teacher is a special calling for her.

Dupree tells her fourth-grade class about teaching as a worthwhile profession.

DUPREE: How many of you think you'd like to be teachers when you grow up?

(A few students raise their hands, all of them girls.)

DUPREE: What about some of you boys?

(Several students snicker.)

DUPREE: Don't you know how important teachers are? Without good teachers, none of the successful people you've read about would have learned the basic things like reading, writing, math, and science that helped them become successful.

MALE STUDENT: But I want to make a lot of money . . . be a basketball star!

DUPREE: That's a good goal, but most basketball players spend more time in classrooms than they do being basketball stars. They have short careers and they have to be prepared to do something afterward. If you're prepared educationally, you could teach. As far as money is concerned, it is true teachers don't earn as much as I think they should but there really is more to work than earning money.

ANOTHER MALE STUDENT: Like what, Mrs. Dupree?

DUPREE: Like getting the chance to work with the most important people in the world.

FEMALE STUDENT: Who?

DUPREE: All of you. Every weekday morning when I wake up I know I'm on my way to work with the most important people in the world. Do you know why you're the most important people in the world?

(Silence.)

DUPREE: Because you represent the future. How you turn out will have consequences for us all. What you decide to do with your lives can help make this community and the world a better place. I hope a few of you will seriously consider teaching. I'll bet quite a few of you would make excellent teachers.

In the midst of unpacking after one of my numerous moves, I came across my college yearbook. In it, I spotted a photo of one of my professors. On it she had written, "Best wishes to a very capable student who will one day go on to pursue doctoral studies." My eyes widened in amazement; my mouth dropped open. Why on earth would she have written that? There was nothing about me as an undergraduate that indicated graduate school material. I didn't even know what I wanted to do with my life back then; I'm not sure I even knew what graduate school was or what it required.

TEACHERS WITH CULTURALLY RELEVANT PRACTICES SEE THEMSELVES AS PART OF THE COMMUNITY, SEE TEACHING AS GIVING BACK TO THE COMMUNITY, AND ENCOURAGE THEIR STUDENTS TO DO THE SAME

This quality is very evident in Julia Devereaux's work. Devereaux is an African American woman who has lived in the school community most of her life. She attended the very school in which she teaches. She is active in the local Catholic church and she serves as the local troop's Girl Scout leader. She is also the president of the district's teachers' association. None of her own three children attended the public schools in the district. Her two daughters went to a local black liberation school where she had once taught (she had been married to a member of the Black Panthers) and later went on to an exclusive white private school. Her son currently attends a Catholic grade school that serves a largely African American and Latino population.

Devereaux's classroom is the portable one next to Dupree's. Both are fourth-grade teachers but there is a tremendous contrast in the classroom climates. Where Dupree's class is neat and orderly, Devereaux's may be described as one of "organized chaos." It is a busy classroom presided over by a busy teacher. Devereaux constantly looks for materials and supplies to purchase for her students. She takes advantage of special offers and bargains for classroom teachers offered by publishers and teacher supply stores. In consequence her room is filled to the brim with books, posters, novelty pencils, pens, erasers, key chains, coffee cups, and other interesting items. Devereaux is a scavenger who does not mind spending time looking for things that can be used in her classroom.

Along the back wall of the classroom are book shelves overflowing with books—some whole-class sets, others with random, single titles. Devereaux keeps her desk at the rear of the classroom. It has probably been some time since she has seen the top of it because it is covered with books and papers. But the condition of the desk is of little consequence to her because, as its placement in the room suggests, she spends little time there.

> This job demands that you be up and active. I don't have time to sit down at a desk. I need to be able to move in and among the children all day. I'm always saying to the kids, "Put that on my desk . . . put this on my desk." By the end of the day, so many things have been put on my desk that I can't even see it. But my teaching is not about paper, it's about people.

Devereaux believes that teaching offers a humane, ethical way for people to give back to the community. Because she is fluent in French, Devereaux could have opted to teach in a more affluent high school district. She reflects on her choice to remain in the African American community.

> I wanted to teach here so much! My first job barely paid the rent. I taught in the private black liberation school where my own kids went too. I just don't believe that you just take, take, take from the community and never give back. That's what I try to tell my students today. You've got to get a good education because the community needs your brain power.

Throughout the school day, Devereaux reminds her students of ways in which they can become more involved in the community. In addition to talking about building community, she demonstrates how to do it. She offers her home phone number to all of her students' parents. She establishes a telephone tree so that important information can get to the parents quickly.

One Friday, one of Devereaux's students did not arrive home. The student's mother called Devereaux in a panic. Devereaux reassured her that they would find the boy. She activated her telephone tree and the parents organized search parties. The student was found at the home of a friend at about 11:30 that night. Devereaux insists that she could never have done such a thing alone but because the parents worked together as a community the whole group helped in the search.

One of the persistent complaints among today's teachers is that parents are not involved enough in the schools. Teachers lament the fact that more and more children come from households where both parents work. One statistic suggests that 75 percent of parents never visit their children's schools.[6] I don't recall my parents going out of their way to come to school. Perhaps once a year they came for a conference or a student performance, but neither my mother nor my father was very visible. They were too busy working. They expected me to do what the teacher told me to do. However, if my teachers needed my parents for something, all they had to do was call.

Ann Lewis, a sixth-grade teacher, also emphasizes the idea of community. Lewis is a white woman who has lived in the community all her life. Her mother is one of the few white residents who did not participate in the "white flight" of the 1950s; she has lived in the community for more than forty years. Lewis says that it was the excellent teachers in the district she had as a child that inspired her to become a teacher. Lewis identifies strongly with the African American community; she has speech patterns similar to African American speakers. For a recent television documentary about the community and the school district, Lewis was asked by community members to be a spokesperson. She was the only white teacher that they saw as a legitimate spokesperson for the district.

Lewis and Devereaux were classmates. Now, both in their early forties, the two attended school together as girls. Like Devereaux, Lewis has been active in school district politics and preceded Devereaux as teacher association president. Indeed, she has been president of the local teachers' association at least four times.

Perhaps because of her own active community involvement, Lewis insists that her students form a viable social community before they can become a viable learning community.

> They have to care about each other and to depend on one another before we can really get anything meaningful accomplished. We have to have a sense of family, of "teamness." When we see ourselves as a team that works together, we can do anything. Having a kind of team spirit helps them to under-

stand that one person's success is success for them all and that one person's failure is failure for everybody.

One of the ways Lewis builds community in her classroom is through her annual camping trip. Every fall semester she arranges a five-day camping trip for her students near the San Francisco Bay coastline. Organized through the county's environmental education program, Lewis and students camp out with several other groups of students. The goals are to teach about the environment, encourage cross-cultural contact, and in Lewis's case, to build a sense of togetherness and team spirit among her students.

Because many parents in the district have had negative experiences with teachers, Lewis must spend almost a month convincing some that the camping trip is a worthwhile experience and that they should grant their permission. Lewis makes sure that each student is prepared with a sleeping bag and any other necessary equipment.

Many inner-city teachers shy away from this kind of intense interaction with their students. The working hours for them are Monday through Friday, 8:30 to 3:00. Lewis's camping trip represents a sacrifice on her part, but she feels that this experience is a necessary one to mold each group of individual students into a cohesive whole.

"Well, Miss Philadelphia, when are you coming to my house for dinner?" boomed my U.S. history professor. Each of us was invited in turn as part of a group of three or four others to his home for dinner and small talk. Many years later I would be invited—actually required—to attend dinner at my graduate adviser's home. By then I understood that such gatherings served as a way to include people on the "team" and build a sense of community. My undergraduate professor was helping us understand the importance of this kind of behavior. Much of what is expected of you comes in informal learning situations. The jobs that are available, the grants being awarded, the committees most helpful for a person's advancement are issues that are not often discussed in the "neutral"

classroom environment. The real business and politics of school often take place among the "community," outside of the classroom.

TEACHERS WITH CULTURALLY RELEVANT PRACTICES SEE TEACHING AS AN ART AND THEMSELVES AS ARTISTS

These teachers do not ignore scientific principles of pedagogy. However, they do not view teaching as a technical skill that requires minimal training and they do not believe that as long as one follows a kind of recipe or prescription one can predict outcomes. On the contrary, teachers like Peggy Valentine exemplify the creative aspect of teaching.

Valentine,[7] an African American woman in her midforties, is relatively new to the district, having come from the Midwest after her husband's company transferred him to the West Coast. She considers herself a strict teacher and she has a flair for the dramatic, waving her arms and rolling her eyes to get a point across. She attended a historically black college and identifies closely with the students because many of them are from single-parent households and her own upbringing was in a single-parent home.

Valentine has taught in both inner-city and suburban schools. Her experiences with teaching more affluent white students has convinced her that African American students have special strengths that are rarely recognized in schools. She is very sensitive to what she perceives as slights made on the basis of race by the school administration. Her principal does not seem to like her personally but he does not hesitate to acknowledge her as one of the best teachers in the school.

Valentine enjoys teaching African American students because she says she identifies so closely with them:

> When I look at my children I see myself. I grew up in a single-parent household. I know what it is not to have the things that other children have. I also know that being smart has nothing to do with skin color. I know that some of our kids are what is called "street smart." They have what black folks call "mother wit"—you know, the kind of sense that keeps you from getting hurt or even killed.

When I taught those white kids in the suburbs, of course many seemed to know "book knowledge" but more often than not some of them don't have sense enough to come in out of the rain.

Valentine creatively engages her fourth-grade students in what could otherwise be a relatively boring lesson about adjectives. To encourage the students to use more descriptive, colorful language in their writing, she has developed an activity to get them to reach for unusual adjectives. This class is held in October and so she benefits from a Halloween atmosphere. She writes a noun on the chalkboard and asks the children to think of as many words as they can to describe it. The first noun is "witch." Tentatively at first, students begin to offer some modifiers. "Old witch," says one student. "Mean witch," says another. "Black witch," offers a third. All of a sudden, Peggy grasps her chest as if she were having a heart attack and rolls her eyes back in their sockets. "Black witch, old witch, mean witch—give me a break! You guys are killin' me! I need some great, fantastic, outstanding, stupendous, magnificent adjectives. I'll even take some compound adjectives. Can anybody save me?" After a few snickers, one boy ventures, "How about a green-faced, hook-nose, evil witch?" "Yes!" shouts Peggy Valentine. "Now you're cookin' with gas. Give me more, more!" The lesson proceeds with students shouting out a variety of compound and complex adjective phrases to revive the "dying" Valentine. The lesson goes on for almost forty minutes.

In our after-lesson briefing, Valentine tells me that she had not planned the dramatic part of the lesson. However, until that point she had not felt that the students were really engaged in the lesson.

They were just trying to get through it and I know they weren't getting anything out of it. So I decided then and there to do something dramatic to get their attention. You have to be something of an actor to be a good teacher, and sometimes you have to overact. You're on stage all of the time. I knew when I went into my "dying" act it would cause some giggles but I also know that my children *want* to please me. They want to do things right because they want my approval. In order to help them develop some motivation, I capitalize on their strong feelings for me. In my acting role, I could be angry without actually scolding them. I really planned to go about twenty-five to thirty minute on this lesson, but once they got the hang of it and seemed to really enjoy it, I knew I couldn't cut them off. You just can't put a time limit on good teaching. You have to go with it and see where it comes out. That's why a good teacher's planning is only tentative. You can write all the behavioral objectives you want. When the dynamic of a good class gets rolling, you can't know where you're going to end up. You just have to trust that the learning has been worth it and that the kids have gotten something out of it.

TEACHERS WITH CULTURALLY RELEVANT PRACTICES BELIEVE THAT ALL STUDENTS CAN SUCCEED

This notion that all students can succeed may seem trite because it is constantly repeated in the pedagogical literature. However, it is not until you see it in action that you know it can be more than a slogan.

In the classrooms of assimilationist teachers—those who seem satisfied with the status quo—there is a belief that failure is inevitable for some students. Thus the teacher develops favorites, or "pets," who are often alienated from their peers. Spindler's discussion of a teacher who operates in this way is very telling about the inability of some white middle-class teachers to recognize the idiosyncratic ways in which they interact with students of different backgrounds.[8]

My fourth-grade teacher, Mrs. Powell, seemed out of place in our largely African American school. She was a middle-aged white woman who rarely smiled. I cannot remember her ever touching any of us. I do recall her saying that nobody could get an A in her class because an A would mean that we were as smart as she was. "What a bizarre notion," I thought. I worked hard to earn the A's she did not intend to give. Despite my perfect spelling, reading, and math papers she only gave me B+. My mother went to see her about the discrepancy between the papers I brought home and the grades on my report card. And from the second reporting period until the time I left her room, I received A's from Mrs. Powell. I don't think she thought I was particularly deserving of those A's, but I don't think she wanted to try to explain her unjust grading system to my mother again. Unfortunately, I don't think my mother's ability to persuade Mrs. Powell to rethink her grading extended to my classmates. My mother was able to act as my advocate but she had little impact on the overall system.

Although all of the teachers in this study demonstrated the belief that all of their students could succeed, Gertrude Winston and Elizabeth Harris will be discussed here to illustrate this quality.

Winston is a teaching veteran of forty years. She attended normal school and began teaching in a one-room school in rural Michigan. After twelve years she decided to join the Peace Corps. She had her first contact with black people as a teacher in West Africa. From West Africa she began teaching in urban schools in Southern California and eventually moved to the San Francisco Bay Area for the final years of her teaching career. She describes her experience of teaching African and African American students as transformative. She believes she has received as much from the students as she has been able to give. She is quick to share things the students have taught her about responsibility and kinship relations. She says she has never married because she has been too busy enjoying her life as a teacher.

Walk into Winston's classroom and you walk into a model of order. The room is brightly painted and there are cubicles for each student's work. All kinds of folders have been prepared to help students keep their various papers organized. Because she has her students sit at large tables rather than at desks as most of the teachers do in her school, Winston's room seems larger. Less of the floor space is taken up by individual desks. The personal touches that she has given her room are indicative of the love and care she feels for her students. She presides over a room that shouts "success." Winston insists that she has never met an unsuccessful student.

You know, they're all successful at something. The problem is that school often doesn't deal with the kinds of things that they can and will be suc-

cessful at. And those tests! Those are the worst things ever. They don't begin to test what the kids really know. That's why my class is a constant search for ways to be successful. That's why we do so many projects in my class. I figure if we do enough *different* kinds of things we'll hit on the kinds of things the kids can be successful with. *Then* I look for ways to link that success with other tasks. For example, when I do my sewing bee, it's linked to my social studies unit but when a number of kids find out they're pretty good at sewing—and I mean boys as well as girls—I can get them interested in reading about sewing and other crafts and then in writing about it. But you know, the tests don't get at this big involved process of moving from a concrete experience to the level of abstraction that writing represents.

Alice Hall became my sixth-grade teacher after our original sixth-grade teacher, Mr. Moses, was promoted to assistant principal. Mr. Moses was a tall white man, one of the few male teachers at our school. While he was our teacher, he seemed to spend an inordinate amount of time chatting with Miss Plunkett, a pretty white teacher across the hall. He sat at his desk a lot. From there he told us what pages to read in our textbooks. Whenever we finished our work we were allowed to draw. I did a lot of drawing while he was our teacher.

I was one of the few students excited about Mrs. Hall's move from fourth to sixth grade. I knew her from flute club and I knew she had many talents and interests. She was a magnificent knitter and she would teach that skill to anyone who was interested. She was a gifted musician and always taught her students to play the flutophone. One of her strongest subject areas was mathematics and she helped students to delve deeply into its mysteries. Some of the students didn't like Mrs. Hall. Unlike Mr. Moses she required us to work—hard. Many students grumbled but everyone learned. Many years later I saw her at a commencement ceremony at a local college where she was a faculty member. She had become a mathematics professor.

Elizabeth Harris is a "fifty-something" African American woman who has lived in the community for more than twenty years. She is active in a local Pentecostal congregation and is accorded the respect of a "mother of the church." Students throughout the school are careful about the kind of language they use around her. She is very gentle and soft-spoken. I describe her approach to teaching as reflective and spiritual. Her religious conviction does not permit her to see her students as failures. She sees them all as creatures of God and, accordingly, "God doesn't make junk!"

Harris, Dupree, and Devereaux all teach in the same school. Although it is situated in a white community, the residents were successful in passing an initiative that allows them to send their children to a school in a neighboring white community. Thus African American, Latino, and Pacific Islander students make the short bus ride across the freeway to attend this school. The school's principal is relatively new to the district and is not seen as effective by either her staff or the community. Harris, Dupree, and Devereaux, with their independent spirits, are not among her favorite staff members. They do not deliberately antagonize her, but neither do they kowtow to her wishes, as some of the newer faculty do.

It is not an easy school in which to teach. The school yards, halls, and a number of the classrooms seem particularly noisy. Students talk loudly and sometimes rudely to one another and to the teachers and teachers' aides. Discipline seems to be a preoccupation for many teachers.

Harris, Dupree, and Devereaux have unusual classrooms for this school; all have a sense of order and student engagement. As you walk into Harris's room you are overcome with a feeling of calm and peace. Unlike Dupree's neat and orderly, no-nonsense classroom, or Devereaux's beehive of activity, Harris's classroom seems to be an oasis in a desert or a calm place in the midst of a storm.

Harris starts her second-grade class each morning with a song. One of her children's favorites is "Peace is Flowing Like a River." She begins instruction by asking "What are we going to be our best at today?" Students start volunteering things, both instructional and noninstructional, at which they intend to excel. "I'm gonna to be good at my math," says one little boy. "I'm gonna

be good at lining up for recess," shouts another. "I'm gonna be good at doin' my own work and minding my own business," says a little girl. As the students recite their goals and expectations for the day, Mrs. Harris encourages them with a smile or a comment, "Oh, you are? Well, that's very good!" or "I just know you can do that."

At the end of the day, Harris reconvenes her students to have them assess how well they met their goals. Each student is given an opportunity to describe what she or he did to be successful during the day. Students report on successes and reflect on ways they could have been even better at some things. Harris constantly tells them how good they are.

> I'm not trying to tell the children that they're something that they're not. Even though they don't all perform on grade level, we have to have a starting point for success. They need to identify for themselves what they know they can do and then do it. They also need to get credit for these accomplishments.
>
> I see a number of our children in church. They demonstrate that they are capable of all sorts of things there. They sing in the choir, they usher, they recite, and they make announcements. I know that if they have the discipline to accomplish these adult tasks, they can certainly do the things that schools ask of them.
>
> I think that children let too many people, like bad teachers, convince them that they are incapable of things. They give them baby work—tons and tons of silly worksheets—and never really challenge them. They need challenges. They can do it!

TEACHERS WITH CULTURALLY RELEVANT PRACTICES HELP STUDENTS MAKE CONNECTIONS BETWEEN THEIR COMMUNITY, NATIONAL, AND GLOBAL IDENTITIES

This chapter began with a discussion of the ways in which some white teachers pretend not to see a child's color. But for teachers with culturally relevant practices, students' diverse cultural backgrounds are central.

Margaret Rossi is relatively new to the district. She is a former Catholic nun who has taught in another urban district and at a white suburban private school. She considers herself a "hard" teacher, and she cultivates that reputation throughout the school. She laughs at the fact that the children refer to her, behind her back, by her surname, as if they were speaking of a drill sergeant.

Rossi says she "hated" teaching at the private school because she felt the children were "neglected": they were given material things but lacked sincere parental involvement. She describes African American children as the one group of children who "will be themselves no matter what" and who will tell you exactly how they feel. "They don't try to deceive you by pretending that something is all right when deep down inside they don't think it is." Her assessment of African American children's frankness is based on experiences in both African American and white school communities. Instead of regarding these perceived differences as deficits, Rossi has called upon them as strengths.

In Rossi's class, *who* students are and how they are connected to wider communities is very important. In the class's current-events lesson, Rossi insists that the students be able to make pertinent connections between the news items they select and themselves. As the tensions increased in the Middle East prior to the Gulf War, many students brought in articles that detailed the impending conflict.

"But what does that have to do with you?" asked Rossi. "We're sitting here in sunny California, thousands of miles away from Kuwait. Why should we care?"

"Because they can drop a bomb on us!" volunteered one of her sixth graders.

"No, they can't," countered another. "We have all kinds of radar and stuff, and if they tried to fly over here, we could shoot them out of the sky."

"Let's say Rashad is right, and no planes could get through the U.S. radar," said Rossi. "What other reasons can you offer as to why these news issues would be important to us here in *this* community?"

The students sat silent for what seemed like a long time but was actually only about a minute and a half. This waiting for an answer was characteristic of Rossi's teaching style. She was not uncomfortable with classroom silence, because she believed that when you posed substantive questions with students, you were obligated to give them time to think about an answer. Finally, Denisha, a small African American girl who was a diligent student but rarely spoke up in class, raised her hand.

"Yes Denisha?"

In a soft and measured voice, Denisha said. "Well, I think it affects us because you have to have people to fight a war, and since they don't have no draft, the people who will volunteer will be the people who don't have any jobs, and a lot of people in our community need work, so they might be the first ones to go."

Before Rossi could comment, an African American boy, Sean, chimed in.

"Yeah, my dad said that's what happened in Vietnam—blacks and Mexicans were like the first ones to go."

"I'm not sure if they were the first to go," remarked Rossi, "but I can say that they were *over-represented*." She writes these words on the board. "Do you know what I mean by this?"

None of the students volunteers a response, so Rossi proceeds with an example.

"If African Americans are 12 percent of the total U.S. population, and Latinos are 8 percent of the total U.S. population, what percent of the armed services do you think they should be?"

"Twenty percent total," calls out James, beaming at his ability to do the arithmetic quickly. "Twelve percent should be black, and 8 percent should be Mexican."

"Okay," says Rossi. "However, I would call that 8 percent Latino rather than Mexican, because we are also including Puerto Ricans, Cuban Americans, and other U.S. citizens who are from Latin America. But in Vietnam their numbers in the armed services far exceeded their numbers in the general population. Often they were among the first to volunteer to go. Does it seem as if Denisha's comments help us link up with this news item?"

A number of the students verbally concur, while others nod in assent. As the discussion continues, students talk about the impact of having young males in particular leave their community. Given the fact that the numbers of African American and Latino males in this community are decreasing due to incarceration and other institutionalization, the prospect of losing even more men to war does not seem appealing.

By the end of the lesson, students are working in cooperative groups and creating "causality charts" where they list a number of current events and their possible impacts on their community.

In Ann Lewis's class, who students are and how they are connected to wider communities is also very important. One Monday morning, Ann writes on the board "Mandela." She asks if anyone recognizes the name. Most of the students' hands go up. South African leader Nelson Mandela has just been released after decades of political imprisonment. "I know who Mandela is," says Jerry, a sixth-grade African American boy who has strong opinions and an impressive cumulative file of school transgressions.

"Who is he, Jerry?" asks Lewis.

"Well, he's this man who was in jail a long, long time in South Africa and he was fightin' for the black people's rights."

"What does Nelson Mandela have to do with us?" asks Ann. Several hands go up. Ann calls on Sugar Ray, a handsome African American boy with a trendy haircut.

"Well, like . . . Nelson Mandela represents, like, black people everywhere, not just in Africa. You know, just like Martin Luther King was a symbol for black people not just here but all over the world."

The conversation continues as students talk about how proud they are of Nelson Mandela and how they hope his freedom will mean freedom and equality for black South Africans. Lewis suggests some books and films that students might consult to learn more about apartheid and the struggles of blacks in South Africa. Students talk animatedly about which of these they will choose to read or view. No student expresses an unwill-

ingness to read. Even if they do not follow through with these commitments, it is clear that it is "okay" to read in this class. Reading is not seen as a "sissy" or effeminate activity.[9] The students understand both reading and film as ways to get information about things that interest them.

TEACHERS WITH CULTURALLY RELEVANT PRACTICES SEE TEACHING AS "DIGGING KNOWLEDGE OUT" OF STUDENTS

One of the commonalities among this diverse group of teachers is an overriding belief that students come to school with knowledge and that that knowledge must be explored and utilized in order for students to become achievers.

Patricia Hilliard is an African American woman in her early fifties who came to teaching after spending several years at home raising her family. After attending the local state university, she began as a long-term substitute teacher in a large urban district. She has taught in African American private schools in urban areas. She describes herself as someone who loves school and learning. Evidence of this claim is the fact that she regularly enrolls in in-service courses and workshops. She has served on statewide curriculum committees and university-funded projects on pedagogy. She sees her role in these activities as ensuring that African American children do not get short-changed when resources are allocated and policy is decided. She came to this school district as a long-term substitute but quickly demonstrated her ability to be effective with the students. The district offered her a teaching contract at the end of her substitute assignment.

Hilliard uses various methods to discover the knowledge that the students bring with them to the classroom. First, she spends time talking with parents about ways that they have educated their children. Then she talks to students about their interests and the things at which they are "experts."

I find that much of what we claim we want to teach kids they already know in some form. I want to know what they know so that we can make some natural and relevant connections to their lives. Sometimes my black children will have information about home remedies or stories and folktales they've heard from their grandparents. We take those stories and remedies and write them up, compare notes, see how their knowledge compares with so-called traditional knowledge. I'm always amazed when students tell me things that I don't know. That happens a lot (the older I get). But it's not just about younger generation versus older generation. My students know about things like community politics and police brutality. I can't feed them a steady diet of cute little animal stories and happy middle-class kids. Their experiences have to be a part of our curriculum, too.

Hilliard's statements reflect her respect for her students' experiences. Rather than treating them as if they do not know anything, their only purpose being to come to school to learn what she wants to teach, she understands teaching as a reciprocal process. By listening and learning from the students, she understands the need to rethink and reenvision the curriculum and what she should do with it.

In sum, a focus on the children's perceptions of self and others is especially important because teachers often express feelings of low self-esteem concerning their own work.[10] These feelings are exacerbated when they work with low-income students and children of color. The pattern for some teachers is to endure a teaching assignment in an inner-city school until they can find a position in a more affluent district with fewer children of color. In contrast, several of the teachers in this study were offered teaching positions in other districts but refused them. Their conceptions of self, students, students' parents, and community are positive. They have made their work in the district their life's work because they love it and are good at it. In the next chapter I will describe how teachers' perceptions of themselves and others affects the ways that they structure their social relations.

STUDY QUESTIONS FOR PART 7

1. What is your vision of a good school; a good classroom?
2. What is the role of a teacher in developing students' understanding of society?
3. What are some examples of the choices teachers make regarding the pedagogical structures and methods they use that can make education transformative (or reproductive) of our society?
4. Modeling participatory pedagogy, rather than following a prescribed curriculum or text, is difficult and time-consuming. What are some of the rewards and benefits of such teaching?
5. How can you make your work in schools transformational? What steps would you actually take to move your teaching in this direction? What challenges can you expect to have to overcome?
6. Who benefits from the types of education we see examples of in Part 7?
7. How should teacher training change to foster the development of transformational educators?
8. What are some of the arguments against transformative education? Assuming you disagree with those viewpoints, what counter-argument can you offer, speaking in support of transformative education?

FIELD EXPERIENCES

SUGGESTED GUIDELINES FOR STUDENTS AND INSTRUCTORS

The activities listed here are very specific and should provide no difficulty of access for students. Experienced teachers are encouraged to think of ways they might facilitate access for classmates not working in schools. These activities are designed to further a teacher's grasp of the many different viewpoints on various issues related to teaching, educational philosophy, school organization, and educational governance.

As veterans know, teaching does not occur in a vacuum. One of the major challenges of teaching involves developing a personal perspective on schooling, teaching, and learning that is at once rooted in what the profession knows about good practice, while at the same time being responsive to the diversity of views within the profession and the school community and providing a *realistic* sense of how schools and classrooms actually work. It is not always clear what is right or good. Judgments must be made, and in the course of making such judgments many different elements need to be considered. Part of what enables due consideration is the ability to anticipate the viewpoints or possible responses of others to a particular decision or course of action. What helps one do this is the breadth and depth of formal learning and experience one brings to the situation.

The field experiences described here can provide the preservice student with an initial glimpse of the diversity of perspectives held by others regarding teaching, learning, schooling, and educational governance, among other concerns. Experienced teachers can also benefit from these experiences, particularly if the school or community context of the interviewee is linguistically, racially, culturally, or socioeconomically different from one's current situation. Even if the experienced teacher must observe or interview others in their own school, the learning to be achieved by this activity can be enhanced to the extent that the person observed or interviewed is someone unfamiliar, or someone with whom you don't normally interact.

The following activities are recommended:

- Interview both a novice and a veteran teacher.
- Interview a school principal or assistant principal; follow one around for part of the day.
- Observe a self-contained classroom for special needs students; interview a special education teacher.
- Attend a school faculty meeting.
- Visit and observe in a school that differs from yours in terms of its student characteristics (more or less heterogeneous, a different social-class composition, culturally different from your experience).
- Visit a classroom implementing inclusive education practices.

- Talk to other professionals involved with youth outside the school (religious leaders, community service agencies, police, or social workers).
- Interview local business leaders regarding their expectations of schools and teachers; what do they expect of teachers and students?
- Attend a site council or PTA meeting.
- Attend a school board meeting.

Interview questions or guides for observation should be developed by the individual students based on class readings and conversations. A general guideline is to ask questions that require either a description or an explanation; try to stay away from questions calling for a yes/no response. Reassure the person with whom you are talking that his or her name and the name of the school and district (or other identifying features) will not be revealed to anyone. Plan for an interview that will last 30–60 minutes. Do your best to make an appointment with the person and set the interview up to be held at a time and in a location convenient for the subject and unlikely to be interrupted by noise or intrusions (people, telephone, etc.). Introduce yourself as a student and tell the subject that your major purpose is to understand things from his or her viewpoint.

Suggested interview questions:

- Tell me about your first year as a teacher. What was your greatest frustration; your greatest accomplishment?
- How are things different (or the same) for you now?
- What do you do when you have children with a very broad range of academic abilities?
- Who decides what gets taught in your school, in your classroom? What are your views about this?
- Should a teacher's personal values and attitudes influence what gets taught or how one teaches? Why?
- What do you like (don't like) about your school? Why?
- What are your greatest sources of reward as a teacher/administrator?
- Tell me what you think about the following: multicultural education, cooperative learning, career or vocational education, bilingual education, prayer in schools, charter schools, school vouchers, nongraded primary schools, gender bias in curricula, instructional technology, AIDS education, parental involvement, site-based decision making that involves teachers and parents, student internships, rewarding teachers based on student performance, (a topic of your choosing).
- What are your beliefs about student grouping for instruction?
- What role do schools have in developing students' attitudes and values?
- We hear a lot about equal educational opportunity. What does that mean in your classroom/school? What would you change, if anything, and why?
- What is the role of school in society?
- Is subject matter important to being a good teacher? Why? What else is important? Why?
- Some people argue that local school boards should be abolished. What do you think?

- What are your thoughts about education funding? What are your thoughts about full-state funding for education?
- What do you look for when hiring a new teacher?

There are many purposes to be served by completion of these field activities. While the general outcome will be a broadening of the individual's perspective, some particular outcomes can include

- exposure to various influences on teachers
- gaining a better understanding of how your colleagues view their work
- hearing firsthand from teachers and administrators about their jobs
- getting a better understanding of who controls the schools
- seeing what role parents and community members play in education
- enabling career exploration and helping students decide if teaching is the *right fit* for them
- gaining a glimpse of the larger reality of teaching—that it's *not* just you and the kids in your classroom, it's other teachers, parents, administrators, school board members (with all of them having somewhat disparate and frequently conflicting views)
- broadening your perspective as a veteran teacher; seeing how others might be successfully responding to many of the challenges raised by the readings

A field experience like those listed here can be very helpful in broadening an individual's view of what *being* a *teacher* is all about. The more such experiences an individual can get, be that person a veteran or a prospective teacher, the more complete will be his or her understanding of what it means to be a teacher. The insights gained will enable teachers to be more reflective about their practice and to be more deliberate and informed in deciding the what, how, and why of their work as a teacher.

PRACTICUM EXPERIENCES

SUGGESTED GUIDELINES FOR STUDENTS AND INSTRUCTORS

A major purpose of this collection of readings is to introduce teachers to the many facets of teaching beyond the child or the subject to be taught. A teacher's work life is influenced by a multitude of factors, ranging from the clarity of the school's curriculum and the availability of the needed instructional resources to the politics of the local community, the cultural and socioeconomic diversity of the children to be taught, and the degree of parental involvement in the classroom or school, to name but a few.

There are many influences on the quality, amount, and focus of a teacher's classroom instruction. A practicum that provides some insight into these various influences can help the veteran as well as the inexperienced or prospective teacher understand the complexity and the challenges faced by the classroom teacher. Too often, teachers enter their first teaching assignment with little understanding of all the forces shaping what occurs in a classroom or school. And frequently, experienced teachers work for years with little else to guide them but their subject-matter expertise and the little they might recall of their preservice class in human growth and development. While many teachers have taken the initiative to keep up with the latest theory and research about good teaching and child development practices, too few veterans have been encouraged to explore the bigger picture—the school and community beyond their classroom.

The purpose of the suggested practicum experiences is to enable beginners as well as veteran teachers to develop their awareness of these factors influencing their work and to give them opportunities to reflect upon their effects in the classroom and to consider courses of action they might take to ameliorate, insulate, or build upon those forces to help them be more effective as a teacher. Being a good teacher involves a lot more than knowledge about child development, teaching methods, and subject matter.

The best practicum for a prospective teacher is one that allows the individual extended opportunities to work directly with school-age children in a school, although it does not have to be limited to a traditional classroom or school setting. There are any number of opportunities to work with children in other community contexts that will introduce individuals firsthand to the myriad forces shaping the teaching and learning that occur in schools. Some suggestions for students in a preservice teacher education program include working with teen parents, Head Start, English as a Second Language (ESL) programs, the Urban League, migrant education programs, youth development programs in the community, a youth outreach center, children with disabilities, 4H youth programs, or a juvenile treatment center. Every community will offer a number of opportunities for individuals to volunteer for one or more programs serving children.

For the experienced teacher, a practicum can take a number of forms, including "trading" assignments for a day or week with a teacher colleague working at a different grade level or in a socioeconomically, linguistically, racially, or culturally different school or community. Although such an experience will require extra effort by the teachers involved, it frequently proves to be both a refreshing and an inspiring experience. Veterans taking advantage of such opportunities often find themselves making major changes in their regular classroom practices—changes that reflect their new understanding of the assumptions they'd been making about children, about teaching, and about the purposes of public education. Sometimes the practicum for a veteran teacher can simply take the form of "shadowing" another teacher, a school administrator, or perhaps a special education specialist or ESL teacher.

The practicum experience for a preservice teacher can occur in a school or in some other setting. A 30-hour experience is recommended. Whatever the nature of the practicum, each individual should be asked to take responsibility for sharing their observations and reflections on their experience with other members of the class and perhaps to prepare a brief report describing their experience and discussing its implications for their future work as a classroom teacher.

A practicum has a number of additional benefits, depending on the audience it serves. It can

- inform admission decisions in a teacher education program
- help experienced teachers gain fresh insights
- help individuals determine whether teaching really is for them
- foster community-based learning that returns something to the community
- serve as an enriching multicultural experience
- introduce the challenges of inclusion models of education
- serve as a confidence builder for the individual
- provide an early experience in teaching and working with children for the prospective teacher.

The suggested practica are a win-win situation. University or college students grow and develop as a result of their teaching experience in the practicum, and they receive additional assistance and support beyond what an individual instructor can provide. In addition, their overall learning experience is more robust and engaging because it provides opportunities for them to experience firsthand the many ideas, cultural and economic influences, and moral dilemmas they will encounter in the selected readings and, eventually for many, in their teaching. For prospective teachers, a practicum experience provides a relatively efficient way to test out some of their understandings of what being a teacher might be like. For veteran teachers, a practicum can be the means for providing insights about the efficacy of their current perspective as a teacher, or about the promises and challenges of teaching in a manner that reflects a deeper understanding of the functions of schools and how schools perpetuate inequalities among children and, ultimately, in our society. For the veteran teacher, a practicum experience can serve as a catalyst for change that results in greater educational equity for all children, particularly for those not well-served by current practices.

SUGGESTED READINGS

Adams, M., Bell, L., and Griffin, P. 1997. *Teaching for Diversity and Social Justice.* New York: Routledge.

Aronowitz, S., and Giroux, H. 1993. *Education Still Under Siege.* Westport, CT: Bergin & Garvey.

Barth, R. 1990. *Improving Schools from Within: Teachers, Parents and Principals Can Make the Difference.* San Francisco: Jossey-Bass.

Berliner, B., and Biddle, B. 1996. *The Manufactured Crisis: Myths, Fraud, and the Attack on America's Public Schools.* Reading, MA: Addison Wesley Longman.

Brice-Heath. S. 1983. *Ways with Words: Language Life and Work in Communities and Classrooms.* New York: Cambridge University Press.

Brown, L., and Gilligan, C. 1992. *Meeting at the Crossroads: Women's Psychology and Girls' Development.* Cambridge, MA: Harvard University Press.

Carnoy, M. 1974. *Education as Cultural Imperialism.* New York: Longman.

Chase-Landsdale, P., and Brooks-Gunn. J. Eds. 1995. *Escape from Poverty: What Makes a Difference for Children?* New York: Cambridge University Press.

Cohen, E. and Lotan, R. Eds. 1997. *Working for Equity in Heterogeneous Classrooms: Sociological Theory in Practice.* New York: Teachers College Press.

Cyrus, V. 1993. *Experiencing Race, Class and Gender in the United States.* Mountain View, CA: Mayfield Publishing.

Darder, A. 1991. *Culture and Power in the classroom.* Westport, CT: Bergin & Garvey.

Duckworth, E. 1997. *Teacher to Teacher: Learning from Each Other.* New York: Teachers College Press.

Fiol-Matta, L., and Chamberlain, M. (Eds.). 1994. *Women of Color and the Multicultural Curriculum: Transforming the College Classroom.* New York: The Feminist Press.

Fordham, S. 1996. *Blacked Out: Dilemmas of Race, Identity and Success at Capital High.* Chicago: University of Chicago Press.

Freire, P. 1970. *Pedagogy of the Oppressed.* New York: The Seabury Press.

Garcia, G. 1994. *Understanding and Meeting the Challenge of Student Cultural Diversity.* Boston: Houghton Mifflin.

Gordon, E. W. 1999. *Education and Justice: A View from the Back of the Bus.* New York: Teachers College Press.

Greene, M. 1988. *The Dialectic of Freedom.* New York: Teachers College Press.

Grusky, D. (Ed.). 1994. *Social Stratification: Class, Race, and Gender in Sociological Perspective.* Boulder, CO: Westview Press.

Hacker, A. 1992. *Two Nations: Black and White, Separate, Hostile, Unequal.* New York: Charles Scribner's Sons.

Hakuta, K. 1986. *Mirror of Language: The Debate on Bilingualism.* New York: Basic Books, Inc.

Kerber, L., and De Hart, J. (Eds.). 1995. *Women's America: Refocusing the Past.* New York: Oxford University Press.

Kochman, T. 1981. *Black and White Styles in Conflict.* Chicago: University of Chicago Press.

Kozol, J. 1991. *Savage Inequalities: Children in America's Schools.* New York: Brown Publishers.

Kuykendall, C. 1992. *From Rage to Hope: Strategies for Reclaiming Black and Hispanic Students.* Bloomington, IN: National Educational Services.

McCarthy, C., and Crichlow, W. 1993. *Race Identity and Representation in Education.* New York: Routledge.

Meier, D. 1995. *The Power of Their Ideas: Lessons for America from a Small School in Harlem.* Boston: Beacon Press.

Miller, L. 1995. *An American Imperative: Accelerating Minority Educational Advancement.* New Haven, CT: Yale University Press.

Nakanishi, D., and Nishida, T. 1995. *The Asian American Educational Experience.* New York: Academic Press.

Nieto, S. 1992. *Affirming Diversity.* New York: Longman.

Oakes, J., and Lipton, M. 1999. *Teaching to Change the World.* Boston: McGraw-Hill College.

Ogbu, J. 1978. *American Education and Caste: The American System in Cross-cultural Perspective.* New York: Academic Press.

Orenstein, P. 1994. *School Girls: Young Women, Self-esteem, and the Confidence Gap.* New York: Doubleday.

Paley, V. 1995. *Kwanzaa and Me: A Teacher's Story.* Cambridge, MA: Harvard University Press.

Philips, S. U. 1983. *The Invisible Culture: Communication in Classroom and Community on the Warm Springs Indian Reservation.* New York: Longman.

Poplin, M., and Weeres, J. 1992. *Voices from the Inside: A Report on Schooling from Inside the Classroom.* "Part One: Naming the Problem." Claremont, CA: The Institute for Education in Transformation at the Claremont Graduate School.

Purpel, D. E. 1989. *The Moral and Spiritual Crisis in Education: A Curriculum for Justice and Compassion in Education.* Granby, MA: Bergin and Garvey.

Rothenberg, P. 1995. *Race, Class, and Gender in the United States: An Integrated Study.* New York: St. Martin's Press.

Sadker, M., and Sadker, D. 1995. *Failing at Fairness: How Schools Short-change Girls.* New York: Simon and Schuster.

Shapiro, H., and Purpel, D. (Eds.). 1993. *Critical Social Issues in American Education: Toward the 21st Century.* New York: Longman Publishing Group.

Tavris, C. 1992. *The Mismeasure of Woman: Why Women Are Not the Better Sex, the Inferior Sex, or the Opposite Sex.* New York: Simon & Schuster.

Thompkins, J. P. 1996. *A Life in School: What the Teacher Learned.* New York: Addison-Wesley.

Thompson, B., and Tyagi, S. (Eds.). 1993. *Beyond a Dream Deferred: Multicultural Education and the Politics of Excellence.* Minneapolis, MN: University of Minnesota Press.

Villegas, A. M. 1991. *Culturally Responsive Pedagogy for the 1990s and Beyond.* Princeton, NJ: Educational Testing Service.

Weis, L., and Fine, M. (Eds.). 1993. *Beyond Silenced Voices: Class, Race and Gender in United States Schools.* Albany: State University of New York Press.

West, C. 1993. *Race Matters.* Boston: Beacon Press.

Wilson, W. J. 1987. *The Truly Disadvantaged: The Inner City, the Underclass, and Public Policy.* Chicago: The University of Chicago Press.

Wood, G.H. 1992. *Schools That Work: America's Most Innovative Public Education Programs.* New York: Dutton.

INDEX

Twofold judgments, as cultural value, 33
Two Nations: Black and White, Separate, Hostile, Unequal (Hacker), 220

Udall, Stewart, 231
Ulithian culture, 8-11
Universalism, as social norm, 77

Valli, Linda, 119
Value governed selections, 112
Value judgments, 18
Van Gennup, Arnold, 13
Vaughn Occupational High School, 242
Vietnam War, 37, 39, 42

Ward, James Gordon, 215
Welcher, William, 235
West, Cornell, 218
White Teacher (Paley), 208, 319
Whiting, John F., 13

Wilkinson, Rupert, 92
Williams, Thomas, 16-17, 18
Wilson, A.B., 177
Winners All: A Call for Inclusive Schools, 242
Wollenberg, Charles, 234, 235
Woman's Consciousness, Man's World (Rowbotham), 162
Women. *See also* Equal educational opportunities; Minorities; Sex roles
  culture of femininity, 157-169
  equal access to economic opportunities, 236
  sex discrimination, 3, 236, 236-241
Woodson, Carter G., 206
Work, as cultural value, 34-35
Working-class schools, 128, 129-133
Worldview, 4, 7

Young, Frank, 13
Youthfulness, as cultural value, 37-38

Zeichner, Kenneth M., 75, 78, 103